HARVARD HISTORICAL STUDIES ♦ 196

Published under the auspices of the Department of History

From the income of the
Paul Revere Frothingham Bequest
Robert Louis Stroock Fund
Henry Warren Torrey Fund

REINVENTING PROTESTANT
GERMANY

RELIGIOUS NATIONALISTS
AND THE CONTEST
FOR POST-NAZI DEMOCRACY

BRANDON BLOCH

HARVARD UNIVERSITY PRESS

Cambridge, Massachusetts

London, England

2025

Copyright © 2025 by the President and Fellows of Harvard College
All rights reserved
Printed in the United States of America

First printing

Library of Congress Cataloging-in-Publication Data

Names: Bloch, Brandon, author.
Title: Reinventing Protestant Germany : religious nationalists and the
    contest for post-Nazi democracy / Brandon Bloch.
Description: Cambridge, Massachusetts ; London, England : Harvard
    University Press, 2025. | Includes bibliographical references and index.
Identifiers: LCCN 2024048465 | ISBN 9780674295438 (hardcover)
Subjects: LCSH: Church and state—Germany (West)—History—
    20th century. | Democracy—Germany (West)—History—20th century. |
    Protestant churches—Germany (West)—History—20th century. |
    Reconciliation—Political aspects—Germany (West)—History—
    20th century. | Nationalism—Germany—Religious aspects—
    History—20th century. | National socialism and religion—
    Germany—History—20th century. | Protestants—Germany—
    Attitudes—History—20th century. | Germany (West)—Politics
    and government—1945–1990.
Classification: LCC DD258.75 .B56 2025 | DDC 943.087—
    dc23/eng/20250113
LC record available at https://lccn.loc.gov/2024048465

EU GPSR Authorised Representative
LOGOS EUROPE, 9 rue Nicolas Poussin, 17000, LA ROCHELLE, France
E-mail: Contact@logoseurope.eu

In memory of my grandparents
HANNAH AND MORTON ADELMANN
SYDNEY AND MORTON BLOCH

CONTENTS

	Abbreviations	*ix*
	Introduction	1
1	A Church in Crisis	22
2	From the Total State to the Limits of Obedience	48
3	Post-Nazi Justice and Protestant Human Rights	81
4	Families, Schools, and the Battle for the Basic Law	119
5	Rearmament and the Myths of Resistance	158
6	The Eastern Border and the Bounds of Reconciliation	197
7	Emergencies of Democracy	234
	Conclusion	274
	Notes	*289*
	Acknowledgments	*369*
	Index	*373*

ABBREVIATIONS

CDU	Christian Democratic Union
CSU	Christian Social Union
CSVD	Christian Social People's Service
DEK	German Protestant Church (1933–45)
DFU	German Peace Union
DNVP	German National People's Party
DVP	German People's Party
EDC	European Defense Community
EKD	Protestant Church in Germany (1945–)
FDP	Free Democratic Party
FEST	Protestant Research Center, Heidelberg
FRG	Federal Republic of Germany (West Germany)
GDR	German Democratic Republic (East Germany)
GVP	All-German People's Party
IMT	International Military Tribunal, Nuremberg
PEL	Pastors' Emergency League
RAF	Red Army Faction
SA	Stormtroopers (Nazi paramilitary)
SDS	Socialist German Student League
SED	Socialist Unity Party (East Germany)
SPD	Social Democratic Party
SRP	Socialist Reich Party
SS	Schutzstaffel (Nazi paramilitary)
WCC	World Council of Churches, Geneva

REINVENTING PROTESTANT GERMANY

INTRODUCTION

ON CHRISTMAS EVE 1967, shortly before 11 P.M., congregants gathered in West Berlin's Kaiser Wilhelm Memorial Church experienced a sudden disruption. Several student activists rose from their seats, while others, who had been demonstrating outside, entered the church through the central aisle. The students unfurled banners plastered with slogans against the Vietnam War: "Support Peace—Support Vietnam" and "What you have done to one of the least of my brothers, you have done to me" (Matthew 25:40). Rudi Dutschke, the famed leader of the Socialist German Student League, mounted the pulpit. His attempt to address the congregation, however, was cut short by cries of disgust. In the ensuing melee, congregants ripped the banners from the students and an elderly war veteran bloodied Dutschke's head with his cane. Ordered by a sexton to leave the church, Dutschke smeared his blood on the sexton's face, shouting "You are a servant of the devil!"[1]

The disruption came at a time of growing conflict between students and West Berlin authorities. On June 2, 1967, a police officer had shot and killed the university student Benno Ohnesorg during a protest against a visit to West Berlin by the Iranian shah. Ohnesorg's death radicalized the burgeoning student movement, including the Protestant Student Communities at West Germany's universities. In the weeks that followed the Ohnesorg shooting, violent clashes between students and police broke out at demonstrations against the Vietnam War, the NATO alliance, and the West German government's proposed emergency laws. Discord quickly spilled into West Berlin's Protestant churches. In mid-June, Rudi Dutschke led a hunger strike at the Neu-Westend Church in the affluent Charlottenburg neighborhood. By October the parish council of the Kaiser Wilhelm Memorial Church banned the local Protestant Student Community from holding worship services in the church's chapel, accusing the students of misusing church spaces for political ends. The resulting tensions boiled over on Christmas Eve.[2]

The West German press reported on the protests in West Berlin's churches as displays of generational rebellion, and not propitious ones at that. Even the left liberal newsmagazine *Der Spiegel,* known for its challenges to conservative West German governments, chastised the disruption of Christmas worship as an example of youthful excess.[3] The response by an older generation of Protestant intellectuals, however, was more varied. Helmut Thielicke, a professor at the University of Hamburg and one of West Germany's most prominent Lutheran theologians, maligned student demonstrators as authoritarians who threatened to bring about "a new Hitler—even if with different colors."[4] Others took the side of the protesters. Helmut Gollwitzer, a professor of theology at West Berlin's Free University and a mentor to Rudi Dutschke, denounced the "unchristian congregation" whose violent response to the students exposed the hollowness of its prayers for peace. For Gollwitzer it was the congregation's refusal to tolerate dissent, and the one-sided coverage of the incident in the press, that conjured the specter of the Nazi past.[5]

At one level the reactions of Thielicke and Gollwitzer represented the divided response of West Germany's liberal–conservative mainstream and radical left to the political upheavals of the late 1960s. But in a longer perspective, the shared experiences of the two Protestant theologians are striking.[6] Born three weeks apart in December 1908, Thielicke and Gollwitzer came of age in Germany's nationalist Protestant milieu at its moment of greatest crisis: the years following the collapse of the German Empire in 1918 and the founding of the Weimar Republic. Each completed his theological education and launched his career after the formation of the National Socialist dictatorship in 1933—Gollwitzer as a pastor in Thuringia and then in the Dahlem district of Berlin, Thielicke as a lecturer in theology at the University of Heidelberg. Both were later dismissed from their positions and faced periodic bans on public speaking due to their engagement in the Confessing Church, an organization of Protestant pastors and laypeople that opposed Nazi efforts to "coordinate" the churches under state auspices. At the same time, neither participated in wartime resistance efforts. Gollwitzer, who in his own words "had voluntarily put on Hitler's uniform, and would probably have done so ten times over with a clear conscience," survived the war as an infantry soldier and medic on the Eastern Front.[7] Thielicke joined the National Socialist Teachers League while at Heidelberg and worked during the war as a pastor in Ravensburg and Stuttgart. His sermons avoided open criticism of the regime and its atrocities.[8]

The formation of the West German state in 1949 brought a change of fortune for Thielicke and Gollwitzer. Both men attained professorships in the newly founded Federal Republic of Germany and achieved national recognition as public intellectuals whose opinions were broadcast to churchgoers and newspaper readers alike. Although they took opposing positions on the most contentious issues of the day, their responses to the events of Christmas Eve 1967 were marked by a deeper commonality. Notwithstanding their own political compromises under the Nazi regime, Thielicke and Gollwitzer concurred that the Protestant church should favor a democratic state and repudiate the Nazi past. By the late 1960s the question was not whether, but how the church should contribute toward the strengthening of West German democracy.

The ideological transformation represented by the Christmas Eve demonstration is also symbolized in its physical location. Perched at the northern tip of Berlin's fashionable Kurfürstendamm, the Kaiser Wilhelm Memorial Church long stood as the architectural embodiment of an imagined link between Protestantism and the German nation. Commissioned in 1891 by the newly crowned Kaiser Wilhelm II, the church was named in honor of Wilhelm I, the first leader of the unified German Empire. Its dedication on September 1, 1895, marked the twenty-fifth anniversary of Prussia's victory over France, which had established the empire. Designated a national monument in 1906, the Kaiser Wilhelm Memorial Church played host to a crowd of thousands for a National Day of Prayer on August 5, 1914, days after the opening of the First World War.[9] The church would register the convulsions of the coming decades. Derided by left-wing critics in the 1920s as a symbol of bourgeois nationalism, the church was devastated by Allied bombers on the night of November 23, 1943. When rededication finally took place in December 1961, the damaged spire left intact after four years of reconstruction, the battered facade no longer symbolized a unified German nation. Instead the church stood as a monument to a defunct empire in the Cold War island of West Berlin.[10] By Christmas Eve 1967, the Kaiser Wilhelm Memorial Church assumed new significance as a battleground to define the role of Protestants in a democracy—a function unthinkable to its architects in the 1890s.

The controversy over the Christmas Eve protest marked the culmination of the half-century ideological transformation that is the subject of this book.

Figure I.1. Kaiser Wilhelm Memorial Church, Berlin-Charlottenburg, ca. 1900. Library of Congress, Prints and Photographs Division, LC-DIG-ppmsca-00341

Figure I.2. The damaged Kaiser Wilhelm Memorial Church in the British zone of Allied-occupied Berlin, July 7, 1945. The ruins of a German anti-aircraft gun sit in front of the church. Photo by Fred Ramage/Keystone Features/Getty Images

Protestant pastors and lay churchgoers were largely hostile toward Germany's first democracy, the Weimar Republic of the 1920s. In the critical elections of 1930 and 1932, German Protestants were twice as likely as their Catholic counterparts to vote for the Nazi Party.[11] Yet during the two decades after 1945, the newly formed Protestant Church in Germany emerged as a locus for political movements that sought to expand West Germans' constitutional rights and pursue reconciliation with Germany's wartime enemies. Pastors and lay parishioners mobilized behind initiatives to reform family law, widen the scope of conscientious objection to military service, recognize Germany's postwar eastern border, and restrain the state's emergency powers. Through participation in these campaigns, Protestants became central actors in national debates about not only major domains of legislation and policy but the nature of democracy itself. In turn, they shaped the Federal Republic's model of constitutional democracy.

A Generation Between the Times

Reinventing Protestant Germany traces the democratic reorientation of German Protestant politics by following the actors at its heart: a cohort of Protestant intellectuals born between 1890 and 1910 whose biographies tracked the political landmarks of the twentieth century. Born into the Protestant bourgeoisie of late Imperial Germany, these men and women belonged to the generation of Helmut Thielicke and Helmut Gollwitzer. They began their careers during the Weimar Republic; participated in the bitter conflict over the role of the Protestant churches in the Nazi state; and emerged as leaders in churches, government, and universities during the early Federal Republic. Some were religious professionals—theologians, pastors, church administrators, and religious educators—while others worked as lay politicians, jurists, and academics. Postwar Protestant intellectuals encountered one another in a *parallel public sphere* forged around Protestant Academies, church commissions, regional and national synods, and a vibrant network of newspapers and journals.[12] In the mainstream press, parliamentary debates, and petitions to West Germany's highest courts, these Protestants also brought their visions of political reform to a broader public. Across diverse venues, midcentury Protestant intellectuals confronted a shared question: How could the theological teachings and institutional hierarchies of Germany's Protestant churches, which lacked a heritage of democratic thought or engagement, be brought to bear on the challenges of political reconstruction after Nazism?

INTRODUCTION 7

This question was a matter not only of theoretical speculation but of political action. It was ultimately through their participation in West German politics, I argue, that a generation of German Protestant intellectuals reconciled an older ideological tradition with a new affirmation of democracy. During the early postwar decades, Protestant political activism rarely deployed the language of democracy, instead drawing upon mentalities rooted in the pre-1933 world. Yet without affirming an affinity between Protestantism and democracy in principle, Protestant intellectuals born around the turn of the twentieth century participated in the practice of postwar democracy.[13] They engaged in contentious debates about their church's relationship to the state; advocated for their ideas in the media, parliament, and court system; and organized movements for political reform both within and beyond their milieu. Against the backdrop of Germany's Cold War division, Protestant initiatives found a surprising degree of success, shaping state policy as well as popular opinion on key issues facing the young Federal Republic. By the mid-1960s, a generation of pastors and lay intellectuals could look upon West Germany's constitutional democracy as a state that reflected their own political tradition.

This argument builds upon recent works of contemporary history and political theory that have recast the trajectory of democratization in post-1945 Western Europe. Rather than narrating the emergence of postwar democracy as a linear march toward a preconceived set of outcomes—whether the safeguarding of individual rights, punishment of fascist collaborators, or pluralist inclusion of minoritized groups—new scholarship conceives of democracy as an open-ended process in which citizens continually contest and remake the terms of their collective life.[14] In this book I situate Protestant intellectuals within a dynamic debate about democracy's scope and meaning, a debate that itself fostered the emergence of a democratic public sphere in postwar West Germany. Yet its open-ended character also means that democracy can have ironic, even antidemocratic origins.[15] In the case of mid-century German Protestant intellectuals, democratic convictions took root in an ideological soil suffuse with an older, deeply illiberal tradition, that of German Protestant nationalism.

Imbued with the cultural codes of the nineteenth century, Protestant nationalist ideology continued to shape and constrain the goals of German Protestant politics into the mid-twentieth.[16] An overview of its contours is therefore critical to understanding the dynamics of West German Protestantism after 1945. Like other forms of nationalism that emerged in nineteenth-century Europe,

German Protestant nationalism had both "official" and "popular" faces.[17] Protestantism was the official confession of the pre-1918 Prussian monarchy, and gained a privileged status in the German Empire formed under Prussian leadership in 1871.[18] The Prussian Union of Churches, established in 1817 by Kaiser Friedrich Wilhelm III, was governed by successive Prussian monarchs down to 1918 under a system of church–state alignment that extended back to the Reformation era.[19] But German Protestant nationalism involved more than a framework for church–state relations; it was also a means of constructing history and identity among a growing Protestant bourgeoisie. During the 1860s wars of German unification, the liberal German Protestant Association (Deutscher Protestantenverein) played a key role in consolidating the Protestant middle classes behind Prussian chancellor Otto von Bismarck and celebrated Prussia's victories over Catholic Austria and secular France.[20] Protestants constituted nearly two-thirds of the new German Empire's population, dominating the nobility, officer corps, civil service, universities, and professions; leading theologians declared the 1870 defeat of France to mark the German nation as God's "chosen people." School textbooks and national holidays narrated German history as the unfolding of a Protestant spirit extending back through Bismarck, Schiller, Goethe, and Luther.[21]

Under these conditions there took root a set of interlocking prejudices that, in evolving iterations, would shape German Protestant politics into the post-1945 decades. Among the most ubiquitous elements of the Protestant nationalist synthesis was a theological hostility toward Judaism, which frequently spilled into political and racial antisemitism. Until the 1960s, Europe's Catholic and Protestant churches alike overwhelmingly excluded Jews from the promise of salvation and held the New Testament to supersede God's covenant with the people of Israel.[22] In German-speaking Europe, Protestant-Jewish relations were long dominated by the *Judenmission,* launched by Pietist theologians in the early eighteenth century with the backing of the Prussian monarchy. Although missionaries reacted with ambivalence to the rise of political antisemitism in the German Empire—a sign that their efforts to promote conversion had failed—Protestant pastors and publicists also played important roles in the nascent antisemitic movement.[23] Germany's first antisemitic political party, the Christian Social Workers' Party, was founded in 1878 by the Berlin court chaplain Adolf Stoecker. Appealing to the economic stresses of artisans and small shopkeepers amid Germany's rapid industrialization, Stoecker railed against secular Jews as agents of a rapacious capitalism; his attacks spiraled into a racial key among

INTRODUCTION 9

his followers.[24] To be sure, antisemitic parties never approached the levers of political power in Imperial Germany, and were in decline by the late 1890s.[25] But antisemitic pressure groups in the German Empire linked traditional anti-Jewish theologies with new political grievances, forging a model for later generations of Protestant pastors.[26]

Even more than German Jews—who were less than 1 percent of Germany's population before 1933—Protestant nationalists in the German Empire defined themselves in opposition to the far larger Catholic minority. Although tensions between Protestants and Catholics persisted long after the early modern wars of religion, confession took on heightened political significance in the mid-nineteenth century. For the Protestant liberals who formed the core constituency behind Prussian-led unification, Germany's Catholic minority, supposedly backward, irrational, and disloyal, formed a foil to a Protestant national identity defined by modernity, science, and patriotism. The founding of the German Empire in January 1871 was quickly followed by the anti-Catholic Kulturkampf, launched by Bismarck with the backing of the Protestant-dominated National Liberal Party. The campaign involved restrictions on Catholic schooling and political activity, confiscations of church property, as well as the imprisonment or exiling of some 1,800 priests. According to the supporters of these measures, Catholics were unfit for full membership in the German state due to their subservience to clerical hierarchies and loyalty to the Vatican. Only the Protestant confession harmonized the private faith of the individual with the public virtues of rationality, hard work, and national duty.[27]

By the late 1870s, amid fierce Catholic resistance, Bismarck abandoned the Kulturkampf in favor of a new alliance with conservatives, right-wing liberals, and the Center Party, formed in 1870 to defend Catholic interests. But anti-Catholicism remained a prominent feature of Imperial German politics well beyond the end of the Kulturkampf. An 1872 law expelling the Jesuit order remained on the books until 1917; an 1890 campaign against its repeal, supported by the Protestant League (Evangelischer Bund), garnered more than a million signatures.[28] A voice of militant anti-Catholicism, the Protestant League became Imperial Germany's fourth-largest voluntary association outside the trade unions, with over 500,000 members in 1913. The group's signature Los von Rom (Away from Rome) initiative, which aimed to convert Catholics in the Habsburg Empire to Protestantism, linked anti-Catholic hostility to the expansionist agenda gaining ground among ethno-nationalist pressure groups.[29]

If late nineteenth-century Protestant nationalists viewed themselves, rather than Catholics or Jews, as the natural leaders of the German Empire, they were less united in a positive political vision. The aftermath of the Kulturkampf brought a hardening division between Protestant liberals and conservatives, with liberals supporting free trade and economic individualism, and conservatives favoring paternalist programs of social reform. Yet across this division, Protestant nationalists defined their church not as the religious arm of a political party but as a source of values uniting the German nation above the divisions of class, region, and even confession.[30] Friedrich Naumann, a leading liberal theologian, celebrated the alignment of a free church and a free state in a 1909 lecture before the German Protestant Association. Whereas freedom of conscience came to England only through protracted civil war, Naumann declared, German liberalism aligned individual conscience with the health of the community; the state formed "the will of all and the will that extends to all."[31] Naumann's most prominent conservative counterpart, the Berlin theologian Reinhold Seeberg, similarly endowed German national identity with religious significance. In a tract of 1911, Seeberg added the *Volk* (people) to Martin Luther's "three estates" of marriage, church, and state, as "positive organs of the highest moral ideals, part of the coming kingdom of God."[32] A pretension to stand above political parties frequently translated into suspicion toward Imperial Germany's parliamentary system altogether.[33] This was all the more so due to the electoral success of the Social Democratic Party (SPD), the largest political party in the German parliament by 1912. The SPD drew its support from a largely unchurched working class, while its most radical wing promoted the renunciation of church membership altogether.[34]

A final, no less significant dimension of Protestant nationalism in Imperial Germany involved a backlash against the growing influence of women within the church. Recent scholarship has challenged the "feminization thesis" as a catch-all description of Christianity in nineteenth-century Europe.[35] For contemporary male church leaders in both confessions, however, the rising proportion of women among parishioners and lay activists was a source of deep anxiety. During and after the Kulturkampf, Protestant publicists disparaged the Catholic Church for the public roles it afforded laywomen and female religious orders, while criticizing Catholic priests for undermining male authority in the household.[36] Yet a stark gender disparity held within Imperial Germany's Protestant churches as well. Women lacked the right to vote in church elections or become ordained clergy members,

INTRODUCTION 11

but they formed the rank and file of a vibrant Protestant associational life. Even as women's subordination remained an expectation of middle-class culture, the church provided a rare space where gender hierarchies could be subverted.[37] In the words of one historian, German Protestant nationalism emerged as an alternative "citizen's religion" through which an urban male bourgeoisie, increasingly distant from village-centric churches, could interpret its own civic engagement as the enactment of God's will.[38]

This ideological constellation—antisemitism, anti-Catholic prejudice, hostility toward the party system, and patriarchal gender attitudes—defined the political outlook of a wide swath of Protestant intellectuals born around the turn of the twentieth century. German defeat in 1918 was this generation's foundational rupture. Protestant pastors overwhelmingly participated in the war frenzy of 1914, viewing the war as an opportunity to achieve the spiritual unity that had eluded Germans since political unification in 1871. Hundreds of wartime sermons assured congregants that God would deliver a German victory over Western decadence and materialism.[39] Leading Protestant theologians, including Friedrich Naumann and Reinhold Seeberg, were among the signatories of the October 1914 appeal by ninety-three German intellectuals defending Germany's invasion of Belgium. Both would support the military's annexationist aims during the war.[40] Even German pastors active in the international Protestant missionary movement, who had previously espoused cosmopolitan alternatives to German nationalism, rallied behind their nation's wartime cause.[41]

Fervent supporters of the war even as military losses and domestic strain soured the popular enthusiasm of 1914, the Protestant churches suffered an "enormous loss of credibility" with German defeat four years later.[42] For churchgoing Protestants, the dissolution of the German Empire and the formation of the Weimar Republic—a secular state whose constitution outlawed an official church—meant the collapse of the ideological coordinates that had framed their worldviews. Amid the shock of defeat and climate of political instability, a generation of Protestant students, alongside their slightly older mentors, joined forces with the republic's enemies. Blaming Catholics, socialists, and Jews for the collapse of Imperial Germany's Protestant political culture, young Protestant writers radicalized the antisemitic, anti-Catholic, and patriarchal strands of prewar Protestant nationalism. Many backed the Nazi assumption of power in 1933 as a catalyst of national and religious revival, and only gradually grew disillusioned with the regime. Unlike the émigré intellectuals who populate many studies of postwar West

German democracy, this Protestant cohort lived out the Nazi years inside Germany—or as soldiers, officers, and military chaplains in Nazi-occupied Europe—and undertook the compromises characteristic of German life under dictatorship. Although the individuals centered in this book include both participants in Nazi crimes and conspirators in anti-Nazi resistance, most occupied a messy middle ground that spanned pragmatic cooperation, passive complicity, and partial, belated opposition.

The turning point of 1945 transformed the conditions in which Protestant politics unfolded. Following Germany's second defeat, the Allies transferred the lands east of the Oder and Neisse Rivers, one-quarter of Germany's pre-1937 territory, to Poland and the Soviet Union. Over 12 million German speakers were expelled from East-Central Europe into Germany's shrunken borders. Germany's remaining territory was partitioned into American, British, French, and Soviet zones of occupation, leading to the formation of the Western-aligned Federal Republic of Germany (FRG) and the Soviet-dominated German Democratic Republic (GDR) in 1949. Under the new arrangement, the Protestant heartlands of Eastern Germany fell behind the Iron Curtain. The GDR, whose ruling Socialist Unity Party aimed to push the churches out of public life, was initially over 90 percent Protestant. From having been two-thirds of the German Empire, Protestants made up just over half the population of the FRG.[43] Unlike their Catholic counterparts, who overwhelmingly backed the Christian Democratic Union (CDU), West German Protestants lacked an obvious political party affiliation. The Protestant Church in Germany (Evangelische Kirche in Deutschland; EKD), the church federation formed in 1945, was the only major German institution during the 1950s and 1960s to span the divide of East and West.

It was amid these upheavals that Protestant intellectuals in West Germany would reconceive of their confession as a bulwark of democracy. From rejecting democracy altogether, or declaring their indifference to it, the Protestant generation born around the turn of the century embraced constitutional democracy by the mid-1960s—indeed, as a form of government that relied upon Protestant traditions. Their affirmation of democracy did not require a complete jettisoning of Protestant nationalism, however. Even though postwar Protestants mollified their most vehement antisemitic, anti-Catholic, and patriarchal rhetoric, these ideologies frequently resurfaced. Moreover, a key tenet of prewar Protestant nationalism continued to underpin their activism: the conviction that the Protestant confession served as a source of shared values that bound together the German political community.

INTRODUCTION 13

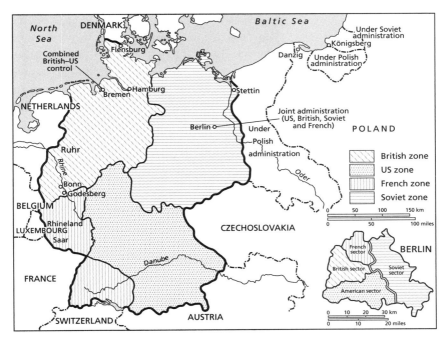

Map I.1. Allied occupation of Germany after German defeat on May 8, 1945. Territory east of the Oder River was later transferred to Polish administration. Hans-Peter Schwarz, "The Division of Germany, 1945–1949," in *The Cambridge History of the Cold War*, vol. 1, *Origins*, ed. Melvyn P. Leffler and Odd Arne Westad (Cambridge: Cambridge University Press, 2010), 138. Reproduced with permission of Cambridge University Press through PLSclear

If German defeat and national division compelled a generation of Protestant intellectuals to reconsider their church's political role, it was hardly inevitable that this cohort would align itself with West German democracy. Instead the trajectory of German Protestant politics after 1945 was molded by a series of personal and intellectual encounters: between Allies and Germans; between competing factions within German Protestantism; and between theologians and lay intellectuals. All three are central to this book. Allied occupation narrowed the political space for expressions of overt hostility toward democracy, while elevating claims of anti-Nazi resistance to a key currency of political life. The US and British occupation governments envisioned the German churches as repositories of anti-Nazi values, a preconception bolstered by the international Christian ecumenical movement. In turn, German Protestant intellectuals refashioned their ambiguous pasts into accounts of fully fledged resistance, a process that had already begun during the war. Resistance claims did not necessarily lead to the embrace of liberal democracy under Western aegis. In the early postwar years, Protestants invoked a legacy of resistance to oppose Allied denazification measures and contest the legitimacy of the West German state itself. But even when deployed instrumentally, resistance narratives enabled postwar pastors and lay intellectuals to frame their political demands within a language of human rights and limited state power, which eventually informed their defense of constitutional democracy.

At the same time that German Protestant intellectuals were forced to adapt to the pressures of Allied occupation, they also faced internal division. The postwar Protestant Church in Germany was a federation of regional Protestant churches affiliated with the Lutheran and Reformed (Calvinist) denominations, as well as the United denomination that merged the two. Although the central administration of the EKD represented all the regional churches before national political authorities, long-standing doctrinal differences endured. A conservative Lutheran majority of the German pastorate followed Luther's distinction between the fallen earthly realm and the coming reign of Christ—the Lutheran doctrine of the two kingdoms—to advance a conservative social and political vision. A smaller, competing camp built upon Reformed traditions that regarded the created world as a harbinger of the kingdom of God. The church, for this group, was less a bedrock of political order than a spiritual community that reminded the state of its higher purpose. But after 1945, both wings of German Protestantism embraced a narrative of anti-Nazi resistance. Competition to represent the legitimate heir to the Protestant opposition against Nazism facilitated a turn to the language of human rights, and ultimately, of democracy, on both sides.

A final set of encounters critical for the reorientation of German Protestant politics involved exchanges between theologians and lay intellectuals. Protestant theologians, whether affiliated with the EKD's Lutheran or Reformed wing, frequently asserted the centrality of their confession as a source of shared political values, yet lamented the lack of a Protestant political theory on par with the social teachings of the Catholic Church. It was lay intellectuals and politicians who translated the abstractions of theology into concrete legislative proposals, and who spearheaded the political successes that would lead church authorities to espouse the Protestant roots of democracy. Because constitutional law emerged as a foundational arena for reworking the relationship between church teachings and politics in postwar West Ger-

INTRODUCTION 15

many, I pay particular attention to jurists and constitutional scholars among lay intellectuals. Moreover, Protestant lay intellectuals were more socially diverse than the ordained clergy. Protestant women activists and Protestants of Jewish descent, shut out of the pastorate by law or convention, opened the door to more inclusive conceptions of political belonging, even as the force of their ideas was often blunted in official church statements.

Certainly the individuals I foreground cannot stand in for all Protestant church members in West Germany. This group included over 26 million people in 1950 and was highly diverse in class, region, and religious practice.[44] Instead I focus on the intellectuals who constructed the discourse of Protestant national identity, and who sought to translate ideas produced within the Protestant public sphere into political and legal decisions. An emphasis on the meeting point of politics and ideas conditions the people and sources at the heart of this study. Individuals who are at most passing characters in surveys of the early Federal Republic, including the CDU parliamentarian Elisabeth Schwarzhaupt, Social Democratic jurist Adolf Arndt, or West Berlin theologian Helmut Gollwitzer, play central roles. On the other hand, Protestant politicians who concentrated their energies on government institutions rather than church-based ones, such as Bundestag presidents Hermann Ehlers and Eugen Gerstenmaier, do not occupy as prominent a position as they would in a conventional political history. Published treatises by individual authors are less central than conferences and commission meetings, speeches and memorandums, and the ideologically diverse Protestant press. At the same time, I consider how the initiatives of Protestant intellectuals were received within the wider political and media landscape.

Locating Protestant Germany

The transformation of Protestant politics in West Germany belongs to the larger story of Europe's political evolution after 1945. Traditionally that story has been told as one of deradicalization, in which the dictatorships, total war, and extremist ideologies of the early twentieth century gave way to the geopolitical standoff of the Cold War, but also to rising prosperity and successful democratization in the continent's western half. More recently, scholars have reexamined this narrative, questioning whether the post-1945 period was indeed one of quiescence and stability in contrast to the hyper-politicization of the previous decades. *Reinventing Protestant Germany* participates in these revisions, while also opening new perspectives.

First, this book joins a wave of studies that have transformed the writing of twentieth-century European history by underscoring the ongoing political salience of religion after 1945. Recent scholarship foregrounds the political movement that, more than any other, brokered Western Europe's transition out of fascism: Christian Democracy. On the ashes of war, newly formed Christian Democratic parties swept to power from France and West Germany to Belgium, Italy, and Austria. While ideologically protean, these parties located the moral basis of politics in the continent's Christian heritage, espousing the "re-Christianization" of postwar societies. Christian Democracy found an indispensable patron in the Catholic Church, which marshaled its vast network of diplomatic posts, lay associations, charities, and newspapers to pave Christian Democrats' roads to victory. In the political vacuum opened by the Second World War, Europe's—and the world's—largest religious organization found itself in an unprecedented position to shape a generation of West European social and foreign policy.[45]

An exclusive focus on Christian Democracy and the Catholic Church, however, conceals national variations, as well as countervailing visions of Christian politics at the postwar moment. Unique among countries where Christian Democrats came to power, West Germany was not predominantly Catholic but confessionally mixed. The Christian Democratic Union, which dominated national politics during West Germany's first two decades, could not but be interconfessional. Historians have shown how the CDU helped reconcile conservative Catholics and Protestants to cooperate with one another, and to participate in democracy.[46] Yet this is only part of the story. The Catholic-Protestant antagonism, long a determinant of how Germans voted, where they lived, and which schools they attended, remained a fault line of West German politics into the 1960s.[47] Moreover, Protestant church leaders and lay intellectuals by no means uniformly supported Christian Democracy. My analysis therefore shifts from a familiar emphasis on cross-confessional alliances within the CDU to cross-party alliances forged through Protestant networks.

Centering Protestants also suggests an alternative chronology of Christian politics in twentieth-century Western Europe. Scholars have traced the height of Christian political power during this century to the early Cold War, arguing that the political influence of churches dissipated with the growth of consumer societies in the 1950s, followed by the youth cultures and sexual revolution of the 1960s.[48] Church attendance indeed fell precipitously across Western Europe by the end of the latter decade. Protestant politics in West Germany, however, complicates narratives of secularization conceived of as religion's confinement to the private sphere.[49] As critical observers have noted, the entire history of German Protestant nationalism unfolded against a decline in popular religiosity since the mid-nineteenth century.[50] But Protestant political engagement in the postwar Federal Republic did not hinge upon widespread religious observance. Instead, a basic tenet of Protestant nationalist ideology—the conviction that the confession served as a source of values uniting the polity as a whole—encouraged pastors and lay intellectuals to frame their interventions in universalist languages of peace, reconciliation, and human rights. Postwar Protestant intellectuals developed new models for operating in and through a society where religious faith was no longer a given, and forged alliances beyond their milieu. Ultimately they influenced policies and legal decisions whose legacies would outlast the 1960s, well beyond the caesura when historians have pronounced the end of Christian Europe.

Reinventing Protestant Germany contributes to scholarship not only on Cold War Christian politics but on the Federal Republic's democratic reconstruction. Indeed, it is hardly the first study to point out that West German democracy did not begin with the student movement of the late 1960s. Historians have demonstrated how German intellectuals born around the turn of the twentieth century, whose political outlook was fashioned against the collapse of the Weimar Republic, played critical roles in forging both West German political institutions and the post-1945 transatlantic order. Frequently the focus has been on individuals, whether of Jewish origin or socialist politics (or both), who went into exile during the Nazi years and returned to Germany after 1945.[51] But although the intellectuals featured in this book belonged to the generation of the émigrés, their experiences diverged in crucial ways. Most significant, they were not racial or political targets of Nazi persecution, and many of them supported the regime early on. Even for the minority of postwar Protestant intellectuals of Jewish descent, reintegration into West Germany meant not donning the uniform of the victorious Americans but working alongside former Nazi collaborators.

This shift in perspective, from émigrés to witnesses and collaborators, supports my argument that West German democratization depended upon the partial, incomplete reorientation of nationalist lineages. In turn, this book participates in broader reassessments of West Germany's democratic transformation. Although interpretations of a "zero hour" at 1945 have long fallen out of fashion, the timing and sources of postwar democratization—as well as the nature of the democracy that emerged—remain subject to debate. Following the end of the Cold War, the first efforts to historicize the Federal Republic described postwar democracy as the result of West Germany's "Americanization," "Westernization," or "re-civilization." West Germans, on this view, gradually overcame the polarization and political violence that plagued the twentieth century's first half, through Allied interventions as well as internal reckonings with the Nazi past.[52] More recently, historians have painted a less hagiographic picture of postwar democratization.[53] American influence, it turns out, involved not only reeducation programs and consumer goods but the importation of US racial hierarchies.[54] Scholars drawing on the history of emotions and everyday life have shown how traumatic memories of the Nazi past continually threatened to upend the façade of postwar stability.[55] Long after the West German Basic Law proclaimed the protection of "human dignity" as the state's foremost task, minoritized groups—including immigrants, queer people, and Black Germans—struggled for equality and inclusion.[56]

I address both sets of arguments, while suggesting new departures. If recent scholarship on the Federal Republic engages critically with the framework of "Westernization," the history of postwar Protestantism cannot escape the question of Western and American influence. German churches—Protestant as well as Catholic—gained privileged positions in postwar society through the favor of the US and British occupation governments. German Protestants were integrated into the international ecumenical movement around the World Council of Churches, dominated in the early postwar years by West European and North American churches, while the Protestant public sphere operated with American funding. But these interactions were not a matter of one-way influence. German Protestants informed, and at times outright manipulated, Western ideas about Nazism. They adapted the language of the ecumenical movement, including the discourse of human rights, toward their own theological traditions and political goals. Moreover, contacts with East German and East European Protestants critically informed how Protestant intellectuals in West Germany understood their political mission. Given its boundary-crossing status, the EKD was in no simple sense a Western institution.[57]

Examining the Protestant role in post-Nazi reconstruction, then, affirms interpretations that have called into question the Federal Republic's successful integration into an idealized West. At the same time, transformations of Protestant politics help account for West Germany's dramatic break from its Nazi precursor. During the postwar decades, German Protestant intellectuals espoused exclusionary conceptions of democracy, constrained by ongoing commitments to elements of Protestant nationalist ideology. But Protestants also strengthened West German constitutional democracy by demanding protections for individual basic rights, limits on executive power, and the mollification of revisionist territorial claims. Protestant political movements point toward neither the successful overcoming of Nazism nor its unbending continuation, but a more ambivalent reality: the building of democracy on illusory narratives about the past.

REINVENTING PROTESTANT GERMANY unfolds over seven chapters. In order to contextualize the full generational trajectory of its protagonists, the narrative begins not in 1945 but at an earlier moment of rupture: the defeat of 1918. Disestablishment, declining membership, and threats to traditional church privileges created unprecedented challenges for German Protestantism. Chapter 1 examines how a generation of theologians and political thinkers who came of age during the First World War struggled to reformulate the place of the churches in the secular state of the Weimar Republic. Among theologians, two proposals predominated: the purification of Christianity from worldly politics altogether, or the creation of a post-liberal "total state." Lay intellectuals who envisioned their confession as the foundation of a democratic culture formed a small minority.

The establishment of Nazi dictatorship in 1933 transformed the debate about the church's political role. Although initial discussions proceeded along the fissures of the Weimar era, Nazi incursions into church administration demonstrated the futility of both solutions envisioned in the 1920s—political disengagement, as well as an authoritarian state that respected church autonomy. Chapter 2 shows how intellectuals affiliated with the Nazi-era Confessing Church, first publicly and then in wartime underground circles, developed a new conception of a church that restrained state power over the individual. While this vision remained imbued with the strands of prewar Protestant nationalism, and few Protestants actively resisted the Nazis, wartime discussions laid the foundation for a powerful myth of Confessing Church opposition.

That myth was abetted by leaders in the international ecumenical movement as well as Western occupation authorities. As both groups looked toward the German churches as sources of moral renewal after 1945, Confessing Church veterans inserted themselves into pan-European conversations about human rights and postwar re-Christianization. These German Protestants were not passive recipients of Western influence but active participants in reshaping the discourses of international postwar planning. Chapter 3 details how the newly formed Protestant Church in Germany marshaled a novel language of Protestant human rights to call for the termination of Allied war crimes trials and amnesty for convicted Nazi perpetrators. The campaign against war crimes trials indicated the long reach of Protestant nationalism after 1945. But it also formed a critical juncture at which German Protestants positioned themselves, however cynically, as avatars of human rights and resistance against unjust state authority.

This new self-image shaped the EKD's political interventions following the founding of the Federal Republic in 1949. During the 1950s, both wings of the church—the conservative Lutheran majority, as well as a minority around the Reformed theologian Karl Barth and dissident pastor Martin Niemöller—sought to influence foundational debates about West Germany's Basic Law. Controversies over family law and education reform became opportunities to contest the perceived Catholic dominance over West German politics and articulate an alternative Protestant vision. As Chapter 4 demonstrates, when Catholic CDU politicians defended patriarchal marriage and confessional schools, a cohort of Protestant theologians and lay intellectuals advocated for legal reform through a language of religious toleration and limited state power. Chapter 5 turns to the Protestant campaign for conscientious objection to military service amid the bitter controversy over West German rearmament. By the mid-1950s, with rearmament an imminent reality, the EKD defended an expansive right of conscientious objection as the outgrowth of an anti-Nazi legacy. On the basic rights issues that preoccupied the church during the 1950s, Protestant petitions resulted in victories at the Federal Constitutional Court. At the same time, both wings of the EKD remained reluctant to address Protestant accommodation and complicity during the Nazi era.

By the early 1960s, political victories fostered a growing sense of identification among Protestant intellectuals with West German constitutional democracy, insofar as democracy could be defined as an expression of Protestant values. The postwar EKD's most impactful political statement, the Eastern Memorandum of 1965, expressed this newfound self-confidence. Marking a sharp break with both its own earlier position and all West German political parties, the EKD called on the Federal Republic to acknowledge the loss of Germany's former eastern territories. Still, as Chapter 6 shows, the Eastern Memorandum, and a key EKD statement on West German Nazi trials that preceded it, recast rather than repudiated the church's historical nationalism.

INTRODUCTION

The moment of unity around the Eastern Memorandum did not mean that divisions within the Protestant public sphere were overcome. New political controversies of the 1960s, especially the issue of proposed emergency laws, provoked bitter debate among Protestant intellectuals born around the turn of the twentieth century, who were now part of the older generation of academics, church leaders, and politicians. But as Chapter 7 demonstrates, the central fault line fell between Protestants who believed that the West German state had already internalized the values of their confession, and those who insisted upon ongoing vigilance against threats to democracy—a rift that defined the divided response to the Christmas Eve protest at the Kaiser Wilhelm Memorial Church. Democracy itself was no longer in question.

Although few Confessing Church veterans remained active in West German politics by the early 1970s, this generation's legacy would extend into and beyond the period of German reunification. In the Conclusion, I consider a successor generation of Protestant intellectuals who rose to prominence during the 1970s and 1980s. In church memorandums and public addresses, members of this second postwar generation lauded the achievements of their predecessors but continued to define democracy in restrictive terms. When migration from outside Europe emerged as a hot-button issue at the end of the Cold War, church leaders questioned the capacity of Muslim immigrants to integrate into Germany's democratic culture, which they linked to its Protestant heritage. The tension between universal rights and religious values—both of which had been espoused by Protestant intellectuals as foundations of German democracy since the postwar years—helps explain the persistence of conflict around religion and migration in a reunified Germany.

CHAPTER ONE

A CHURCH IN CRISIS

IN A TRACT of October 1917, on the eve of the 400th anniversary of the Protestant Reformation, the twenty-nine-year-old military chaplain Paul Althaus celebrated Martin Luther as a "German prophet," the "embodiment of German inwardness and spirituality."[1] The towering liberal theologian Adolf von Harnack waxed equally grandiose in a Luther biography for schoolchildren: Luther was the greatest of all Germans, without whom Leibniz, Goethe, and even Bismarck would be unthinkable.[2] In a public lecture at the University of Berlin, the church historian Karl Holl extolled Luther's "German qualities": "The courage to take personal responsibility, the determination to go to the end, an equal sense for the heroic and for the delicate."[3] Amid mounting military losses, devastating food shortages, and growing political unrest, Protestant theologians seized on the Reformation anniversary to renew the nationalist appeals that had defined their pro-war pronouncements three years earlier. As a Catholic observer noted, the Luther literature of 1917—from academic treatises to children's books—was overwhelmingly untheological. Dogmatics appeared beside the point for Protestant preachers seeking a symbol for a nation in disarray. Instead they lauded Luther's religiosity, conscience, and German spirit.[4]

A year later, military defeat and domestic revolution laid waste to German Protestant visions of a divinely ordained victory, bringing irreversible changes to the churches' position in public life. The abdication of Kaiser Wilhelm II on November 9, 1918, and then of the territorial monarchs throughout the German states, ended the system of monarchical rulership that had defined church–state relations in the German-speaking lands since the Reformation. Germany's transformation into a republic threatened traditional church privileges, while defeat exposed the hollowness of pastors' wartime pronounce-

22

A CHURCH IN CRISIS   23

ments. Their prophecy discredited, the Protestant churches experienced record-shattering declines in membership, with over 260,000 Germans exiting each year from 1919 to 1921, and tens of thousands annually in the years after. For Germany's Protestant leadership—and the 11 million Germans who formed the core of the churchgoing laity—defeat and revolution marked an unmitigated disaster.[5]

Like virtually every other aspect of the Weimar Republic's turbulent history, the role of the Protestant churches in the republic's brief lifespan and dramatic collapse has become the subject of a vast, often polemical literature. Certain facts are now beyond doubt. Statistical studies demonstrate that Protestant church affiliation was a strong predictor of the Nazi vote in the elections of 1930 and 1932, even when accounting for region and class—though scholars debate whether this correlation reflects ideological affinity, economic interests, or simply the lack of an effective Protestant counterpart to the Catholic Center Party.[6] Prominent theologians and church leaders aligned themselves with National Socialism before 1933, with several pastors running as Nazi parliamentary candidates as early as 1924.[7] The pro-Nazi German Christian movement, which would support the "coordination" of the Protestant churches under the Nazi state, was founded in the summer of 1932.[8] Lest such findings paint a lopsided picture of Nazism as a Protestant movement, historians have also shown how Catholic nationalists in Munich formed the core constituency of the early Nazi Party. Right-wing Catholic politicians and intellectuals had long espoused an antidemocratic and anti-secular ideology that facilitated an alliance with Nazism in 1933.[9]

This chapter moves beyond long-running debates about confessional culpability for the republic's fall. Instead I revisit Weimar Protestantism as a laboratory of ideas about the church's relationship to a newly secular, democratic state that would continue to shape German Protestant politics after 1945. I turn to three protagonists who defined a wide-ranging debate among Protestant intellectuals about the church's political role: the Swiss Reformed theologian Karl Barth, the Erlangen Lutheran theologian Paul Althaus, and the Berlin jurist and constitutional scholar Rudolf Smend. Together, these three thinkers represent the generational transformation at the heart of Weimar Protestant intellectual life.

While leading prewar theologians continued to write and teach after 1918, the works of Adolf von Harnack, Karl Holl, and Reinhold Seeberg retreated from political declarations toward academic themes of dogmatics and church history. The new pacesetters of Protestant theology and social thought were contemporaries of the "front generation" born in the 1880s and 1890s. Although only Althaus (b. 1888) served in the military, Barth (b. 1886) and Smend (b. 1882) also saw decisive challenges to the preconceptions in which they had been educated. In turn, this cohort served as teachers and mentors to members of the "war youth" generation born in the first decade of the twentieth century. Drawn to heroic mythologies of a war they experienced only as children, and deprived of professional opportunities by the republic's perennial economic instability, Weimar students frequently gravitated to the political extremes. Students of Protestant theology were no exception.[10]

Like many Weimar intellectuals, Barth, Althaus, and Smend perceived their moment as one of "crisis," a crossroads that demanded a fundamental decision about society's direction.[11] But they were also driven by a distinct preoccupation: the concern that the Protestant confession—in contrast to German Catholicism—lacked firm principles on which to confront the rupture of 1918. Each tried to fill the normative void. Barth called on the church to return to the bedrock truths of revelation, while Althaus elevated the nation itself to a divine creation. Smend, unusually among Weimar Protestant intellectuals, came to view the church's lack of a fixed social doctrine as a source of democratic potential. None, however, defended the Weimar parliamentary system or individual basic rights. Althaus and his circle espoused a radical critique of Weimar democracy that turned the strands of prewar Protestant nationalism—including its antisemitic, anti-Catholic, and patriarchal impulses—against the state itself. Barth's theology did not allow for a Christian defense of any political form, while Smend affirmed democracy only within the limits of Protestant nationalist ideology. The failure of any faction to realize its vision of religious renewal in Germany's first democracy in turn shaped the political outlook of the Protestant "war youth" generation that came of age during the 1920s. Not what their church did during Weimar, but what it failed to do—secure a prominent political voice—became the basis for this generation's foundational myths.

An Uncertain Revolution

The revolutionary events of 1918–1919 cast a shadow over Protestant efforts to redefine the confession's public role in the Weimar Republic. The founding of the republic unfolded in a turbulent Europe where the Bolshevik Revolution and subsequent Communist uprisings in Berlin, Munich, Budapest, and other cities sent shock waves through church hierarchies across the conti-

A CHURCH IN CRISIS   25

nent. By 1919, the Vatican launched a vigorous anti-Communist campaign, concluding treaties over the following years to secure the public rights of Catholics and stem the spread of Communism in the new states of Central and Eastern Europe.[12] European Protestant pastors were no less hostile to the perceived tidal wave of atheistic Communism.[13] Although no Weimar cabinet would adopt an overtly anti-Christian stance, fears rooted in the early postwar months imbued Protestant discussions of church–state relations throughout the republic's short-lived history.

Prussia formed the ground zero of contests over religious authority in revolutionary Germany. After a coalition of Social Democrats and more radical Independent Socialists announced a provisional government on November 10, 1918, the Prussian Ministry of Culture, co-led by Independent Socialist Adolph Hoffmann, embarked on an ambitious effort to reverse the churches' public privileges. A longtime activist in the socialist church-leaving movement, Hoffmann demanded a complete separation of church and state, seeking to overturn centuries of intertwinement. By the end of the month, a series of decrees spelled out the new policies: the expropriation of church property, stripping of the churches' status as public corporations, and elimination of compulsory religious instruction in public schools. Protestant church leaders joined with the German Catholic bishops to mobilize the faithful against these measures. A petition circulated by the Prussian Union of Churches opposing the new government's educational policies quickly garnered nearly 7 million signatures. The departure of the Independent Socialists from the governing coalition in January 1919 did not end the conflict—in part because Hoffmann's successors in the Ministry of Culture continued to oppose compulsory religious instruction, in part because the churches found anti-secular agitation a useful way to expand their political voice.[14]

The constitution adopted by the elected National Assembly, convened in bucolic Weimar to escape the violence in Berlin, was a far cry from the worst fears of church leaders. The Center Party alongside the left liberal German Democratic Party, represented at the National Assembly by the liberal Protestant theologian Friedrich Naumann, mediated a settlement that restored many of the churches' prewar privileges. To be sure, the collapse of the German monarchies upended church–state relations. The Prussian Constitution of 1850, which remained valid down to 1918, had provided that "the Christian religion shall be taken as the basis for state institutions which are connected to the practice of religion."[15] In contrast, the Weimar Constitution concluded in August 1919 announced that "there is no state church."

The preamble derived the constitution's authority solely from the German people, without reference to God.[16] But the new constitution did not wholly break from precedent. The document secured "the undisturbed practice of worship" and the admission of clergymen to military barracks, hospitals, and prisons. Sunday was established as a day of "rest and spiritual edification." On the controversial school question, the constitution guaranteed that students would receive religious instruction in accordance with the tenets of their confession, while permitting teachers and parents to opt out. Moreover, churches would remain "public corporations," retaining the right to collect revenue through state taxes. While any religious group could apply for this status, the provision favored the Protestant and Catholic churches, which had been organized as public bodies in the German Empire.[17] As a whole, the legal arrangement was consonant with a German tradition of church–state partnership rather than French state secularism or American church–state separation, let alone Soviet atheism.

Despite this favorable settlement, the republic received at best a lukewarm endorsement by Protestant pastors and church leaders. Many resigned themselves to working within the new constitutional order, defending the privileges they retained while recognizing that closer integration with a state that no longer recognized itself as Christian was neither possible nor desirable. This hardly meant principled support of democracy, the stance of only a minority.[18] Instead the Protestant clergy formed a key constituency of the conservative nationalists for whom the widely reviled Versailles Treaty discredited the republic altogether. Reluctantly ratified by the National Assembly in June 1919, the treaty stripped Germany of its colonies along with 13 percent of its European territory, demanded billions of marks in reparations to the Allies, and compelled Germans to accept sole responsibility for the war. The Berlin pastor Otto Dibelius spoke for many of his counterparts in a 1921 tract denouncing Allied hypocrisy: "Under the pretext of the nationality principle and the right of self-determination of peoples, everything was taken away from the defeated states that could be taken away . . . And all of this as a rule without in any way asking the people, whose right of self-determination was so loudly proclaimed to the world, its own wishes."[19]

The influence of Dibelius and likeminded Protestant nationalists was compounded by an ironic twist of fate. Several leading prewar Protestant liberals, including the politician Friedrich Naumann, theologian Ernst Troeltsch, and sociologist Max Weber, died in the republic's early years before reaching the age of sixty.[20] The intellectual life of German Protantism

A CHURCH IN CRISIS   27

devolved to a younger generation, whose formative experience was that of national defeat.

The Crisis in Theology

"Your concepts were strange to us, always strange," wrote the Lutheran theologian Friedrich Gogarten in a 1920 manifesto published in the leading journal of liberal theology, *Die Christliche Welt.* "Where we heard you, we heard the best and truest of intentions, but they sounded hollow, hollow, to our ears ... We could not find ourselves (we sought ourselves in you—we did indeed) and you left us empty ... We received much that was scholarly, much that was interesting, but nothing that would have been worthy of this word."[21] Born in 1887, Gogarten exemplified the generational rupture that would transform Protestant theology in post-1918 Germany. A student of the liberal theologians Adolf von Harnack and Ernst Troeltsch before the war, Gogarten belonged to a group of young pastors and theologians who assailed liberal Protestantism for its unwarranted optimism about human progress and its seamless integration of religion and culture. Gogarten would soon become a leading figure in the intellectual revolt that transformed not only theological debate but also the response by a cohort of influential pastors to the political revolution.[22]

The giant of the new theology was indisputably Karl Barth, whose trajectory demonstrates the profound impact of the war. Born in Basel in 1886 and trained in both Switzerland and Germany, Barth had absorbed critiques of liberal theology well before 1914. As a student, Barth was drawn to the teachings of the heterodox Marburg theologian Wilhelm Herrmann, who cut against the grain of the period's dominant historicist theologies. Led by the liberal Heidelberg theologian Ernst Troeltsch, the "history of religions" school represented the apex of nineteenth-century rational-critical methods, rejecting claims to supernatural revelation and insisting on a historical analysis of early Christianity. Herrmann countered with a radical alternative: The truths of Christianity were not historical, dependent on the evolution of a particular people, but absolute, grasped by the believer through the experience of revelation.[23]

The war would spur Barth's most creative period. Although he likely exaggerated in tracing his final break with liberal theology to the October 1914 pro-war appeal of German intellectuals—only three of Barth's teachers signed the document—it was during the war that Barth moved decisively beyond the premises of historicist biblical criticism.[24] As a pastor at the working-class Swiss parish of Safenwil, Barth was politically sympathetic to the religious socialist movement around the theologian Leonhard Ragaz, who called on Christians to join with anti-war socialists and pacifists. Yet Barth came to perceive in religious socialism an error analogous to the nationalist theologies that promised a divinely willed German victory. Both, Barth believed, conflated Christian revelation and human history, yoking the Christian message of salvation to a political agenda. From his confrontation with wartime theologies, Barth reached a radical conclusion: Christian faith had to be purified of worldly impulses. Even Wilhelm Herrmann's appeal to experience introduced a subjective element into knowledge of God that vitiated the objective truth of revelation.[25]

Barth took the decisive step in his landmark commentary on Paul's Epistle to the Romans, first published in December 1918 and reissued in a thoroughly revised edition in early 1922. The text won Barth a professorship at the University of Göttingen before his later moves to Münster and Bonn, launching his career at the forefront of European Protestant theology. The work's fundamental message, radicalized in the second edition, expressed the conclusion Barth had reached during the war: A vast epistemic gulf separated divinity from humanity. Appealing to the Danish theologian Søren Kierkegaard, who had confronted the progenitors of liberal theology in the mid-nineteenth century, Barth rejected the liberal characterization of the Bible as a document of humanity's religious illumination meant to be verified through historical methods. Instead, Scripture stood as a repository of divine revelation. This revelation occurred only in the moment of Christ's resurrection, standing outside history to constitute a "breakthrough" in time. The great error of liberal theology, Barth argued, was to conflate the human being's religious experience, which remained subject to the limits of human knowledge and perception, with the authentic event of divine self-disclosure.[26] Still, God's absolute otherness did not imply a divine retreat from the world: "What Kierkegaard called the 'infinite qualitative distinction' between time and eternity . . . possess[es] negative as well as positive significance."[27] God's revelation negated the present human world but also affirmed humanity through the promise of salvation. These tensions—between fallenness and salvation, the impossibility and necessity of speaking of the divine, God's "No" and "Yes" to humanity—formed the dialectical motor of Barth's early writings.[28]

The political implications of Barth's Weimar-era writings have been subject to controversy since the republic's demise. According to his critics, the

A CHURCH IN CRISIS　　　29

Swiss pastor's "dialectical theology," as contemporaries termed Barth's movement, joined a litany of radical intellectual currents that refused the values of compromise and pluralism necessary to sustain a liberal democracy.[29] Barth's defenders, in contrast, warn against mistaking Barth's critique of liberal theology for hostility toward liberal democratic politics. Instead they point toward Barth's lifelong sympathy for Social Democracy and his private disagreements with his Göttingen colleagues—above all the ultranationalist Lutheran theologian Emanuel Hirsch, whose political diatribes advanced the "stab-in-the-back" myth that blamed domestic saboteurs for the lost war. Barth would later attribute his reluctance to publicly criticize Hirsch to his status as a Swiss citizen, an explanation that carries some weight in light of the nationalist climate at German universities. On the most charitable reading, Barth emphasized the disjuncture between salvation and human works in order to deny the redemptive pretensions of secular politics and thereby encourage sober acceptance of the Weimar Republic.[30]

Barth's own dialectical approach provides a key to unlocking this impasse. Rejecting both a total separation of faith and politics as well as their total equation, Barth's *Epistle to the Romans* held that political engagement remained part of a responsible Christian life, even if it did not bring salvation. In his commentary on chapter 13 of Paul's Epistle, which famously enjoins Christians to "be subject to the governing authorities," Barth followed Paul's condemnation of political resistance, even against an illegitimate ruler. God had denied the righteousness of the human world; for human beings to overthrow their government was to take God's task upon themselves, an act that could lead only to an equally unjust order. God's simultaneous affirmation of humanity was expressed not through political revolution but in the timeless event of revelation.[31] Christians could participate in the life of the state, Barth concluded, but with a view to the limits of worldly politics. Suspicious of revolutionary energies of any political stripe, Barth's theology hardly lent itself to agitation against the Weimar Republic. He was a theological, not a political, radical.

Still, to suggest that Barth deployed theology to defend the Weimar Republic goes too far. The heterogeneity of the circle he attracted points instead toward a movement whose theological preoccupations obscured questions of politics, to the point that outright detractors of the republic were not barred from participating. The editor of dialectical theology's central organ, *Zwischen den Zeiten* (Between the times), was a stalwart of the monarchist German National People's Party. The journal's contributors included writers active on opposite sides of the political spectrum: the religious socialists Günther Dehn and Alfred de Quervain, as well as Emanuel Hirsch and the future National Socialist philosopher Alfred Bäumler.[32] Other members of Barth's circle abjured politics altogether. One of Barth's closest colleagues at the University of Bonn was the church historian and theologian Ernst Wolf, who joined the faculty in 1931 at age twenty-nine. Wolf's early publications centered on the young Martin Luther, in whom Wolf found a precursor to Barth's call for a return to the bedrock truths of revelation. At no point before 1933 did Wolf address whether such a call entailed political consequences.[33] What united Barth's disparate circle was the promise of a return to the authentic Reformation message after centuries of syncretism.

For some of Barth's followers, moreover, dialectical theology dovetailed directly with hostility toward liberal democracy. The young Lutheran theologian Hans Joachim Iwand, who commenced a lifelong friendship with Barth after the two met in late 1924, aligned with far-right currents of the Weimar-era youth movement. As a theology student in Breslau, Iwand had participated in the Kapp Putsch of 1920, an attempted coup d'état by the paramilitary Freikorps; he later joined the anti-Catholic Protestant League.[34] At the height of Weimar's political crisis, Iwand would take to the pages of the ultranationalist *Jungnationale Stimmen* (Young national voices) to issue a Barth-inspired critique of liberal theology.[35] The Bavarian-born theology student Helmut Gollwitzer, who joined Barth's seminar at Bonn in 1930, later recalled that dialectical theology had appealed to his classmates because it embodied "the clash of generations, the youth against the establishment." Gollwitzer himself had spent a decade in the nationalist youth movement, including a stint in the Nazi paramilitary stormtroopers. Upon beginning his studies in Bonn, Gollwitzer left his youth organization and quickly moved toward the political left. Still, he acknowledged that "the irrationalism to which the youth movement also paid homage disposed us toward the paradoxes of the new theology, even before we could recognize its objective necessity on biblical grounds."[36] Dialectical theology's irreverence for tradition appealed to the same sense of disillusionment that sparked antidemocratic radicalisms.

To be sure, Barth himself never voiced opposition to the Weimar Republic, and *Zwischen den Zeiten* did not publish articles calling for the overthrow of democracy. Barth's closest young followers, including Gollwitzer, Iwand, and Wolf, went on to join the Nazi-era Confessing Church and spearheaded movements for the expansion of constitutional rights in post-1945 West Germany. Nevertheless, in the context of the 1920s, dialectical theology reinforced two preoccupations of Protestant nationalist politics. Resolutely opposed to Catholic theologies of mediation between God and humanity, dialectical theology's call to renew Christian authenticity resonated with long-standing Protestant polemics against political Catholicism. For some of Barth's adherents, theological anti-liberalism also bled into its political counterpart. Politically agnostic, dialectical theology provided little recourse for linking Protestant values to a democratic state.

Protestant Nationalism Reborn

Dialectical theology was hardly the only player in the intellectual field of Weimar theology. *Die Christliche Welt*, founded in 1886 by the Marburg theologian Martin Rade, remained the flagship journal of liberal Protestantism throughout the republic and a locus of intergenerational debate.[37] The theologian and philosopher Paul Tillich led a Berlin-based circle responsible for the journal *Blätter für religiösen Sozialismus*, which aimed to draw the working classes back to the church and criticized Karl Barth's abstract, otherworldly concept of revelation.[38] Yet liberal theology and religious socialism remained minority currents that found little resonance within the younger generation of Protestant theologians, and even less among the wider laity.

Instead the major challenge to Barth and his circle emerged from the right. Conservative theologians who saw their faith standing in direct opposition to the republic, rather than liberals or members of Barth's camp, found their views reflected among the Protestant rank and file. During the 1920s, churchgoing Protestants predominantly supported the conservative-nationalist German National People's Party (DNVP), Germany's second-largest party before the Nazi breakthrough in 1930.[39] The DNVP had agitated for the restoration of the monarchy at the National Assembly and voted against the Weimar Constitution. Even during two brief stints as a government coalition party in the mid-1920s, DNVP leaders insisted that their cooperation with the republic was merely pragmatic.[40]

Conservative Weimar theologians coalesced around Luther studies, a field ripe for nationalist mobilization. Revived before the war by an older generation of conservatives, including Karl Holl, Adolf Schlatter, and Reinhold Seeberg, the study of Luther's theology took inspiration from a German national hero who had espoused a hierarchical vision of social order. At the same time, younger academics of the 1920s infused Lutheran theology with the spirit of radical critique and search for utopian solutions that permeated the postwar intellectual climate.[41] In its denunciations of nineteenth-century liberalism and historicism, as well as the youth of its leading proponents, the Weimar-era Luther renaissance mirrored dialectical theology. Contemporaries of Karl Barth and Friedrich Gogarten, its protagonists called for a return to the essentials of Christianity. As the veteran military chaplain Werner Elert put the point in his 1921 tome, *The Struggle for Christianity*, the efforts of nineteenth-century liberal Protestants to amalgamate "Christianity and general spiritual life" had resulted in an anemic Christianity evacuated of faith.[42] But conservative Lutherans also revived a central idea of nineteenth-century Protestant nationalism: The church served as a source of shared values and identity, standing above divisions of ideology and class.

At the outset of the Weimar Republic, conservative Lutherans waxed nostalgic for a lost unity of throne and altar. The theologian Friedrich Brunstäd, a leading spokesperson for the DNVP, exemplified this view. Born in 1883 and trained at Heidelberg and Berlin, Brunstäd took up a professorship in 1917 at the University of Erlangen, the center of the Luther renaissance. He would be joined by Elert six years later.[43] Brunstäd's major works, *The Idea of Religion* (1922) and *Germany and Socialism* (1924), espoused a nineteenth-century vision of a "national cultural state" in which Protestantism served as a source of national unity. Such a state, constructed in the tradition of idealist philosophy rather than the "atomistic individualism" of the Enlightenment, molded its people into a shared "community of conscience" loyal to the nation rather than self-interest. The state ruled over its subjects not through brute force but by awakening their religious feelings; its authority stood "in service to values, which demand and inspire commitment."[44] For Brunstäd, the Protestant state took the form of a constitutional monarchy, which embodied the good of the whole, rather than a "representative democracy" governed by a merely numerical and easily misguided majority.[45] Speaking at the DNVP Congress in 1928, Brunstäd described his party's aspirations toward a "national, Christian, and social" state that overcame the fragmentation of Weimar politics.[46]

Brunstäd's backward-looking monarchism reached a limit, however. The prewar theologians whom Brunstäd followed had adopted Luther's doctrine of the two kingdoms to distinguish a this-worldly realm, ruled by the sword of the earthly sovereign, from the coming kingdom of God, governed solely by divine grace. God created the state to preserve order in a fallen, sinful world; Christians therefore owed obedience to worldly rulers. But prewar conservatives such as Holl, Schlatter, and Seeberg had in mind the officially Christian state of Imperial Germany, which had promoted patriarchal, conservative social policies and staunchly resisted secularism and socialism. With the German revolution and formation of a secular state—one with a socialist party in government, no less—these assumptions came into question. Simply leaving the spheres of politics, economics, and law to the governing authorities was no longer sufficient. Instead younger Lutheran theologians embraced an active view of the church's responsibility for worldly affairs.

The most influential scholar who pushed Lutheran theology toward a new, more aggressive brand of Protestant nationalism was Paul Althaus, who succeeded Brunstäd at Erlangen in 1925. Born in 1888 to a pastor's family outside Hanover, Althaus studied under Adolf Schlatter and Karl Holl before the war, imbibing his teachers' critiques of liberal theology. Althaus's formative experience, however, was his service as a military chaplain in German-occupied Łódź, where he joined the Deutscher Verein and preached to the local German minority. Althaus's wartime sermons defended Germany's eastern conquests and assailed the nation's victimization by Allied aggressors. Like many Protestant pastors, Althaus greeted the postwar republic with ambivalence. Convinced that church independence from the state presented an opportunity for the renewal of Christian faith, he nevertheless railed against the Versailles Treaty and rejected the presumption that Christians should pursue democracy and individual rights.[47]

Althaus's postwar writings addressed the same problem that confronted the dialectical theologians around Barth: How could the eternal truths of revelation be related to the contingent realm of politics, when the war had rendered established models obsolete? On the one hand, Althaus shared with Barth a suspicion of any theology that collapsed divinity and humanity onto one another. His first postwar tract, a 1921 critique of religious socialism, criticized the fallacy of seeking to realize God's kingdom on earth.[48] On the other hand, Althaus contended that radical separation, whether in the guise of the two-kingdoms theology or Barth's dichotomy between benighted human "experience" and the revelatory divine "event," was equally insufficient in the face of a secular state and increasingly unchurched society. Instead Althaus rejected an absolute disjuncture of the two realms, adopting from his teacher Adolf Schlatter the concept of divine "self-revelation" in human history. In addition to scriptural revelation, Althaus argued, God imprinted his will upon culture and institutions, such that the divine light penetrated into the fallen, human world.[49] In practice this theology allowed Althaus to claim a divine imprimatur for a conservative, patriarchal vision of social order. Protestants should seek to secure "the Christian moral idea of marriage," while women's suffrage—introduced to Germany in the Weimar Constitution—belonged to an "individualist and inorganic" conception of society.[50]

Althaus's next major work, *The Idea of the State and the Kingdom of God* (1923), continued to move in a radically nationalist and antidemocratic direction. In addition to emphasizing the divine foundations of marriage, property, law, and the state, Althaus added "nation" and "Volk" as institutions through which God revealed his will for human social organization.[51] The key linking concept was Luther's notion of the *Beruf,* or worldly "calling," through which the believer achieved his—Althaus had a male laity in mind—divinely ordained purpose. According to Althaus, God also endowed each nation with its distinct *Beruf,* a calling whose "recognition . . . can only be the thing of the few."[52] Extending the theology he had preached as a military chaplain, Althaus believed that war allowed the nation to realize its calling most fully. Nations inevitably faced conflict, leaving political leaders with the responsibility to discern whether war was justified in the fulfillment of a divine mission.[53] War remained legitimate, even necessary, so long as it was fought for the good of the people, in the conscientious judgment of the Christian statesman, and without "murderous spirit."[54]

Althaus's writings of the early 1920s did not reflect a complete break with prewar Protestant conservatism. The church's long-standing opposition to socialism, secularism, and women's equality rang through in his work. At the same time, Althaus did not call for the restoration of monarchy. Although Bismarck remained his exemplar of Christian leadership, Althaus's unapologetic militarism, and his ruminations on the divine purpose of nation and Volk, pointed the way to more overtly authoritarian alternatives.[55] By mid-decade, Althaus's strident nationalism brought him into proximity with *völkisch* organizations that promoted nationalist alternatives to institutional Christianity, such as writer Kurd Niedlich's League for the German Church and former general Erich Ludendorff's Tannenbergbund. Decrying the division of Protestants and Catholics as detrimental to national unity, völkisch associations called for a "German church" that defined membership on racial rather than confessional principles. Among their demands was the removal of the Hebrew Bible as a foreign imposition on Christian Scripture.[56]

A CHURCH IN CRISIS

35

Such calls for a radical reformulation of the faith were a bridge too far for conservative Lutherans such as Althaus. Niedlich's and Ludendorff's associations were also competitors to the institutional Protestant churches, to which academic theologians such as Althaus owed their careers. Nevertheless, Althaus's response to the völkisch challenge revealed his close affinity with the movement's racism and antisemitism. Speaking before the 1927 Kirchentag in Königsberg, the triennial lay assembly organized by the German Protestant Church Federation, Althaus maintained that the church could remain a bulwark against the völkisch movement only if Protestants recognized the legitimate concerns that motivated its adherents. The threat to the German Volk was not simply biological or racial, as the völkisch organizations believed, but political. Eugenics and racial hygiene alone could not solve Germany's problems, for the Bolshevik Revolution and spread of socialism meant that "the front line between spirit and spirit runs through our German-blooded Volk."[57] Nevertheless, the church must join the burgeoning "national struggle against foreign infiltration," which was directed not against Jewish "blood" or religion, but against "the very particular destructive and destroying urban spirit, whose carriers in the first instance are the Jewish people."[58]

The Kirchentag's concluding "Fatherland Declaration," adopted nearly unanimously by the participants and discussed in both the church and mainstream press, aimed at a similar amalgamation of Lutheran conservatism and völkisch nationalism. On the one hand, the statement was clear that the message of Christianity was universal, not to be replaced by worship of the Volk: "God is the God of all peoples, Jesus Christ the redeemer of the entire world." On the other hand, the declaration followed the theology of Althaus and other Protestant nationalists, who had argued that each people received the gospel through its own language and national culture. "We reject a cosmopolitanism that is indifferent toward its own people. Jesus our Lord, also Paul and Luther, each of them had a heart for his Volk, mourned for its misery and sin and fought for its well-being." This was not simply a paean to the equality of the world's diverse peoples before God but a call for the German church to enter the political arena on behalf of national interests. As much as the church sought "peace among peoples," so too did it "champion the freedom and right of its own people" at a time when the German "fatherland" found itself "oppressed from the outside, divided and fractured from the inside."[59] The Fatherland Declaration described not only a theory of Protestant nationalism but the attitude of German church leaders toward international cooperation. Two years earlier, the German delegation to the Stockholm conference of the ecumenical Life and Work movement had used the occasion to broadcast its grievances against the Versailles Treaty, and opposed a resolution praising the League of Nations.[60]

Like Barth's dialectical theology, the blend of Lutheranism and völkisch nationalism popularized by Althaus exerted a strong influence on the generation of Protestant students who came of age during the 1920s. Nationalist Protestant students gravitated toward the Young National League (Jungnationaler Bund). The organization conceived of itself as the vanguard of a spiritual revolution above political parties but in practice gravitated toward the antisemitic, antidemocratic extremes of the German youth movement.[61] Several authors for the group's journal, *Jungnationale Stimmen*, would rise to prominence in Protestant intellectual life in Nazi and postwar Germany, among them the Berlin law student Hans Dombois, the theologian Hans Joachim Iwand, and the young pastor Heinz-Dietrich Wendland. Wendland, a former student of Friedrich Brunstäd, opened the first issue with a manifesto that braided religious themes with revanchist nationalism in a style that became typical of the journal. German history, Wendland explained, was determined by the nation's position between East and West, the "Asiatic" Soviet Union and the "human rights" doctrines of the French Revolution. The "German idea" born of the Reformation "must be thrown into the struggle for the world," for "a Volk of pacifists means nothing in humanity, only a spiritually powerful nation."[62] For the Young National League, the church served as a seedbed not of postwar reconciliation but of nationalist commitment.

Protestant Jurisprudence between Integration and Totality

The Protestant reckoning with the place of the church in Weimar politics was not confined to theology. Lay intellectuals, in particular jurists and constitutional scholars, became critical interlocutors in the discussion. The new dialogue of theology and law, facilitated by organizations such as Friedrich Brunstäd's Protestant-Social School in Berlin and the DNVP-aligned Society for the German State, was in part pragmatic.[63] As the guarantees of the imperial system washed away, church leaders in both confessions relied on jurists, and on diplomats with legal training, to renegotiate the terms of church–state relations.[64] But the motivations ran deeper. The problem for both Karl Barth and Paul Althaus—the challenge to Christian beliefs in a world ravaged by war and revolution—was equally at stake for Protestant

A CHURCH IN CRISIS   37

constitutional theorists. For critics of parliamentary democracy among both theologians and jurists, the dysfunction of Weimar government signaled a deeper spiritual crisis. At the same time, Weimar-era exchanges laid the groundwork for a renewed dialogue of theology and law after 1945 that would shape the Protestant Church's interventions on questions of constitutional rights, and ultimately, its rapprochement with constitutional democracy.

Weimar constitutional theory saw a methodological dispute that paralleled the rupture in Protestant theology. In both disciplines, established practitioners grounded in the ideas of German liberalism confronted younger scholars disillusioned by the experience of war. This division was not only generational but political. In the legal academy, a group of older liberal jurists sought to adapt a prewar tradition of statutory positivism, which regarded valid legal procedure as the source of the law's legitimacy. For legal positivists such as Gerhard Anschütz, Hugo Preuss, and Richard Thoma—all born in the 1860s and 1870s—laws passed by the republic's elected Reichstag were by definition legitimate. The law required no further grounding than the Weimar Constitution's guarantee that "supreme power emanates from the people."[65] In contrast, a bevy of younger critics argued that the upheavals of war and revolution had given the lie to the positivist view of the law as an autonomous, self-contained system of rules. Anti-positivist constitutional scholars, including Erich Kaufmann, Carl Schmitt, and Rudolf Smend, emphasized the new constitution's internal contradictions—the tension, for instance, between the procedural guarantees of its first part and the social and economic rights adumbrated in the second. For detractors of legal positivism, the Weimar Constitution reflected a jumble of compromises that could be overcome only by locating the foundations of law outside the legal order itself. Frequently, anti-positivist jurists looked toward religion as a source of authority above democratic debate.[66]

Efforts to forge new links between law and theology were not restricted to Protestants. For German Catholics, however, the rupture of 1918 was less extreme. Not only did Catholics lack an umbilical connection to the pre-1918 German state, but Weimar-era Catholic intellectuals could draw upon a longer tradition of modern Catholic social theory. That tradition began with the 1891 social encyclical of Pope Leo XIII, *Rerum Novarum,* issued in response to Europe's rapid industrialization and burgeoning socialist movements. The encyclical spearheaded a modern revival of the social teachings of the thirteenth-century theologian Thomas Aquinas, in particular the concept of natural law. The divine law given in revelation, the encyclical taught, harmonized with the natural law discernible to human reason. From natural law flowed a second pillar of Catholic social teaching: the principle of subsidiarity. Against the centralizing impetus of the modern nation-state, Leo XIII called for the provision of social welfare to be devolved, where possible, to families, local communities, trade unions, and the church. In contrast to a rapacious capitalism or leveling socialism, *Rerum Novarum* envisioned a Catholic alternative based upon harmony and solidarity across social classes. For the pontiff, these ideals corresponded to the divine will as well as the natural ordering of human society.[67]

Catholic social teachings were put to diverse uses in the politics of the Weimar Republic. The Catholic trade union movement, well represented in the Center Party, supported social policies based on the principle of subsidiarity. Its leaders championed cooperative bargaining between workers' and employers' associations, as well as the empowerment of Catholic welfare organizations.[68] Catholic trade unionists did not reject the republic. Indeed, both *Rerum Novarum* and *Quadragesimo Anno*, the 1931 social encyclical by Pope Pius XI, made it explicit that Catholics were free to work within any political system, "provided that the proper regard is had for the requirements of justice and of the common good."[69]

Catholic detractors of the Weimar Republic, in contrast, molded Catholic social doctrine toward antidemocratic ends. Among the most prominent was Carl Schmitt, a young law professor at the University of Bonn who later gained notoriety as the Nazi regime's leading legal defender. Schmitt shared with conservative Protestants a deep hostility toward liberalism, socialism, and secularism, railing against the liberal-parliamentary state for its inability to articulate the underlying foundations of its authority. But his proposed solutions during the early 1920s contained a distinctly Catholic flair. In *Roman Catholicism and Political Form*, a 1923 essay that gained a wide reception in German Catholic intellectual circles, Schmitt hailed the Catholic Church as the sole contemporary institution to model an authentic expression of authority. The pope's claim to represent God on earth contrasted with the legitimacy gap of the liberal state and allowed the church to survive the corrosive forces of modernity.[70]

The Protestant dialogue of law and theology both mirrored and intersected with the Catholic one. Like their Catholic counterparts, conservative Protestant jurists criticized the Weimar Constitution as an assemblage of compromises that betrayed a lack of shared principles, and looked toward Christian visions of social order as an alternative basis of political legitimacy. Shared

A CHURCH IN CRISIS   39

frustrations with the secular state fostered interconfessional alliances in parliamentary politics. During the mid-1920s, Protestant DNVP and Catholic Center parliamentarians cooperated in a failed effort to pass a national school law safeguarding confessional schools and the requirement of religious instruction.[71] However, Protestant jurists also faced specific confessional constraints. Catholic social teaching invoked natural law as a code available to human reason, accessible to Christians and non-Christians alike. In contrast, both Lutheran and Reformed theology regarded human reason as corrupted by the Fall and dependent upon divine grace for illumination. Moreover, given German Protestantism's long pre-1918 association with the Prussian monarchy, conservative Protestants were more inclined to envision a "national cultural state," rather than subsidiary institutions, as the worldly guarantor of Christian values.[72]

The most significant attempt to surmount these impasses was articulated by Carl Schmitt's friend and intellectual rival, Rudolf Smend. Born in 1882 as the son of an eminent Reformed theologian, Smend progressed rapidly through his legal studies, attaining a professorship at the University of Tübingen at age twenty-nine. From his earliest writings on the high court of the Holy Roman Empire and the 1850 Prussian Constitution, Smend adapted nineteenth-century "organic" theories of the state that emphasized the primacy of historically accumulated wisdom over abstract legal principles. True to his conservative convictions, Smend spent the war defending the Prussian Constitution, including its system of three-class voting, against calls for democratic reform. In 1922 Smend took up the prestigious chair in public law at the University of Berlin, where he joined the DNVP. He also became active in lay Protestantism, serving on the synod of the Prussian Union of Churches.[73] Smend's constitutional theory offered a point of contrast to the Barth circle's indifference to questions of political form, as well as the Althaus camp's outright hostility toward the Weimar Republic. Although he remained ambivalent about parliamentary democracy during the 1920s, Smend opened a path toward a Protestant reading of the constitution that he would advance during the republic's final years and again after 1945.

Smend's Weimar-era magnum opus, the 1928 treatise *Constitution and Constitutional Law,* appeared at an inflection point in the debate about the Weimar Constitution. In the previous year Carl Schmitt had published his comprehensive *Constitutional Theory,* a text that marked Schmitt's departure from Catholic political theology and move toward authoritarian solutions. Even as he recognized the Weimar Constitution's decision for a liberal parliamentary state,

Schmitt treated the constitution's central function as the delineation of executive authority.[74] Smend, in contrast, adopted a more holistic view. Rather than taking executive power as its essence, Smend regarded the constitution as a document that expressed the unity of the state as a whole. Building on his long interest in "organic" state theories, Smend explained that the state was not made up simply of "laws, diplomatic acts, judgments, [and] administrative procedures." Instead the state was "present in these individual expressions of life only insofar as they form its spiritual unity."[75] At the core of Smend's work lay an effort to identify the means of forging a shared political community out of a heterogeneous citizenry. Smend distinguished three forms of "integration" available to the modern state: "personal" (executive authority as well as bureaucracy); "functional" (procedures such as elections and parliamentary debates); and "factual" (symbols such as flags, ceremonies, and holidays).[76] The role of the constitution was less to delineate a single moment of sovereign authority than to serve as an "integrating reality" across these disparate offices, institutions, and symbolic forms.[77]

Smend's *Constitution and Constitutional Law* did not explicitly invoke Protestantism or directly address the place of religion in the Weimar Constitution. Nevertheless, Protestant undertones infused his legal theory. Smend's emphasis on integration reflected a critique of the fragmentation of Weimar politics, which he shared with conservative Christians from both confessions. However, Smend did not appeal to supra-positive natural law or offload the task of integration onto subsidiary institutions. Instead he assigned the state the task of unifying the polity. Smend's description of the state as a "life-community" that cultivated the individual's "spiritual development" reflected his inculcation in Calvinist theology, which emphasized the individual's formation through the community of believers.[78]

More broadly, Smend shared with conservative Protestant theologians such as Friedrich Brunstäd and Paul Althaus a predilection for a strong state standing above competing ideologies and interest groups. Although Smend distanced himself from Carl Schmitt's reduction of the state to an organ of executive sovereignty, his 1928 treatise did not defend the Weimar Republic.[79] Instead Smend praised Benito Mussolini's fascist Italy for "see[ing] this necessity of all-sided integration with great clarity."[80] Authoritarian states were better poised than democracies to embody the unitary system of values that Smend viewed as the basis of political life. Parliaments served, at best, to represent "political unity" and "values that transcend the state," rather than individual rights or the will of the majority.[81]

Protestantism and Democracy at the Republic's Demise

The global economic collapse of late 1929, which in Germany culminated with one-quarter of the workforce unemployed, infused new urgency into the Protestant debate about the church's political role. Controversy over unemployment benefits precipitated the fall of the Social Democratic–led Grand Coalition government in March 1930. President Paul von Hindenburg then named the economist and Center Party politician Heinrich Brüning as German chancellor, a turning point that proved to be the beginning of the end of Weimar democracy. Unable to secure a compromise between labor leaders and industrialists, Brüning quickly came to rely on presidential emergency powers to enact unpopular budget reductions.[82] In elections of September 1930, the Nazi Party catapulted from less than 3 percent of the national vote to 18 percent at the expense of the center-right parties that backed Brüning's coalition. National Socialists saw their greatest gains in rural Protestant regions.[83] At this critical juncture, the Protestant intellectual currents that had emerged out of war and revolution—Karl Barth's dialectical theology, Paul Althaus's nationalist Lutheranism, and Rudolf Smend's theory of constitutional integration—lacked the resources to confront the threat to the republic. Clashes among these factions served instead to fragment any coalition among pastors and lay intellectuals in the face of Nazi ascendancy.

The Lutheran nationalist camp was the most vocal in greeting the challenges to the Weimar Republic. As the economic downturn reached its nadir, young Protestant nationalists grew even more bellicose in their attacks on democracy, joining a chorus of far-right critiques. "The current state, built on the ideas of 1789, must be radically overcome," declared Heinz-Dietrich Wendland in a 1931 address before the German Christian Student Union of Mannheim. True community could be realized only in an "objective authoritative order," which "the state receives beyond itself, from the unconditional link to God."[84] Writers for *Jungnationale Stimmen* effused over Hitler's rallies at the Berlin Sports Palace and determined that the Weimar Republic was not an authority Christians were bound to obey.[85]

Such ideas facilitated a further rapprochement between conservative Protestant nationalists and the völkisch movement. In a 1932 pamphlet for Berlin's Central Apologetic Institute, a branch of the German Protestant Church Federation active in the struggle against secularism, the young Lutheran theologian Walter Künneth criticized völkisch religious organizations for reducing God to the national community. Yet the proliferation of völkisch groups also spoke to their inner truth: the failure of the established churches to speak to the needs of the German people. Going beyond Paul Althaus's address at the 1927 Kirchentag, Künneth concluded that even "the völkisch call for racial hygiene and eugenics" demanded serious consideration by theologians.[86]

For Karl Barth and his circle, all of this was anathema. Instead of addressing the political dangers to the republic, however, Barth approached the Luther renaissance from the perspective of his own critique of liberal theology. On Barth's view, neo-Lutheranism recapitulated prewar liberalism's basic error of regarding history as an arena of divine revelation. Rather than acknowledge the either/or decision that revelation demanded, Paul Althaus believed the Christian could choose both divine love *and* the "elementary necessity of law and the State," both the "righteousness of God" *and* "the 'organic laws' of history."[87] At a February 1931 lecture before Berlin's Schleiermacher Hochschule, Barth unleashed a more aggressive attack against the pastor and church administrator Otto Dibelius. Appointed superintendent of the Brandenburg church province of Kurmark in 1925, Dibelius had published *The Century of the Church* to wide acclaim the following year. Released in six editions and the subject of more than one hundred reviews, Dibelius's manifesto maligned the Center Party's alliance with Social Democracy and called on the German Protestant church to restore the "conscience of the nation." This church, Dibelius effused, must remain "as God had determined it: a church in which Martin Luther is involved, in which Jesus Christ is seen with German eyes and believed with a German heart."[88] For Barth, however, Dibelius's Protestant nationalism abandoned the "essence" of gospel, a message of repentance and salvation. Dibelius celebrated the "publicity" of the church, but without asking what the church was meant to proclaim. Only a short path, Barth warned, separated Dibelius and his ilk from the idolatrous völkisch movement.[89]

Although Barth exposed the theological flaws of the revived Protestant nationalism, his alternative—restricting the church to the proclamation of salvation—offered little by way of a political response. Efforts in *Zwischen den Zeiten* to address church-based völkisch movements evinced similar limits. Barth's student Richard Karwehl declared Nazi racial ideology to be incompatible with Christian fellowship but acknowledged that the church did not align itself with any political form. Indeed, "it may be that the age of democracy in Germany will be replaced by an age of dictatorial discipline."[90] The Westphalian pastor Joachim Beckmann, who had studied theology with Barth, attacked the Nazis' "divinization of the nation" while remaining equally clear that "the Protestant confession is incompatible with the ideology of the Enlightenment."[91] Instead writers for *Zwischen den Zeiten* traced völkisch errors back to the Enlightenment and liberal theology. As late as the fall of 1932, Friedrich Gogarten took to the journal to defend "peoplehood [*Volkstum*]" as a source of mediation between church and state, while criticizing the deification of the Volk as a reflection of "the true core of liberal thought . . . the belief of human beings in themselves."[92]

Certainly the Barth circle's critique of liberal theology did not entail unthinking opposition to the Weimar Republic. In May 1931 Barth himself joined the Social Democratic Party, the final bastion of Weimar democracy.[93] But the group's theology offered little basis for a defense of the republic. What divided the circle around *Zwischen den Zeiten* from partisans of the Luther renaissance was the theological question of revelation, a competition to espouse a more authentic Christianity. Neither side engaged head-on the presidential dictatorship, erosion of parliamentary authority, or advance of the extreme right.

Like their counterparts in theology, conservative Protestant jurists embraced increasingly radical ideologies as the Weimar Republic entered its final crisis. As right-wing German Catholics looked toward the corporatist regimes of Benito Mussolini's Italy, Miguel Primo de Rivera's Spain, and Engelbert Dollfuss's Austria, Protestants found an ally in an even more uncompromising critic of liberal democracy: Carl Schmitt. By the early 1930s, Schmitt's writings treated the republic's dysfunction as symptomatic of the legitimacy gap faced by parliamentary democracy itself.[94] Schmitt's concept of the "total state," introduced in 1931, resonated with Protestant critics of the Weimar Republic. According to Schmitt, the classical liberal distinction between state and society had eroded under the conditions of twentieth-century mass democracy, in which the state increasingly intervened to manage economic life. The choice was no longer between an expansive or limited state, but between the "quantitative" total state monopolized by parties and special interests—the danger Schmitt saw in the Weimar Republic—and the "qualitative" total state that consolidated authority over questions of war and peace, while protecting the institutions of society and economy from political interference.[95]

Schmitt's ideas held deep appeal for Lutherans steeped in a theology of worldly orders overseen by a divinely ordained sovereign. In the pages of *Jungnationale Stimmen,* Heinz-Dietrich Wendland lauded Schmitt's call for overcoming "parliamentarism" and advocated for an authoritarian alternative to democracy.[96] Even the Social Democrat Otto Piper, Karl Barth's successor at Münster, used his 1931 address before the Protestant Social Congress to praise Schmitt's account of emergency authority and voice skepticism of political parties.[97] For Schmitt and his Protestant backers, the alternative to a defenseless legal positivism was not the devolution of authority to subsidiary institutions but a strong executive capable of making decisions in a crisis.

Schmitt's advocacy for the total state was not universally embraced by conservative Protestants. In the late 1920s the nationalist right wing experienced a crisis of its own. Under its new chair, the media magnate Alfred Hugenberg, the DNVP lurched to the far right and moved into open alignment with the Nazis. In December 1929, a group of Protestant DNVP parliamentarians disillusioned with this shift split off to form the Christian Social People's Service (CSVD) as a rendezvous party for a politically homeless Protestant bourgeoisie. Among its members were Protestants who would become active in democratic politics after 1945, including the young lawyer Gustav Heinemann.[98] Yet in the overheated politics of the early 1930s, the CSVD found little resonance. The party gained only 14 (of nearly 600) Reichstag seats in September 1930, and just 3 in July 1932. Its calls for spiritual renewal were too tepid to win over unchurched workers; middle-class Protestant voters increasingly shifted from the conservative and liberal parties to the Nazis.[99] Moreover, Protestant politicians and religious leaders alike criticized the CSVD for violating a core tenet of Protestant nationalism: The confession formed the backbone of the nation as a whole, not a political interest group smacking of clericalism.[100]

Rudolf Smend shared this concern. Although he too left the DNVP in 1930, in protest against the party's authoritarian direction, the leading Protestant voice in Weimar constitutional debates declined to join the CSVD. Instead Smend outlined a defense of the republic that harmonized with his theory of constitutional integration, and ultimately shared the premises of Protestant nationalist ideology. In early 1932, Smend contributed an essay on "Protestantism and Democracy" to a volume by leading academics, writers, and civil servants defending Brüning's cabinet as the government stood on its last legs. In what was Smend's first explicit defense of democracy, the essay emphatically rejected Carl Schmitt's theory of the total state. But Smend defined democracy in restrictive terms reminiscent of the homogeneous and hierarchical society envisioned by Althaus, Brunstäd, and Dibelius. Eschewing Catholic "natural law" as a front for "papal politics," as well as the CSVD— hardly representative of "the diversity of all German Protestantism"—Smend instead defined the Protestant confession as a repository of values for the polity as a whole.[101] Protestants could represent the general interest of the nation, Smend argued, precisely because they lacked a party on the model of the Center Party. Not a political or legal doctrine, Protestantism was instead "a diffuse element, spread and effective through all spiritual, political, and religious circles in contemporary Germany." It alone could provide the "measure of spiritual homogeneity that is the prerequisite of an inwardly adopted democracy."[102]

Smend recognized the desperation of the moment. In a subtle rebuke to his friend and intellectual sparring partner, he sent Carl Schmitt a copy of the essay with a laconic note: "A tired product, full of crises!"[103] Decades later Schmitt would observe that the tract lacked a positive solution, instead reflecting a mere critique of the existing political situation.[104] This observation was correct—Smend not only eschewed the total state but avoided calls for a broad-based anti-Nazi coalition that included the Social Democrats, the only realistic possibility for salvaging Weimar democracy by the spring of 1932. Although Smend would not follow Schmitt to become a Nazi supporter, significant overlap remained between the two jurists during the crisis years of the republic. Both insisted that democracy rested on a basis of uniformity: for Smend, religious and cultural; for Schmitt, increasingly ethnic and racial. Only after the Nazi defeat would Smend reframe his political Protestantism as a defense of constitutional rights rather than an apologia for cultural homogeneity.

Smend found a rare ally in the thirty-one-year-old jurist Gerhard Leibholz, a young professor at the University of Göttingen and a rising star in constitutional law. Born in 1901 to upper-middle-class converts from Judaism, Leibholz studied with Smend in the mid-1920s and adopted his mentor's theory of constitutional integration. Leibholz's early publications developed a staunch defense of judicial review, on the grounds that a strong judiciary was crucial for defending the constitution's foundational values of liberty and political equality.[105] For Leibholz, these values were rooted in a religious basis that transcended the positive law. In a November 1932 lecture, Leibholz followed Smend in attributing the crisis of democracy to the Weimar Constitution's "break with the connection to Protestantism" on which prewar German parliamentarism had rested.[106] Myths such as Schmitt's total state arose to fill the spiritual void left by the secularization of European politics, yet invariably led to despotism. Instead Leibholz proposed a revival of Protestantism, with its "powerful religious-metaphysical foundation for ideas of freedom and personality," as a prophylactic against the "development of a mythical-total state." The "Protestant state" was "a state conscious of its boundaries," which safeguarded profession, family, and church without claiming transcendent authority.[107]

Smend and Leibholz cut through the lines of Protestant political debate, eschewing both the disavowal of politics by the circle around *Zwischen den Zeiten* and the attack on parliamentary democracy advanced by Lutherans like Paul Althaus and Heinz-Dietrich Wendland. Instead these jurists affirmed the salience of Protestantism as a source of shared political values, while rejecting the instrumentalization of theology to endow the state with "religious-absolute" authority.[108] However, their concept of democracy overlapped with authoritarian alternatives. Rather than advocating for a state that could accommodate a plurality of ideologies and social groups, Smend and Leibholz presupposed cultural uniformity as a prerequisite for democracy. Both favored collective integration around pre-political institutions over individual rights. Ultimately Smend and Leibholz shared the animating assumption of Protestant proponents of the total state, one that seemed only too obvious in the face of the republic's paralysis—that liberal democracy could not withstand the conflicts of the modern age.

KARL BARTH, PAUL ALTHAUS, AND RUDOLF SMEND did not represent the entirety of Protestant social thought in the Weimar Republic, nor the weight of lay opinion. Nevertheless, each spearheaded a novel current that critically shaped twentieth-century debates about the role of the church in the political world. These debates were transformed with the dramatic events of early 1933. On January 30, following the collapse of the Brüning cabinet and the short-lived chancellorships of archconservatives Franz von Papen and Kurt von Schleicher, President Hindenburg appointed Adolf Hitler as German chancellor at the helm of a Nazi-DNVP coalition. The military and business elites who negotiated the deal notoriously believed they could control Hitler's movement. But the total state that arrived proved radically different from the bastion of stability envisioned by conservative Protestant nationalists. The visions for the church advanced by Barth, Althaus, and Smend during the Weimar era—of disentanglement from worldly concerns, partnership with a Christian authoritarian state, and representation of shared political values— could hardly be realized under the Nazi dictatorship. Instead, fresh debates about the sources of state authority and the limits of obedience would give rise, already by the late 1930s, to narratives of Protestant anti-Nazi resistance, laying the foundation for a new set of postwar myths.

CHAPTER TWO

FROM THE TOTAL STATE TO THE LIMITS OF OBEDIENCE

"BECAUSE YOU BELIEVE, we too want to believe; because you fight, we too want to fight so that the sun may rise again over Germany." Spoken by the Protestant pastor Joachim Hossenfelder at Berlin's St. Mary's Church, before a packed congregation of over 2,000, these words expressed the aspirations of Germany's most ardent Protestant nationalists four days after Adolf Hitler's appointment as chancellor.[1] In the ensuing weeks, the Nazi stormtroopers (Sturmabteilung; SA) and newly deputized auxiliary police arrested and detained thousands of Communists and Social Democrats, raiding their homes, offices, and gathering places. President Hindenburg announced emergency decrees that banned criticism of the new regime and curtailed the civil liberties guaranteed under the Weimar Constitution. When the Nazi-led government was confirmed in national elections of March 5—neither free nor fair, held under the watchful eye of the newly minted Gestapo—the Brandenburg church superintendent Otto Dibelius greeted the regime in an enthusiastic letter to his subordinates. "What a contrast between the new parliament and . . . the National Assembly of Weimar! There will be only very few of us who do not celebrate this turn with all our hearts."[2] The Berlin pastor Martin Niemöller, who voted for the Nazi Party on the morning of March 5, returned to his parish in suburban Dahlem to deliver a sermon heralding the church's role in the national revival. The nation's "outward rise and inward health," Niemöller declared, depended on the "fateful connection of peoplehood [*Volkstum*] and Christianity."[3]

In the heady days of early 1933, the statements of Hossenfelder, Dibelius, and Niemöller gave voice to the far-reaching enthusiasm across Protestant

Germany. Having outperformed in Protestant regions in 1932, Hitler's party was widely welcomed by pastors and lay churchgoers as a solvent to the economic blight, cultural decline, and diplomatic humiliation associated with the Weimar Republic. Many greeted the Nazi takeover as a catalyst of religious revival, the alliance of church and Volk heralded by Protestant nationalists since the collapse of the German Empire. At least in the early months of 1933, such hopes appeared to be realized. Following years of declining membership, the Protestant churches gained 325,000 new members in 1933 alone. Enthusiastic pastors organized mass weddings of party members complete with SA banners, lending a Christian imprimatur to the new regime.[4]

This early show of unity would not last. As the regime pursued its vision of "coordinating" the church under state auspices, pastors and parishioners quickly divided into competing factions. Hossenfelder, Dibelius, and Niemöller emerged as leaders in what contemporaries termed the "church struggle" (*Kirchenkampf*). Hossenfelder was the early head of the pro-Nazi German Christian movement; Dibelius served as a church administrator who sought out a cautious approach to the regime; Niemöller became a fierce opponent of Nazi church policy and founder of the Confessing Church who would spend seven years in concentration camps.

To be sure, the contest between these groups did not entail a political struggle against the Nazi state. Since critical scholarship on the Nazi-era churches took off in the 1980s, historians have roundly rejected that conceit. Instead scholars have shown how the church struggle involved a conflict for leadership *within* German Protestantism, driven less by opposition to the regime than by internal rivalries. Divided on questions of theology and church organization, all sides hastened to stress their political loyalty.[5] Aid to Jews and to Christians of Jewish descent was carried out only at the margins of organized Protestantism, disproportionately by laywomen with little support from church authorities.[6] A small number of theologians and lay intellectuals participated in the military conspiracy to overthrow the Nazi regime, but this effort came late in the war without the backing of the institutional churches.

In this chapter, I concur with the scholarly consensus against hagiographic narratives of Confessing Church resistance. At the same time, I locate the contest to define the place of the church in the new political order on a longer chronological arc than is typical of studies of the church conflict. Scholars have suggested that the churches' accommodationist stance under Nazism brought the Protestant nationalist tradition to a dead end by 1945, demanding a rethinking of the Protestant relationship to the German state and nation.[7] Instead I argue that such a rethinking commenced already during the mid-1930s, but in conformity with, rather than in conflict against, long-standing assumptions of German Protestant nationalism. As hopes for a Nazi-inspired religious renewal soured, Protestant intellectuals representing a range of theological positions—not only the small group around Karl Barth but also members of the Confessing Church's conservative Lutheran wing—re-imagined Christian conscience as a bulwark against overreaching state power. But this new vision did not entail the rejection of deep-rooted anti-semitism, anti-Catholicism, or hostility toward liberal democracy. Protestant plans for post-Nazi Germany continued to frame the Protestant confession as a source of shared political values that transcended the divisions of class, party, and ideology, a core tenet of the Protestant nationalist tradition.

Likewise, I argue that the myth of Protestant anti-Nazi resistance was not simply a post-1945 creation, retrofitted to gloss over a compromised past, but a product of the Nazi era itself. The contacts of the Confessing Church in the international ecumenical movement played critical roles in formulating this myth, reinterpreting limited statements of discontent with Nazi church policy as broadsides against the regime. In turn, ecumenical Protestants shaped the self-perceptions of Confessing Church leaders. By the final years of the war, as German defeat appeared inevitable, underground Protestant circles asserted that a basic incompatibility between Christianity and National Socialism had been present from the outset. Armed with the conviction of their own resistance, theologians and lay intellectuals who had begun their careers during the Weimar Republic, and navigated the pressures of the Nazi era, claimed an expansive public role immediately upon the onset of the postwar Allied occupation. Twelve years of Nazi rule led to not the dethroning of Protestant nationalism but its recasting.

Orders of God and the Total State

In the early months and years of Nazi rule, the debate about the church's response to the national revolution fractured along the lines of the Weimar era. For Protestant conservatives who had participated in the interwar Luther renaissance and welcomed the republic's demise, the total state remained a key concept. The Nazi state appeared to promise what Carl Schmitt had described as the "qualitative" total state: a state that consolidated absolute authority in order to establish clear boundaries between politics and society and safeguard institutions such as church, marriage, and family. Schmitt's student Ernst Forsthoff, the son of a Lutheran pastor who joined the leadership of the German Christians, defined the total state for the Nazi era in a widely circulated text of May 1933: a state anchored in both an "order of authority" that divided rulers from the ruled, as well as an "order of the people" that established a racially homogeneous community.[8] Theologians and lay intellectuals who had adapted a Protestant theory of the total state since the early 1930s revised their Weimar-era theologies only slightly to interpret the Nazi revolution through the language of Protestant nationalism.

The Erlangen theologian Paul Althaus remained the pacesetter among conservative Protestant nationalists. His *The German Hour of the Church*, published in October 1933 and then in two more editions during its first year in print, built on his Weimar-era theology of "self-revelation" to lay the foundations for a political theology of the Nazi state.[9] Divine revelation in human history, Althaus wrote, represented "the testimony of the living God in the reality of historical life." Althaus described fatherhood, motherhood, and state, as well as Volk, Führer, and fatherland, as "orders of God," instruments through which individuals experienced the divine presence in the human world.[10] Althaus's metaphor of "orders" resonated with an emergent corpus by pro-Nazi intellectuals across the humanistic disciplines seeking to demonstrate their usefulness for the new regime.[11] At the same time, Althaus's effort to perceive a divine will behind the Nazi takeover reflected the nationalist, antidemocratic convictions that had animated Protestant attacks on the Weimar Republic. The following year Althaus would describe the "totalitarian features" of the Nazi state as a "therapeutic intervention" to rescue the German Volk in its time of need—that is, as anything other than a threat to Christianity.[12] The "total state" should be welcomed inasmuch as it overcame the "anomie in the liberal state" and supported "the life of the people according to God's will."[13]

Althaus's synthesis appealed to younger Protestant pastors who had participated in nationalist youth organizations during the Weimar Republic. In the first phase of the church conflict, this group coalesced around the Young Reformation movement. Founded in May 1933 by Walter Künneth, the director of the Central Apologetic Institute in Berlin, and Hanns Lilje, a leader in the International Christian Student Federation, the movement emphasized the centrality of a strong church for national revival. While rejecting radical assaults on church doctrine by the German Christians, this group largely shared the Nazis' politics. The Young Reformation movement's most outspoken figure, the forty-one-year-old Berlin pastor Martin Niemöller, exemplified its accommodationist stance. A decorated naval veteran who had participated in the paramilitary Freikorps and far-right student organizations during the early 1920s, Niemöller backed the conservative-nationalist DNVP before voting for the Nazi Party in March 1933.[14] The Königsberg theology lecturer Hans Joachim Iwand, a close ally of Niemöller who organized the opposition against the German Christians in East Prussia, was similarly a Freikorps veteran and ultranationalist critic of the Weimar Republic.[15]

Walter Künneth, the intellectual leader of the Young Reformation movement, laid out a theology of Protestant nationalism for the Nazi state in *The Nation before God*, a collective volume by young Protestant nationalists that went through five editions between 1933 and 1937. The first edition, published in June 1933, appeared as the Nazi suppression of the political left reached an apex. Künneth neglected the rampant SA violence and makeshift concentration camps that characterized the early months of Nazi rule, instead defending the regime. Künneth's opening essay characterized marriage, family, state, and profession as divine "orders of preservation." Echoing Paul Althaus, Künneth maintained that the Volk also constituted such an order: The "fateful integration and differentiation of humanity into peoples and races" manifested "the will of God." Therefore, Künneth continued, the "principled Yes of the church to the 'national revolution'" followed from "the question of the order of God."[16] The Heidelberg theologian Heinz-Dietrich Wendland, an activist in the Weimar-era Young National League, explained in his contribution that Christians preferred an "authoritarian" state that stood "in a relationship of responsibility and service to the other orders: marriage and family, education and profession, nationhood and scholarship." Only such a state preserved community and guarded against the human tendency toward self-destruction.[17]

Beyond their hostility toward liberalism and democracy, shared antisemitism formed another means for Künneth's circle to prove its loyalty to the new regime. In a chapter titled "The Jewish Problem and the Church," Künneth supported legislation of April 1933 that banned Germans with at least one Jewish grandparent from employment in the Reich civil service. Künneth parroted Nazi logic: The dismissal of Jews from the German civil service was merely compensation for Jews' long-standing overrepresentation in prominent positions, which threatened "the foreign infiltration of German public life." Künneth's antisemitism was not only a matter of personal prejudice but followed from a political theology that defined race and nationhood as divinely endowed orders. The Nazi effort to safeguard "the unique characteristics of the German people," Künneth declared, "is to be greeted by the church in accordance with its Yes to the orders of God."[18]

The pro-Nazi apologias produced by Künneth and like-minded theologians proved equally appealing to lay Protestant intellectuals, above all jurists, who had drawn on theology in their attacks against the Weimar Republic.[19] Beginning with its third edition, Künneth's *The Nation before God* included the inaugural lecture of Erik Wolf, a young professor of criminal law at the University of Freiburg handpicked as dean of the law faculty by the pro-Nazi rector Martin Heidegger.[20] Wolf's December 1933 lecture took up the problem that had preoccupied Protestant jurists during the Weimar Republic: the inadequacy of both legal positivist and natural law doctrines for defining the purpose and legitimacy of the state. For Wolf, National Socialism opened a path beyond these alternatives. Rather than treating law as the realization of abstract principles—whether legal procedure or pre-political norms—Nazism rooted law in the "existence" of the "German *Volksgemeinschaft* [national community] in which we live." Wolf's conclusion echoed the defense of the authoritarian state proffered by Künneth and Wendland. The role of the church was not to establish "supra-state law" but to preserve the divinely mandated institutions of "marriage, family, and community as fundamental elements of the order of the Volk." A "fundamentally necessary connection between National Socialism and Christianity" resided in their common mission to defend the divine orders of "race and peoplehood."[21] For Wolf as much as his counterparts among theologians, no daylight could come between Protestantism and Nazism.

Preserving Christian Purity

The early enthusiasm for the Nazi state by conservative Protestant nationalists went largely unreciprocated. For the Nazi Party's paganist faction, led by the ideologue Alfred Rosenberg, Christianity was irredeemably corrupted by its Jewish origin, to be replaced by a völkisch religion based on the principle of racial purity. Many Nazi elites, in contrast, believed that Christian faith, if not the institutional churches, had an important role to play in the new Germany. Point 24 of the Nazi Party program, which remained official doctrine down to 1945, described the party's allegiance to a "positive Christianity" that "does not bind itself in the matter of creed to any particular confession" and "combats the Jewish-materialist spirit."[22] The twin goals of positive Christianity—overcoming the confessional divide and excluding Jews from German life—resonated with the sensibilities of many Protestant nationalists.

But this was Christianity on the Nazis' terms. For all the credibility that right-wing intellectuals provided the regime during its early months, party leaders demanded the ruthless subordination of the institutions of German society, even sympathetic conservative ones. The Catholic Church and Protestant regional churches, to which 95 percent of Germans belonged in 1933, were potential sources of independent moral authority and therefore prime targets of Nazi "coordination."[23] Assurances by the Young Reformation movement that church independence would serve the state and Volk were of little use to the regime.

The party's attempt to contain the churches proved straightforward on the Catholic side. During the spring of 1933, Vice Chancellor Franz von Papen negotiated a Concordat with Vatican foreign minister Eugenio Pacelli, the future Pope Pius XII, modeled on a similar treaty between the Holy See and Mussolini's Italy. Concluded on July 20, the so-called Reich Concordat guaranteed the existence of Catholic confessional schools, religious instruction, and welfare associations in the Nazi state. In exchange, the Catholic hierarchy agreed to a prohibition on clerical political activity. The Center Party had dissolved itself two weeks earlier, the final such act of self-destruction by a democratic party before Hitler's official ban on non-Nazi parties. The Vatican's unitary structure and fervent anti-Communism facilitated this swift rapprochement. A minority of Catholic priests attempted to synthesize Catholic and National Socialist ideas and even joined the Nazi Party; others welcomed the Concordat in the hope that the church could retain its traditional privileges and continue its work unimpeded. Although German Catholics had voted for the Nazi Party in smaller proportion than their Protestant counterparts, the regime's promise to overcome class and confessional conflicts in a shared *Volksgemeinschaft*—and not least, the collapse of political alternatives—proved sufficient for many German Catholics to make their peace with the new authorities.[24]

No such agreement was forthcoming with German Protestantism, divided into twenty-eight regional churches of Lutheran, Reformed, and United denominations. The state's first aim was to form a national Protestant church that aligned with Nazi goals, a move welcomed by Walter Künneth and his allies. The terms of church unification, however, proved controversial. The regime initially backed the German Christian movement, a group of Protes-

FROM THE TOTAL STATE TO THE LIMITS OF OBEDIENCE

tant pastors and laypeople formed in the summer of 1932 that fused a racially defined Christianity with loyalty to the Nazi Party. The German Christians shared the antisemitism of the völkisch religious organizations that had sprung up in the 1920s, including the rejection of the Hebrew Bible as a "Jewish" text. Following Hitler's appointment as chancellor, the German Christian movement quickly outgrew its precursors, ballooning to encompass 600,000 members and one-third of the Protestant clergy at its peak in late 1933.[25]

The most bitter point of disagreement involved German Christian efforts to implement an "Aryan paragraph" in church constitutions. Following the passage of the Nazi civil service law in April 1933, some German Christian leaders demanded the adoption of parallel legislation in the church. "Non-Aryans"—which the Nazi law defined to encompass not only Jews but baptized Christians of Jewish descent—would be excluded from serving as pastors and church officials.[26] The Young Reformation movement rejected the proposal, not out of principled opposition to antisemitism but on the supersessionist doctrines that had long guided the Protestant mission to the Jews. As Martin Niemöller put the point in the movement's newly founded journal, *Junge Kirche,* the admission of converted Jews into the church bespoke the validity of God's promise of salvation for Israel.[27] Dietrich Bonhoeffer, a young lecturer in theology at the University of Berlin, was a lone voice suggesting that the imposition of the Aryan paragraph might lead the church into political opposition. Bonhoeffer's time as a visiting student at New York's Union Theological Seminary during the early 1930s had provided him with an alternative model of Christian social engagement. He was unique among German Protestant theologians in stressing the state's responsibility for protecting individual rights. Still, at this stage even Bonhoeffer addressed only threats to the integrity of the church and to baptized Christians of Jewish descent, not Nazi antisemitism as such.[28]

Conflict between the church factions spiked in the summer of 1933, just after the publication of Künneth's *The Nation before God.* In late June the Young Reformation movement's candidate for the new position of Reich bishop, the pastor and Inner Mission leader Friedrich von Bodelschwingh, resigned from consideration under pressure from the Prussian Ministry of Culture. During July church elections, intensive voter mobilization and propaganda campaigns by Nazi officials secured the appointment of German Christians to majorities in local synods throughout Prussia. At the Prussian General Synod meeting on September 5, German Christian delegates donned

SA uniforms to appoint the Nazi-backed naval pastor Ludwig Müller as Reich bishop, "with quasi-dictatorial powers." Müller quickly set about establishing a national church under German Christian auspices, reaching shotgun agreements with regional churches throughout Northern and Eastern Germany to secure their incorporation into the Prussian structure. German Christians implemented the Aryan paragraph in each church they took over.[29]

Karl Barth became the theological lodestar of the opposition to the German Christian takeover. While the extent to which Barth privately rejected the Nazi regime has been hotly debated, the concerns of his Weimar-era dialectical theology, rather than political opposition to Nazi dictatorship, shaped his earliest published responses.[30] For Barth, the rise of Nazism confirmed the urgency of purifying the church from worldly ideologies. In his first statement on the church conflict, published in *Zwischen den Zeiten* in July 1933, Barth recapitulated the charge he had laid out against Paul Althaus and Otto Dibelius during the Weimar years: Völkisch Christianities, with their immanent theology of divine revelation in German history, were continuous with the errors of prewar liberal theology. A national Reich Church, Barth argued, would become a political body subordinated to the state, while a Reich bishop was a political office, not an ecclesiastical one.[31] If German Christians sought to replace the gospel with Nazi ideology, the Young Reformation movement offered only half measures: "a new, perpetual adjustment and compromise (Creation *and* Redemption, Nature *and* Grace, Nationalism *and* Gospel)."[32] Notably, Barth did not address the regime's anti-Jewish legislation, even though his essay was published three months after the civil service law and a spate of antisemitic ordinances that followed it.

Barth rightly recognized that the Young Reformation movement, at the outset of the Nazi regime, was an accommodationist group sharing little with his own call for Christian purification. Yet as the German Christian takeover continued, Barth's call for resolute theological opposition gained traction. In September 1933 Martin Niemöller and his Berlin colleague Gerhard Jacobi formed the Pastors' Emergency League (PEL), a new initiative to halt the German Christians that quickly expanded to include 6,000 pastors. By February 1934 pastors and lay congregants from throughout the Rhineland met in Barmen as a free Protestant synod, quickly merging with the PEL—the first step toward the formation of the Confessing Church.[33] Lutheran bishops Hans Meiser of Bavaria, August Marahrens of Hanover, and Theophil Wurm

FROM THE TOTAL STATE TO THE LIMITS OF OBEDIENCE 57

Figure 2.1. Reich Bishop Ludwig Müller (front row, center) and other members of the Protestant clergy, escorted by SS guards, at the synod of the Protestant Reich Church in Wittenberg, September 27, 1933. The Castle Church, where Martin Luther is believed to have posted his ninety-five theses in 1517, is visible in the background. Süddeutsche Zeitung Photo / Alamy Stock Photo

of Württemberg, whose churches had avoided coordination into Müller's Reich Church, declined to side with Niemöller and the PEL for fear of losing their own independence.[34] The bishops of the "intact" Lutheran churches would lead a third faction in the church conflict unaligned with either the German Christian movement or the PEL. Still, cooperation among the groups opposed to the German Christians remained possible. On April 22 Bishop Meiser read out a statement at a church service in the Württemberg town of Ulm. The entire spectrum of Protestant groups that rejected the German Christians, Meiser declared, represented the "lawful German Protestant church." It was the new body's "first founding document."[35]

In late May 1934, 138 delegates from both the "intact" Lutheran and the "destroyed" Prussian churches convened in Barmen for the first national synod of the Confessing Church. In addition to electing an all-male leadership committee known as the Brethren Council—the gendered term reflecting that only one woman delegate attended the synod—the body adopted a set of theses that became the foundational creed of the church opposition. Although the statement was drafted principally by Karl Barth, the synod worked to achieve consensus across delegates from the Lutheran, Reformed, and United regional churches. Adopted on May 31 with near unanimity, the Barmen Declaration encapsulated the synod's rejoinder to German Christian theology.[36]

The opening thesis laid the foundation for this critique: Scripture formed the sole source of the church's knowledge of God. "Jesus Christ, as he attested to us in Holy Scripture, is the one Word of God which we have to hear, and which we have to trust and obey in life and in death. We reject the false doctrine that the church could and should recognize as a source of its proclamation, beyond and besides this one Word of God, yet other events, powers, historic figures, and truths as God's revelation." The mission of the Christian church, the Barmen statement continued, "consists in delivering the message of the free grace of God to all people in Christ's stead." The church could not perform this divinely appointed mission "in the service of any arbitrarily chosen desires, purposes, and plans," or relinquish its message "to changes in prevailing ideological and political convictions." These admonitions contained thinly veiled attacks on the heresies of the German Christians: treating the Volk as a source of revelation and adapting the gospel to fit Nazi ideology. Other parts of the declaration addressed the Nazi state itself. According to the second thesis, "God's mighty claim on our whole life" led Christians to "reject the false doctrine as though there are areas of life in which we would not belong to Jesus Christ but to other lords." The fifth thesis put the point most explicitly: "We reject the false doctrine, as though the state, over and beyond its special commission, should and could become the single and totalitarian order of human life, thus fulfilling the church's vocation as well."[37]

With its invocation of the "totalitarian" state, the Barmen Declaration joined a transatlantic Christian response to the rise of dictatorships across Europe. But the document was hardly an announcement of political resistance. Scholars have long shown that the synod participants regarded the declaration as a purely theological statement, a claim about biblical principles intended to challenge the German Christians.[38] But even in its theology, the Barmen statement moved little beyond Protestant conceptions of church–state relations during the Weimar Republic. The controversial fifth thesis reiterated familiar assumptions about the state's role in preserving worldly order. The state was endowed with "the task of providing for justice and peace," toward which it marshaled the "threat and exercise of force, according to the measure of human judgment and human ability." In turn, the church was limited by its "special commission"—the proclamation of Scripture—and should not appropriate "the characteristics, the task, and the dignity of the state."[39] While insisting upon the autonomy of the church from state interference and expropriation— the same demand issued in 1918—the document had little basis to address the Nazi regime's effort to remold institutions, from courts to professional associations to the press, around its radically exclusionary vision. Nazi antisemitism and racial doctrine went equally unmentioned.

Barth's own activities following the Barmen synod underscored the extent to which the declaration was driven by theological rather than political concerns. Amid the events of mid-1934 that consolidated Hitler's grip on power—the assassination of the dictator's intraparty rivals in the "Night of the Long Knives," the death of President Hindenburg, and the expansion of the concentration camp system—Barth became caught up in a dispute with his fellow Swiss Reformed theologian, Emil Brunner, over the problem of "natural theology." The category had already been at issue in Weimar-era debates about the church's political role. Catholic social teaching pointed toward supra-positive natural law as a basis for social organization. Protestant theologians, in particular Barth's faction, questioned whether nature could be regarded as a source of revelation at all.

Barth and Brunner had cooperated around *Zwischen den Zeiten* in the early days of dialectical theology. With the onset of the church conflict, however, long-standing tensions between them boiled over into a pitched rhetorical battle. The instigating event was the May 1934 publication of Brunner's tract,

Nature and Grace, which took up the problem of divine revelation in the natural world. Revelation, Brunner argued, unfolded not only through the Bible but also in God's creation; at the same time, a sinful humanity required biblical revelation in order to recognize its natural counterpart. Whatever the nuances of Brunner's position, Barth believed his colleague had moved too far toward the theology of the German Christians, which found an arena of divine revelation in the history of the German Volk. Barth's reply, curtly titled *No!,* called on Protestants to dispense with the category of natural theology entirely. Brunner, Barth declared, "has been unable to adhere to *sola fide—sola gratia* [by faith alone, by grace alone]."[40]

Certainly the natural theology debate, which drew the attention of Protestant readers on both sides of the Atlantic, was not without political connotations. Brunner's *Nature and Grace* was reviewed favorably in the German Christian press, and Paul Althaus made his sympathy for Brunner's position known.[41] The month after the appearance of Brunner's text, Althaus, Werner Elert, and six of their Lutheran colleagues issued the Ansbach memorandum, a rejoinder to the Barmen Declaration that invoked Volk and race as orders of divine revelation and praised Hitler as a "pious and faithful sovereign."[42] By rejecting any path toward natural revelation, Barth sought to subvert the deification of the Volk by German Christians as well as conservative Lutherans like Althaus. But on Barth's reasoning, the central error of Brunner and other Protestant expositors of "natural theology" was less proximity to Nazism than to Catholicism and liberal theology.

The controversy that followed the initial statements by Brunner and Barth similarly centered on issues of theological purity. Ernst Wolf, a church historian and Luther scholar who had taught alongside Barth at the University of Bonn since 1931, became a key ally of his senior colleague. As the founder and editor of the Confessing Church monthly *Evangelische Theologie,* Wolf criticized nationalist theologies not for lending support to the Nazi state but for committing an error shared with Catholicism: neglecting the interdependence of law and gospel at the heart of the Reformation. Catholic neo-Thomism linked salvation to the natural law, apart from the intervention of divine grace; conversely, German Christian sympathizers made law entirely unnecessary to salvation, which instead emerged as the fulfillment of the "German hour." Brunner, Wolf averred, had failed to overcome this impasse.[43]

Yet the dividing lines were not as sharp as the polemics in *Evangelische Theologie* suggested. In the second edition of his *Theology of Orders,* Paul Althaus attempted to smooth over the fissures, emphasizing the assumptions

FROM THE TOTAL STATE TO THE LIMITS OF OBEDIENCE 61

he shared with the Confessing Church. His own framework, Althaus contended, did not accord essential priority to any one of the "orders of creation," nor did it deify merely human institutions. If today German Protestants were called to defend the Volk, tomorrow their highest duty may change. It was not a rigid law that determined Christian ethical action in the world but the discernment of God's active command.[44] Like Barth, Althaus emphasized the Christian's ethical responsibility to heed God's word in the absence of the guiding precepts of natural law. This assertion could be marshaled to defend virtually any political regime, including the Nazi state.

Law and Conscience in the Confessing Church

Despite the limits of the Confessing Church's early position, events of late 1934 challenged the narrow framing of the Barmen Declaration and the natural theology debate. At the second Confessing Church synod, held at Martin Niemöller's Berlin-Dahlem parish in October, the fragile truce between the destroyed Prussian church and the intact Lutheran churches of Bavaria, Hanover, and Württemberg, broke down. Conservative Lutherans favored ongoing cooperation with the national Reich Church; in contrast, Niemöller's wing of the Brethren Council called for the implementation of a church emergency law that would devolve all governing authority to Confessing Church institutions. When the emergency law failed to pass, Niemöller's "Dahlemite" faction formed an alternative leadership body that split off from the Provisional Church Administration directed by Hanover bishop August Marahrens.[45] After a subsequent meeting of Niemöller's group in March 1935 produced a statement denouncing Alfred Rosenberg's paganism, the Gestapo arrested and briefly imprisoned 715 Prussian pastors, including Niemöller himself, in the first such mass action against the Protestant clergy.[46]

Growing pressures on the churches were felt in other ways as well. With efforts to unify German Protestantism at an impasse, the state violated the churches' legal privileges in welfare and education, incursions that, the Concordat notwithstanding, also affected the Catholic Church. By mid-1935 a campaign for the "German community school" barred clergy members of both confessions from offering religious instruction, cut the weekly hours of religion classes, and attempted to remove crucifixes from school buildings.[47] Nazi elites increasingly shifted from Protestant or Catholic affiliation to the more acceptable *gottgläubig*—a catch-all term for a vaguely defined theism outside the institutional churches, which could encompass pagan beliefs as much as "positive

Christian" ones.[48] Private seminaries established by Confessing Church theologians to ordain young pastors outside of Nazified theology faculties lost official church recognition in late 1935, thereby becoming "illegal de facto."[49]

For the Confessing Church Dahlemites—a term coined to refer to the entire faction aligned with Niemöller, not simply members of the Dahlem parish—state repression forced a reckoning with political questions downplayed in the first stage of the church conflict. For the first time, Karl Barth, and the larger theological movement he led, questioned whether calls for Christian purification were an adequate response to the Nazi regime. When a new oath for civil servants in late 1934 demanded personal loyalty to Hitler, Barth agreed to sign only if an additional clause were added: "so far as I can answer for this as a Protestant Christian." Quickly removed from his professorship at Bonn, and finding himself with little support from the Provisional Church Administration under Marahrens, Barth departed for his native Switzerland in the summer of 1935.[50]

From the safety of a new position at the University of Basel, Barth developed the outlines of a revised political theology, first formulated in a farewell address to the Confessing Church. Read out to an "overfilled" Barmen congregation by the Confessing Church pastor Karl Immer, Barth's lecture took up a core topic of Protestant theology: the relationship between law and gospel.[51] In the conventional Lutheran ordering, God first communicated his law through biblical revelation to a sinful humanity, which could never fully obey. God then offered forgiveness to the faithful through the salvific message of gospel. Titling his lecture "Gospel and Law," Barth reversed the terms. The law, Barth argued, was founded on the gospel's promise of grace; divine law was the mere "form" of God's message, of which gospel was the "content." Because God's law stemmed directly from gospel, it could not be replaced by human forces—whether "natural law, or an abstract 'reason,' or history, or, in these recent troubled times, the '*Volksnomoi.*'"[52] More clearly than the Barmen Declaration, Barth's 1935 tract established that there was no escaping God's all-encompassing sovereignty, even in matters of politics. The Christian response to Nazism could not be limited to theological critique.

The extent to which Barth's lecture presented an open confrontation with the regime can be gauged through the contents of *Evangelische Theologie,* the leading expositor of Barth's theology in Germany. In the mid-1930s the journal published a series of articles teasing out the implications of Barth's framework, daring to criticize the state in more open terms than prior statements by the Confessing Church. God's rule over the political world meant that Christians could make independent judgments about the state's violations of divine law, rather than obeying the state unquestioningly. But the extent to which such judgments could authorize outright defiance remained, for the journal's authors, highly limited. Ernst Wolf cited an obligation to suffer the consequences of one's disobedience rather than actively resist the state, even when the state violated biblical precepts.[53] The Bavarian pastor and jurist Karl-Heinz Becker, a frequent contributor to *Evangelische Theologie*, similarly emphasized the inward nature of Christian freedom. A "total state" that demanded "particular ideological theories and impulses in its subjects" violated the sphere of Christian conscience. At the same time, while preaching the "true free obedience" bestowed by God's grace, the church should instruct its members to fulfill their obligations to the state.[54] Departing from the Barmen Declaration, which continued to delineate the separate spheres of church and state, articles in *Evangelische Theologie* stressed the limits of state authority over Christians. But the journal's prescriptions remained narrowly framed, both in demanding that Christians passively suffer the state's transgressions and in declining to name the Nazi policies that violated divine law.

The narrow discourse of inner, "Christian" freedom found its greatest challenge not in theological periodicals but within lay Confessing Church circles, above all among women denied access to the pastorate. This divided response reflected the gendering of the church conflict itself. In Berlin, the organization's national center, women made up 70 to 80 percent of registered Confessing Church members, to the point that the Confessing Church has been described as a "Protestant women's movement led by male theologians." Martin Niemöller's Berlin-Dahlem congregation became an important meeting place for laywomen who demanded a more robust response against Nazi antisemitism.[55] The nurse Margarete Meusel, who directed a Berlin Protestant welfare office under Niemöller's supervision, organized an aid service for "non-Aryan" Christians beginning in 1934. In advance of the June 1935 Confessing Church synod at Augsburg, Meusel penned a statement that appealed to the body to provide "spiritual and material aid" to Christians of Jewish descent. After the enactment of the Nuremberg laws in September, which stripped "non-Aryans" of their German citizenship, Meusel added an addendum: "We must note that obedience may not be rendered in contradiction to God's command."[56] The Provisional Church Administration refused to discuss or publicize Meusel's statement, despite it appearing numerous times on the committee's agenda.[57]

64   REINVENTING PROTESTANT GERMANY

The Berlin secondary school instructor Elizabeth Schmitz, who had studied theology with Adolf von Harnack and maintained close friendships with Jewish colleagues, issued an even more forthright response to the plight of German Jews. A member of Niemöller's congregation, Schmitz compiled a memorandum in the summer of 1935, updated following the Nuremberg laws, that moved beyond the question of "non-Aryan" Christians to detail the exclusion of Jews from citizenship, schools, economic life, welfare aid, and freedom of marriage. Schmitz concluded by calling on the Confessing Church to take an active stance against the persecution of Jews.[58] Without the backing of influential theologians, however, her plea could have little impact. Walter Künneth, to whom Schmitz appealed in July 1935, proved unwilling to help despite his critique of the Nazi ideologue Alfred Rosenberg in a widely publicized tract earlier that year.[59] Schmitz also maintained a correspondence with Karl Barth, who continued to identify the German Christians' central error as a theological liberalism that lost sight of the essence of the church.[60] Arguably, their exclusion from positions of church authority sensitized laywomen like Schmitz to the limits of the Confessing Church's theology.

The tensions between a more confrontational stance and appeals to passive suffering came to the fore following the final break of the Confessing Church. At the body's fourth synod in February 1936, held at the Westphalian town of Bad Oeynhausen, the Dahlemite faction severed ties with the Lutheran churches of Bavaria, Hanover, and Württemberg once and for all. At issue was the newly formed Reich Ministry for Church Affairs, created by Hitler under the cabinet minister Hanns Kerrl following the failure of previous efforts to bring about a unified national church. When delegates from the "intact" churches advocated for participation in church committees directed by Kerrl's ministry, the Dahlemite wing, which rejected such cooperation, split off to form a second Provisional Church Administration.[61] Buoyed by the hardening divisions, the most radical members of the new leadership body, later joined by Confessing Church pastors including Hans Asmussen, Franz Hildebrandt, and Heinz Kloppenburg, embarked on a memorandum to Adolf Hitler himself.[62] The more fervently nationalist Martin Niemöller joined the final phase of revisions, demanding a mollifying of the draft's most severe criticisms of the Nazi regime.[63]

The Provisional Church Administration's memorandum to Hitler, submitted to the Reich Chancellery on June 4, 1936, stopped short of Elisabeth Schmitz's call for a public denunciation of the Nuremberg laws. Still, the statement moved beyond the Dahlemites' earlier defense of church autonomy to question a strict demarcation of faith and politics. According to the authors, not only German Christian theology but Nazi ideology itself—including racial antisemitism—contradicted Christian principles. "If here blood, race, and *Volkstum* attain the level of eternal values, then the Protestant Church will be forced through the first commandment to reject this valuation." The Nazi "hatred of Jews" violated "the Christian command of love of the neighbor."[64] Without demanding open disobedience, the memorandum described Nazi lawlessness in a level of detail absent from earlier statements of the Confessing Church: "Protestant conscience, which knows itself to be co-responsible for Volk and government, is most severely burdened by the fact that in Germany, which always described itself as a state governed by the rule of law [*Rechtsstaat*], there are still concentration camps; the measures of the Gestapo are removed from any judicial oversight."[65] Christian conscience blurred the line between religious and political judgments, allowing the believer to condemn grave breaches of legality on Christian grounds.

The memorandum's aftermath, however, attested to the limits of Confessing Church solidarity. Twelve days after its delivery to Hitler's Chancellery, the document was reprinted in the *New York Herald Tribune,* an international embarrassment as the regime attempted to soften its image abroad in preparation for the Berlin Olympics. The Gestapo concluded that the document had been leaked by a young Confessing Church vicar, who in turn had received it from the jurist Friedrich Weissler. A baptized Protestant of Jewish descent, Weissler found employment as a Confessing Church legal adviser after his expulsion from the German civil service and served as one of the memorandum's principal authors. Following the Gestapo investigation, however, Weissler was quickly stripped of his affiliation with the Provisional Church Administration. Martin Niemöller led the charge, demanding at a meeting of the Confessing Church Brethren Council that "against Weissler, a *clear* line must *immediately* be drawn."[66] Taken into custody on October 7, Weissler was murdered at Sachsenhausen on February 18, 1937. During his interrogation, Weissler invoked a biblical verse that had gone unmentioned in the memorandum itself: "In the Confessing Church, the view prevails that the Christian must obey God more than man."[67]

No member of the Provisional Church Administration would issue such a bold declaration. Instead Weissler's execution had a chilling effect. Not until the final years of the war, amid plans for a military coup d'état, would statements by Confessing Church members approach the condemnation of the

66   REINVENTING PROTESTANT GERMANY

Nazi regime attempted by a radical minority in 1936. Instead the Confessing Church Dahlemites retreated to a more comfortable position, both ideologically and practically: the proclamation of the Christian's spiritual freedom from worldly ideologies.

Ecumenical Myths, German Realities

Developments of late 1936 and 1937 further effaced the expansive critique of Nazi racial policy put forth in the memorandums of Margarete Meusel, Elisabeth Schmitz, and the Provisional Church Administration, confirming the dominance of Niemöller's more restrictive line. The galvanizing event of European Protestant intellectual life during this period was the ecumenical conference organized by the Geneva-based Christian Council for Life and Work, scheduled for July 1937 in Oxford. The association's first international meeting since the Stockholm assembly of 1925, the Oxford conference was planned amid the rise of authoritarian regimes across the continent. The organizers expressed deep concern over the divide between German Protestants and their West European counterparts, already an issue at Stockholm.[68] But the Oxford conference did less to clarify the German church conflict for Christians abroad than to spur a myth of Confessing Church resistance, which German Protestants would embrace long into the post-1945 period.

The Protestant ecumenical response to Nazism was shaped by a theology of Christian personalism that gained ground among both European Catholic and Protestant intellectuals during the turbulent 1930s. Within the Catholic public sphere, personalism emerged out of a critique of totalitarianism spearheaded by lay Catholics who had grown disillusioned with Carl Schmitt's theory of the total state. Linking fascist Italy, Nazi Germany, and the Soviet Union, Catholic theorists of totalitarianism, including the influential French Catholic philosopher Jacques Maritain, drew upon the theology of natural law revived by the papal social encyclicals. The totalitarian state, on this view, transgressed its rightful limits by seeking to dominate "natural communities" such as family and church. At the heart of the Catholic critique of totalitarianism stood not liberal democracy but the human person, a core category of neo-Thomist theology that signified the transcendent human being created in God's image.[69]

The Protestant pastors who spearheaded the Oxford meeting embraced a similar theology of the human person, defined in terms of the individual's divine creation and embeddedness in community. The conference's lead organizer, the Scottish missionary and longtime Life and Work activist Joseph H. Oldham, exemplified this orientation. Like his Catholic counterparts, Oldham rejected both liberal individualism and authoritarian collectivism as the Janus faces of secular modernity. The flaw of the secular totalitarian state was that it claimed the whole of the individual and left no room for the development of the Christian "person," especially in the spheres of education and the family.[70] But Oldham remained indebted to a statist tradition of Protestant theology that departed from Catholic notions of subsidiarity. Echoing German Lutherans such as Paul Althaus and Walter Künneth, Oldham did not criticize authoritarian states as such but only their incursions into private life. "It is conceivable," Oldham wrote in a 1935 pamphlet for the Life and Work movement, "that the aims of an authoritarian state might be inspired by, or in large measure consistent with, the Christian view of life." Such a state, "while exerting its authority to put an end to the disorders of society ... might accord to religious, cultural and other activities the largest freedom compatible with what it believed to be the requirements of the general good."[71]

In line with their authoritarian sympathies, Oldham and other organizers of the Oxford conference insisted on accepting delegates from both the official German Protestant Church (DEK), coordinated under Hanns Kerrl's Ministry for Church Affairs, as well as the Provisional Church Administration.[72] The ecumenical movement refused to acknowledge the Confessing Church's claim to be the sole legitimate representative of German Protestantism. Scholars have rightly pointed toward ecumenical leaders' paramount concern with preserving church unity and preventing war.[73] Equally significant, they prioritized a critique of secularism and liberal individualism over one of dictatorship.

The invitation to participate at the Oxford conference was a boon for the DEK, which could present itself to German authorities as a loyal arm of the Nazi state and to ecumenical leaders abroad as a voice of Christian witness. To prepare, the DEK's Foreign Office convened a series of working groups on the relationship between the church and the political world. Participants included theologians and jurists who had defended the Nazi state, among them Paul Althaus, Walter Künneth, Heinz-Dietrich Wendland, Erik Wolf, and the Halle theologian Friedrich Karl Schumann.[74] DEK authors concurred with Joseph Oldham's critique of secular totalitarianism, while defending the total state in terms even more adamant than their pro-Nazi pronouncements of 1933. In his contribution to a working group on "Church and Volk," Althaus abandoned the hesitancy toward völkisch racial theories voiced in his

Kirchentag address a decade earlier. Eugenics, Althaus now declared, was necessary to preserve "the bodily and spiritual heritage of our Volk."[75] The Freiburg jurist Erik Wolf, who joined the Nazi Party when the opportunity for membership reopened in May 1937, echoed Oldham's assertion that Christians could retain "co-responsibility for the formation of public life" in a totalitarian state.[76] For Heinz-Dietrich Wendland, the "total state" remained a welcome solvent to the threats of factionalism and social disintegration.[77] The constitutional law scholar Rudolf Smend, who had been forced to resign his Berlin chair in 1935, issued a rare word of caution at a meeting on "Religion and Law," urging the church to maintain its political independence.[78]

In the spring of 1937 a committee of the Provisional Church Administration met at Martin Niemöller's Berlin-Dahlem parish to prepare an alternative statement for the Oxford conference, challenging the DEK's defense of the total state. The authors represented the most critical wing of the church opposition that remained active in theological discussions. In addition to Niemöller, they included the Freiburg agricultural economist Constantin von Dietze, who had been dismissed from his Berlin professorship due to his engagement in the Confessing Church; the pastor Otto Dibelius, who had joined the leadership of the Confessing Church in Brandenburg after being removed as a church superintendent in June 1933; as well as the theological prodigy Dietrich Bonhoeffer, now the director of an illegal Confessing Church seminary.[79] Yet in the aftermath of Weissler's execution, and amid ongoing state harassment of Confessing Church pastors, the Provisional Church Administration avoided mention of Nazi racism or antisemitism. Instead its statement returned to the principle of divine sovereignty voiced in the Barmen Declaration. Obedience to the state and service to the Volk were "grounded in our salvation by Jesus Christ [and] determined and delimited through the commandment of God." By recognizing "the claim of authority of Jesus Christ in their whole lives," Christians could free themselves of "all false claims of the state to bind conscience."[80]

The consequences that could be drawn from such formulations were uncertain. In cases of conflict between the state's laws and God's word, the Provisional Church Administration urged individual Christians to determine the appropriate course of action based on "a careful examination of the particular situation." The church offered at most "spiritual advice and help," not clear directives.[81] Centering humanity's dependence on divine grace, the authors could not rely on natural law as a vantage point from which to challenge the state. Instead the statement accepted National Socialist rule while charging individual conscience to determine whether obedience should be denied in particular instances. Even at its most confrontational, the report of the Provisional Church Administration endorsed only passive disobedience, in witness to the sins of the world and coming kingdom of God.

As it turned out, no German participant would attend the Oxford ecumenical conference. With German Protestantism still divided, Nazi leaders abandoned the strategy of church unity under the umbrella of positive Christianity, instead resorting to the overt repression of dissidents. By mid-1937 the Gestapo had arrested over 800 Confessing Church pastors on suspicion of making oppositional statements and holding intercession services for other arrestees. Amid the regime's rearmament drive, the possibility that pastors could stir up criticism abroad appeared as a growing threat. In the weeks leading up to the Oxford meeting, Hitler banned the entire German delegation from attending after the Gestapo seized the passports of Confessing Church participants. Then, eleven days before the conference was set to open, Martin Niemöller was arrested at his Dahlem home and incarcerated in Berlin's Moabit prison on charges of "giving inflammatory lectures and sermons" and "incit[ing] resistance against governmental laws and decrees." Although Niemöller's prior detentions had resulted in quick releases, the Gestapo would hold him until the opening of his criminal trial in February 1938.[82]

Among leaders in the international ecumenical movement, the regime's actions reinforced an incipient narrative of Protestant resistance. George Bell, the English Bishop of Chichester and a key figure in the Life and Work movement, wrote to the London *Times* the day after Niemöller's arrest: "The question is not only a question of the fate of a particular minister, but of the whole attitude of the German State to Christianity and Christian ethics."[83] The most influential interpreter of the German church conflict for the British public, Bell had met Niemöller on several visits to Germany and became a leading propagator of the view that Christians were the primary targets of the Nazi regime.[84] The official report of the Oxford conference struck a similar chord, lauding Confessing Church members "who have stood firm . . . for the freedom of the church of Christ to preach his gospel."[85] Such expressions of sympathy did not prevent the conference's published volumes from including contributions by pro-Nazi theologians, such as Heinz-Dietrich Wendland, alongside representatives of the Confessing Church Dahlemites.[86] Divisions among the German church factions paled before the ecumenical movement's larger theory of totalitarianism, which regarded any

70   REINVENTING PROTESTANT GERMANY

presence of Christianity as a challenge to the Nazi state's all-encompassing claim.

The ecumenical misapprehension of the German church conflict was in part an effect of breakdowns in communication, as well as Niemöller's ability to project himself internationally as the leader of German Protestantism as a whole. But it also reflected a basic compatibility with both sides. The Oxford conference could affirm the harmony of Christian personalism and political authoritarianism, while accepting the Provisional Church Administration's critique of a state that contravened biblical precepts. From the perspective of Oldham, Bell, and other leading ecumenists, the distinctions between the German theological camps were less significant than their common hostility toward liberalism and secularism. All detractors of the German Christians could be regarded as opponents of the spirit of totalitarianism, regardless of their actual political stance. As Nazi Germany plunged Europe into war, these commitments became the basis for a vision of postwar Christian renewal, one that decentered the state while leaving Protestant acquiescence during the early Nazi years unquestioned.

Protestant Political Thought in Wartime

Even before Germany's invasion of Poland, the months leading up to the war saw an ever-expanding crackdown on ideological dissenters, including critical Protestant pastors. After being acquitted on charges of treason, Martin Niemöller was rearrested in March 1938 on Hitler's personal orders and imprisoned at Sachsenhausen, and then at Dachau, for the remaining years of Nazi rule.[87] Private seminaries directed by Confessing Church pastors were declared criminal and shut down in 1937, including Dietrich Bonhoeffer's seminary at the Pomeranian town of Finkenwalde and the theologian Hans Joachim Iwand's in the East Prussian village of Bloestau.[88] Authorities banned the public reading of lists of imprisoned church members, a common practice at Confessing Church worship services, leading to further arrests of pastors and parishioners.[89] The Confessing Church periodical *Evangelische Theologie* suspended its circulation in 1938, followed by *Junge Kirche* in 1941. The critical voices of Protestants of Jewish heritage were also cut out. In September 1938 Rudolf Smend's former student Gerhard Leibholz escaped to England, where he would spend the war on an Oxford lectureship arranged by George Bell.[90]

At this critical juncture, it was again lay church members who spearheaded resistance and rescue efforts at the margins of institutional Protestantism.

The Dahlem parish continued to stand out. Following Martin Niemöller's imprisonment, the twenty-nine-year-old Confessing Church pastor Helmut Gollwitzer, who had completed his doctorate at Basel with Karl Barth, took over the leadership of Niemöller's circle. One week after police, SA militias, and eager civilians carried out the Kristallnacht pogrom of November 9, 1938, terrorizing Jews across Germany and deporting tens of thousands to concentration camps, Gollwitzer issued one of the only sermons in all of Germany to address the events. Speaking at the urging of Elisabeth Schmitz, Gollwitzer denounced the conflation of "God's justice" with "the justice of one's own nation," and pilloried the "self-justification and self-excuse" of Germany's Christians.[91] Although Gollwitzer did not adopt Schmitz's request to include Jewish victims in the congregation's prayers, one congregant, a Christian of Jewish descent, recalled the "great experience that this man unwaveringly spoke the words that had to be said to the community on that day."[92] Following Kristallnacht, the Berlin Confessing Church pastor Heinrich Grüber organized an aid office that helped nearly 2,000 Jews and "non-Aryan" Christians emigrate from Germany. Laywomen in the Dahlem community were critical participants in the informal networks that sustained its work.[93]

The beginning of the war in September 1939 made public criticism altogether impossible, and rescue efforts yet more dangerous. The war was not greeted with the boisterous enthusiasm of 1914—by the Protestant clergy or the wider German population. Nevertheless, pastors from across the camps of the church conflict implored their congregants to back the military effort as a valiant struggle against the Versailles Treaty, and, after the German invasion of the Soviet Union in June 1941, against godless Bolshevism.[94] Remaining embers of dissent could be dealt with expeditiously. In late 1940 Heinrich Grüber and most of the employees of his office were arrested and deported to concentration camps. Few would survive the war.[95] Of the 2,000 pastors ordained in illegal Confessing Church seminaries, 1,500 had been conscripted into the military by mid-1941.[96] Some, like Helmut Gollwitzer, served reluctantly but willingly under a state that had made conscientious objection a capital crime.[97] Others actively abetted the regime's genocidal warfare. Approximately 500 Protestant pastors, among them Confessing Church members, served as military chaplains in the Wehrmacht (Nazi armed forces). While rarely commenting on wartime atrocities, chaplains' sermons frequently echoed the regime's anti-Communist rationalizations and heralded the revival of Christianity in the occupied Soviet Union.[98] Even Martin Niemöller, to the consternation of his ecumenical interlocutors, volunteered from his Sachsenhausen cell to resume his naval service.[99]

The war did not entirely eclipse the debate about Protestantism's relationship to the secular state that had preoccupied theologians and lay intellectuals since 1918 and continued after 1933. Instead, with the closure of Confessing Church seminaries and periodicals, the discussion was pushed into private homes and clandestine meetings. Increasingly, the dominant figures to emerge were intellectuals aligned with the conservative wing of the Confessing Church who had escaped the purges of 1937–1938 and were too old to be conscripted into military service. Some participated in interconfessional networks, such as the Kreisau circle around the Silesian military intelligence officer Helmuth James von Moltke or the Düsseldorf circle organized by the former DNVP politician Robert Lehr. These groups brought together Protestants and Catholics to develop shared visions of postwar re-Christianization. Protestant members, including the theologian Eugen Gerstenmaier and Lehr himself, would become leading figures in postwar Christian Democracy.[100] Yet even as the war fostered new opportunities for dialogue, theological differences, as well as deep-rooted social prejudice, continued to color the views of Protestant intellectuals on their Catholic counterparts. Confessional tensions with roots long before 1945 would pervade the early Christian Democratic Union and spill over well beyond its boundaries.

A network of pastors and lay academics around the University of Freiburg formed the most significant group to extend discussions of Protestant responsibility for law and politics during the war. The origins of the Freiburg circle extended back to the mid-1930s, when Gerhard Ritter, a leading conservative historian who had written an acclaimed biography of Martin Luther, organized a series of seminars on the question of Christian obedience to the state. The group quickly expanded to include the economists Walter Eucken and Adolf Lampe, as well as several Freiburg pastors. The economist and Confessing Church member Constantin von Dietze joined following his arrival in Freiburg. By the beginning of the war, the Freiburg circle had become a center of Protestant planning for a post-Nazi Germany that brought together intellectuals from competing camps of the church conflict. Erik Wolf, whose wartime writings continued to echo Nazi tropes of racial superiority, joined the meetings in 1942. Helmut Gollwitzer maintained connections to the circle with the dissolution of Dahlemite networks.[101]

The writings of the Freiburg circle aimed to move beyond the antinomies that had structured Protestant political debate since the Weimar era. In closed-door discussions and privately circulated memorandums, the group refused a posture of Christian distance from the world, whether on the grounds of the Lutheran two-kingdoms doctrine or a Barthian faith in the purity of revelation. Its discussions illuminate how Nazi pressures catalyzed a political reorientation not only among Confessing Church Dahlemites but within conservative Protestant networks. Yet as much as the Freiburg circle challenged long-standing impasses of Protestant social thought, it did not address the preconceptions that structured the entire field of debate. The very charge of political passivity, which would become a central trope of German Protestant discourse after 1945, elided the active roles of pastors and laypeople—well beyond the German Christian movement—in abetting the Nazi regime.[102] Moreover the Freiburg circle's post-Nazi plans reflected deep continuities with the tenets of Protestant nationalism that had made Nazism appealing to many Protestants early on, setting a model for postwar Protestant conservatives.

The group's first memorandum, composed in December 1938 with a view to the recent Kristallnacht pogrom, already displayed these tensions. The principal author, Gerhard Ritter, implored Christians to serve as witnesses to God's commandments by refusing to participate in "the sinful doings of the world." In his most direct reference to Nazi crimes, Ritter sought to narrow the cleft between the Christian message and the political world: "The experience of recent years has made fully apparent to us how enormously important it is that the teachings of revelation are preached again and again *with concrete application to our times.*" But for Ritter the problem of Nazism remained one of human "self-justification," the absence of responsibility before God, rather than antisemitism or the destruction of democracy. Like Helmut Gollwitzer's sermon a month earlier, Ritter's memorandum made no reference to the Kristallnacht pogrom itself.[103] The Freiburg economist Constantin von Dietze similarly framed the problem of Protestant political engagement around the church's otherworldliness. In lectures before the Freiburg circle and the Society for Protestant Theology, founded in 1940 by Ernst Wolf, Dietze urged audiences to embrace their political responsibility despite the tensions between biblical teachings and the contingent realm of power politics. If they lacked "a similarly exhaustive doctrine of natural law and its requirements as Catholics have," Dietze argued in a June 1941 address, Protestants remained accountable for determining "what resulted from God's word for the fundamental order of human life."[104]

But what would such a Protestant social order look like? Dietze's wartime lecture and the responses he received—from interlocutors including military chaplains Karl-Heinz Becker and Heinz-Dietrich Wendland, as well as the Lutheran theologian Helmut Thielicke—only exposed the fact that the Freiburg circle lacked a robust source of social teachings on par with the Catholic papal encyclicals.[105] A crucial impetus for bridging the gap between Protestant doctrine and the imperatives of postwar planning came from Dietrich Bonhoeffer, who had established contact with the Kreisau group around Helmuth von Moltke after obtaining a civilian position in the Wehrmacht intelligence service. In May 1942 Bonhoeffer met with George Bell in Sweden to request the Anglican bishop's support for the Kreisau circle, which had begun plotting a coup d'état against Hitler. Although Bell's entreaties to a skeptical British Foreign Office proved futile, contacts with the German resistance increased the ecumenical leader's convictions in the anti-Nazi credentials of the Confessing Church.[106] At the behest of the Confessing Church Provisional Administration, Bonhoeffer traveled to Freiburg in the fall of 1942 to request from Constantin von Dietze a memorandum outlining the Freiburg circle's vision for a post-Nazi political order. The memorandum was intended to serve as a German contribution to a postwar ecumenical conference planned by Bishop Bell and the Anglican Church.[107]

The core document of the wartime Freiburg circle therefore served a dual purpose. The authors aimed both to formulate a comprehensive Protestant vision for a post-Nazi Germany, and to convince church leaders abroad of the Germans' constructive contributions to international ecumenical community. Over a series of covert meetings at his home, Dietze convened a group of theologians and lay intellectuals to produce the memorandum. In addition to the Freiburg professors Gerhard Ritter, Adolf Lampe, and Erik Wolf, participants included the Brandenburg Confessing Church leader Otto Dibelius; the theologian and pedagogue Friedrich Delekat; as well as Helmut Thielicke, who attended as a representative of Württemberg bishop Theophil Wurm.[108] Completed in January 1943, the memorandum included chapters on law, economy, education, and church affairs, and would become a cornerstone of postwar narratives of Protestant resistance. The Freiburg memorandum indeed warned against "excessive demands of state authority that become a tyranny over conscience," and called for "legally secured freedom of conscience" as the first principle of a postwar German constitution.[109] But the authors did not eschew the antisemitic, illiberal, and patriarchal currents that had long shaped German Protestant social thought. Instead the document prescribed a corporate social order strikingly resonant with prewar nationalist theologies.

Entitled "The Political Order of the Community," the Freiburg memorandum opened with a historical overview by Gerhard Ritter that reinforced the assumptions of conservative Protestant nationalism. The rise of Nazism and other forms of totalitarianism, according to Ritter, was the product of the secularizing impulses of the Enlightenment. Not the Reformation but the French Revolution had torn asunder the civilization of Christian Europe, leading individuals to seek false gods in state and nation. It was Napoleon who inaugurated an age of total warfare that destroyed the distinction between civilian and combatant, culminating in the catastrophe of the First World War. Although Ritter did not treat nation and Volk as divine "orders of creation," he hardly broke with the assertions of German victimhood that had fueled the intensification of Protestant nationalism during the Weimar Republic. The Versailles Treaty, Ritter wrote, had "deprived the Germans, of all the nations of Europe, the right of political self-determination of their people." Without this decision, "the National Socialist revolution would not have been possible." For Ritter, the Nazi regime was less the product of German history than of Allied chauvinism and long-running secularization.[110]

The path forward, then, was the return of Christianity. Like his Freiburg colleagues, Ritter avoided discussing the active participation of Protestants in the Nazi state, instead blaming a heritage of Protestant otherworldliness for the church's distance from politics and society. Through wartime contacts with Freiburg Catholics, Ritter became "sensitized to the riches of natural law traditions" as one means for traversing this cleft, and references to "natural communities" appeared throughout the memorandum.[111] Yet Ritter's vision for a post-Nazi Germany was adamantly Protestant. Appeals to natural rights, the historian held, too often led to the deification of mere worldly communities, providing justification for revolutionaries and fanatics claiming to act on the side of God.[112] Instead Ritter followed a line of argument shared by Lutheran church leaders and Confessing Church Dahlemites alike: Because the human world was necessarily fallen and sinful, no political order deserved an absolute Christian sanction, least of all liberal democracy. The church could only hold the state accountable to its divine purpose of "protecting the good and punishing evil," navigating between the twin threats of anarchic individualism and totalitarian collectivism.[113] By this logic, Ritter's co-confessionals who had supported Nazism as a manifestation of divine will were guilty, at most, of falling into Catholic or secular patterns of thought. Like earlier statements of the Confessing Church—with the exception of the 1936 memorandum to Hitler—Ritter did not directly address the crimes of the Nazi regime.

The Freiburg circle's own outlines for a post-Nazi society echoed the theology of orders advanced by conservative Lutherans like Paul Althaus, with the exception that the state no longer appeared as an order of creation in itself. The memorandum contained a pointed critique of the "totalitarian" state, which, the authors argued, made an authentic Christian life impossible—a reflection of their connections to ecumenical Protestants like George Bell, as well as the very real experience of church fragmentation during the Nazi years. But neither did they believe liberal democracy to be appropriate for an era of mass politics. Ritter's historical overview made this point clear. If the "'general human rights' of the liberal age" reflected an effort to preserve the human being's transcendence, the expansion of human rights to include "a political separation of powers," "popular sovereignty," and "equal political rights for all" marked a decisive "weakness."[114] Instead the Freiburg circle envisioned a strong state that presided over a society organized into autonomous, hierarchically constructed institutions, such as marriage, family, church, and workers' and employers' associations. The first priority of such a state was to protect not individual rights but pre-political institutions, whether those ordained in Scripture or those necessary to preserve social peace in a class-based society. As Erik Wolf wrote in an appendix on the legal order, a written constitution that delimited "the legal rights and obligations of citizens" was less important than the formation of "a moral community of responsible people." Political parties should limit their goals in respect of this larger structure.[115]

Foreshadowing the arguments of Protestant conservatives in the early Federal Republic, the Freiburg circle gave pride of place to gender hierarchy in its vision of moral community. Erik Wolf called for the law to preserve the "sacral character of marriage and the moral significance of the family," while Constantin von Dietze listed "family and Volk" as communities that the economic order was bound to protect.[116] The memorandum's program for social policy was even more explicit: "The natural foundation of every social order that supports organic, true community is the family." Criticizing the Nazi state for promoting procreation outside of marriage, the authors described the "deplorable confusion and dissolution of elementary moral concepts" as the "foundational evil of our time."[117]

Not only did the memorandum reserve harsher words for the Nazis' supposed assault on the family than the regime's wartime atrocities; its calls for the restoration of marriage and family came at a moment when women had begun to expand their roles in the Confessing Church. With the onset of the war and the conscription of male pastors, the Confessing Church Brethren Council was forced to open the question of women's ordination, a matter it had dismissed earlier in the church conflict. Since 1927 the Prussian Union of Churches had permitted women to be ordained as vicars but not as full pastors, who alone were permitted to lead worship services and administer the sacraments. In October 1942, however, the national Confessing Church synod authorized women vicars to deliver sermons if no qualified man were present, a function some had already begun to take on. Although the compromise disappointed women theologians, several hundred women vicars performed pastoral functions during the war, often as parish leaders.[118] The Freiburg memorandum helped prepare the ground for the reassertion of masculine authority in the postwar church.

Antisemitism also remained central to the post-Nazi plans of the Freiburg circle. A final section of the memorandum written by Dietze, "Suggestions for the Solution of the Jewish Question in Germany," indicated the group's knowledge of wartime atrocities against Jews. But while Dietze recognized German responsibility for the murder of "hundreds of thousands" of Jews—a vast understatement already by early 1943—he located the roots of Nazi antisemitism in the excessive political influence of Jews after Emancipation, a product of "the doctrine of general human rights." Dietze's proposed solutions reflected an equally antisemitic animus, accepting the legitimacy of the Nuremberg laws. Dietze outlined three possibilities: Restrictions on Jewish rights could be lifted if the number of postwar returning Jews were small; an international commission could determine "the rights and obligations of Jews"; or an "international Jewish statute" could reduce Jews to the status of "foreign nationals" throughout Europe. Christians were commanded to love all their neighbors, Dietze wrote, but "for the love of one's own Volk, Christians must still keep their eyes open to whether closer contact or even mixing with other races can only be damaging for body and soul."[119] Since the memorandum was kept hidden from Nazi authorities, distributed in only three copies during the war, such statements cannot be dismissed as efforts to placate the regime.[120] The Freiburg circle adopted a racialized understanding of religion on its own terms, underscoring its proximity to the conservative Protestant nationalism of the interwar era.

The Freiburg memorandum revealed both the extent and the limits of conservative Protestant reorientation as the tide of the war turned against Germany. As much as the document repudiated Nazi dictatorship, it continued to express underlying beliefs that had led many Protestant nationalists to embrace Nazism: racialized antisemitism, a critique of parliamentary democracy, and a patriarchal vision of society. In turn, the Freiburg authors' condemnation of secularism, suspicion toward party politics, and preference for a corporate, authoritarian state gained resonance among conservative opponents of Nazism. Carl Goerdeler, the former mayor of Leipzig and a leading figure in the Kreisau circle around Helmuth von Moltke, joined the Freiburg discussions. Although not directly involved in plotting the assassination attempt on Hitler, the Freiburg professors provided economic expertise for the conspirators through frequent correspondence.[121] The Kreisau circle's own memorandums similarly emphasized the centrality of Christian beliefs and ethical traditions, while its post-Nazi plans envisioned a constitutional dictatorship under Carl Goerdeler, not a return to liberal democracy.[122]

Neither the Freiburg nor the Kreisau circle, moreover, took action against the ongoing destruction of European Jewry. In July 1943 Bishop Wurm issued the only word of protest from within the high ranks of the Protestant churches. In a private letter to Hitler's Chancellery, the Württemberg bishop warned against threats to "privileged non-Aryans"—Christians of Jewish descent who now faced deportation—only to fall silent after receiving a menacing reply.[123] Initiatives to rescue Jews and "non-Aryan" Christians remained confined to the margins of the Confessing Church. With the closure of Pastor Grüber's office, the attorney Franz Kaufmann gathered a group of Dahlem parishioners, including congregants Helene Jacobs and Gertrud Staewin, to arrange hiding places and falsify passports.[124]

On July 20, 1944, the long-awaited coup d'état failed. Colonel Claus von Stauffenberg planted a bomb in Hitler's "Wolf's Lair" field headquarters in East Prussia, but Hitler survived the explosion. Within several days, over 170 suspected conspirators, including Constantin von Dietze, Gerhard Ritter, and Adolf Lampe, were arrested. Dietze faced trial before the Nazi People's Court; unlike many conspirators, he was spared an almost certain death sentence with the killing of the notorious Nazi judge Roland Freisler during an Allied bombing raid in February 1945. The Freiburg professors were released only with the arrival of Soviet troops in Berlin.[125] Dietrich Bonhoeffer was not so lucky. Imprisoned already in the spring of 1943 on suspicion of involvement in resistance activities, Bonhoeffer was accused of treason after Gestapo investigators discovered documents that tied him to the failed assassination plot. Hitler personally ordered Bonhoeffer's execu-

FROM THE TOTAL STATE TO THE LIMITS OF OBEDIENCE

tion on April 5, 1945. The thirty-nine-year-old theologian was hanged at Flossenbürg, after a court martial found him guilty, four days later.[126]

IN THE YEARS before his execution, Dietrich Bonhoeffer despaired over the ineffectiveness of Christian witness under National Socialism. Bonhoeffer's essay "After Ten Years," written on Christmas 1942 for a close circle of friends, presented an account of his confession's failures through a critique of received Protestant theologies. The central problem, Bonhoeffer, argued, was the German Protestant conflation of "freedom" and *Beruf*—a category deployed by Luther to signify the Christian's worldly "calling" in service to God. Yet the *Beruf* could become perverted when the world forgot its divine moorings; indeed, Paul Althaus had used the term in 1923 to justify war and authoritarian rulership. Protestant Germans, Bonhoeffer asserted, "lacked one decisive and fundamental idea: that of the need for the free, responsible act, even against *Beruf* and commission."[127] Bonhoeffer presented a powerful indictment of the Confessing Church. Its statements, including the Freiburg memorandum, pronounced the Christian's inviolable freedom of conscience. Yet this freedom was understood to entail inward resilience against state indoctrination, or at most passive disobedience against unbiblical laws, rather than the decisive act for which Bonhoeffer called. Bonhoeffer himself struggled to derive a theological justification for his resistance activities, maintaining that even the assassination of a tyrant confronted the Christian with an irresolvable dilemma.[128]

Constantin von Dietze offered a more apologetic view, one that papered over the gap between thought and action. Writing to his wife and brother from prison in October 1944, Dietze presented his own stance in Nazi Germany as one of consistent, principled resistance: "Attitude toward National Socialism? Here I have very often avowed that as a Christian, I regard contempt toward divine commandments (lawlessness, mendacity, anti-church, yes anti-Christian politics) as evil and calamitous; because God does not allow himself to be defied. This I also shared with [Carl] Goerdeler. We are both in agreement that this power, established through injustice and crime, has been the greatest national catastrophe; it must come to a dire end."[129] Contrasting with Bonhoeffer's ambivalence about his own role, Dietze's self-congratulation evoked more common attempts at whitewashing and erasure. Belated critiques were read onto attitudes held throughout the Nazi years. Conscience, for so much of the regime's history a justification for inaction, became a bulwark of resistance. Christianity was held to be inherently opposed to Nazism, effacing not only the close connections between Protestantism and Nazi ideology at the outset of the regime but the acquiescence of Confessing Church pastors even during the war.

Dietze's narrative, rather than Bonhoeffer's, came to dominate postwar depictions of the Protestant churches under Nazism. This narrative omitted marginalized figures—laywomen and Christians of Jewish heritage who demanded that the Confessing Church take a stronger stance, as well as the few theologians like Bonhoeffer who engaged in direct resistance—while elevating a conservative, only belatedly anti-Nazi faction. Whitewashed accounts of the Nazi era would continue to take shape in the crucible of the Allied occupation that succeeded Germany's surrender in May 1945. With the National Socialist regime defeated—not by German resistance, but by Allied arms—Protestant intellectual life emerged from the shadows of secret meetings and privately circulated tracts, rising to the forefront of debates about the political reconstruction of a post-Nazi Germany.

CHAPTER THREE

POST-NAZI JUSTICE AND PROTESTANT HUMAN RIGHTS

EIGHT WEEKS AFTER Allied troops entered Stuttgart, where he had served as a pastor during the final years of the war, the Lutheran theologian Helmut Thielicke submitted a memorandum to a US press officer outlining his church's vision for a post-Nazi Germany. At the center of that vision stood a revived Christianity. In a narrative crafted for an American audience, Thielicke characterized National Socialism as "the final and most terrible product of secularization." Postwar reconstruction, the Freiburg circle veteran announced, could only proceed from the foundation laid by the Christian anti-Nazi opposition. The wartime activities of the Freiburg circle demonstrated that "the Confessing Church did not restrict its work to the 'ghetto' purely internal to the church, but understands the commanding and guiding word that its model has set for all domains of life." Although the Confessing Church could not alone determine the political course of post-Nazi Germany, its members had important roles to play in media, education, and culture. "What ultimately amounts to a religious crisis," Thielicke concluded, "can only be rectified through religious means."[1]

Thielicke's admonition joined a burgeoning discourse of re-Christianization at the end of the Second World War. Across Europe, church leaders ascribed the destruction of war to the failures of secular modernity and called on Christians to reengage in public life. The Catholic Church, Pope Pius XII wrote in 1947, had emerged "strengthened and purified" through its "ordeal by fire."[2] The 1948 Amsterdam Assembly that officially inaugurated the World Council of Churches (WCC) chastised churches that limited themselves to "a purely spiritual or other-worldly or individualistic interpretation of their message."[3] Calls for re-Christianization were especially resonant in Allied-occupied Germany. As political institutions and the German state itself ceased to function, the British press reported "a religious revival like none Europe had seen in a hundred years." Churches not only provided spiritual solace to a war-torn population but distributed food aid and welfare services, especially to the millions of German refugees expelled from their homes in Eastern Europe.[4] If short-lived, the German "Hour of the Church" convinced the Catholic and Protestant clergy alike of their responsibility as guides to the nation's moral, material, and political reconstruction.

Despite consensus on the imperative of public engagement, Christian intellectuals and religious leaders in postwar Europe remained split along national, confessional, and ideological lines. Across the continent, Christians mobilized behind a dizzying array of visions for Europe's future. On both sides of the incipient Iron Curtain, a radical minority went so far as to seek out cooperation with Communists, building on relationships forged in the wartime resistance.[5] Even Europe's newly founded Christian Democratic parties were ideologically protean, drawing together social Catholics who sought a high degree of economic planning with market-leaning liberals.[6]

In Germany, Christian politics were further complicated by the Catholic–Protestant divide. As a transnational institution whose hierarchy survived the war intact, the Catholic Church could claim a safe distance from National Socialism, throwing its weight behind the Christian Democratic Union. The Protestant churches faced greater uncertainty and fragmentation. Although pastors who had joined the pro-Nazi German Christians frequently found their way back to church employment, leadership positions fell to those who had affiliated with the Confessing Church as well as the unaligned Lutheran churches of Bavaria, Hanover, and Württemberg.[7] But even among the broad cohort that had opposed the German Christians, fissures dating to the Weimar and Nazi years remained pervasive. Deep theological and political clefts continued to divide conservative Lutherans from Dahlemites inspired by the political theology of Karl Barth. A contest between these groups to represent their confession on the national and international stage set the fault lines for German Protestant politics into the 1960s.

While that contest was invariably shaped by the Allied presence, pastors and lay intellectuals continued to pursue goals anchored in the traditions of German Protestant nationalism. Each faction staked its claim to leadership over German Protestantism on its ability to represent German interests against the depredations of the Allied occupiers. Moreover, German

Protestant intellectuals adapted the terms of international postwar planning toward their own, frequently nationalist commitments. Paramount among these was the category of human rights. Mobilized by Christians, liberals, socialists, and conservatives alike, human rights emerged in the mid-1940s as a ubiquitous language in the battle to define Europe's future. The category possessed no single accepted definition; instead, human rights formed a contested terrain that actors across the ideological spectrum sought to claim as their own.[8] Postwar German Protestants developed a distinctive theological iteration of human rights, which they marshaled toward a seemingly unlikely cause. In their first major political campaign, clergy members and lay intellectuals across both wings of the church petitioned occupation authorities for amnesties or sentence reductions on behalf of hundreds of former Nazis convicted in Allied war crimes trials. They argued that misguided justice had violated the human rights of the accused, and of the German people more broadly.[9]

The German Protestant campaign against war crimes trials embodied the antisemitic and anti-liberal ideologies that were paramount of prewar Protestant nationalism. Advocacy for convicted war criminals overlooked German atrocities against Jews and other occupied populations, and flouted the liberal assumption that the rule of law was a prerequisite for Germany's reintegration into the community of nations. Yet the campaign also built upon departures undertaken in the Confessing Church. The Confessing Church Provisional Administration, as well as the wartime Freiburg circle, had described Christian conscience as a bulwark against state overreach—however much this image overlooked the realities of compromise and cooperation with the Nazi regime. Now, postwar conservative Lutherans and Dahlemites alike cast the church in a similar role using the language of human rights.

If initially deployed to discredit the occupation governments, the discourse of rights would reverberate through Protestant politics in 1950s West Germany. Church leaders and lay activists would continue to style their church as a defender of individual rights in campaigns for family law reform, interconfessional schools, and conscientious objection to military service. Protestant politics during the occupation years therefore challenges the dichotomies around which West German history has been written—either a process of "re-civilization" by which Germans gradually repudiated Nazi legacies, or a continuation of Nazi-era ideologies under the auspices of America's Cold War empire. Instead, German Protestants recast long-standing nationalist traditions as a basis for new values that they would seek to incorporate into

84   REINVENTING PROTESTANT GERMANY

the West German constitution, and that they would come to describe as democratic. Ambitions toward restoration and reorientation reinforced one another in the twilight of German defeat.

Visions of Christian Renewal

Allied occupation set the conditions for Christian politics in postwar Germany. At the Yalta Conference of February 1945, US, British, and Soviet leaders agreed to the division of Germany into zones of occupation, with France included as a fourth occupying power. The jointly administered Allied Control Council, established following the conclusion of the Potsdam Conference in August, would serve as the executive authority across occupied Germany. Early Allied planners, convinced that the Nazi regime was the product of deep social pathologies, envisioned a transformative occupation summed up in the "4 D's" announced at Potsdam: demilitarization, denazification, democratization, and decentralization. By late 1945, however, ideological differences and the opening shots of the Cold War led to widening policy disparities across the occupation zones.[10]

Allied treatment of the churches was exemplary of these divides. In the Protestant-majority Soviet zone, a brief period of toleration gave way to a restrictive religious policy following the formation of the Communist-dominated Socialist Unity Party in April 1946. A series of directives worked to exclude churches from public life: quashing the Soviet zone's Christian Democratic Union, eliminating religious instruction in schools, restricting the flow of funds to Christian hospitals, and banning church-based women's and youth organizations. These measures reflected the anti-religious ideology of Soviet leaders and bolstered Soviet authorities' efforts to establish Communist rule in their zone.[11] French officials, jaundiced by the experience of wartime occupation, similarly rejected the German churches' claims to an expansive public presence.[12] In the view of French and Soviet authorities alike, the churches were little more than pillars of the reactionary coalition that had upheld the Nazi regime.

British and US occupation authorities took a more conciliatory approach, due in part to the sway of domestic church leaders with ties to their German counterparts. George Bell, the influential Bishop of Chichester, quickly renewed his connections to Confessing Church networks and lent his moral stature to relief campaigns that highlighted the suffering of ordinary Germans. In press conferences and published reports following his first visit to occupied Germany in October 1945, Bell recounted how German churches had served as the sole sources of sustained anti-Nazi resistance. The Anglican bishop then painted a dire picture of postwar starvation, homelessness, and disease.[13]

The Pennsylvania Lutheran clergyman Stewart Herman concurred. The pastor of the American Church in Berlin from 1936 to 1941, Herman returned to Germany in July 1945 as a delegate of the Geneva-based World Council of Churches. Herman's reports detailed the desperate conditions in occupied Germany, while his 1946 account of the Nazi-era church conflict, the first published in English, extolled the "seven thousand" pastors—corresponding to the entire Confessing Church—who had "actively resisted the Nazi Party and its totalitarian pretensions."[14] This sanguine view of the German churches found another proponent in the Michigan Congregationalist pastor Marshall Knappen, the head of religious affairs for the US military government. Under Knappen's guidance, US and British religious policy would include the reestablishment of religious education, return of confiscated church property, and restoration of the church tax. The churches would become the only German institutions permitted to carry out the denazification of their own ranks.[15]

The revived German Protestant debate about the political role of the church took place in the shadow of Allied occupation. Church leaders, pastors, and lay intellectuals did not simply conform to Allied expectations, however, whether occupation authorities' goal of political cleansing or ecumenical leaders' vision of international reconciliation. Instead they dug deep in their theological heritage, drawing upon postwar plans put forward during the Nazi era itself. The debate took on different tenors in the Western and Soviet zones. Whereas Western German Protestants could appeal to Christian sensibilities in their interactions with British and US authorities, Soviet zone Protestants confronted a regime that was fundamentally hostile to the presence of independent organizations, let alone religious ones. It was the debate in the Western zones that would ultimately inform Protestant conceptions of democracy in the early Federal Republic of Germany. But this discussion was shaped by contrasting perceptions of Communism, which quickly emerged as a fault line among Protestants in the West.

Veterans of the Confessing Church Dahlemites continued to look toward Karl Barth for guidance. Barth's departure for Switzerland in the summer of 1935 had cut him off from participation in the German church conflict. However, Barth continued to teach German students from his new perch at the University of Basel, including the young pastor Helmut Gollwitzer, until the Reich Ministry for Church Affairs forbade such contacts in 1937. During the war, Barth remained apprised of plans for a coup d'état against Hitler through contacts with Dietrich Bonhoeffer, whose position as a Wehrmacht intelligence officer enabled travel to Switzerland.[16] Postwar conservatives dismissed Barth as a foreigner ignorant of the situation inside Nazi Germany; his Dahlemite allies, however, embraced the Swiss theologian's connections to the anti-Nazi resistance.

The theological writings Barth produced following his return to Switzerland laid the foundation for political discussions among postwar Dahlemites. Whereas Barth's exhortations during the early Nazi years stressed the preservation of gospel from political ideologies, his distance from Germany, as well as the deepening political crisis, led Barth to place new emphasis on the church's responsibility for worldly affairs. Barth first set out this perspective in a June 1938 lecture, "Justification and Justice," which he composed with a view to the escalating Nazi threat. Building on his 1935 address "Gospel and Law," Barth now insisted upon an inherent linkage between the Protestant principle of divine justification by faith and the establishment of justice in the human world. The authority of human law derived from the higher authority of gospel, and served as an expression and fulfillment of divine love.[17]

Underlying these abstractions was a decidedly political message. Conservative German Lutherans had long cited chapter 13 of Paul's Epistle to the Romans—which implored Christians to "be subject to the governing authorities"—as evidence of the divine sanction of state power. According to the Lutheran doctrine of the two kingdoms, God ruled the fallen worldly realm through the sword of state authority, whereas the gospel's message of grace reigned only in the church. Barth turned the relationship between law and gospel on its head, prioritizing the authority of gospel even over the political world. Paul's injunction did not grant the state a free hand to rule under the cover of divine right, but established "the duty of authority to reward the good and to punish the evil."[18] By proclaiming the state's "divine justification" and its responsibility for securing "human justice," the church had a vital role to play in the political sphere.[19] But the converse was also true. If the state failed to preserve justice, Barth argued, then "it cannot be honored better than by this *criticism* which is due to it in all circumstances."[20] The Christian owed loyalty to the God-given purpose of the state, not the existing political order.

Barth's vision exerted a powerful influence on surviving members of the Confessing Church Dahlemites. Most prominent among them was the Confessing Church leader Martin Niemöller, who was rescued from seven years of Nazi imprisonment by US Army troops in early May 1945. Tensions between the Swiss Reformed theologian and German Lutheran pastor remained pronounced. During a widely publicized press conference shortly after his liberation, Niemöller shocked his British and American interviewers by defending his early enthusiasm for National Socialism and his 1939 request to rejoin the German navy. The interview came as no surprise to Barth, who would lament Niemöller's recalcitrant nationalism in their earliest postwar correspondence. Nevertheless, the two emerged as allies following Niemöller's release from US Army custody. Against the view of theological conservatives, Barth and Niemöller believed that the Confessing Church Dahlemites, the only contingent in the church conflict to refuse cooperation with the official Reich Church, had gained the moral legitimacy to lead postwar German Protestantism. In a memorandum to US occupation authorities, Niemöller maligned the "neutral" Lutheran churches of Bavaria, Hanover, and Württemberg, while exaggerating his own faction as representative of the "great majority" of German Protestants.[21] Barth recognized postwar Germans' temptation to deny their complicity with Nazism, yet believed that Niemöller and his allies offered the best chance for church renewal.[22]

The vision of Niemöller's circle took shape at the first postwar meeting of the Confessing Church Brethren Council, the leadership body formed at the 1934 Barmen synod. Convened at Frankfurt in August 1945, the gathering brought together forty pastors, along with Karl Barth on his inaugural postwar visit to Germany. Participants advocated for the radical reform of church administrations, including the replacement of ecclesiastical hierarchies with elected Councils of Brethren on the model of the Confessing Church.[23] The meeting's concluding "Message to the Pastors" reflected Barth's call for the church to serve as a witness to the state's divine mandate. Lutheran orthodoxy, the Brethren Council announced, with its tradition of church subordination to the state, had paved the way for Protestants' helplessness before the Nazis. Railing against "the dominance of bureaucracy in the church," the statement challenged Protestants to ask themselves "to what degree does the church bear responsibility for the whole of public life—state, society, and culture—and how far it has in fact carried out this responsibility."[24]

The "Message to the Pastors" surpassed Nazi-era statements of the Confessing Church in its willingness to identify authoritarian tendencies within

Figure 3.1. Martin Niemöller preaching at Saint Anne's Church in Berlin-Dahlem, October 28, 1945. The majority-women congregation is representative of the gendered dynamics of church participation after the end of the war, as well as the demographic imbalance in Germany. Photo by George Konig / Keystone / Hulton Archive / Getty Images

German Protestantism. At the same time, the announcement had a self-serving aim. By pinning the Nazi rise on the inaction of Lutheran conservatives, delegates exaggerated their own opposition and reduced the problem of Christianity and Nazism to one of passive complicity rather than active cooperation.[25] The conference also told a gendered story that would shape later Dahlemite narratives of resistance. While the Brethren Council met to call the church to account, women theologians who had taken on pastoral functions in the Confessing Church were being relegated to the traditional roles of social work and religious education—even though laywomen fueled the postwar increase in church attendance.[26]

Leaders of the conservative Lutheran faction of German Protestantism, grouped around the Nazi-era "intact" churches of Bavaria, Hanover, and Württemberg, grounded their own vision of postwar renewal in an alternative account of anti-Nazi resistance. Rejecting calls for a bottom-up transformation of church life, church officials led by the Württemberg bishop

Theophil Wurm sought instead to revive the governance structures of the regional churches and unite the disparate wings of German Protestantism under conservative auspices. Although lacking a resistance symbol on the order of Martin Niemöller, this group reconceived the Lutheran distinction between political and religious affairs to recount its own opposition against Nazism. In a letter to the Archbishop of Canterbury, the conservative Confessing Church pastor Hans Asmussen claimed that the "inward turn" of the wartime churches had reflected not a capitulation to Nazism but a spiritual refortification, prefiguring their postwar rebirth.[27] For Lutheran conservatives, the Brethren Council's call to reorient all domains of public life around the message of gospel reflected a dangerous conflation of worldly and spiritual authority, reminiscent of the German Christians.

On August 27, eighty-eight German Protestant leaders met at the Hessian town of Treysa to reorganize the postwar church, with battle lines already drawn. Wurm was infuriated upon learning of the Brethren Council meeting that had taken place days earlier, while Bishop Hans Meiser of Bavaria called for the formation of an independent Lutheran Church rather than uniting German Protestants in a single organization.[28] Only Wurm's personal diplomacy saved the conference. The resulting compromise created a national-level church federation, the Protestant Church in Germany (Evangelische Kirche in Deutschland; EKD). According to the Treysa agreement, the Protestant regional churches would maintain autonomy over their internal affairs, while the EKD would represent German Protestantism before government authorities and churches abroad. Wurm was elected chair of the EKD Council, the federation's twelve-member executive body. Conservatives including Meiser, Asmussen, Otto Dibelius, and the Hanover church administrator Hanns Lilje dominated the group. In view of his credibility abroad, Martin Niemöller was elected to head the EKD's Foreign Office, leading a minority faction of the EKD Council associated with the Confessing Church Dahlemites. The body included only two lay members: the Essen attorney and industrialist Gustav Heinemann, a participant at the Barmen synod and member of the Rhineland Confessing Church Brethren Council; and the jurist Rudolf Smend, named rector of the University of Göttingen after the war.[29] On one point, the two factions agreed. Until 1970 no woman was appointed to the EKD Council.[30]

Competing visions of Protestant renewal coalesced in the ensuing years. As each wing of the EKD forged its own associations, periodicals, and international contacts, church leaders and lay intellectuals developed elaborate proposals for postwar reconstruction. Yet the conflict within the EKD served

90   REINVENTING PROTESTANT GERMANY

less to encourage confrontation with the Nazi past than to reinforce a shared narrative of resistance. As tensions between the churches and the occupation governments mounted, Protestants on both sides of the divide drew on this narrative to channel popular discontent against the Allied occupation. In campaigns against post-Nazi justice, shot through with the assumptions of prewar Protestant nationalism, Protestant leaders would embrace a new language of human rights.

Postwar Lutheranism and the Protestant Academies

Following the Treysa gathering, the postwar vision of the EKD's conservative wing took shape around a parallel public sphere of Protestant conference centers, church commissions, and periodicals. At the center of this web stood the newly founded Protestant Academies, the first launched in September 1945 in the Württemberg village of Bad Boll and quickly followed by successors across the Western zones. Constructed in country towns far from postwar urban ruins, the Protestant Academies pursued a conservative vision of re-Christianization in harmony with the views of ecumenical leaders as well as US occupation authorities. Indeed, the US military government supplied critical funding. At the same time, the academies served as sites of political rehabilitation for former Nazis, members of the paramilitary SS (Schutzstaffel), and German Christians, who sought to whitewash their biographies by establishing connections with the postwar churches. The theologian Paul Althaus and jurist Ernst Forsthoff, both proponents of the total state who were suspended from their university positions after the war, were among the early speakers at Bad Boll.[31] Moreover, the plans for political reconstruction outlined at the Protestant Academies echoed the authoritarian constitutionalism of the wartime Freiburg circle, only slightly removed from the antidemocratic political theologies of the Weimar and Nazi eras.

The founder of the Protestant Academy at Bad Boll, the pastor Eberhard Müller, exemplified postwar continuities in conservative German Lutheranism. Born in Stuttgart in 1906, Müller studied theology at the Lutheran bastions of Tübingen and Erlangen and was ordained in the Württemberg regional church. With the rise of the Nazi dictatorship, Müller joined the Young Reformation movement around the conservative Confessing Church theologians Walter Künneth and Hanns Lilje, becoming general secretary of the Union of Christian German Students (Deutsche Christliche Studentenvereinigung) before the organization was banned in 1938.[32] Müller would later describe the

Figure 3.2. Visit of an American education commission to the Protestant Academy in Bad Boll during a conference for "Poets and Thinkers," September 1946. Eberhard Müller (front, right) is pictured next to Eugene Anderson, deputy director of the US State Department's Office of Occupied Areas. Archiv der Evangelischen Akademie Bad Boll

Bad Boll academy as the outgrowth of a new ethos of public responsibility cultivated in the Nazi-era Christian student movement and the wartime Freiburg circle.[33] Yet Müller's own role in the Third Reich was one of participation rather than resistance. As a Wehrmacht chaplain on the Eastern Front, Müller had preached field sermons that mourned German victimhood and framed the war around a narrative of Christian salvation.[34] After the war, however, Müller and other academy leaders presumed that Protestants had erred under Nazism by withdrawing from public life.

The most important drivers of the agenda at Bad Boll were veterans of the Freiburg circle, including the historian Gerhard Ritter and economist Constantin von Dietze. Returning to Freiburg at the end of the war, Dietze and Ritter worked to secure their status as spokespersons of the anti-Nazi resistance. In July 1945 Ritter circulated copies of the Freiburg memorandum alongside a preface highlighting the group's connections to the July 20 plot. Passages blaming Jewish political influence for the rise of Nazism were reproduced unaltered, while only overt attacks on the Western Allies were eliminated.[35] Soon afterward the jurist Erik Wolf, whose writings under Nazism had embraced the total state, inaugurated a book series documenting the "witness of the Confessing Church."[36] By September the pastor Hans Asmussen, appointed at Treysa to lead the EKD chancellery, solicited Ritter, Dietze, and Wolf to establish church commissions on law and social policy.[37] As shapers of the emergent Protestant public sphere, the three continued to espouse the vision of the 1943 Freiburg memorandum: a corporate social order based on hierarchically organized institutions.

This vision structured the first conference of the Protestant Academy in Bad Boll, a "Meeting for Men of Law and Economy" that opened on September 30, 1945. Over two weeks of prayer, Bible study, and excursions to the surrounding countryside, the 158 lawyers, industrialists, and academics in attendance—including just five women—imbibed lectures imploring them to bring Christian tenets to bear on their professional lives.[38] An inaugural address by Bishop Wurm established the conference's narrative of the Nazi era, centered on silences rather than active participation. Protestants' lack of a sustained tradition of social thought, Wurm declared, had led the church to "take unclear and disunified positions on questions of law and economy." As a result, the Protestant bourgeoisie had lacked the resources to confront the "power-hungry total state."[39] Wurm and subsequent speakers assumed that Nazism had emerged in a religious vacuum, and they neglected the role of Protestant pastors and intellectuals in backing the Nazi state early on. Instead the conference's final report called for the church to assume political responsibility beyond "the proclamation of gospel to believers," opening a path for the return of Protestant nationalism under the guise of reform.[40]

Keynote lectures by Freiburg circle veterans operated within a similar dichotomy of passivity and engagement. Gerhard Ritter's address built on his contribution to the Freiburg memorandum by suggesting an alternative to a supposed Lutheran heritage of political quietism. Placing himself within a Protestant lineage that denied "the ability of human reason to form a proper understanding of the world," Ritter nevertheless refused a posture of world denial. Christian efforts to shape political life, Ritter argued, reflected not human "self-assertion" but a striving "for God's cause."[41] Constantin von Dietze's lecture on economic order gave concrete shape to these exhortations, imploring Protestants to work with Catholics to seek a middle path between liberal individualism and totalitarian collectivism. Dietze favored economic competition to prevent the overconcentration of state power, while insisting that competition be constrained by the institutions of a "well-ordered soci-

POST-NAZI JUSTICE AND PROTESTANT HUMAN RIGHTS   93

ety": family, profession, and employers' and employees' associations.[42] At the same time, Dietze's vision shared features with authoritarian political theologies of the Nazi era. While calling for a "democracy fitting German conditions," Dietze had little to say about constitutional basic rights or popular representation in government. Instead Christians were obliged to "search for and realize the order corresponding to divine commands and factual necessities."[43] His key departure followed the Freiburg memorandum. Rather than a total state, Christian precepts encoded in the constitution, above the popular will or competition among interest groups, would serve as the guarantors of social order.

The inaugural Bad Boll conference established the pattern by which Lutheran conservatives would confront the occupation powers in subsequent years: insisting on a break with their church's past while continuing to affirm their nationalist commitments. This strategy shaped the EKD Council's first public statement. In the months after the war, representatives of the World Council of Churches—including George Bell, Stewart Herman, and WCC general secretary Willem Visser 't Hooft—urged German church leaders to release a public acknowledgment of wartime guilt in order to facilitate their reintegration into the international Christian community. Karl Barth issued similar exhortations in his correspondence with Martin Niemöller.[44] Despite its initial reluctance, the EKD Council had little choice but to comply. Meeting at Stuttgart in October 1945, the EKD Council concluded a statement expressing the church's "solidarity of guilt" with the German people. "Through us," the council acknowledged, "has endless suffering been brought to many peoples and countries." Yet the Stuttgart Declaration also conveyed an apologetic narrative of anti-Nazi resistance. German Protestants had struggled "in the name of Jesus Christ against the spirit which found its terrible expression in the National Socialist regime of tyranny." This narrative was linked to an announcement of public responsibility, mirroring the lectures at Bad Boll: "Our hope is in the God of grace and mercy that He will use our churches as His instruments and will give them authority to proclaim His word, and in obedience to His will to work creatively among ourselves and among our people."[45]

Just how little the Stuttgart Declaration marked a reckoning with the tradition of German Protestant nationalism became apparent in the controversy that ensued after reports on the statement appeared in the press. The EKD chancellery and regional churches were flooded with petitions protesting the declaration's supposed recognition of "collective guilt," which parishioners

Table 3.1. Percentage of Germans in the American zone who believed that the Nuremberg International Military Tribunal and the subsequent Nuremberg trials had been conducted in a manner that was fair or unfair, based on surveys conducted by the Office of the Military Government, United States and the Office of the US High Commissioner for Germany

	Fair	Unfair
October 1946	78%	6%
October–November 1950	38%	30%

Source: Anna J. Merritt and Richard L. Merritt, eds., *Public Opinion in Semisovereign Germany: The HICOG Surveys, 1949–1955* (Urbana: University of Illinois Press, 1980), 11, 101.

feared would legitimize vindictive occupation policies.[46] Responding to these criticisms, leading conservative theologians fell back on a distinction between spiritual and political affairs. The Stuttgart Declaration, Hans Asmussen argued in the EKD Council's official defense of the statement, had offered an acknowledgment of repentance addressed to fellow Christians, not a political message to the occupation governments. While admitting its failure to proclaim the gospel, the church could not be held responsible for Nazi policies.[47] Other theologians went as far as to equate German and Allied crimes. In a widely publicized open letter to Karl Barth, whose postwar lectures had called for an expansive acknowledgment of German guilt, Helmut Thielicke decried the guilt of the Allies for the "dictate of Versailles" and the postwar expulsions of millions of ethnic Germans from Eastern Europe. Specific responsibility dissolved in Thielicke's call for universal forgiveness.[48]

The EKD's attacks on the Allies grew only louder as the occupation governments moved to implement an ambitious agenda of post-Nazi justice. The centerpiece of that program, the International Military Tribunal (IMT) at Nuremberg, opened in November 1945 following the indictment of twenty-four Nazi leaders on charges of crimes against peace, war crimes, crimes against humanity, and criminal conspiracy. While surveys found that a large majority of Germans initially believed the IMT to be fair, popular opinion soured against the subsequent trials conducted under the auspices of Allied Control Council Law No. 10 (see Table 3.1). Issued in December 1945, the ordinance permitted Allied authorities to try suspected war criminals in their respective occupation zones, leading to indictments of thousands of military and SS officers, concentration camp guards, diplomats, industrialists, and

POST-NAZI JUSTICE AND PROTESTANT HUMAN RIGHTS 95

Table 3.2. Percentage of Germans in the American zone who expressed satisfaction with the denazification program, based on surveys conducted by the Office of the Military Government, United States

November 1945	50%
March 1946	57%
December 1946	34%
September 1947	32%
May 1949	17%

Source: Anna J. Merritt and Richard L. Merritt, eds., *Public Opinion in Occupied Germany: The OMGUS Surveys, 1945–1949* (Urbana: University of Illinois Press, 1970), 304.

professionals. The US occupation government alone conducted twelve additional military tribunals at Nuremberg between 1946 and 1949, while the US Army tried over 1,600 defendants at the former Nazi concentration camp in Dachau.[49] Even more far reaching—and less popular—was the denazification program announced at Potsdam (see Table 3.2). In all four occupation zones, denazification required every German adult seeking employment in the civil service and other professional positions to complete a questionnaire reporting on their political activities under Nazism. By 1949, more than 20 million Germans had responded to what amounted to "likely, the largest survey in history to that point."[50] Although denazification tribunals categorized the majority of defendants as "followers," conviction as an "offender" carried a heavy burden, up to loss of employment and forced labor.[51]

War crimes trials and denazification were met with not only popular distrust but vociferous critiques from the German legal establishment as well as the Allied side. Winston Churchill and Joseph Stalin initially favored summary executions of the leading Nazis instead of potentially knotty trials.[52] Even as plans for a tribunal crystallized, lawyers in the British Foreign Office and their French counterparts questioned the legality of new criminal categories.[53] Indeed, of the accusations detailed in the August 1945 Nuremberg Charter, only the category of war crimes was firmly rooted in existing international law. Crimes against peace, crimes against humanity, and criminal conspiracy made their first appearance in an international criminal indictment at Nuremberg, largely at the behest of Soviet jurists.[54] German defense attorneys at the IMT—as well as legal scholars from the disgraced Nazi jurist Carl Schmitt to the liberal émigré Hans Kelsen—echoed the

96   REINVENTING PROTESTANT GERMANY

charge of retroactive law. The Allies, these critics added, had committed equivalent crimes, while Soviet participation at the tribunal violated any pretense of impartial justice.[55]

Protestant leaders advanced similar arguments. At a meeting of the EKD Council in December 1945, Bishop Wurm and his Bavarian counterpart Hans Meiser assailed the crimes against humanity charge as an application of ex post facto law.[56] Wurm, whose Württemberg church fell in the US zone, launched a parallel campaign against denazification, which aroused similar outcries of victors' justice and retroactivity. After a March 1946 ordinance transferred the proceedings in the US zone to German oversight, Wurm sent a petition to US military governor Lucius Clay that denounced the denazification program as a perversion of the rule of law. Denazification, according to the bishop, criminalized political decisions that had been legal, even necessary, in the Nazi era, and failed to recognize that "many party members joined at the beginning out of idealistic motives." Moreover, the program ignored the fact that German soldiers and civil servants had felt obliged to obey the chain of command—the classic superior orders defense that was banned at Nuremberg but reappeared with vigor at denazification proceedings.[57]

Protestant attacks on war crimes trials and denazification went beyond a critique of retroactive lawmaking, however. Bolstered by contacts with ecumenical Protestants such as George Bell and Stewart Herman, who publicly assailed denazification as an indiscriminate attack on the German people, Wurm and other EKD leaders elaborated upon the narrative of wartime resistance and postwar responsibility outlined at Bad Boll.[58] As Wurm asserted in his petition to Lucius Clay, the churches had launched the "only publicly visible serious resistance" against Nazism, an act undertaken in obedience not to the state but to God. By punishing Germans who had failed to resist, denazification proceedings overstepped the bounds of human authority, judging what "counts as injustice only under divine law."[59] A week after Wurm's petition, the EKD Council released a public statement against denazification that lambasted the program for "preventing the hearing of the proclamation of the divine command and divine mercy." Faith alone would ensure "a true new beginning."[60]

With Wurm's campaign against denazification in full swing, the second Bad Boll jurists conference in October 1946 saw the convergence of legal and theological arguments against post-Nazi justice. A small number of attendees recognized what the dominant discourse eluded: individual, human responsibility for betrayals of law in Nazi Germany. One participant, a district court judge from Stuttgart, lamented, "We should all feel guilty that we did not react sufficiently against all breaches of law that occurred." Perhaps, this jurist argued, denazification might make his profession more politically aware in the future. But such a perspective was in a distinct minority. Instead the discussion at Bad Boll was dominated by church administrators such as Eberhard Müller and Theophil Wurm. These conservatives continued to call on the occupation powers to be guided by "the spirit of God's wisdom and righteousness" that "far exceeded human ability alone."[61] The conference's concluding statement similarly demanded, "Because all human law is dependent on divine mercy, criminal law does not lose any of its force if the idea of retribution in law is not exercised without limits." Protestant jurists would practice political responsibility by calling attention to the bounds of human law.[62]

The attacks on post-Nazi justice leveled at Bad Boll reflected the sense of victimization widespread among the German public, but also a specific political theology rooted in the preceding decades. After 1945 Protestant conservatives ceased to describe Volk, nation, and race as divine orders, and they distanced themselves from theories of the total state. But speakers at Bad Boll continued to characterize marriage, family, and property as divinely ordained institutions, organized on the basis of "biblical guidelines."[63] The basic break from pro-Nazi "orders of creation" theologies had already been anticipated in the wartime Freiburg memorandum: Christian conscience, rather than the state, would serve as the final arbiter over the limits of human law. This vision shaped the campaign against denazification and war crimes trials led by Bishop Wurm and his conservative counterparts, and would soon inflect the human rights language adopted at the Bad Boll academy.

The Christian Community and the Civil Community

If Protestant conservatives sought to reestablish regional church administrations and guide the reconstruction of political institutions, the Dahlemite-led Brethren Council, incorporated as an official organ of the EKD following the Treysa conference, espoused an alternative vision of re-Christianization. Rather than a restoration of pre-1933 church bureaucracies, this group sought a democratically organized church that served as a check on state power. However, polemics between the competing Protestant factions served less to promote a critical reckoning with the Nazi past than to buttress the resistance narratives of both sides. By attacking Lutheran conservatives for their political quietism, the Brethren Council fostered its own account of anti-Nazi resistance, one that centered a few male heroes while neglecting the disproportionately women-led rescue networks at the margins of the Confessing Church. Questions of antisemitism and Christian–Jewish relations, which were central to those networks, remained equally neglected. Moreover, conservative Lutherans and Dahlemites alike concurred that a legacy of Christian resistance had relativized the claims of state authority. Even as they proposed competing models of church–state relations, the two factions aligned in the campaign against war crimes trials and denazification.

Surviving pastors affiliated with the Confessing Church Dahlemites worked quickly to reestablish their networks. The theologian Ernst Wolf, one of Karl Barth's closest allies during the church conflict, again played a key organizational role. Appointed to a professorship at the University of Göttingen upon his return from military service, Wolf refounded the Confessing Church journal *Evangelische Theologie* and the wartime Society for Protestant Theology.[64] Hans Joachim Iwand, who became Wolf's colleague at Göttingen shortly thereafter, emerged as another leading voice in postwar efforts to elevate the Dahlemite faction. A member of the far-right Young National League during the Weimar Republic, Iwand had joined the Confessing Church and led an illegal seminary in the East Prussian village of Bloestau. He survived the war as a pastor in Dortmund following several rounds of speaking bans and imprisonment.[65] The Protestant church in the western German Rhineland, whose members had been prominently represented at the Barmen and Dahlem synods, formed a critical node of the postwar Dahlemite network. After the war the regional Confessing Church leadership council was refounded as the Rhineland Church Brethren Society. The group's chair, the Düsseldorf pastor Joachim Beckmann, was a former student of Karl Barth who had been active in the Confessing Church throughout the Nazi era. The Church-Theological Working Group in Württemberg, the only pastors' association that had urged Confessing Church leaders to speak out against the Nazi persecution of Jews, also aligned with the postwar Dahlemites.[66]

Karl Barth continued to serve as a theological mentor to this network. During the summers of 1946 and 1947, Barth returned to the University of Bonn as a visiting professor, rekindling his German connections. Barth's lecture "The Christian Community and the Civil Community," delivered before numerous German audiences in 1946, outlined the Dahlemite vision for the postwar church in its most influential form. Barth again argued that Paul's Epistle to the Romans did not mandate absolute deference to the state, but expressed the Christian obligation to bear witness to the state's divinely appointed mission. In turn, Christians relied on the state to secure their freedom to preach the gospel. The "Christian community" was a fellowship that proclaimed a message of justice, grace, and reconciliation *within* the polity, or "civil community," rather than an institution standing *alongside* the state to ensure social stability.[67] This was a bottom-up, rather than top-down vision of Christian renewal.

Most significant, Barth's postwar lecture marked a new departure in his normative vision for politics. In light of the experience of Nazism and war, Barth threw off the political ambivalence that had characterized his writings of the 1920s and 1930s to cast his lot with democracy. In what became the most controversial portion of the lecture, Barth proposed a series of analogies between the message of gospel and political life. Because Jesus ministered to the poor and dispossessed, the church should advocate for social justice; because Christians formed "a fellowship of those who live in one faith under one Lord," they must demand political equality regardless of race, gender, or religion; because God's mercy outlasted his anger, the state should exhaust peaceful solutions to international conflict before turning to violence.[68] A similar analogy existed between the freedom of the Christian community to preach the gospel and the political freedom enjoyed by citizens of a constitutional democracy. The church, Barth argued, should favor the "constitutional state" over anarchy or tyranny, for only such a state protected the church's freedom while maintaining the state's divinely ordained purpose: "the limiting and preserving of man by the quest for and establishment of law."[69] To be sure, Barth continued to stress the contingency of all political formations, in light of the Christian's ultimate loyalty to God. The Christian community "will be aware of playing off one political concept—even the 'democratic' concept—as *the* Christian concept, against all others."[70] Nevertheless, Barth affirmed "an affinity between the Christian community and the civil communities of the free peoples"—even if "the so-called 'democracies,'" as currently constituted, did not live up to their ideals.[71]

Other elements of Barth's lecture, however, could be interpreted by his German interlocutors to reinforce long-standing elements of Protestant nationalism. As in his earlier writings, Barth rejected efforts to bridge Christian revelation with secular politics through the concept of natural law, which he regarded as a merely human creation that blurred the church's true mission.[72] In the postwar context, Barth's critique of Catholic social teaching spiraled into a broadside against political Catholicism, which Barth saw at the root of the interconfessional Christian Democratic parties emerging across Western Europe. These parties, Barth feared, would sacrifice the message of gospel for the accumulation of power, invoking a divine mandate on behalf of worldly interests: "How can Christians mass together in a political party at all in these circumstances? The thing is only possible—and the suspicious alliance of the Protestants with the Romans in the French M.R.P. [Mouvement républicain populaire] and the German C.D.U. [Christian Democratic Union] shows that it becomes successful only where the Kingdom of God is interpreted as a human goal founded on natural law, where an allegedly Christian law, which is in fact a mere amalgam of humanitarian philosophy and morality, is set alongside the gospel in the political sphere."[73] In a letter to Gustav Heinemann, a cofounder of the Christian Democratic Union in Essen, Barth suggested instead that Christians work within the existing parties, or form a new one "without the title or claim to be Christian!"[74] Nevertheless, Barth's published writings cast doubt altogether on the mediating institutions of parliamentary democracy. Instead he called on Christians to build up democracy in their religious communities and spread the message of gospel across the divisions of party and ideology.

For the pastors who rebuilt the network of Confessing Church Dahlemites, Barth enabled a confrontation with the legacies of conservative Protestant nationalism through comfortable critiques of Catholic political theology and the party system—critiques that, ironically, were deeply rooted in the Protestant nationalist tradition. The manifold writings and speeches of Barth's German interlocutors said little about democracy and far more about the Protestant mission to engage with the world regardless of the political form of the state. In this, Dahlemites were not far off from their conservative counterparts, who similarly emphasized the need to overcome a supposed legacy of political quietism. In October 1946, on the heels of Barth's famous lectures, eighty pastors affiliated with Ernst Wolf's Society for Protestant Theology and the Württemberg pastor Hermann Diem's Church-Theological Working Group gathered at Bad Boll to take stock of the Lutheran legacy in German politics. In a plenary lecture, Ernst Wolf rehearsed a familiar attack on conservative Lutheranism, whose doctrine of "orders of creation" perverted Martin Luther's theological breakthrough. Whereas Luther had preached the direct responsibility of the laity before God, modern Lutheranism separated the preaching of gospel from the organization of worldly institutions, which supposedly operated according to their own autonomous laws. The resulting "apolitical ghetto church," Wolf averred, had retreated into political passivity, abandoning its role as a "guardian office" over state power.[75]

Attacks on the conservatives' alleged quietism also advanced Dahlemites' own narrative of anti-Nazi resistance. Most dramatically, a lecture by Hans Joachim Iwand invoked the Barmen statement of May 1934 as the basis for full-blown Christian opposition to Nazism. Even the Confessing Church's conservative wing, Iwand claimed, had recognized the "need to resist" due to "the freedom of the grace of God ... that made the protest against the total state and its paganism necessary." However, the united Protestant front broke apart by 1936, when the Dahlemites established an autonomous Provisional Church Administration. Iwand blamed this fissure squarely on the side of conservative Lutherans, who fell back toward a doctrine of obedience to worldly "orders" and forgot the alliance of the Lutheran and Reformed confessions "against scholastic theology."[76]

Iwand's account accomplished several purposes. By establishing the Dahlemites as the sole heirs to the Confessing Church resistance, Iwand asserted his faction's rightful leadership over postwar German Protestantism. At the same time, following the Brethren Council's 1945 "Message to the Pastors," he elided the roles of women in the Confessing Church as well as the organization's reaction to the Nazi persecution of Jews. Iwand also covered over his own past as an activist in the ultranationalist youth movement of the Weimar Republic. These omissions, alongside Iwand's attempt to pin the failures of his church on Catholic influence, bespoke the ongoing imprint of Protestant nationalism on his thinking.

In July 1947 the Brethren Council met with Karl Barth in Darmstadt to lay out its vision for the postwar church. Drafted by Iwand a month later, the resulting declaration, "On the Political Course of Our People," reflected the sweeping reorientation envisioned by postwar Dahlemites as well as its limits. Signed only by a radical minority even within the Brethren Council, the document advanced a scathing attack on the tradition of conservative Protestant nationalism. German Protestants had erred in "dreaming about a special German mission" and in "prepar[ing] the way for the unrestricted exercise of political power." Reflecting the influence of Barth, the Darmstadt statement condemned the reduction of the German church to a mouthpiece for conservative ideologies, in "alliance ... with the forces which clung to everything old and conventional." Instead the authors expressed a new opening to the left: "We went astray when we failed to see that the economic materialism of Marxist teaching ought to have reminded the Church of its task and its promise for the life and fellowship of men."[77] In the view of a commentary authored by Joachim Beckmann, Hermann Diem, Martin Niemöller, and Ernst Wolf, the long-standing Protestant vilification of socialism had not only alienated the German working class but abandoned the church's universal mission.[78]

As much as the Darmstadt statement criticized the church's traditional conservatism, it also extended a core tenet of German Protestant nationalism: the conviction that the church stood above the fray of political parties and ideologies to guide the nation as a whole. For the signatories, the growing rift between the Western and Soviet zones was a matter of paramount concern that demanded the church's message of reconciliation in the political world. Particularly Iwand, a native of the Silesian territories transferred to Poland under the terms of the Potsdam Agreement, feared the growing divide between East and West Germans.[79] Considerations of German unity superseded those of democracy. While acknowledging that conditions in the West proved more favorable for Protestants to exercise their "positive public responsibility," Iwand and his coauthors worried that the promise of political privilege would lead the churches in the Western occupation zones to a dogmatic anti-Communism—the same kind of submission to state ideology that had proven fateful in the Nazi years. East German Protestants, who faced no such temptation to become lackeys of Soviet ideology, were better positioned to forge a new model of Christian witness in the political world.[80]

In the overheated atmosphere of the early Cold War, conservative detractors accused the Brethren Council of Communist apologetics. Even for sympathetic critics, the Darmstadt statement demonstrated profound ignorance of the repression of the churches in the Soviet zone.[81] Yet the criticisms that Protestant conservatives launched against the Brethren Council mirrored the Darmstadt statement's attacks on the EKD establishment. Each side charged the other with politicizing theology, misunderstanding Luther's two-kingdoms doctrine, and reverting to Catholic patterns of thought. In the Lutheran journal *Zeitwende,* Gerhard Ritter retorted that Luther had never preached thoughtless obedience to the state, a charge invented by the reformer's Anglo-Saxon critics.[82] According to Helmut Thielicke, it was Barth who had sullied the purity of the gospel by reasoning directly from Scripture to politics.[83] These polemics reinforced the shared assumptions of both groups: their hostility to liberal theology, skepticism toward party politics, and insistence on the human propensity toward sin. Conservative Lutherans and Dahlemites alike invoked the church's responsibility to remind the political world of the human being's dependence on divine grace—and thereby to warn against political hubris. At stake was a conflict not between passivity and engagement but between competing visions of re-Christianization.

The shared nationalist convictions of the Brethren Council and the conservative Protestant mainstream facilitated these groups' cooperation in the campaigns against denazification and war crimes trials. Martin Niemöller emerged as the most vociferous critic of denazification on the Dahlemite side, lobbying Allied authorities and WCC representatives against the program's continuation with language no less vitriolic than Bishop Wurm's. The US Army's Counter Intelligence Corps, Niemöller told Stewart Herman in a private conversation, was no different from the Gestapo.[84] As the newly appointed president of the regional Protestant church of Hesse-Nassau, Niemöller organized a statement that lambasted Allied "vengeance" and urged pastors not to testify at denazification proceedings.[85] Hermann Diem's Church-Theological Working Group distinguished itself in 1946 as the only German Protestant association to defend denazification.[86] But by early 1948 even Diem's organization conceded that the proceedings had been so compromised by a collapse in popular legitimacy that the only choice was a "generous amnesty" for all but the most egregious perpetrators.[87] The Dahlemites' theology of reconciliation could be aimed equally to criticize denials of guilt by conservative German Lutherans, as well as demands for denazification by occupation authorities. For both camps, confrontations with Allied authorities became a testing ground for narratives of anti-Nazi resistance and visions of a renewed, publicly oriented church.

Human Rights and German Protestant Internationalism

While German Protestants' early opposition to denazification and war crimes trials was carried out primarily through private petitions, the campaign quickly became embedded in broader efforts to reestablish the EKD's international credibility. Most significant, the inaugural assembly of the World Council of Churches, held in Amsterdam over two weeks in August 1948, provided an opportunity for both German church factions to advance their visions of re-Christianization on an international stage. Proposed at the 1937 Oxford conference of the Life and Work movement but delayed until after the war, the WCC assembly marked an effort to unite the world's non-Catholic churches in a common organization. Eager to reintegrate the German church into the fold of ecumenical Protantism, organizers established a central ecumenical office in Frankfurt prior to the Amsterdam conference and invited German theologians and lay intellectuals to participate in the conference preparations.[88] The lead-up to Amsterdam formed the first juncture at which German Protestants linked their criticisms of the Allied occupation to questions of human rights, a discourse that the WCC actively promoted as a basis for postwar international order.

At one level the German Protestant adoption of human rights language fit with broader Christian and conservative uses of human rights. Although human rights took on manifold meanings at the postwar moment, the language gained particular resonance among West European conservatives, who invoked human rights as constraints on mass politics and democratic sovereignties—in particular the power of national legislatures to enact the nationalizations and social welfare programs demanded by the postwar left.[89] But German Protestants from both wings of the EKD also invoked human rights language in ways that were self-consciously set off from their nearest rivals: West European Catholics and Anglo-American ecumenists. Indeed, it was precisely because these intellectuals articulated their human rights claims within a familiar Protestant semantic that they could avoid engaging the potential challenges of human rights ideas to deeply held nationalist worldviews.

Catholic human rights discourse in 1940s Europe was rooted in the neo-Thomist theology of natural law that had gained ground in Catholic social thought since the late nineteenth century. Although the Church had traditionally dismissed human rights as a product of the secular Enlightenment, an influential cohort of wartime Catholic intellectuals sought to reclaim the concept. The most prominent was the French philosopher Jacques Maritain, whose *The Rights of Man and Natural Law* (1942), penned in American exile, redefined human rights as the epitome of Catholic teachings. The key linking concept was the "dignity of the human person," a category that took shape in Catholic critiques of totalitarianism during the mid-1930s. According to Maritain, a wide range of rights—to life, bodily integrity, freedom of conscience and association, but also to political participation and a just wage for one's labor—flowed from the human being's God-given dignity. Maritain's formulation of human rights followed the neo-Thomist synthesis of natural law and revelation. Although human rights emerged through "natural law and the light of moral conscience within us," it was "the message of Gospel" that "awakened this consciousness, in a divine and transcendent form."[90]

POST-NAZI JUSTICE AND PROTESTANT HUMAN RIGHTS 105

Maritain's text gained influence at the highest ranks of the Catholic Church. In his 1944 Christmas Eve address, Pope Pius XII himself invoked human rights as a basis for the postwar settlement, even linking human rights to a conservative vision of democracy that instantiated the natural law.[91] For German Protestant critics, however, this model was flawed. From both Lutheran and Reformed perspectives, Maritain seemed to place too much emphasis on innate human dignity, rather than humanity's fallenness and dependence on salvation. The presumption that human rights could be known absent the light of grace was also beyond the pale.

The human rights advocacy of American ecumenical Protestants presented a more complex problem of filiation and distance. Personalist ideas had also gained ground in Protestant ecumenical circles in the 1930s, especially at the 1937 Oxford conference, where the human person was counterposed against the menacing "totalitarian" state. During the war American participants at Oxford turned to the language of human rights. While they lacked a specific vision of natural law and tended to envision a stronger role for the state in securing individual rights, ecumenical Protestants similarly viewed human rights as a Christian moral basis for postwar reconstruction. The US Federal Council of Churches' Commission on a Just and Durable Peace, founded in 1940 by the Presbyterian attorney, ecumenical activist, and future secretary of state John Foster Dulles, championed the incorporation of human rights into the UN Charter of 1945. A member of Dulles's committee, the Philadelphia pastor Frederick Nolde, would go on to represent the WCC at the UN Commission on Human Rights. Yet German Protestants could not fully assent to the work of the Dulles commission. As he came to embrace a militant Cold War anti-Communism, Dulles braided together human rights and American nationalism, emphasizing human rights promotion as a pillar of America's global mission. For his part, Nolde viewed human rights as a basis for Protestant cooperation with states and international organizations rather than a domain of the church's exclusive authority.[92]

At the outset of the Allied occupation, then, German Protestant intellectuals tended to share a jaundiced view of human rights. Conservative Lutherans and Dahlemites alike criticized the idea of human rights as theologically faulty and, more pointedly, a tool of foreign domination. On the side of the Confessing Church Dahlemites, Ernst Wolf opened the first postwar issue of the refounded *Evangelische Theologie* with a polemic against "humanism." Wolf's attack on the precepts of the Christian human rights revival was steeped in Barthian theology: The human being was redeemed through God's grace alone, while the world of human affairs could attain its ideals of justice only through the message of gospel. In contrast, ideologies that insisted upon the transcendence and autonomy of reason fueled self-aggrandizing visions of human mastery, culminating in social Darwinism and, finally, "the racial theory of recent years."[93] While participating in the broader discourse that saw secularization at the root of the Nazi regime, Wolf went a step further than his Catholic and Anglo-American counterparts, perceiving the same danger in attempts to amalgamate Christianity and human rights.

Gerhard Ritter, the most outspoken conservative German Lutheran on the issue of human rights, was more circumspect in his judgment. In a 1947 memorandum submitted to the WCC Study Department, the historian acknowledged that he shared a concern for excessive state power and unbridled nationalism with Christian human rights proponents across postwar Europe. But like Wolf, Ritter feared that human rights discourse, even in its Christian guise, concealed agendas of domination under the patina of universal principles. Statements produced at Anglo-American ecumenical conferences, Ritter wrote, assumed "the recognition of general human rights as the moral foundation of world peace," but neglected the plural understandings of human rights around the world. Moreover, Germans had been shut out entirely from discussions of international human rights principles, reduced to "a mere object of Great Power politics."[94]

These critical assessments notwithstanding, the groundwork for the EKD's human rights swerve was laid already before the 1948 WCC assembly. With Germany's loss of sovereignty, intellectuals from both wings of the church needed international credibility, which they sought to gain by adapting a language that was fast becoming a dominant idiom of international postwar planning. Within Dahlemite circles, the French jurist and philosopher Jacques Ellul provided the most influential reformulation of human rights. Ellul would later become known as a pioneer of Cold War–era technology critique. His earliest works, however, were contributions to Protestant political theology inspired by the writings of Karl Barth, whose dialectical theology he discovered as a law student in the early 1930s.[95] Politically distant from the German nationalist milieu that dominated the EKD, Ellul had been an early opponent of the Vichy regime and joined a network that passed false papers to Jews threatened with deportation.[96] Nevertheless, Ellul's postwar writings, published when he was a young member of the law faculty at the University of Bordeaux, offered a powerful answer to the dilemmas faced by Protestants in post-Nazi Germany.

Ellul's first text to appear after the war, a slim volume entitled *The Theological Foundation of Law,* aimed to rethink the Protestant contribution to postwar legal reconstruction. Ellul built on the premise of Barth's 1938 "Justification and Justice." Although the natural law remained concealed from a fallen humanity, Scripture revealed points of intersection between God's "justification of the sinner through Jesus Christ" and "the problem of human justice."[97] According to Ellul, "human rights" represented one such conjuncture. Like Catholic natural law theorists, Ellul understood human rights as a means of mediating between liberal individualism and totalitarian collectivism. He attributed rights not to the atomized individual but to "man in relationship." However, Ellul diverged from neo-Thomists such as Jacques Maritain in two respects, which became foundational for German Protestant discussions of human rights. First, Ellul emphasized that the source of rights lay in the undeserved gift of divine grace, not natural law. If rights were not conferred by grace, then rights claims would reflect mere self-aggrandizement, collapsing the distinction between justice and power. Second, in the absence of universal principles of natural law, the "content" of human rights was "contingent and variable," "granted to man by God for a specific purpose."[98] In practice, Ellul's formulation allowed the church wide latitude in discerning the scope and limits of human rights.

Ellul's tract resonated with central beliefs of the Confessing Church Dahlemites. Like German theologians influenced by Karl Barth, Ellul stressed the authority of gospel in the political world and the insufficiency of natural law as a basis for reorganizing the postwar legal order. Even before the work's 1948 translation into German, Ernst Wolf and other reviewers hailed its significance.[99] For a German audience, Ellul's appeal was not only theological but political: His theory of human rights could be readily mobilized behind an attack on war crimes trials. Ellul's 1946 treatise stressed the church's responsibility to "watch the legal affairs of a society," especially to "*affirm the limits of law.*"[100] Writing for a French ecumenical journal the next year, Ellul followed this reasoning to join the chorus of German jurists attacking the Nuremberg category of crimes against humanity. The Nuremberg IMT, Ellul held, propagated a dangerous illusion by arrogating to itself the authority to speak on behalf of all humanity. Exceeding the bounds of human law, the tribunal replicated the hubris at the root of the Nazi catastrophe.[101]

Not only Dahlemites but also German Protestant conservatives sought to make the discourse of human rights their own. The exemplar of human rights language at the Protestant Academies, the jurist Hans Dombois, had a far more compromised past than Ellul. Born in 1907, Dombois had been active in the Young National League during the Weimar Republic. After completing his legal training in 1933, Dombois worked as a prosecutor at Berlin and Potsdam criminal courts, subsequently joining the SA and the Nazi Party. In one instance he prosecuted a Jewish attorney, Alfred Lehmann, for violating Nazi miscegenation laws, leading to Lehmann's death at the Gross-Rosen concentration camp. Upon his return from wartime military service, Dombois sought to minimize his Nazi past and conceal his role in Lehmann's conviction. During his denazification hearing, Dombois managed to be classified as a "follower" rather than the more severe "offender," partly on account of his membership in the Confessing Church and the recommendation of his former pastor. He took a position as a legal adviser to the EKD chancellery following his release from postwar custody, quickly becoming active in the church's campaigns against denazification and war crimes trials.[102]

Dombois's first statement on human rights, subsequently submitted to the WCC Study Department, was delivered in September 1947 at Bad Boll before an audience that included Gerhard Ritter, Helmut Thielicke, and numerous prominent jurists.[103] Dombois echoed a widespread conservative discourse that linked human rights to the struggle against Communism and the recovery of Europe's Christian foundations. On this view, human rights were not a project of human emancipation but a mission to salvage "the final unconditional law from the devouring jaws of the modern state." Only a return to authentic Christianity could save Europe from the "pseudo-religions" of National Socialism and Bolshevism.[104] At the same time, Dombois gave voice to the specific premises undergirding the German Protestant discussion, tracing human rights to a Calvinist tradition that viewed the human being's religious, political, and economic freedoms as signs of divine grace.[105] Grace, rather than reason, natural law, or the state, served as the ultimate source of human rights—a point on which Dombois converged with Jacques Ellul. On this basis, Dombois attacked the pretension of Allied governments to represent a universal standard of morality. Instead the expulsions orchestrated by the Soviets and Western Allies alike were violations of "the right to life of the German people," expressions of the "radical self-justification of the modern human being."[106]

The encounter between German Protestant and ecumenical discourses of human rights culminated at the 1948 Amsterdam Assembly of the WCC. The meeting displayed the ongoing tensions between German Protestants and their Anglo-American counterparts, but also marked a moment of reconciliation. At the conference, which brought together delegates from 147 churches in forty-four countries, American speakers had the primary word on human rights. Frederick Nolde's contribution contained a characteristic expression of ecumenical human rights thinking. Christians, Nolde pronounced, should promote "principles which will be universally applicable and which can be reasonably expected to find endorsement by men of goodwill everywhere."[107] Memorandums submitted to the WCC by Hans Dombois, Gerhard Ritter, Erik Wolf, and Ernst Wolf, which contained a more sober account of human dependency on divine grace, were not included in the meeting's official record.[108] Nevertheless, the forty EKD delegates in attendance at Amsterdam—a who's who of church leaders and lay intellectuals, including Otto Dibelius, Constantin von Dietze, Hans Joachim Iwand, Hanns Lilje, Martin Niemöller, Gerhard Ritter, Rudolf Smend, Erik Wolf, Ernst Wolf, and Theophil Wurm—could find speakers who affirmed their perspectives.[109] Most significant, German participants welcomed the conference's ambition to work toward Christian unity in the face of unprecedented global challenges, not least the rise of the "modern total state."[110]

The German Protestant press even celebrated the WCC's human rights work. The EKD biweekly *Evangelische Welt* reprinted the official conference statement, "The Church and the International Disorder," which stressed that human rights derived from the Christian "freedom to obey God rather than men."[111] Following the adoption of the UN Universal Declaration of Human Rights in December 1948, reports in *Evangelische Welt* and the revived Dahlemite organ *Junge Kirche* applauded the UN's expansive definition of religious freedom.[112] This was the direct result of ecumenical activism. At the UN Commission on Human Rights, Frederick Nolde had successfully defended a concept of religious liberty that included not only freedom of belief, the narrow definition proposed by the Soviet delegation, but freedom of "teaching, practice, worship and observance."[113] Acknowledging that the UN declaration did not derive human rights from God, the German Protestant press nevertheless urged that human rights "be defended through national and international measures."[114]

The Limits of Human Jurisdiction

While bringing EKD delegates into dialogue with new interlocutors, the Amsterdam Assembly did not entirely overcome national and confessional differences among member churches. Following the conference, German

Protestants would continue to espouse their own version of human rights language, marshaling human rights behind the campaign against war crimes trials in newfound appeals to Christians abroad. The linkage between human rights and anti-trial polemics was not unique to the EKD. Already at the Nuremberg IMT and the subsequent Nuremberg proceedings, German defense attorneys invoked human rights to contest the supposed application of retroactive law against their clients.[115] Still, the EKD's deployment of human rights arguments reflected the parameters of the German Protestant discussion. Human rights, on this view, were founded on God's grace alone and constituted a domain of the church's unique authority. Moreover, its usage of human rights language had two specific consequences for the EKD. First, German Protestants could mobilize international support for the cause of amnesty without calling into question their own theological framework, including its historical elisions. Second, church leaders, theologians, and lay intellectuals cemented the promotion of rights as an objective of the EKD's public interventions. They thereby established a new model for Protestant engagement in the public sphere that would extend beyond the anti-trial campaign.

The EKD's campaign against war crimes trials gained momentum as preparations for the Amsterdam Assembly were underway. While Bishop Wurm had made his debut as a trial opponent during the Nuremberg IMT, he threw himself into anti-trial advocacy in the spring of 1948 after receiving reports of torture and witness tampering from defense attorneys in the Malmédy massacre trial at Dachau. The trial, which sentenced seventy-two Waffen-SS members—including forty-three death sentences—for the murder of disarmed American soldiers, had sparked international controversy. Like other activists in the transatlantic lobby to overturn the convictions, Wurm refused to recognize, or to admit, that claims of irregularities were outright fabrications.[116] In June Wurm expanded his offensive by releasing to the press a series of letters he had exchanged with Robert Kempner, a German-Jewish lawyer who had escaped to the United States in 1939 and later joined the prosecutorial team at Nuremberg. With barely concealed antisemitic undertones, Wurm decried the use of "criminal methods and hideous cruelties" in war crimes investigations, which ultimately amounted to "acts of vengeance cloaked in legal form."[117]

Wurm's campaign for the Malmédy defendants, which quickly spiraled into an attack on the entire program of US trials, fostered alliances across confessional and national divides. The appearance of the Malmédy allegations coincided with the consolidation of Germany's Western occupation zones under a single administration and the ensuing Soviet blockade of West Berlin, a standoff that would culminate in the founding of the West German state in May 1949. The mounting Cold War tensions eroded any pretense of cooperation in the Allied Control Council. As West German integration into the emergent Western alliance became the primary aim of the US occupation, Wurm's office expertly exploited divisions in American public opinion. By early 1949 the bishop forwarded reports from war crimes defense attorneys to US senators William Langer and Joseph McCarthy, who had opened a Senate investigation into the alleged abuses at the Dachau trials.[118] EKD officials also launched joint initiatives with their Catholic counterparts. In the fall of 1948 Wurm and Munich auxiliary bishop Johannes Neuhäusler issued a statement calling for a review of the Dachau convictions.[119] Soon afterward the German Catholic and Protestant churches cofounded the Committee for Church Aid to Prisoners, which funded a pair of defense attorneys who together represented over 800 convicted war criminals.[120]

Despite these newfound alliances, the EKD's anti-trial advocacy had distinctive aims and outcomes. Neuhäusler, the most active Catholic opponent of war crimes trials, adopted a less confrontational posture than Wurm, assuring occupation authorities that he did not reject punishment altogether but sought only to ensure the trials' impartiality.[121] Moreover, whereas Catholic advocacy centered on defendants who had undergone prison conversions, Protestant trial opponents rejected the very premise that Nazi crimes could be brought before human courts.[122] In turn, the EKD's mobilization of theological resources in its attack on war crimes trials—including the language of human rights—would reverberate beyond the occupation years.

The EKD administrator Hansjürg Ranke led the Protestant effort to marshal a theology of human rights behind the amnesty campaign. Appointed in 1948 as the EKD's commissioner for postwar questions—a euphemism for his role overseeing the initiatives against denazification and war crimes trials—Ranke belonged to the generation of ex-Nazi Protestant intellectuals who sought political expiation in the EKD. Born in 1904 and trained in law, Ranke had served as a secretary in the Nazi-era Reich Church. Like Hans Dombois, Ernst Forsthoff, and Erik Wolf, he had joined the Nazi Party. Captured during the final months of the war after five years of military service, Ranke landed at Norton Camp, England, where he directed a theological school for his fellow POWs.[123] The experience of internment reinforced Ranke's apologetic view of the German military's conduct and his subordination of specific guilt to universal reconciliation. Imprisonment "destroyed our illusions that we had behaved rightly, and that we could have behaved rightly," Ranke recalled in a 1948 report for the World Council of Churches. Nevertheless, "the word of God led us in the Protestant prison community to repentance."[124]

Shortly following the WCC Amsterdam Assembly, Ranke launched a project that would form the linchpin of the EKD's amnesty appeal: a memorandum assembling affidavits, defense attorneys' reports, dissenting judicial opinions, and church leaders' petitions against war crimes trials, intended for presentation to US occupation authorities. Ranke received authorization from the EKD Council to compile the memorandum in February 1949, as Bishop Wurm's office strengthened its connections with American trial opponents.[125] At the same time, Ranke inaugurated a commission of theologians and jurists to address ongoing debates about the church's role in the legal order, a theme the EKD synod had taken up a month prior without a resolution.[126] The two initiatives were closely linked. Ranke's commission on "Church and Law," which met for two days in May at the University of Göttingen, quickly evolved into a network promoting the release of convicted war criminals.

The "Church and Law" commission helped to heal the rift between the Lutheran and Dahlemite factions of the EKD and unite both sides around a shared conviction: that the Protestant church possessed unique knowledge of the purpose and limits of human law. The sixteen participants spanned the church's theological divide. Ernst Wolf attended alongside the Freiburg circle theologian Friedrich Delekat, as well as jurists including Ranke, Hans Dombois, the Göttingen rector Ludwig Raiser, and Rudolf Smend, whose Institute for Protestant Church Law hosted the meeting.[127] As a common text, Ranke selected Jacques Ellul's *The Theological Foundation of Law*. Ellul's contentions about the divine sources of grace and the paramount role of the church resonated across the commission. Controversies over occupation policy were never far from the surface. In a lecture to the group, Ernst Wolf pointed out that Ellul's critique of "natural law ideology" found its practical expression in the French jurist's "confrontation with the Nuremberg trials"—a reference to Ellul's 1947 excoriation of the crimes against humanity charge.[128]

The second plenary speaker, the jurist Ulrich Scheuner, was, like Dombois and Ranke, a beneficiary of the EKD's postwar apologetics. A member of the Nazi Party and the SA who published a 1934 defense of the "national revolution," Scheuner went on to serve as a Wehrmacht lieutenant. After the war he obtained employment at the Evangelisches Hilfswerk, the EKD relief organization that doubled as a clearinghouse for aid to convicted war criminals.[129] At the "Church and Law" conference, Scheuner followed a familiar formula of trial opponents, noting that Ellul's text offered a path toward Protestant engagement with law despite "the time-boundedness and imperfection of the human pursuit of justice."[130] The lectures and discussions at Göttingen, as well as the commission's concluding theses, resolved on two basic points. On the one hand, no fixed blueprint could guide Christian interventions in the world of law, for Protestants were aware of the "helplessness of all natural law programs and evasions." On the other hand, Christians "may not abdicate from concrete decisions toward the realization of justice on earth."[131]

Despite its theological abstraction, this call to public responsibility could be mobilized behind the anti-trial campaign. During the summer of 1949, as he worked to compile the war crimes memorandum, Ranke received advisory briefs from Dombois and Scheuner that reiterated the Göttingen meeting's warnings against human "self-justification."[132] Ranke also joined the Heidelberg jurists circle, a group of war crimes defense attorneys formed to coordinate the newly founded West German state's clemency appeals. As one of the group's leaders argued at its first meeting, whereas secular jurists could petition only for an impartial review of the convictions, the churches could seek "total mercy."[133] The final version of Ranke's report, submitted to the office of the newly appointed US High Commissioner for Germany as well as church leaders abroad, similarly invoked the limits of human law: "We wish to call attention in the name of the righteous and merciful God to the fact that the highest expression of justice is not necessarily sentence and punishment. As servants of God, we ask that in suitable cases, mercy be shown."[134]

Shortly after the completion of the memorandum, ecumenical contacts prompted the network around Ranke to frame their clemency appeals even more directly around the language of human rights. In August 1949 Frederick Nolde, who remained the WCC liaison to the UN Commission on Human Rights, solicited a response from the EKD Foreign Office to the Covenant on Human Rights drafted by the UN committee.[135] The EKD Foreign Office quickly convened a second meeting of the "Church and Law" commission, whose invitees included Hans Dombois, Ludwig Raiser, Ulrich Scheuner, Rudolf Smend, and Ernst Wolf, to produce the reply.[136] The group's final report, submitted to Nolde in March 1950, defined human rights in opposition to "a doctrine of natural law that ignores the sinful nature of fallen man." If human rights originated from cognizance of human limitation, then "human states and institutions" alone could not "guarantee" them. Instead human justice must guard against overextension and hubris. Following this framing, the commission mobilized the language of human rights to underscore the EKD's critique of Allied occupation policy. The UN Covenant on Human Rights should be expanded to incorporate a "prohibition on retroactive penal laws" and a guarantee of human rights in occupied territories. Moreover, "cases that involve guilt that can be judged by God alone may not be brought before human courts." In a barely concealed reference to war crimes trials, the commission asserted that a proper understanding of human rights nullified any attempt to judge wartime atrocities under human law.[137]

The immediate impact of the EKD's recommendations to the Commission on Human Rights was slim, in part because UN work on human rights had stalled amid mounting Cold War tensions.[138] But at the same time, Protestant leaders received an increasingly favorable reception by US occupation authorities. Meeting with Ranke and other EKD officials over dinner at his home, US high commissioner John J. McCloy acknowledged inconsistencies in the Nuremberg judgments and welcomed Ranke's recommendation for the establishment of a German-American commission to review the sentences.[139] Certainly Cold War calculations played a role in McCloy's thinking, as hawkish American legislators pressured the high commissioner to accede to German demands. But McCloy's willingness to consider a review of the convictions suggested a deeper affinity for his German interlocutors, likely fostered by American diplomatic circles' growing knowledge of the failed July 20 plot.[140] The EKD also found support from influential figures in the WCC, including George Bell and the American theologian Reinhold Niebuhr. Both had joined the EKD's amnesty campaigns out of a concern for reintegrating West Germany into the Western fold. In his correspondence with McCloy, Niebuhr went so far as to echo Bishop Wurm's accusations against the "refugee resentment" of German-Jewish prosecutors.[141]

By March 1950 McCloy partially fulfilled his promise to Ranke, establishing an Advisory Board on Clemency for War Criminals. The panel of three American judges spent the summer reviewing thousands of pages of files, issuing a final report that recommended reductions for the majority of the ninety-three outstanding Nuremberg sentences.[142] Seizing this apparent momentum, the EKD Foreign Office planned a third conference on the relationship between theology and law to be held in November. This time organizers were transparent about their aims. By elucidating "the limits of state jurisdiction," the conference invitation noted, the church would contribute toward "a resolution of the war criminals complex through a generous amnesty."[143] In addition to ongoing participants such as Hans Dombois, Ulrich Scheuner, and Ernst Wolf, the attendees included the Heidelberg circle jurist Erich Kaufmann.[144]

An address by the Reformed theologian Otto Weber, the German translator of Jacques Ellul's *The Theological Foundation of Law*, set the tenor of the meeting. A former Nazi Party member, Weber had joined the German Christians in 1933, and he later worked toward conciliation between German Christians and the Confessing Church.[145] Like Protestant ex-Nazi jurists including Dombois, Ranke, and Scheuner, Weber now followed Ellul to position the church as the arbiter over the limits of law. Because National Socialism resulted from humanity's fall away from God, attempts to resolve the ensuing crisis by political means would only reinforce the pretension to "self-justification" that precipitated the collapse. Instead the church should "call on the justice and obligation of the sovereign act of mercy."[146]

The following day the assembled theologians and jurists composed statements for delivery to the governments and churches of the fifteen countries where accused or convicted German war criminals remained imprisoned. Both reflected the language of human rights that the EKD had adopted in the lead-up to the Amsterdam conference and perfected in its amnesty campaign. The petition to government officials called for amnesty for old, young, and sick prisoners; sentence reductions for those convicted based on laws applied unequally to Germans; and the creation of mixed clemency commissions. Stressing the "limits of human jurisdiction," the petition appealed to the UN Universal Declaration of Human Rights, through which the "principles" allegedly violated in the trials—such as retroactive convictions and selective prosecution based on the defendant's nationality—"have been newly advanced in the consciousness of humankind."[147] The message "to the churches of the participating countries," drafted by Ulrich Scheuner, similarly evoked the overextension of human justice. If the war had resulted from Europe's fall away from Christianity, then "the Christian longing for justice" could not stop at ascertaining individual violations of law. Instead guilt was an existential matter involving the whole of society, "which surely does not stand within the domain of the human judge." Citing calls by the World Council of Churches for a "just peace," the message to the churches welcomed the ecumenical movement's "friendly understanding of our particular hardships and readiness to help."[148]

The reports were distributed in December 1950, and their reception indicated the success of the German church's ecumenical efforts. The EKD Foreign Office received sympathetic replies from Protestant church officials in Britain, Denmark, France, and the Netherlands. All promised to lobby their respective governments for amnesties and sentence reductions.[149] Shortly before Christmas, the French high commissioner to West Germany, André François-Poncet, informed the EKD Council of the early release of 123 convicted war criminals and the reduction of thirty-one sentences.[150] The EKD remained a vocal presence in the final stage of public debate. In early January 1951, Bavarian bishop Hans Meiser rallied the leaders of the regional Protestant churches to send a new petition to John McCloy, while the conservative Protestant weekly *Christ und Welt* called for a "general amnesty."[151] Ranke was convinced, based on their meeting a year prior, that the US high commissioner was "attempting ... to make the German standpoint plausible in America."[152]

Such expectations proved vindicated. On January 31, 1951, under pressure to resolve the war criminals issue amid covert negotiations over West German rearmament, McCloy announced his decision to reduce sixty-nine of seventy-four outstanding prison terms and commute ten of fifteen death sentences. General Thomas Handy, who oversaw the prisoners convicted in the US Army trials at Dachau, commuted eleven of the thirteen death sentences under his authority.[153] McCloy denied that his decisions had been influenced by the anti-trial lobby, but he acknowledged considering the large numbers of "letters and petitions for clemency." His report on the matter emphasized the efforts of American authorities to find "mitigating circumstances."[154] This was not enough for some trial opponents. Bavarian bishop Hans Meiser and Catholic auxiliary bishop Johannes Neuhäusler launched a final, unsuccessful effort to halt the executions of the five prisoners whose death sentences McCloy confirmed: four SS-Einsatzgruppen commanders who were responsible for organizing massacres of Jews and other civilians on the Eastern Front, as well as Oswald Pohl, the overseer of the Nazi concentration camp system.[155]

The majority of the EKD leadership, however, believed that McCloy's extensions of clemency reflected a Christian ethos. Two days after the decisions were announced, the Stuttgart prelate Karl Hartenstein, a member of the EKD Council, wrote to McCloy on behalf of the church leadership, thanking the high commissioner for his display of leniency. McCloy had allowed mercy to prevail over law, signaling his "sense of justice." In Hartenstein's remarks, the antisemitic underpinnings of the EKD's anti-trial campaign rose to the surface. McCloy could do no less in the name of justice precisely because "the image of man" had been so gravely violated in the concentration camps and the "mass murder of Jews."[156] At the same time that Hartenstein acknowledged the reality of Jewish victimhood, so often obscured in German Protes-

POST-NAZI JUSTICE AND PROTESTANT HUMAN RIGHTS   117

tant guilt discourses, he posited an equivalence of suffering with German society, and even with the architects of Nazi genocide, as the basis for Christian reconciliation. On March 6, satisfied with Hartenstein's report, the EKD Council resolved to refrain from issuing further statements on war crimes trials.[157]

MCCLOY'S AMNESTIES MARKED the cessation only of the EKD's public advocacy for convicted war criminals. Privately the Protestant Church continued to petition Allied officials for sentence reductions, participating in a covert campaign that spanned the West German political spectrum from Social Democrats to the extreme right. Hansjürg Ranke remained the EKD's leader in these efforts. Well into the 1950s the church administrator collaborated with Stille Hilfe, an organization of SS wives dedicated to the release of the remaining prisoners. Ranke also continued to participate in the Heidelberg jurists circle.[158] By 1953, amid negotiations over West German rearmament, the Heidelberg circle secured the creation of a parole board that included West German, American, British, and French representatives. British and French war crimes prisons were closed in 1957, two years after the end of the Allied occupation. US authorities released their four remaining inmates the following year.[159] After the success of the Nuremberg IMT—in mobilizing international public opinion, and in securing convictions for the highest-ranking Nazi leaders—subsequent trials in the Western zones concluded with mixed results.

The EKD's criticisms of Allied war crimes trials were not unique to the church. Arguments about retroactive lawmaking, collective guilt, and war crimes committed by the Allies all belonged to a transatlantic debate about the post-Nazi trials. Indeed, the EKD's cooperation with the Catholic Church, Anglo-American ecumenists, and US politicians is indicative of widespread skepticism about the trials by the late 1940s. Cold War polarization, recrudescent nationalism, personal networks, as well as Christian ideas of grace all motivated German—and Allied—efforts to obtain the release of convicted Nazi war criminals. German jurists brought to bear all manner of legal theories in their efforts to delegitimize the trials. Even Social Democratic and liberal politicians joined the lobby for sentence reductions, especially in death penalty cases.[160]

German Protestant petitions against the trials were distinct, however, in the ways they leveraged a specific theology of human rights, rooted in both the

Protestant Academies and the EKD Brethren Council. While participating in a broader postwar discourse of re-Christianization, German Protestants' language of human rights exhibited distinctive features: a critique of "natural law"; a preoccupation with grace as the sole source of rights; and, the conviction that the Protestant community alone perceived the boundary demarcating the coercive power of law from the inviolable sphere of the human. This usage of human rights arguments did not require a critique of the church's historical antisemitism but instead relied upon a timeworn theme of Jewish vengeance and Christian grace. German Protestants also did not link human rights to a defense of democracy—not even the limited vision of democracy that Pius XII had affirmed in 1944. However, human rights discourse did signal a decisive break with the political theologies that had characterized Protestants' early reactions to the Nazi regime, whether Lutheran apologias for the total state or Barthian attempts to preserve the purity of the Christian message. By mobilizing the language of human rights, postwar German Protestant intellectuals not only sought the sympathy of occupation authorities and ecumenical interlocutors but situated their church as a check on state power.

The EKD's campaign against war crimes trials, as much as it reflected continuities with a long tradition of Protestant nationalism, therefore marked a moment of transition. Far more than in the Nazi period, German Protestant church leaders, pastors, and lay intellectuals styled themselves as arbiters over the limits of law and critics of overbearing state power. Embedded in antisemitism and anti-Allied sentiment, the initiative also shaped a new self-image that extended beyond the early occupation years. Following the formation of the West German state in 1949, leaders of the Protestant campaign against war crimes trials would bring their vision of a politically engaged church to bear on pivotal debates about the relationship among state, church, and individual under the West German Basic Law.

CHAPTER FOUR

FAMILIES, SCHOOLS, AND THE BATTLE FOR THE BASIC LAW

FOUR YEARS TO THE DAY after the defeat of Nazi Germany, the Parliamentary Council meeting at the Koenig Museum in Bonn adopted a constitution for the Federal Republic of Germany. After approval by the Western Allies the new constitution went into effect on May 23, 1949, once two-thirds of West Germany's states had voted for ratification.[1] Despite its unusual title—the name "Basic Law" was chosen to underscore the Federal Republic's provisional status—the document answered fundamental questions about Germany's future. At least in the immediate term, Germany would not form a neutral buffer between the Cold War blocs. Created out of the American, British, and French zones, the Federal Republic was instead a semi-sovereign state that remained under three-power military occupation; its creation was quickly answered by the founding of the Soviet-backed German Democratic Republic in October. The Basic Law also established the Federal Republic's state form: a capitalist democracy on a Western model, rather than the socialist state or mixed economy for which some German intellectuals had called.[2] But the moment of constitutional genesis was also replete with doubt. How could democracy take root in a country whose recent experience was shaped by dictatorship, war, and military occupation, and whose professional and political classes had been widely complicit with National Socialism? Could the Federal Republic gain the loyalty of its population, or was it merely a mirage of American power, destined to be swallowed into the Communist bloc if the US commitment to postwar Europe waned?

For churchgoing Protestants, the founding of the Federal Republic created an added layer of uncertainty. Whereas Protestants made up two-thirds of the pre-1945 German Reich, they were only a slim majority in postwar West Germany. Historic centers of German Protestantism in Brandenburg, Pomerania, Saxony, and Thuringia fell on the other side of the Iron Curtain. The GDR's population was 90 percent Protestant, yet the East German churches faced land expropriations and state repression, causing West German Protestant leaders to fear for the future of their confession. The establishment of the West German capital at Bonn, in the heart of the Rhineland, along with the election of the Catholic Christian Democrat Konrad Adenauer as West Germany's first chancellor, confirmed the spatial and confessional re-centering of the Federal Republic. The mayor of Cologne during the Weimar Republic, Adenauer remained an inveterate skeptic of Protestant-Prussian militarism, to which he attributed Nazism's rise. Instead the chancellor and his closest political allies viewed West Germany as a pillar of a West European *Abendland* (Occident), a term that gained ground in postwar Catholic political discourse to call for closer West European integration.[3]

Confessional division therefore remained a wellspring of political conflict during the Federal Republic's early decades. Certainly the Communist threat to the east, as well as the perceived dangers of secularization and "materialism" at home, helped unite Catholics and Protestants who joined the Christian Democratic Union (CDU) around a conservative vision of constitutional democracy.[4] Konrad Adenauer, notwithstanding his strongly held Catholic identity, worked to achieve confessional parity among party leaders and parliamentarians. At the same time, the CDU, like the pre-1933 Center Party, drew its politicians and voters disproportionately from the Catholic milieu.[5] Confessional divisions on key issues such as school policy and German reunification rent West German society, fueling a vocal minority of Protestant pastors and politicians who shunned the CDU and encouraged their followers to do the same. Historians increasingly recognize early postwar West Germany as a period of confessional tension, as well as one of reconciliation.[6] In this chapter and in Chapter 5, I go a step further by foregrounding Protestant political actors and their internal rifts. Not only Christian Democratic interconfessionalism but also competition among the wings of German Protestantism worked to foster the democratization of the Federal Republic.

This dynamic emerged forcefully in conflicts over the reform of family and education law. Although both major churches had long looked to families and schools as key domains for propagating their influence, postwar conditions raised the stakes of debate. The war transformed the gendered structure of German society, with over 5 million men killed and women serving as

FAMILIES, SCHOOLS, AND THE BATTLE FOR THE BASIC LAW

workers and heads of household in unprecedented numbers. Divorce rates spiked in the late 1940s, as hasty wartime marriages broke apart. The German situation was extreme but also symptomatic of a broader European crisis. Across the continent, war laid waste to traditional family structures while fueling feminist demands for reform around marriage and divorce law, freedom of employment, and the rights of unmarried mothers.[7] Nazi school policies and postwar demographic transformations equally disrupted patterns of religious education.

Within the academies, church commissions, and periodicals that remained at the center of the Protestant public sphere, pastors and lay intellectuals continued to draw on the lexicon of German Protestant nationalism. Yet as in the campaign against war crimes trials, Protestant efforts to claim the mantle of anti-Nazi resistance fostered a language of individual rights and limited state authority. Moreover, both wings of the postwar EKD, conservative Lutherans and veterans of the Confessing Church Dahlemites alike, looked toward West Germany's Federal Constitutional Court as a check on Catholic political influence. Divisions among Protestant leaders allowed those who were outside the Protestant mainstream—including women activists and Protestants of Jewish descent—to gain clout in calling for legal reforms. By the end of the decade, the Federal Constitutional Court would draw on arguments introduced by Protestant jurists to rule against Adenauer's government in cases involving family law and confessional schools.

To be sure, Protestant intellectuals and politicians shaped domestic policy in the early Federal Republic well beyond the reform of family and education law. Most notably, Protestant economists including Walter Eucken, Alfred Müller-Armack, Wilhelm Röpke, and Adenauer's economics minister, Ludwig Erhard—all of whom had ties to the wartime Freiburg circle—were key thinkers behind West Germany's "social market economy." Calling for a market economy tempered by a strong state, these economists drew on the Freiburg circle's dual critique of laissez-faire liberalism and state socialism.[8] But whereas proponents of the social market economy operated at the edges of institutional Protestantism, the churches and their affiliated organizations occupied the front lines of pitched battles over family law and confessional schools. Moreover, family law and education reform were key *constitutional* domains in which the Protestant churches intervened during the 1950s. An emphasis on these issues is in keeping with this book's larger argument that practical engagement with constitutional politics facilitated a Protestant affirmation of constitutional democracy.

During the postwar campaign against war crimes trials, Protestant church leaders and lay intellectuals adumbrated a language of human rights untethered to democracy. In disputes over family and education, these Protestants first sought to achieve their vision of rights within West Germany's existing political institutions. While few Protestant writers or church authorities would explicitly defend constitutional democracy during the 1950s, participation in public debate—and not least, victories before the Federal Constitutional Court—prepared an influential cohort of West German Protestants to locate the roots of constitutional democracy in their own confession by the mid-1960s. This project of political reinvention extended back to the drafting of the Basic Law.

Confessional Polemics and the Basic Law

The sixty-five delegates who convened the Parliamentary Council, the convention that drafted the West German Basic Law between September 1948 and May 1949, represented the eleven postwar West German states and the major reconstituted parties. The body was composed of twenty-seven Christian Democrats, including members of the CDU and its Bavarian counterpart, the Christian Social Union (CSU); twenty-seven Social Democrats; five liberals; and two delegates each from the Communist Party of Germany, the conservative German Party, and the revived Center Party.[9] Political parties were not the only groups that sought to shape the new constitution; the major churches were also closely involved. Whereas relations between the churches and the Weimar National Assembly of 1919 had been characterized by mistrust, the creation of the Basic Law was altogether different. The unique circumstances of German defeat—the destruction of other major institutions, a presumed legacy of anti-Nazi resistance, and the support of the American and British occupation governments—strengthened the churches' claim to participate in the constitution-making process.

Developments in legal theory also worked in the churches' favor. During the second half of the 1940s, a host of German legal writers blamed a tradition of legal positivism for the failures of their profession under the Nazi regime. In the words of this argument's most influential expositor, the Social Democratic legal philosopher Gustav Radbruch, the positivist doctrine that law derived from the state alone had left German judges "defenseless" against "laws of arbitrary and criminal content." Anti-positivist polemics were often self-serving; German jurists were not simply pawns of the Nazi regime but had actively

FAMILIES, SCHOOLS, AND THE BATTLE FOR THE BASIC LAW   123

abetted the creation and enforcement of its racial legislation.[10] Nevertheless, the drafters of the Basic Law, including delegates from the left-wing parties, widely agreed that the new constitution required a grounding in values that preceded the state.[11] Protestant and Catholic intellectuals, who had articulated a similar critique of legal positivism since the 1920s, were poised to position Christianity as the very source of the constitution's authority.

The matter on which church officials sought the most direct influence over the Parliamentary Council involved religious education and confessional schooling. The issue was highly emotional, as the recent past sharpened long-standing passions. In most of Germany, primary education was traditionally provided by the Protestant or Catholic confessional school (*Bekenntnisschule*). Students and teachers belonged to a single confession, while instruction was, at least in principle, organized around confessional precepts. In the mid-nineteenth century, German states with strong liberal traditions, such as Baden and Hesse, introduced the confessionally mixed "community" school (*Gemein-schaftsschule*), where students were divided by confession only for religious instruction. Twentieth-century upheavals challenged these patterns. To the chagrin of Protestant and Catholic church leaders, the Weimar Constitution called for the standardization of the community school throughout the country. However, Weimar-era legislators failed to pass a national school law, despite numerous attempts by the left-wing and liberal parties, leaving the confessional schools intact in much of Germany. The Nazi regime brought further pressures. The Concordat of July 1933 guaranteed the autonomy of Catholic institutions in Nazi Germany, including confessional schools, in exchange for a ban on political activity by the Catholic clergy. The regime, however, quickly violated these provisions, launching a campaign for the "German community school" by 1935 and banning confessional schools in 1939. After 1945, Soviet occupation authorities shuttered confessional schools in their zone once and for all, whereas the Americans and British signaled a willingness to reopen them. However, mass population movements caused by bombings and forced displacements meant that once largely homogeneous regions of Germany were now confessionally mixed. The demographic basis, if not the political will, for confessional schools appeared in jeopardy.[12]

If both churches sought to protect their privileges in education, the issue did not catalyze a unified Christian front. For the Catholic clergy, and many lay activists, reestablishing confessional schools was a matter not only of the Catholic Church's position in society but its foundational teachings. In the view of the German Catholic hierarchy, the "parents' right" to determine the religious education of their children followed from the principles of natural law and subsidiarity. Writing to the Parliamentary Council shortly after its opening, Cologne cardinal Josef Frings, the chair of the Fulda Bishops Conference and the most visible representative of Catholic interests in the Western occupation zones, warned that the "parents' right" to confessional schools was the product of "God-given human nature." Excluding this right from the Basic Law would set West Germany on the path toward Soviet totalitarianism.[13] Frings's closest ally on the Parliamentary Council was the Rhineland-Palatinate CDU delegate and Catholic jurist Adolf Süsterhenn, whose record of defending Center Party politicians during the Nazi years ensured his smooth reintegration into public life. A long-standing veteran of Catholic politics, Süsterhenn put forth a classic Catholic defense of subsidiarity in his postwar writings, calling for the devolution of authority to the natural orders of family, community, and church.[14] Süsterhenn secured the addition of the "parents' right" to the CDU platform and, in November 1948, introduced a motion for its incorporation into the Basic Law.[15]

Protestant positions on the school question were more complex, reflecting two intersecting dynamics. On the one hand, Protestant church leaders feared losing leverage to the better-organized Catholics. On the other hand, the Lutheran and Dahlemite wings of the EKD promoted competing visions for postwar Protestantism. For veterans of the Confessing Church Dahlemites, the school controversy offered an opportunity to achieve Karl Barth's ideal of the Christian community as a witness to the divine message within the political world. Looking to Barth's wartime and postwar lectures, this group prioritized the revival of Christian faith at the local level rather than the reconstruction of church–state alignment. The pastor and pedagogical theorist Oskar Hammelsbeck, who had endured multiple arrests for his work in illegal Confessing Church seminaries, exemplified the Dahlemites' educational agenda. In an address before the first postwar meeting of the EKD Brethren Council, Hammelsbeck argued that the social basis for confessional schools had been eroded in a process of "de-Christianization" that had been underway long before 1933. Demanding the reintroduction of confessional schools would not only impinge on the conscience of nonreligious families but implicate the Protestant church in party politics, abandoning its universal mission. Instead Hammelsbeck encouraged Protestants to accept interconfessional schools, while advocating for one crucial change: the introduction of true "Christian instruction," rooted in confessional and biblical tenets, rather than liberalized "religious education."[16]

FAMILIES, SCHOOLS, AND THE BATTLE FOR THE BASIC LAW

Conservative Lutherans proved more divided. Some conservative church leaders, including Bavarian bishop Hans Meiser as well as Otto Dibelius, named bishop of Berlin-Brandenburg in 1948, joined their Catholic counterparts in the fight for confessional schools.[17] Others, however, favored a more flexible policy. The Lutheran pastor Hanns Lilje, a cofounder of the Young Reformation movement and a Confessing Church veteran who was appointed bishop of Hanover in 1947, adopted a conciliatory posture in a petition to the Parliamentary Council. "Parents' rights," Lilje argued, required less a particular legal arrangement than parental responsibility for taking an active role in children's education. Reestablishing "the relationship between church and school in 'freedom and responsibility'" meant curtailing both the state's monopoly over education as well as "the unreservedly absolute demand for confessional schools" by the churches.[18] A 1948 report by Lilje's Hanover church acknowledged the practical difficulties of reestablishing confessional schools and joined the Brethren Council's call for ensuring Christian instruction even in "community" schools.[19]

In the fractious landscape of postwar constitutional politics, Protestants' abdication of expansive political claims ironically enhanced their influence. The staunchest defenders of confessional schools at the Parliamentary Council, Adolf Süsterhenn and the Center Party delegate Helene Weber, found their strong formulation of parents' rights rebuffed by deputies of the Social Democratic Party (SPD) and the liberal Free Democratic Party (FDP).[20] By contrast, Protestant delegates positioned themselves as mediators prepared to save the constitutional project. By early 1949, Protestant CDU members of a compromise committee formed to address the issue refused to take the hard-line position of their Catholic colleagues.[21] When Adolf Süsterhenn and the Catholic bishops rejected a proposed agreement, the EKD's representative to the Parliamentary Council, the Rhineland church leader Heinrich Held, met with CDU delegates to negotiate a final arrangement.[22] In early May, Süsterhenn relented. The compromise, codified in Article 7 of the Basic Law, ensured that religious education would remain a mandatory subject in public schools, while affording parents and teachers the possibility of opting out. But Article 7 did not stipulate a parents' right to confessional schools, guaranteeing only "the right to establish private schools" with the permission of the states.[23]

A similar dynamic emerged in the Basic Law's broader compromise around church–state relations, as Protestants urged moderation in response to the perceived threat of Catholic clericalism. In October 1948 a commission of the Protestant churches in the British zone submitted a petition to the Parliamentary Council that recommended incorporating the provisions of the Weimar Constitution into the Basic Law, with the notable addition of a guarantee of church property. Like its 1919 precursor, the new constitution should designate religious communities as "corporations of public law," guarantee religious instruction in public schools, and recognize Sundays and Christian holidays as "days of public worship." At the same time, the state should allow all religious groups an equal right of free association and refrain from establishing a "state church."[24]

For the Confessing Church jurist and Oldenburg church administrator Hermann Ehlers, who helped draft the petition, the appeal of these compromises stemmed from confessional anxieties.[25] Despite joining the CDU in 1946, Ehlers remained concerned that a resurgent political Catholicism could further divide a fractured society. Speaking before the lay Protestant Week in Bremen, Ehlers invoked theological differences behind a call for humility in the application of Christian precepts to law. The Catholic belief in an "unambiguous and clearly prescribed natural law," which could be directly translated into legislation, neglected "the highly relevant story of the Fall."[26] Ehlers's own formulation came closer to that of Karl Barth. Today's state was "at best an ideologically neutral, tolerant one" rather than a "Christian state." Still, the state should open itself to Christian participation in areas such as schools, welfare services, and the protection of human rights, "for the sake of its own existence."[27]

The formulations of the Protestant commission held sway at the Parliamentary Council. When the proposal of Ehlers's group came before the Basic Rights Committee, Adolf Süsterhenn presented an alternative set of recommendations supported by the CDU, German Party, and Center Party. The conservative parties sought an explicit invocation of the churches' role in "the protection and securing of the religious and moral foundations of human life," beyond the religious freedom guaranteed in the Weimar Constitution.[28] FDP delegate Theodor Heuss fell back on the principle of federalism, holding that church–state relations should be addressed only at the state level.[29] Süsterhenn and Heuss eventually reached a compromise that accorded with Ehlers's Protestant commission, adopting the Weimar Constitution's articles on church–state relations into the Basic Law.[30] Liberals and conservatives could agree to acknowledge the churches' claim to participation in public life, so long as their privileged status did not hinder the recognition of religious freedom and state neutrality in religious affairs. Protestants welcomed other aspects of the constitution as well, even if these were matters more of general consensus than spe-

FAMILIES, SCHOOLS, AND THE BATTLE FOR THE BASIC LAW 127

cific Protestant influence. Unlike the Weimar Constitution, the basic rights that made up the Basic Law's first nineteen articles were formulated not as guidelines for future legislation but as guarantees binding the legislature and safeguarded by a Federal Constitutional Court. The preamble invoked the German people's "responsibility before God and man."[31]

The positive reception of the Basic Law in the Protestant press reflected the church's role in drafting the new constitution. Hermann Ehlers, who was elected to the West German Bundestag (parliament) in August 1949 and as Bundestag president the following year, lauded the constitution's combination of official religious neutrality with a strong public role for the churches. Writing for the revived Confessing Church journal *Junge Kirche*, Ehlers noted that the basic rights did not rest on any one confession or ideology, and therefore could help Germans overcome their long-standing divisions. At the same time, the Basic Law created the opportunity and responsibility for Christians to become politically engaged.[32] The EKD newspaper, *Evangelische Welt*, similarly greeted the Parliamentary Council's positions on religious education, church–state relations, and pre-political basic rights.[33] Even the conservative Freiburg historian Gerhard Ritter, who lamented that "Christian social ethics" could no longer form the basis for a German constitution, praised the Basic Law for recognizing the importance of "moral community."[34] In contrast, Cardinal Frings and the West German Catholic bishops announced that they could "regard this Basic Law only as a preliminary one that requires amendment as soon as possible," noting the disregard for parents' rights.[35] This divided response would provide a template for confessional polemics over the Basic Law in the decade to come.

A Protestant Constitutional Theory

Efforts to define the relationship of the churches to the Basic Law continued during the early 1950s in debates among constitutional lawyers. As in the 1920s, Catholic and Protestant jurists alike viewed their moment as one of crisis, at which political upheaval had opened new possibilities for the churches' reengagement in public life but also threatened their exclusion. Constitutional debates of the 1950s did not merely rehash their 1920s precursors. In the aftermath of the Radbruch thesis, Catholic as well as Protestant attacks on legal positivism found a stronger reception in the mainstream of constitutional law.[36] At the same time, Protestant jurists lacked a tradition of social thought on a par with Catholic natural law teachings. Although they had

128   REINVENTING PROTESTANT GERMANY

faced this challenge during the Weimar Republic, the political stakes were raised with the formation of the CDU as an interconfessional but Catholic-majority party. Key participants, however, remained the same. Rudolf Smend, whose theory of constitutional integration had inserted a Protestant perspective into Weimar-era debates, returned to the center of the discussion on the Protestant side.

Sixty-seven years old at the time of the Basic Law's enactment, Smend had an ambivalent record under National Socialism. As a conservative scholar from the older generation, Smend could not retain his prestigious chair at the University of Berlin even after joining the League of National Socialist German Jurists. In 1935 he was replaced by the thirty-year-old Nazi Party member Reinhard Höhn and took up a new post at the University of Göttingen. Smend would subsequently resign from the editorial board of the *Archiv des öffentlichen Rechts* (Archive of public law) in rejection of its total coordination by the regime.[37] Although he continued to lecture throughout the Nazi years, Smend moved into the apparently nonpolitical field of administrative law and published only two minor, historical essays during the war.[38] Smend also remained on the sidelines of Protestant opposition. He served as a member of the Reformed Church Committee of the Confessing Church and was questioned repeatedly by the Gestapo during the final years of the war, but by his own postwar admission had not participated in the July 20 movement. However, Smend never joined the Nazi Party itself. His church engagement and comparatively clean political record allowed him to be selected by British occupation authorities as the first postwar rector of the University of Göttingen.[39]

After the war, Smend recovered his role as an influential figure in constitutional law. As a professor in Göttingen, he directed a seminar on public law that produced some of West Germany's leading politicians, judges, and political scientists.[40] Most significant, Smend made explicit the religious underpinnings of his constitutional theory, which were only latent in his Weimar-era masterwork, *Constitution and Constitutional Law*. As a member of the EKD Council, he founded the EKD's Institute for Protestant Church Law in late 1945 and the field's flagship journal in 1951, publishing extensively on church–state relations. Smend's postwar writings extended his call for Protestantism to serve as a foundation for shared political values, a view he had first advanced in his 1932 essay "Protestantism and Democracy." But whereas Smend's late Weimar appeal was a cry in the wilderness, new political conditions lent his postwar writings outsize influence.

FAMILIES, SCHOOLS, AND THE BATTLE FOR THE BASIC LAW

Smend's "State and Church under the Bonn Basic Law," published in the first issue of the *Zeitschrift für evangelisches Kirchenrecht* (Journal of Protestant church law) two years after the new constitution's enactment, quickly became the authoritative interpretation on the subject among Protestant jurists. Smend framed his essay around a long sweep of German history. The era from the Reformation to the mid-nineteenth century remained a "Constantinian" age in which church and state recognized each other as "commensurable" powers, whether they sought cooperation or separation. The Kulturkampf of the 1870s, which led the Catholic Church to demand freedom rather than privileges from the state, inaugurated a second phase in which the churches retreated to the private sphere, culminating in the liberal Weimar Constitution. The Nazi-era "church struggle," according to Smend, marked a final turning point. Whereas the Catholic Church looked back to the first era, seeking to regulate its relationship to the Nazi state through the 1933 Concordat, the Confessing Church's Barmen Declaration of 1934 broke new ground by calling on the regime to recognize the churches' "public claim." Following Barmen, the Confessing Church aimed not at attaining political power for itself but at securing the authority and limits of the state. Although the Bonn Basic Law had adopted verbatim the Weimar Constitution's articles on religion, Smend concluded, these articles should be reinterpreted on a new foundation in light of the Confessing Church's struggle against Nazism.[41]

Smend's 1951 essay appealed to Protestant jurists above all because it linked a narrative of Christian anti-Nazi resistance with a call for postwar political engagement. The Nazi-era church opposition, Smend argued, had counterposed the "universal claim of the kingdom of Christ" against the "demonization of all domains of life in the total state."[42] At the same time, Smend omitted the Confessing Church's early enthusiasm for Nazism, its contribution of soldiers and military chaplains to the German war effort, and its silence during the destruction of European Jewry. His narrative of Confessing Church opposition inflated the scope of the Barmen Declaration, from a theological critique of the pro-Nazi German Christians to a new doctrine of the state's purpose and limits.

Smend's reappropriation of Barmen had a second advantage for Protestant jurists. Although he insisted that "the churches were unified in opposition to the Third Reich," Smend also criticized a "static," Catholic approach to church–state relations that sought to return to a premodern era of corporate privileges.[43] The Basic Law, Smend contended, allowed church–state conflicts to be resolved through a "foundation of discussion," not contracts or treaties.[44] At the same time, the churches' "public claim" required their exclusion from the exercise of state power: "The fundamental guarantee of the liberties of the churches requires their simultaneous fundamental delimitation through state sovereignty."[45] While articulating Protestants' new role in public life, Smend revived old canards against Catholic clericalism in the context of a perceived alliance between the Catholic clergy and the CDU. Following Smend, Protestant jurists could characterize their own bids to shape law and policy as expressions of Christian political responsibility while denouncing parallel Catholic efforts as illegitimate power grabs.

Smend's essay quickly became a touchstone for discussions on church–state relations. The 1952 Marburg meeting of West Germany's Association of Constitutional Law Scholars brought the competing possibilities to the fore. In a plenary lecture, the Cologne jurist and Catholic CDU politician Hans Peters described the church as the "source of the religious and moral life of the people," charged to "fill all private and public life with the Christian spirit." Consistent with Catholic notions of subsidiarity, Peters invoked the church's participation in the "implementation of public services taken on by the state," including the overseeing of confessional schools.[46] Peters's counterpart, Smend's younger Göttingen colleague Werner Weber, took a contrary approach. A student of Carl Schmitt in the 1920s, Weber belonged to a far-right school of ex-Nazi jurists who bemoaned the collapse of unitary state sovereignty into a cacophony of competing interest groups. The churches, Weber argued, had taken their place among various "parties, unions, and similar pressure groups" that colonized the state and threatened its capacity for decision making. For Weber, the expanded role of the churches in the postwar education and welfare systems reflected less a welcome devolution of state power than the dangerous evacuation of executive authority.[47]

Whereas Peters and Weber rejected Smend's theory of church–state relations from opposite vantage points—Catholic teachings of subsidiarity and a Schmitt-inspired doctrine of executive sovereignty—a cohort of Protestant jurists born in the early twentieth century championed Smend's mediating position. One of Smend's most ardent expositors was the jurist Ulrich Scheuner, who in 1950 left the Evangelisches Hilfswerk for a chair in administrative law at the University of Bonn. Although a former Nazi Party member and an activist in the campaign against war crimes trials, Scheuner embraced a new political vision as a member of Smend's circle. In a commentary on the Marburg conference for the *Zeitschrift für evangelisches Kirchenrecht*, Scheuner criticized Werner Weber's outdated view of the state as a "unitary" authority

FAMILIES, SCHOOLS, AND THE BATTLE FOR THE BASIC LAW

standing over society. In a democracy, Scheuner argued, the state could only derive its legitimacy through public opinion, channeled through "intermediate powers" such as parties, unions, and indeed, churches.[48] The legal scholar Ludwig Raiser, Smend's successor as rector at Göttingen, noted in a Festschrift for Smend's seventieth birthday that Christianity could not function as an immediate basis for law in West German democracy. Still, the shared values on which judges relied "derive overwhelmingly from a Christian source, albeit a buried one."[49] Smend's former student Gerhard Leibholz, appointed as a judge on West Germany's Federal Constitutional Court shortly following his return from wartime British exile, lauded the court's newly won power of judicial review as a means of preserving such values.[50]

Scheuner, Raiser, and Leibholz were all close to the CDU. Scheuner wrote for the journal of the party's Protestant Working Group.[51] Raiser would align with CDU Protestants to oppose the EKD Brethren Council's campaign against West German rearmament.[52] Leibholz served on the Constitutional Court's Second Senate, the "Black" chamber whose members were appointed by the Christian Democrats.[53] For these conservative Protestants, the CDU offered the only realistic political alternative to the left, however uneasy they may have felt about Catholic predominance in the party. Yet all three argued for a distinctively Protestant understanding of the Basic Law that went beyond interconfessional paeans to re-Christianization. The church, in their view, should serve as a source of shared values—implicitly coded as Protestant—rather than legislative authority. Catholic calls for "parents' rights" and church–state alignment appeared as illegitimate attempts to hijack the state in the service of Catholic interests. Protestant identity was not only baked deeply into these jurists' self-understanding; it was also a means of laying claim to a narrative of anti-Nazi resistance.

The EKD and the Equal Rights Debate

Confessional battles over the Basic Law took concrete shape as Protestants and Catholics entered controversies about the basic rights following the new constitution's enactment. The earliest such debate involved provisions of the German Civil Code relating to marriage and the family. For Protestant church leaders, politicians, and lay activists, Civil Code reform brought into sharp relief questions about the EKD's role in the new political system. Three concerns dominated the discussion. First, Protestants sought consistency with their theological traditions. Second, they confronted the enormous changes to the structure of the family since the promulgation of the Civil Code in 1900, transformations that accelerated during the war. Finally, fears that Catholics would dominate the Federal Republic remained palpable, even among Protestant Christian Democrats. Combined, these factors fueled reformist arguments. While a patriarchal current pervaded the EKD in the early 1950s, proponents of Civil Code reform advanced an alternative view. Precisely because their church lacked a strong natural law tradition, reformists argued, Protestants not only could adapt to the current moment but were required to do so to counteract the threat of Catholic ascendancy.

The Basic Law guaranteed that issues of marriage and the family would spark contention in the young Federal Republic. At the Parliamentary Council, Social Democratic and liberal delegates had demanded a robust guarantee of women's equality. Christian Democratic deputies, however, sought to maintain the model of the Weimar Constitution, which provided for women's equality in civil and political, but not social and economic, rights. Under pressure from popular opinion and feminist organizations—as well as competition with the German Democratic Republic, which promised to grant women full equality in its own constitution—the Parliamentary Council ultimately recognized women's equality in Article 3, Paragraph 2, of the Basic Law. Eliminating the qualifiers initially favored by conservatives, the clause stated simply, "Men and women shall have equal rights."[54]

Upon its ratification in May 1949, the Basic Law immediately came into conflict with numerous provisions of the Civil Code, which, despite efforts by feminist reformers, had remained virtually unchanged since its enactment in 1900. Under this legislation, husbands retained the right to make final decisions in marital conflicts; fathers were granted the sole right to legally represent their children and to exert final authority over matters involving their children's welfare or education; wives were obliged to obtain permission from their husbands to work outside the home; and husbands administered property their wives acquired before or during marriage.[55] The Basic Law stipulated a deadline of March 31, 1953, for the Bundestag to revise the Civil Code in compliance with the guarantee of equal rights.[56]

Confessional divisions in the debate about Civil Code reform mirrored those of the earlier controversy over parents' rights. Catholic church leaders and jurists framed their interventions around the language of natural law, emphasizing the husband's place at the head of marriage and the family. A long patriarchal tradition in Catholic social thought buttressed the injunc-

FAMILIES, SCHOOLS, AND THE BATTLE FOR THE BASIC LAW

tion in Paul's Epistle to the Ephesians that wives "be subject to your husbands as to the Lord."[57] The early twentieth-century Catholic moral theologian Joseph Mausbach, whose treatise on social ethics remained the "standard work" into the postwar years, put the point succinctly: "The parents stand as bearers of authority together over children and servants. Of the marriage partners, the man is, according to his natural aptitude and according to the general moral and legal tradition, the true head of the family."[58] Pope Pius XI reaffirmed the Church's patriarchal teachings in his 1930 encyclical on marriage and sexuality, *Casti Connubii.*[59]

After 1945 the restoration of the patriarchal family remained a key goal of conservative Catholic politics across Western Europe, however tempered by a new affirmation by some Catholic writers of emotional ties and sexual pleasure within marriage.[60] The Federal Republic was no exception. With strong support from the CDU, the Parliamentary Council adopted as Article 6 of the Basic Law the promise that "Marriage and family shall enjoy the special protection of the state."[61] Following its enactment, Catholic activists cited the Basic Law's protection of marriage as a limiting condition for the equal rights clause of Article 3. The most common argument held that Article 3 guaranteed the equal treatment of men and women relative to natural sexual differences, not absolute equality. A typical expression of this view was voiced by the conservative Catholic jurist Frank Bosch, who served on the family law commission of the Catholic Office in Bonn. The elimination of "unjust discrimination against the wife and mother," Bosch wrote in the *Süddeutsche Juristen-Zeitung,* required neither dismantling the "holy order" of marriage and family nor "mechanical equalization." Instead the principle of equality should be interpreted according to the natural law tenet of *suum cuique:* to each their own.[62]

To be sure, Catholic commentators in the new Federal Republic did not universally espouse the Vatican's position. Catholic women's organizations issued counter-proposals to the recommendations of the Catholic Office, demanding the elimination of the husband's right of the final decision.[63] Opinions in the Catholic journals *Hochland* and *Frankfurter Hefte* stressed the disjuncture between biblical pronouncements and worldly law—an argument that would echo in Protestant writings as well.[64] However, given the Catholic Church's stronger institutional coordination, as well as the absence of a legacy of Nazi-era division, the clerical hierarchy could assert greater control over official statements. A 1953 pastoral letter, signed by West Germany's Catholic bishops and widely distributed at the parish level, confirmed the husband's prerogative as a nonnegotiable matter of church teaching.[65] These dynamics—and similar ones in the case of religious education—would shape Protestant critiques of the Catholic Church as an authoritarian institution.

Different theological and political concerns motivated the discussion within the Protestant camp. Unlike Catholic teaching, both Lutheran and Calvinist theology regarded marriage not as a sacrament but as a domain regulated by civil law. Protestant churches had largely accepted the requirement for civil marriage introduced in the German Empire in 1875.[66] But the social theory laid out in the wartime Freiburg memorandum, and taken up at the postwar Protestant Academies, demanded that Christian precepts assume a stronger role in shaping civil institutions to counteract the threats of Communism and secularism. Early postwar statements by Protestant conservatives, attempting to thread the needle between church authority and state oversight, fell close to the position of the Catholic hierarchy. The ex-Nazi jurist Hans Dombois, who joined the EKD's Christophorus-Stift research institute following his stint coordinating the Protestant campaign against war crimes trials, noted that marriage was "founded by God": "The core of each institution, despite a certain mutability, lies in its pregivenness, its indispensability."[67] The Lutheran theologian Paul Althaus, restored to his position at the University of Erlangen in 1948, similarly warned in an opinion for the EKD chancellery that "the contemporary deviations from the essence of marriage, of the woman, of the mother, must be recognized as an *emergency*."[68]

While appealing to biblical tenets, these arguments joined larger currents of West German conservative thought. If the reception of Smend's ideas on church and state would soon reorient the Protestant discussion of civil law, another possibility beckoned in the early 1950s: the social theory of right-wing intellectuals around Carl Schmitt. Beyond Werner Weber, an influential cohort of Schmitt's disciples, including the jurist Ernst Forsthoff, philosopher Arnold Gehlen, and sociologist Helmut Schelsky, described prepolitical institutions, rooted in deep anthropological structures, as the basis of social order. Without explicitly invoking Nazi racial theory, these ex-Nazi thinkers recycled key concepts of their Nazi-era social thought, seeking to displace fundamental decisions about the organization of society from the pressures of democratic legislatures.[69] Marriage and family proved a central domain for their defense of immutable institutions. Along with Protestants such as Althaus and Dombois and Catholics like Frank Bosch and Josef Frings, secular conservatives painted the restoration of gender hierarchy as a

FAMILIES, SCHOOLS, AND THE BATTLE FOR THE BASIC LAW

critical task of postwar reconstruction—a convenient argument that enabled them to ascribe Nazi crimes to the regime's supposed sexual anarchy.[70]

These assumptions were reflected in the work of the EKD's official marriage law commission, which met at the Christophorus-Stift in the Westphalian town of Hemer. Founded in 1947 by the Lutheran theologian Friedrich Karl Schumann, the Christophorus-Stift shared the politics of the wider Protestant Academy movement. While aiming to expand the church's voice in politics and academic research, the institute served as a vehicle of political rehabilitation for ex-Nazi Protestants.[71] Schumann himself was a former Nazi Party member, as was the Münster judge Karl August Bettermann, who drafted the memorandum considered by the all-male marriage law commission over the first half of 1950. Bettermann's memorandum exemplified conservative discourses on marriage and the family in the early Federal Republic, proposing to interpret the constitutional guarantee of equality in light of men's and women's "natural differences" and "different functions in state and society."[72] The final version, which Schumann submitted to the West German Interior and Justice Ministries in July 1950, called for preserving the most contested clauses of the Civil Code: the right of the husband to make final decisions in marital conflicts, and the obligation of wives to perform housework.[73] Reflecting the political vision of postwar conservative Lutherans, the memorandum envisioned a paramount role for the church, rather than the state, in preserving hierarchical institutions. "The church," Schumann concluded in a theological introduction, "must unconditionally defend, from its understanding of marriage as a holy status and divine order, the fundamental independence of the institution of marriage from state and political authority."[74]

Another interpretation of marriage, however, gained ground in Dahlemite circles. Karl Barth's theology of "Gospel and Law" pointed toward the impermanence of human institutions and insisted that the law ultimately served the gospel's promise of grace. As the French Reformed jurist Jacques Ellul wrote in his 1946 treatise, *The Theological Foundation of Law*, the law "is not static. We have seen that it is always an act of God. It is living, progressing, and aimed at a certain goal."[75] The third volume of Barth's *Church Dogmatics*, published in 1951, applied this perspective to the question of marriage. While maintaining traditional assumptions about the fixity of gender—"Man never exists as such, but always as the human male or human female"— Barth described marriage not as a hierarchy but as a source of "freedom in fellowship." Marriage reflected humanity's essence as a being in community, modeled on the relationship between Christ and the church.[76] The theologian Ernst Wolf, who had supported women's ordinations in the wartime Confessing Church, cited extensively from the *Church Dogmatics* in an opinion commissioned by the EKD chancellery as a counterweight to Paul Althaus's proposal.[77] The contested passages from Paul's epistle, Wolf argued, signified not the subordination of the wife to the husband but the "covenant" by which husband and wife merged into one spiritual body. Analogous to the union of Christ and the Christian community, a "Christian understanding of marriage" was rooted in "mutual consensus," a "parity of man and woman in reciprocal dependence."[78]

Like the conservative Lutherans around the Christophorus-Stift, Dahlemites drew on longer theological discourses about marriage and participated in a broader revaluation of the institution underway in the early Federal Republic. Already in the mid-1930s, the German-speaking Reformed theologians Emil Brunner and Otto Piper criticized the use of Scripture to justify the oppression of wives by their husbands and described marriage using biblical metaphors of partnership.[79] Over the 1950s a growing number of voices within both Catholic and Protestant periodicals, academies, and lay organizations argued for a more "democratic" conception of marriage as central to the building of a democratic society. By the end of the decade, journals such as the Protestant *Kirche und Mann*, as well as family associations in both churches, called on fathers to break with militaristic models of masculinity and take a more active role in childrearing, if they continued to imagine a "married and heterosexual" father who was committed at most "part-time" to his family.[80]

It was the Evangelische Frauenarbeit (Protestant Women's Association), however, that introduced a Christian critique of patriarchal marriage into the debate about Civil Code reform before such ideas gained broader traction. Founded in 1918 as an umbrella organization of regional Protestant women's societies, the Evangelische Frauenarbeit was reorganized in 1945 as an affiliate of the EKD.[81] Like nearly all postwar Protestant organizations, its past was shrouded in compromise. As much as their male counterparts, many conservative Protestant women had embraced the Nazi promise of national renewal, even as they resented the state's interference in church affairs. Meta Eyl, the chair of the Evangelische Frauenarbeit from 1934 to 1947, was a Nazi Party member who celebrated the regime's eugenics laws.[82] Anna Paulsen, who in 1951 was appointed the EKD's speaker on women's issues, had taken a more cautious stance that typified the Confessing Church. As the director of the Berlin-Dahlem Burckhardthaus for young women's education, Paulsen criti-

FAMILIES, SCHOOLS, AND THE BATTLE FOR THE BASIC LAW 137

cized the subsumption of Protestant youth organizations into their Nazi counterparts but avoided publicly addressing the regime's persecution of Jews, or even its anti-feminist policies.[83] Nevertheless, the gender politics of wartime Protestantism, when emergency legislation allowed women to take on pastoral functions in the Confessing Church, left a mark on the Frauenarbeit. Despite postwar attempts to restore masculine authority within both the Lutheran regional churches and the Brethren Council, the Frauenarbeit would play a key role in reshaping the EKD's position on marriage and the family.

The politics of the Evangelische Frauenarbeit shifted in the late 1940s, after British occupation authorities compelled Meta Eyl's resignation.[84] The organization's new director, the lawyer and women's rights activist Elisabeth Schwarzhaupt, came from a background that set her apart from the dominant trajectory of German Protestant nationalism. A product of the Frankfurt bourgeoisie rather than the Weimar Republic's conservative nationalist milieu, Schwarzhaupt joined the liberal German People's Party (DVP) in 1928 after encountering Hitler's *Mein Kampf.* Her interest in Civil Code reform was awakened already during the 1920s, when she worked as an attorney representing unmarried mothers for a Frankfurt legal aid office.[85] Although Schwarzhaupt recognized the Nazi threat to the women's movement early on, lecturing on the topic for the DVP, her record under Nazism was not one of opposition.[86] Deposed from her position as an appeals court judge in March 1933, Schwarzhaupt joined the League of National Socialist German Jurists in an effort to preserve her career. She later took a position as a legal adviser to the state-backed German Protestant Church.[87] Schwarzhaupt continued her church employment after 1945 as a secretary in the EKD Foreign Office, where she helped coordinate the campaign against war crimes trials.[88] But if her early career involved close cooperation with Protestant conservatives, Schwarzhaupt issued a strong challenge to patriarchal models of family law.

In July 1950 the Evangelische Frauenarbeit submitted its recommendations for Civil Code reform to the EKD chancellery. The proposals fell short of complete equality. Like nearly all participants in the debate, including Social Democrats, the Frauenarbeit continued to stipulate that "The wife is the leader in household matters." However, the recommendations also called for the elimination of special privileges for husbands and fathers, the reform of marital property laws, and the authorization of either spouse to represent the household in legal matters.[89] Frauenarbeit leaders marshaled theological as well as sociological arguments to defend their proposals. As Schwarzhaupt maintained in *Stimme der Gemeinde* (Voice of the community), a journal founded by Martin Niemöller and other veterans of the Confessing Church Dahlemites, women's growing prominence in the labor force and as heads of household had rendered the Civil Code's assumption of patriarchal marriage obsolete. Civil Code reform should seek less to preserve a timeless structure of marriage than to fulfill the Christian ideals of "dignity, freedom, equality, and justice."[90] Anna Paulsen echoed the theological reflections of Karl Barth. Even if "the emphasis on the fundamental equality of the sexes must always remain connected to the emphasis on functional difference," the Bible placed women and men in equal responsibility toward the community.[91]

In the opening stages of the debate over Civil Code reform, representatives of the Frauenarbeit on the EKD marriage law commission stood at loggerheads with the group's conservative majority. Controversy erupted in response to proposals of the FDP-led Federal Justice Ministry, an outlier in the socially conservative Adenauer government. The ministry's first recommendations on the issue, released to the EKD chancellery in 1951, called for the equal right of husbands and wives to legally represent the household and make decisions "in all areas affecting common life."[92] The official report of the Protestant commission, authored by the conservative faction around Friedrich Karl Schumann, warned that such reforms would endanger the "essence of marriage."[93] In turn, the Frauenarbeit issued alternative recommendations that challenged the use of Scripture to justify women's "subordination."[94] The two sides clashed over the theological underpinnings of marriage as well as the correct response to postwar social transformations.

Yet the third pole of the Protestant family law debate—fears of Catholic dominance in the Federal Republic—brought the two sides closer together. Even Protestant conservatives increasingly acknowledged that civil law could not directly translate Christian precepts, the demand advanced by Catholic jurists. Rudolf Smend's constitutional theory offered a middle path: The Basic Law protected marriage as a shared, pre-political value but not as a specific institutional structure. The discourse of values cut both ways. In an address to the marriage law commission, Ulrich Scheuner insisted that Article 3 be interpreted in relationship to "value judgments that depend upon the historical-social moment," which to his mind ruled out "absolute formal equality." Nevertheless, the state should not interfere in the "inner sphere of the marital community." Scheuner contrasted his own proposals, which rejected the husband's right to the final decision, against the more stringent formulations of Catholic jurists.[95] Even Friedrich Karl Schumann conceded

FAMILIES, SCHOOLS, AND THE BATTLE FOR THE BASIC LAW 139

that the EKD could "agree to the elimination of the general power of decision of the husband," since the relationship between spouses was not accessible to "legislation and adjudication."[96]

West Germany's Catholic hierarchy would not go even this far. Headed by Prelate Wilhelm Böhler, the family law commission at the Catholic Office in Bonn advocated for the preservation of both husbands' and fathers' rights, as well as the requirement that wives obtain the permission of their husbands to work outside the home.[97] At an April 1952 meeting of representatives of both churches with Justice Ministry officials, the Catholic delegation found its proposals rebuffed, while the Protestants agreed not to intervene in the government's handling of husbands' rights. The Lutheran theologian Edo Osterloh, an official in the EKD chancellery, reported that "the Protestant side felt it had been largely understood," whereas "the Catholic representatives bid farewell in an obviously somewhat depressed mood."[98]

Political developments quickly overtook the initial debate. Despite support for the Justice Ministry's proposal by Protestant interior minister Robert Lehr, Adenauer's cabinet advanced a draft law that hardly made concessions to reformist demands. The ensuing parliamentary debate, which pitted conservative Christian Democrats against Social Democrats and liberals, resulted in a stalemate. The Bundestag failed to reform the Civil Code by the March 1953 deadline.[99] Meanwhile, the Federal Republic's second national election in September enhanced the conservative position. The election brought to power an emboldened coalition led by the CDU, whose share of the vote shot up from 31 percent in 1949 to 45 percent in 1953. The conservative party made ample use of gendered appeals in its campaign and, as in the 1949 election, found its most reliable voter base among Catholic women.[100]

Adenauer took the results as a mandate for his party's conservative family law agenda. In his second cabinet, Adenauer appointed the archconservative Catholic parliamentarian Franz-Josef Wuermeling to the newly created position of federal family minister. A staunch partisan of conservative natural law rhetoric, Wuermeling had staked out a position to the right even of Adolf Süsterhenn during the negotiations over the Basic Law.[101] To the chagrin of the Women's Department of the Interior Ministry, Adenauer delegated the task of Civil Code reform to Wuermeling's ministry. The new draft, concluded in late 1953, granted even greater authority to husbands and fathers.[102]

The Protestant response divided along familiar lines. In a statement signed only by the conservatives Friedrich Karl Schumann and Hans Dombois, the EKD marriage law commission largely assented to the government's

Figure 4.1. CDU electoral poster, 1953. "Protect us! Be ready for defense—Vote CDU." The Communist threat to women and children was a common motif in the CDU's campaign. The poster's visual metaphors were familiar from Nazi propaganda, and also evoked the sexual violence against German women by Soviet soldiers during the postwar occupation. Konrad-Adenauer-Stiftung / Archiv für Christlich-Demokratische Politik, 10-001-414

FAMILIES, SCHOOLS, AND THE BATTLE FOR THE BASIC LAW   141

proposals.[103] But when the Civil Code draft came up for debate in the Bundestag, Elisabeth Schwarzhaupt dominated Protestant contributions. Elected in 1953 as a CDU Bundestag delegate from Frankfurt, Schwarzhaupt personified the conservative party's gender and confessional dynamics. In advance of the election, party leaders aimed to increase the number of women deputies without disrupting the party's efforts toward confessional parity. Schwarzhaupt's identity as a Protestant woman pushed her near the top of the Frankfurt party list. Although initially suspicious of a party that openly mixed religion and politics, Schwarzhaupt embraced the CDU's interconfessionalism, while also joining the party's Protestant Working Group under Hermann Ehlers.[104] On the issue of husbands' and fathers' prerogatives, she joined with the party's Women's Committee, consisting of Protestant and Catholic women who had long dissented from the CDU mainstream.[105]

Notwithstanding her cooperation across the confessional divide, Schwarzhaupt's views on family law reform remained steeped in the Protestant discussion. In a plenary speech before the Bundestag at a February 1954 debate about the Civil Code, her first as a deputy, Schwarzhaupt invoked the interpretation of Scripture advanced by Karl Barth and Ernst Wolf. The biblical analogy between marriage and the Christian community was one not of hierarchy but of partnership: "Christ was not the head of the community as a man who demanded a right of decision." At the same time, Schwarzhaupt insisted that civil law was a social formation, reflecting contemporary realities rather than a timeless order. Industrialization, the separation of home from work, and not least, the war, had undermined patriarchal structures and made demands for husbands' and fathers' privileges obsolete.[106]

It was Protestantism itself that authorized a pragmatic focus. Echoing the critique of Catholic clericalism advanced in both Lutheran and Dahlemite circles, Schwarzhaupt distinguished between "what is to be said in pastoral care and sermons" and matters of "the law set by the state." Rather than imposing Christian precepts through law, the state should use social policy to foster the conditions of a Christian life. Lamenting the decline of the family, Schwarzhaupt advocated for tax relief for large families and state-subsidized aid to mothers, policies that had garnered support across the political spectrum. She justified her proposal to refer marital disagreements to a family court on the grounds that such a solution would yield "a better chance of allowing a broken marriage to emerge without further damage." Citing the EKD's recommendations to eliminate the "husband's right" and allow both spouses to represent the family, Schwarzhaupt echoed the approach to church–state relations set out by Rudolf Smend. Rather than an immediate source of law, the church would serve as a repository of the shared values underlying state policies.[107]

Cold War dynamics lent Schwarzhaupt's position cross-party appeal. Against the backdrop of heightening East–West polarization, the SPD sought to uphold a tradition of support for gender equality while distancing itself from East Germany's Socialist Unity Party, which had actively encouraged women's entry into the full-time workforce.[108] The liberal FDP, for its part, remained in Adenauer's coalition but chafed at the CDU's conservative social policies. Schwarzhaupt's parliamentary address allowed members of both minority parties to uphold the mantle of Christian values while contesting the CDU's position. At the February 1954 Bundestag debate, SPD and FDP deputies rejected claims by the conservative Catholic parliamentarians Franz-Josef Wuermeling and Helene Weber to represent the sole Christian position. The Darmstadt parliamentarian Ludwig Metzger was exemplary of a new group of Social Democrats who espoused religious convictions. A veteran of the Weimar-era religious socialist movement, Metzger had served as a legal adviser to the Confessing Church and participated in postwar exchanges between the SPD and the EKD Brethren Council. Addressing the Bundestag in support of Civil Code reform, Metzger cited the recommendations of the Evangelische Frauenarbeit: "There are not only Christians in the CDU and FDP, there are also very serious Christians in the SPD."[109] The Protestant FDP delegate Marie-Elisabeth Lüders, a longstanding leader in the liberal feminist movement, referenced Scripture to call for the overturning of patriarchal privileges: "There are neither fathers' rights nor mothers' rights, but parents' rights."[110]

A similar constellation of concerns shaped the debate about family law reform at the EKD synod meeting the next month, where the annual theme, "The Family in Modern Society," reflected the urgency of the issue. On the first day of discussion, delegates convened in West Berlin's Spandau neighborhood remained divided between conservative proponents of patriarchal marriage and reform-minded Dahlemites.[111] But the following day's presentation by Helmut Schelsky, a sociologist who had written influential studies of the postwar West German family, helped unify the competing camps. Like Elisabeth Schwarzhaupt, Schelsky traced a long process of industrialization and secularization that had weakened family bonds. The clock

FAMILIES, SCHOOLS, AND THE BATTLE FOR THE BASIC LAW

could not be turned back to a preindustrial age when the family formed the basis for economic life, Schelsky argued, let alone before a war that had left millions widowed and homeless. Schelsky's lecture, which both upheld the family as a pillar of the anti-Communist West but expressed skepticism toward expansive legislative initiatives to "save" it, resonated with Protestant concerns about Christian Democratic uses of family law to expand the Catholic Church's imprint.[112]

Following Schelsky's address, the synod's family law committee drafted a report that would be adopted by the full body. The report continued to describe marriage and parenthood as "endowments of God." In contrast to Wuermeling and the Catholic hierarchy, however, the Protestant synod agreed upon the preservation of civil marriage and the legitimacy of divorce, as well as the elimination of the husband's right of the final decision.[113] The committee chair, the jurist Ludwig Raiser, summed up the group's reasoning: "We cannot immediately make Holy Scripture into valid worldly law."[114]

Even as the EKD synod reached consensus on critical issues, the Bundestag remained deadlocked. Unable to conclude a revised Civil Code following the February 1954 debate, deputies voted to send the issue back to committee, where it languished for three years. When the Equal Rights Act finally came up again for plenary debate in May 1957, the Bundestag narrowly passed a compromise bill introduced by the government. This version adopted some reformist proposals, including eliminating the husband's right of the final decision and allowing wives full control over property acquired during marriage. However, the bill upheld the father's authority over a child's welfare and continued to restrict wives' employment outside the household, despite the protests of Elisabeth Schwarzhaupt and Ludwig Metzger at the final parliamentary reading.[115]

While the statute came as a disappointment to reformers, the Protestant discussion of family law was not without consequence. Although both the EKD marriage law commission and the synod remained divided over fathers' rights, the synod committee modified the patriarchal language of its initial proposals in response to protests by women members.[116] Moreover, the Evangelische Frauenarbeit introduced a language for reconciling Christian values with equal rights that would prove influential during a later stage of debate. When feminist activists rose to contest the constitutionality of the new family law, the Federal Constitutional Court would take up the critique of conservative natural law doctrines laid out by the Frauenarbeit.

Protestant Jurists and the Concordat Case

Alongside the debate about family law reform, the 1950s controversy over confessional schooling lent practical urgency to questions of church–state relations under the Basic Law. The two controversies shared key features. Both centered on the role of the churches in shaping domestic policy, and on the meaning of a Christian social order. In each case, competition among the Lutheran and Dahlemite wings of the EKD was complicated—at times mollified—by shared suspicion over the political power of the Catholic Church. The debate about confessional schools, however, brought a new dynamic to the fore. In light of its intertwinement with the 1933 Concordat, this controversy invariably raised thorny questions about the churches' actions during the Nazi dictatorship. Lutherans and Dahlemites clashed not only over their own visions, but to define themselves as exemplars of anti-Nazi resistance against the complicity of the Catholic Church.

As much as the patriarchal family, confessional schooling was foundational to conservative Catholic visions of re-Christianization in 1950s West Germany. Following the defeat of "parents' rights" at the Parliamentary Council, the Catholic hierarchy remained adamant in its defense of the confessional school, a key front in the battle to preserve the Catholic milieu against the tide of de-Christianization. This front was hardly impenetrable. Mirroring its dissident position in the family law debate, the left-wing Catholic *Frankfurter Hefte* called for the creation of interconfessional community schools that anchored Germany's Christian as well as secular traditions.[117] Nevertheless, the conservative Catholic hierarchy reigned supreme in the early 1950s, and official church statements hardly permitted a word of opposition—again fueling Protestant efforts to link Catholic clericalism with authoritarian politics.

The Concordat between the Vatican and the Nazi state, which guaranteed the protection of confessional schools, was central to the controversy from the outset. The nub of the issue was the treaty's ongoing validity. Should the Concordat be regarded as a Nazi document rendered void with the regime's defeat, or did the 1933 agreement remain binding on the Federal Republic? Legal history provided no clear answer. The Allies had set to work eliminating German laws considered to express a Nazi worldview, but the Federal Republic acknowledged itself as the legal successor to the Nazi Reich.

Since a "parents' right" was not included in the Basic Law, Catholic proponents of confessional schooling had no choice but to insist that the Concordat remained valid law. Adolf Süsterhenn, appointed president of the Rhineland-

FAMILIES, SCHOOLS, AND THE BATTLE FOR THE BASIC LAW   145

Palatinate state constitutional court in 1951, reemerged as the most outspoken Catholic advocate on the issue. Writing for the Catholic weekly *Rheinischer Merkur* in 1952, Süsterhenn unequivocally denied any link between the Concordat and National Socialist ideology. Instead the Concordat followed the pattern of church–state treaties during the Weimar Republic, which both the Catholic and Protestant churches had concluded at the regional level. Moreover, Süsterhenn pointed out, Article 123 of the Basic Law obliged the Federal Republic to fulfill the terms of preexisting treaties.[118] In contrast, Protestant church leaders tended to favor the compromise of the Parliamentary Council. The Protestant churches of both Baden and Württemberg supported the introduction of "community" schools in the new state of Baden-Württemberg, objecting only when an initial draft of the state constitution did not specify the Christian character of secondary schools.[119] In Hesse, the regional Protestant church led by Martin Niemöller focused its efforts on training Protestant religious educators, without contesting the reestablishment of interconfessional schools by the Social Democratic state government.[120]

Although the issue of confessional schools sparked debate throughout West Germany, nowhere else did the controversy reach the fever pitch of Lower Saxony. Created in 1946 out of a patchwork of formerly separate territories, the northwestern state was 77 percent Protestant, with a Catholic minority concentrated around the city of Oldenburg.[121] Beginning in 1951 the state government under SPD minister president Hinrich Wilhelm Kopf embarked on an effort to standardize school administration, in line with the long-standing SPD preference for interconfessional schools. Soon after, the ruling SPD-FDP coalition proposed new legislation that would require confessional schools to maintain a student population of at least 120, effectively outlawing such schools in the largely rural state.[122]

The proposed legislation polarized opinion around Lower Saxony's churches. Catholic parents staged over one hundred rallies during the early months of 1952, culminating in a letter to the Lower Saxony government by the state's Catholic bishops threatening to oppose the reforms "with all means available to us."[123] Surely Nazi legacies were on the minds of these Oldenburg Catholics. During the mid-1930s, the region had been at the center of a Nazi initiative to ban the display of crucifixes in schools; protests by local priests and Catholic parishioners had prevented the measures from going through.[124] In a sign of coming confessional disagreements, the Hanover Protestant church under Bishop Hanns Lilje announced its willingness to cooperate with the state government, so long as education policy recognized that "the cultural

146   REINVENTING PROTESTANT GERMANY

assets of our people are decisively determined by Christian belief."[125] Affirming that the region's Lutheran congregations did not desire to engage in "ecclesiastical power politics," Lilje positioned his church as a bastion of moderation against a creeping Catholic clericalism.[126] In turn, the Catholic rallies were met by Protestant protests portending a "counter-Reformation."[127]

The conflict came to a head in the spring of 1954. The CDU minority in the Lower Saxony parliament denounced the state government's proposed legislation, while the Catholic archbishop of Osnabrück called for open resistance were the school law promulgated. Demonstrations organized by the Catholic hierarchy brought tens of thousands of lay Catholics to the streets of Hanover and Lingen.[128] After a final round of deadlocked discussions, the school law was passed on September 14 with the support of the SPD-FDP coalition. During the following weeks, over three-quarters of the state's confessional schools were converted into interconfessional community schools, a veritable Kulturkampf in the eyes of Adolf Süsterhenn.[129] Konrad Adenauer initially avoided engaging in the conflict, for fear of upsetting the fragile confessional balance in the national CDU. However, popular protests, along with pressure from the Catholic bishops, ultimately led the federal government to file a petition against the Lower Saxony school law with the Federal Constitutional Court. The continued validity of the 1933 Concordat formed the linchpin of the government case. Soon afterward, the SPD-led states of Hesse and Bremen, whose own state constitutions had standardized the interconfessional school, joined Lower Saxony in a counter-petition against the federal government.[130]

The impending case before the Constitutional Court catalyzed an acrimonious national debate. The legal issues at stake were already contentious: the continuity of the Third Reich with the Federal Republic; the relationship between the federal government and the states; and the competing claims of parents, churches, and government over education. However, the controversy became even more explosive for how it threatened to expose the churches' tarnished legacies under National Socialism. Protestant participants, conservative Lutherans as well as Dahlemites, sought to use the Concordat issue toward their own advantage. The confessional anxieties articulated in the family law debate quickly spilled into outright anti-Catholic polemics, as Protestants pointed toward Catholic cooperation with the Nazi state in order to conceal their own compromises.

Martin Niemöller's circle pioneered these denunciations. Given the long-standing rejection of an interconfessional Christian party by veterans of the

FAMILIES, SCHOOLS, AND THE BATTLE FOR THE BASIC LAW

Confessing Church Dahlemites, as well as this group's confrontations with CDU Catholics over issues from "parents' rights" to West German rearmament, attacks on Catholic complicity with Nazism were not a far step. The Dahlemite journal *Stimme der Gemeinde,* which had perfected its denunciations of Catholic "clericalism" during the early 1950s, lambasted the Concordat in a series of feature articles.[131] The author, Matthäus Ziegler, had worked as a propagandist under the Nazi ideologue Alfred Rosenberg, retraining as a Lutheran pastor after church connections facilitated his early release from postwar imprisonment. With Niemöller's help, Ziegler took up a pastorate in the regional Protestant Church of Hesse-Nassau. He later joined the Institute for Confessional Research, founded in 1947 under the auspices of the nationalist Protestant League.[132] Ziegler's exposé for *Stimme der Gemeinde* centered on documents uncovered by the Hessian investigative team, which revealed a secret clause of the Concordat that had made Catholic priests liable for military service. The signing of the secret clause while the Versailles Treaty was still in effect, Ziegler argued, stood in patent violation of international law, making the Catholic Church complicit in the outbreak of the war.[133]

Ziegler not only maligned the Vatican's actions under Nazism. He went further, identifying the Protestant-coded values of pluralism and tolerance with the Basic Law. Conjuring the specter of Catholic canon law coming to replace the laws of the Federal Republic, Ziegler declared, "The community school is tolerant and corresponds in its ideological foundations, which determine its spirit, to the requirements of the basic rights; the Catholic confessional school is, in its innermost essence, intolerant, and contradicts a range of basic rights."[134] Whatever the legal merits of his argument, Ziegler's implied hierarchy of Christian culpability flew in the face of historical realities, not least his own past. Wolfgang Sucker, the director of the Institute for Confessional Research and himself a former member of the SA and the German Christians, similarly denounced the Concordat in a lecture before the Hesse-Nassau synod. The Concordat was nothing less than a Catholic bid at the "clericalization of the world"; by contrast, Protestants had an "unsurpassed interest in the modern confessionless state that leaves the freedom of conscience of its citizens untouched."[135]

It was not only Niemöller's Hesse-Nassau church that attacked the Concordat. Protestant Christian Democrats as well proved reluctant to back the federal government's case. At a meeting of Protestant jurists and church administrators convened by the EKD chancellery in late 1955, attendees—including Hansjürg Ranke, Ulrich Scheuner, and Elisabeth Schwarzhaupt—concluded

148   REINVENTING PROTESTANT GERMANY

that a decision in favor of the Concordat would be unfavorable for Protestant interests. Such a ruling could bring about protests against "clericalism" in subsequent elections and threaten the efforts of Protestant regional churches to conclude treaties with West German state governments. But an alternative account of the Nazi past was also at stake. While their statements lacked the vitriol of *Stimme der Gemeinde,* the jurists accentuated the divide between the churches' postwar trajectories. Whatever cooperation may have occurred between Protestant churches and the Nazi state, the meeting report concluded, the EKD had "distanced itself" from this past with the Stuttgart Declaration of October 1945. By contrast, the Concordat represented a fundamental continuity, because "the recognition of National Socialism in Germany was the price the [Catholic] Curia paid for accommodations that remained denied in the Weimar Republic."[136] After considering the meeting's recommendations, the EKD Council decided against publicly taking a side on the issue, a blow to Christian Democratic interconfessionalism.[137]

Rudolf Smend advanced on these arguments in a pair of commentaries for West Germany's *JuristenZeitung,* distributed to attorneys on both sides just prior to the hearings before the Federal Constitutional Court.[138] Even as he stressed the legitimate public rights of the Catholic Church, the doyen of West German constitutional law questioned the Concordat's compatibility with the Basic Law. In one of the few explicit appeals to democracy to surface in the Concordat debate, Smend noted that education policy belonged to the "political core" of the Basic Law, given the centrality of reeducation programs to "democratic reconstruction after 1945." Therefore, "it must be asked whether self-determination in matters of school type, which is fundamentally necessary . . . can endure such restrictions as the school article of the Concordat, when these restrictions stem from the authoritarian past." Following his larger theory of constitutional integration, Smend insisted that the values underpinning new political order took precedence over treaty obligations inherited from the Third Reich.[139]

If Scheuner, Schwarzhaupt, and Smend made the case against the Concordat at the level of legal theory, the Social Democratic parliamentarian Adolf Arndt put it into practice as the lead attorney representing the state of Hesse before the Constitutional Court. Born in 1904 to a Prussian civil servant who had converted from Judaism, Arndt was, like Elisabeth Schwarzhaupt, an outsider among Germany's postwar Protestant intellectuals. Stripped of his judgeship on the Berlin-Moabit criminal court in 1933, Arndt established a private law practice in Berlin that defended the rights of trade unionists

FAMILIES, SCHOOLS, AND THE BATTLE FOR THE BASIC LAW   149

and Jews, coming to sympathize with the underground Social Democratic opposition. Arndt was spared from deportation due to his marriage to a non-Jewish wife, but he was conscripted into forced labor at an armaments factory during the final year of the war. Despite his marginalized status as a Protestant of Jewish descent, Arndt found solace at the edges of the church. Throughout the war, the Dahlemite pastor Gerhard Salzsieder remained one of Arndt's closest friends and interlocutors. The jurist embraced the idea of a Confessing Church set apart from the institutional Christianity that had so readily complied with the regime.[140]

Arndt's postwar career diverged from both conservative Lutherans who moved toward the CDU, as well as Confessing Church Dahlemites who rejected the party system altogether. Instead Arndt joined the SPD, identifying with the party's legacy of anti-Nazi opposition and convinced that a nationalist stance "above parties" was no longer tenable.[141] He rejected the EKD's campaign against denazification, and his postwar legal writings emphasized the law's roots in a common humanity that transcended religious divides.[142] Nevertheless, Arndt forged connections to the Protestant churches, in part through his friendship with Ludwig Metzger, a fellow SPD member and a Confessing Church veteran. Arndt participated in early meetings of EKD and SPD representatives and remained a mediator between the Social Democratic and Protestant milieus following his 1949 election to the Bundestag.[143] Ultimately Arndt adopted the position on church–state relations proposed by Rudolf Smend, whom Arndt first met during his student days in Berlin and whose constitutional theory remained a profound source of influence. Like Smend, Arndt rejected any direct role for the churches in the process of lawmaking, regarding Christian natural law claims as a veneer for conservative politics. Still, he continued to view the churches as repositories of shared political values.[144]

Arndt's arguments in the Concordat case reflected this synthesis of Protestant and Social Democratic legal theories. Arndt never denied that religion had a place in public schools, but he regarded the Catholic position as too narrow to accommodate the Basic Law's vision of religious tolerance and freedom of conscience. Implicitly, this values consensus was Protestant. In a published exchange with Adolf Süsterhenn, Arndt accused the federal government of fostering a Kulturkampf of its own with its one-sided partisanship for the Catholic position.[145] A March 1956 parliamentary query, submitted by a group of Social Democratic and liberal deputies including Arndt and Ludwig Metzger, argued that the government's stance disregarded "the new historical and constitutional-legal situation" and had aroused "concern in circles of the Protestant population."[146] In the weeks before the court hearings began, Martin Niemöller furnished Arndt with a copy of the secret clause obliging priests to perform military service. The revelation likely furthered Arndt's conviction that the Concordat was a document of Nazi collusion.[147]

The proceedings at the Federal Constitutional Court, held over five days in June 1956, renewed the confessional polemics that had structured the press and parliamentary debates. The Catholic CDU jurist Hans Peters, who represented the federal government, advanced an argument from the principle of subsidiarity that reversed the Protestant discourse of conscience and toleration. According to Peters, responsibility for a child's education lay first and foremost with parents and family, and then with the school. By usurping the alignment of "teacher, school, and home," the contested Lower Saxony school laws infringed upon the conscience of Catholic parents and practiced intolerance toward the state's Catholic population.[148] Attorneys for the state governments of Lower Saxony, Hesse, and Bremen countered that confessional schools necessarily violated the freedom of conscience of nonmembers.[149]

In keeping with Protestant discussions of law, however, defense attorneys did not seek to vitiate the Christian underpinnings of West German institutions. An exchange between Hans Peters and Lower Saxony state secretary Eckhard Koch revealed the opposition parties' alternative understanding of a nonconfessional Christianity as a basis for public schools. Asked by Peters whether Lower Saxony would require non-Christian "dissidents" to attend Christian interconfessional schools, Koch replied that practical realities prohibited the state from forming separate schools for the 2 percent of students who were non-Christians. However, the Christian community school was "tolerant" and therefore equally open to all students, including nonbelievers.[150] Adolf Arndt similarly rejected the CDU government's equation of confessional schools with Christian values. Martin Niemöller along with the Protestant regional synod of Hesse-Nassau, Arndt assured the court, had endorsed the community school as the standard school type in the state of Hesse.[151]

Rudolf Smend's commentaries on the Concordat came in for scrutiny in debates about religious freedom and the scope of church claims in public life. Federal government attorneys contended that Smend's rejection of the Concordat's school articles violated his own theory of church–state cooperation. According to this line of reasoning, Smend failed to acknowledge the legitimate claim of the churches in the sphere of education, instead asserting

FAMILIES, SCHOOLS, AND THE BATTLE FOR THE BASIC LAW 151

one-sided state control.[152] In a rebuttal to the government side, however, Adolf Arndt captured the crux of Smend's argument: the fundamental nature of the post-1945 constitutional change. Smend, Arndt contended, recognized that concordats rested on a reciprocal relationship between state and church, not the "unilateral lawmaking" of either entity. Smend's critique of the 1933 Concordat reflected not the arbitrary assertion of state power but the transformation of the German state's "value order" after 1945.[153]

Arndt, whose grasp of the legal details and wider stakes "dominated" the proceedings, gave a rousing speech on the final day of the hearings that made clear the Protestant underpinnings of the defense case.[154] Drawing together Rudolf Smend's theory of the Basic Law with a narrative of Christian anti-Nazi resistance, Arndt went beyond a critique of the Concordat to champion the Christian interconfessional school as the foundation of a new, post-Nazi Germany. Government representatives, he insisted, were wrong to accuse his side of proposing "value-free" schools. The Hesse state constitution charged schools with "forming the moral personality." Moreover, Hesse's interconfessional schools inculcated the values of "education, reverence, altruism, respect, tolerance, uprightness, and truthfulness," as well as "professional virtue and preparation for political responsibility." Invoking the anti-Nazi "resistance" of both churches, Arndt asserted that Protestants and Catholics alike had rejected the National Socialist dictatorship as an "anti-Christian" state. By insisting upon the continued legality of the Concordat, Catholic leaders now undermined their own legacy. Instead, Arndt noted in a nod to Smend, the reorganization of church–state relations must correspond to the "new value order" of the post-1945 Federal Republic.[155]

Although he appealed to a shared resistance narrative, Arndt's interventions in the Concordat case reflected the efforts of Protestant intellectuals in 1950s West Germany to reinvent their confession as a pillar of the new constitutional order. Following leaders of the EKD Brethren Council such as Martin Niemöller and Oskar Hammelsbeck, Arndt not only accepted the compatibility of the Christian interconfessional school with the state's religious neutrality but celebrated its contributions to political responsibility and civic life. His invocations of an unmarked, non-Catholic Christianity as the basis for virtues of altruism, reverence, and tolerance suggested, against a long historical backdrop, that a tradition of cultural Protestantism would nourish the Federal Republic. Arndt's expressions of Christian loyalty were doubtless framed to sway conservative judges and disentangle his Social Democratic Party from associations with its Marxist past and the East

152   REINVENTING PROTESTANT GERMANY

German present. But Arndt's arguments before the Constitutional Court, which underscored the Christian roots of the Basic Law, also reflected his immersion in Protestant discussions.

Protestant Jurisprudence at the Federal Constitutional Court

The arguments advanced by Protestant jurists in commentaries, parliamentary debates, and legal hearings shaped the judgments of the Federal Constitutional Court on both the Concordat and family law cases. Backchannels linked the Constitutional Court to Protestant networks. Gerhard Leibholz had studied with Smend during the 1920s and was Smend's colleague at the University of Göttingen before his appointment as a judge in 1951.[156] Shortly before the start of the hearings on the Concordat, Smend sent twenty copies of his commentary in the *JuristenZeitung* to Leibholz, whose Second Senate would hear the case.[157] Yet the court's adaptation of Protestant arguments did not simply reflect personal connections or the judges' institutional investment in the Protestant churches. Instead, Protestant jurists and theologians provided conservative judges with a language for articulating the values underlying the West German constitution at a time when the German judiciary widely accepted the need for such norms as bulwarks against democratic collapse. At the same time, judges could safely avoid claims of Christian natural law that violated the Basic Law's prohibition against establishing a state religion.

The Concordat decision, released on March 18, 1957, formed a landmark of Protestant influence on West German constitutional law. Although the Constitutional Court did not release its vote, and would not publish dissenting opinions until 1971, Vatican diplomats obtained on the word of a Catholic judge that the court had split five to four along confessional lines.[158] Gerhard Leibholz stood with the ruling majority, which rejected the government's argument for preserving the school clauses of the Concordat. The decision largely accorded with the opinions advanced by Adolf Arndt and Rudolf Smend. On the one hand, the Second Senate recognized the ongoing validity of the Concordat, based on the legal continuity of the Federal Republic with the pre-1945 German Reich. But on the other hand, the court concluded that only the federal government was a party to the treaty—the states were not. Because the Basic Law had made education a domain of state rather than federal policy, the provisions of the Concordat mandating Catholic confessional schools were nonbinding. The principle of federalism enshrined in the Basic Law took precedence over treaties signed by the Nazi regime.[159]

FAMILIES, SCHOOLS, AND THE BATTLE FOR THE BASIC LAW 153

The Constitutional Court followed another part of Arndt's argument as well. While denying that the federal government could mandate confessional schools, the decision upheld states' right to define public schools as interconfessional Christian institutions. The contested Lower Saxony school law itself stated that "schools have the task of educating the students entrusted to them ... on the foundation of Christianity, Western culture, and German educational heritage, to become independent and responsible citizens of a democratic, social rule-of-law state."[160] The statute thereby echoed the Basic Law's own description of the Federal Republic as a "democratic and social federal state."[161] The majority found no reason to question the Lower Saxony law's linkage between Christianity and the democratic values of the Federal Republic. Indeed, the shared acceptance of such a connection had characterized the parliamentary debate about family law reform as well. If a state's failure to offer confessional schools did not violate parents' constitutional rights, neither did the provision of interconfessional Christian schools. Religious freedom, according to the court, was not so expansive as to interpret the basic rights in line with church demands, but not so narrow as to confine religion to the private sphere.

The decision confirmed a newfound alliance between Protestant jurists and the Federal Constitutional Court. Writing privately to Smend, Gerhard Leibholz noted that he would have preferred "to have gone a step further and declared the Concordat as nonbinding in international law." Nevertheless, Leibholz expressed satisfaction that the court had recognized the legal break between the Nazi regime and its postwar successor.[162] Smend concurred with much of the majority's analysis, holding open the possibility of publishing a defense of the decision in the *JuristenZeitung* in response to the inevitable "Catholic critique."[163] Even Ulrich Scheuner, who had served as an attorney for the CDU government, believed that a transfer of responsibility for church affairs to the state level was a positive development, allowing the federal government to extricate itself from a "frustrating dispute."[164] While CDU parliamentarians called for further negotiations with the Vatican, the SPD's defense of the decision echoed Smend's foundational writings: "The relationship between state and church must be rethought to take into account not only the federalist structure of our constitution but the historical changes in Germany since 1945."[165]

The Constitutional Court's decision also offered Protestant critics of the Concordat an opportunity to affirm their loyalty to the Basic Law. Pronouncing a victory against the "theocratic" goals of the Catholic Church, the

EKD's Institute for Confessional Research concluded that Catholic freedom of conscience and religious practice would be guaranteed by the Basic Law, not the Concordat.[166] Adolf Süsterhenn, by contrast, decried the Concordat decision for violating the federal government's authority to enforce international treaties, as well as basic norms of tolerance and parity.[167] The Holy See's ambassador to Germany, American bishop Aloisius Muench, threatened to expose the court's dissenting opinion in the Catholic press.[168] These polemics confirmed an implicit narrative of Protestant resistance and Catholic conformity under Nazism as a basis of Protestant support for the Basic Law. The controversy over the Concordat would recede over the following decade. Confessional schools became casualties of education reform initiatives across West Germany, while the Vatican itself recognized education as a government function by the mid-1960s.[169] However, the debate exerted an enduring impact on the self-image and political strategies of Protestant intellectuals, who could view their church as a source not only of individual rights but of political integration around fundamental values.

The alliance between Protestant jurists and the West German judiciary was confirmed two years later in the Federal Constitutional Court's decision on the Equal Rights Act. Shortly after the statute's passage, the FDP parliamentarian Marie-Elisabeth Lüders and Social Democratic attorney Helmut Ridder organized a group of four young mothers, who submitted a petition to the Constitutional Court challenging the fathers' privileges retained in the 1957 law. Feminists had their own backchannel to the court. Erna Scheffler, a Protestant of Jewish descent and the Constitutional Court's only woman judge, had privately encouraged Lüders to file a constitutional case after the SPD declined to bring the statute for judicial review.[170] Scheffler's First Senate decided in favor of the petitioners. But the ruling against the government reflected less a feminist argument for women's complete equality than a compromise between secular egalitarianism and a conservative Christian defense of patriarchy. Like the compromise that underlay the Second Senate's earlier judgment on the Concordat, this position had been brokered within the Protestant public sphere.

Protestant influence, implicit and explicit, suffused the judgment on the Equal Rights Act. Released in July 1959, the Constitutional Court's decision flatly rejected claims about natural law by federal government attorneys, on the grounds that the court could hardly decide among the "variety of natural law doctrines." The ruling equally eschewed the Justice Ministry's appeal to the "Christian-Western" structure of marriage.[171] Instead, drawing on a re-

FAMILIES, SCHOOLS, AND THE BATTLE FOR THE BASIC LAW 155

cent article published by Elisabeth Schwarzhaupt, the court concluded that privileging the father would infringe upon the free decision of husbands and wives over the division of family responsibilities. An "ideologically plural state such as the Federal Republic of Germany" must grant its citizens the freedom to form "their marital and family lives" according to "their [own] religious and ideological commitments."[172] Ulrich Scheuner was one of the jurists the court cited to strike down the father's prerogative.[173]

Yet this appeal to pluralism hardly meant that constitutional interpretation was without guiding principles. Instead the court echoed the arguments of Rudolf Smend and his cohort of Protestant jurists, citing its obligation to protect the "value order" of the Basic Law. These values included the Article 6 protection of marriage, which the court defined as an "institution . . . come down from time immemorial" grounded in the "objective biological or functional . . . differences" between the sexes.[174] On this basis, the court upheld Civil Code provisions that expected wives to manage the household and husbands to work outside the home.[175] Even the elimination of fathers' prerogatives was justified on the biological argument that the "essence" of women was "deeply rooted" in "motherhood."[176] Like the Concordat decision, the ruling on the Equal Rights Act enacted incremental, not radical, change. Judges could wield the language of a values-based constitution to challenge conservative conceptions of natural law, but also to oppose more thoroughgoing reforms.

The reception of the family law ruling, like the Concordat case, split largely along confessional lines. The conservative Catholic *Rheinischer Merkur* lamented the rise of the "fatherless society." The dismantling of fathers' prerogatives, wrote one author, marked a step toward "the wild beginnings of socialism."[177] Protestant assessments proved more sanguine. Defending the ruling in the Protestant weekly *Christ und Welt*, Elisabeth Schwarzhaupt flipped the Catholic argument for fathers' rights on its head. Precisely the principle of subsidiarity, Schwarzhaupt argued, required the state to remove itself from regulating the structure of authority within the family.[178] The EKD-supported Protestant Action Committee for Family Issues made it clear that its interest lay in pro-family housing, taxation, and welfare policies, rather than legalized patriarchy.[179] Even the conservative legal scholar Günther Beitzke, a member of the EKD's marriage law commission who had previously supported fathers' privileges, distanced himself from Catholic jurists like Frank Bosch who questioned the validity of the Constitutional Court's decision.[180] Certainly there was diversity within the confessions as well. Lay Catholic family associations welcomed the ruling, consistent with their support for a more egalitarian vision of the family.[181] But ongoing confessional divisions mirrored the debate that had led up to the decision, and affirmed an emergent Protestant narrative linking confessional values to the norms of constitutional democracy.

THE WRITINGS OF Protestant jurists formed only one influence on the decisions of the Constitutional Court, which did not reference the confessional backgrounds of the authors it cited. Unlike parliamentarians, who were free to appeal to the churches as participants in social policy debates, judges were bound by the Basic Law's guarantee of the state's religious and ideological neutrality. Yet West German judges overwhelmingly shared the consensus of post-Nazi jurisprudence that the constitution rested on a set of shared values, and was not simply an act of state authority. In this political context, Protestants were well equipped to challenge both Catholic natural law doctrines that positioned the churches as arbiters of social order, as well as liberal conceptions of religious freedom as the absence of religion from the public sphere. Protestant jurists affiliated with both the CDU and SPD, including Adolf Arndt, Ulrich Scheuner, Elisabeth Schwarzhaupt, and Rudolf Smend, argued for a nondoctrinal Christianity as a source of values underlying constitutional interpretation.

This newfound synthesis had wide-reaching consequences for Protestant conceptions of democracy. Although Protestant interlocutors in the debates over family and education law only rarely invoked the language of democracy, their interventions participated in the shaping of constitutional democracy in the early Federal Republic. Democracy as practiced by these church leaders, pastors, jurists, and lay intellectuals did not require the abandonment of traditions of Protestant nationalism. Critiques of Catholic theologies of natural law, which at times spiraled into outright diatribes against Catholic "clericalism," suffused both controversies and helped outsiders such as Schwarzhaupt and Arndt gain conservative support for reformist initiatives. Anti-Catholic polemics were enlivened by an ambition to tout Protestants' ostensibly cleaner record under National Socialism and more complete break with the Nazi past. Rather than enact a rapprochement between Protestant and Catholic conservatives, postwar debates about education and the family united the conservative Lutheran and Dahlemite wings of the EKD in shared confessional anxieties and efforts at political rehabilitation.

An emergent consensus on family law and confessional schools did not mean that divisions among the factions of postwar Protestantism were overcome. Protestant conservatives, as well as a growing number of moderate Social Democrats, welcomed the EKD's newfound alliance with the Federal Constitutional Court as a means of translating Protestant values into social policy. Veterans of the Confessing Church Dahlemites also backed the reform of education and family law. Another issue, however, made this group's relationship to the West German state more tortuous: the question of rearmament within the US-led Cold War alliance. Even more than the controversies over civil law reform, the possibility of West German rearmament ignited impassioned disagreement across the political spectrum and laid bare the selective resistance narratives and enduring nationalism that pervaded Protestant circles. This debate, too, would foster new appeals to democracy among Protestant theologians and lay intellectuals—but rather than a straightforward matter of individual rights and constitutional checks on state power, democracy itself became a bitterly contested term.

CHAPTER FIVE

REARMAMENT AND THE
MYTHS OF RESISTANCE

THE TENTH ANNIVERSARY of the July 1944 assassination attempt on Hitler brought a wave of commemorations that confirmed the centrality of the resistance movement for Protestant memories of the war. Yet these remembrances also underscored the plot's divided legacy. In an address on July 20, 1954, delivered before Konrad Adenauer and other dignitaries at West Berlin's Free University, Federal President Theodor Heuss lauded the politicians and military officers who had followed the demands of conscience over their oaths to the Nazi state. Nevertheless, Heuss declared, the "border case" of resistance became thinkable only under the extreme circumstance of tyranny. The modern state remained a "legal order" that rested on "the power of commands and the claim of obedience."[1] The Freiburg historian Gerhard Ritter echoed these conclusions in an essay for the Lutheran journal *Zeitwende*. The conspirators were not traitors but patriots who had sought to save Germany—and all of Europe—from the clutches of Communism.[2] In contrast, the pastors and lay congregants who forged the EKD Brethren Council invoked the legacy of anti-Nazi resistance as an ongoing model of opposition to political authority. In a November 1954 address commemorating Germany's national day of mourning, Karl Barth interpreted anti-Nazi resistance as a broad-based, democratic act. Beyond the elites of the July 20 movement, "many nameless people" had been targeted for opposition against the regime. These victims could not be honored through "empty sighs, wishes, and hopes," but only through "actions" taken to prevent a future war.[3]

At stake in these competing narratives of July 20 was not simply the theological division of conservative Lutherans and Confessing Church Dahlemites,

REARMAMENT AND THE MYTHS OF RESISTANCE   159

but the explosive controversy over West German rearmament. Upon assuming the chancellorship in September 1949, Konrad Adenauer made rearmament a pillar of his agenda, first through covert negotiations with the Western Allies and soon after in a public campaign. For Adenauer and like-minded anti-Communists, rearmament within a US-backed alliance was critical to the security of the fledgling West German state; only a Western show of strength would force the Soviet Union to abandon its aspirations to dominate Europe. Among the broader population, however, the rearmament issue was deeply contentious. Would Germans again don soldiers' uniforms, so soon after the calamity of total war and in a world where nuclear destruction had become possible? For Theodor Heuss and Gerhard Ritter, who backed Adenauer's defense policy, the anti-Communist West German state stood as the spiritual heir to the wartime resistance. In Karl Barth's estimation, by contrast, the gravest threat to world peace, ten years on, came less from Soviet Communism than from "West German rearmament in the framework of an anti-Eastern military alliance."[4] Opposition to West German foreign policy became the true fulfillment of the resistance legacy.

This chapter turns to the rearmament controversy and its impact on Protestant conceptions of democracy in 1950s West Germany.[5] While conservative Lutherans and veterans of the Confessing Church Dahlemites divided over the government's plans, neither group articulated a democratic understanding of the state at the outset of the debate. Whereas conservatives stressed the duty of military obedience, Dahlemites invoked the obligation of resistance, each side drawing on its own narrative of the Nazi era. A constitutional issue reoriented the debate toward questions of democracy. Upon its ratification in May 1949, the West German Basic Law became the world's only constitution to guarantee a right of conscientious objection to military service, ensconced in Article 4, Paragraph 3. Beginning with the first leaks of Adenauer's intentions, and extending beyond the introduction of conscription in 1956, this constitutional right became a flashpoint in West German discussions of rearmament. The Adenauer government sought to construe the right of conscientious objection as narrowly as possible; its detractors angled for an expansive reading of Article 4. Alongside the Social Democratic Party, trade unions, and left-wing intellectual circles, the Protestant Church—spurred on by its Dahlemite faction—became a central actor in the coalition demanding a far-reaching right of conscientious objection.

As in the concurrent battles over family law and confessional schools, practical engagement with West Germany's political institutions preceded an explicit defense of democracy. Without needing to affirm a linkage between Protestantism and democracy in principle, pastors and lay intellectuals who appealed to Article 4 of the Basic Law spoke the new language of individual rights and limited state power that had shaped Protestant politics since the early occupation years. In this instance, however, the question of whether the Basic Law was sufficient to secure Protestants' political vision became hotly contested. For some Protestant conservatives and reformist Social Democrats, favorable rulings by the Federal Constitutional Court in the early 1960s marked a successful effort to actualize a Protestant defense of conscience rights within constitutional democracy. For members of the Dahlemite camp, by contrast, the shortcomings of the campaign for conscientious objection illustrated the limits of rights-based, legalistic strategies and the need to conceive of democracy in more radical, participatory, and confrontational terms. By the beginning of the 1960s, both sides framed their arguments about conscientious objection in terms of expanding democracy—but this category was itself at stake.

At the same time, the political reorientation of the 1950s EKD continued to be inflected and facilitated by older ideologies of Protestant nationalism. The Protestant campaign for the right of conscientious objection did not demand a forthright confrontation with the Nazi past. Instead it relied on the partial, exaggerated accounts of anti-Nazi resistance espoused by both wings of the church. Dahlemite supporters of conscientious objection were frequently nationalists in a more literal sense as well. Although members of this group participated in an international peace movement that transcended narrowly German concerns, they also aimed to restore Germany's role as a mediator between East and West, a long-standing conceit of German Protestant nationalism. With Germany divided, representatives of the only major institution to operate across East and West Germany continued to figure their church as a bulwark of national values above the divisions of ideology and confession. Like their conservative Lutheran counterparts, veterans of the Confessing Church Dahlemites found their way to democracy by recasting, not entirely abandoning, their church's political heritage.

Resistance and the Politics of Rearmament

The question of rearmament proved more divisive than any other political issue facing the newly founded West German state. Demilitarization was a pillar of the occupation policy announced at Potsdam. The Allied governments not only disbanded the Wehrmacht and closed weapons factories but prohibited displays of militarism through flags, uniforms, monuments, parades, and even library books.[6] Suspicion of German military power was hardly restricted to the Allies. After the defeat of 1945, with more than 5 million German soldiers and 1 million German civilians killed, many West Germans remained wary of future military service. Asked by the EMNID Institute for Public Opinion Research in 1949 whether "you [would] consider it right to become a soldier again, or for your son or husband to become a soldier again," nearly three-quarters of respondents replied in the negative.[7] While only a minority of West Germans committed themselves to principled pacifism, many more feared that rearmament within a Western military alliance would increase their country's vulnerability to Soviet aggression. An EMNID survey of August 1950 found that 54 percent of West Germans "believed that if the Soviets attacked, the Western powers would simply abandon the [Federal Republic]." Moreover, many West Germans viewed rearmament as a hindrance to the speedy reunification of West and East Germany.[8]

The controversy over rearmament raised charged questions about not only German division but the Nazi past. The East German Socialist Unity Party (SED), the self-styled heir to the Communist anti-fascist resistance, could justify its militarized People's Police as a defensive measure against the neofascist capitalist powers.[9] Rearmament presented a more complex problem of legitimacy for the Federal Republic, which acknowledged itself as the legal successor to the Nazi Reich. In their negotiations with the Allies, West German leaders stressed the distance between the Nazi-era Wehrmacht and a planned postwar military. But a West German military would necessarily rely on former Wehrmacht officers and soldiers. The Association of German Soldiers and other veterans' organizations insisted upon the "rehabilitation" of the Wehrmacht in exchange for their support of rearmament, including the "equal treatment" of German soldiers in a future West European army.[10] The example of officers who had joined the resistance against Hitler proved especially problematic. Central to West German elites' search for an anti-Nazi military tradition, the legacy of July 20 nevertheless fit uncomfortably with the reestablishment of military discipline. In the early 1950s, public opinion remained divided over the attempt to overthrow Hitler's dictatorship; many West Germans continued to view wartime resistance as an act of treason.[11]

Widespread fears of a future war, as well as the contested legacy of anti-Nazi resistance, formed the backdrop to the postwar debate about conscientious objection. Unlike Britain, Canada, and the United States, which created tribunals to adjudicate conscientious objector claims during both world wars, no German government had established a legal mechanism for authorizing draft refusal before 1945.[12] Following German unification in 1871, Mennonite conscripts were permitted to serve in noncombatant roles or obtain exit visas from Germany. In practice, however, German Mennonites had widely abandoned their church's traditional pacifism by the turn of the twentieth century.[13] German soldiers who refused to perform military service during the First World War were frequently labeled not conscientious objectors but "war neurotics," subjected to psychiatric rather than criminal confinement.[14] In August 1939 the Nazi regime radicalized the German state's long-standing nonrecognition of conscientious objectors by making the refusal of military service a capital crime. The majority of men executed for the offense during the Second World War belonged to the Jehovah's Witnesses, unique as a Christian community that refused to abandon its principled pacifism in the face of Nazi terror.[15]

The end of the war brought an opening to radically revise the German state's traditional position on the issue. Postwar Social Democrats, buoyed by their anti-Nazi credentials, took the lead. Under the indefatigable party leader Kurt Schumacher, the SPD positioned itself in staunch opposition to German division and roundly rejected rearmament prior to negotiations for a militarily—if not ideologically—neutral Germany between the Cold War blocs.[16] The right of conscientious objection would both symbolically differentiate postwar Germany from its Nazi past and form a bulwark against renewed militarism. By 1948, Social Democratic state legislators shepherded the enactment of a right to conscientious objection in Baden, Bavaria, Hesse, and Württemberg-Baden.[17] At the Parliamentary Council, Social Democrats supported such a guarantee in the Basic Law. At the most ambitious, one SPD delegate proposed that the right of conscientious objection would serve a "pedagogical function," educating post-Nazi Germans to question the commands of their state and become critical, democratic citizens.[18] An expansive vision of conscientious objection, however, raised the specter of resistance. Could the state authorize individuals to take their legal obligations into their own hands?

Ultimately, a narrower definition found its way into the Basic Law. In an effort to convince skeptical liberals and conservatives—who argued for regulating conscientious objection as a matter of administrative law on the Anglo-American model—Social Democrats restricted the purview of the proposed constitutional right. A right to conscientious objection, SPD deputies argued, would serve primarily to acknowledge the suffering of religious pacifists who had refused military service in Nazi Germany.[19] CDU and FDP delegates backed such a right after the CDU jurist Hermann von Mangoldt suggested its incorporation into an article on freedom of religion. The final text, based on von Mangoldt's formulation, appeared as Article 4, Paragraph 3, of the Basic Law: "No person shall be compelled against his conscience to render military service involving the use of arms."[20]

Although West Germany's right of conscientious objection broke new ground in democratic constitutions worldwide, its placement underscored the Parliamentary Council's restrictive understanding of religious conscience. Aside from members of the tiny "free churches" of Mennonites, Quakers, and Jehovah's Witnesses—which were independent from the state-supported Protestant churches that made up the EKD—young men would be expected to perform military service. Moreover, the Basic Law's restriction of conscientious objection to "military service involving the use of arms" left open the possibility of induction into a medical or auxiliary service, or even conscription into the armed forces during peacetime. The constitutional article stipulated that "details shall be regulated by a federal law," potentially allowing for further constraints.[21]

The debate about conscientious objection entered the Protestant public sphere early on. Questions about the scope of state authority and the legacy of anti-Nazi resistance that had animated the Parliamentary Council proved even more contentious among Protestants seeking to redefine their church's role in political life. For all the challenges to a supposed tradition of political quietism underway at the Protestant Academies, Protestant conservatives continued to invoke the two-kingdoms distinction on matters of military service, in line with a long history. Luther himself had distinguished between the fallen world and the coming kingdom of God in order to justify the Christian vocation of the soldier. Military service was an unavoidable, if regrettable, necessity, Luther wrote in his 1526 treatise "Whether Soldiers, Too, Can Be Saved": "For the very fact that the sword has been instituted by God to punish the evil, protect the good, and preserve peace is powerful and sufficient proof that war and killing . . . have been instituted by God."[22] The EKD chancellery's first statement on conscientious objection, issued in September 1948, reflected the same reasoning: "In this world, the reclamation of a true kingdom of peace cannot occur." For postwar Protestant conservatives, conscientious objection reflected a utopian pacifism, the

164   REINVENTING PROTESTANT GERMANY

purview of Mennonites, Quakers, and Jehovah's Witnesses rather than hard-nosed Lutherans.[23]

This view on conscientious objection was bolstered by an emergent narrative of anti-Nazi resistance among Lutheran conservatives. Its most prominent expositor, Walter Künneth, belonged to the cohort of Lutheran theologians who had backed Nazism early on and later joined the conservative wing of the Confessing Church. Künneth continued his postwar career uninterrupted, appointed to a chair at the University of Erlangen with the support of the erstwhile Nazi sympathizer Paul Althaus. While mobilizing opposition to denazification at Erlangen, Künneth published his first postwar tract, *The Great Decline*.[24] The 1947 text, a sprawling account of the clash between Christianity and National Socialism, posited a close link between conscience and resistance. "God-given conscience," Künneth wrote, had led millions of Germans to mark an inward break with the Nazi regime. But acting upon conscience to oppose the state represented a crossing from ordinary politics to Christian witness, demanding "a readiness for martyrdom." While figuring Christianity as the final source of opposition to a tyrannical state, Künneth rendered the conditions for conscientious objection so extreme as to absolve the millions of Germans who had faithfully obeyed the state's dictates, whatever their inner convictions. Moreover, by situating the "resistance of conscience" within the exceptional circumstances of a tyrannical regime, Künneth laid the ground for the postwar return of state authority.[25] Künneth prefigured the reflections of Theodor Heuss and Gerhard Ritter on the tenth anniversary of the July 20 plot. All three sought to recover the conspiracy as an act of Christian conscience while confining its legitimacy to the Nazi past.

Veterans of the Confessing Church Dahlemites sharply disagreed—both on the issue of conscientious objection and on the broader meaning of anti-Nazi resistance. The most influential statement of political ethics within this group, Karl Barth's 1946 tract "The Christian Community and the Civil Community," challenged the Lutheran two-kingdoms doctrine for reducing the church to a lackey of state power. Blurring the bounds of spiritual and political affairs, Barth instead called upon Christians to bear witness to the gospel's message of justice, peace, and reconciliation in the political world. For some members of the Dahlemite faction, motivated both by German nationalism and by newfound anti-militarism, this message meant opposition to the division of Germany and the looming Cold War. Signatories of the EKD Brethren Council's 1947 Darmstadt statement, including Martin Niemöller and the theologian Hans Joachim Iwand, had already rejected the

REARMAMENT AND THE MYTHS OF RESISTANCE 165

amalgamation of "Christianity and Western culture" in favor of a message of reconciliation across the East–West divide.[26] In the view of this group, the legacy of resistance was not confined to the Nazi past—or to the campaign against war crimes trials and denazification—but retained ongoing relevance in a divided present where ideology and state repression again threatened the bonds of solidarity.[27]

Niemöller's wing of the Brethren Council therefore required its own account of anti-Nazi resistance, one that was even more ambitious than Walter Künneth's. Martin Niemöller's younger brother, the pastor Wilhelm Niemöller, laid the foundation for such an account. A fervent German nationalist like his brother, Wilhelm Niemöller had joined the Nazi Party in 1923 but later participated in the Dahlemite wing of the church opposition. After the war, the younger Niemöller established an archive of the Confessing Church at his Bielefeld parish that formed the basis for early research on the organization. Wilhelm Niemöller's postwar histories of the Confessing Church recounted a succession of male heroes who had boldly challenged the regime's claim to total authority and the heresies of the German Christians. The Nazi persecution of the Jews occupied a marginal place in his writings, as did the roles of women, such as Margarete Meusel, Elisabeth Schmitz, and Helene Jacobs, who had challenged the Confessing Church to speak out against the Nuremberg laws and participated in wartime rescue efforts.[28] Naturally, Wilhelm Niemöller also sought to bolster the standing of the Dahlemite faction within the postwar EKD. His 1948 tome, *Struggle and Witness of the Confessing Church*, concluded with a call to action: The Confessing Church should not "keep silent and die" but remain a "light to the world."[29]

The network of pastors and lay Protestants around Martin Niemöller sought to bring this vision to bear in the debate about rearmament that broke open shortly after the founding of the Federal Republic. For Martin Niemöller and his allies, opposition to West German rearmament was the natural extension of the Confessing Church's resistance against Nazism. In December 1949, after Adenauer's plans for a West German defense contribution surfaced in an interview with the *Cleveland Plain Dealer*, Niemöller emerged as the CDU chancellor's most outspoken critic. In a subsequent interview with the *New York Herald Tribune*, widely reported in the West German press, the pugilistic pastor argued that Germans would prefer a unified state, even under Soviet domination, to Cold War partition. "The present West German government," Niemöller declared, "was conceived in the Vatican and

166   REINVENTING PROTESTANT GERMANY

born in Washington. The continuance of the West German state means the death of Continental Protestantism."[30]

Niemöller's biographers debate his motivations. On the one hand, Niemöller had increasingly gravitated toward pacifism since encountering members of the Anglo-American Fellowship of Reconciliation at the 1948 World Council of Churches Assembly in Amsterdam. Like many West Germans, he feared that rearmament could provoke war on German soil. On the other hand, the echoes of Niemöller's long-standing Protestant nationalism are undeniable. He continued to view the Protestant church as the representative of German national interests, and his attack on rearmament was laden with anti-Catholic rhetoric.[31] Ultimately, under the conditions of the early Cold War, pacifism and nationalism reinforced one another. Niemöller's fears of war and potential nuclear attack were doubtless genuine, but he framed his initial opposition to West German rearmament around Germany's national integrity rather than global demilitarization.

The emergent rearmament controversy led the EKD synod to address the issue of conscientious objection for the first time at its April 1950 meeting in the East Berlin borough of Weissensee. In a concluding "Word on Peace," the body sought to steer between the two Protestant camps, welcoming the Basic Law's right of conscientious objection without condemning Adenauer's rearmament plans. "Whoever refuses military service on grounds of conscience," the synod announced, "should be certain of the advocacy and intercession of the church."[32] Yet the Weissensee statement remained vague on critical questions. The declaration did not clarify who counted as a conscientious objector, whether principled pacifists alone or individuals who refused military service in a divided Germany. The synod also left open the precise role of the church. Advocacy for individual objectors was a different proposition from entering the political fray in controversies over rearmament and conscription.

Such questions broke open with the beginning of the Korean War in June 1950. Adenauer and his political allies believed that the Soviet-backed North Korean invasion of US-aligned South Korea demonstrated the Federal Republic's vulnerability to a similar attack, a fear heightened by the formation of the East German People's Police. By August, Adenauer met covertly with members of the Allied High Commission to discuss the establishment of a West German paramilitary reserve, still prohibited under the occupation statute. The following month, Adenauer's government submitted a memorandum to the NATO foreign ministers calling for a "federal police force."[33] Protestant CDU parliamentarians and conservative church leaders widely accepted the need for a West German defense contribution, even if they tended to view rearmament as a means toward German reunification rather than a long-term security arrangement.[34] At the same time, the Korean War drew together the fractious coalition that would oppose West German rearmament over the next five years: Protestant pastors and laypeople as well as the Social Democratic Party, trade unions, Communist-adjacent peace movement, nationalist intellectuals, and neo-Nazi far right. Although vast ideological gulfs prevented sustained cooperation among these factions, opponents of rearmament broadly shared Martin Niemöller's concern that West German remilitarization would increase the likelihood of a European war and prolong Germany's division.[35]

The debate about conscientious objection within the EKD reflected these larger fissures, as well as the competing Protestant narratives of anti-Nazi resistance. As issues of defense emerged as the government's first priority, Interior Minister Gustav Heinemann asked the EKD's Commission on Public Responsibility to take a position on the right of conscientious objection.[36] Created in 1949 to coordinate the church's statements on political affairs, the commission divided along the lines of the wider Protestant public sphere. Walter Künneth quickly emerged as the most outspoken representative of the group's conservative wing, which also included Gerhard Ritter, the jurist Ulrich Scheuner, and the CDU parliamentarian Robert Tillmanns.[37] In an August 1950 memorandum Künneth approached the problem of conscientious objection through the concept of conscience laid out in *The Great Decline*. The refusal of military service, on this view, was a matter of resistance in the name of a higher power, stepping beyond the purview of ordinary politics to bear witness to "Christ's reign of freedom." Like the resister against Nazism, the true conscientious objector had to demonstrate "readiness for martyrdom." For Künneth and other conservative Lutherans, the state held absolute authority to compel its subjects to military service, short of the extreme case of a tyrannical regime. A legally secured right of conscientious objection made little sense within this framework.[38]

Heinemann himself took a different position. A lawyer and industrialist who had served as a lay leader in the Rhineland Confessing Church, Heinemann was appointed interior minister in Adenauer's first cabinet in an effort by the chancellor to expand Protestant representation in the CDU. As a member of the EKD Council and president of the EKD synod, Heinemann was the highest-ranking layperson in the church and could potentially mobilize a wide laity behind the CDU agenda. But Heinemann did not share the chancellor's foreign policy views. Although insisting that he did not reject rearmament in principle, Heinemann believed that such a step required negotiations between the Western Allies and a sovereign West German state on an equal footing, impossible under the conditions of occupation. Without taking German interests into account, rearmament threatened to lead to a German-German war and the reduction of German soldiers to "cannon fodder" for Western defense.[39]

Conflict erupted in late August 1950 when Adenauer disclosed to his cabinet his secret communications with US authorities on rearmament. Heinemann abruptly announced his resignation and embarked on a speaking tour with Martin Niemöller, who seized the opportunity to achieve a public victory against the chancellor.[40] On October 4, representatives of West Germany's Church Brethren Societies, the successor organizations to the regional Confessing Church leadership councils, released a leaflet declaring their opposition to any form of rearmament and demanding strict neutrality in the Cold War. While recalling the Weissensee synod's support for the right of conscientious objection, the statement went a step further, raising the prospect of disobedience against the state: "In the current situation of Germany, we object to military service, *whether or not this right remains secured in the constitution.* We encourage everyone of good conscience to do the same."[41] In a public letter to the chancellor, Niemöller invoked a legacy of Protestant resistance against Nazism. If the right to conscientious objection were repealed, "then we will again have to announce that one must obey God more than human beings."[42]

The controversy surrounding Heinemann's resignation sparked national attention in both Germanies. Niemöller's open letter was reprinted in East German newspapers and circulated in hundreds of thousands of copies by the SED. The East German Communist party quickly followed up by launching a public opinion poll of West Germans under the auspices of the West German Peace Committee, aiming to illustrate the unpopularity of rearmament.[43] While they did not defend the Communist regime's attempt to instrumentalize their campaign, neither did Adenauer's Protestant detractors speak out in support of West German constitutional democracy. For Heinemann, writing in the Brethren Council monthly *Stimme der Gemeinde* shortly following his resignation, the rearmament controversy illustrated the problems of representative democracy. The CDU had come to power in 1949 on a platform that did not include rearmament, and the public would not have the opportunity to weigh in on the issue again until new federal elections in 1953. Heinemann proposed to rectify this democratic deficit through a plebiscite on rearmament, despite the fact that the Parliamentary Council had excluded referenda from the Basic Law.[44] This was not the last time that Protestant critics of the Adenauer government would counterpose West Germany's constitutional system against a more authentic democracy.

Other writers for *Stimme der Gemeinde* had little to say about democracy altogether, instead adhering to Martin Niemöller's nationalist neutralism and justifying their dissent through the language of resistance. In a series of articles for the journal, the Göttingen theologian Hans Joachim Iwand, one of the leading expositors of Karl Barth in West Germany, continued to distinguish Catholic, liberal, and "natural" theologies from the gospel's authentic message of freedom before God. Declaring that "the Confessing Church remains in opposition," Iwand likened Christian Democratic interconfessionalism to the Nazis' "positive Christianity" and Adenauer's program of Western integration to Hitler's continental expansion. The role of the church was to limit, not augment, state power.[45] The Brethren Council pastor Theodor Dipper, the author of the Weissensee synod statement on conscientious objection, similarly argued that individual conscience stood beyond the bounds of state authority.[46] Even Gustav Heinemann harkened back to the Barmen Declaration to assert that "the experiences of the Third Reich made the question of the limits of obedience toward authority immediate for German Protestants."[47]

The Brethren Council continued to mobilize narratives of anti-Nazi resistance as the Protestant debate about rearmament turned to the issue of conscription policy. In the course of 1951, the EKD chancellery established communications with West German defense officials involved in drafting a conscription statute.[48] In line with the conservative position at the Parliamentary Council, the CDU government aimed to restrict the right of conscientious objection to absolute pacifists, especially members of minority Christian sects. In contrast, the government's Protestant critics called for the recognition of selective conscientious objectors who rejected military service on the grounds of Germany's division and the possibility of nuclear war. Conservative Lutherans saw this move as an illegitimate mixing of gospel and politics. For Protestant proponents of selective objection, however, particular circumstances, rather than abstract principles, motivated an authentic Christian decision of conscience—a point that could be justified by invoking anti-Nazi resistance. The EKD administrator Hansjürg Ranke, who continued to lead the church's amnesty campaign for convicted war criminals, noted that at the Nuremberg trials and during the Nazi period itself, Protestants had confronted the same problem: the limits of the human judge over decisions of conscience.[49]

The Protestant defense of selective conscientious objection was also rooted in ongoing confessional polemics. As early as 1947, Vatican diplomats made their support for West German and Italian rearmament known to US authorities, while the 1948 Christmas Eve address of Pope Pius XII left no question as to which side in the Cold War the Catholic hierarchy supported. As the Soviet Union consolidated its rule over Eastern Europe, the pontiff mobilized a traditional doctrine of just war toward the anti-Communist cause: Christians were permitted, indeed obliged, to take up arms in defense "against unjust aggression."[50] West Germany's Fulda Bishops Conference, led by the Cologne cardinal Josef Frings, elaborated its own position in a November 1950 statement submitted to the Catholic press. Catholics, the bishops concluded, were obliged to perform military service in the case of a just, defensive war. Judgments of conscience—including the decision to refuse military service—were not matters of subjective opinion but should reflect the "objective norms of morality," in line with church teachings.[51]

Protestant detractors seized on these pronouncements to contrast a hidebound Catholic hierarchy against a reform-minded Protestant community, a distinction familiar from contemporary debates about family law and confessional schools. Whereas Catholic conscience was ostensibly subservient to the dictates of clerical authority and the church's interpretation of natural law, Protestant conscience was free to discern the meaning of divine commandments for the present moment and could be judged only by God. As so often happened, theological argument spilled into political polemic. Following an October 1951 meeting of Protestant and Catholic church representatives with West German defense officials, Hansjürg Ranke quipped that the Catholics took a "reluctant" stance toward conscientious objection "after the Pope spoke out against [it] once."[52] When Ulrich Scheuner defended the CDU position on military service at the Protestant Academy in Bad Boll, Martin Niemöller decried the conservative jurist's confessional disloyalty: "It seems to me ever clearer that these so-called Protestant Academies are sometimes wholly Catholic academies."[53]

Such a divide was largely an artifact of postwar Protestant invention. Martin Luther himself tied the judgment of conscience to the objective truths of the Bible—narrowing the definition of conscience from medieval Scholastic sources, which obliged the individual to follow the dictates of conscience when the law remained unclear.[54] During the First World War, German Protestant

REARMAMENT AND THE MYTHS OF RESISTANCE 171

theologians had invoked the alignment of individual conscience with national community to justify the duty of military service.[55] Even in the pronouncements of the Confessing Church Dahlemites during the mid-1930s, conscience served at most to authorize noncompliance when the state contravened narrowly conceived biblical precepts.

Moreover, military service remained a contentious issue for Catholics across postwar Western Europe. As in the contest over family law, a left-wing Catholic contingent around the *Frankfurter Hefte* challenged the German bishops' position on rearmament.[56] The German Catholic theologian and war veteran Bernhard Häring, whose experience of the Eastern Front led him to question doctrines of military obedience, delinked decisions of conscience from natural law in his influential 1954 tract, *The Law of Christ*.[57] In France a cohort of left-leaning priests rejected the Catholic hierarchy's anti-Communism and laid the groundwork for a Catholic conscientious objector movement during the Algerian War, in dialogue with their Protestant counterparts.[58] By reducing the Catholic debate to the pronouncements of Pius XII and Cardinal Frings, the Brethren Council invoked a timeworn opposition between Catholic obedience and Protestant freedom. In doing so, the circle around Heinemann, Niemöller, and Iwand asserted its own claim to national leadership.

Democratizing Conscience

By late 1951 the discussion of conscientious objection within the Commission on Public Responsibility broke down. Whereas the conservative faction around Walter Künneth insisted upon a sharp delineation between political decisions and matters of conscience, Dahlemites argued that Cold War conditions could lead to a decision of conscientious objection.[59] But even as the EKD Council gave up on releasing a public statement on the issue, a basic commonality united the two camps. Each side conceived of the relationship between individual and state through the binary categories of authority and resistance, a dichotomy sharpened in their accounts of the Nazi past. In the years leading up to West German rearmament, however, the debate underwent a marked transformation. Moving beyond calls for absolute obedience or outright opposition, both camps increasingly appealed to the status of conscientious objection as a constitutional basic right. This shift was not rooted in a newfound defense of constitutional democracy per se. Dahlemites were concerned primarily to distance their campaign against rearmament from views

172   REINVENTING PROTESTANT GERMANY

espoused by the neo-Nazi far right and the Communist left, while conservatives sought to gain traction for their own resistance narratives. Nevertheless, Protestant appeals to the language of constitutional rights formed the basis for a later defense of constitutional democracy.

For Protestant opponents of rearmament, the first challenge came from the far right. Fueled by Wehrmacht veterans, including many former Nazis, the postwar ultranationalist right rejected West German rearmament as an affront to German sovereignty and the honor of the wartime military. The largest of the new far-right groups, the Socialist Reich Party (SRP), called instead for a revived Reich that would restore Germany's role as a "third force" spanning East and West, echoing third-way visions common across the anti-rearmament coalition.[60] Shared opposition to rearmament brought the neo-Nazi party into uncomfortable proximity with Protestant networks. In late 1950 Martin Niemöller and Gustav Heinemann met in Wiesbaden with the historian Ulrich Noack, the founder of the neutralist Nauheim circle that had emerged as a forum for nationalist intellectuals opposed to Western integration. The resulting "Call for Peace," which demanded the disarmament of East and West Germany as a basis for "mutual security," aimed to serve as a shared statement of principles for the anti-rearmament movement. The document, however, caused considerable embarrassment for its Protestant backers. Heinemann and Niemöller retracted their support after Noack garnered signatures from three high-ranking representatives of the SRP, including party leader Otto Ernst Remer, a former Wehrmacht officer who had commanded the unit that defeated the July 20 coup attempt.[61]

The tensions between the Brethren Council and the neo-Nazi far right reached a turning point at Remer's criminal trial the following year. Following the SRP's strong showing during 1951 state elections in Lower Saxony, Remer delivered a series of speeches denouncing the July 20 conspirators as "traitors to their country." The Protestant CDU politician Robert Lehr, Heinemann's successor as interior minister and himself a veteran of the July 20 conspiracy, brought defamation charges against Remer to the state prosecutor's office at Braunschweig. The prosecutor to take the case, the German-Jewish attorney and returned émigré Fritz Bauer, would soon gain national fame as a pioneer of West German efforts to bring Nazi criminals to justice. Although Remer would be sentenced only to three months' imprisonment, Bauer turned the trial into a broader referendum over the legitimacy of the July 20 movement. "Disobedience to inhumane laws," Bauer contended in his closing argument, constituted a "Christian" act; the July 20 plotters had demonstrated patriotism by aiming to rescue the "fatherland" from impending defeat; and Germanic law since medieval times had recognized a right of resistance against tyranny.[62]

Confessing Church Dahlemites echoed the SRP's hostility toward the Western Allies in the debate about West German rearmament but disagreed profoundly with the far-right party's condemnation of anti-Nazi resistance. The March 1952 trial provided an opportunity to defend an alternative vision. A centerpiece of Bauer's case against Remer involved a series of expert opinions on the right of resistance, solicited from historians as well as Protestant and Catholic theologians. No member of the EKD's conservative wing agreed to provide such an opinion, which would have called into question conservatives' own conduct under the Nazi regime and might have been instrumentalized by the anti-rearmament campaign.[63] Instead Bauer turned to Hans Joachim Iwand and Ernst Wolf, who elaborated a theological justification of resistance based on Luther's 1539 disputation "On the Right of Resistance against the Emperor." His most radical statement on the subject, Luther upheld the obligation of Christians—in particular those in positions of authority—to resist a tyrant who sought to destroy the church and become the Antichrist itself. Luther referred to the 1530s alliance of the pope and the Habsburg emperor against the Protestant Schmalkaldic League. Wolf and Iwand, however, whose report was published for a broader audience in *Junge Kirche*, found in Luther's text a potent lesson for assessing resistance against the Nazi state. Even though they were unsuccessful, and their intervention came too late, the conspirators of July 20 had acted justly and in accordance with Christian conscience.[64]

While they defended the organizers of the July 20 plot, Wolf and Iwand no longer presented anti-Nazi resistance as a direct model for the campaign against rearmament. Ironically, casting the Federal Republic as illegitimate would have echoed the rhetoric of the SRP. But neither did the theologians circumscribe the resistance legacy to the Nazi past, on the model of conservatives such as Walter Künneth and Gerhard Ritter. Instead their expert opinion advanced a new possibility: The resistance movement formed the basis of a more critical citizenship after 1945. The assassination attempt of July 20 had provoked "a new evaluation of law and the limits of political power," leading to the "true reconstruction of our political system, until then shattered to the ground."[65] Judgments of conscience now took on greater importance, militating against a return to uncritical obedience to state authority. "Tyrannicide," Iwand conceded in an exchange with Remer's defense attorneys, was permissible for Christians only in the extreme condition that

174   REINVENTING PROTESTANT GERMANY

the state had become a "beast out of the abyss." Still, Iwand acknowledged his own failure to speak out against Nazi breaches of legality in 1933, when public criticism was still possible.[65] A vision of conscience that reinforced rather than undermined the rule of law would reappear in Dahlemites' later defense of conscientious objection.

If a confrontation with the far right led Dahlemites to downplay calls for resistance against the Federal Republic, proximity to the Communist left demanded sharper attention to the differences between the West and East German political systems. Like the SRP, Communist front organizations such as the West German Peace Committee were a consistent presence in the anti-rearmament coalition, which frequently led to charges that prominent Dahlemites had Communist sympathies.[67] In January 1952 Martin Niemöller provoked a firestorm of criticism in the West German press after visiting Moscow on the invitation of the Russian Orthodox patriarch.[68] Accusations of Communist loyalties continued to dog Niemöller's circle when negotiations for a European Defense Community (EDC) opened the following month. Seeking to scuttle plans for a West European military, Joseph Stalin issued notes to Washington, London, and Paris proposing a neutral, reunified Germany. While the veracity of the Soviet dictator's overture has been widely debated, the entire anti-rearmament camp—including the SPD, the neutralist circle around Ulrich Noack, the Communist-aligned peace movement, and the Church Brethren Societies—urged the Adenauer cabinet to seriously consider Stalin's offer. Undeterred, the chancellor forged ahead with the Western defense agreement, joining his West European counterparts for the signing ceremony in Paris on May 27.[69]

Although the EDC treaty was a setback for opponents of rearmament, the first dispute over conscientious objection that broke out in its aftermath illustrated the efforts of Protestant detractors to distance themselves from Communist apologetics. In July 1952 ten pastors in the Rhineland city of Duisburg, members of the regional Church Brethren Society, distributed leaflets inviting young men of conscription age to register as conscientious objectors with their local pastor's office. The leaflets reflected the expansive conception of conscientious objection defended by the anti-rearmament movement: Respondents could choose to identify themselves either as absolute pacifists, or as selective objectors until the "enactment of a just, all-German peace treaty." At one level the ensuing controversy reenacted the fault lines that had followed the Brethren Council's October 1950 leaflet and Martin Niemöller's visit to Moscow. The West German Communist press celebrated the pastors' call for conscientious objection, while CDU Bundestag president Hermann Ehlers accused the Duisburg pastors of inciting "resistance" against the Federal Republic.[70] In a statement defending the action, however, the Rhineland Church Brethren Society appealed to conscience as an alternative, rather than a complement, to resistance. Acknowledging the likelihood of conscription, the group noted that military service and conscientious objection both remained legitimate decisions for Christians. The role of the church was not to oppose the state but to protect the judgment of conscience, which "cannot be taken away from us by any political entity."[71]

The Confessing Church pastor Helmut Gollwitzer emerged as a prominent voice within the Church Brethren Societies to advocate for a critical rapprochement with the West German state. A student of Karl Barth at Basel and an ally of Martin Niemöller during the church conflict, Gollwitzer had taken over Niemöller's Berlin-Dahlem parish following the senior pastor's imprisonment. Conscripted into the Wehrmacht in late 1940, Gollwitzer was captured by the Red Army near the Czech–German border at the end of the war. He eventually reached a prisoner of war camp in the Moscow suburb of Krasnogorsk, where he would remain until his repatriation to West Germany in December 1949. After taking up a position in Protestant theology at the University of Bonn, Gollwitzer renewed his Confessing Church contacts, including the circle around Martin Niemöller, Hans Joachim Iwand, and the Rhineland Church Brethren Society. Unlike his Dahlemite colleagues, however, Gollwitzer returned from postwar imprisonment firmly disillusioned with Soviet Communism.[72] As Gollwitzer remarked before an audience of East and West Germans at the August 1950 Kirchentag, the lay Protestant assembly founded the year prior, if Christians could not seek salvation in politics, neither should they remain politically indifferent. Christians in the West could continue to fight for personal and religious freedoms, however imperfectly realized in practice, an opportunity foreclosed in the East.[73]

Gollwitzer addressed the question of conscientious objection in his groundbreaking contribution to the debate about the political role of the church, the 1953 manifesto *The Christian Community in the Political World*. Widely reviewed in West Germany and abroad, Gollwitzer's text applied the political theology of Karl Barth, whose 1946 tract his title echoed, to the challenges facing Protestants in the Federal Republic. By empowering the Christian community to bring the message of gospel into the political world, Gollwitzer argued, Barth and his followers had prepared the ground for a modernization of the two-kingdoms doctrine.[74] Whereas Luther restricted a right of resistance to individuals in positions of power, the "democratization of political life" had devolved "a political office in Luther's sense to every citizen."[75] Dietrich Bonhoeffer and the conspirators of July 20 gave the most radical expression to this ethic of political responsibility. Bonhoeffer had recognized that the extreme situation of Nazism required obedience to God alone, releasing "the command to truth from the rigidity of principles."[76] But Gollwitzer insisted upon distinguishing the conditions of anti-Nazi resistance from those confronting postwar West Germans. On the one hand, Gollwitzer defined conscience in terms that paralleled his description of Bonhoeffer's resistance: an "internal dialogue" that takes place "in the hearing of God's word."[77] On the other hand, Gollwitzer suggested that West German Protestants turn to law, rather than resistance, to seek the protection of conscience. Based on their understanding of conscience, Protestants could sooner support selective conscientious objectors than absolute pacifists. If the government continued to discount selective objectors, then "the church will have to intervene before the state to demand legal protection, because the state is not master over conscience."[78]

At the time that Gollwitzer's text was published, the Church Brethren Societies had not fully shifted from their frontal assault against rearmament to more narrowly defending the rights of conscientious objectors in a constitutional democracy. Federal elections of September 1953 would hasten that shift. Again the Protestant anti-rearmament movement found itself in uncomfortable proximity to neutralists of the far right and left. The previous year Gustav Heinemann had cofounded the All-German People's Party (GVP) alongside his Essen law partner Diether Posser and the Catholic politician Helene Wessel. The party platform opposed the EDC and backed negotiations with the Soviet Union for a united, neutral Germany. Strapped for funds, Heinemann reluctantly entered a coalition with Ulrich Noack's neutralist Free Social Union as well as the SED-backed Federation of Germans. The perception of Communist infiltration proved disastrous. Even some of Heinemann's closest allies, including Helmut Gollwitzer, refused to join the GVP, and the party's returns fell well below the 5 percent threshold required for entry into the Bundestag.[79] At the same time, the SPD, which opposed rearmament but remained adamantly anti-Communist, proved unable to break out of its working-class base. Adenauer's CDU expanded its share of the vote to an unprecedented 45 percent as the result of a booming economy, and quickly ushered in the necessary constitutional amendments to authorize military conscription.[80]

With the anti-rearmament coalition suffering a crippling electoral blow, Gollwitzer's call for the expanded legal recognition of conscientious objectors gained new traction. Although the GVP platform had not even addressed the issue, defending the right of conscientious objection appeared urgent as the prospect of rearmament became imminent.[81] Even the most vociferous detractors of rearmament shifted their attention to conscientious objector rights. Following the 1953 election, Martin Niemöller's Hesse-Nassau church presented a petition to the EKD Council recommending that young men be permitted to register as conscientious objectors, either "fundamentally or under particular conditions."[82] When the French parliament voted against the EDC treaty the following year, creating an unexpected opening for the anti-rearmament movement, oppositional pastors redoubled their commitment to the language of the Basic Law. Meeting in November 1954 the Rhineland Church Brethren Society drafted a statement that invoked the constitutional inviolability of Article 4 to justify its opposition to rearmament. Signed by over 1,400 pastors, the declaration admonished the government that "the coming conscription legislation cannot restrict this basic right."[83]

Not only Dahlemites but also Protestant conservatives increasingly embraced a rights-based argument for conscientious objection, spurred on by efforts to advance their own narrative of anti-Nazi opposition. The Bonn jurist Ulrich Scheuner, who initially defended the CDU's restrictive proposals, exemplified this transformation.[84] Beginning in 1953 Scheuner participated in a commission at the Westphalian Christophorus-Stift that aimed to reevaluate Lutheran political teachings in light of a lecture at the Lutheran World Congress by the Norwegian bishop Eivind Berggrav. Rewriting his own complex history under Nazism as one of faith-bound resistance, Berggrav had called on postwar Lutherans to restrict their allegiance to a *Rechtsstaat*, a state bound by the rule of law.[85] Scheuner adopted a similar position at the Christophorus-Stift commission. Because Protestants had been forced to reckon with a state that asserted itself as a "quasi-religious totality," they now sought the "limitation of state power" and the "protection of human freedoms and rights."[86]

This seamless narrative flew in the face of Scheuner's own past as a Nazi Party member and advocate for convicted war criminals. But his newfound defense of the rule of law led Scheuner to call for the expansion of conscience rights. In a 1954 essay for the Mainz Institute for Statecraft and Politics, Scheuner acknowledged for the first time that selective objection "against service in a particular war" could reflect "true concerns of conscience." Drawing upon Helmut Gollwitzer's *The Christian Community in the Political World,* as well as the writings of Karl Barth, the conservative jurist acknowledged the confessional distinction central to the Dahlemite defense of selective objectors. Protestants were less concerned than the Catholic Church with "objective truth and tradition" as the measure for decisions of conscience.[87]

Even as Protestant theologians and lay intellectuals increasingly embraced a right to conscientious objection, the problem of national division—rather than West Germans' constitutional rights—remained their central concern. Behind closed doors Hans Joachim Iwand lamented to the Rhineland Church Brethren Society that Protestants faced a "leaderless [*führerlos*]" Germany and a fight against both "East *and* West," sentiments that continued to resonate within the Dahlemite opposition.[88] Tensions between nationalist and democratic aims resurfaced at the culminating event of the anti-rearmament campaign. On January 29, 1955, more than 900 activists—including SPD leaders, Protestant pastors, as well as representatives of trade unions, youth groups, and academia—crowded into the Paulskirche (Saint Paul's Church) in Frankfurt amid new negotiations for West Germany's entry into NATO. Broadcast on the radio, the event drew national press attention and sparked a wave of anti-rearmament protests that brought tens of thousands of West Germans to the streets.[89] In his address at the Paulskirche, Gustav Heinemann described the rally as an expression of democratic will, insisting that popular opinion—including "the most loyal members of our Protestant communities"—opposed rearmament.[90] Helmut Gollwitzer greeted a movement driven by humanitarian concerns for East Germans, rather than nationalist or pro-Soviet sympathies.[91] At the same time, the rally's concluding "German Manifesto" gave voice to underlying nationalist aims. Signed by the Confessing Church pastors Hermann Diem, Helmut Gollwitzer, Oskar Hammelsbeck, Hans Joachim Iwand, Heinz Kloppenburg, Martin Niemöller, and Ernst Wolf, as well as Gustav Heinemann and the SPD parliamentarian Adolf Arndt, the manifesto declared opposition to rearmament a matter of "resistance" against the division of the Volk. The language of democracy and basic rights remained absent from the statement.[92]

Figure 5.1. Flyer of the Paulskirche movement displaying photographs of the rally of January 29, 1955, as well as the text of the German Manifesto. The flyer's warning against nationalism was belied by its content. "Secure Unity, Freedom, and Peace: Against Communism and Nationalism!" Friedrich-Ebert-Stiftung / Archiv der sozialen Demokratie, 6/PLKA020038

From the Bundestag to the Federal Constitutional Court

The protests that followed the Paulskirche rally could not halt the government's push toward rearmament. The anti-rearmament coalition continued to experience the fissures that had pervaded the earlier debate, with SPD leaders wary of extra-parliamentary activism and the ongoing threat of Communist infiltration.[93] Meanwhile, following British threats to remove troops from the European continent, the French parliament finally relented and approved of West German membership in NATO, the alternative solution brokered by the British Foreign Office. The Bundestag ratified the Paris Treaties on February 27, 1955, with the support of the CDU-FDP coalition, followed by the upper house of West Germany's legislature on March 18. President Heuss's signature cleared the way for West German entry into NATO on May 5.[94]

The demise of the anti-rearmament campaign placed the Church Brethren Societies at a crossroads. Meeting in March 1955, the EKD synod voted against reinstating Gustav Heinemann as president, replacing the anti-rearmament stalwart with the conservative economist and Freiburg circle veteran Constantin von Dietze. The language of resistance had clearly failed, as West Germany joined NATO and conservative EKD leaders signaled that the church would no longer stand in the way of Adenauer's foreign policy. But the rearmament debate of the first half of the 1950s had opened a new possibility as well. The Dahlemite camp had already begun to advocate for an expansive right of conscientious objection. This cause only became more important as the government began preparing a conscription statute. At the same time that it ousted Heinemann, the EKD synod voted unanimously to recommend the formation of a commission on the right of conscientious objection, reaffirming its commitment at the Weissensee synod five years earlier. The commission members represented a broad political and theological spectrum. Both the conservative Ulrich Scheuner and the Dahlemite Helmut Gollwitzer participated, alongside the leader of the Rhineland Church Brethren Society, Joachim Beckmann; the EKD liaison to the Bonn government, Hermann Kunst; as well as representatives of the West and East German regional churches.[95] Buoyed by support from the SPD and even some Protestant conservatives, Dahlemites would come to describe the right of conscientious objection not as a matter of regaining national sovereignty but as a fundamental value of West German democracy.

The commission's discussions made plain the shared understanding that came out of the preceding years of debate. Freedom of conscience, members agreed, was a Protestant tenet recovered in a legacy of anti-Nazi resistance. Moreover, the Protestant understanding of conscience widened the scope of individual freedom and responsibility beyond Catholic doctrine. At its final meeting in November 1955, the synod commission determined to support Martin Niemöller's "evangelical" concept of conscience, a situational judgment made before God alone and "not justiciable" by human law. A "Catholic and moralist understanding"—which regarded conscience as a matter of obedience to pregiven laws—had to be foregone.[96] Without using the language of democracy, the commission also underscored that the West German constitution was better suited to protecting conscientious objectors than East German Communism was. Whereas the challenge in West Germany was to ensure that Article 4 of the Basic Law did not become a "false paragraph," one member noted, the East German government had not addressed the issue at all.[97]

The commission's concluding memorandum, approved by the EKD Council in December 1955 and distributed to both German governments, urged the two German states to recognize selective conscientious objectors as well as absolute pacifists. Although constitutional law required a universal standard applicable across confession and ideology, the law should not exclude the "Protestant teaching."[98] The memorandum proved divisive within the Protestant laity. However, church leaders and pastors tended to echo the more laudatory appraisals. In the Protestant press, the theologian and pacifist activist Friedrich Siegmund-Schultze welcomed the memorandum as much as the Hamburg-based *Sonntagsblatt,* founded by Lutheran bishop Hanns Lilje.[99]

The legislative campaign that followed the memorandum further aligned the EKD's case for conscientious objection with the language of constitutional rights. Amid ongoing demonstrations against military service, the CDU government announced a highly restrictive conscription law in early June 1956.[100] Conscientious objection would be limited to absolute pacifists, with no legal provisions for selective objectors. While the president of the East German Volkskammer (People's Chamber) refused to consider the EKD's petition to amend the East German constitution, the Bundestag Defense Committee invited the Protestant church diplomat Hermann Kunst to speak at a hearing on the proposed statute alongside the Jesuit theologian Johannes Hirschmann.[101] A former Wehrmacht chaplain and standard-bearer of the EKD's conservative Lutheran wing, Kunst nevertheless defended the right of conscientious objection through the confessional narrative that had come to dominate the debate. The EKD's support for selective objectors, Kunst told the Defense Committee, followed from Protestant principles recovered by the Confessing Church. The

Barmen Declaration of 1934 demonstrated that decisions of conscience lay outside the bounds of the state. Moreover, whereas "the genuine Catholic countries, like Italy and Spain" did not permit conscientious objection, Protestant Sweden, England, and America had long recognized the practice. Rather than calling for the extension of anti-Nazi resistance into the postwar era, Kunst sought to guarantee freedom of conscience through the expansion of a constitutional right. Although conscience might well set the individual against the expectations of government, "it is not good for a state when it does not respect the conscience of its citizens." Hirschmann did not go quite so far. While arguing that even an "errant" conscience deserved to be respected, the Catholic theologian linked judgments of conscience to an "objective moral order" that permitted just, defensive wars.[102]

The EKD's advocacy also deepened the partnership between the Protestant Church and the Social Democratic Party. Following West Germany's entry into NATO, the SPD pivoted from opposition against rearmament to support for conscientious objector rights. While the EKD Brethren Council first initiated a dialogue with the SPD during the drafting of the Basic Law, shared support for conscientious objection brought the party into alignment with a wider group of Protestant leaders.[103] Moreover, a rising cohort of reformist Social Democrats, who sought to transform the SPD from a sectarian working-class party into a catch-all "people's party," aimed to overcome the historical adversity between the SPD and the churches. New lines of cooperation obscured a legacy of division, as Social Democrats who had been in exile or imprisoned found themselves working alongside former Nazi Party members and Wehrmacht chaplains. Nevertheless, the vision of constitutional democracy that emerged out of the EKD's petitions, rooted in freedom of conscience rather than class-based economic demands, resonated with SPD reformers who sought to broaden their party's appeal.

The Protestant campaign for conscientious objector rights echoed in the final parliamentary reading of the conscription statute on July 6. At the hearing, the Protestant SPD delegates Adolf Arndt, Fritz Erler, and Ludwig Metzger cited the EKD memorandum as well as Hermann Kunst's address before the Bundestag Defense Committee to call for expanding the rights of selective objectors. Incensed that the government press office had published a statement by Walter Künneth as evidence of the "Protestant" position, these SPD parliamentarians sought to present the church instead as an avatar for freedom of conscience.[104] The most outspoken was Arndt, the SPD jurist who four weeks earlier had represented the state government of Hesse at the Federal

Figure 5.2. Demonstration against military conscription outside the military district command office in Munich, organized by the West German branch of the pacifist War Resisters International, March 24, 1956. The banners read, "Command of Conscience" and "We Refuse Military Service." Photo by Gerhard Rauchwetter/picture alliance via Getty Images

Constitutional Court in its case against the Concordat. While Arndt had served as a leading voice in the SPD's campaign against rearmament during the early 1950s, his defense of conscientious objection was not a capitulation to CDU foreign policy.[105] Instead Arndt's address to the Bundestag reflected the interpretation of the Basic Law he had developed in his postwar writings and arguments before the Constitutional Court. Seeking to bridge a Social Democratic theory of law with a Protestant ethical foundation, Arndt continued to regard Germany's Protestant tradition as a key source of the values underlying the constitution. The proposed conscription statute, Arndt warned, "aimed to replace the decision of conscience with a doctrine," at odds with Protestant principles. As Hermann Kunst had explained, "According to Protestant teaching, the voice of conscience becomes audible in taking a stance toward a particular concrete act or decision."[106]

The Protestant-SPD alliance did not succeed at the legislative level. After a debate that stretched into the early morning hours, the CDU-led coalition voted down an SPD amendment to acknowledge selective objectors. Instead the final legislation affirmed the efforts of the Adenauer cabinet to sharply limit conscientious objection.[107] The conscription statute, which came into effect three weeks later, established that conscientious objectors must oppose "*any* use of weapons between states," restricting the right to absolute pacifists.[108] Among the authors of the EKD memorandum, reactions were decidedly negative. Not only did the Dahlemite organ *Junge Kirche* denounce the conscription statute, but Ulrich Scheuner commented on the law's borderline constitutionality and failure to consider the EKD's position.[109] The Catholic journal *Herder Korrespondenz,* which had provided a critical perspective on the clerical hierarchy in the conscription debate, noted a fundamental cleavage between the confessions. Whereas Catholic theologians such as Johannes Hirschmann defended an "errant" conscience from state interference, Protestants had questioned just-war teachings altogether.[110]

Despite its failure, the parliamentary campaign for an expansive right of conscientious objection deepened the EKD's allegiance to constitutional principles. While continuing to cite anti-Nazi resistance as a source of moral legitimacy, Protestant church leaders, politicians, and lay intellectuals sought to harmonize their vision of conscience with the freedoms guaranteed in the Basic Law. Protestant notions of conscience rights would find a more successful reception before the Federal Constitutional Court. Conscientious objection remained a limited phenomenon in the first decade of conscription. On average, only 4,000 men applied for conscientious objector status each year from 1956 to 1966, fewer than 1 percent of conscripts; 80 percent of this group were recognized by draft boards as absolute pacifists.[111] Nevertheless, between 1956 and 1960, over 270 conscientious objectors whose claims were denied by draft boards filed appeals with the Federal Constitutional Court. The claimants relied on a provision in the Constitutional Court's statute that enabled individual citizens to directly petition the court over violations of basic rights.[112] Protestant jurists, including Adolf Arndt, Gustav Heinemann, and the former GVP leader Diether Posser, would rep-

Nuclear Politics

resent conscientious objectors before the Constitutional Court. Their case reflected the Protestant argument for conscientious objection since the early 1950s: The conscription of selective objectors contravened these young men's rights under Article 4 of the Basic Law, as well as the Protestant conception of conscience.

Nuclear Politics

While a broad Protestant coalition came together behind the EKD memorandum and legislative campaign, a new controversy following the introduction of conscription exposed ongoing conflict over the political role of the church. In December 1956, West German defense minister Franz Josef Strauss joined his West European counterparts to request that NATO armies be outfitted by the United States with mid-range nuclear weapons, a centerpiece of NATO's "New Look" plan. Four months later, Adenauer announced the government's intention to equip the newly formed West German military (Bundeswehr) with delivery systems to launch US-controlled nuclear warheads. In a press statement that quickly gained notoriety, Adenauer deemed the move "basically nothing but the further development of artillery."[113]

As the missiles began to arrive, a national debate broke out that rivaled in ferocity the earlier controversy over rearmament. The opening salvo was issued in April 1957 by eighteen prominent nuclear physicists, whose cooperation Strauss had sought in implementing the plan. Led by the Göttingen nuclear engineer and lay Protestant Carl Friedrich von Weizsäcker, the Göttingen Manifesto deplored the euphemism of "tactical" nuclear arms and warned of the weapons' destructive potential against "the entire population of the Federal Republic." The manifesto echoed similar statements by British and American physicists, and helped spark a West German movement that joined a burgeoning transnational campaign for nuclear disarmament.[114] In the ensuing debate, Church Brethren Societies throughout West Germany emerged as leaders in the coalition against nuclear armament. Conservative Lutherans, in contrast, continued to back the CDU's foreign policy.

The controversy over nuclear weapons did not simply mirror the rearmament debate of the early 1950s, however. Conservative Lutherans as well as the Church Brethren Societies upheld the right of conscientious objection, and neither group returned to a demand for the absolute duty of military conscription. The Lutheran theologian Helmut Thielicke, recently appointed to a chair in theology at the University of Hamburg, emerged as the most outspoken Protestant representative of the conservative position. In his first lecture on the subject, delivered before the national conference of the CDU, Thielicke maintained that modern nuclear defense capabilities belonged to a realistic and responsible West German defense policy in light of the Soviet acquisition of atomic weapons. Nevertheless, Thielicke did not call into question the individual right to dissent from government policy.[115] The significance of the Protestant campaign against nuclear weapons was instead its exposure of a new tension within the coalition that opposed the CDU. Protestant SPD politicians espoused the rights-based understanding of democracy reflected in the campaign for conscientious objector rights before the Federal Constitutional Court; the Church Brethren Societies moved toward a more radical, participatory vision.

The initial alliance between the Church Brethren Societies and the SPD was the product of pragmatic consensus. SPD leaders sought to mobilize popular antinuclear sentiment to revive their party's electoral fortunes after federal elections of September 1957 resulted in an absolute majority for the CDU.[116] In contrast, regional Church Brethren Societies throughout West Germany issued statements of immediate, principled opposition to nuclear weapons, in alignment with the Göttingen Manifesto.[117] Gustav Heinemann formed a bridge between the two groups. Two years after West Germany's entry into NATO, Heinemann dissolved the All-German People's Party on recognition that its campaign for immediate reunification had no plausible path forward. Instead the longtime anti-rearmament champion urged his colleagues to follow him into the SPD, now the only realistic option for opposing Adenauer's CDU.[118] After the CDU-FDP coalition predictably voted in favor of the government plan for nuclear armament, the SPD joined with the German Trade Union Confederation and the Church Brethren Societies to launch the Fight Against Atomic Death (Kampf dem Atomtod) movement. During the spring and summer of 1958, local branches of the campaign organized rallies that brought thousands to the streets throughout West Germany. The largest, in Hamburg, drew an estimated 150,000 demonstrators.[119]

From the outset, tensions pervaded the coalition. While the SPD sought an issue on which to challenge the CDU's electoral hegemony, the Church Brethren Societies used the campaign against nuclear weapons to promote an understanding of the church as not merely an advocate for individual rights but also a check on state power. Helmut Gollwitzer spoke for many in the antinuclear movement when he denounced the government's foreign policy in a September 1957 lecture on South German Radio. Gollwitzer rejected the theory of the just war, the basis for both Lutheran and Catholic arguments in favor of military service. The advent of atomic weapons, Gollwitzer argued, made this traditional doctrine obsolete. Atomic wars could not be limited engagements, fought defensively to rectify a specific injustice, but would necessarily lead to mass civilian casualties as well as harm to the physical environment and future generations. The only possible Christian response to this looming catastrophe was to completely refuse nuclear weapons.[120] A month after Gollwitzer's address, the regional Church Brethren Societies convened a joint conference in Wuppertal, where the concluding statement called on the EKD synod to publicly condemn NATO's nuclear defense program.[121] In April 1958, at the height of the antinuclear protests, the conservative majority in the synod declined to adopt the proposal, leaving decisions about military service to the individual Christian.[122] Undeterred, representatives of the Brethren Societies reconvened in Frankfurt to form a national-level Working Group, aiming to serve as an alternative voice for Protestants disaffected with the EKD leadership.

The antinuclear campaign led the Church Brethren Societies to turn to a different aspect of Karl Barth's political theology. The Swiss theologian had emphasized not only the state's obligation to protect the individual's freedom of conscience but also the role of the Christian community as the voice of gospel in the political world. While the EKD Brethren Council had embraced the right of conscientious objection as a means of signaling its dissent against rearmament, this viewpoint no longer appeared sufficient to confront the prospect of nuclear destruction—especially because the synod had called for the protection of individual conscience rights while avoiding a position on the issue of nuclearization.[123] Instead the Brethren Societies described a collective expression of conscience by the Christian community. According to the concluding statement at Frankfurt, the advent of atomic weapons established a binding confessional stance. The Christian community was obliged to oppose the proliferation of atomic weapons, an existential threat to humanity that "stood in factual contradiction" against God's will.[124] While the Nazi past was not invoked directly, attendees would have recognized a parallel to the church emergency law declared at the Dahlem synod of October 1934.

The principled antinuclear position of the Brethren Societies entailed a rethinking of two other key terms of the rearmament debate: resistance and democracy. If the anti-rearmament campaign of the early 1950s looked to individual resistance heroes like Dietrich Bonhoeffer, the Working Group of Church Brethren Societies conceived of itself as an extension of the collective opposition voiced at Barmen and Dahlem. Ernst Wolf's address at the Wuppertal conference recalled the fifth thesis of the Barmen Declaration, which warned against the state's "totalitarian" overextension. Although the text originally had been an effort to protect the sphere of church administration from Nazi incursions, Wolf reread it to justify the Brethren Societies' expansive, critical voice on state policy.[125] On this view, anti-Nazi resistance was not simply the basis of a constitutional democracy that protected individual rights but an impetus to popular participation. Christians had the "freedom and obligation ... to support the construction of a true democracy and protect it from the threat of particular ideologies or attempts at its depletion." Energized by the Göttingen Manifesto, the Brethren Societies denounced calls for the shifting of responsibility on matters of nuclear weapons to "experts," and demanded a critical questioning of "Christian anti-Communism" and "the re-Catholicization of public life."[126] In Barthian fashion, the Christian community, rejuvenated through participation at the local level, would become a model of political responsibility.

The SPD took a different approach. While backing the demonstrations of the Fight Against Atomic Death movement, party leaders also sought to advance their aims through legal channels. To be sure, the SPD interpreted the Basic Law to authorize expansive forms of direct democracy. In early 1958 Social Democratic jurists led by Adolf Arndt petitioned the Federal Constitutional Court to permit the Bundestag to call a popular referendum on the nuclearization of the Bundeswehr. On Arndt's view, the popular will stood as the legitimating force behind parliamentary authority, even if the Basic Law had not explicitly created provisions for referenda. However, the SPD's support for direct democracy was tempered by its deference to the established division of powers. When the Constitutional Court turned down the SPD's referendum petition in July 1958, the party quickly exited the Fight Against Atomic Death campaign.[127] This shift was hastened by a mediocre showing in the state election of North Rhine-Westphalia, the region at the center of NATO's nuclear initiative, as well as the campaign's inability to keep out Communist front groups.[128] The effort to appeal to popular opposition against nuclear weapons had failed to win over a mass base of voters.

The Protestant debate about atomic weapons concluded with an impasse in 1959, by which point the outfitting of the Bundeswehr with nuclear delivery systems was a foregone conclusion. Seeking common ground between the competing factions, the EKD Council authorized the formation of an "atomic commission" at the Protestant Research Center in Heidelberg, founded the previous year as the successor to the Westphalian Christophorus-Stift. Like the 1955 synod commission on the right of conscientious objection, the group brought together participants representing a cross-section of the Protestant debate. Led by the Tübingen law professor Ludwig Raiser, members included Helmut Gollwitzer, Ulrich Scheuner, and Carl Friedrich von Weizsäcker.[129]

This commission, however, was unable to reach consensus. After meeting for over a year, members could agree only on the Christian's "special contribution to the preservation of peace." The group's summative theses rested on the concept of "complementarity" proposed by Weizsäcker, concluding that the countervailing viewpoints, for and against nuclearization, "support each other." The seventh of the eleven theses announced, "The church must recognize a right of conscientious objection." The eighth followed, "A Christian can believe that nuclear weapons safeguard peace and freedom."[130] The Heidelberg theses represented at most a "Pyrrhic victory" for the conservative majority, since the EKD neither endorsed nor opposed nuclear pacifism.[131] Instead the Protestant Church opted to preserve a tenuous unity rather than take a principled stance.

Despite this deadlock, the debate about atomic weapons reflected the ongoing reorientation of both sides. Protestants who favored West German rearmament, including Ludwig Raiser, Ulrich Scheuner, and Helmut Thielicke, affirmed the decision of individual conscience over military service. Even as the Heidelberg theses refused to condemn nuclear weapons, they also maintained the EKD's ongoing support for conscientious objectors. The Brethren Societies articulated a more radical, participatory vision of democracy, in which the Christian community inspired a broader mobilization against unchecked state power. By the late 1950s, no major voice in the Protestant press or EKD synod advocated for the unconditional duty of military service. Increasingly, the debate in the EKD revolved around competing visions of democracy, rather than its desirability. Both sides angled to advance a narrative of resistance against Nazism and expand the church's political voice.

Conscientious Objection and the Road to Godesberg

While the Church Brethren Societies continued their campaign against nuclear weapons past the summer of 1958, Protestant SPD politicians maintained the legalist strategy spearheaded after the enactment of the conscription law. The Social Democrats' exit from the Fight Against Atomic Death movement accelerated a reform process within the SPD that culminated in the moderate party program issued at the Bonn suburb of Bad Godesberg in November 1959.[132] The Godesberg program was long in the making. Since the early postwar years, a group of younger reformers, many of whom spent the war in exile in Western Europe, had advocated for jettisoning the SPD's Marxist commitments. With the death of party leader Kurt Schumacher in 1952, returned émigrés such as Willy Brandt, Willi Eichler, and Herbert Wehner gained growing influence. The "action program" concluded at the 1954 party congress in West Berlin already described the SPD's foundations in "Christianity, humanism, and classical philosophy," language that would find its way into the Godesberg platform.[133]

The CDU's absolute majority in the 1957 election proved the final straw for the party's traditional Marxist doctrine. Protestant networks played a critical, under-recognized role in the reform process. SPD parliamentarians with close connections to the Protestant churches, including Adolf Arndt, Fritz Erler, Gustav Heinemann, and Ludwig Metzger, belonged to the group of influential reformers.[134] Not only did Protestants draft key sections of the Godesberg program, but the platform itself reflected a vision of democracy that had taken shape in the Protestant public sphere.

Adolf Arndt was a pioneer of the new course, bridging the campaign for the right of conscientious objection with broader currents of party reform. In lectures and writings leading up to the Godesberg Congress, Arndt continued to develop the legal theories that had informed his arguments in the Concordat case, constructed in dialogue with Rudolf Smend. Speaking before the Munich-based Association of Social Democratic Academics as well as the Protestant Academies in Loccum and Arnoldshain, Arndt sought to mediate between CDU visions of a Christian party and traditional Social Democratic demands for the separation of religion and politics. While denying that any one party could declare a monopoly on Christian virtue, Arndt cited Ernst Wolf to affirm that church representatives could speak on politics "in the name of the church" when moved toward a political position by religious convictions. Churches could not set policy, but they remained important interlocutors in articulating the fundamental values on which the constitution rested.[135]

Arndt's defense of selective conscientious objectors at the Federal Constitutional Court provided another opportunity for applying these ideas, laying the groundwork for his interventions at Godesberg. Beginning in August 1956, weeks after the enactment of the conscription law, Arndt filed a series of petitions with the court on behalf of five university students—one of them Martin Niemöller's son—who refused military service "only in a divided Germany."[136] Arndt's petitions drew liberally on Protestant sources, including the EKD memorandum, Karl Barth's *Church Dogmatics*, and Hermann Kunst's speech to the Bundestag Defense Committee. These sources, Arndt claimed, revealed a Protestant understanding of conscience as a realm of individual decision subject only to the judgment of God, not human authority. Arndt also cited several Catholic writers who emphasized the inviolability of individual conscience.[137] Nevertheless, Arndt followed the confessional orientation of the Protestant conscientious objector campaign, warning that the dominant Catholic notion of "objectively correct conscience" would make the exercise of the individual right of conscientious objection altogether impossible.[138] A basic continuity linked Arndt's petitions for conscientious objectors with his argument in the Concordat case: Protestant values formed a basis for the norms of democratic citizenship more generally.

Arndt's petitions to the Constitutional Court also affirmed the resistance narrative that had gained ground in the Protestant conscientious objector campaign. A new relationship between individual and state, Arndt implored the court, had emerged on the basis of an anti-Nazi legacy. Article 4 of the Basic Law was "an answer to the crisis of conscience in the years of National Socialist tyranny and total war."[139] Even if the church could call on its members to "suffer in the fulfillment of its commands"—an implicit reference to the Nazi past—it did not follow that "the state is also authorized to require a believer to incur suffering . . . on account of his belief."[140] Arndt conjured an ecumenical history of resistance that went beyond hagiographies of the Confessing Church, invoking the suffering of Jehovah's Witnesses as well as Catholic priests who had refused military service. Nevertheless, Arndt's petitions restated the myth of West German democracy's anti-Nazi origins, prominently articulated by his Protestant contemporaries. Freedom of conscience, Arndt wrote, "is, according to the Basic Law, the very first requirement of the community, which legitimizes its communality. The free *Rechtsstaat* is thereby fundamentally distinguished from an authoritarian and totalitarian political system."[141]

Even as the antinuclear protest movement collapsed, the campaign for conscientious objector rights became a vehicle for a wider cohort of Protestant SPD jurists to advance a new vision of democracy. Gustav Heinemann and his law partner Diether Posser had filed a petition with the Constitutional Court on behalf of four plaintiffs—a union secretary, architect, university student, and typesetter—all of whom rejected "military service under the current circumstances." Like Arndt, Heinemann and Posser cited the EKD memorandum as a basis for the conscription law's unconstitutionality, and they called for Protestant representatives to speak at the court's oral proceedings.[142] The Stuttgart Protestant attorney Martin Löffler drew on Rudolf Smend's argument for the inalterability of the basic rights in order to advance a similar case against the conscription law.[143] Although not directly involved in the campaign before the Constitutional Court, the Protestant SPD parliamentarians Fritz Erler and Ludwig Metzger also defended selective conscientious objection in their Bundestag addresses and writings for the Social Democratic press.[144] Protestant legal theories formed a broad basis for SPD leaders to affirm the constitutional order of the Basic Law. From moderates like Erler to oppositional figures such as Heinemann, these politicians could underscore their loyalty to the values of West German democracy while contesting the government's conscription policies.

As petitions for conscientious objector rights accumulated before the Federal Constitutional Court, Social Democrats gathered in November 1959 for the party congress at Bad Godesberg. The meeting marked a watershed for the SPD. The platform concluded at the congress's end, approved by all but 16 of the 340 delegates, abandoned a Marxist vision of class struggle, which had been party doctrine since the Erfurt program of 1891. Instead the Godesberg platform unequivocally embraced constitutional democracy. Rather than a working-class party aiming to abolish wage labor and individual ownership of the means of production—long-standing commitments of German Social Democracy, in theory if not in practice—the SPD rebranded itself as a "people's party" that represented all sectors of society.[145]

The Protestant public sphere was well represented at Godesberg. Adolf Arndt drafted the new party platform's section on politics and law, drawing nearly verbatim from his petitions to the Constitutional Court on behalf of conscientious objectors. The fundamental rights outlined in the Basic Law not only guaranteed "the freedom of the individual against the state" but served as "rights that co-found the state and build community."[146] Gustav Heinemann took responsibility for the platform's statement on the churches, which jettisoned long-standing SPD demands for a strict separation of religion and politics. Instead the Godesberg program recognized the claim of the churches to participation in public life.[147] On the contentious issue of foreign policy, the platform accepted the fundamentals of West German rearmament and NATO integration while continuing to call for a reunified Germany at the heart of a nuclear-free Europe. Not only absolute pacifists but also opponents of atomic weapons should be recognized as conscientious objectors.[148] As a whole, the new SPD platform echoed the vision of constitutional democracy formulated within Rudolf Smend's circle, charting a path between the CDU's vision of Christian politics and Social Democracy's history of militant atheism.

The Godesberg Congress widened the rift within the postwar Protestant left descended from the Confessing Church Dahlemites. *Stimme der Gemeinde* published a mixed evaluation by the Confessing Church pastor Herbert Werner, who noted that the Godesberg platform was no different from past SPD programs in reflecting the conditions of its time. Commitment to pragmatism over principle, however, had led to vagueness on critical issues of economic organization and labor power.[149] Some of Werner's colleagues now moved toward the left socialist opposition that had long challenged the SPD's course toward moderation. This group continued to envision economic democracy, including the eventual abolition of private industry, as a prerequisite to its political counterpart, and rejected the Godesberg platform's acquiescence to West German rearmament.[150] Left-wing Protestants were strongly represented in the annual Easter Marches launched in 1960, a nationwide antinuclear movement modeled after the Campaign for Nuclear Disarmament in Britain.[151] Increasingly, more direct forms of democracy became a tempting option.

The Constitutional Court Decides

Over the late 1950s and early 1960s, as the SPD embraced a reformist path, the legal campaign for conscientious objection held sway at West Germany's federal courts. The Federal Administrative Court first took up the issue in October 1958, ruling in favor of a twenty-one-year-old locksmith from Düsseldorf who had belonged to his local Protestant youth association. He declared himself an absolute objector to military service on the basis of his childhood experience of war, but his claim had been rejected by his local draft board for lack of adequate proof. In overturning the draft board's decision, the Federal Administrative Court drew on the writings of Protestant jurists, including Adolf Arndt and Ulrich Scheuner. Because conscience represented "the most inward ... experience" of the individual's "freedom and responsibility," draft boards could not require "unfulfillable demands of proof." The Basic Law had defined conscientious objection not as a "right of exception" but as a "fundamental right" that placed conscientious objection "at least on the same level as the obligation of military service." Moreover, the right established in Article 4 extended beyond religious pacifists. Political and ideological, as well as religious or ethical convictions, the court concluded, could give rise to the "emotional considerations" characteristic of a decision of conscience.[152]

The Federal Constitutional Court soon followed suit. In December 1960 the court ruled on the case of a twenty-two-year-old selective objector from Schleswig-Holstein. Four months later the judges issued a collective decision on the cases brought by Arndt, Heinemann, Posser, and other attorneys.[153] While affirming the validity of the conscription law, the majority in both decisions followed the Federal Administrative Court to widen the scope of conscientious objector rights. The conscription statute, the Constitutional Court concluded, had acknowledged pacifists who "reject war itself in every historical situation" but neglected another category of legitimate conscientious objectors: individuals whose decision of conscience was "driven by experiences or considerations that are valid only for the immediate historical-political situation, without needing to be valid for every time and for every war." The judges thereby opened a path for young men who refused military service in a divided Germany to register as conscientious objectors. In its decisions, the Constitutional Court echoed the petitions of Adolf Arndt. The state's "protection of the free self-determination of the individual," the court concluded, also served as a "community-building value."[154]

The federal court decisions on conscientious objection followed the logic of earlier judgments shaped by Rudolf Smend and his school, including the Concordat decision and the ruling on the Equal Rights Act. In each of these instances, Protestant jurists appealed to the Basic Law not simply as a catalogue of individual rights against the state but as a repository of principles that undergirded post-Nazi democracy. Freedom of conscience, like federalism and the protection of marriage and family, formed a shared norm of political life that transcended divisions of confession and ideology. Federal courts, in the view of Protestant constitutional lawyers, had a central role to play in guarding the fundamental values of the postwar political order from the polarizing ideologies that had prevailed before 1933.

The emergent alliance between Protestant politicians and the federal courts remained rooted less in a shared religious identity than the politics of the postwar judiciary. The principle of judicial review, ensconced in the Basic Law, was novel to German legal tradition and widely distrusted by cabinet members and legislators during the early postwar years.[155] As federal judges struggled to validate their newfound authority, Protestant jurists provided the courts with a key tool of legitimation. By appealing to the universal values codified in the Basic Law, judges could adopt a pre-political justification for their role without violating the constitution's standard of religious neutrality. The fact that the Protestant roots of this legal theory remained suppressed in the court's decisions only served to vindicate the pretensions of Protestant intellectuals to reclaim their role as guides to national politics.

At the same time, the Constitutional Court's rulings exacerbated fissures within the Protestant conscientious objector movement. In the view of SPD reformers, the court had vindicated the rights-based conception of democracy outlined in the Godesberg platform. Although the decisions did not go as far as Protestants would have liked, Gustav Heinemann opined in *Junge Kirche*, they marked a "fundamental step toward the restoration of freedom of conscience."[156] The Church Brethren Societies, by contrast, continued to insist that protecting democracy required citizens' ongoing vigilance. An article for *Stimme der Gemeinde* by Theodor Michaltscheff, a leader in the West German branch of the War Resisters International, attacked the Constitutional Court's decision to uphold the general obligation of conscription. If conscientious objectors did not find their claims recognized by West German courts, then "there remains for them their final and highest authority—their conscience."[157]

This very division reflected how participation in the campaign for conscientious objector rights reshaped Protestant attitudes toward constitutional democracy. At the outset of the rearmament controversy, the faction around Niemöller and Heinemann looked toward anti-Nazi resistance as a model of opposition to government policy. By the late 1950s, Protestant SPD reformers, the Church Brethren Societies, and even a growing number of Protestant conservatives accepted that a resistance legacy had authorized detractors of government policy to advance expansive rights claims within the framework of the Basic Law. The disagreement centered on whether the federal courts had adequately protected the Federal Republic's constitutional values, and whether law alone was enough to secure citizens' basic rights.

No Protestant camp, however, contested the inflated account of anti-Nazi resistance on which the conscientious objector campaign had rested. Dahlemites' activism for conscientious objection bolstered, if inadvertently, the parallel narrative of anti-Nazi resistance advanced by conservative Lutherans. During the 1960s, new encounters across confessional and Cold War divides forced a broader reckoning with the traditions of Protestant nationalism. But intellectuals across the EKD's political divide would continue to claim a resistance legacy to assert an expansive role in West German democracy.

CHAPTER SIX

THE EASTERN BORDER AND THE
BOUNDS OF RECONCILIATION

ON OCTOBER 15, 1965, the EKD Council released a forty-page memorandum that set off a storm of debate in both the church and the mainstream press. Titled "The Fate of the Expellees and the Relationship of the German People to Its Eastern Neighbors," known colloquially as the Eastern Memorandum, the document became the most widely discussed political statement issued by the postwar EKD. Published in over 200,000 copies by the end of 1965, the memorandum touched a third rail of West German politics: the status of the former German territories east of the Oder and Neisse rivers. These lands, comprising one-quarter of Germany's prewar territory, had been transferred to Polish and Soviet control under the Potsdam Agreement of August 1945 (see Map I.1). Two decades after the end of the war, the West German government and all major political parties refused to acknowledge the losses, officially recognizing Germany's borders of 1937 that preceded Hitler's expansions. The EKD became the first major institution in West Germany to challenge the national consensus. Germans, the Eastern Memorandum declared, must "respect the right to life of the Polish people, and give them the space necessary for its development."[1] While maintaining that a final territorial settlement awaited a treaty with the four occupation powers, the Eastern Memorandum urged the West German government to pursue a foreign policy of reconciliation, rather than revanchism, toward Eastern Europe.

The furor over the Eastern Memorandum reflected the emotional tenor of the issues at stake, which involved not only territorial loss but mass crimes perpetrated against Germans. The final stages of the war and early postwar years witnessed the movement of over 12 million German speakers from

Eastern Europe into Germany's post-1945 borders. They included both *Volksdeutsche*—ethnic Germans who had lived in Poland, Czechoslovakia, and other East European countries before the war—as well as *Reichsdeutsche*, citizens of Germany's pre-1937 eastern territories. Many ethnic Germans fled their homes from the advancing Red Army beginning in 1944, while political authorities in Eastern Europe organized the expulsions of remaining Germans immediately after the end of Nazi occupation. The Potsdam Agreement officially sanctioned these policies and created a legal process for registering, transporting, and resettling ethnic Germans.

The Allied leaders at Potsdam declared that the population transfers should proceed in an "orderly and humane" manner; in practice, though, the expulsions were anything but. Especially at the early stages, flight was frequently accompanied by violence perpetrated by local governments that targeted ethnic Germans indiscriminately as Nazi collaborators. At least 500,000 ethnic Germans, disproportionately children and the elderly, died in internment camps or along the journey. By the late 1940s, the lobby formed to represent the 8 million ethnic German refugees living in the Federal Republic exerted a powerful political influence, calling for the restoration of Germany's prewar borders and the return of the expellees to their homelands. These demands resonated with the narratives of German victimhood that dominated public memory of the war and reflected popular resentment against the imposition of Communist rule in Germany's former eastern territories.[2]

The Eastern Memorandum formed a remarkable rupture. It departed not only from the dominant rhetoric on the border in West German politics but from the German Protestant churches' own alignment with revanchist nationalism since the 1920s. To be sure, the EKD memorandum belonged to a landscape of postwar German–Polish reconciliation initiatives that extended well beyond the Protestant churches. Progressive German Catholics, liberal media outlets, and dissident Polish intellectuals all contributed to a counter-discourse that promoted reconciliation between Poland and West Germany and challenged the West German consensus on the eastern border.[3] Moreover, their integration into West German society and the resettlement of the Oder-Neisse territories by Communist regimes diminished the interest of expellees themselves in a literal return to the homeland.[4]

Still, the Eastern Memorandum was distinct not only in its broad reception but the ways it signaled the reorientation of a major political milieu. The memorandum marked a crucial node in the Protestant rapprochement with West German constitutional democracy. All three sets of encounters highlighted in this book—between German Protestants and their interlocutors abroad, between the conservative Lutheran and Dahlemite wings of the church, and between theologians and lay intellectuals—flowed into the EKD statement. In particular, the Eastern Memorandum was linked to an incipient process of dialogue between Christians and Jews that provoked a broader reassessment of responsibility for Nazism amid West German trials of Holocaust perpetrators. The positive media reception of the memorandum, as well as its proximity to the *Ostpolitik* (Eastern policy) of the early 1970s—which culminated with West Germany's provisional acknowledgment of the Oder-Neisse Line—encouraged Protestant intellectuals to identify their confession with the Federal Republic's democratic values.

At the same time, the shifts represented by the Eastern Memorandum became possible only through abiding continuities. The authors belonged not to a new generation but to the cohort born around the turn of the twentieth century, which had participated on the front lines of the Nazi-era church conflict and after the war reimagined the Confessing Church as having been a resistance organization. Basic premises of the Protestant discussions on the family, confessional schools, military service, and even war crimes trials continued to inform debates about the eastern border within the Protestant public sphere. The memorandum envisioned the Protestant church as a source of Germans' shared political values, consistent with long-standing traditions of German Protestant nationalism. The very concept of human rights that the EKD developed in its campaign against war crimes trials—based on the limits of human law and the church's role as the arbiter over state power—motivated Protestant intellectuals' critical engagement with the expellee lobby. As in debates about family law and military service, outsiders to the Protestant mainstream helped to drive political change. But reckonings with the legacies of Protestant nationalism during the early 1960s remained partial and halting.

The Right to the Homeland in Postwar Protestant Politics

The EKD's early work with expellees was dominated by urgent matters of humanitarian relief. With the German state destroyed and the United Nations expressly forbidden from aiding ethnic German refugees, the Evangelisches Hilfswerk (Protestant Relief Agency) alongside its Catholic counterpart, Caritas, played a critical role in meeting the food, shelter, employment, and religious needs of the new arrivals. By the early 1950s the Evangelisches Hilfswerk had set up its own housebuilding agency, and along with Caritas

Figure 6.1. Aid workers from the Evangelisches Hilfswerk distribute donations to a refugee family in Stuttgart, September 1951. A refugee barrack is visible in the background. Photo by Hermann Weishaupt/Evangelisches Hilfswerk via Landeskirchliches Archiv Stuttgart, Bildarchiv, Best.-Nr. 8434

established a resettlement office to support the neediest expellees who fell through the cracks of government programs.[5] This aid was hardly politically neutral, drawing Christian leaders and humanitarian workers from both confessions into the debate about Germany's postwar borders long before the 1965 Eastern Memorandum. During the immediate postwar years, isolated voices in both churches urged expellees to accept their resettlement. But as frustrations with the occupation authorities mounted, the public statements of Protestant and Catholic officials more often stressed the expellees' right of return and the need for territorial revisions.[6]

The church-based narrative of German victimhood flowed into a broader discussion of the expulsions in postwar West Germany. This discussion was quickly dominated by the "homeland societies" that sprung up throughout the early Federal Republic after the Basic Law superseded the occupation governments' ban on expellee organizing. Headed by local notables from ethnic German communities, many of whom were former Nazi Party activists,

THE EASTERN BORDER AND THE BOUNDS OF RECONCILIATION 201

Figure 6.2. CDU electoral poster, 1947. "Never the Oder-Neisse Line." Konrad-Adenauer-Stiftung / Archiv für Christlich-Demokratische Politik, 10-009-21

Figure 6.3. SPD electoral poster, 1949. "With the SPD for a free, social, and united Germany—from Bonn through Berlin." Friedrich-Ebert-Stiftung/Archiv der sozialen Demokratie, 6/PLKA009982

these associations aimed not only to secure the expellees' well-being but to shape the public discourse about the war. By the late 1940s, leading expellee politicians and writers had streamlined the refugees' diverse experiences into a uniform narrative of "flight and expulsion," one that downplayed the link between German atrocities in Eastern Europe and the subsequent movements of people and borders. By emphasizing Communist aggression against helpless civilians, expellee associations sought to legitimize their demands for territorial restitution as well as reparations from the West German state.[7] Given their claim to represent the 8 million expellees living in the Federal Republic, the homeland societies exerted a strong impact on party politics. Both the CDU and the SPD made the recovery of the "lost territories" central to their postwar platforms. When the German Democratic Republic recognized its border with Poland in the July 1950 Treaty of Görlitz, only the West German Communist party acknowledged the treaty's validity.[8]

From the late 1940s, the expellee lobby centered its advocacy around a category that resonated with the human rights language advanced by the postwar EKD: the "right to the homeland" (*Recht auf die Heimat*). The concept was anchored in the Charter of Expellees concluded at the first national conference of the homeland societies in August 1950, and popularized in the writings and speeches of West Germany's leading international lawyers.[9] The right to the homeland also featured prominently in the activism of the two principal Protestant expellee organizations: the Eastern Church Committee, the branch of the EKD that represented the churches of the former Eastern Germany and German-speaking communities in Eastern Europe; and the Convention of Dispersed Eastern Protestant Churches, an independent association of expellee pastors.[10]

In the hands of the expellee lobby and its supporters, the right to the homeland contained two interlocking demands. First, the expellees possessed the right to return to their territories of origin. Second, based on a correlate right of self-determination, expellees gained the prerogative to determine the political status of the Oder-Neisse territories, effectively restoring these lands to German sovereignty. Like Protestant defenders of convicted war criminals, expellee advocates mobilized the language of human rights in order to delegitimize the postwar settlement. West German international lawyers grounded the right to the homeland in the United Nations Universal Declaration of Human Rights, which guaranteed that "Everyone has the right to leave any country, including his own, and to return to his country."[11]

Despite early affinities between the churches and the expellee lobby, Protestant discussions of the postwar border broke down during the 1950s along the fissure between the EKD's conservative Lutheran and Dahlemite wings. For Lutheran conservatives, the homeland was a divinely endowed order, like marriage, family, and church, whose timeless structure Christians were charged to defend before political authorities. This view resonated across the confessional divide. If they quibbled over the underlying theology, conservative Protestants concurred with the political conclusions of Pope Pius XII and the German Catholic hierarchy, who affirmed West German claims to the Oder-Neisse territories as a matter of natural law.[12] Beginning in 1958 the Protestant Academy in Arnoldshain held a series of biconfessional conferences advancing the expellee lobby's case for the right to the homeland. As in the concurrent discussions of family law and military service, conservative Protestant networks enabled Nazi collaborators and sympathizers to reinvent themselves as advocates for individual rights. The organizer of the Arnoldshain conferences, the Munich jurist Kurt Rabl, was a former SS officer and administrator in the Nazi-occupied Sudetenland who emerged after the war as a proponent of the "right of self-determination of peoples."[13] The lead Protestant theological speaker, the Erlangen theologian Walter Künneth, offered a barely updated version of his Nazi-era theology. The homeland was a "divine order of preservation," Künneth declared, expulsion from which constituted an "indignation" against God's will.[14]

An alternative conception of the right to the homeland, however, was available to veterans of the Confessing Church Dahlemites. Certainly these Protestants were not the only group to challenge the government consensus on the Oder-Neisse Line. The postwar Catholic Pax Christi movement, including its West German branch, dissented from the papacy's revisionism.[15] Left Catholic intellectuals, including Walter Dirks, the founding editor of the *Frankfurter Hefte,* developed close contacts with Polish counterparts who supported German–Polish reconciliation.[16] Nevertheless, in light of the sharp lines of intra-Protestant conflict extending back to the 1930s, as well as the more diffuse structure of German Protestantism, minority positions could gain greater traction within the Protestant public sphere.

Again Karl Barth served as the theological pacesetter. In the 1951 volume of his *Church Dogmatics,* Barth rejected the view of the national homeland as a divine "order of creation." Division into nations, he argued, did not belong to the essence of humanity but reflected a contingent formation of the modern age. Inherent to the nation's very existence was its duty of solidarity with other peoples, analogous to the fellowship practiced by the Christian community.[17] Barth's critique of the right to the homeland flowed from his larger vision of postwar Christian renewal. This vision centered less on the restoration of fixed institutions than on modeling the virtues of gospel regardless of the state or territory in which the church found itself.

Barth's framework offered a powerful alternative for the minority of Protestant expellee pastors who dissented from the revisionist mainstream of the expellee lobby. The most prominent of these was the Hungarian-German pastor Friedrich Spiegel-Schmidt, who first met Barth during the Swiss theologian's visit to the Hungarian Reformed Church in 1936.[18] During the final year of the war, Spiegel-Schmidt volunteered as a chaplain in the Hungarian army to avoid conscription into the paramilitary Waffen-SS, arriving in Bavaria in late 1944. After his regiment's surrender, Spiegel-Schmidt served as a pastor to ethnic German expellees from Hungary and founded an aid organization for Protestant refugees, eventually becoming the administrative director of the EKD's Eastern Church Committee. Spiegel-Schmidt urged his congregants to accept their fate as a sign of their guilt before God, an admonition that gained sharper orientation through the ongoing influence of Barth.[19]

In 1953 Spiegel-Schmidt delivered a lecture before a conference of one hundred Eastern German pastors that was quickly reprinted in the revived Confessing Church journal *Evangelische Theologie*. Spiegel-Schmidt's lecture became a foundational statement for Dahlemite critics of the expellee lobby. Drawing from Barth's *Church Dogmatics,* Spiegel-Schmidt argued that Christians found their homeland not in a specific territory but in freedom before God. Like his theological mentor, Spiegel-Schmidt held nineteenth-century liberal theologies responsible for conflating historical categories such as nation, Volk, and *Heimat* (homeland) with the content of divine revelation. The "false development of the Heimat concept" resulted from this error. Like virtually every commentator in 1950s West Germany, Spiegel-Schmidt denounced the crime of the expulsions, and he did not foreclose the possibility of a future return to the homeland. Nevertheless, the church was responsible for illuminating "the path of reconciliation" rather than insisting upon the recovery of a static, divinely endowed homeland. "Taking the Heimat from God's hand," Spiegel-Schmidt concluded, "also means to take Heimat how and where God gives it to us. We do not resist when he leads us to a new Heimat."[20]

Spiegel-Schmidt's lecture found wide assent within the ranks of Dahlemite intellectuals and critical expellee pastors. For theologians who had joined postwar Protestant discussions on law and human rights, the Barthian critique of the right to the homeland resonated with wider concerns over the political instrumentalization of natural law doctrines. According to the Tübingen theologian Heinz-Horst Schrey, who had participated in several ecumenical conferences on the issue, Christians were not bound to "blood and soil" but found their homeland in "church and society." Schrey cautioned against the "idolization" of territory and calls for retributive justice.[21] The expellee pastor Herbert Girgensohn, a Baltic German who served as the first chair of the Eastern Church Committee, concurred in a reply to Spiegel-Schmidt published in the Protestant expellee journal *Der Remter*. The homeland, Girgensohn wrote, existed not principally in a territory but "in human relationships with one another." There was "no right from God to demand the fate of returning to the Heimat."[22] Although such arguments departed from the nationalist demands advanced in the EKD's campaign against war crimes trials, they also rehashed tropes of the postwar Protestant language of human rights. Followers of Karl Barth asserted that human rights were not fixed and timeless but instead the products of divine grace, whose content could be discerned only by the Christian community.

Beyond theological reflection alone, new encounters across the Iron Curtain were critical for reshaping Dahlemites' views on the right to the homeland. The question of Communism had dogged Barth's German advocates since the early postwar years. The EKD Brethren Council provoked accusations of political naïveté after calling for engagement with Marxism in its 1947 Darmstadt statement, and Martin Niemöller's 1952 visit to the Soviet Union drew condemnation even from his political allies. However, events of the following years raised new hopes for reconciliation. Joseph Stalin died in 1953, and the Soviet leader's successor, Nikita Khrushchev, denounced Stalinist crimes at the Soviet Communist Party Congress of 1956. The "Thaw" that accompanied the early years of Khrushchev's rule saw contradictory developments for the churches. In the German Democratic Republic, de-Stalinization proceeded more slowly than elsewhere in the Eastern bloc. Protestant pastors clashed with the state over the elimination of religious instruction from schools and the mandatory *Jugendweihe*, a secular coming-of-age ceremony instituted by the Socialist Unity Party in 1955.[23] In Communist Poland and Czechoslovakia, however, as in the Soviet Union itself, the mid-1950s brought a temporary relaxation of anti-religious campaigns, in part as a propagandistic effort to project a more sympathetic image to the West.[24] West Germany's Church Brethren Societies, the key organizations for veterans of the Confessing Church Dahlemites, would find some of their closest Eastern bloc interlocutors in these countries.

The first contacts between West German and Polish Protestants took shape amid the "Polish October" of 1956, which brought the return to power of the Communist politician Władysław Gomułka. Removed from the Polish Politburo in 1948 after calling for an independent political course, Gomułka was greeted by West German correspondents in Poland, as well as left-wing German Catholics, as a harbinger of European peace.[25] In the months following Gomułka's return, Martin Niemöller made his first visit to Poland as a guest of the tiny Polish Protestant Church, alongside the Darmstadt pastor Herbert Mochalski and a small circle of their Dahlemite colleagues. The visit brought a shift in consciousness for the German participants. Their tour of Poland, which included stops at the Warsaw Ghetto memorial, the barracks of Auschwitz, and the former German territory of Upper Silesia, fostered a new acknowledgment of the connection between Nazi atrocities and the expulsions of ethnic Germans—a link obscured in the rhetoric of the West German expellee lobby. As Mochalski reminded readers of the Brethren Societies' journal, *Stimme der Gemeinde,* upon the group's return: "All of Poland was a German 'blitz' beginning on September 1, 1939 . . . Or have we really not absorbed and understood what is connected with our name?"[26]

The Poland visit also resulted in the first public statement by a prominent West German church figure challenging the government position on the eastern border. Asked by the press about the Oder-Neisse Line following his return, Niemöller recognized that the border would be the subject of a future peace treaty but admonished that changes remained unlikely. Christians were obliged to search for a solution based on peace rather than vengeance.[27] Amid the inevitable backlash from the expellee lobby, the Wuppertal pedagogy professor Renate Riemeck, a prominent activist in the campaign against nuclear weapons, penned the first exposé in *Stimme der Gemeinde* supporting the Oder-Neisse Line.[28]

If the delegation to Poland sparked the initial calls by West German Protestants for recognition of the Oder-Neisse Line, these were quickly amplified by a larger gathering, the Prague-based Christian Peace Conference. Established in 1958 by the Czech Protestant theologian Josef Hromádka, the organization drew together pastors from across the Iron Curtain to oppose nuclear proliferation and promote Khrushchev's calls for "peaceful coexistence." Although Eastern bloc pastors predominated among attendees at the annual conference, which counted over 700 participants in 1961, approximately one-third came from the West.[29] Indeed, the conference built upon longer cross-border ties. Hromádka had established connections to Karl Barth and the Confessing Church before the war, and Hromádka, Niemöller, and the Bonn theologians Hans Joachim Iwand and Helmut Gollwitzer crossed frequently between West Germany and Czechoslovakia beginning in the mid-1950s.[30] The Christian community, these theologians believed, was obliged to seek out modes of cooperation and coexistence in order to propagate its message within the Communist world. Dialogue with Communists, and among Christians across the Iron Curtain, would unearth shared commitments to social justice. East–West exchanges gained new urgency following the stationing of American nuclear warheads in West Germany. West German participants at the Christian Peace Conference were frequently active in the Working Group of Church Brethren Societies formed to oppose the Bundeswehr's nuclearization.

To be sure, Communist states aimed to mobilize ecumenical encounters for their own agendas. The Czechoslovak regime funneled funds to the Christian Peace Conference as a counterweight to international Christian organizations, whether the Vatican or the World Council of Churches, that criticized the suppression of religious freedom in the Communist bloc. The prospect of further dividing the West German churches, between proponents of East–West dialogue and conservative skeptics, proved equally appealing to Communist authorities.[31] Hromádka himself had been one of several Czech Protestant leaders to support the Communist takeover in Czechoslovakia a decade earlier, reflecting both his anti-Nazi fervor and his misjudgment of the Czechoslovak party's subordination to the Soviet line.[32]

But West German attendees at the Christian Peace Conference were not simply lackeys for the Eastern bloc regimes, and their speeches at the congress were not reducible to Communist apologetics. Instead their participation reflected a commitment to a Barthian theology of the Christian community. On this view, the role of Christians was not to provide a religious justification for any political order but to model the virtues of peace, solidarity, and reconciliation regardless of the state in which they lived. Speaking before the Christian Peace Conference in 1959, the West Berlin theologian Heinrich Vogel condemned nuclear armament in the socialist as well as the Western states.[33] Helmut Gollwitzer similarly used the gathering as a platform to espouse his nuclear pacifism and critique of the just-war doctrine in an atomic age.[34]

THE EASTERN BORDER AND THE BOUNDS OF RECONCILIATION   209

For all these departures, the reconciliation work of the Church Brethren Societies reflected the legacies of traditional German Protestant nationalism. Martin Niemöller and his counterparts in the Poland delegation viewed West Germany's ongoing claim to the Oder-Neisse territories as an antagonizing gesture that hindered the prospects for German reunification. This perspective was affirmed by Władysław Śliwka-Szczerbic, the group's Polish guide and a German affairs correspondent for Warsaw Radio, in his own contributions to *Stimme der Gemeinde*.[35] Niemöller accepted the loss of the eastern territories as a price for reunification, extending the nationalist neutralism his circle had advanced in the campaign against rearmament. At the Christian Peace Conference, the Silesian native Hans Joachim Iwand similarly presented West German recognition of the border as a necessary step toward reunification, "a question of life and death for the German nation."[36] The Brethren Societies continued to position themselves as defenders of all-German interests above the divides of confession, class, and ideology—and now, above Germany's Cold War partition as well.

As the relaxation of East–West conflict after Stalin's death gave way to renewed tensions, the Brethren Societies' vision of reconciliation flowed into an increasingly public debate about the Oder-Neisse Line. After elections of September 1957 resulted in significant losses for the All-German Bloc/League of Expellees, the three larger parties redoubled their efforts to attract newly available expellee voters. Now represented by the Federation of Expellees, an umbrella group formed after the election, the expellee lobby flexed its power to stymie any diplomatic engagement with the Eastern bloc. The lobby reached the height of its influence in advance of the July 1959 Geneva Foreign Ministers Conference, after plans leaked of a proposal by the West German Foreign Ministry to conclude bilateral nonaggression treaties with Poland and Czechoslovakia. Claiming that the agreements would mark the first step toward recognition of the Oder-Neisse border, the Federation of Expellees forced the government to retreat.[37] When Khrushchev provoked a breakdown in East–West relations by threatening to turn over Soviet control of East Berlin to the GDR, the Adenauer cabinet reaffirmed its refusal to recognize the GDR or the Oder-Neisse Line.[38] An address by federal expellee minister Theodor Oberländer at the September 1959 Tag der Heimat (Homeland Day) celebration took the government's hardline rhetoric a step further, suggesting that Germans maintained an ongoing territorial claim against Poland.[39]

Bolstered by these developments, conservative leaders of the Protestant expellee associations sought to consolidate their authority in the debate about the right to the homeland. At its September 1959 meeting the Convention of Dispersed Eastern Protestant Churches departed from its traditional focus on expellee welfare and integration to address the politically charged theme "The Right to the Homeland and the Right of Self-Determination." Theologians who questioned a fixed right to the homeland, including Herbert Girgensohn and Friedrich Spiegel-Schmidt, found their position in the minority.[40] Instead Kurt Rabl's keynote address dispensed with the categories of repentance and reconciliation altogether, arguing that a right to the homeland was rooted in positive international law as well as "the objective idea of justice."[41] To support its demand for territorial revisions, the Convention of Dispersed Eastern Protestant Churches turned back to the theses of the Göttingen "Church and Law" conference a decade earlier. In 1949 theologians and jurists gathered at Rudolf Smend's Institute for Protestant Church Law cited Christian responsibility for law to justify their attack on Allied war crimes trials. The expellee group now invoked the same language to demand territorial revisions. The Göttingen principle of "respect for human beings as a fundamental element of legal order" could be realized only through individuals' "claim to an unchallenged life" in their homeland. To defend the homeland, the convention announced, the church should "raise a voice of warning in preservation of its guardian office."[42]

By 1959, however, this use of the Göttingen theses was controversial. Since the Göttingen meeting itself, Protestant theologians and lay intellectuals had argued that human rights were dependent upon the discernment of God's word in particular situations, not fixed in natural law. Moreover, Dahlemite circles resisted calls for a reconfiguration of borders that would destabilize initiatives toward reconciliation with Protestants across the Iron Curtain. Hans Joachim Iwand and Friedrich Spiegel-Schmidt denounced the Protestant expellee organizations in published articles and private petitions, while the Working Group of Church Brethren Societies submitted a rejoinder to the EKD synod.[43] The right to the homeland, Iwand believed, could be assessed only in its historical context: "Whoever stomped so mercilessly on the right to the homeland of others should here at least remain silent, if he is not able to understand what must follow from such behavior from the standpoint of a higher justice." Although individuals possessed the right to a dignified life in *a* home, neither international law nor Protestant teachings promised nations the right to a specific territory.[44] Karl Barth himself contributed a short piece to *Der Remter,* noting simply, "'Heimat' is an unearned gift. There is no absolute 'right' to the homeland."[45]

In the fall of 1959, six months before his premature death of a stroke, Iwand brought another issue to the debate about the right to the homeland: German responsibility for the destruction of European Jewry. Iwand had participated in nascent initiatives among the Confessing Church Dahlemites to rethink the place of Jews in Protestant theology, including the annual Weeks of Brotherhood organized by the postwar Societies for Christian–Jewish Cooperation.[46] In a controversial letter to the daily *Die Welt,* penned in response to Theodor Oberländer's Tag der Heimat address, Iwand linked Christian–Jewish and East–West reconciliation. "Where was the right to the homeland," Iwand asked, "when we expelled our Jewish co-citizens, who had been present in Germany for centuries, often doing great service to our fatherland in science, art, and business?"[47] While framed in terms of expulsion rather than genocide, and couched in the nationalist language of "service to our fatherland," this question would grow only more pertinent as the Church Brethren Societies deepened their engagement in Christian–Jewish dialogue.

Origins of the Eastern Memorandum

Early postwar discussions of the right to the homeland led the small group of expellee pastors aligned with the Confessing Church Dahlemites to diverge from the dominant view within the expellee lobby. By the early 1960s, Protestant expellee organizations were riven with contention over whether the homeland should be regarded as a divine right or as a gift that could be granted and rescinded by the will of God. The Eastern Memorandum, however, did not emerge solely from the milieu of expellee pastors and their Dahlemite allies. Instead the EKD Council's decision to release the controversial document reflected a consensus among a broader cohort of Protestant intellectuals, including those who affiliated with the church's conservative Lutheran wing.

Protestant conservatives remained adamant anti-Communists, and shared little of the Cold War neutralism popular within the Church Brethren Societies. But by the early 1960s, exchange between conservative theologians and lay intellectuals around the Protestant Academies fostered new openness to reformist ideas. Many conservative Protestants, like their Dahlemite colleagues, viewed their church as a source of shared political values rather than an arbiter over fixed institutions. This vision was critical to Protestant advocacy for the reform of family law as well as the right of conscientious objection, in which members of both wings of the EKD had participated. Ultimately, lay–theological exchange found its way into Protestant discussions of the eastern border as well. Adopting the new Protestant language of human rights, and seeking to maintain their church's distance from the Catholic hierarchy, Protestant conservatives increasingly followed their Dahlemite counterparts to question a divinely endowed right to the homeland.

The Tübingen jurist Ludwig Raiser, who would chair the EKD commission that authored the Eastern Memorandum, both exemplified and shaped the reorientation of conservative Protestant politics. Born in 1904 into a Stuttgart merchant family, Raiser shared the experiences of war and upheaval that marked his generation. Raiser's roots in the Württemberg bourgeoisie insulated him from the most aggressive currents of interwar Protestant nationalism. Unlike other prominent intellectuals in the postwar EKD, including Hans Dombois, Walter Künneth, Hans Joachim Iwand, and Ulrich Scheuner, he had not taken part in the Weimar Republic's nationalist youth movement or joined paramilitary organizations like the Freikorps and the SA. Nevertheless, Raiser shared the prejudices of his milieu, including what he termed its "'latent' antisemitism." He would later recall his mistrust of a "certain type of Jew who very strongly shaped cultural life, journalism, and so forth in Berlin during the 'Golden Twenties.'" At the same time, Raiser maintained friendships with Jewish classmates, and several of his teachers in the law faculty at Berlin were of Jewish origin—one of whom, according to Raiser's recollections, shared Raiser's suspicions of his urban co-religionists.[48]

After successfully defending his postdoctoral thesis in December 1933, Raiser sought to pursue an academic career. This was forestalled, however, by regulations that made obtaining an academic lectureship contingent upon completing a training course at a military sports camp. Raiser was refused admission due to his lack of membership in a National Socialist organization and his work with Jewish teachers. Through a connection of his father, Raiser found employment as an agent for the Magdeburg Insurance Society, a position that afforded travel abroad and relative protection from political pressures.[49] This distance from the regime would not last. In the fall of 1942, Raiser was appointed to a professorship at the University of Strasbourg. The position required an oath to Hitler, which on his own account Raiser swore "free[ly]." The following spring, with the war squeezing out the private economy, Raiser accepted an offer to join Alfred Rosenberg's Reich Ministry for

THE EASTERN BORDER AND THE BOUNDS OF RECONCILIATION   213

the Occupied Eastern Territories as an economic administrator. Despite his acquaintance with members of the Kreisau circle, Raiser did not join the July 20 plot against the Nazi dictator. He later reasoned that he had opted for "inner emigration, since I took open resistance, in any case as an individual, for useless suicide."[50] Whether this account reflected his genuine motivation or a retrospective rationalization, Raiser's participation in the military effort was consistent with his conformity throughout the Third Reich.

Like many in his generation, Raiser benefited after the war from his Protestant connections. Captured by the US Army, he was released in early October 1945 and immediately invited to take up an academic position at the University of Göttingen by the newly installed rector, Rudolf Smend.[51] With the recommendation of an influential and politically unencumbered jurist, whom he had known since his student days in Berlin, Raiser assumed a professorship in civic and economic law. As a member of the university's denazification board, Raiser followed a broad Protestant milieu in interpreting National Socialism as a period marked by widespread passivity rather than active participation. While avoiding the extreme rhetoric of the EKD's campaign against war crimes trials, Raiser took to the *Göttinger Universitäts-Zeitung* to deplore the denazification program as a violation of due process and the principle of individual criminal responsibility.[52] As the West German state took shape after 1949, Raiser poured his efforts into the revival of academic scholarship. He would ultimately succeed Smend as rector at Göttingen and become president of the reestablished German Research Foundation. For Raiser, a German tradition of scientific expertise, rather than a direct confrontation with the Nazi past, formed an alternative source of national identity and political education.

Raiser's postwar political vision, built on continuity rather than rupture with conservative legacies, fit in with the wider network of Lutheran theologians and lay intellectuals who coalesced around the Protestant Academies. Across a postwar academic career that took him from Göttingen to Bad Godesberg to Tübingen, the Lutheran bastion in his home state of Württemberg, Raiser became a frequent speaker at the newly formed institutions.[53] Although Raiser was a mediator and reformist by temperament, his political convictions were firmly on the conservative side of the EKD's political divide. During the controversy over West German rearmament, Raiser declined to join Gustav Heinemann's All-German People's Party, instead signing on to a statement by Protestant CDU politicians that accepted the government's prerogative to decide the issue.[54] Like his fellow Protestant jurists Hans

214   REINVENTING PROTESTANT GERMANY

Dombois, Ulrich Scheuner, and Rudolf Smend, Raiser looked toward the Protestant Church as an institution that could set the moral parameters of national policymaking while remaining above the everyday compromises of party politics. As Raiser frequently claimed, he sought to embody "the political responsibility of a nonpolitician."[55]

This outlook was anything but nonpolitical, however. Instead, their professed independence from ideologies and participation in the parallel public sphere around the Protestant Academies enabled Raiser and his circle of lay intellectuals to gain political influence across party lines. The early 1950s controversy around family law reform helped move this group from the patriarchal vision of re-Christianization espoused by postwar Protestant conservatives toward a more moderate stance. At the outset of the debate about Civil Code reform, the marriage law commission at the Westphalian Christophorus-Stift had called on the state to safeguard marriage and family as divinely ordained, hierarchical institutions, departing only in name from prewar "orders of creation" theologies. Yet in response to the interventions of the Evangelische Frauenarbeit, the commission's conservative Lutherans adopted a more flexible approach, ultimately breaking with Catholic hardliners in the CDU by the mid-1950s. While continuing to demand state protection for the "essence" of marriage, conservatives acknowledged that as a human institution, marriage adapted to its historical and social contexts. Ludwig Raiser himself led the EKD synod commission that advocated for eliminating the husband's right of the final decision.[56]

Members of the Protestant marriage law commission recognized that their discussions had wider implications for the church's relationship to law and politics. By January 1955 the group's leaders, the jurist Hans Dombois and theologian Friedrich Karl Schumann, organized a more broadly framed "institution commission." This group soon found a home at the Heidelberg-based Protestant Research Center (Forschungsstätte der evangelischen Studiengemeinschaft; FEST), the successor institute to the Christophorus-Stift formed in 1958. Among the participants numbered theologians from both wings of the EKD, including the conservative Lutheran Walter Künneth and Dahlemite Ernst Wolf, as well as the jurists Ludwig Raiser, Hansjürg Ranke, Ulrich Scheuner, and Rudolf Smend.[57]

During the second half of the 1950s, the institution commission emerged as a center of Protestant social thought, building on the departures of its predecessor in a series of meetings on marriage, property, and the state. Positioning itself in opposition to a Catholic social theory based on divinely ordained natural law, the commission called upon the individual to assume active "responsibility" for worldly institutions.[58] Raiser's lecture to the group in 1959 summed up its ambition: the search for a "supra-positive ground of law" that nevertheless undertook a "critical confrontation with natural law doctrines." Rather than the template for a fixed legal order, Protestant ethics provided ideals of human personality and community that could be translated into positive law only through an "act of will," responsive to the conditions of the immediate moment.[59]

The FEST network entered the debate about the Oder-Neisse Line through its discussions of property rights. The pastor Wolfgang Schweitzer, a professor of theology at the Kirchliche Hochschule in Bethel, first addressed the theme at a 1957 lecture before the Christophorus-Stift, whose attendees included the veteran conservatives Hans Dombois, Hansjürg Ranke, and Friedrich-Karl Schumann. Schweitzer's own formation reflected the influence of the Confessing Church Dahlemites. Dismissed from military service due to his father's Jewish heritage, Schweitzer served in the World Council of Churches Study Department after the war and joined the Protestant campaigns against rearmament and nuclear weapons, becoming active in the Christian Peace Conference.[60] At the Christophorus-Stift, however, Schweitzer spoke to shared preoccupations with human responsibility and historical contingency. Property regimes, Schweitzer noted, were constructed historically through shifting relations among state, society, and economy. Rather than declaring one particular property regime as divinely endowed, Protestants were responsible for ensuring that any property order respected the "Christian image of the human being," even when this required the curtailment of property rights in pursuit of larger ethical goals.[61] If unspoken, Schweitzer's political message was plain: The Protestant church should serve as a moral guide to West German politics not by advancing unbending claims on the Oder-Neisse territories but by subjecting these claims to considerations of history and justice.

New initiatives toward Christian–Marxist dialogue at the FEST provided a further impetus for rethinking the Oder-Neisse border. In 1952 the Christophorus-Stift spearheaded a commission on Marxism that brought together theologians and lay intellectuals within and beyond the Protestant milieu. This group hardly shared the neutralist ambitions of the Christian Peace Conference, and focused on scholarly examination, rather than advocacy, of Marxist thought. Nevertheless, from its founding the Marxism commission aimed to establish "contact points for a common dialogue" across

216   REINVENTING PROTESTANT GERMANY

Western and Eastern Europe, moving beyond simplistic conceptions that reduced Marxism to Soviet totalitarianism.[62] By the early 1960s the commission brought together left-wing Social Democrats such as the jurist Wolfgang Abendroth, theologian Helmut Gollwitzer, and philosopher Jürgen Habermas with conservatives including Friedrich Delekat, Hans Dombois, Hansjürg Ranke, and Heinz-Dietrich Wendland.[63]

Property rights were also a frequent theme for this group, which sought to overcome the polarities of West German political debates. In a March 1961 lecture Ernst Wolf noted that the "ideology" of neither private nor collective property adequately grasped the role of property as an arena of active responsibility before God. Instead the hallmark of Protestant social ethics was its openness before changing historical circumstances: "The Reformation sermon, with its emphasis on the sharpening of social obligations and evangelical freedom from bonds, as well as its admonition toward renunciation, stands in conflict with a Catholic doctrine of property that is built upon the laws of realization of the divinely willed natural social order."[64] Although Wolf's reference to the Oder-Neisse Line remained oblique, it would not have been lost on participants. The Catholic Church understood property rights as a matter of unchanging natural law and therefore could not accept border revisions; Protestants, in contrast, maintained a more flexible approach, seeing all human laws and institutions as provisional.

The ideas espoused at the Christophorus-Stift and the FEST prepared Protestant participants across the EKD's divide to mount a forceful challenge to West German foreign policy. The FEST had already served as a site of foreign policy discussions during the late 1950s, when Ludwig Raiser headed a commission that attempted to mediate the debate about West German atomic armament. But in 1961 mounting Cold War tensions catalyzed a more forceful statement. That August the East German regime began construction of a thirteen-foot concrete barrier through the center of Berlin, seeking to stem the flight of East Germans across the border following the failure of negotiations to resolve the status of the divided city. In the long run, the Berlin Wall would stabilize relations between the two Germanies and help facilitate the détente of the 1970s. More immediately, however, the Adenauer government upheld its foreign policy orthodoxies: commitment to the Oder-Neisse territories and refusal to establish diplomatic relations with any country that recognized the GDR.

For Protestant intellectuals around the FEST, these positions had reached a dead end and failed to recognize international realities. Shortly following

THE EASTERN BORDER AND THE BOUNDS OF RECONCILIATION   217

the construction of the Berlin Wall, Hermann Kunst, the EKD's liaison to the West German government, gathered a group of eight intellectuals affiliated with the research center to address the tense political climate. The participants included Ludwig Raiser; the physicist Carl Friedrich von Weizsäcker, who had initiated the antinuclear Göttingen Manifesto; the theologian Joachim Beckmann, the president of the Rhineland Church Brethren Society; as well as Klaus von Bismarck, the director of the Cologne-based West German Radio and an advocate for German–Polish reconciliation.[65] The circle reflected a growing consensus among Protestant elites against the government's intractable stance on the Oder-Neisse Line. The ethos of moral discernment and situational judgment exhorted at the FEST offered an alternative solution.

The group completed its final statement at Raiser's home in Tübingen in November 1961, following an election that left the CDU in power while seeing significant gains for Social Democrats. The statement addressed issues ranging from nuclear armament to social policy to education, in each case advocating for compromise between extremes—a rearmament policy determined by "rational military planning" rather than "national nuclear armament," for instance. The Tübingen Memorandum, as the press termed the statement, spoke out most provocatively on the Oder-Neisse Line. Decrying the "irresponsible rhetoric" of all three major parties, the authors criticized West German politicians for linking reunification with the recovery of Germany's 1937 borders: "We do not say anything new when we express the view that certainly freedom for those living in Berlin is an internationally recognized right, but that the national demand for reunification in freedom cannot today be realized, and that we will have to give up the claim of sovereignty over the territories beyond the Oder-Neisse Line."[66] This was wildly out of step with the political mainstream—including the SPD, which remained publicly committed to recovering the eastern territories—but consistent with the discussions of the FEST institution commission. Rather than demand an eternal right to the Oder-Neisse territories, Germans should determine the responsible reaction to the immediate situation. For all the political divisions within German Protestantism, the FEST intellectuals ultimately reached the same conclusion as Hans Joachim Iwand and the Church Brethren Societies.

The release of the Tübingen Memorandum put the authority of Protestant elites to the test. Initially intended as a private statement for distribution to Protestant Bundestag members, the explosive call for recognition of the Oder-Neisse Line inevitably was leaked to expellee activists. By mid-February 1962 the signatories elected to publish the entire document in the Hamburg newspaper *Die Zeit,* igniting a controversy in both the mainstream press and the Protestant Church.[67] Newspapers stretching from the CDU-aligned *Christ und Welt* to the far-right *Deutsche National-Zeitung,* as well as the Federation of Expellees and the EKD's Eastern Church Committee, predictably denounced the memorandum. The leader of the parliamentary advisory committee of the Federation of Expellees summed up this reaction: The Tübingen Memorandum "stands in contradiction to the right of self-determination and homeland, the international legal prohibition against annexation, and the idea of Europe."[68]

Notably, however, public support for the memorandum was not restricted to the milieu of the Church Brethren Societies, typified by Helmut Gollwitzer's call for "the recognition of an irreversible loss and a politics proceeding from this recognition."[69] Instead the left liberal weeklies *Die Zeit* and *Der Spiegel,* as well as the Munich-based *Süddeutsche Zeitung,* lauded the signatories for their responsibility and reasonableness.[70] The Protestant authors not only joined a growing chorus of West German journalists calling for reconsideration of the Oder-Neisse Line. Their largely conservative backgrounds and anti-Communist bona fides endowed this call with greater legitimacy.

By the time of the Tübingen Memorandum, Protestant discussions of the right to the homeland had moved beyond the standoff between Protestant expellee groups and the minority of pastors affiliated with the Church Brethren Societies. Ecumenical encounters across the Iron Curtain, the work of the FEST institution commission, as well as the public debate about the Tübingen statement itself led a broad Protestant milieu to recognize the untenability—political, legal, and theological—of rigid claims on Germany's 1937 borders. This consensus was reflected in the new composition of the EKD's Commission on Public Responsibility, revived under the leadership of Ludwig Raiser amid the fallout of the Tübingen statement. The group's administrative director, the Lutheran theologian Erwin Wilkens, hoped the commission would adopt a mediating position on contentious foreign policy questions.[71] In practice, however, the revived Commission on Public Responsibility reflected the views of the Tübingen signatories more than Protestant expellee groups. In addition to Raiser and Wilkens, West German members included Hermann Kunst, Elisabeth Schwarzhaupt, the SPD parliamentarian Ludwig Metzger, as well as Dietrich Goldschmidt, a sociologist at West Berlin's Pedagogical Academy.[72]

THE EASTERN BORDER AND THE BOUNDS OF RECONCILIATION   219

The Commission on Public Responsibility would not immediately discuss Germany's eastern border. Following its reestablishment in November 1962, the EKD Council rebuffed Raiser's request to address the "right to the homeland" for fear of exacerbating the growing divide between the church and the expellee lobby.[73] Instead the commission turned to a different issue galvanizing public debate in the early 1960s: the opening of a new round of West German trials of Nazi perpetrators. This departure had fortuitous consequences. Through its work on Nazi trials, the commission expanded its conception of reconciliation in ways that would enable the groundbreaking stance of the Eastern Memorandum.

An Amnesty Campaign Redux?

Along with the Berlin crisis, West German Nazi trials belonged to a set of events that galvanized intellectuals critical of the CDU government around the turn of 1960. US, British, and French occupation authorities had concluded their own war crimes trials by the late 1940s, and all but abandoned their commitment to upholding prison sentences following the termination of the occupation statute in 1955.[74] But new pressures at mid-decade drew attention to the ongoing presence of Nazi perpetrators in West German public life—embarrassing revelations from the GDR, but also advocacy by a small group of determined prosecutors, including the German-Jewish attorney Fritz Bauer.

The first major case came in the fall of 1957, when the Munich District Court found Wehrmacht field marshal Ferdinand Schörner guilty of ordering the executions of deserters. A high-profile trial of SS-Einsatzgruppen members who had participated in massacres of Lithuanian Jews followed soon after. In November 1958 the West German government established a central office for the investigation of Nazi crimes in Ludwigsburg that spearheaded a series of trials over the ensuing years, culminating with the Frankfurt Auschwitz trial that opened in 1963.[75] Unlike the war crimes trials conducted by the Allied occupation powers, West German trials of Nazi perpetrators were carried out under the domestic criminal code. Due to statutes of limitation, only the charge of murder could be prosecuted by the late 1950s, and many defendants received light sentences.[76] But for all the restrictions imposed by West German criminal law, its application negated the familiar charge of victors' justice, allowing for a more critical discussion of Nazi atrocities to emerge in the press.[77]

Given the EKD's central role in the campaign against Allied war crimes trials, the new round of Nazi trials posed a particular challenge for Protestants. In the late 1940s, church leaders and lay intellectuals had mobilized the language of human rights in defense of convicted Nazi war criminals. Certainly the passage of time, as well as the shift from international to domestic criminal law, softened Protestant critiques of Nazi trials by the early 1960s. Two sets of encounters proved equally crucial in fostering an evolution of the church's position. Ongoing East–West dialogue gave new meaning to an insight that had belonged to German Protestants' earlier discussion of war crimes trials: rights claims reflected not eternal truths but the demands of the concrete situation. At the same time, initiatives toward Christian–Jewish dialogue challenged the dichotomy of grace and retribution central to postwar Protestant discourses of human rights.

The Protestants most active in promoting Christian–Jewish relations were pastors who had participated in prewar missions to German Jews. Dating back to the eighteenth century, the Protestant *Judenmission* was outlawed by the Nazi regime in 1933 as part of the bid to define Judaism as a biological category, thereby making conversion impossible. Dahlemite pastors who had rejected the Nazi racialization of religion, including Martin Niemöller and Hermann Diem, were also the most enthusiastic proponents of reviving the *Judenmission* after the war. Despite their hostility toward the Nazis' racial antisemitism, these pastors continued to affirm the supersessionist teachings that traditionally accompanied missionary work.[78]

Such teachings were reflected in the EKD Brethren Council's 1948 "Message concerning the Jewish Question," the first statement on Christian–Jewish relations released by any postwar German Protestant group. According to the Brethren Council, God's biblical covenant with the people of Israel had been superseded in Christ's resurrection; Jews could partake in divine salvation only through conversion to Christianity. The "fate of the Jews" was a sign of their punishment for refusing to accept the divinity of Christ—an explanation for the Holocaust that resonated with centuries-old Christian justifications for anti-Jewish violence. Nevertheless, the statement rejected racial discrimination against Jews, a far cry from conservative groups like the wartime Freiburg circle, and acknowledged that "we Christians helped to bring about all the injustice and suffering inflicted upon Jews in our country."[79] For all its limitations, the Brethren Council statement opened a path toward new engagement with German Jews.

THE EASTERN BORDER AND THE BOUNDS OF RECONCILIATION 221

That engagement took shape through postwar Societies for Christian–Jewish Cooperation, the first founded in Munich, Stuttgart, and Wiesbaden in 1948 with support from US occupation authorities. By 1952 the West German federal and state governments took over the funding of the local societies, now established in fourteen cities, as well as the national-level Coordinating Council.[80] Recent scholarship has emphasized the instrumentalization of Christian–Jewish relations by a CDU government eager to secure West Germany's legitimacy abroad and establish a moral basis for neoliberal reforms at home.[81] But at the local level the Societies for Christian–Jewish Cooperation provided opportunities for postwar Protestants and Catholics alike to encounter members of West Germany's Jewish community, a tiny minority that numbered just over 20,000 by the late 1950s.[82] Often for the first time in their lives, Christian interlocutors were forced to confront Jewish perspectives on antisemitism and the claim of Jewish participants to represent an autonomous, living faith. As the returned German-Jewish rabbi Robert Raphael Geis noted at a conference of the German Protestant Committee for Service to Israel, authentic religious tolerance required "not merely patience for the other's convictions, but recognition of the reality of their beliefs."[83]

Although discussions of antisemitism operated at the margins of organized Protestantism during the 1950s, Christian–Jewish dialogue received a boost in prominence with the 1961 election of Kurt Scharf, a former leader in the Confessing Church Dahlemites, as chair of the EKD Council. A member of Martin Niemöller's Pastors' Emergency League, Scharf had participated in the Barmen, Dahlem, and Bad Oeynhausen synods, serving as president of the Confessing Church Brethren Council in Brandenburg and enduring numerous detentions during the Nazi years. As the EKD Council chair, Scharf supported the expansion of Christian–Jewish dialogue and joined a coalition of Confessing Church veterans, including Helmut Gollwitzer, Heinrich Grüber, and Heinz Kloppenburg, who lobbied the West German government to recognize the state of Israel.[84] The year of Scharf's election, Gollwitzer participated as a founding member of the Working Group on Jews and Christians at the biennial German Protestant Kirchentag (lay assembly).[85] The group's first meeting included a controversial address by Robert Raphael Geis that reversed the traditional missionary gaze: The Jewish people, which retained its unbroken covenant with God, remained charged to proclaim God's redemption of the world.[86]

222   REINVENTING PROTESTANT GERMANY

The deepening of Christian–Jewish dialogue during the early 1960s coincided with the expansion of West German trials of Nazi perpetrators. Protestants of Jewish descent played key roles in linking the two issues. When the EKD Council began planning a public statement on the trials in the fall of 1962, the West Berlin sociologist Dietrich Goldschmidt emerged as a staunch advocate for the punishment of convicted war criminals and a critic of the church's long-standing defense of amnesty. Born in 1914 to an academic family, Goldschmidt was classified as "mixed-race" under the Nazi regime due to his father's Jewish heritage and conscripted into forced labor during the final year of the war. After completing his studies in sociology at the University of Göttingen, where he worked with Ernst Wolf and other Confessing Church theologians, Goldschmidt took up a position at West Berlin's Pedagogical Academy, quickly becoming active in Christian–Jewish dialogue.[87]

At the Dortmund Kirchentag of January 1963, shortly after work on the EKD Council statement began, Goldschmidt organized a discussion of the Nazi trials at the Working Group on Jews and Christians. The meeting culminated in letters to Ludwig Raiser and Kurt Scharf targeting the theology behind the EKD's postwar amnesty campaigns. Rather than uphold forgiveness as the pathway toward re-Christianization, the petitions cautioned that "acts of mercy can only take place where justice has been done."[88] This admonition paid off when the Commission on Public Responsibility took up the trials the following month. The guest speaker, Barbara Just-Dahlmann, was an attorney at the Ludwigsburg investigative office whose recent condemnation of mild sentences for convicted war criminals had attracted national media attention.[89] At the most radical, the Commission on Public Responsibility suggested petitioning judges directly to ensure fair punishment.[90]

In the end the EKD Council statement on Nazi trials, released on March 13, 1963, did not go as far as the commission's recommendations. The EKD Council reiterated familiar allusions to the gap between divine law and human justice in language hardly distinguishable from the amnesty campaigns of the late 1940s. Courts should consider the circumstances in which Nazi crimes were committed, including "what a powerful influence was exerted at that time by the terror of the party and the State." Nevertheless, the statement broke from the EKD's postwar anti-trial campaign by refusing to obscure individual guilt behind invocations of universal human sin. Perpetrators should be held individually accountable before the law, "especially given the even greater responsibility of those entrusted with authority over others." The trials also had a pedagogical function, "to restore respect for the law among our people, which has been destroyed in the past, and thus to help restore our country to spiritual health." Moreover, by calling attention to Christian complacency—albeit not complicity—in the destruction of European Jewry, the EKD statement contained an unprecedented acknowledgment of German guilt. "Whereas it would have been the duty of all Christians to confront us with the Word of truth entrusted to us, by publicly confessing the irrevocable Lordship of God over every sphere of life, thus protecting the victims of [the Nazi] system, especially the Jews living in our midst, very few had the insight or the courage to resist."[91]

The EKD's statement on war crimes trials garnered a positive response in the West German press, with one newspaper hailing it as a "new high point" of Protestant politics following the Tübingen Memorandum.[92] The document also found a significant reception at the parish level, especially in the Dahlemite-led Rhineland and Westphalian churches. The Rhineland Protestant church alone ordered 500,000 copies from the EKD chancellery for distribution at Sunday services. In Westphalia, church president Ernst Wilm instructed pastors to present and explain the statement to their congregations on Palm Sunday.[93] The EKD Foreign Office commissioned English and French translations for distribution throughout the member churches of the World Council of Churches.[94] Nevertheless, the reaction from Protestant parishioners, especially in the Lutheran churches, was largely critical. As a jurist writing to the Hamburg *Sonntagsblatt* complained, the statement's insinuation of collective German responsibility was equivalent to holding all East Germans accountable for the actions of the ruling forces in the "Soviet occupation zone."[95]

Although the EKD statement did less to transform lay opinion than entrench existing divides, the hostile public reaction compelled the Commission on Public Responsibility to sharpen its defense of the trials. In writings and speeches clarifying the statement, commission members advanced the theology that had emerged out of Christian–Jewish dialogue. Only the acknowledgment of guilt, on this view, could precipitate reconciliation. In a broadcast on North German Radio, Ludwig Raiser praised the trials as a means to foster introspection about the Nazi past among a wider public. Surely, Raiser acknowledged, Nazi trials could hold only individuals, not an entire society, liable for the perpetration of atrocities. Nevertheless, the trials forced each German to confront their own conscience and ask themselves "how much of his own guilt each individual, even if only through allowing the reversal of fundamental concepts of morality and law, has contributed toward making possible such crimes."[96] The church administrator Erwin Wilkens, a Confessing Church veteran who directed the press office of the United German Lutheran Church, similarly defended the EKD statement in a lecture on the twenty-fifth anniversary of the Kristallnacht pogrom: "Punishment is the final and most extreme worldly aid toward recognition of guilt before God; it should not be withheld from the criminal for the sake of his humanity and the offer of forgiveness."[97] Rather than unlink divine and human justice, Wilkens underscored that the principle of Christian grace applied only after the punishment of sin.

The advancement of Christian–Jewish dialogue during the early 1960s was intimately linked to the rethinking of Protestant positions on the eastern border. EKD Council chair Kurt Scharf embodied the intersection of the two projects of reconciliation. A native of eastern Prussia, Scharf had served as the director of church administration in Brandenburg since the end of the war. He lived in East Berlin until East German authorities barred him from entering the GDR, as a punishment for writing to Communist party chief Walter Ulbricht to protest the Berlin Wall. Scharf's election to lead the EKD Council, six months prior to the wall's construction, was intended to signal the unity of the EKD against the pressures of national division.[98]

The issues were also closely connected for West German Protestants such as Ludwig Raiser and Erwin Wilkens. As members of the EKD's conservative mainstream, Raiser and Wilkens belonged to a political milieu that only a decade earlier had campaigned for the release of convicted Nazi war criminals. Yet Christian–Jewish dialogue, as well as political discussions at the FEST and the Commission on Public Responsibility, fostered a shift from the abstractions of early postwar Protestant human rights discourse to a deepened recognition of the dynamics of wartime violence. Reconciliation was no longer a Christian obligation that could be achieved through the suspension of law but a guiding principle of law itself. This framework informed the views of Raiser and Wilkens as they drafted the Eastern Memorandum.

The Eastern Memorandum: Reconciliation and Amnesia

In March 1963, at the same time that it released the statement on war crimes trials, the EKD Council reversed its decision to prohibit the Commission on Public Responsibility from discussing the Oder-Neisse border. Philipp von Bismarck, a spokesperson for the Pomeranian homeland society, requested that the group undertake a "clarifying conversation" on the issue, providing

THE EASTERN BORDER AND THE BOUNDS OF RECONCILIATION   225

the EKD Council with the cover to maintain neutrality between the Protestant expellee lobby and its critics.[99] The commission was certain to invite Bismarck and other expellee activists to its meetings.

Nevertheless, the marginalization of the expellee societies was a foregone conclusion. Numerous members of the reconstituted commission—including Ludwig Raiser, Erwin Wilkens, Elisabeth Schwarzhaupt, Hermann Kunst, and Dietrich Goldschmidt—had participated in reformist initiatives over the previous decade and favored a shift toward reconciliation with Eastern Europe. The Hungarian-German theologian Friedrich Spiegel-Schmidt, while not a member, continued to pen articles that formed a basis for the commission's discussions.[100] Longtime critics of West German foreign policy were invited to participate as guests: the journalist Marion Dönhoff, who as editor of *Die Zeit* had orchestrated the publication of the Tübingen Memorandum, and the Bethel theologian Wolfgang Schweitzer, whose defense of the Tübingen statement had stirred up controversy in the *Zeitschrift für evangelische Ethik*.[101] Moreover, the commission's prior consideration of Nazi trials prepared members to recognize the law's responsiveness to historical contexts, as well as its role in confronting German wartime atrocities.

In its first conversation on the Oder-Neisse Line, held in November 1963, the Commission on Public Responsibility discussed a set of theses produced by Wolfgang Schweitzer and other representatives of the Church Brethren Societies. In keeping with the Brethren Societies' prior initiatives toward East–West reconciliation, the theses contained a striking acknowledgment of German responsibility for "the destruction of the old legal order in Eastern Europe" and questioned the wisdom of demanding a return to the homeland, especially for the second generation.[102] While the majority in the commission welcomed this perspective, further months of discussion did little to bridge the cleft with representatives of the expellee lobby.[103] In an October 1964 lecture to the commission, Erwin Wilkens sought to mediate between the two sides. Neither of the competing theological positions on the homeland, Wilkens noted, yielded an unambiguous political conclusion. Instead Wilkens followed Ludwig Raiser in calling for a "historical assessment" of the conditions that would enable a final settlement of the border.[104] The commission agreed to forward Wilkens's memorandum on to the EKD Council as the basis for a volume on the right to the homeland.[105]

For all its pretensions to mediation, the Eastern Memorandum hardly presented a compromise position. Composed in the spring of 1965, the memorandum reflected the views of the reformist group around Raiser, Schweitzer, and the majority in the Commission on Public Responsibility. In order to gain broader public acceptance for their position, the authors agreed to avoid referencing the "renunciation" of territory, instead viewing "the 'right to the homeland' principally under the sign of reconciliation between Germany and the peoples of the East."[106] In practice, the distinction between renunciation and reconciliation meant little; both concepts signified that the EKD would accept the Oder-Neisse Line. But the discourse of reconciliation enabled the commission to claim the moral high ground from the expellee lobby and articulate a theological rationale beyond mere acceptance of a fait accompli—the accusation leveled by the expellee lobby against its Protestant critics.

Raiser's chapter on international law framed the issue as one of history and ethics rather than natural rights, following his lectures and publications over the previous years. The "right of self-determination of peoples," Raiser noted, remained a contested concept, not an inflexible principle. Poland's loss of its own eastern regions was the product of the Nazi regime's expansionist machinations that culminated in the Nazi–Soviet pact of August 1939. This historical reality, alongside the extraordinary victimization of Poland during the war, had created a novel legal situation. The Polish state could now claim the Oder-Neisse territories as legitimate compensation for its losses. Moreover, the legacy of German atrocities on Polish soil strengthened the Polish people's rights to "life" and "security" in their new territories. Consistent with his writings on Nazi trials, Raiser demanded that the acknowledgment of historical injustice serve as the foundation of international law.[107]

The Eastern Memorandum's discussion of "Ethical and Theological Considerations," whose final version was prepared by Erwin Wilkens, reinforced Raiser's treatment of international law. While criticizing the absolutist stances of both the Eastern Church Committee and the Church Brethren Societies, the memorandum described Protestant political ethics as a matter of "historical orders," not "orders that are pre-given by nature in eternal, unchanging design." In a modern, "mobile society," the notion of a permanent homeland had lost its meaning. Clinging to a "false understanding of homeland" would prevent the expellees from "turning to the new tasks of their lives without resignation." Following the critical expellee pastors around Friedrich Spiegel-Schmidt, Wilkens described the homeland as a gift of God, who could equally choose to take away what he had provided. Acknowledgment of the reality of divine mastery relativized human claims to property and territory. The task of the church was not to restore a prior state

THE EASTERN BORDER AND THE BOUNDS OF RECONCILIATION   227

of affairs but to bring about a new order, one rooted in a "foundation of reconciliation."[108]

At the same time, the Eastern Memorandum did not fully depart from nationalist preconceptions. The authors focused on the crime of expulsion rather than Nazi atrocities, and expressed gratitude to the German people for bearing its territorial losses without "the danger of nationalistic radicalization"—a statement that downplayed the role of the expellee lobby in West German politics and elided the churches' long history of denouncing Allied occupation policies.[109] The concept of reconciliation had a double-edged meaning, signaling atonement for the Nazi era but also the imputation of mutual guilt. Wilkens's advocacy for "partnership, in which the other side must also reexamine their own standpoint and make their own contribution to a new beginning," placed the burden of reconciliation equally on the Polish side and even suggested an equivalence of wartime suffering.[110]

Such arguments were part and parcel of the German-centric war memories espoused by the expellee lobby. Nowhere did the memorandum call for reparations or material restitution to Poland beyond the recognition of territorial realities. Indeed, it was only within the comfortable frame of German victimhood that the authors invoked the salvific power of reconciliation. The Eastern Memorandum was a signal contribution to the slow transformation of memory in postwar West Germany, composed by an older generation working in and through the traditions of German Protestant nationalism.

From the Eastern Memorandum to Ostpolitik

The Eastern Memorandum was published on October 15, 1965, with a glowing foreword by EKD Council chair Kurt Scharf. Although representatives of the East German churches had played a secondary role in the Commission on Public Responsibility—the Berlin Wall made travel between the two Germanies increasingly difficult, while the GDR had already recognized its eastern border—the memorandum was issued the name of the entire EKD, enhancing its claim to represent an ethic of reconciliation.[111] The document proved immediately contentious, provoking a wider press reception than any prior, or future, statement by the postwar German Protestant Church. Certainly the memorandum was not the driving force behind West Germany's official Ostpolitik of the late 1960s. The policy shift was catalyzed by security concerns as well as the expectation that rapprochement would weaken the East German regime and pave the way toward reunification.[112] Nevertheless, the

Eastern Memorandum allowed for a public debate on the eastern border unprecedented in scope since the end of the war.[113] Public opinion also shifted rapidly in its aftermath. According to one survey, only 22 percent of West Germans accepted the postwar border in 1964, whereas this number more than doubled, to 47 percent, by 1967.[114] The memorandum's broad and largely positive reception had another consequence crucial for the EKD's rapprochement with West German democracy. The authors, and their successors in a subsequent generation of Protestant intellectuals, could celebrate the alignment between Protestant values and West German foreign policy, downplaying the document's limits and elisions.

The Eastern Memorandum's widespread acclaim owed to its appearance at an inflection point in West German politics. The SPD experienced a revival of its electoral fortunes beginning in 1961, a sign of the appeal of the reforms enacted at the Godesberg party congress two years earlier as well as broader secularizing trends that eroded the CDU's stronghold among Catholic women. Critical journalism and movements for university reform also gained momentum in the early 1960s. After sixteen years of Christian Democratic rule, the conservative party's monopoly on political discourse was beginning to fade. The reception of the Eastern Memorandum reflected the momentum of reformist currents in West German politics. Although it had dominated public discussions of the border since the late 1940s, the expellee lobby found itself increasingly isolated. Falling back on its strategy of linking territorial revision to German unity, the Federation of Expellees quickly denounced the Eastern Memorandum as an act of "political dilettantism" that "ignores the goal of reunification anchored in the Basic Law and cements atheist rule in Eastern and Central Europe."[115]

Mainstream liberal media and even conservative press outlets proved more receptive. Periodicals that had welcomed the Tübingen Memorandum three years earlier hailed the Eastern Memorandum as another step toward a more rational and secure foreign policy. The left-leaning weeklies *Der Spiegel* and *Die Zeit* opened their pages for Raiser to defend the document against its critics.[116] Even the center-right *Christ und Welt* and *Rheinischer Merkur*, published by conservative Protestants and Catholics, respectively, issued laudatory appraisals.[117] Across ideological divides, journalists recognized that the EKD statement represented not a naive pacifism but the more realistic policy on the Oder-Neisse territories after twenty years of Polish resettlement.

At the same time, the press reception reinforced the limits of Protestant discussions. Journalists welcomed the memorandum's refusal to call for the "renunciation" of territory, underscored Soviet as well as German responsibility for the expulsions, and accepted the Protestant concept of reconciliation uncritically. Writing for *Rheinischer Merkur,* the journalist Paul Wilhelm Wegner opined, "True peace can only come about when Germany, Poland, and Russia bring a common willingness to suffer compromise." While Poland could expect "restitution" for its wartime losses, no one side should be overburdened by concessions.[118] Another writer for the same newspaper lauded the EKD for exercising "its prophetic guardian office" against "the approval of public opinion."[119] Like the Eastern Memorandum itself, the press neglected the question of accountability for Nazi crimes raised by Dietrich Goldschmidt and the Kirchentag Working Group on Jews and Christians. Instead press coverage affirmed Protestant intellectuals' narrative of postwar political responsibility.

The major political parties proved equally amenable to the Eastern Memorandum, departing from years of acquiescence to the expellee lobby. Leading CDU politicians, including Foreign Minister Gerhard Schröder, Expellee Minister Johann Baptist Gradl, and Bundestag president Eugen Gerstenmaier gave press interviews praising the EKD's commitment to reconciliation. These politicians faulted the memorandum for failing to insist upon German reunification as a condition for negotiations with the Soviet Union. Still, their public statements abandoned pretensions to restoring Germany's 1937 borders. The participation of Elisabeth Schwarzhaupt in the Commission on Public Responsibility, following her appointment as minister of health in 1961, helped bridge the cleft between the EKD and Christian Democrats, as did the theologian Eugen Gerstenmaier's long-standing participation at the EKD synod.[120] Even more than CDU politicians, Social Democrats signaled their openness to the EKD's position. Without going as far as to endorse the Oder-Neisse Line, influential SPD politicians including Willy Brandt and Helmut Schmidt abandoned their party's earlier mimicry of expellee polemics and sought to correct the expellee lobby's distortion of the memorandum.[121]

Beyond the laudatory reception by the press and political parties, developments on the Catholic side bolstered Protestant celebrations of the Eastern Memorandum. The small German Catholic peace movement backed the EKD's stance on German–Polish reconciliation and subsequently issued its own call for recognition of the Oder-Neisse Line.[122] West Germany's Catholic hierarchy, however, was reluctant to break from the official government standpoint. In November 1965, shortly after the memorandum's release, a commission of Polish Catholic bishops initiated a parallel process of reconciliation in a letter to their West German counterparts. Organized by Archbishop Bolesław Kominek, the missive invited the German Catholic bishops to a Warsaw ceremony honoring the 1,000th anniversary of the arrival of Christianity in Poland. The Polish bishops pleaded for West German recognition of the Oder-Neisse Line as a matter of "our existence," in light of Poland's territorial losses to the Soviet Union. Nevertheless, the letter concluded with a striking statement that broke with the official anti-Western rhetoric of the Polish government: "We grant forgiveness, and we ask your forgiveness."[123]

Even framed in these conciliatory terms, the Polish request was too bold for Germany's conservative Catholic hierarchy. On December 5, German Catholic bishops led by the Cologne Cardinal Josef Frings released a response that fell short of the EKD memorandum. While accepting the Polish invitation, the German bishops offered no gesture of concession. Instead their reply retreated to the language of reconciliation in its most abstract form: "The Christian spirit will contribute, therefore, to the reaching of a solution to all the unhappy consequences of the war, a solution satisfactory and fair to all sides." Expellees' demands for the "right to a home," the bishops insisted, contained, "aside from a few exceptions . . . no aggressive intention."[124]

The German Catholic bishops may well have adopted this cautious posture to avoid the appearance of celebrating the "re-Catholicization" of the Oder-Neisse territories under Polish auspices.[125] Still, their statement was consistent with a pattern of postwar Catholic political interventions, whether on questions of family law, confessional schools, or military service. Across these disparate issues, conservative Catholic leaders emphasized the fixed norms of natural law rather than the ethical demands of concrete situations. By contrast, Archbishop Kominek had maintained contact with Martin Niemöller and the West Berlin pastor Martin Albertz since the late 1950s. In a subsequent interview, Kominek even credited the Eastern Memorandum for inspiring his own letter.[126]

While German Catholic bishops refused to compromise on the Oder-Neisse Line, a broad consensus in support of the Eastern Memorandum took hold among Protestant church leaders and lay intellectuals. Writers in the Protestant press, from the conservative theologian Helmut Thielicke to the pacifist activist Renate Riemeck, celebrated the memorandum as an exemplary contribution of Protestant ethics to a burning political question.[127]

THE EASTERN BORDER AND THE BOUNDS OF RECONCILIATION   231

At the EKD synod in March 1966, a commission formed to take stock of the debate reiterated the injustice suffered by the expellees while affirming the Eastern Memorandum's call for reconciliation. Unlike prior synod debates on family law and nuclear weapons, there was no great divide between conservative Lutheran and Dahlemite factions. Both sides had undertaken a process of reorientation, in dialogue with each other and with interlocutors beyond their milieu.[128]

West German recognition of the Oder-Neisse Line would take new elections that brought the SPD to power for the first time in four decades. In 1969 the former West Berlin mayor Willy Brandt, a stalwart of the Godesberg program, became the Federal Republic's first Social Democratic chancellor on a promise to expand democracy at home and secure peace abroad. The August 1970 Treaty of Moscow between West Germany and the Soviet Union marked the opening gambit of the new government's Ostpolitik, committing both sides to the stability of postwar borders. Four months later Brandt and Polish prime minister Józef Cyrankiewicz signed the Treaty of Warsaw, the first agreement by the West German government to officially recognize an Eastern bloc state. The treaty entrusted both countries with maintaining peace and provisionally recognized the Oder-Neisse Line as the German–Polish border. The Bundestag ratified the agreement in May 1972.[129] Although Germany's eastern border was finalized only during German reunification in 1990, the Ostpolitik of the early 1970s effectively put the matter to rest.

Arguably the Eastern Memorandum only made public a political reality that was already recognized in private by most West German politicians, and by many expellees themselves.[130] But given the proximity between the Protestant memorandum and the Eastern treaties, the document entered the collective memory of German Protestant intellectuals as an emblem of the church's moral courage. The day after the Bundestag ratified the Treaty of Warsaw, Ludwig Raiser received a telegram from Willy Brandt: "Honored professor, on this day I gratefully remember the pioneering work that you and your friends accomplished through the memorandum."[131]

Official recognition confirmed the self-image of Raiser and his coauthors, paving the way for laudatory assessments over the coming decades. In an essay published on the document's twentieth anniversary, Wolfgang Schweitzer pronounced what had become a well-established tenet in Protestant circles: "Without the memorandum, the détente with the East, for which there were the first signs in 1965, would not have progressed as far as it did from 1969."[132] Speaking in Warsaw on the fortieth anniversary of the Eastern Memorandum, Berlin-Brandenburg bishop Wolfgang Huber praised the EKD's "fundamental contribution to the reorientation of German politics." West Germany's Catholic leaders, Huber noted, had failed to act with the courage of their Protestant counterparts.[133] Such narratives reduced the complex and contentious path by which the memorandum emerged, and most significantly, overlooked the currents of German Protestant nationalism that had made the document possible.

THE EASTERN MEMORANDUM marked a rare moment of consensus in the postwar EKD. Across the church's Lutheran and Dahlemite wings, a broad cohort of pastors and lay intellectuals upheld reconciliation rather than retributive justice as the foundation of the church's witness in the political world. The memorandum reflected a culmination of political shifts since 1945, fostered in a series of encounters: with East European and Jewish interlocutors, between theologians and lay intellectuals, and across the factions of the church. At the same time, the statement also rested upon the reimagining, rather than abandonment, of older nationalist traditions. The Eastern Memorandum advanced a familiar conception of Protestantism as a source of shared political values, and it hardly questioned postwar commonplaces of German victimhood and Christian anti-Nazi resistance. The document's positive public reception fostered a celebration of the role of the Protestant churches in Germany's moral renewal, rather than a self-critical engagement with the church's past. But for all its limits, the Eastern Memorandum contributed to the stabilization of liberal democracy in post-1945 Western Europe, which depended upon the cessation of the revisionist claims that had proven disastrous in the interwar era. Reconciliation between the Federal Republic and its western neighbors took place largely under Catholic auspices, and was closely bound up with West European political and economic integration.[134] The EKD, for its part, pushed the West German state toward a rapprochement with the Communist regimes to its east.

The Eastern Memorandum appeared at a hinge point of Protestant politics in postwar West Germany. Although rates of church attendance fell over the 1950s and early 1960s, both major churches maintained close connections to the federal government. Political parties and the mainstream press continued to regard church statements as important contributions to public debate. In retrospect, however, the pivotal Protestant documents of the first half of the 1960s—the Tübingen Memorandum, the EKD statement on Nazi trials, and the Eastern Memorandum—represented the apex of a form of church politics centered on the public exhortation of state authorities. As the FEST and the EKD Commission on Public Responsibility debated the merits of West German foreign policy, the forces of generational change, economic prosperity, and sexual revolution had already challenged the political influence of the churches in ways unprecedented since 1945, or even 1918. The secularization of West German society was the backdrop to the final set of political controversies that confronted veterans of the Nazi-era church conflict, concerning the scope of executive power in the face of burgeoning New Left protest movements.

CHAPTER SEVEN

EMERGENCIES OF DEMOCRACY

UNFURLING BANNERS EMBLAZONED with the slogans "1933 Enabling Act—1968 NS Constitution," "For the Basic Law—Against National Socialist Laws," and "Never Again—Throne and Altar," 500 Protestant pastors and church employees gathered for a demonstration in Bonn on May 8, 1968.[1] The rhetorical intensity of the protest matched what supporters and critics alike perceived as its high stakes: a set of proposed constitutional amendments to expand executive power and limit basic rights during state-declared emergencies. Protestant intellectuals born around the turn of the twentieth century, now in the final stages of their careers, remained vocal actors on both sides of the national debate about emergency laws, which became a galvanizing cause of the 1960s West German New Left. The executive board of the Committee on the Emergency of Democracy, the opposition movement's central organization, included the former Confessing Church pastors Helmut Gollwitzer, Heinz Kloppenburg, and Martin Niemöller, as well as the theologian Ernst Wolf and Protestant sociologist Dietrich Goldschmidt.[2] At the same time, Gustav Heinemann served as justice minister of the Grand Coalition government that passed the emergency laws in May 1968, while Adolf Arndt and Ludwig Raiser were outspoken in their support of the measures.

The contest over emergency laws came amid the most significant challenges the German Protestant churches had experienced since 1945. Longterm factors fostering the secularization of West European societies, including postwar prosperity, the growth of consumer cultures, and the relaxation of traditional attitudes toward sexuality, had become impossible for churches to ignore by the mid-1960s. Among West German Protestant church members under age forty-five, only 11 percent regularly attended

Sunday worship by 1963; this dropped to 6 percent in 1967.[3] Most dramatic, the middle of the decade saw the explosive rise of student movements that challenged the privileged status churches had enjoyed in postwar politics across the western half of the continent. Yet West German Protestants also exemplified the dynamic stance adopted by many West European Christians at this pivotal moment. Rather than retreat to a reactive posture—the assumption of much of the scholarship on 1960s protest movements, which tends to regard the West European New Left as wholly secular—Protestant intellectuals remained on the front lines of debates about the future of West German democracy.[4] Key figures of the Confessing Church generation joined a broader group of left liberal and left socialist intellectuals who engaged in critical dialogue with, rather than wholesale rejection of, the students.[5]

Protestant reactions to the ruptures of 1960s West Germany contrasted sharply with the responses of leading theologians and lay intellectuals to earlier periods of crisis. In 1918 and 1945, retrenchment to the tenets of Protestant nationalism and sharp opposition to the forces of secularism were the rule. To be sure, generational change helps account for this shift. By the early 1960s a transitional cohort born in the 1920s, whose political formation took place during the years of post-1945 reconstruction rather than the Weimar Republic, had begun to enter the Protestant public sphere. But members of the older generation continued to be key interlocutors in political debates both within and beyond the church. Instead of rejecting democracy as an incubator for the hostile forces of secularism, theologians and lay intellectuals across the EKD's divisions increasingly looked to their own political engagement since 1945 for evidence of their church's standing as a bulwark of democratic values.

Democracy, however, had no singular meaning for Protestant intellectuals in 1960s West Germany. Three competing models emerged in the debate about emergency laws, reflecting not only the ideological fissures of the preceding decades but the disparate results of political advocacy. On the one hand, church leaders and lay intellectuals who had helped bring about the victories in the family law and conscientious objector cases of the late 1950s—moderate conservatives as well as reformist Social Democrats—could see their own initiatives reflected in West German institutions. This group adopted a discourse of militant democracy, which regarded emergency laws as essential to protecting the constitutional democracy that had already been established. On the other hand, the left wing of the Church Brethren Societies, whose demands for the renunciation of nuclear weapons had gone unfulfilled, rallied behind an alternative conception of neutralist democracy that regarded emergency laws as a threat to democracy itself. Nevertheless, both groups coalesced around the narrative of their confession's recent history that took hold after 1945: The Confessing Church had served as an anti-Nazi resistance organization, endowing its heirs with the moral credibility to articulate the shared values undergirding postwar politics. This minimal consensus allowed for Protestant proponents and opponents of emergency laws, members of the EKD's conservative and Dahlemite wings alike, to affirm the concept of a democratic *Rechtsstaat* (rule-of-law state) as a Protestant creation and value.

It was this third model of democracy that would outlast the tumultuous events of 1968, when student protests reached their height. Even as the West German New Left splintered into competing factions, a successor generation of Protestant church leaders and lay intellectuals would continue to promote the tenets of a Protestant Rechtsstaat: a state based on expansive basic rights protections, where the Basic Law encoded the religious values underpinning democracy. The German Protestant defense of constitutional democracy marked the culmination of a long transformation. Both the Lutheran and Dahlemite wings of the EKD emerged out of intellectual traditions that had rejected the mobilization of theology behind any political form. Rather than an explicit confrontation with the church's Nazi past, political engagement against the backdrop of the Cold War and West German confessional tensions shaped the democratic reorientation of the Protestant public sphere. But the Protestant visions of democracy that emerged in the 1960s remained rooted in exaggerated accounts of anti-Nazi resistance, and in a discourse of Protestant values that took one confession to represent West German democracy itself.

Emergency Laws and Militant Democracy

Although the controversy over emergency laws reached its height amid heady protests of the late 1960s, the debate had its origins following West Germany's accession to NATO. After the occupation statute expired in May 1955, the United States, Britain, and France retained the authority to deploy military force within the Federal Republic during a domestic or international emergency. As a prerequisite for lifting this prerogative, the Allies stipulated that West Germany demonstrate the capacity to govern itself in emergency situations. Proposals for emergency laws took shape amid the ensuing efforts to restore West German sovereignty. CDU interior minister Gerhard Schröder, who prepared the government's earliest drafts, suggested a constitutional amendment authorizing a simple parliamentary majority to declare a state of emergency in response to an internal or external threat. If the parliament were subsequently unable to convene, the chancellor could unilaterally suspend the freedoms of the press, assembly, and movement, the right to choose or leave one's profession, and the right of workers to strike. Most dramatically, Schröder's proposal permitted the chancellor and federal cabinet to deploy the military on West German soil.[6]

The controversy over emergency laws was never simply about West German sovereignty, however, but went to the heart of the viability of a post-Nazi democracy.[7] Only a generation earlier, Heinrich Brüning and his successors had relied on presidential emergency powers under the Weimar Constitution's Article 48 to subvert parliamentary authority, effectively ending German democracy even before Hitler's appointment as chancellor. Aware of the issue's volatility, Schröder waited until October 1958, a year after the CDU's overwhelming electoral victory, to publicly announce his proposal. The outcry proved swift and furious. Critics from the entire political spectrum left of the CDU assailed the government plan as a ruse to undermine democracy and silence opposition, with ominous echoes in recent German history.[8] Military simulations of the mid-1950s further demonstrated that government plans for a Soviet invasion or nuclear attack—including the creation of civilian militias, construction of bunkers, and mass evacuations— were at odds with West Germany's actual defense capabilities. Instead of providing a sense of security, the proposed emergency laws, as well as the civil defense law passed by a simple parliamentary majority in 1957, exposed West German vulnerabilities and stoked popular fears.[9]

Within Protestant political networks, the discussion of emergency laws exacerbated fissures taking shape around the late 1950s. Alongside the failed campaign against the nuclearization of the West German military and the SPD's 1959 Godesberg Congress, the proposed legislation raised a fundamental question. Had West Germans already succeeded in establishing a secure democracy, or did the young state remain threatened by the residues of Nazi ideology? The EKD Council sought to maintain harmony within the church's ranks by avoiding the issue's contentious politics. Its recommendations to the government focused on narrowly church-based concerns: ensuring clerical exemptions from mandatory civilian defense service and the freedom of religious practice during emergencies.[10] But questions about the nature of West German democracy infused the controversy between Protestant SPD politicians who championed the Godesberg platform and members of the Church Brethren Societies who sought to continue their antinuclear advocacy.

The Protestant debate about emergency laws belonged to a national contest over the scope and meaning of democracy by the early 1960s. Proponents of the legislation, who spanned the political spectrum from the CDU to the post-Godesberg SPD, drew heavily on the concept of "militant democracy" (*wehrhafte Demokratie*). Proposed during the mid-1930s by the German-Jewish émigré legal scholar Karl Loewenstein, militant democracy was popularized by a cohort of liberal jurists and politicians in postwar West Germany. Loewenstein himself returned to Germany in 1945 as an adviser to the US occupation government. Pointing to the collapse of the Weimar Republic, Loewenstein and his followers warned that democracies remained vulnerable to cooptation by antidemocratic parties, which sought to abolish the very procedures they used to gain power. Democracies, Loewenstein argued, must implement constitutional safeguards to exclude antidemocratic groups, even if this meant restricting political freedoms during national emergencies.[11]

In the early 1950s these ideas became the basis for a series of measures that aimed to defend the West German state from internal adversaries. Konrad Adenauer's cabinet created the Federal Office for the Protection of the Constitution in October 1950. In July 1951 the Bundestag passed, with both CDU and SPD support, the Law Against the Enemies of Democracy. The act imposed stiff penalties against both government officials and private citizens charged with attempting to undermine the constitutional order. The government's most aggressive interventions involved the banning of the neo-Nazi Socialist Reich Party and the Communist Party of Germany. The prohibitions were confirmed in Federal Constitutional Court decisions of 1952 and 1956, which cited the Basic Law's outlawing of "parties that . . . seek to undermine or abolish the free democratic basic order."[12]

Protestants who could see their own political interventions reflected in the nascent state's legislation and judicial decisions embraced the concept of militant democracy. The model's most vocal Protestant advocate, the SPD jurist and politician Adolf Arndt, helped negotiate the 1951 Law Against the Enemies of Democracy.[13] Arndt's advocacy before the Federal Constitutional Court in cases on the Reich Concordat and the right of conscientious objection strengthened his identification with West German institutions. In both instances Arndt successfully adapted the theories of the Protestant constitutional lawyer Rudolf Smend. West German courts, Arndt argued, could not directly translate religious precepts into law, but should acknowledge the pre-political values that served as the foundation of the basic rights.

The Constitutional Court formalized this principle in a landmark decision of 1958 involving the head of the Hamburg state press office, Erich Lüth, and the famed ex-Nazi filmmaker Veit Harlan. The constitutional basic rights, the court concluded, were not simply a domain of personal autonomy from the state but reflected an "objective order of values" that bound all members of the political community. The critical brief in the case, which defended Lüth's call for a boycott of Harlan's postwar films, was composed by Adolf Arndt's assistant Wilhelm Hennis, himself a student of Rudolf Smend.[14] For Arndt and other members of the Smend school, the series of constitutional rulings that culminated in the Lüth decision demonstrated the durability of West German democracy. On the one hand, the Constitutional Court had removed threats to democracy from both the extreme left and right. On the other hand, the court ensured that democracy was rooted not simply in naked state power but in shared values.

Ideas of militant democracy suffused Arndt's proposals for emergency laws. As early as 1955 Arndt and his fellow SPD jurist Carlo Schmid expressed concern that the Basic Law was unequipped to defend itself in "crisis situations."[15] For Arndt and other reformist Social Democrats, emergency laws were essential for protecting West Germany's parliamentary system from antidemocratic attacks. After the SPD's voter share increased from 32 to 36 percent in the federal elections of 1961, a clear victory for the Godesberg reformers, Arndt took the lead in charting his party's moderate course. In a position paper published shortly after the election, Arndt linked emergency laws to his larger theory of the Basic Law. Against the prevailing wisdom among the legislation's critics, Arndt denied that presidential emergency powers were alone the reason for the Weimar Republic's collapse. Instead the Weimar Constitution had proven unsustainable because it rested on fragile compromises rather than a core of shared values. No basic rights protections had constrained the aspirations of antidemocratic actors. Even the republic's supporters had failed to agree on fundamental values: Whereas the Catholic Center Party played off "natural law" against laws that had "'only' arisen historically," the socialist left counterposed the constitution's merely formal democracy against true democratic socialism.[16] In contrast, the Basic

240   REINVENTING PROTESTANT GERMANY

Law introduced what its Weimar precursor lacked: a framework in which the shared values underpinning political life formed the organizing and inalienable principles of the constitution itself.[17]

Arndt and his SPD colleagues were convinced that emergency laws were both legitimate and necessary to defend the Basic Law's value system. At the same time, they averred that the CDU proposals for the dramatic expansion of executive authority contravened the postwar constitution's democratic core. Arndt criticized the government draft's conflation of internal and external emergencies, as well as its provisions enabling the executive to bypass parliamentary oversight.[18] In early 1962 Arndt participated in an SPD commission that took up negotiations with the Interior Ministry, laying out an alternative draft of emergency legislation. The SPD version guaranteed the right to strike and maintained the authority of the Bundestag and the Constitutional Court.[19] Emergency laws should be activated only in response to a foreign threat, because unlike its Weimar precursor, the Basic Law protected democratic values from domestic subversion and banned "anticonstitutional parties."[20]

Concepts of militant democracy and the Basic Law's value order, honed by a predominantly Protestant milieu around Rudolf Smend, came together in the SPD's defense of emergency laws. The SPD's alternative legislation presupposed the strength of West Germany's democratic institutions and assumed that democracies were obliged to defend their values, forcefully when necessary, against antidemocratic threats. Yet Arndt's was hardly the only Protestant response to proposed emergency laws.

Neutralist Democracy and the Return of Resistance

While Protestants aligned with the West German political mainstream defended a modified version of emergency laws, the Church Brethren Societies spearheaded the national opposition against the government proposals. The fissure reflected divergent responses to political events of the late 1950s and early 1960s. Whereas Protestant Social Democrats could celebrate their own influence on the Godesberg program and the Constitutional Court's rulings on conscientious objection, these developments left members of the Brethren Societies even more disaffected with the West German state. Many aligned with the left socialist wing of the SPD that had opposed the Godesberg reforms and split from the party following the expulsion of its more radical youth organization, the Socialist German Student League, in late

1961.[21] By the early 1960s *Stimme der Gemeinde* and *Junge Kirche* joined a slate of oppositional journals that positioned themselves outside the parliamentary system, including the left Catholic *werkhefte* and the GDR-backed *konkret*. Leading left socialist intellectuals, including the jurist Wolfgang Abendroth and the political scientist Ossip K. Flechtheim, contributed to the Brethren Societies organs.[22] Protestant peace activists were also well represented in the antinuclear Easter March movement, launched in the spring of 1960 following the collapse of the SPD-backed Fight Against Atomic Death.[23]

Like SPD reformers, members of the Church Brethren Societies understood emergency laws as a matter that raised fundamental questions about the meaning of democracy. This group's discussion of democracy, however, was complicated by an additional tension stemming from its commitment to East–West reconciliation and Christian–Marxist dialogue. Democracy, even if never precisely defined, had belonged to the political lexicon of the Confessing Church Dahlemites since the early postwar years. As early as 1946, Karl Barth's lecture on "The Christian Community and the Civil Community" affirmed an affinity between Christian ideas of equality before God and the democratic state. Protestant opponents of rearmament and nuclear weapons had criticized the West German government for preventing the formation of a genuine popular will. At the same time, expressing an overt preference for democracy, certainly in its parliamentary form, would threaten their access to East European contacts on which the Brethren Societies pinned their hopes for German reunification.

The tightening grip on the East German churches by the Socialist Unity Party (SED) made the question of democracy even more acute for the Church Brethren Societies. Church–state conflict in the GDR spiked after the EKD signed a military chaplaincy treaty with the Federal Republic in early 1957, leading East German officials to declare the church a fifth column against the socialist state. In July 1958, following a year of mutual recriminations, a subset of the East German clergy led by Thuringian bishop Moritz Mitzenheim signed a declaration of loyalty drafted by party officials. In exchange for freedom of religious practice, the church leaders recognized the military treaty's invalidity in the GDR, affirmed their commitment to peace, and promised that East German Christians would respect the laws of the Communist state.[24]

Protestant conservatives in West Germany quickly denounced the capitulation of their East German counterparts. In contrast, Karl Barth defended the loyalty declaration in a widely publicized letter to East German pastors the following month. Barth's letter advised East German Christians to form a "loyal opposition" oriented toward improvement of the Communist state.[25] Unlike the anti-Christian Nazi regime, Barth believed, East Germany was merely an "a-Christian" state that did not pursue the destruction of Christianity as a central tenet of its ideology.[26] If Barth's position indicated his political naïveté, or his sympathy toward the SED's social message, it was also consistent with a basic impulse of his postwar theology: the search for Christian community that could thrive in secular European societies. Such a theology could only ever accord secondary importance to the political form of the state, whether democracy or dictatorship.

Posed in the controversy over Barth's letter, the question of the Church Brethren Societies' loyalty to democracy returned in a yet more public dispute the following year, this one launched by Otto Dibelius. A leader in the conservative wing of the Confessing Church, after the war Dibelius was named bishop of the Protestant church in Berlin-Brandenburg, the only postwar regional church to cross the intra-German border. He quickly emerged as a combative opponent of East German church policy and upbraided his colleagues who signed the 1958 loyalty declaration.[27] In August 1959, Dibelius raised the stakes of the standoff in a letter to his Hanoverian counterpart, Hanns Lilje, on the occasion of Lilje's sixtieth birthday. The letter concerned the proper translation of Paul's command to obey state authority in the Epistle to the Romans, a passage at the center of German Protestant debates about church–state relations since 1918. Paul's injunction, Dibelius opined, had to be again rethought in Communist East Germany: "If in the so-called free world, I see a street sign that requires me to drive only fifteen kilometers per hour, then I will follow it straight away. Because I know that this rule is valid for all, that therefore there is a reason for it, and certainly a reason that will protect me directly or indirectly from harm ... But if I see the same sign on the highway in East Germany, already a Russian car rushes past me at one hundred, followed by an East-zone authority's car. They can do it; I cannot, because I am not a party functionary. And not only that! Why shouldn't I drive faster?"[28]

The seemingly trivial example of traffic rules illustrated Dibelius's broader point. The bishop questioned whether East German Christians were obliged to obey even the most rudimentary laws of their government. Dibelius himself was hardly a democrat, but a traditional Protestant nationalist for whom the loss of the political "authority" invoked by Paul was the great tragedy of the modern world. Nevertheless, the letter set up Dibelius's critics to be targeted as Communist sympathizers disloyal to West German democracy.

Leaked to the press after Dibelius distributed 500 copies to pastors throughout Berlin and Brandenburg, the letter was quickly excerpted in leading West German weeklies, with Dibelius's photograph splashed on the cover of *Der Spiegel.*[29] During the inevitable intra-Protestant polemics that followed, the Church Brethren Societies sided with Karl Barth in refusing to endow one or the other German state with a Christian sanction.[30] The Brethren Societies' Heidelberg statement of July 1960, drafted by pastors Herbert Werner of Württemberg and Herbert Mochalski of Hesse-Nassau, declared that Christians are "freed, either in the East or the West, from participating in the Cold War and in agitation against other states … From the point of view of the Bible, there is no reason to stand in the way of a mutual recognition of the two partial German states."[31] Such expressions of Cold War neutrality allowed Dibelius and his allies to reclaim the mantle of anti-Nazi resistance in the name of anti-Communism. In a conversation with Hanns Lilje and the conservative jurist Ulrich Scheuner on West Berlin radio shortly following the release of his letter, Dibelius described the GDR as a "total state" on par with the Nazi regime, recalling that he had hidden two "non-Aryans" in his office during the war. The three agreed that a state that sought to impress itself upon the "thoughts" and "convictions" of its subjects lost the claim of obedience. Implicitly they linked the Confessing Church's discourse of Christian freedom to the dilemmas facing Christians in the GDR. The problem of resistance arose most clearly in a total state, Lilje noted, whereas democracy offered Christians the "orderly means of expressing one's will."[32]

However evasive the arguments of their critics—in light of the long history of antidemocratic agitation by Protestant conservatives—the Church Brethren Societies struggled to reconcile their commitment to Cold War neutrality with an alternative vision of democracy. Nevertheless, as the structures of militant democracy placed Cold War neutralism beyond the bounds of legitimate political discourse, the societies adumbrated their own language of democracy to safeguard their ability to propagate neutralist ideas. Pressure to take a clear stance on democracy became acute with the founding of the German Peace Union (DFU), a political party that aimed to renew the neutralist coalition outside the SPD. Formed in December 1960, the DFU drew together the groups that had rallied around Gustav Heinemann's All-German

People's Party seven years earlier: the nationalist Federation of Germans, former members of the banned Communist party, disaffected Social Democrats, as well as the Church Brethren Societies.[33] Martin Niemöller and Herbert Mochalski were two of the party's founding members.[34] Party chair Renate Riemeck was an active lay Protestant who had taken a professorship at the Pedagogical Academy of Wuppertal through the invitation of pastor Oskar Hammelsbeck, and deepened her contacts with Niemöller's circle in the campaign for recognition of the Oder-Neisse Line.[35]

Like its predecessors among third-way, neutralist organizations, from the outset the DFU faced questions about its democratic credibility. The DFU's funding by the East German SED was an open secret. Protestant party leaders were active in the Christian Peace Conference, which was backed by the Communist regime in Prague; their extensive Eastern bloc contacts drew suspicion even if Protestant East–West dialogue was not motivated by a Communist agenda. The DFU's platform focused almost exclusively on demands for nuclear disarmament and peace negotiations with the Soviet Union.[36] The election of 1961 proved the limited appeal of this agenda. Whereas the SPD received its strongest returns since the founding of the Federal Republic, the DFU gained just 1.9 percent of the national vote, below the 5 percent threshold needed to enter the Bundestag.[37]

In the aftermath of the election, DFU leaders made new appeals to the language of democracy, aiming to turn the logic of militant democracy on its head. The 5 percent threshold that had kept the DFU out of the Bundestag was itself an artifact of postwar militant democracy, adopted in West German electoral law to limit the influence of splinter parties and prevent the political fragmentation that had hobbled the Weimar Republic.[38] The DFU, however, saw the rule as a constraint on democracy that stifled dissenting voices. Such criticisms were amplified following the 1961 election, when SPD parliamentarians, including Adolf Arndt, signaled their willingness to compromise on emergency laws. In *Stimme der Gemeinde,* which became a hub of opposition against emergency laws, the left socialist political scientist Ossip K. Flechtheim worried that a parliamentary emergency committee authorized to act in lieu of the full Bundestag would shut out smaller parties, let alone those barred from representation.[39] The most damning rebuke was delivered by Renate Riemeck, who panned emergency laws as a greater danger to democracy than the 1933 Enabling Act that had granted Hitler dictatorial powers.[40] Riemeck's attack on the institutions of militant democracy must be understood, at least in part, as personally motivated. Briefly a Nazi

Party member as a student in Jena, Riemeck turned to the far left after the war through her involvement in anti-rearmament and antinuclear politics. By mid-1960 the Interior Ministry had placed Riemeck's publications under censorship for her alleged Communist connections, while the Cultural Ministry of North Rhine-Westphalia barred her from conducting academic examinations.[41]

Yet Protestant critics of the SPD's Godesberg turn also moved toward a more principled defense of a neutralist democracy, rooted in their own narrative of anti-Nazi resistance. Rather than trace a line from the Confessing Church to the "value order" of the Basic Law, neutralist democrats connected their wartime legacy to the unfulfilled promise of the antinuclear protests, extended after the 1961 election to the campaign against emergency laws. On their view, genuine democracy entailed a radical sphere of individual liberties that included the right to fundamental criticism of, and even resistance against, the existing political order. As the reformed SPD released its own proposals for emergency laws, resistance reemerged as a watchword within the Church Brethren Societies—articulated not against the Allies or West German rearmament but in defense of individual expression and conscience.

In November 1961, two months after the DFU's electoral rout, the Church Brethren Society in Martin Niemöller's Hesse-Nassau regional church gave voice to an alternative democratic vision at a meeting in honor of the Dahlemite leader's seventieth birthday. The meeting's core question had already been asked by the conscientious objector movement of the 1950s: "Does the state have the right to seduce, coerce, and control the conscience of the individual?"[42] But conscience rights, rather than simply a means to express opposition to rearmament, were now linked to a defense of democracy. As the attorney Fritz Bauer put the point, "critique and opposition are not tiresome troubles, but the life principle of a democratically organized people." Especially in a "constantly endangered Rechtsstaat," resistance remained a legitimate possibility to prevent a turn to an "*Unrechtsstaat.*"[43] Another speaker at the Frankfurt meeting, the younger jurist Heinrich Hannover, concluded that the right of conscientious objection expressed a wider "obligation to oppose or to resist" orders by the state that would result in mass destruction.[44] Although he gained notoriety during the 1950s as a defense attorney for alleged Communists accused of political crimes, Hannover forthrightly aligned himself with the values of the "free democratic Rechtsstaat." The "political defamation" of government opponents, Hannover argued, presented a graver threat to West German democracy than East German spies themselves, for such persecution undercut democracy's own values.[45]

When the Bundestag began its first reading of the emergency laws in October 1962, the Church Brethren Societies continued to define conscientious objection as the basis for a broader right of resistance. In a pamphlet for West Germany's Association of Conscientious Objectors, Heinrich Hannover praised a vote by the German Trade Union Confederation to deny support to the proposed amendments. If public opposition failed to prevent the passage of emergency laws, then "one day resistance against the civil service law—similar to the right of conscientious objection—will be restricted to a small circle of citizens who are ready, at least for their own persons, to bear the consequences of their conscience."[46] In January 1963 the leadership committee of the Working Group of Church Brethren Societies convened its annual meeting on the theme "The Limits of Obedience." Organized by the former Confessing Church pastor Heinz Kloppenburg, who since 1959 had chaired the Central Office for the Rights and Protection of Conscientious Objectors, the meeting included lectures by Wolfgang Abendroth and the theologian Otto Bauernfeind on the problems of emergency laws and oath swearing.[47] In a formulation that drew a quick rejoinder from Adolf Arndt, the meeting's concluding statement invoked the specter of the Weimar Constitution's presidential emergency powers. Emergency laws, the statement contended, would hollow out West Germany's "free democratic order."[48]

The Church Brethren Societies belonged to the broader milieu of left socialists disillusioned with the Godesberg platform. With its parliamentary opposition eclipsed, this group called for extra-parliamentary activism through strikes and civil disobedience, and held out the possibility of resistance—a category from which violence was never explicitly excluded—as the backstop of democracy.[49] Yet Protestants also brought their own narratives and experiences to bear on defending neutralist democracy. Like Protestant supporters of emergency laws, neutralist democrats rooted their postwar political engagement in an ostensible anti-Nazi legacy. The Brethren Societies also appealed to a set of shared political values standing above the written law, playing into a long-standing German Protestant discourse. Whether such values had already been fulfilled in the institutions of the Federal Republic became the key bone of contention in the Protestant debate about emergency laws.

A Theology of the Rechtsstaat

By early 1963 the Protestant discussion of emergency laws stood at an impasse. Defenders of militant democracy believed that the Basic Law and subsequent decisions by the Federal Constitutional Court had firmly anchored the values of their confession in West German institutions. Partisans of neutralist democracy, in contrast, perceived a backsliding toward authoritarianism that could be combatted only from outside the party system. Yet a third group endeavored to synthesize these perspectives—holding out the possibility of civil disobedience as a final resort while recognizing the progress toward democracy that had been made since 1945. For Protestant intellectuals who aimed to push beyond entrenched binaries, the Basic Law served as both the embodiment of Protestant values *and* an unfulfilled promise. This group's watchword was an unusual amalgam: the democratic Rechtsstaat.

The Rechtsstaat was an unlikely candidate for integrating a broad Protestant milieu, from Christian Democrats through the Church Brethren Societies, around an affirmation of democracy. Literally a "state governed by the rule of law," the concept had long been associated with a legal formalism that admitted no consideration of the law's social and economic consequences, an anathema for the left. From the early 1950s, legal scholars such as Ernst Forsthoff and Werner Weber, who remained in close contact with the ex-Nazi jurist Carl Schmitt, mobilized the concept behind an attack on West German democracy. For these far-right stalwarts, the Rechtsstaat principle—the protection of individual rights from state interference—stood in contradiction with modern mass society, which relied upon an interventionist administrative state to meet basic social needs. The Federal Republic's attempt to create a "social Rechtsstaat" was therefore a contradiction in terms, opening a path toward rule by special interests.[50]

However, another concept of the Rechtsstaat had become available through the writings of Rudolf Smend. Building on the Federal Constitutional Court's 1958 Lüth decision, Smend and his circle emphasized that the formal, positivist doctrine of the Rechtsstaat had been supplanted by a new idea of the "substantive Rechtsstaat." For Smend's followers, including Ulrich Scheuner and the younger Protestant jurist Konrad Hesse, the legitimacy of the West German Rechtsstaat derived not simply from its adherence to legal procedure. Instead the state was charged to uphold the values encoded in the Basic Law. Not only the political rights outlined in the West German constitution, but also the social welfare state (*Sozialstaat*) anchored in Article 20, expressed precisely such a value.[51]

The idea of the substantive Rechtsstaat aligned closely with that of militant democracy. It is no coincidence that both were championed by members of Smend's circle, who believed that the constitution required safeguards against the subversion of its core values. But a cohort of Protestant intellectuals born in the 1920s adapted the Rechtsstaat concept to accommodate the possibility of radical dissent voiced by the Church Brethren Societies. Situated between their elders socialized in the Weimar Republic and the "'68er" generation born during and after the war, members of this cohort, who included the philosopher Jürgen Habermas, jurist Jürgen Seifert, and journalist Ulrike Meinhof, described themselves as "'58ers." This was both an ironic statement of the tensions with their younger counterparts and an acknowledgment that the antinuclear protests of the late 1950s, rather than the student movement of the late 1960s, had posed the first large-scale challenge to postwar West Germany's conservative government.[52] The landmark Lüth decision of the Federal Constitutional Court formed another important marker of 1958. For young observers of the court, the decision offered evidence that constitutional law, by elaborating the democratic and social values immanent in the Basic Law, could serve as a catalyst for the deepening of democracy.[53]

The most influential Protestant member of this transitional cohort was the jurist Helmut Simon, a leader in the Rhineland Church Brethren Society and future judge on the Federal Constitutional Court. Born in a Rhineland village in 1922, Simon's formative political experience involved not the collapse of the Weimar Republic but the challenges of post-1945 occupation and reconstruction. Simon approached the democratic concerns of his generation through the lens of his Protestant upbringing. Both of his parents were active in the Confessing Church, and he had refused to join the Nazi Party as a member of an illegal Christian youth organization. After returning from wartime naval service, Simon attended the University of Basel as a visiting law student, where he was profoundly influenced by encounters with Karl Barth. Barth's vision of the Christian community offered a powerful alternative to the authoritarian church of Simon's youth. Simon quickly embraced Barth's insistence that the world could not stand on "autonomous laws" impermeable by the Christian message.[54]

Simon's early legal writings sought to apply Barth's ideas to the core problem of Protestant politics in West Germany: how Protestants could shape the political and legal order in a state where re-Christianization was frequently synonymous with Catholic visions of a West European *Abendland* (Occident). His 1952 Bonn dissertation, completed under Ulrich Scheuner, echoed Barth's polemic against "natural law" as both a theological construct and a political program.[55] Over the 1950s Simon would instead adopt the position of the Smend school. Railing against the "Catholicization of law," Simon celebrated the Constitutional Court rulings that overturned CDU-backed legislation on family law, confessional schools, and conscientious objection. For Simon, these decisions, alongside the Lüth judgment, had affirmed the values-driven character of the Basic Law, while defining these values broadly enough to accommodate the religious and ideological pluralism of West German society.[56] Against the backdrop of postwar confessional conflict as well as his own religious upbringing, Simon's equation of Protestantism with West German constitutional values becomes evident.

Bridging the worlds of Barthian theology and Rudolf Smend's values jurisprudence, Simon emerged as a moderating figure within the Church Brethren Societies. As a Düsseldorf law clerk during the mid-1950s, Simon joined the Protestant campaign for an expansive right of conscientious objection. He participated as a founding member of the Working Group of Church Brethren Societies during the antinuclear protests of 1958.[57] At the same time, Simon eschewed the rhetoric of resistance that increasingly permeated the Brethren Societies after the antinuclear movement's failure. Without going as far as to assert that the West German state had already fulfilled the democratic promise of the Basic Law—the position adopted by the drafters of the Godesberg platform, such as Adolf Arndt—Simon held out the expectation that the legal order remained perfectible through the engagement of the Protestant laity.[58] Simon thereby opened a path between reformist Social Democracy and pacifist neutralism.

Simon first positioned himself as a mediator within the Church Brethren Societies amid the fallout from Otto Dibelius's 1959 letter on the concept of political authority. The Heidelberg statement, issued by Karl Barth's followers in response to the controversy, called for strict neutrality in the conflict between East and West. Simon, however, contended that this declaration did not go far enough toward recognizing the political role that Protestants had already played in West German democracy. In September 1960 Simon served as the lead author of a rejoinder composed on behalf of the Baden Theological Society, a dissenting group within the Church Brethren Societies that adopted a more critical stance toward the GDR. The counterproposal concurred that

Christian politics should not be reduced to Cold War anti-Communism. However, "the assumption of co-responsibility for the state by Protestant Christians in the [Federal Republic of Germany] was and is with historical necessity connected to a decision against the Communist state form." The affirmation of "parliamentary, rule-of-law democracy" required a "calm and hate-free decision against a Communist state order."[59]

Simon advanced his defense of the democratic Rechtsstaat amid another public controversy that sparked debate about the relationship of the West German state to its Nazi precursor. On October 10, 1962, as the Bundestag prepared for its first reading of the emergency laws, West German police carried out a nighttime raid on the Hamburg office of the left liberal weekly *Der Spiegel* and arrested two editors. The move, ordered by CSU defense minister Franz Josef Strauss, retaliated against the magazine's report on a secret military simulation that had revealed the Federal Republic's unpreparedness for nuclear war. In a letter to the *Frankfurter Allgemeine Zeitung*, the conservative historian Gerhard Ritter, now retired from the University of Freiburg, chastised the "sensationalism" of *Der Spiegel* and defended restrictions on press freedom in the name of protecting the state: "Freedom of the press only makes sense insofar as there are still responsible editors."[60] By contrast, *Stimme der Gemeinde* spoke for many within the Church Brethren Societies, and the West German left more broadly, in describing the raid as a "crisis of political leadership that goes to the roots of our democracy." The *Spiegel* editors, the journal noted, had been charged under a treason statute dating to 1934, a portentous link between the Nazi state and things to come under emergency laws.[61]

In published commentaries and radio lectures reacting to the controversy, Simon pleaded for a moderating course. Although himself a critic of emergency laws as well as the *Spiegel* raid, Simon rejected the insinuation that the time for resistance had arrived. Instead Simon reframed the crisis as an opportunity to affirm the principles of constitutional democracy. To be sure, Simon held fast to the Protestant truism that no merely human order could be rendered sacred by the church. The Rechtsstaat was only a provisional good, the "relatively better, for which Christians decide both according to the measure of human insight and human capability, as well as on the basis of their convictions of belief."[62] Nevertheless, core features of the Rechtsstaat harmonized with Protestant ethics: its binding of power to law; its protection of a "dignified existence" and other fundamental rights; and its "respect for personal freedom as the foundation of community."[63] Protestants, Simon believed,

EMERGENCIES OF DEMOCRACY 251

should work toward the fulfillment of the Basic Law's ideals—not simply because Christians were called upon to take responsibility for political life, but because Christian moral teachings bore an affinity with the democratic Rechtsstaat. "The 'Yes' to a free, rule-of-law democracy," Simon admonished his DFU-supporting colleagues, "has not been sufficiently loud among us."[64]

Simon's effort to work out a Protestant theory of the Rechtsstaat shaped the next stage of the Brethren Societies' agenda. After threatening to resign from the Working Group of Church Brethren Societies, Simon reversed course, helping to organize the next conference of its leadership committee.[65] Set for January 1964 in the Hessian town of Friedrichsdorf, the meeting would take up "The Theological Problem of the Rechtsstaat," a significant departure from the previous year's theme, "The Limits of Obedience." Rather than interrogating the obligations of Christians when the state overstepped its authority, the conference would focus on the state Christians should strive to establish in the first place. Participants spanned the ideological spectrum, from the CDU-aligned jurist Ulrich Scheuner to the SPD politician Gustav Heinemann and DFU cofounder Herbert Mochalski.[66] For all their disagreements, a convergence among proponents of militant and neutralist democracy was made possible by a common tenet: Protestants shaped politics not by advancing partisan positions but by articulating shared values to guide the political community, above the divisions of class, ideology, and confession.

The keynote lectures at the Friedrichsdorf meeting laid out this agenda. The speakers, Ulrich Scheuner and the theologian Ernst Wolf, had been paired earlier at the 1949 Göttingen conference on "Church and Law." Reflecting the immediate context of the campaign against war crimes trials, that meeting had emphasized the gap between human law and divine justice. Fifteen years later, the two academics reached very different conclusions. Scheuner summarized the Smend school's conception of the "substantive Rechtsstaat" as an alternative to the positivist and authoritarian models of the German past. Carl Schmitt and his students were wrong to dismiss the Rechtsstaat as an "unpolitical realm of bourgeois security"; instead, the Rechtsstaat was animated by a political principle, "the preservation of personal freedom as the foundation of political freedom."[67] The Basic Law, Scheuner argued, had expanded, not subverted the Rechtsstaat principle by incorporating social as well as political rights.[68]

Ernst Wolf's lecture made explicit the theological background of these ideas, self-consciously moving beyond prior neutralist statements of the

252   REINVENTING PROTESTANT GERMANY

Church Brethren Societies. On the one hand, the West German Basic Law, unlike its Weimar precursor, acknowledged that basic rights preceded the state. The new constitution thereby aligned with the Christian recognition of God-given human dignity. On the other hand, the "substantive Rechtsstaat" defined the basic rights not simply as restrictions on state power but as shared values that bound together the citizenry. Although Christians could practice their faith under any political regime, they should prefer to live in a "democratic Rechtsstaat," which they could recognize as "the mature product of the Christian education of the Abendland."[69]

Of course, this new affirmation of the Basic Law reflected the political and economic stability of the mid-1960s. But the model of the Rechtsstaat touted at the Friedrichsdorf meeting also resulted from Protestants' active roles in shaping West German constitutional law. A report by Helmut Simon appended to the published conference volume centered the cases on which Protestant jurists had exerted direct influence. For Simon, both the restrictive and expansive elements of democracy belonged to the Basic Law's essence. Not only did the Federal Constitutional Court's bans of the SRP and the Communist party reflect the Rechtsstaat principle, but so too did the 1958 Lüth decision. Of particular importance was the court's 1960 decision extending the right of conscientious objection to military service, which secured both an individual right and a shared value of the political community.[70]

By bridging the SPD's concern for the Rechtsstaat with the Brethren Societies' emphasis on Christians' active political engagement, the Friedrichsdorf meeting helped heal the rift between the two groups. Gustav Heinemann, a key author of the Godesberg platform whose participation in the Church Brethren Societies had grown contentious, now drew upon the Friedrichsdorf lectures to advance his own vision of Social Democracy.[71] In a March 1965 address before a conference of SPD jurists, Heinemann spoke on "The Rechtsstaat as a Theological Problem," a theme that would have been unthinkable at a convention of Social Democrats a decade earlier. Promising his audience that he did not advocate for the imposition of Christian privileges in law, Heinemann instead invoked a Protestant genealogy of the West German constitution. Unlike their Catholic counterparts, Heinemann averred, Protestants did not believe that "God could be grasped in timeless norms of order or determinations of essences." Instead Protestants embraced the responsibility of interpreting divine commands for the concrete moment: "True obedience happens in the always novel dare to answer correctly the question of what God wants from us in the present situation."[72]

On its face, Heinemann's insistence upon a radically situational political ethics had little to do with the institutions and procedures of constitutional democracy. Yet Heinemann smoothed over the tension between theology and politics with a tool so often wielded in the postwar Protestant arsenal: a narrative of anti-Nazi resistance. The 1934 Barmen Declaration, according to Heinemann, marked a moment when Protestants abandoned their old ethics of "throne and altar" to recover the "higher justice" that limited state lawmaking. The Christian heritage of the Basic Law reflected this transformation: "Our democratic Rechtsstaat ... can be interpreted in a Christian manner not only in the fundamental rights, but also as a whole as the effort to achieve a good relationship between law and power, that is the mitigation of power through law and through civic responsibility for the benefit of the dignity of humanity." For Heinemann, responsible citizenship provided the mediating link between the Rechtsstaat and democracy, infusing the "mere formal system of legal technicalities" with a moral basis rooted in a shared Christian culture.[73]

Heinemann's address reflected a new consensus within the Working Group of Church Brethren Societies. Wolf, Simon, Heinemann, Heinz Kloppenburg, and others connected to the association defined the Federal Republic not as an unquestionable fact or a precursor to a reunited Germany but as a state rooted in a distinctive value system.[74] Without engaging in polemical anti-Communism, they laid out a Protestant case for defending, not merely accepting, the Rechtsstaat. These Protestant intellectuals celebrated the state's guarantees of pluralism and religious freedom, while Ernst Wolf went so far as to invoke a shared Christian Abendland that transcended confessional divisions.[75] Still, the Church Brethren Societies remained deeply embedded in Protestant discussions. Their insistence upon confessional distinctions, polemics against "Catholic" jurisprudence, and debt to the legal theories of Rudolf Smend made plain their association of the "substantive Rechtsstaat" with Protestant virtues.

If two decades of Protestant political engagement shaped the theology of the Rechtsstaat advanced at Friedrichsdorf, the new theology informed the resurgent campaign against emergency laws that followed the federal election of September 1965. The election left in power the CDU-FDP coalition under Konrad Adenauer's successor, the Protestant economist Ludwig Erhard, but gave the SPD an unprecedented 39 percent of the vote. Keen to end their tenure as a perpetual opposition party, Social Democratic leaders entered negotiations over emergency laws, a "price" for their party's eventual admission into government.[76] The Church Brethren Societies, while remaining opposed to any version of emergency laws, now anchored their criticisms in an explicit defense of constitutional democracy. When East Germany revealed covert plans by the West German Interior Ministry for an emergency civil service law—even after its rejection by the Bundestag—over 900 Protestant pastors and church officials signed an open letter to all members of parliament. One of the first such missives to follow the 1965 election, the petition framed emergency laws as a piece of Erhard's program for undermining the "democratic-pluralist order of the Federal Republic."[77] Heinrich Hannover subsequently filed a lawsuit with the Federal Constitutional Court alleging that civil defense laws passed by the new government violated the Basic Law's prohibition of forced labor and guarantee of occupational freedom.[78]

At a time when the institutional churches faced mounting challenges to their authority, and more potently the threat of disengagement from the wider society, the emphasis on democratic rights—rather than church privileges or the dangers of secularism—enabled Protestant intellectuals to speak beyond their milieu. Protestants were key participants at the Congress on the Emergency of Democracy, a mass meeting planned during the summer of 1966 to coincide with the Interior Ministry's release of a new round of the proposed amendments. Helmut Gollwitzer, Heinz Kloppenburg, Martin Niemöller, and Ernst Wolf served on the organizing committee alongside some of West Germany's most prominent left-wing and liberal intellectuals, including the jurists Wolfgang Abendroth and Jürgen Seifert, philosopher Ernst Bloch, and political scientist Karl Dietrich Bracher.[79] Writing privately to pastors they hoped to recruit to the organizing committee, congress chairs Helmut Ridder and Heinz Maus echoed the language of the Smend school, counterposing the written law against the higher values underpinning the "democratic constitutional order."[80] Certainly Protestant pastors and lay intellectuals were not the sole group behind the Congress on the Emergency of Democracy. In addition to several hundred church employees, attendees included academics, students, trade unionists, and others with slim or no connection to organized Protestantism.[81] But precisely for that reason, the congress gave dissenting pastors a wider platform to share their ideas.

Held at the University of Frankfurt on October 30, 1966, the Congress on the Emergency of Democracy drew more than 8,000 participants from across the Federal Republic. Three times that number gathered for the day's final rally.[82] Although no session focused directly on religion, tropes of the

Protestant opposition to emergency laws echoed throughout the conference. At the session "Freedom of Conscience and the Right of Resistance," the Kiel jurist Ekkehart Stein noted that no fixed principle regulated the relationship between individual conscience and the dictates of law. Nevertheless, "resistance" became a legitimate possibility in defense of the constitution's core values, and might become necessary against an "abuse of emergency powers."[83] A union representative spoke up to note that organized labor would always support a "right of political strike in defense of a rule-of-law democracy," while another participant proposed "civil disobedience" as an underutilized political strategy in West Germany.[84] The day after the conference, the Working Group on Church and Democracy, formed by signatories of the previous spring's open letter, marched on Bonn under the slogan "The Church Takes Responsibility for Democracy." Speakers—including Helmut Gollwitzer, the left-wing jurist Helmut Ridder, and the former Confessing Church pastor Walter Kreck—criticized the EKD's failure to speak out against emergency laws, which they ascribed to their confession's long tradition of subordinating the individual to political authority.[85]

This was the language not of militant democracy that viewed extraparliamentary activism as a threat, but of a democratic Rechtsstaat that permitted expansive possibilities for political protest. To be sure, the Congress on the Emergency of Democracy expanded the concept of democracy beyond the written constitution to incorporate a right of disobedience in defense of higher democratic values. Not law and the state but the active citizenry served as democracy's ultimate guardian. This distinction would appear untenable to "militant" democrats who believed that democratic ideals had already been actualized through the laws and institutions of the Federal Republic. But the older generation that spearheaded the campaign against emergency laws, including many active Protestants, no longer voiced doubt that West Germans should adopt a principled democratic stance.

The Student Movement and the Ends of Resistance

Through the mid-1960s, the Protestant discussion of emergency laws remained dominated by intellectuals born around the turn of the twentieth century, with several participants, including Heinrich Hannover, Renate Riemeck, and Helmut Simon, from the cohort born in the 1920s. In the decade's second half, however, the debate became far more volatile as student protesters across the Federal Republic took up the fight against emergency laws as a central cause—alongside the Vietnam War and university reform. The West German student movement belonged to a moment of generational rupture across Western Europe and the United States fueled by transnational and transatlantic alliances.[86] Yet historians have tempered a simplistic picture of conflict between youth raised amid postwar prosperity and parents hardened by Depression, fascism, and war. Instead intergenerational dialogue formed a motor of the 1960s student movement, in West Germany and beyond.[87]

This is equally true of the student movement's presence within, and impact on, the German Protestant churches. Certainly many West German students, like their counterparts abroad, decried the Protestant and Catholic churches as bastions of regressive politics, in particular on matters of sex.[88] But students did not simply challenge the Protestant public sphere; they also participated in it, and in turn altered the terms of its debate about democracy. Protestant students played an underappreciated role in West German student organizing. The movement's figurehead, Rudi Dutschke, had come of age in East Germany's embattled Protestant youth organizations, while the extra-parliamentary activist and future left-wing terrorist Ulrike Meinhof was the foster daughter of DFU party chair Renate Riemeck. Older pastors and lay intellectuals who entered into dialogue with the students eschewed apologias for either East German Communism or revolutionary violence. Instead they sought to orient student radicals toward the democratic and social Rechtsstaat that had emerged out of their own political discussions. For their part, Protestant detractors of student protests criticized the students as enemies not of Christianity—the earlier strategy of Protestant conservatives confronting left-wing, secularist movements—but of democracy.

Ground zero of the student movement in general, and of Protestant student organizing in particular, was the Free University in West Berlin. Located in the suburban Dahlem neighborhood where Martin Niemöller's splinter wing of the Confessing Church had challenged the accommodationist mainstream, the Free University was founded in 1948 as a paragon of liberal education on the doorstep of the Communist world. Several factors accounted for its uniqueness. The university's "Berlin Model" of governance allowed elected student assemblies unprecedented input into administrative decisions. This structure was intended by postwar education reformers to foster liberal democratic sensibilities, and in practice it would aid the students who revolted against the "system" altogether. Given the city's status as the front line of the Cold War, political events in Berlin could command wider international attention than those elsewhere in Germany.[89] Moreover, West Berlin became a haven for conscientious objectors, as residents of the divided city were exempt from West German military conscription.[90]

The Free University's Protestant theology faculty was also unusually politically engaged. The former Confessing Church pastor and anti-rearmament activist Helmut Gollwitzer moved to the Free University from the conservative University of Bonn in 1957. His seminar became a testing ground for radical ideas about Christian politics, and served as a bridge between the student movement and the comparatively progressive West Berlin church administration.[91] Gollwitzer mentored a number of students active in the protest movement, including the sociology graduate student Rudi Dutschke, who rose to national fame as the leader of the Socialist German Student League (SDS) during the mid-1960s.[92] The young pastors who advised the Free University's Protestant Student Community, a group that included only 1 percent of the student body but played an outsize role in student protests, equally aligned themselves with left-wing politics.[93]

A close examination of the events at the Free University illustrates how Protestant students, as well as the older generation of theologians and lay intellectuals, sought to enact competing visions of West German democracy. The first controversy that drew in Protestant faculty members and the Protestant Student Community centered on liberal values of free expression and procedural fairness. In May 1965 university administrators banned the journalist Erich Kuby from speaking at a panel discussion due to his critique of the Free University's Cold War politicization several years prior. The next month the political science lecturer Ekkehart Krippendorff was denied renewal of his contract after publishing an article critical of the rector's handling of the Kuby affair. Both decisions flew in the face of the "Berlin Model" and drew the quick condemnation of the student assembly. Conservative faculty members, including the ex-Nazi Protestant jurist Karl August Bettermann, defended the university's position. But Bettermann was not representative of all faculty active in the Protestant public sphere. Confessing Church veterans, including Helmut Gollwitzer and the political scientist Otto Heinrich von der Gablentz, criticized the speaking bans as symptomatic of a broader "democratic deficit in West Germany and the university."[94] For the first time, the university's Protestant Student Community signed on to leaflets criticizing the administration.[95]

Events at the Free University quickly moved beyond debates about academic freedom. The year 1966 saw Rudi Dutschke cement his place as the leader of the SDS amid an upsurge of activism against the Vietnam War. The son of an East German civil servant, Dutschke had arrived in West Berlin in August 1961 as a conscientious objector from the East German National People's Army. Dutschke enrolled at the Free University shortly afterward, seeking to bridge the vision of social justice nurtured in the Protestant youth movement with the revolutionary theory he learned from Marxist luminaries Ernst Bloch, Richard Löwenthal, and Herbert Marcuse. Although the SDS had adopted an extra-parliamentary stance since its involvement in antinuclear protests of the late 1950s, Dutschke spearheaded a more aggressive strategy of direct action modeled on his experience in the militant group Subversive Action.[96] Most significant, Dutschke and his cohort moved the focus of the SDS from issues of university governance to international events, above all the Vietnam War.[97] In their first major protest against the war, Dutschke and his fellow SDS leader Bernd Rabehl orchestrated the plastering of posters across West Berlin that denounced Chancellor Erhard for "Murder through Napalm Bombs!" By the spring of 1967 the SDS had begun raising funds for arming the Communist Viet Cong, likening US-backed South Vietnam to Nazi Germany.[98]

Antiwar protest radicalized the students' interpretations of domestic events. On December 1, 1966, the CDU and SPD announced the formation of a Grand Coalition government and quickly resumed negotiations over emergency laws. The move, which left only the liberal FDP in opposition, was denounced by students as a step toward renewed fascism—an accusation magnified by the appointment of Kurt Georg Kiesinger, a former Nazi propaganda official, as chancellor.[99] Dutschke now christened the loose coalition of activists to the left of the SPD as an "Extra-Parliamentary Opposition," a term that stuck in the coming years.[100]

Veterans of the Nazi-era church conflict divided in response to the radicalization of the students' rhetoric and tactics. Through participation in the international ecumenical movement, which increasingly focused on the problems of decolonization, the older generation of Protestant intellectuals had become aware of demands for economic justice within the emergent postcolonial world. But for many, ecumenical engagement reaffirmed the West German Rechtsstaat as an exemplar of democratic development. In July 1966 the World Council of Churches convened the World Conference on Church and Society in Geneva, where participants from Latin America, Asia, and Africa outnumbered those from the ecumenical movement's traditional European and North American strongholds. In a widely discussed plenary

EMERGENCIES OF DEMOCRACY   259

lecture, the American theologian Richard Shaull called upon Western churches to address the rapid political transformations in postcolonial countries, refusing to rule out violence as a strategy of the revolution "necessary for the humanization of modern society."[101] West German attendees, who included Helmut Gollwitzer, Eberhard Müller, Ludwig Raiser, Hansjürg Ranke, Helmut Simon, and Heinz-Dietrich Wendland, widely rejected such calls for revolutionary violence.[102] Instead they looked toward the Federal Republic as an alternative model of social transformation. Simon participated in a working group at Geneva on law and the state, which concluded that law itself served as a medium of encoding Christian values in political institutions. Rather than promoting revolution, Christians should "press in their own societies for effective implementation of internationally accepted standards of human rights through constitutional provisions, laws, and administration."[103] Such formulations evoked Protestant narratives of the role their confession had played in West German democratization.

Not all West German participants at the WCC conference were content to laud the Rechtsstaat and human rights. Helmut Gollwitzer pursued an active dialogue with the student movement and embraced its goal of social transformation. A long-standing participant in Christian–Marxist dialogue as well as the ecumenical movement, by the late 1960s Gollwitzer had become convinced that the message of gospel obliged Christians to pursue the Marxian vision of a classless society.[104] EKD Council chair Kurt Scharf also sought to foster exchange with student protesters after being elected bishop of Berlin-Brandenburg in 1966, succeeding Otto Dibelius.[105] Although Scharf did not subscribe to Gollwitzer's socialism, he had long resisted doctrinaire anti-Communism as a proponent of East–West dialogue who oversaw the writing of the Eastern Memorandum. These mediators viewed West German democracy less as a set of fixed institutions to be upheld as a global model than a work in progress to which the students could offer fundamental contributions.

The watershed events of June 2, 1967, provided the impetus for Scharf and Gollwitzer to put their vision of dialogue into practice. That evening, during a mass demonstration against a visit by the shah of Iran to West Berlin, a police officer shot and killed Benno Ohnesorg, a twenty-six-year-old graduate student active in the Free University's Protestant Student Community. The killing transformed the little-known Ohnesorg into a martyr for the extraparliamentary cause and led to a sharp radicalization of the student movement. Over the following months, sit-ins, marches, and demonstrations erupted in

Figure 7.1. Helmut Gollwitzer addressing a student assembly in the Auditorium Maximum of West Berlin's Free University, May 5, 1967. Photo by Konrad Giehr/dpa/picture alliance via Getty Images

every major West German city, spurring heightened debate about resistance and the legitimate use of violence.[106] Kurt Scharf positioned himself as a mediator between the students, police, and city authorities. In a public statement released four days after Ohnesorg's death, the bishop offered church rooms as spaces of dialogue that would "bring all together, who in their different perspectives and responsibilities depend upon one another."[107] Speaking at Ohnesorg's burial service and on television the following week, Helmut Gollwitzer similarly defended the students' freedom of expression and called for reconciliation between students and authorities.[108]

Tensions within West Berlin's Protestant community flared when the protest movement entered the church itself. On the evening of June 20, a group of approximately one hundred students led by Rudi Dutschke streamed into the Neu-Westend Church of Berlin-Charlottenburg to stage a hunger strike

EMERGENCIES OF DEMOCRACY   261

in protest of the imprisonment of Fritz Teufel. The leader of West Berlin's notorious Kommune I, Teufel had been charged with "incitement to arson" after publishing a leaflet that described a deadly department store fire in Brussels as the first time Europeans had felt "the crackling feeling of Vietnam that we have thus far missed in Berlin. When will the Berlin department stores burn?"[109] Contrary to the later accusations of angered congregants, Scharf and the congregation's pastor, Manfred Engelbrecht, had not invited the students into the Neu-Westend Church. Students meeting the prior evening at West Berlin's Technical University had announced the hunger strike even though parish leaders had not yet replied to their request to use the church rooms. Nevertheless, when students began arriving late the following afternoon, Scharf and Engelbrecht refused to call the police. Instead they invited the protesters to engage in dialogue with local pastors, ultimately convincing the students to move the strike to a Dahlem dormitory the next morning. For Scharf and Engelbrecht—himself a former student of Karl Barth and Hans Joachim Iwand—the Protestant Church served as a site not of partisanship but of reconciliation. As Scharf wrote to his critics in the Neu-Westend community, the students' concerns for social injustice were sincerely held and should be engaged by the church, lest the isolation of the most radical wing lead to further escalation.[110]

Scharf's mediation efforts continued in attempts to negotiate with West Berlin authorities on the students' behalf. Convinced that the release of Fritz Teufel would quell the rising tensions, Scharf offered to provide the imprisoned radical with church-sponsored housing in exchange for the city dropping the additional charges of squatting and trespassing. West Berlin's attorney general agreed to the solution, as did Teufel himself, though it was turned down by the other members of Kommune I.[111] Meanwhile, Scharf appealed to the West Berlin mayor, the fifty-two-year-old Social Democrat and ordained Protestant pastor Heinrich Albertz. Scharf and Albertz had known each other since their days in the Confessing Church, and the bishop, thirteen years the mayor's senior, helped move Albertz toward a moderating stance. Whereas Albertz had initially backed the police following the June 2 protests, denouncing the "extremist minority" that threatened the "free democratic order," he would soon lift a temporary ban on public demonstrations. By September the mayor issued an impassioned plea for mutual understanding. The students, he argued before an SPD conference, had rightly grown to mistrust "a population ... that thinks in the categories of the early 1950s," categories that "no longer correspond to reality." According to Albertz's biographer, his meetings with Scharf brought the mayor back to his pastoral vocation, helping Albertz to recognize the dangers of a "front city" mentality.[112]

This message was not sufficient to quell the divided city's tensions. On September 26, Heinrich Albertz resigned as mayor of West Berlin, caught between students who continued to blame him for Benno Ohnesorg's death and the right wing of his own party incensed over his loss of control.[113] But as tensions deepened within West Berlin's Protestant community, church leaders continued to seek out modes of reconciliation and refused to condemn the students' actions. When student protesters against the Vietnam War disrupted worship services at the Kaiser Wilhelm Memorial Church on Christmas Eve 1967 and again on New Year's Eve, West Berlin church authorities distanced themselves from the outcry among lay congregants, who compared the students to the Nazi stormtroopers in letters that poured into Kurt Scharf's office.[114] In a statement released following the New Year's Eve protest, church administrators clarified their opposition to demonstrations during church services but noted the "many possibilities for conversation" within the Christian community.[115] Scharf went a step further in an interview with the *Berliner Abendscheu,* calling on pastors to speak with even the most radical wing of the student groups.[116] Writing for the Dahlemite journal *Junge Kirche,* Helmut Gollwitzer criticized bias in the media's coverage of the demonstrations, as well as attempts by the council of the Kaiser Wilhelm Memorial Church to bury Scharf's call for dialogue.[117]

Yet the language of Confessing Church veterans did not match that of student radicals themselves. Increasingly, Protestant Student Communities throughout West Germany presented confrontation rather than dialogue as the essence of Christian politics, criticizing not only conservative parishioners but also the mediation efforts of church leaders. Instead students demanded direct action to expose structures of power and injustice. A letter to the parish community of the Kaiser Wilhelm Memorial Church by an organizer of the Christmas Eve demonstration summed up the student perspective: "Dear Protestants, you have forgotten how to protest against your clerics, you have forgotten to hate your friends and love your enemies. You have shat on Christ in order not to shut out the church, but you should have shut out the church in order not to shut out Christ."[118]

Conflict between protesters and sympathetic church authorities continued during the International Vietnam Congress, a gathering of 5,000 student activists from Western Europe and beyond held at West Berlin's Technical University in February 1968. When the West Berlin Senate refused to grant the SDS organizers a permit to march along the fashionable Kurfürstendamm, Kurt Scharf offered to open church services on the morning of the planned Sunday demonstration to students wishing to pray for "peace in Vietnam."[119] After the demonstration went ahead regardless, the West Berlin Protestant leadership could only issue a statement thanking the protesters for remaining peaceful.[120] This reaction exemplified the dialectic that had come to characterize the relationship between student demonstrators and their Protestant elders. The Confessing Church generation sought to defend the students through the language of nonviolence—clashing with the ambitions of the students themselves, especially the revolutionary rhetoric of the SDS. Scharf and his colleagues were in a reactive mode, not in control of events. In turn, members of the older generation found themselves cornered into positions they could not support.

Ironically, such tensions allowed Protestant conservatives to present themselves as stalwarts of democracy. The Hamburg theologian Helmut Thielicke, long a vocal defender of West German foreign policy, became the public face of the conservative Protestant response to the student protests. After facing regular SDS-backed demonstrations at his monthly Saturday evening sermons at the St. Michael's Church, Thielicke invited a group of Hamburg-based military officers to provide security at his sermon of January 13, 1968, days after the disruptions at the Kaiser Wilhelm Memorial Church. Fifty officers positioned themselves throughout the church, while several hundred students demanded that Thielicke engage in a discussion of the Vietnam War at the conclusion of the service. Thielicke first offered to meet with the students at the parish hall the following Monday. When protesters demanded that the exchange occur during worship services, Thielicke quickly revoked the offer, claiming that he had "no partners capable of discussion."[121]

During the ensuing controversy, reported in the pages of *Der Spiegel*, Thielicke took up the mantle of dialogue and reasonableness against students unprepared for democratic debate. In a statement for the EKD's press service, the conservative theologian argued that Christian students seeking dialogue had been outmaneuvered by SDS radicals whose only aim was to create chaos.[122] Thielicke's counterparts were less discreet. Echoing the conservative press, the new Lutheran bishop of Hamburg, Hans-Otto Wölber, compared student "terror" to that of the Nazis.[123] Such statements conveniently neglected the symbolism of uniformed military officers surrounding the church, but illustrated the equal purchase of democratic rhetoric on the conservative side.

Student protests in West Berlin reached a climax with the events of April 11, 1968. That afternoon Rudi Dutschke was shot three times in the head upon exiting his apartment on the Kurfürstendamm. His assailant was an anti-Communist worker inspired by the assassination of Martin Luther King several days prior. The nearly fatal attack inflamed tensions in the city. Within hours after the shooting, students occupied the Technical University's Auditorium Maximum. Later that evening, more than 5,000 students marched to the offices of the Springer press, the publisher of the right-wing *Bild-Zeitung* that for months had vilified the protests. Demonstrators shattered the glass entrance and set Springer cars on fire. A discussion at the Auditorium Maximum the next day concluded that whereas violence against persons should be deployed only during emergencies, in defense of self or others, the destruction of property, including the infrastructure of the Springer press, was a legitimate response to state violence.[124] Over the following days, students in cities throughout West Germany constructed barricades to disrupt Springer deliveries and set fire to Springer vehicles, in demonstrations that left two dead and hundreds injured. Police responded violently with water cannons and rubber truncheons, ultimately making nearly 400 arrests in West Berlin alone.[125]

This time disagreements between West Berlin students and their Confessing Church interlocutors were aired more openly. Shortly after midnight on April 14, Kurt Scharf and Helmut Gollwitzer addressed 2,000 students who had gathered in the Technical University's Auditorium Maximum to press for "further actions." Scharf drew whistles and boos from the crowd when he spoke out against the use of violence, even in the face of "police measures" against demonstrators.[126] Gollwitzer did not go quite as far, rejecting violence against persons while defending violence against property insofar as this could be "rationally justified." But Gollwitzer also expressed frustration with the demonstrators' use of violence, calling on the Extra-Parliamentary Opposition to move beyond protest to "put forward suggestions on how a 'democratic society' could be organized."[127]

In response to backlash from West Berlin politicians, Gollwitzer attempted to retreat. In a letter to the *Tagesspiegel*, he claimed that he had hardly "endorsed" the "riots" of the previous days. Those who condemned violence against property only had a leg to stand on if they also spoke out against "mass crimes of inhumanity" in the postcolonial world.[128] Even as Gollwitzer sought to translate the demonstrations for West Berlin's political elite, his nuanced position was hardly shared by student radicals themselves. Amid the April demonstrations, the Free University's Protestant Student Community released a solidarity statement, which concluded, "As long as the responsible [authorities] will not 'risk' a public discussion with the [Extra-Parliamentary Opposition], we see no possibility to oblige the members of the [Extra-Parliamentary Opposition] to the principle of nonviolence." Criticizing the ongoing demonstrations on the grounds of "Christian belief" would only play into the hands of those responsible for atrocity in Vietnam.[129]

The debate about nonviolence now split Protestants between detractors of extra-parliamentary protest, critical interlocutors of the student movement, and the demonstrating students themselves. These divides permeated the final conflict over emergency laws that culminated in May 1968. In March a new round of debate opened in the Bundestag, the first since the SPD's entry into government. The revised legislation made significant concessions to Social Democrats: a parliamentary "joint committee" would represent the Bundestag in an emergency, and guarantees of the right to strike and freedom of assembly would be preserved.[130] Gustav Heinemann, serving as justice minister in the Grand Coalition government, now defended emergency laws before the Bundestag as a bulwark of democracy in emergency situations.[131] The Church Brethren Societies, for their part, continued to reject emergency laws while remaining committed to nonviolence. Along with West Germany's Protestant Student Communities, they formed a strong presence at the culminating event of the Committee on the Emergency of Democracy, a peaceful demonstration on May 11 that drew at least 60,000 participants to the West German capital of Bonn.[132]

The radical wing of the student demonstrators sought a more confrontational approach. During the final week of May, students staged strikes and occupations at universities across the country, railing against the transformation of "formal democracy into a state of totalitarian class rule."[133] For student radicals, the measures promoted by the Committee on the Emergency of Democracy—marches, moments of silence at work, and signature campaigns—appeared tame.[134] By occupying physical space instead, students sought to expose the underlying violence of West German institutions, with the hope of generating a systemic crisis as the precursor to revolutionary transformation.[135]

This was not the view held by the older Protestant generation. Even for its farthest-left members, the achievements of the West German Rechtsstaat marked a sharp difference from postcolonial countries, where revolutionary violence remained a legitimate option. During the Bundestag's final reading of the emergency laws, Helmut Gollwitzer returned to the theme that had guided the Protestant discussion of the Rechtsstaat: the values undergirding the Basic Law. In a "funeral oration for the Basic Law" read over Hessian radio

Figure 7.2. Protestant pastors walk in a protest march against emergency laws. Photo by Klaus Rose / picture alliance via Getty Images

on May 28, Gollwitzer warned of the Basic Law's replacement by a new "emergency constitution." Emergency laws, Gollwitzer argued, conflicted fundamentally with the goal of the Basic Law: to bring the German people "into a process of democratization ... and to prepare for emergency situations such that the cooperation of citizens conscious of their rights and freedoms, and therefore democracy, has a chance to prove itself." Echoing the 1964 conference of the Church Brethren Societies, Gollwitzer told a story of his confession's emerging democratic consciousness. German Protestants had finally overcome their "all too long authoritarian tradition" to uphold a "society of free, mature citizens, who are guided by the form of their institutions and are put in the position to become the designers of their common life."[136] Gollwitzer's vision of democracy emphasized the safeguarding of individual autonomy and dignity, values threatened with the introduction of emergency powers. His language remained that of constitutionalism and the rule of law, undergirded by Christian values, not a call for violent revolution.

As it turned out, no such destruction of the constitutional order occurred. The Bundestag passed the emergency laws on May 30, with only the FDP remaining in opposition. The amendments have never been in-

EMERGENCIES OF DEMOCRACY   267

voked in the decades since, remaining a relic of Cold War fears of nuclear attack. But the campaign against emergency laws, including its Protestant wing, was not without impact. The concessions that the SPD negotiated for its support of the amendments were in large part the product of activism by West Germany's unions and their allies in the Extra-Parliamentary Opposition. Moreover, the Protestant controversy around emergency laws engendered a rethinking of civil disobedience and resistance on both sides of the debate. For Protestant members of the extra-parliamentary left, the category of resistance took on meaning beyond the narrative of elite opposition to National Socialism that had been dominant during the early postwar years. Theologians such as Helmut Gollwitzer, Heinz Kloppenburg, and Kurt Scharf, as well as their lay allies, including Wolfgang Abendroth, Helmut Ridder, and Helmut Simon, moderated the demands of more radical student activists by framing the concept of resistance in terms of not the overthrow but the buttressing of constitutional democracy.

Even Protestant SPD parliamentarians moved toward this understanding of resistance. In the final stages of negotiation over emergency laws, Social Democrats won an important concession that addressed concerns of the Extra-Parliamentary Opposition: the incorporation of a constitutional right of resistance against breaches of democracy. Adopted by the Bundestag alongside the passage of emergency laws, the new clause read, "All Germans shall have the right to resist any person seeking to abolish this constitutional order, if no other remedy is available." Its placement in Article 20 of the Basic Law, one of two articles whose "principles" could not be amended, made the right of resistance a pillar of West Germany's "democratic and social federal state."[137] Adolf Arndt himself participated in the commission that formulated the amendment, drawing on a Protestant tradition of constitutional thought.[138] Against the view that the right of resistance pertained solely to natural law, Arndt insisted that the underlying values of West German democracy be made manifest in the constitution itself. As Arndt put the point to one of his SPD colleagues, constitutional law was "the art of completeness."[139] Even the post-Godesberg SPD concurred that resistance, under extreme circumstances, became the final means of preserving democracy.

From Resistance to Protest: Legacies of the Protestant 1968

The coalition that opposed emergency laws, which was already under strain during the spring 1968 protests, would not survive the legislation's passage. With Dutschke sidelined following the assassination attempt, and the aim

268   REINVENTING PROTESTANT GERMANY

of forestalling emergency laws scuttled, more radical currents of the Extra-Parliamentary Opposition rose to the fore. In the weeks following the legislation's enactment, occupations of campus buildings dissipated and regular administration resumed. Adrift with the loss of its leader, the SDS crumbled into competing factions by the beginning of 1969 and dissolved the following year.[140]

At the same time, a radical minority called for moving beyond the distinction between violence against persons and violence against property, the final guardrail of the student movement. This demand received its most influential articulation by Ulrike Meinhof, whose May 1968 manifesto, "From Protest to Resistance," called on the Extra-Parliamentary Opposition to embrace "counterviolence" against police repression.[141] Meinhof had strong connections to the left-wing Protestant milieu. She had been adopted by Renate Riemeck following the early death of her mother, a close friend of Riemeck's since their student days, and wrote for *Stimme der Gemeinde* as a young journalist.[142] In 1970 Meinhof cofounded the Red Army Faction (RAF) with the Communist militant Andreas Baader, becoming the figurehead of the notorious terrorist organization that carried out deadly attacks on business leaders and politicians through the mid-1970s. Meinhof was not the only RAF member with a Protestant background. Baader's partner, Gudrun Ensslin, was the daughter of a Confessing Church pastor who had been active in Protestant youth organizations before her radicalization in the Extra-Parliamentary Opposition.[143] The RAF drew the consternation of erstwhile Protestant sympathizers of student protests such as Helmut Gollwitzer, Gustav Heinemann, Renate Riemeck, and Kurt Scharf, who simultaneously warned against an overreaching state response.[144]

While a minority made the shift to physical violence, a larger strand of the Protestant student movement responded to political defeat by retreating from legislative demands, instead seeking to bring the antiauthoritarian spirit of the protests into the church itself. In late 1968 a group of sixty radical theologians close to the SDS, including several members of the Free University's Protestant Student Community, formed a "conference on critical theology" that recast the message of gospel as intimately tied to struggles against capitalism and colonialism.[145] In Cologne the Political Night Prayer led by the theologian Dorothee Sölle held weekly services from 1968 to 1972 that integrated worship with political discussions on topics ranging from the Vietnam War to South African Apartheid. Both organizations drew inspira-

EMERGENCIES OF DEMOCRACY 269

tion from the July 1968 conference of the World Council of Churches in Uppsala, Sweden, where the global economic divide of North and South again took center stage. By the 1970s, critical theological movements promoted deeper knowledge of the postcolonial world within the German Protestant churches, looking beyond the East–West divide that had preoccupied Confessing Church veterans.[146]

Within the older cohort that came of age during the Weimar Republic and Third Reich, these new theological currents, not only student violence, remained controversial. The basic question posed by the Protestant student movement went to the heart of this generation's debates: Was the church restricted to the proclamation of gospel and the saving of souls, or did it bear responsibility for the direction of the wider society—the "political social work [*politische Diakonie*]" espoused by some student pastors?[147] Both wings of the postwar EKD had moved beyond a traditional doctrine of the two kingdoms that delineated a strict separation of the Christian mission and worldly affairs. But equally significant, members of the older generation widely insisted that the church remain a source of shared values rooted in gospel, rather than a servant of partisan politics.

Even though the Church Brethren Societies had viewed nuclear weapons as an existential matter that transcended partisan divisions, calls for the church to take a stance on the Vietnam War or postcolonial liberation movements were a bridge too far even for many veterans of the Confessing Church Dahlemites. The student protests therefore created strange bedfellows. In March 1966 the conservative theologian Walter Künneth served as the keynote speaker at the inaugural assembly of the "No Other Gospel" movement, which opposed the new political theology and called for a return to the church's biblical foundation. Prominent Dahlemites also criticized what they viewed as syncretic attempts to bring politics into the church. Joachim Beckmann, the longtime president of the Rhineland Church Brethren Society, went as far as to compare the Political Night Prayer to the Nazi-era German Christians. Local branches of the "No Other Gospel" movement gained a strong presence in the Reformed and United, not only Lutheran regional churches.[148]

Efforts to bridge these divisions following the height of the student protests quickly collapsed. A special synod convened by the West Berlin Protestant church in June 1968 failed to reach consensus on the issue of "political social work." The synod's concluding resolution determined that while Christians took a legitimate interest in political matters, the content of gospel could not be replaced with a "political-social program"—a compromise that left nobody satisfied.[149] The West German section of the EKD synod, which convened in West Berlin in October 1968, found itself similarly divided. In a controversial plenary lecture, Helmut Gollwitzer now invoked the experience of the Confessing Church to justify his embrace of religious socialism, a move beyond even the more radical currents of the Church Brethren Societies over the previous two decades. The Barmen Declaration demonstrated that the service of the church extended to "all domains of life"; Dietrich Bonhoeffer had shown how to "translate the religious, the Christian, into the political," a model taken up by Protestant students. In an era of postcolonial transformation, Gollwitzer argued, developing nations similarly required the revolutionary message of Christianity to overcome unjust structures.[150] Helmut Thielicke and Hamburg bishop Hans-Otto Wölber spoke for the synod's majority in presenting the counterpoint. The gospel's injunction to stand with the downtrodden, the conservatives argued, did not justify partisan posturing. Taking sides on controversial political issues would extend the church beyond its domain of expertise and alienate parishioners who disagreed with its stance.[151]

But if certain matters remained up for debate in the late 1960s—notably, which issues counted as "partisan"—the older generation's commitment to a democracy guided by Protestant values was not. Helmut Gollwitzer sharply criticized SDS violence amid new protests in the fall of 1968.[152] His synod address concurred that the church could not become the mere arm of a political party or ideology.[153] For his part, Hans-Otto Wölber insisted that the church's nonpartisanship did not mean neutrality toward social problems. Instead the church served as a source of reconciliation across social divisions.[154]

More pointedly, prominent lay intellectuals drew on the model of the democratic Rechtsstaat to move beyond the binaries of praise and condemnation of the student movement. The jurist Ludwig Raiser, who served briefly as rector of the University of Tübingen at the height of the student protests, was an ardent supporter of emergency laws.[155] Nevertheless, in an August 1968 statement drafted on behalf of the EKD's Commission on Public Responsibility, Raiser expressed sympathy for student demonstrators. Although revolutionary violence could not be justified against the Federal Republic—"a state that may perhaps have deficiencies but is committed to [the rule of] law"—the protests had aired legitimate grievances that demanded "reform" rather than mere "calls for peace and order."[156] Helmut Simon, now a judge on the Federal Court of Justice, shared this assessment in a January 1969 lecture before the Association of Protestant Academics in Berlin. Nonviolent demonstrations, Simon contended, opened opportunities for the critique and improvement of the political order in democratic states. As steps toward the strengthening of constitutional democracy, Simon called for the extension of amnesty to participants in nonviolent civil disobedience as well as the liberalization of West Germany's laws on political demonstration, which dated to the 1870s.[157]

When the EKD Council declined to publish the full version of Raiser's statement, a meeting of the national-level Association of Protestant Academics in Germany addressed the student protests in the spring of 1969.[158] The resulting resolution echoed Simon's call for amnesty, as well as Raiser's plea for intergenerational understanding. The Protestant academics ascribed student radicalism not to antidemocratic animus but to the fact that the students had not experienced the rupture of 1945 and "all that has been achieved in twenty years." Engaging with the students was "uncomfortable," but could ultimately lead to the "renewal of the institutions of parliamentary democracy." These institutions' openness to reform was a hallmark of democracy itself:

> This state is imperfect. We are all to blame for the fact that democracy has not been taken as seriously as it should have been. But the Basic Law offers an opportunity for everyone who wants to take it seriously. It is worth fighting for the Basic Law. We understand the resignation of those who, after endless fruitless attempts to achieve reform through democratic means, believe that the inconclusiveness of their efforts is due to the "system." We understand it, but we don't believe it. We are sure that our own past failures are to blame. But that can be changed![159]

This concluding call summarized a shared narrative of West German democratization developed within the Protestant public sphere over the 1960s. Across a broad political spectrum, Protestant intellectuals celebrated their own role in the creation of democracy since 1945. Equally important, the Association of Protestant Academics defined democracy not as a set of fixed institutions but as a complex of values—such as pluralism, tolerance, and openness to reform—that infused public debate. This was hardly a model of militant democracy cast in the shadow of the Weimar Republic. Instead, for Raiser, Simon, and other members of the older generation, extra-parliamentary protest signaled an opportunity for the improvement of the democratic Rechtsstaat rather than a threat to its security.

In seeking out a critical dialogue with the student movement, rather than simply dismissing its most radical manifestations, Protestants such as Helmut Gollwitzer, Ludwig Raiser, Renate Riemeck, and Helmut Simon joined a broader trend among West German intellectuals. But their origins within the Protestant public sphere are nevertheless significant, illuminating how ideological change in post-Nazi Germany was produced through and within older traditions. Protestant writings on student protest remained suffused with references to the legacies of Confessing Church resistance. Conservative-leaning Protestants like Raiser stressed the disjuncture between resistance against a dictatorship and civil protest in a democracy; Helmut Gollwitzer grounded the theology of revolution in the Barmen Declaration.[160] Neither side called into question the resistance narrative itself, or its role in legitimizing the church's postwar political engagement. By realigning their confession with the values of the democratic Rechtsstaat, Protestant intellectuals redefined the mission of their church for a secular society—but a society in which, on their view, Protestantism would continue to play a central role.

BY THE MID-1960S, the EKD faced a transformed landscape from the rubble of 1945. Visions of postwar "re-Christianization" had not materialized, while rates of religious participation declined in East as well as West Germany. Despite its contributions to *Ostpolitik*, the EKD also failed to overcome the divide of the two German states. In 1969 the regional churches of East Germany would officially establish the League of Protestant Churches in the GDR, formalizing a division that had grown increasingly stringent since the Berlin crisis ten years earlier.[161]

Yet amid these challenges to their authority—and their self-image as representatives of national unity—the cohort of theologians and lay intellectuals born around the turn of the twentieth century did not retreat to the sidelines of 1960s debates. Instead veterans of the Confessing Church, conservatives such as Helmut Thielicke as well as Dahlemites like Helmut Gollwitzer, positioned themselves at the forefront of contests over the nature of West German democracy. Across political camps, Protestant intellectuals came to affirm a vision of the democratic Rechtsstaat that aligned with, and proceeded from, Protestant values. By the end of the 1960s this vision had already taken concrete form. The final version of emergency laws significantly modified Gerhard Schröder's original draft in order to secure basic rights, including a constitutional right of resistance. Calls for an expanded right of political demonstration would be taken up by the Federal Constitutional Court following Helmut Simon's appointment as a judge in 1970.

Even as Protestant intellectuals in 1960s West Germany abandoned anti-parliamentary frameworks and declared their fealty to constitutional democracy, they undertook only a limited reckoning with the legacies of German Protestant nationalism. The controversy over emergency laws centered on the turning point of 1933, the Enabling Act, and the creation of political dictatorship. Protestant collaboration during the twelve years afterward was not mentioned in the debate. Discussion of Protestant antisemitism during the 1960s remained confined to small circles engaged in Christian–Jewish dialogue, not even reaching the agenda of the Working Group of Church Brethren Societies. The discourse of Protestant values that underpinned the EKD's rapprochement with West German constitutional democracy also echoed long-standing Protestant critiques of Catholicism. Ideological continuities were perhaps most evident in the realm of gender politics. Women activists participated widely in the Easter March movement and the Extra-Parliamentary Opposition, but were frequently relegated to subordinate roles and seldom permitted to appear as spokespersons.[162] Only the following decade would bring about the widespread ordination of women pastors and public discussion of institutional sexism in the Protestant churches.

The democratic turn among Protestant intellectuals therefore exemplified wider contradictions of the West German 1960s. This decade was characterized more by intergenerational dialogue and selective engagement with the Nazi past than the wholesale revolution espoused by the SDS. Instead of fading into irrelevance, members of the older Protestant generation sought new paths for engaging with an increasingly secular society, and described the Federal Republic's democratic development as a product of their own values and initiatives. In turn, legacies of the Confessing Church generation would persist in West, and then reunified Germany, even beyond its passing from public life.

CONCLUSION

DURING THE TWO decades after the Second World War, Protestant politics in West Germany underwent a swift and dramatic transformation. Facing the instability of the 1920s and new challenges to church authority, the generation of Protestant theologians and students who came of age in the Weimar Republic widely rejected constitutional democracy. Along with churchgoing Protestants throughout Germany, many looked toward the Nazi Party as a vehicle of religious revival. In the 1950s and 1960s, however, this same cohort of intellectuals, now ensconced as church leaders, politicians, and academics, laid the groundwork for a new approach to Protestant engagement in the political world. Rather than seek direct influence over law and policy, the church would serve as a source of shared democratic values and articulate the limits of state power. As leaders in West Germany's earliest movements for constitutional and human rights, Protestant pastors and lay intellectuals denounced militarism and executive overreach, promoted reconciliation with Eastern Europe, and advocated for the expansion of individual freedom in the domains of family structure, military service, and political demonstration.

At the same time, the midcentury transformation of German Protestant politics was mediated by important continuities. By the late 1960s the EKD had only partially confronted the traditions of German Protestant nationalism. Engagement in democratic politics did not require a full reckoning with the church's Nazi past. Instead Protestant pastors and lay intellectuals could legitimize their self-proclaimed role as arbiters of state authority through distortive accounts of Confessing Church resistance. These narratives masked the ways in which Protestant elites—including individuals who would later reinvent themselves as champions of human rights and democracy—had rejected

CONCLUSION   275

the Weimar Republic and backed the Nazi regime early on. Moreover, the political initiatives of both the mainstream EKD and the Church Brethren Societies rested on the contention that the Protestant confession, with its cultivation of conscience and public responsibility, was uniquely equipped to prepare Germans for exercising their citizenship. The very successes of Protestant political campaigns in the early Federal Republic—whether for the invalidation of the Concordat, widening of conscientious objector rights, or recognition of the Oder-Neisse Line—reinforced timeworn confessional narratives.

Retirements and deaths thinned the ranks of Confessing Church veterans active in West German politics by the early 1970s. Karl Barth died in 1968 in Basel at the age of eighty-two, the final volume of his *Church Dogmatics* still uncompleted. Ernst Wolf died three years later, having continued as the editor of *Evangelische Theologie* until the end of his life. Martin Niemöller lived until 1984 but retreated from public engagement during his final decade, serving more as a figurehead of the international ecumenical movement than the pugilistic pastor of the early postwar years.[1] In 1969 Adolf Arndt and Elisabeth Schwarzhaupt retired from the Bundestag and eighty-seven-year-old Rudolf Smend concluded the final semester of his influential seminar on public law at the University of Göttingen.[2] Among Protestant conservatives, in 1969 Ludwig Raiser stepped down from a stint as the Tübingen rector and Helmut Thielicke retired from the editorship of the *Zeitschrift für evangelische Ethik*. Ulrich Scheuner retired from the University of Bonn in 1972. Gerhard Ritter died in Freiburg in 1967, and Constantin von Dietze died in 1973; both had long been retired from their professorships.

Several members of the older generation remained active in public life beyond the eclipse of the 1968 protest movements. Gustav Heinemann reached the height of his political career as federal president during the SPD chancellorship of Willy Brandt from 1969 to 1974. Others regained the national spotlight during the terrorist attacks of the Red Army Faction. Renate Riemeck publicly called on her foster daughter Ulrike Meinhof to renounce violence, a plea echoed by Helmut Gollwitzer and Kurt Scharf in controversial pastoral visits to imprisoned RAF members during the mid-1970s.[3]

In the 1970s, however, a new generation of Protestant theologians, pastors, and lay intellectuals, who had not participated in the Nazi-era church conflict, took over the leadership of the Protestant public sphere. These included individuals born in the 1920s and early 1930s, and increasingly those born during and after the war. Members of this second postwar generation faced a far more favorable political and economic situation than their predecessors had. West Germany had become a prosperous constitutional democracy, and fears of Cold War annihilation had given way to a stable détente, though tensions still periodically flared. Yet the visions of re-Christianization espoused at earlier moments of crisis, whether 1918, 1933, or 1945, were by now decisively obsolete.

The years following 1968 saw the continuing decline of church attendance and membership in West Germany and across Western Europe. This was the result not only of the student and New Left movements that had explicitly challenged the churches, but of wider social changes. For the generation that had grown up with postwar West Germany's consumer culture, weekends were a chance for shopping, playing sports, or visiting the cinema rather than Sunday worship.[4] New possibilities for spiritual experience abounded for those seeking individualized alternatives to the institutional churches—though whether the proliferation of New Age, yoga, or Zen meditation amounted to a "resacralization" of West German society is doubtful.[5] Most significant, the sexual revolution that took off in the 1960s, and transformed West European societies by the 1970s, challenged churches in the final domain over which they sought to retain authority.[6] Statistical evidence, collected with increasing sophistication by panicked church officials, bore out a reality of secularization that was clear to Protestant pastors and Catholic priests who found themselves preaching to emptying pews.[7]

These transformations took a toll on the social foundations of German Protestant nationalism. While the founding of the CDU in 1945 sparked new efforts toward cooperation among some conservative Protestants and Catholics, the secularizing tendencies of the 1960s and 1970s brought down the final barriers between the Christian confessions. If attacks on political Catholicism helped Protestants of the Confessing Church generation conceal their own compromised pasts and embrace a new democratic identity, the rivalry between Protestants and Catholics appeared out of step with a society that no longer took Christian affiliation for granted. Rather than confessional enemies, Protestants and Catholics across Western Europe increasingly looked to one another as allies in a larger struggle against de-Christianization. By the mid-1960s the World Council of Churches as well as the Catholic Church's Second Vatican Council issued statements recognizing members of the other confession as "brethren in faith." As European Protestants and Catholics cooperated to coordinate missionary and development work around the globe, the confessional polemics of Martin Niemöller or Josef Frings were increasingly confined to the past.[8]

CONCLUSION   277

Challenges to Protestant antisemitism were driven less by trends of secularization than by the deliberate efforts of Protestant pastors and scholars who came of age after the war. The boldest members of this new generation opened a critical confrontation with the Nazi era to address the myths of the "church struggle," and of Dahlemite resistance against the Nazi state. In 1970 the young Essen theologian Wolfgang Gerlach completed a pioneering dissertation at the University of Hamburg that demonstrated for the first time how Confessing Church leaders had declined to take action against the isolation, deportation, and mass murder of German Jews, including Christians of Jewish descent. To be sure, these conclusions were too radical for many even in the 1970s. Gerlach spent years without an academic appointment, while the longtime EKD chancellery president Heinz Brunotte, whose compromised past Gerlach had exposed, sought to prevent the publication of the young pastor's study.[9] Its eventual publication in 1987, however, brought new energy to the field. Further inspiration for confronting Protestant antisemitism came from the internationalization of Christian–Jewish dialogue. In 1975, four years before the airing of the American miniseries *Holocaust* on West German television, the International Council of Christians and Jews hosted an international conference in Hamburg on the theme of "The Holocaust and Its Teachings Today." The first such gathering in the Federal Republic, the conference brought together West German participants, including Gerlach, with pioneering American Jewish scholars. The resulting resolution called for expanded Holocaust education and responsibility for preventing a "similar genocide."[10]

Developments of the years after 1968 also challenged the patriarchal foundations of German Protestant nationalism. Laywomen had been prominent in Protestant social movements throughout the twentieth century, from initiatives on the margins of the Confessing Church to rescue Jews and "non-Aryan" Christians to the antinuclear campaign and the Easter Marches. However, their efforts were rarely recognized publicly. For male church leaders, conservative Lutherans as much as Dahlemites, postwar re-Christianization was a matter of restoring masculine authority in the church and cementing a legacy of male Confessing Church resistance. During the early 1970s, mounting challenges to the traditional gender dynamics of German Protestantism arose from a number of factors: the sexual revolution and burgeoning West German feminist movement; new discussions of women's roles within both the Catholic Church and the World Council of Churches; a shortage of male pastors; as well as critical theological movements such as the Political Night Prayer, in which women theologians occupied leadership positions. The entry of women into the pastorate proceeded haltingly, but women's ordinations were recognized in all but one Protestant regional church by 1978. The presence of women pastors fostered new currents of feminist theology as well as critical discussions on divorce, abortion, and homosexuality, going beyond the limited parameters of postwar family law reform.[11]

The decades after 1968 therefore indelibly changed the face of the German Protestant Church. But the legacies of the Confessing Church generation continued to shape Protestant politics in West—and reunified—Germany long after its departure from the political stage. The successor generation that took over the leadership of the Protestant public sphere continued to advance a central element of their predecessors' vision: the view that the role of the church was not to dictate laws or blueprints for institutions, but to represent the shared values of political life. A full account of the Protestant impact on German politics past the late 1960s is beyond the scope of this book. But two examples illuminate the Janus-faced consequences of the church's postwar self-understanding. On the one hand, by rooting democracy in a set of pre-political values, the EKD maintained a powerful discourse for challenging state overreach, the quelling of dissent, and ongoing militarism. But on the other hand, the language of Protestant values could become a cudgel wielded against immigrant groups that ostensibly stood outside Europe's Christian history.

AMONG THE SOCIAL movements that galvanized the Protestant public sphere after 1968, antinuclear issues again took center stage. The initial wave of protests died down following the Fight Against Atomic Death campaign of the late 1950s. An even larger protest movement appeared in the mid-1970s, however, in response to the launching of a domestic nuclear energy program as well as NATO proposals for new deployments of American medium-range nuclear missiles on West German soil. Although the authority of the church to speak out on political controversies remained contentious, a subset of pastors and lay activists emerged as ardent supporters of grassroots antinuclear initiatives. Issues of international peace and freedom of conscience raised by the first postwar antinuclear movement remained central. Protestant activists also identified environmental protection as a value demanding Christian defense from the apocalyptic threat of nuclear weapons.[12]

Protestants shaped not only the rhetoric and goals of antinuclear protest but also the state response. Over the course of 1980, antinuclear activists

CONCLUSION 279

organized a demonstration in the Schleswig-Holstein village of Brokdorf, where the site of a planned nuclear reactor had experienced multiple occupations since construction began in the mid-1970s. Despite the organizers' failure to register the protest with district authorities, and a subsequent ban by the regional administrative court, the demonstration went ahead in February 1981. Police officers clashed with approximately 100,000 protesters who convened on the construction site.[13] The largest of the antinuclear protests, the Brokdorf demonstration polarized West German society as much as earlier waves of extra-parliamentary activism had. Except for the nascent Green Party, West Germany's political parties rejected the antinuclear movement. It was an SPD-led government under Helmut Schmidt that initially sought the NATO missile deployments, while Helmut Kohl's CDU government shepherded their authorization by the Bundestag in 1983.[14]

When the Brokdorf protesters' appeal reached the Federal Constitutional Court, however, the First Senate ruled against the state ban and in favor of the demonstrators. Helmut Simon played a key role in the 1985 decision. Appointed as a judge on the Constitutional Court in 1970, Simon remained active in the Protestant public sphere, serving as Kirchentag president in 1977 and again in 1989.[15] With key contributions from Simon and two other judges who held strong connections to lay Protestantism—Roman Herzog and Konrad Hesse—the Constitutional Court affirmed the right of assembly, guaranteed under Article 8 of the Basic Law, as a crucial avenue of democratic engagement. Peaceful demonstrations, the court ruled, remained legitimate even if a minority of demonstrators adopted violent tactics. Only an entirely violent demonstration could be prohibited, and even then authorities should prioritize citizens' fundamental rights.[16] By expanding the purview of legitimate protest, the Brokdorf decision addressed a demand advanced by Protestant activists since the 1950s campaign for the right of conscientious objection.

During a Kirchentag lecture shortly following the ruling, and in subsequent writings, Helmut Simon linked the principles undergirding the Constitutional Court's decision to the evolution of the Protestant public sphere. The Federal Republic, Simon argued, should not subvert its own democratic values in the name of state security. Instead the capacity to tolerate "dissenting minorities, through youth rebellion and civil disobedience," was a sign of democratic resilience. The Protestant churches could aid the state in upholding this expansive vision of civil protest: "By contrast to the Weimar period, Protestantism now shows readiness for a constitutional patriotism . . . The astute part of Protestantism tends toward neither uncritical adaptation nor complacent idealization of our constitutional order. It practices its constitutional patriotism as a critical solidarity with an order that is improvable and deserving of improvement; it grasps the gap between constitutional norm and constitutional reality, and the necessity of alternative reforms."[17] Simon's choice of language is telling. Introduced in 1979 by the liberal political theorist Dolf Sternberger, the concept of constitutional patriotism describes a form of national belonging rooted in shared allegiance to the principles of the constitutional state—the only kind appropriate in the post-Nazi Federal Republic, Sternberger believed. If Sternberger built upon Rudolf Smend's theory of constitutional integration, his concept excluded shared religion as a basis for national loyalty.[18] But influential Protestant intellectuals quickly deployed constitutional patriotism to characterize their church's relationship to West German democracy. Rather than situate itself in total support for government policies or total opposition, the church would hold the Federal Republic to the ideals embedded in its constitution—values that Protestants assumed credit for inspiring.[19]

Practice continued to fold back onto theory. In 1985, the year of the Brokdorf decision, the EKD Commission on Public Responsibility released a pamphlet titled "The Protestant Church and Free Democracy: The State of the Basic Law as Opportunity and Task." Marking the first time that the EKD officially recognized an alignment between Protestantism and democracy, the so-called Democracy Memorandum reflected the vision of expansive basic rights and a publicly engaged church long championed in Protestant political campaigns. Renouncing "special rights for Christians," the document insisted that the Protestant church could not "declare its own political program." Instead Protestants were called to "special responsibility" for public life.[20] Rehashing a ubiquitous argument in Protestant circles, the authors portrayed the church less as a direct lawmaker than a bedrock of democratic values, which accepted the limitations on its political interventions required by a pluralist society. Yet by encouraging the laity to carry their Christian convictions into politics, the Commission on Public Responsibility also elevated Protestants to a privileged status as arbiters over the acceptable public role of religion. The "citizens' initiatives" for environmental protection, in which many lay Protestants participated, came in for special praise.[21]

Critics could argue that the memorandum came too late, and that to affirm West German democracy in the mid-1980s was hardly a bold act.[22] But

CONCLUSION   281

this misses the document's wider significance. It was not only the case, as Helmut Simon pointed out to the EKD synod, that the Church Brethren Societies had already declared a Protestant affinity for the democratic Rechtsstaat at the Friedrichsdorf meeting of 1964.[23] Rather, the Democracy Memorandum formalized what had become a broadly shared understanding of the church's role in a democracy: to be a source of common political values, rather than partisan legislation. First articulated by postwar theologians and lay intellectuals, this vision came of age in debates about constitutional patriotism and civil disobedience during the 1970s and 1980s.

EVEN THOUGH THE EKD of the 1980s affirmed constitutional democracy and defended the right to political assembly, the exclusionary legacies of the Confessing Church generation continued to be felt as well. The limits of the EKD's democratic vision emerged most clearly in the church's efforts to broker the integration of a growing Muslim minority into West German society. "Guest worker" treaties with Mediterranean countries, concluded amid the economic boom of the 1950s and 1960s, transformed the overwhelmingly white, Christian, German-speaking society of the early postwar years into one of increasing diversity. Yet it was only in the 1970s, with economic recession and the subsequent termination of labor agreements, that migration became a matter of national debate. The decision by millions of migrant workers to remain in West Germany, the arrival of hundreds of thousands of family members, as well as a sharp increase in asylum claims, confronted policymakers with the emergence of permanent ethnic and religious minorities. Immigrants' religious backgrounds were largely ignored during the initial phase of the labor migration. However, the 1979 Iranian Revolution and global rise of political Islam drew attention to the Muslim faith practiced by much of the Federal Republic's Turkish minority, the largest immigrant community by the early 1980s.[24]

Amid a new national discussion of religious diversity, Protestant churches redefined themselves as sites of interreligious dialogue and stewards of Muslim integration. The EKD Foreign Office formed a Muslim–Christian Working Group in 1976. Two years later the EKD spearheaded the first nationwide "Day of the Foreign Fellow Citizen," an annual day of festivities that included "information sessions and performances that celebrated foreigners' cultural traditions." Over the 1980s, Christian–Muslim discussion circles were formed throughout North Rhine–Westphalia, the state with the largest Muslim population. The Protestant Academy in Arnoldshain was especially active in hosting programs on the concept of multiculturalism.[25]

Such efforts cut two ways. By replacing the label "guest worker" with "foreign fellow citizen," Protestant organizers recognized Islam as a permanent presence in Germany. Theological discussion across religious divides supplanted conversion efforts. At the same time, church initiatives arguably contributed to the public perception that new social cleavages were primarily the product of religious difference. But a "fellow citizen" (*Mitbürger*) was not a citizen; until the citizenship reforms of 2000, it was nearly impossible for immigrants and their descendants, even those born in Germany, to become German citizens. Protestant churches formed part of a reformist block that challenged overtly racist calls for the departure of Turkish immigrants, without acknowledging how citizenship laws based on ethnic descent entrenched discrimination and inequality.[26] Instead the EKD's discourse of integration reflected a basic tenet of postwar Protestant politics: Christian values underlay the principles of Germany's constitutional order. The Muslim minority would achieve acceptance not through the dismantling of legal barriers to inclusion but by adapting its own traditions to these values.[27]

Judicial decisions on religious freedom formed an even more direct link between the political vision of the Confessing Church generation and later policies toward Germany's Muslim minority. For decades after its enactment, the 1956 Concordat decision of the Federal Constitutional Court provided a framework for reconciling the Basic Law's prohibition on religious establishment with a commitment to the Christian foundations of civil society. The original decision refused to mandate the provision of Catholic and Protestant confessional schools, upholding the Basic Law's devolution of education policy to the states. But the decision did not establish public schools as wholly secular institutions. In agreement with Adolf Arndt and Rudolf Smend, the Constitutional Court affirmed the legality of interconfessional "community" schools, on the view that such schools accorded with the values of the Basic Law. Subsequent rulings on religious education extended this second element of the Concordat precedent. In 1975 the Federal Constitutional Court upheld Baden-Württemberg's mandate of interconfessional schools, against a complaint submitted by parents who objected to their children being educated in Christian schools at all. Four years later the court maintained the legality of school prayer. In the absence of a constitutionally protected "parents' right"—which was kept out of the Basic Law due to Social Democratic as well as Protestant lobbying—the states retained wide latitude to determine the religious orientation of public schools. Although parents shared responsibility for their children's education, the court determined, parental rights did not override states' prerogative to imbue schools with a Christian character.[28]

These principles remained the basis for German policies on religious freedom as the end of the Cold War and German reunification in 1990 intensified the national debate about migration. The early 1990s saw eruptions of anti-foreigner violence throughout the former East and West Germany, as well as a growing civil rights movement demanding equal treatment for migrants and their descendants.[29] German courts were quickly forced to take up claims for equal rights. On the issue of religious expression in the public sphere, the foundational case was launched in 1997 by Fereshta Ludin. An Afghan-born German citizen who had completed teacher training, Ludin was denied a position as a public-school teacher in Baden-Württemberg due to her refusal to remove her headscarf in school. Her appeal to Baden-Württemberg's Higher Administrative Court was rejected on the grounds of a provision in the state constitution establishing that "children will be raised on the basis of Christian and Western educational and cultural values." Religious freedom, according to the Mannheim court, pertained not only to the individual's right to practice their religion but even more to the state's right to define its fundamental values.[30]

Ludin's case eventually made its way to the Federal Constitutional Court. In September 2003 the high court found that no law in Baden-Württemberg prohibited a public-school teacher from wearing an Islamic headscarf. However, the ruling went on to permit state legislators to pass such legislation. "The social change connected with rising religious pluralism," read the decision's key statement, "can be cause for a new determination of the permissible extent of religious coverings in the school."[31] Several months later the state parliaments of both Baden-Württemberg and Hesse enacted bans on the conspicuous display of religious symbols by teachers. These laws made exceptions for "Judeo-Christian symbols and clothing," including explicitly, in the case of Baden-Württemberg, head coverings for nuns.[32]

German headscarf bans mirrored similar legislation in France and other West European countries, where national governments went even further in the 1990s and early 2000s to prohibit not only teachers but students from donning the headscarf in schools. Across Western Europe, the Muslim headscarf was characterized as a symbol of women's subjugation at odds with Western norms of gender equality—a claim that ironically negated the agency of the wearers.[33] However, the Constitutional Court ruling on Ludin's case also expressed distinctive elements of Germany's postwar constitutional culture. In keeping with the 1956 Concordat decision, and its subsequent rulings on the presence of Christianity in public schools, the court determined that the individual right of religious freedom was not the only issue at stake. Instead the German states retained latitude to prohibit teachers from wearing the Muslim headscarf, in light of their prerogative to establish the "ideological-religious character of the public school."[34] The court's decision reflected not French state secularism or US separation of church and state but a German Protestant tradition that regarded Christianity as the basis for shared democratic values.

The EKD reaffirmed this tradition even as formal religious affiliation continued to decline. The response to the 2003 headscarf decision by Wolfgang Huber, the EKD Council chair and bishop of Berlin-Brandenburg, illustrated the deep roots of the exclusions that imbued Protestant visions of German democracy. Born in 1942 as the son of a leading Nazi jurist, Huber did more than any Protestant intellectual of his generation to extend the dialogue of theology and politics pioneered by the Confessing Church generation. As the associate director of the Heidelberg-based Protestant Research Center during the 1970s, Huber published prolifically on themes of human rights, peace theology, and the public role of the church.[35] As Kirchentag president during the early 1980s, he spoke out in favor of nuclear disarmament and defended the right of civil disobedience. Huber was also a principal contributor to the EKD's Democracy Memorandum of 1985.[36] Yet the equal right of religious expression did not extend to the Muslim minority. In an interview with the Berlin *Tageszeitung*, Huber concurred with the Constitutional Court's 2003 ruling. The headscarf, Huber claimed, "symbolizes an attitude in gender relations that is incompatible with our constitution."[37] Huber's statement was less a product of conservative Islamophobia than the apogee of a tradition that identified the progressive values of the German constitution as the product of Protestant teachings.

The EKD's most comprehensive statement on Islam in Germany, issued during Huber's tenure as chair of the EKD Council, extended the trope of Muslim incompatibility with German constitutional culture. Entitled "Clarity and Good Neighborliness: Christians and Muslims in Germany," the 200-page "guidebook" was issued in 2006 amid controversies about the presence of Islam in Western Europe that followed the attacks of September 11, 2001, in the United States and the July 2005 train bombings in London. Ostensibly an invitation to dialogue, the document expressed skepticism about the preparedness of Muslims for democracy. At the core of the report, authored by a commission of the EKD Council, stood the elision between Christianity and democracy that had taken root in postwar Protestant politics. Contemporary German society was "influenced by Christianity" yet still "secular and pluralist," marked by "religious and ideological diversity." Muslims allegedly regarded such a society with fear: "Muslim identity is rooted in a cultural world that has not completed the transformation of religion under the conditions of the scientific-technical age and a secular state, as has the West."[38]

According to the EKD Council, such distinctions in democratic preparedness were rooted not only in history but in theology. Protestants practiced religious tolerance because they recognized that God allowed non-Christians "space and time to recognize [Jesus Christ's] love." Their respect for the dignity of the individual human being followed from the biblical teaching of humanity's creation in God's image.[39] Islam's failure to recognize the values of dignity and tolerance was manifest not only in its views about gender but in Mohammad's injunction to murder apostates and the unequal rights accorded to nonbelievers under Sharia law.[40] On this view, Protestant values blended seamlessly with constitutional democracy. Islam, in contrast, constituted a problem for democracy and therefore an object of state intervention.

As if to counter the objection that their church's own recent history had hardly been marked by pluralism and tolerance, the EKD Council framed the Christian embrace of Germany's democratic "value order" as the result of a historical process, one, however, that was rooted in the very tenets of Protestant Christianity. Through a "long historical path," the Protestant Church had "learned" to "critically engage with elements of its own tradition"— certainly an understatement of the conflicts that pervaded the EKD after 1945, but also a misapprehension of those conflicts, which centered on competing resistance narratives rather than critical engagement with the Nazi past.[41] Moreover, the report argued, Protestants had contributed to German democracy the fundamental values of human dignity, tolerance, and "likeness to God." In contrast to the Muslim headscarf, a "mere piece of clothing" that was hardly a "religious symbol" but a sign of gender inequality, the "identifying symbols of the Jewish–Christian tradition do not represent beliefs that come into tension with the value decisions underlying the German constitutional order. Rather, the Jewish–Christian tradition has contributed decisively to the cultural and spiritual foundations of liberal democracy."[42]

Therefore, the EKD Council demanded that Muslims living in Germany undertake a process of self-critique, mirroring the postwar Protestant churches. The Muslim rapprochement with democracy would entail greater deviation from tradition, however, insofar as democratic principles remained inherent, if sometimes historically unrealized, in Protestant thought.

To be sure, Muslim immigrants to Germany and their descendants in the late twentieth century were not subjected to the explicitly racist theologies that German Protestant theologians deployed against Jews during the 1920s and 1930s. Instead the connection to the long trajectory of German Protestant nationalism is more subtle. Members of the second postwar Protestant generation invoked a liberalizing, self-congratulatory narrative of their confession's successful secularization to call into question Muslims' democratic loyalties. This narrative affirmed the contributions of Confessing Church veterans to the constitutional democracy of the Federal Republic, in sharp contrast with earlier iterations of Protestant nationalism. Church leaders now criticized members of a religious minority for being insufficiently liberal and democratic, rather than for their racial or confessional difference—a critique that indicates the transformation of German Protestant politics over the mid-twentieth century, as well as its limits.

ASSERTIONS OF PROTESTANTISM'S democratic telos have remained common in the German public sphere since the EKD's 2006 memorandum on Islam. Events from the European migration crisis of 2015–2016 to the 500th anniversary of the Protestant Reformation to the rise of the far-right Alternative for Germany became occasions for church leaders like Wolfgang Huber and Protestant politicians such as Angela Merkel, Wolfgang Schäuble, and Frank-Walter Steinmeier to invoke the centrality of their church as a repository of democratic values.[43] The history traced in this book complicates such assertions. A broad swath of German Protestant intellectuals did come to affirm constitutional democracy by the mid-1960s, but the road was more circuitous than deterministic narratives of the Federal Republic's democratization allow. Confessing Church veterans perpetuated exaggerated accounts of Protestant resistance under Nazism, while impeding the prosecution of Nazi perpetrators. They facilitated the expansion of constitutional rights, from gender equality to conscientious objection to public assembly, but claimed that such rights were the product of their confession's own deep-rooted values. In fact, an alternative set of continuities can be traced through the careers of Protestant intellectuals born around the turn of the twentieth century: ideologies that figured the Protestant as the avatar of responsible citizenship and sought cultural uniformity as a basis of political life. These Protestants embraced democracy as a vehicle for pursuing their political goals, whether contesting government policies, achieving reconciliation across the Cold War divide, or enhancing the public voice of the church, but not for expanding the religious sphere to include minority faiths.

This ambivalent legacy speaks to the dynamics of religion and secularization in modern societies more broadly. That modernity is not fully secular has become a truism of recent studies on the history of religion. Yet attempts to grapple with the presence of religious beliefs, communities, and institutions in the modern world often operate within a binary opposition between the religious and the secular. Either religious groups have succeeded in asserting themselves against countervailing secular forces, or secular actors have mimicked the logics of religious discourses. Protestant Germany presents a different case: a church that sought to sustain its public presence by writing itself into the history of secularization. According to the view that became dominant within the postwar EKD, the Protestant church was not antithetical to constitutional democracy; rather, the democratic state, including its commitments to religious freedom and neutrality, could not be conceived of in the absence of Germany's Protestant heritage. Expanding this narrative to acknowledge the limits of the EKD's democratic vision does not negate the remarkable transformation of Protestant politics in the Federal Republic of Germany, or suggest that religious groups can play no role in sustaining democratic, pluralist societies. Instead it is to recognize that democracy itself is a work in progress, one that can become more inclusive only through reflection on its origins.

NOTES

Biblical citations refer to the *New Revised Standard Version,* updated edition: https://www.biblegateway.com/versions/New-Revised-Standard -Version-Updated-Edition-NRSVue-Bible/.

Citations of the German Basic Law (Grundgesetz) refer to "Basic Law for the Federal Republic of Germany," trans. Christian Tomuschat, David P. Currie, Donald P. Kommers, and Raymond Kerr, https://www.btg -bestellservice.de/pdf/80201000.pdf.

Abbreviations in Notes

ACDP	Archiv für Christlich-Demokratische Politik, Sankt Augustin
AdsD	Archiv der sozialen Demokratie, Bonn
AEKR	Archiv der Evangelischen Kirche im Rheinland, Düsseldorf
BArch	Bundesarchiv
BBKL	*Biographisch-Bibliographisches Kirchenlexikon*
EABB	Archiv der Evangelischen Akademie Bad Boll
EvTh	*Evangelische Theologie*
EvW	*Evangelische Welt*
EZA	Evangelisches Zentralarchiv in Berlin
FEST	Forschungsstätte der evangelischen Studiengemeinschaft (Protestant Research Center), Heidelberg
JK	*Junge Kirche*
KJ	*Kirchliches Jahrbuch der Evangelischen Kirche in Deutschland*
Protokolle	*Protokolle des Rates der Evangelischen Kirche in Deutschland*

290   NOTES TO PAGES 1–6

SdG *Stimme der Gemeinde*
SUBG Staats- und Universitätsbibliothek Göttingen
UAF Universitätsarchiv Freiburg
WCC World Council of Churches, Geneva
VDBT *Verhandlungen des Deutschen Bundestages*
ZEE *Zeitschrift für evangelische Ethik*

Introduction

1. For accounts of this event, see Gemeindekirchenrat der Kaiser-Wilhelm-Gedächtnis-Kirche, *Was ist geschehen? Dokumentation zu den Störungen der Gottesdienste in der Kaiser-Wilhelm-Gedächtnis-Kirche in Berlin am Heiligen Abend und in der Silvesternacht 1967* (Berlin: Büxenstein, 1968), 4–6; and Wolf-Dieter Zimmermann, *Kurt Scharf: Ein Leben zwischen Vision und Wirklichkeit* (Göttingen: Vandenhoeck und Ruprecht, 1992), 138–139. The translation of the biblical citation is my own.
2. Zimmermann, *Scharf,* 132–138.
3. "Sache der Elenden," *Der Spiegel,* December 31, 1967. Other press reports are included in Gemeindekirchenrat der Kaiser-Wilhelm-Gedächtnis-Kirche, *Was ist geschehen?,* 17–20.
4. Quoted in Hans-Georg von Studnitz, *Ist Gott Mitläufer? Die Politisierung der evangelischen Kirche: Analyse und Dokumentation* (Stuttgart: Seewald, 1969), 167. See also Helmut Thielicke, *Kulturkritik der studentischen Rebellion* (Tübingen: Mohr Siebeck, 1969).
5. Helmut Gollwitzer, "Noch einmal: Heiligabend in der Kaiser-Wilhelm-Gedächtniskirche," *JK* 29, no. 2 (1968): 103–105.
6. For biographical profiles from which details in the following paragraphs are drawn, see Benedikt Brunner, "Avantgardi Christ? Helmut Gollwitzer als Prototyp eines progressiven Protestanten im 20. Jahrhundert," *Kirchliche Zeitgeschichte* 35, no. 2 (2022): 351–369; and Friedrich Wilhelm Graf, *Helmut Thielicke und die "Zeitschrift für Evangelische Ethik": Zur Ideengeschichte der protestantischen Bundesrepublik* (Tübingen: Mohr Siebeck, 2021), 11–151.
7. Helmut Gollwitzer, *Unwilling Journey: A Diary from Russia,* trans. E. M. Delacour (London: SCM Press, 1953), 20.
8. Graf, *Thielicke,* 35–47.
9. Vera Frowein-Ziroff, *Die Kaiser-Wilhelm-Gedächtniskirche: Entstehung und Bedeutung* (Berlin: Mann, 1982), 331; Hannelore Kuna, *Erster Weltkrieg: Kriegssplitter aus Berlin in Wort und Bild* (Grambin: Haff, 2019), 72.
10. Frowein-Ziroff, *Kaiser-Wilhelm-Gedächtniskirche,* 333–338.
11. Jürgen Falter, *Hitlers Wähler: Die Anhänger der NSDAP 1924–1933,* rev. ed. (Frankfurt: Campus, 2020), 223–225.
12. On the significance of Protestant lay–theological networks in postwar West Germany, see also Sabrina Hoppe, *Der Protestantismus als Forum und Faktor:*

NOTES TO PAGES 7–8   291

Sozialethische Netzwerke im Protestantismus der frühen Bundesrepublik (Tübingen: Mohr Siebeck, 2019).

13. On democracy as a practice, see also Margaret Lavinia Anderson, *Practicing Democracy: Elections and Political Culture in Imperial Germany* (Princeton, NJ: Princeton University Press, 2000).

14. See especially Warren Breckman, *Adventures in the Symbolic: Post-Marxism and Radical Democracy* (New York: Columbia University Press, 2013), 96–138; Martin Conway, *Western Europe's Democratic Age: 1945–1968* (Princeton, NJ: Princeton University Press, 2020); Jan-Werner Müller, *Contesting Democracy: Political Ideas in Twentieth-Century Europe* (New Haven, CT: Yale University Press, 2011); and Till van Rahden, *Demokratie: Eine gefährdete Lebensform* (Frankfurt: Campus, 2019).

15. Here I draw upon William Sewell's contention that transformative "events"—a description that certainly applies to Germany's defeat in 1945—involve less the creation of new social structures wholesale than the transposition of established symbols and concepts toward new purposes. See William H. Sewell Jr., *Logics of History: Social Theory and Social Transformation* (Chicago: University of Chicago Press, 2005), esp. 197–270. Other adaptations of Sewell in modern European intellectual history include Sean A. Forner, *German Intellectuals and the Challenge of Democratic Renewal: Culture and Politics after 1945* (Cambridge: Cambridge University Press, 2014); and Samuel Moyn, "Imaginary Intellectual History," in *Rethinking Modern European Intellectual History,* ed. Darrin M. McMahon and Samuel Moyn (New York: Columbia University Press, 2014), 112–130. On the transposition of religious discourses across social and political contexts, see Sarah Shortall, "Lost in Translation: Religion and the Writing of History," *Modern Intellectual History* 13, no. 1 (2016): 273–286.

16. This description owes to Shulamit Volkov's classic essay "Antisemitism as a Cultural Code: Reflections on the History and Historiography of Imperial Germany," in *Interpreting Antisemitism: Studies and Essays on the German Case* (Berlin: De Gruyter, 2023), 61–84.

17. The terms derive from Benedict Anderson, *Imagined Communities: Reflections on the Origin and Spread of Nationalism,* rev. ed. (London: Verso, 2006), 86–87. In the German context, see Helmut Walser Smith, *German Nationalism and Religious Conflict: Culture, Ideology, Politics, 1870–1914* (Princeton, NJ: Princeton University Press, 1995), 8–9.

18. I use "confession" and "confessional" to refer to the division between Protestants and Catholics, in the German sense of *Konfession.* I use "denomination" to refer to "religious groups within Protestantism," including the state-sponsored regional churches: Lutheran, Reformed, and United. This usage follows Smith, *German Nationalism,* xv.

19. For a historical overview of church–state relations in the German lands, see Christoph Link, *Staat und Kirche in der neueren deutschen Geschichte: Fünf Abhandlungen* (Frankfurt: Peter Lang, 2000), 11–42.

292   NOTES TO PAGES 8–9

20. Claudia Lepp, *Protestantisch-liberaler Aufbruch in die Moderne: Der deutsche Protestantenverein in der Zeit der Reichsgründung und des Kulturkampfes* (Gütersloh: Kaiser, 1996), 294–319.

21. Rebekka Habermas, "Piety, Power, and Powerlessness: Religion and Religious Groups in Germany, 1870–1945," in *The Oxford Handbook of Modern German History*, ed. Helmut Walser Smith (Oxford: Oxford University Press, 2011), 455–460; Hartmut Lehmann, "'God Our Old Ally': The Chosen People Theme in Late Nineteenth- and Early Twentieth-Century German Nationalism," in *Many Are Chosen: Divine Election and Western Nationalism*, ed. William R. Hutchison and Hartmut Lehmann (Harrisburg, PA: Trinity Press International, 1994), 85–107. While there is no single-author overview of Protestant nationalism in nineteenth-century Germany, the topic is mapped out in Manfred Gailus and Hartmut Lehmann, eds., *Nationalprotestantische Mentalitäten: Konturen, Entwicklungslinien und Umbrüche eines Weltbildes* (Göttingen: Vandenhoeck und Ruprecht, 2005). For approaches that situate Protestants in the wider religious field of the German Empire, see Olaf Blaschke and Frank-Michael Kuhlemann, eds., *Religion im Kaiserreich: Milieus—Mentalitäten—Krisen* (Gütersloh: Kaiser, 1996); Rebekka Habermas, ed., *Negotiating the Secular and the Religious in the German Empire: Transnational Approaches* (New York: Berghahn Books, 2019); and Helmut Walser Smith, ed., *Catholics, Protestants, and Jews in Germany, 1800–1914* (Oxford: Berg, 2001). On the limits of nineteenth-century German Protestant nationalism, however, see Jeremy Best, *Heavenly Fatherland: German Missionary Culture and Globalization in the Age of Empire* (Toronto: University of Toronto Press, 2020).

22. On the Catholic case, see John Connelly, *From Enemy to Brother: The Revolution in Catholic Teaching on the Jews* (Cambridge, MA: Harvard University Press, 2012).

23. Christopher M. Clark, *The Politics of Conversion: Missionary Protestantism and the Jews in Prussia, 1728–1941* (Oxford: Oxford University Press, 1995), esp. 271–278.

24. Martin Ohst, "Antisemitismus als Waffe im weltanschaulichen und politischen Kampf: Adolf Stoecker und Reinhold Seeberg," in *Protestantismus, Antijudaismus, Antisemitismus: Konvergenzen und Konfrontationen in ihren Kontexten*, ed. Dorothea Wendebourg, Andreas Stemann, and Martin Ohst (Tübingen: Mohr Siebeck, 2017), 275–292.

25. See the chart in Peter Hayes, *Why? Explaining the Holocaust* (New York: Norton, 2017), 45. Antisemitic parties and the German Conservative Party received their highest combined vote total in 1893, with 16.9 percent.

26. This argument is indebted to a large body of scholarship that has rejected a sharp distinction between "traditional" Christian anti-Judaism and "modern" political antisemitism. For a foundational work, see Uriel Tal, *Christians and Jews in Germany: Religion, Politics, and Ideology in the Second Reich, 1870–1914*, trans. Noah Jonathan Jacobs (Ithaca, NY: Cornell University Press, 1975);

NOTES TO PAGES 9–11

more recently, Susannah Heschel, *The Aryan Jesus: Christian Theologians and the Bible in Nazi Germany* (Princeton, NJ: Princeton University Press, 2008).

27. For an overview, see Anthony J. Steinhoff, "Christianity and the Creation of Germany," in *The Cambridge History of Christianity*, vol. 8, *World Christianities, c. 1815–c. 1914*, ed. Sheridan Gilley and Brian Stanley (Cambridge: Cambridge University Press, 2005), 293–300. Studies of the influence of liberal Protestantism on the Kulturkampf include Wolfgang Altgeld, *Katholizismus, Protestantismus, Judentum: Über religiös begründete Gegensätze und nationalreligiöse Ideen in der Geschichte des deutschen Nationalismus* (Leiden: Brill, 1992), 195–211; Michael B. Gross, *The War against Catholicism: Liberalism and the Anti-Catholic Imagination in Nineteenth-Century Germany* (Ann Arbor: University of Michigan Press, 2005), 240–291; and Smith, *German Nationalism*, 19–49. Catholics themselves vigorously contested these characterizations. See Rebecca Ayako Bennette, *Fighting for the Soul of Germany: The Catholic Struggle for Inclusion after Unification* (Cambridge, MA: Harvard University Press, 2012).

28. Róisín Healy, *The Jesuit Specter in Imperial Germany* (Leiden: Brill, 2003), esp. 88–93 on the 1890 repeal effort.

29. Smith, *German Nationalism*, 102, 136, 206–232.

30. On the liberal–conservative divide within Protestantism, however, see Gangolf Hübinger, *Kulturprotestantismus und Politik: Zum Verhältnis von Liberalismus und Protestantismus im wilhelminischen Deutschland* (Tübingen: Mohr Siebeck, 1994), 291–302.

31. Friedrich Naumann, "Liberalismus und Protestantismus," in *Geist und Glaube* (Berlin: Reimer, 1911), 29.

32. Reinhold Seeberg, *System der Ethik im Grundriss* (Leipzig: Deichert, 1911), 146.

33. The title of Jonathan Wright's study of Protestant politics in the Weimar Republic could apply equally to Imperial Germany: J. R. C. Wright, *"Above Parties": The Political Attitudes of the German Protestant Church Leadership, 1918–1933* (London: Oxford University Press, 1974).

34. Todd H. Weir, *Red Secularism: Socialism and Secularist Culture in Germany, 1890 to 1933* (Cambridge: Cambridge University Press, 2024), 160–167, 176–183.

35. Patrick Pasture, Jan Art, and Thomas Buerman, eds., *Beyond the Feminization Thesis: Gender and Christianity in Modern Europe* (Leuven: Leuven University Press, 2012).

36. Gross, *War against Catholicism*, 185–239; Healy, *Jesuit Specter*, 149–150, 162–172.

37. Lucian Hölscher, *Geschichte der protestantischen Frömmigkeit in Deutschland* (Munich: Beck, 2005), 300–305. On parallel gender dynamics in German Catholicism, see Rebecca Meiwes, "Catholic Women as Global Actors of the Religious and the Secular," in Habermas, *Negotiating the Secular*, 171–191.

38. Lucian Hölscher, "Die Religion des Bürgers: Bürgerliche Frömmigkeit und protestantische Kirche im 19. Jahrhundert," *Historische Zeitschrift* 250 (1990): 595–630.

294   NOTES TO PAGES 11–16

39. Frank Becker, "Protestantische Euphorien: 1870/71, 1914 und 1933," in Gailus and Lehmann, *Nationalprotestantische Mentalitäten*, 30–36. For a catalog of wartime sermons and theological tracts, see Günter Brakelmann, *Protestantische Kriegstheologie 1914–1918: Ein Handbuch mit Daten, Fakten und Literatur zum Ersten Weltkrieg* (Kamen: Spenner, 2015), 203–294.

40. Bernhard vom Brocke, "'Scholarship and Militarism': The Appeal of 93 'to the Civilized World!,'" German History in Documents and Images, https://ghdi .ghi-dc.org/sub_document.cfm?document_id=938. See also Günter Brakelmann, *Protestantische Kriegstheologie im Ersten Weltkrieg: Reinhold Seeberg als Theologe des deutschen Imperialismus* (Bielefeld: Luther, 1974), 89–99; and Friedrich Naumann, *Mitteleuropa* (Berlin: Reimer, 1916).

41. Best, *Heavenly Fatherland*, 206–210.

42. Doris L. Bergen, "'War Protestantism' in Germany, 1914–1945," in Gailus and Lehmann, *Nationalprotestantische Mentalitäten*, 119.

43. Thomas Großbölting, *Losing Heaven: Religion in Germany since 1945*, trans. Alex Skinner (New York: Berghahn Books, 2017), 22.

44. Detlef Pollack, "Religiöser und gesellschaftlicher Wandel in den 1960er Jahren," in *Religion und Lebensführung im Umbruch der langen 1960er Jahren*, ed. Claudia Lepp, Harry Oelke, and Detlef Pollack (Göttingen: Vandenhoeck und Ruprecht, 2016), 37.

45. Recent studies of Catholic politics in twentieth-century Europe include Giuliana Chamedes, *A Twentieth-Century Crusade: The Vatican's Battle to Remake Christian Europe* (Cambridge, MA: Harvard University Press, 2019); James Chappel, *Catholic Modern: The Challenge of Totalitarianism and the Remaking of the Church* (Cambridge, MA: Harvard University Press, 2018); Marco Duranti, *The Conservative Human Rights Revolution: European Identity, Transnational Politics, and the Origins of the European Convention* (Oxford: Oxford University Press, 2017), 255–320; Wolfram Kaiser, *Christian Democracy and the Origins of the European Union* (Cambridge: Cambridge University Press, 2007); Piotr H. Kosicki, *Catholics on the Barricades: Poland, France, and "Revolution," 1892–1956* (New Haven, CT: Yale University Press, 2018); Samuel Moyn, *Christian Human Rights* (Philadelphia: University of Pennsylvania Press, 2015); and Sarah Shortall, *Soldiers of God in a Secular World: Catholic Theology and Twentieth-Century French Politics* (Cambridge, MA: Harvard University Press, 2021). On the place of Christian Democracy in modern European political thought, see Carlo Invernizzi Accetti, *What Is Christian Democracy? Politics, Religion, and Ideology* (Cambridge: Cambridge University Press, 2019); and Müller, *Contesting Democracy*, 132–146.

46. Frank Bösch, *Die Adenauer-CDU: Gründung, Aufstieg und Krise einer Erfolgspartei 1945–1969* (Stuttgart: Deutsche Verlags-Anstalt, 2001); Maria D. Mitchell, *The Origins of Christian Democracy: Politics and Confession in Modern Germany* (Ann Arbor: University of Michigan Press, 2012); Noah Benezra Strote, *Lions and Lambs: Conflict in Weimar and the Creation of Post-Nazi Germany* (New Haven, CT: Yale University Press, 2017), 175–196. On postwar

NOTES TO PAGES 16–18   295

conservative interconfessionalism beyond West Germany, see Udi Greenberg, *The End of the Schism: Catholics, Protestants, and the Remaking of Christian Life in Europe, 1880s–1970s* (Cambridge, MA: Harvard University Press, 2025), 172–227.

47. On the persistence of the confessional divide in modern German history, see Mark Edward Ruff and Thomas Großbölting, eds., *Germany and the Confessional Divide: Religious Tensions and Political Culture, 1871–1989* (New York: Berghahn Books, 2022).

48. In addition to the works cited above, see Nancy Christie and Michael Gauvreau, eds., *The Sixties and Beyond: Dechristianization in North America and Western Europe, 1945–2000* (Toronto: University of Toronto Press, 2013); Großbölting, *Losing Heaven;* Hugh McLeod, *The Religious Crisis of the 1960s* (Oxford: Oxford University Press, 2007); and Mark Edward Ruff, *The Wayward Flock: Catholic Youth in Postwar West Germany, 1945–1965* (Chapel Hill: University of North Carolina Press, 2005).

49. Here I am indebted to a wide scholarship that shows how moments of perceived religious crisis can also open opportunities for renewal. A foundational work is José Casanova, *Public Religions in the Modern World* (Chicago: University of Chicago Press, 1994). On the German case, see Wilhelm Damberg, ed., *Soziale Strukturen und Semantiken des Religiösen im Wandel: Transformationen in der Bundesrepublik Deutschland 1949–1989* (Essen: Klartext, 2011); and Michael Geyer and Lucian Hölscher, eds., *Die Gegenwart Gottes in der modernen Gesellschaft: Transzendenz und religiöse Vergemeinschaftung in Deutschland* (Göttingen: Wallstein, 2006).

50. See Gailus and Lehmann, *Nationalprotestantische Mentalitäten,* especially the chapters by Frank Becker, Doris L. Bergen, and Frank-Michael Kuhlemann.

51. See especially Udi Greenberg, *The Weimar Century: German Émigrés and the Ideological Foundations of the Cold War* (Princeton, NJ: Princeton University Press, 2014); on left-wing émigrés, see Terence Renaud, *New Lefts: The Making of a Radical Tradition* (Princeton, NJ: Princeton University Press, 2021). Works that depict interactions between émigrés and intellectuals who survived the war in Germany include Forner, *German Intellectuals;* Fabian Link, *Demokratisierung nach Auschwitz: Eine Geschichte der westdeutschen Sozialwissenschaften in der Nachkriegszeit* (Göttingen: Wallstein, 2022); and Strote, *Lions and Lambs.* For an interpretation that foregrounds a younger generation of German intellectuals born in the 1920s and 1930s, see A. Dirk Moses, *German Intellectuals and the Nazi Past* (Cambridge: Cambridge University Press, 2007).

52. Major works include Anselm Doering-Manteuffel, *Wie westlich sind die Deutschen? Amerikanisierung und Westernisierung im 20. Jahrhundert* (Göttingen: Vandenhoeck und Ruprecht, 1999); Konrad Jarausch, *After Hitler: Recivilizing Germans, 1945–1995,* trans. Brandon Hunziker (Oxford: Oxford University Press, 2006); and Heinrich August Winkler, *Germany: The Long Road West,* vol. 2, *1933–1990,* trans. Alexander J. Sager (Oxford: Oxford University Press, 2007). For a recent work that critically engages the concept of "civilization" in

NOTES TO PAGES 18–22

postwar Europe, see Paul Betts, *Ruin and Renewal: Civilizing Europe after World War II* (New York: Basic Books, 2020).

53. For programmatic statements, see Frank Biess and Astrid M. Eckert, "Introduction: Why Do We Need New Narratives for the History of the Federal Republic?," *Central European History* 52, no. 1 (2019): 1–18; and Lauren Stokes, "The Protagonists of Democratization in the Federal Republic," *German History* 39, no. 2 (2021): 284–296. For a similarly critical look at post-1945 West European democracy in transnational perspective, see Conway, *Western Europe's Democratic Age*.

54. Rita Chin et al., *After the Nazi Racial State: Difference and Democracy in Germany and Europe* (Ann Arbor: University of Michigan Press, 2009).

55. Frank Biess, *German Angst: Fear and Democracy in the Federal Republic of Germany* (Oxford: Oxford University Press, 2020); Monica Black, *A Demon-Haunted Land: Witches, Wonder Doctors, and the Ghosts of the Past in Post-WWII Germany* (New York: Metropolitan Books, 2020); Daniel Fulda et al., eds., *Demokratie im Schatten der Gewalt: Geschichten des Privaten im deutschen Nachkrieg* (Göttingen: Wallstein, 2010).

56. Basic Law, art. 1, para. 1. See Tiffany N. Florvil, *Mobilizing Black Germany: Afro-German Women and the Making of a Transnational Movement* (Urbana: University of Illinois Press, 2020); Samuel Clowes Huneke, *States of Liberation: Gay Men between Dictatorship and Democracy in Cold War Germany* (Toronto: University of Toronto Press, 2022); Michelle Lynn Kahn, *Foreign in Two Homelands: Racism, Return Migration, and Turkish-German History* (Cambridge: Cambridge University Press, 2024); and Lauren Stokes, *Fear of the Family: Guest Workers and Family Migration in the Federal Republic of Germany* (Oxford: Oxford University Press, 2022).

57. I thereby offer a different perspective from works focused on the "Westernization" of postwar German Protestantism. For instance, see Thomas Sauer, *Westorientierung im deutschen Protestantismus? Vorstellungen und Tätigkeit des Kronberger Kreises* (Munich: Oldenbourg, 1999); and Axel Schildt, *Zwischen Abendland und Amerika: Studien zur westdeutschen Ideenlandschaft der 50er Jahre* (Munich: Oldenbourg, 1999).

1. A Church in Crisis

1. Paul Althaus, *Luther und das Deutschtum* (Leipzig: Scholl, 1917), 3, 5.

2. Adolf von Harnack, *Martin Luther und die Grundlegung der Reformation: Festschrift der Stadt Berlin zum 31. Oktober 1917* (Berlin: Weidmannsche Buchhandlung, 1917), 63–64.

3. Karl Holl, *Was verstand Luther unter Religion?* (Tübingen: Mohr, 1917), 38. For the context, see James M. Stayer, *Martin Luther, German Saviour: German Evangelical Theological Factions and the Interpretation of Luther, 1917–1933* (Montreal: McGill-Queen's University Press, 2000), 41.

NOTES TO PAGES 22–25

4. Helmut Grisar, "Die Literatur des Lutherjubiläums 1917: Ein Bild des heutigen Protestantismus," *Zeitschrift für katholische Theologie* 42, no. 3 (1918): 591–628.

5. Friedrich Wilhelm Graf, *Der heilige Zeitgeist: Studien zur Ideengeschichte der protestantischen Theologie in der Weimarer Republik* (Tübingen: Mohr Siebeck, 2011), 6–7. See also Benedikt Brunner, "The Revolution of 1918 / 19: A Traumatic Experience for German Protestantism," in *Germany and the Confessional Divide: Religious Tensions and Political Culture, 1871–1989,* ed. Mark Edward Ruff and Thomas Großbölting (New York: Berghahn Books, 2022), 75–100.

6. The standard work in the field emphasizes the role of the Center Party as a bulwark against Nazi support within the Catholic milieu. See Jürgen Falter, *Hitlers Wähler: Die Anhänger der NSDAP 1924–1933,* rev. ed. (Frankfurt: Campus, 2020), 215–238. For arguments about ideology and economic interests, respectively, see Richard Steigmann-Gall, "Apostasy or Religiosity? The Cultural Meaning of the Protestant Vote for Hitler," *Social History* 25, no. 3 (2000): 267–284; and Gary King et al., "Ordinary Economic Voting Behavior in the Extraordinary Election of Adolf Hitler," *Journal of Economic History* 68, no. 4 (2008): 951–996.

7. Richard Steigmann-Gall, *The Holy Reich: Nazi Conceptions of Christianity, 1919–1945* (Cambridge: Cambridge University Press, 2003), 47–49, 66–76.

8. Doris L. Bergen, *Twisted Cross: The German Christian Movement in the Third Reich* (Chapel Hill: University of North Carolina Press, 1996), 5.

9. Derek Hastings, *Catholicism and the Roots of Nazism: Religious Identity and National Socialism* (Oxford: Oxford University Press, 2010); Christoph Hübner, *Die Rechtskatholiken, die Zentrumspartei und die katholische Kirche in Deutschland bis zum Reichskonkordat von 1933: Ein Beitrag zur Geschichte des Scheiterns der Weimarer Republik* (Berlin: Lit, 2014); Klaus Große Kracht, "'Time to Close Ranks': The Catholic *Kulturfront* during the Weimar Republic," in Ruff and Großbölting, *Germany and the Confessional Divide,* 51–74.

10. I follow the framework of "political generations" outlined in Detlev J. K. Peukert, *The Weimar Republic: The Crisis of Classical Modernity,* trans. Richard Deveson (New York: Hill and Wang, 1992), 14–18. On generations in Weimar Protestant theology, see Graf, *Der heilige Zeitgeist,* 29–45.

11. On the language of crisis in the Weimar Republic, see Rüdiger Graf, "Either-Or: The Narrative of 'Crisis' in Weimar Germany and in Historiography," *Central European History* 43, no. 4 (2010): 592–615. On "crisis" in Weimar theology, see Peter E. Gordon, "Weimar Theology: From Historicism to Crisis," in *Weimar Thought: A Contested Legacy,* ed. Peter E. Gordon and John P. McCormick (Princeton, NJ: Princeton University Press, 2013), 150–178.

12. Giuliana Chamedes, *A Twentieth-Century Crusade: The Vatican's Battle to Remake Christian Europe* (Cambridge, MA: Harvard University Press, 2019), 34–68.

NOTES TO PAGES 25–29

13. Udi Greenberg, "The Rise of the Global South and the Protestant Peace with Socialism," *Contemporary European History* 29, no. 2 (2020): 205–208; Mirjam Loos, *Gefährliche Metaphern: Auseinandersetzungen deutscher Protestanten mit Kommunismus und Bolschewismus (1919 bis 1955)* (Göttingen: Vandenhoeck und Ruprecht, 2020), 27–53.

14. Daniel R. Borg, *The Old Prussian Church and the Weimar Republic: A Study in Political Adjustment, 1917–1927* (Hanover, NH: University Press of New England, 1984), 58–66; Todd H. Weir, *Red Secularism: Socialism and Secularist Culture in Germany, 1890 to 1933* (Cambridge: Cambridge University Press, 2024), 216–221; on Hoffmann, see also 83–88, 164–167, 208–216.

15. "Verfassungsurkunde für den Preußischen Staat vom 31. Januar 1850," art. 14, Verfassungen der Welt, https://www.verfassungen.de/preussen/preussen50 -index.htm. See also Christoph Link, *Staat und Kirche in der neueren deutschen Geschichte: Fünf Abhandlungen* (Frankfurt: Peter Lang, 2000), 54–57.

16. "The Constitution of the German Federation of August 11, 1919," in Heinrich Oppenheimer, *The Constitution of the German Republic* (London: Stevens and Sons, 1923), 219, 249.

17. "Constitution of the German Federation," 249–253. On the constitutional settlement, see also Borg, *Old Prussian Church,* 83–97; and Link, *Staat und Kirche,* 104–116.

18. Benedikt Brunner, *Volkskirche: Zur Geschichte eines evangelischen Grundbegriffs (1918–1960)* (Göttingen: Vandenhoeck und Ruprecht, 2020), 47–61.

19. Otto Dibelius, *Staatsgrenzen und Kirchengrenzen: Eine Studie zur gegenwärtigen Lage des Protestantismus* (Berlin: Engelmann, 1921), 68.

20. Graf, *Der heilige Zeitgeist,* 32.

21. Friedrich Gogarten, "Between the Times," in *The Beginnings of Dialectical Theology,* ed. James M. Robinson (Richmond, VA: John Knox Press, 1968), 277.

22. On Gogarten, see D. Timothy Goering, *Friedrich Gogarten (1887–1967): Religionsrebell im Jahrhundert der Weltkriege* (Berlin: De Gruyter, 2017).

23. Bruce L. McCormack, *Karl Barth's Critically Realistic Dialectical Theology: Its Genesis and Development, 1909–1936* (Oxford: Clarendon Press, 1995), 40–42, 49–68.

24. Christiane Tietz, *Karl Barth: A Life in Conflict,* trans. Victoria Barnett (Oxford: Oxford University Press, 2021), 68–69.

25. McCormack, *Dialectical Theology,* 117–125.

26. For a detailed exposition of Barth's theology of revelation in the first edition of his Romans commentary, see McCormack, *Dialectical Theology,* 141–162. On revelation as experience and event, see also Gordon, "Weimar Theology," 159.

27. Karl Barth, *The Epistle to the Romans,* 6th ed., trans. Edwyn C. Hoskyns (London: Oxford University Press, 1968), 10.

28. Tietz, *Barth,* 133–136.

29. Graf, *Der heilige Zeitgeist,* 425–459; Paul Silas Peterson, *The Early Karl Barth: Historical Contexts and Intellectual Formation, 1905–1935* (Tübingen: Mohr Siebeck, 2018), 410–430.

NOTES TO PAGES 29–32   299

30. Christophe Chalamet, "Karl Barth and the Weimar Republic," in *The Weimar Moment: Liberalism, Political Theology, and Law,* ed. Leonard V. Kaplan and Rudy Koshar (Lanham, MD: Lexington Books, 2012), 241–268; Rudy Koshar, "Demythologizing the Secular: Karl Barth and the Politics of the Weimar Republic," in Kaplan and Koshar, *Weimar Moment,* 313–334. On Hirsch, see Robert P. Ericksen, *Theologians under Hitler: Gerhard Kittel, Paul Althaus and Emanuel Hirsch* (New Haven, CT: Yale University Press, 1985), 124–141.
31. Barth, *Epistle to the Romans,* 475–502. The biblical verse is Romans 13:1.
32. Graf, *Der heilige Zeitgeist,* 85; Emanuel Hirsch; "Zum Problem der Ethik (an Friedrich Gogarten)," *Zwischen den Zeiten* 1, no. 3 (1923): 52–57.
33. Ernst Wolf, "Johannes von Staupitz und die theologischen Anfänge Luthers," *Luther-Jahrbuch* 11 (1929): 43–86. On Wolf's connection to Barth, see Tietz, *Barth,* 199.
34. Graf, *Der heilige Zeitgeist,* 461–463.
35. Hans Joachim Iwand, "Religion und Kultur," *Jungnationale Stimmen* 6, no. 6 (1931): 164–173.
36. On Gollwitzer's student years, see Friedrich-Wilhelm Marquardt, Wolfgang Brinkel, and Manfred Weber, eds., *Helmut Gollwitzer: Skizzen eines Lebens* (Gütersloh: Kaiser, 1998), 26–64, quotes at 42.
37. Hans Manfred Bock, "Die *Christliche Welt* 1919 bis 1933: Organisierte Akteure und diskursive Affinitäten in der kulturprotestantischen Zeitschrift," in *Das evangelische Intellektuellenmilieu in Deutschland, seine Presse und seine Netzwerke (1871–1963),* ed. Michel Grunewald and Uwe Puschner (Bern: Peter Lang, 2008), 341–382.
38. Barbara Picht, "Religiöse Sozialisten in der Weimarer Republik: *Der Religiöse Sozialist* und die *Blätter für religiösen Sozialismus,*" in Grunewald and Puschner, *Das evangelische Intellektuellenmilieu,* 383–408.
39. Contemporaries estimated that 70 to 80 percent of Protestant pastors supported the DNVP: Karl-Wilhelm Dahm, *Pfarrer und Politik: Soziale Position und politische Mentalität des deutschen evangelischen Pfarrerstandes zwischen 1918 und 1933* (Cologne: Westdeutscher Verlag, 1965), 147–148. See also Brunner, *Volkskirche,* 39; Graf, *Der heilige Zeitgeist,* 8; and Weir, *Red Secularism,* 220.
40. Larry Eugene Jones, *The German Right, 1918–1930: Political Parties, Organized Interests, and Patriotic Associations in the Struggle against Weimar Democracy* (Cambridge: Cambridge University Press, 2020), 81–87, 361–362, 377–378.
41. For a detailed study of the interwar "Luther renaissance," see Stayer, *Martin Luther, German Saviour.*
42. Werner Elert, *Der Kampf um das Christentum seit Schleiermacher und Hegel* (Munich: Beck, 1921), 4.
43. On Brunstäd's role in the DNVP, see Julius Trugenberger, *Neuhegelianisches Kulturluthertum: Friedrich Brunstäd (1883–1944)* (Berlin: De Gruyter, 2021), 63–74.
44. Friedrich Brunstäd, *Die Idee der Religion: Prinzipien der Religionsphilosophie* (Erlangen: Niemeyer, 1922), 192–212, quotes at 195, 201, 203–204.

NOTES TO PAGES 32–36

45. Friedrich Brunstäd, *Deutschland und der Sozialismus,* 2nd ed. (Berlin: Elsner, 1927), 122–130.
46. Friedrich Brunstäd, "Die Weltanschauung der Deutschnationalen Volkspartei," in *Der nationale Wille: Werden und Wirken der Deutschnationalen Volkspartei 1918–1928,* ed. Max Weiss (Essen: Kamp, 1928), 56.
47. On Althaus's early life, see Tanja Hetzer, *"Deutsche Stunde": Volksgemeinschaft und Antisemitismus in der politischen Theologie bei Paul Althaus* (Munich: Allitera, 2009), 33–109.
48. Paul Althaus, *Religiöser Sozialismus: Grundfragen der christlichen Sozialethik* (Gütersloh: Bertelsmann, 1921), 31–42.
49. Hetzer, *"Deutsche Stunde,"* 37–40.
50. Althaus, *Religiöser Sozialismus,* 47, 49.
51. Paul Althaus, *Staatsgedanke und Reich Gottes* (Langensalza: Beyer, 1923), 16–18.
52. Althaus, *Staatsgedanke,* 38–39.
53. Althaus, *Staatsgedanke,* 44.
54. Althaus, *Religiöser Sozialismus,* 68.
55. Althaus, *Staatsgedanke,* 39–40.
56. Stefan Breuer, *Die Völkischen in Deutschland: Kaiserreich und Weimarer Republik* (Darmstadt: Wissenschaftliche Buchgesellschaft, 2008), 252–264; Kurt Meier, "Der 'Bund für deutsche Kirche' und seine völkisch-antijudaistische Theologie," in *Protestantismus und Antisemitismus in der Weimarer Republik,* ed. Kurt Nowak and Gérard Raulet (Frankfurt: Campus, 1994), 177–198.
57. Paul Althaus, *Kirche und Volkstum: Der völkische Wille im Lichte des Evangeliums* (Gütersloh: Bertelsmann, 1928), 14–15.
58. Althaus, *Kirche und Volkstum,* 33–34.
59. "Vaterländische Kundgebung des Königsberger Kirchentages," in *Verhandlungen des zweiten Deutschen Evangelischen Kirchentages 1927* (Berlin: Evangelischer Presseverband für Deutschland, 1927), 338–340. On the 1927 Kirchentag, see also Daniel Bormuth, *Die Deutschen Evangelischen Kirchentage in der Weimarer Republik* (Stuttgart: Kohlhammer, 2007), 229–243.
60. Kenneth C. Barnes, *Nazism, Liberalism, and Christianity: Protestant Social Thought in Germany and Great Britain, 1925–1937* (Lexington: University Press of Kentucky, 1991), 43–47; Justin Reynolds, "Against the World: International Protestantism and the Ecumenical Movement between Secularization and Politics, 1900–1952" (PhD diss., Columbia University, 2016), 104–113.
61. On the Young National League, see Marion E. P. de Ras, *Body, Femininity, and Nationalism: Girls in the German Youth Movement, 1900–1934* (New York: Routledge, 2007), 167–186.
62. Heinz-Dietrich Wendland, "Nation und Welt," *Jungnationale Stimmen* 1, no. 1 (1926): 7–10. See also Hans Dombois, "Schrifttum," *Jungnationale Stimmen* 4, no. 7 (1929): 230–231; and Iwand, "Religion und Kultur."
63. For a detailed study of exchanges between German Protestant theologians and jurists during the Weimar Republic, see Klaus Tanner, *Die fromme Verstaatlichung des Gewissens: Zur Auseinandersetzung um die Legitimität der Weimarer*

NOTES TO PAGES 36–40   301

Reichsverfassung in Staatsrechtswissenschaft und Theologie der zwanziger Jahre (Göttingen: Vandenhoeck und Ruprecht, 1989), esp. 194–195.

64. Chamedes, *Twentieth-Century Crusade*, 81–91; Marcus Rehtmeyer, *Die Staatskirchenverträge Preußens 1929 und 1931: Vor dem Hintergrund der Entwicklung des Staats-, Staatskirchen- und Staatskirchenvertragsrechts im 19. und 20. Jahrhundert* (Baden-Baden: Nomos, 2024), 462–471.

65. "Constitution of the German Federation," 219.

66. On the Weimar-era debate about legal positivism, see Peter C. Caldwell, *Popular Sovereignty and the Crisis of German Constitutional Law: The Theory and Practice of Weimar Constitutionalism* (Durham, NC: Duke University Press, 1997); and John P. McCormick, "Legal Theory and the Weimar Crisis of Law and Social Change," in Gordon and McCormick, *Weimar Thought*, 55–72.

67. On the encyclical, see James Chappel, *Catholic Modern: The Challenge of Totalitarianism and the Remaking of the Church* (Cambridge, MA: Harvard University Press, 2018), 79, 82–83; and Rudolf Uertz, *Vom Gottesrecht zum Menschenrecht: Das katholische Staatsdenken in Deutschland von der Französischen Revolution bis zum II. Vatikanischen Konzil (1789–1965)* (Paderborn: Schöningh, 2005), 278–284, 294–295.

68. Chappel, *Catholic Modern*, 47–49. On Catholic trade unions in the Weimar Republic, see also William L. Patch, *Christian Democratic Workers and the Forging of German Democracy, 1920–1980* (Cambridge: Cambridge University Press, 2018), 9–45.

69. "Quadragesimo Anno," para. 86, The Holy See, https://www.vatican.va/content /pius-xi/en/encyclicals/documents/hf_p-xi_enc_19310515_quadragesimo -anno.html. See also Uertz, *Gottesrecht*, 279, 298.

70. Carl Schmitt, *Roman Catholicism and Political Form*, trans. G. L. Ulmen (Westport, CT: Greenwood Press, 1996). On the text's reception, see Manfred Dahlheimer, *Carl Schmitt und der deutsche Katholizismus 1888–1936* (Paderborn: Schöningh: 1998), 115–144.

71. Borg, *Old Prussian Church*, 123–167.

72. On the ideal of a "national cultural state" in Weimar Protestantism, see Tanner, *Die fromme Verstaatlichung*, 186–262.

73. Caldwell, *Popular Sovereignty*, 121–123; Konrad Hesse, "In Memoriam Rudolf Smend," in Hesse, *Ausgewählte Schriften*, ed. Peter Häberle and Alexander Hollerbach (Heidelberg: C. F. Müller, 1984), 576. On Smend's early writings, see Stefan Korioth, *Integration und Bundesstaat: Ein Beitrag zur Staats- und Verfassungslehre Rudolf Smends* (Berlin: Duncker und Humblot, 1990), 16–91.

74. The shift in Schmitt's approach was hastened by his excommunication from the Catholic Church after being refused an annulment of his first marriage. See Dahlheimer, *Schmitt*, 453–455. For an overview of Schmitt's constitutional theory, see Benjamin A. Schupmann, *Carl Schmitt's State and Constitutional Theory: A Critical Analysis* (Oxford: Oxford University Press, 2017), 135–152.

75. Rudolf Smend, "Verfassung und Verfassungsrecht," in *Staatsrechtliche Abhandlungen und andere Aufsätze*, 3rd ed. (Berlin: Duncker und Humblot, 1994), 136.

302 NOTES TO PAGES 40–43

76. Smend, "Verfassung," 142–170.
77. Smend, "Verfassung," 192.
78. Smend, "Verfassung," 131, 161. On Protestant connections in Smend's constitutional theory, see also Caldwell, *Popular Sovereignty*, 122; and Stefan Korioth, "Evangelisch-theologische Staatsethik und juristische Staatslehre in der Weimarer Republik und der frühen Bundesrepublik," in *Konfession im Recht: Auf der Suche nach konfessionell geprägten Denkmustern und Argumentationsstrategien in Recht und Rechtswissenschaft des 19. und 20. Jahrhunderts,* ed. Pascale Cancik et al. (Frankfurt: Klostermann, 2009), 130–134.
79. Smend, "Verfassung," 186.
80. Smend, "Verfassung," 175.
81. Smend, "Verfassung," 204.
82. Patch, *Christian Democratic Workers,* 19–25.
83. Falter, *Hitlers Wähler,* 227.
84. Heinz-Dietrich Wendland, "Sozialismus und Nationalismus," *Neue kirchliche Zeitschrift* 42, no. 8 (1931): 412, 436–437.
85. Winfried Wendland, "Adolf Hitler spricht," *Jungnationale Stimmen* 5, no. 5 (1930): 158–159; Gustav Giere, "Wider die Autorität Brünings," *Jungnationale Stimmen* 6, no. 11 (1931): 326–330.
86. Walter Künneth, *Die völkische Religiosität der Gegenwart,* 2nd ed. (Berlin: Wichern, 1932), quote at 16. On the Central Apologetic Institute, see Weir, *Red Secularism,* 304.
87. Karl Barth, "Basic Problems of Christian Social Ethics: A Discussion with Paul Althaus," in Robinson, *Beginnings of Dialectical Theology,* 46–57, quotes at 52–53.
88. Otto Dibelius, *Das Jahrhundert der Kirche: Geschichte, Betrachtung, Umschau und Ziele* (Berlin: Furche, 1927), 241, 256, see also 142–148. On Dibelius's text and its reception, see Lukas Bormann, "Vom *Jahrhundert der Kirche* (1926) bis *Friede auf Erden?* (1930): Otto Dibelius und die misslungene politische Neupositionierung der Evangelischen Kirche in den guten Jahren der Weimarer Republik," in *Otto Dibelius: Neue Studien zu einer protestantischen Jahrhundertfigur,* ed. Lukas Bormann and Manfred Gailus (Tübingen: Mohr Siebeck, 2024), 117–129.
89. Karl Barth, "Die Not der evangelischen Kirche," in Barth, *Vorträge und kleinere Arbeiten 1930–1933,* ed. Michael Beintker, Michael Hüttenhoff, and Peter Zocher (Zurich: Theologischer Verlag Zürich, 2013), 86–144, quotes at 140, 142. On the debate between Barth and Dibelius, see also Brunner, *Volkskirche,* 93–104.
90. Richard Karwehl, "Politisches Messiantum: Zur Auseinandersetzung zwischen Kirche und Nationalsozialismus," *Zwischen den Zeiten* 9, no. 6 (1931): 519–543, quote at 538.
91. Quoted in Christoph Weiling, *Die "Christlich-deutsche Bewegung": Eine Studie zum konservativen Protestantismus in der Weimarer Republik* (Göttingen: Vandenhoeck und Ruprecht, 1998), 234. See also Chalamet, "Barth," 253.
92. Friedrich Gogarten, "Staat und Kirche," *Zwischen den Zeiten* 10, no. 5 (1932): 390–410, quotes at 393–394. For a similar critique of völkisch theologies, see

NOTES TO PAGES 43–46 303

Gerhard Gloege, "Zur deutschkirchlichen Christologie," *Zwischen den Zeiten* 9, no. 5 (1931): 421–450.

93. Tietz, *Barth*, 210.

94. See especially Carl Schmitt, *Legality and Legitimacy*, trans. Jeffrey Seitzer (Durham, NC: Duke University Press, 2004). On Catholic enthusiasm for authoritarian corporatist regimes, see Chappel, *Catholic Modern*, 78–92.

95. Carl Schmitt, "Die Wendung zum totalen Staat," and "Weiterentwicklung des totalen Staates in Deutschland," in *Positionen und Begriffe im Kampf mit Weimar—Genf—Versailles 1923–1939*, 4th ed. (Berlin: Duncker und Humblot, 2014), 166–178, 185–190.

96. Heinz-Dietrich Wendland, "Demokratie und Diktatur," *Jungnationale Stimmen* 6, no. 8 (1931): 229–234.

97. Otto Piper, "Demokratie in Kirche, Staat und Wirtschaft," in *Die Verhandlungen des 38. Evangelisch-Sozialen Kongresses in Duisburg 26.–28. Mai 1931* (Göttingen: Vandenhoeck und Ruprecht, 1931), 89, 106–107. See also Tanner, *Die fromme Verstaatlichung*, 190n261.

98. Jörg Treffke, *Gustav Heinemann: Wanderer zwischen den Parteien: Eine politische Biographie* (Paderborn: Schöningh, 2009), 58–69. On the formation of the CSVD, see Jones, *German Right*, 517–523; and Günter Opitz, *Der Christlich-soziale Volksdienst: Versuch einer protestantischen Partei in der Weimarer Republik* (Düsseldorf: Droste, 1969), 137–155.

99. The Protestant shift from the DNVP and liberal parties to the Nazis— especially among domestic workers, self-employed workers, and the working poor—is demonstrated in King et al., "Ordinary Economic Voting Behavior," 977, 980–981. On the CSVD's electoral returns, see Opitz, *Der Christlich-soziale Volksdienst*, 181, 279–280.

100. Jones, *German Right*, 579–580; Opitz, *Der Christlich-soziale Volksdienst*, 112–113.

101. Smend, "Protestantismus und Demokratie," in *Staatsrechtliche Abhandlungen*, 297–308, quotes at 302, 306. The essay originally appeared in Oskar Müller, ed., *Krisis: Ein politisches Manifest* (Weimar: Lichtenstein, 1932). Smend's departure from the DNVP is noted in Caldwell, *Popular Sovereignty*, 123.

102. Smend, "Protestantismus," 307–308.

103. Smend to Schmitt, undated, in *"Auf der gefahrenvollen Strasse des öffentlichen Rechts": Briefwechsel Carl Schmitt—Rudolf Smend 1921–1961*, ed. Reinhard Mehring, 2nd ed. (Berlin: Duncker und Humblot, 2012), 87.

104. Carl Schmitt, *Political Theology II: The Myth of the Closure of Any Political Theology*, trans. Michael Hoelzl and Graham Ward (Cambridge: Polity, 2008), 40.

105. Noah Benezra Strote, *Lions and Lambs: Conflict in Weimar and the Creation of Post-Nazi Germany* (New Haven, CT: Yale University Press, 2017), 27–34.

106. Gerhard Leibholz, *Die Auflösung der liberalen Demokratie in Deutschland und das autoritäre Staatsbild* (Munich: Duncker und Humblot, 1933), 43.

107. Leibholz, *Auflösung*, 74.

108. Leibholz, *Auflösung*, 60.

304 NOTES TO PAGES 48–50

2. From the Total State to the Limits of Obedience

1. Quoted in Manfred Gailus, *Im Bann des Nationalsozialismus: Das protestantische Berlin im Dritten Reich* (Freiburg: Herder, 2023), 45.
2. Quoted in Hartmut Fritz, *Otto Dibelius: Ein Kirchenmann in der Zeit zwischen Monarchie und Diktatur* (Göttingen: Vandenhoeck und Ruprecht, 1998), 386.
3. Quoted in Benjamin Ziemann, *Martin Niemöller: Ein Leben in Opposition* (Munich: Deutsche Verlags-Anstalt, 2019), 176.
4. Manfred Gailus, *Gläubige Zeiten: Religiosität im Dritten Reich* (Freiburg: Herder, 2021), 21–23; Ziemann, *Niemöller*, 177.
5. Early works to challenge postwar narratives of Confessing Church resistance included Klaus Scholder, *The Churches and the Third Reich*, vol. 2, *The Year of Disillusionment, 1934: Barmen and Rome*, trans. John Bowden (London: SCM Press, 1988); and Wolfgang Gerlach, *Als die Zeugen schwiegen: Bekennende Kirche und die Juden*, 2nd ed. (Berlin: Institut Kirche und Judentum, 1993). Since the 1990s, numerous revisionist studies have extended the picture with greater attention to gender, lay responses, and the full range of church factions beyond the Confessing Church. Major works include Victoria Barnett, *For the Soul of the People: Protestant Protest against Hitler* (New York: Oxford University Press, 1992); Doris L. Bergen, *Twisted Cross: The German Christian Movement in the Third Reich* (Chapel Hill: University of North Carolina Press, 1996); Olaf Blaschke and Thomas Großbölting, eds., *Was glaubten die Deutschen zwischen 1933 und 1945? Religion und Politik im Nationalsozialismus* (Frankfurt: Campus, 2020); Robert P. Ericksen, *Complicity in the Holocaust: Churches and Universities in Nazi Germany* (Cambridge: Cambridge University Press, 2012); Manfred Gailus, *Protestantismus und Nationalsozialismus: Studien zur nationalsozialistischen Durchdringung des protestantischen Sozialmilieus in Berlin* (Cologne: Böhlau, 2001); Susannah Heschel, *The Aryan Jesus: Christian Theologians and the Bible in Nazi Germany* (Princeton, NJ: Princeton University Press, 2008); Richard Steigmann-Gall, *The Holy Reich: Nazi Conceptions of Christianity, 1919–1945* (Cambridge: Cambridge University Press, 2003); and Ziemann, *Niemöller*. For an up-to-date survey, see Gailus, *Gläubige Zeiten*. A concise overview of the Protestant church conflict in English is Matthew D. Hockenos, *A Church Divided: German Protestants Confront the Nazi Past* (Bloomington: Indiana University Press, 2004), 15–41.
6. This topic is only beginning to be researched. See Manfred Gailus and Clemens Vollnhals, eds., *Mit Herz und Verstand: Protestantische Frauen im Widerstand gegen die NS-Rassenpolitik* (Göttingen: Vandenhoeck und Ruprecht, 2013).
7. Doris L. Bergen, *Between God and Hitler: Military Chaplains in Nazi Germany* (Cambridge: Cambridge University Press, 2023), 226–228; Barnett, *Soul of the People*, 284–309; Hartmut Lehmann, "'God Our Old Ally': The Chosen People

NOTES TO PAGES 51–53   305

Theme in Late Nineteenth- and Early Twentieth-Century German Nationalism," in *Many Are Chosen: Divine Election and Western Nationalism,* ed.
William R. Hutchison and Hartmut Lehmann (Minneapolis: Fortress Press,
1994), 107; Clemens Vollnhals, "Im Schatten der Stuttgarter Schulderklärung:
Die Erblast des Nationalprotestantismus," in *Nationalprotestantische Mentalitäten: Konturen, Entwicklungslinien und Umbrüche eines Weltbildes,* ed. Manfred
Gailus and Hartmut Lehmann (Göttingen: Vandenhoeck und Ruprecht,
2005), 379–432.

8. Ernst Forsthoff, *Der totale Staat* (Hamburg: Hanseatische Verlags-Anstalt,
1933), 34–50. On Forsthoff, see Florian Meinel, *Der Jurist in der industriellen
Gesellschaft: Ernst Forsthoff und seine Zeit* (Berlin: Akademie, 2011).

9. Robert P. Ericksen, *Theologians under Hitler: Gerhard Kittel, Paul Althaus, and
Emanuel Hirsch* (New Haven, CT: Yale University Press, 1985), 85.

10. Paul Althaus, *Die deutsche Stunde der Kirche* (Göttingen: Vandenhoeck, 1933),
8–15, quotes at 11, 13.

11. Frieder Günther, "Ordnen, gestalten, bewahren: Radikales Ordnungsdenken
von deutschen Rechtsintellektuellen der Rechtswissenschaft 1920 bis 1960,"
Vierteljahreshefte für Zeitgeschichte 59, no. 3 (2011): 353–384; Lutz Raphael,
"Radikales Ordnungsdenken und die Organisation totalitärer Herrschaft:
Weltanschauungseliten und Humanwissenschaftler im NS-Regime," *Geschichte
und Gesellschaft* 27, no. 1 (2001): 5–40.

12. Paul Althaus, "Totaler Staat?," *Luthertum* 45, no. 5 (1934): 129–135, quote at
134.

13. Paul Althaus, "Zum gegenwärtigen lutherischen Staatsverständnis," in
Die Kirche und das Staatsproblem in der Gegenwart, ed. Forschungsabteilung
des Oekumenischen Rates für Praktisches Christentum (Berlin: Furche,
1934), 7.

14. Ziemann, *Niemöller,* 174–188.

15. Friedrich Wilhelm Graf, *Der heilige Zeitgeist: Studien zur Ideengeschichte der
protestantischen Theologie in der Weimarer Republik* (Tübingen: Mohr Siebeck,
2011), 467–471. On Iwand's connection to Niemöller, see Jürgen Seim, *Hans
Joachim Iwand: Eine Biografie* (Gütersloh: Gütersloher Verlagshaus, 1999),
167–169.

16. Walter Künneth, "Die biblische Offenbarung und die Ordnungen Gottes," in
Die Nation vor Gott: Zur Botschaft der Kirche im dritten Reich, ed. Walter
Künneth and Helmuth Schreiner (Berlin: Wichern, 1933), 1–23, quotes at 16,
20.

17. Heinz-Dietrich Wendland, "Staat und Reich," in Künneth and Schreiner, *Die
Nation vor Gott,* 174–193, quotes at 183, 187.

18. Walter Künneth, "Das Judenproblem und die Kirche," in Künneth and
Schreiner, *Die Nation vor Gott,* 90–105, quotes at 94.

19. For instance, Hans Gerber, *Das ewige Reich* (Tübingen: Mohr, 1935). Gerber, a
professor of administrative law at Leipzig and the president of the Protestant
Gustav Adolph Association, had been active in exchanges with Lutheran

306 NOTES TO PAGES 53-58

theologians during the Weimar Republic. See Gerber, *Die Idee des Staates in der neueren evangelisch-theologischen Ethik: Eine Studie* (Berlin: Junker und Dünhaupt, 1930).

20. On Wolf's connection to Heidegger, see Emmanuel Faye, *Heidegger: The Introduction of Nazism into Philosophy in Light of the Unpublished Seminars of 1933–1935*, trans. Michael B. Smith (New Haven, CT: Yale University Press, 2009), 174–183.

21. Erik Wolf, "Richtiges Recht und evangelischer Glaube," in *Die Nation vor Gott: Zur Botschaft der Kirche im dritten Reich*, ed. Walter Künneth and Helmuth Schreiner, 3rd ed. (Berlin: Wichern, 1934), 241–266, quotes at 246, 249, 257.

22. "NSDAP Party Program (1920)," German History in Documents and Images, https://ghdi.ghi-dc.org/sub_document.cfm?document_id=4625. On leading Nazis' religious views, see Steigmann-Gall, *Holy Reich;* and Todd Weir, "Hitler's Worldview and the Interwar Kulturkampf," *Journal of Contemporary History* 53, no. 3 (2018): 597–621.

23. Statistics on church membership are found in Bergen, *Twisted Cross,* 259n2.

24. Gailus, *Gläubige Zeiten,* 39–50; Klaus Große Kracht, "Katholischer Glaube zwischen 'Volksgemeinschaft' und 'Reich Gottes': Kirchlich-konfessionelle Großveranstaltungen in Berlin im Jahr 1933," in Blaschke and Großbölting, *Was glaubten die Deutschen,* 267–292. On pro-Nazi Catholic priests, see Kevin P. Spicer, *Hitler's Priests: Catholic Clergy and National Socialism* (DeKalb: Northern Illinois University Press, 2008). On anti-Communism and Nazi–Vatican relations, see also Giuliana Chamedes, *A Twentieth-Century Crusade: The Vatican's Battle to Remake Christian Europe* (Cambridge, MA: Harvard University Press, 2019), 137–143.

25. Bergen, *Twisted Cross,* 21–42, 143–154, 178.

26. Bergen, *Twisted Cross,* 88.

27. Martin Niemöller, "Sätze zur Arierfrage in der Kirche," *JK* 1, no. 17 (1933): 269–271.

28. Dietrich Bonhoeffer, "The Church and the Jewish Question," in *Dietrich Bonhoeffer Works,* vol. 12, *Berlin: 1932–1933,* ed. Larry L. Rasmussen (Minneapolis: Fortress Press, 2009), 361–370; Charles Marsh, *Strange Glory: A Life of Dietrich Bonhoeffer* (New York: Knopf, 2014), 101–135, 165–170.

29. Hockenos, *A Church Divided,* 18–19; Ziemann, *Niemöller,* 188–197, quote at 196.

30. For a highly critical assessment, see Paul Silas Peterson, *The Early Karl Barth: Historical Contexts and Intellectual Formation, 1905–1935* (Tübingen: Mohr Siebeck, 2018), 255–298. More balanced is Christiane Tietz, *Karl Barth: A Life in Conflict,* trans. Victoria Barnett (Oxford: Oxford University Press, 2021), 211–214, 223–226.

31. Karl Barth, *Theological Existence To-Day! A Plea for Theological Freedom,* trans. R. Birch Hoyle (London: Hodder and Stoughton, 1933), 30–34.

32. Barth, *Theological Existence To-Day,* 70.

33. Hockenos, *A Church Divided,* 21–22; Ziemann, *Niemöller,* 197–200, 233.

34. Ziemann, *Niemöller,* 219–223.

NOTES TO PAGES 58–63   307

35. Ziemann, *Niemöller,* 235.
36. For a detailed overview of the statement's origin and reception, see Scholder, *Churches,* 2:122–171. The only dissenter, Hermann Sasse, left Barmen before the final vote. The sole woman delegate was Stephanie von Mackensen, who represented the Brethren Council of Pomerania.
37. "Theological Declaration of Barmen (Confessing Church, May 1934)," in Hockenos, *A Church Divided,* 179–180.
38. Scholder, *Churches,* 2:149–150.
39. "Theological Declaration of Barmen," 180.
40. Emil Brunner and Karl Barth, *Natural Theology: Comprising "Nature and Grace" by Professor Dr. Emil Brunner and the Reply "No!" by Karl Barth,* trans. Peter Fraenkel (Eugene, OR: Wipf and Stock, 2002), quote at 90. On the conflict, see Alister E. McGrath, *Emil Brunner: A Reappraisal* (Malden, MA: Wiley Blackwell, 2014), 90–132.
41. McGrath, *Brunner,* 92–93, 128.
42. Quoted in Ericksen, *Theologians under Hitler,* 87.
43. Ernst Wolf, "'Natürliches Gesetz' und 'Gesetz Christi' bei Luther," *EvTh* 2, no. 8 (1935): 305–330, quote at 307; see also Wolf's critique of Brunner in, untitled note, *EvTh* 1, no. 5 (1934): 215–216.
44. Paul Althaus, *Theologie der Ordnungen,* 2nd ed. (Gütersloh: Bertelsmann, 1935), 20–25; see also 13–16 for Althaus's concept of "orders of creation."
45. Hockenos, *A Church Divided,* 28–31; Ziemann, *Niemöller,* 249–256.
46. Ziemann, *Niemöller,* 259–260.
47. Ernst Christian Helmreich, *Religious Education in German Schools: A Historical Approach* (Cambridge, MA: Harvard University Press, 1959), 162–178.
48. Gailus, *Gläubige Zeiten,* 65–70.
49. Barnett, *Soul of the People,* 87.
50. Tietz, *Barth,* 239–248, quote at 239.
51. Tietz, *Barth,* 272.
52. Karl Barth, "Gospel and Law," in Barth, *Community, State, and Church: Three Essays,* ed. David Haddorff (Eugene, OR: Wipf and Stock, 2004), 71–100, quote at 91.
53. Ernst Wolf, "'Natürliches Gesetz,'" 327.
54. Karl-Heinz Becker, "Über das theologische und politische Problem der Versöhnung," *EvTh* 2, no. 4 (1935): 127–140, quotes at 129, 135. See also Becker, "Der Christ als Untertan nach lutherischem Bekenntnis," *EvTh* 3, no. 7 (1936): 276–288.
55. Gailus, *Gläubige Zeiten,* 36–37. See also Manfred Gailus and Clemens Vollnhals, "Protestantische Frauen mit viel Empathie und klugem Eigensinn: Zur Einführung," in Gailus and Vollnhals, *Mit Herz und Verstand,* 7–20.
56. Quoted in Gerlach, *Zeugen,* 139, 143. On Meusel, see Barnett, *Soul of the People,* 130–133; and Hansjörg Buss, "Couragierter Einsatz für die Christen jüdischer Herkunft: Margarete Meusel," in Gailus and Vollnhals, *Mit Herz und Verstand,* 129–146.

NOTES TO PAGES 63–67

57. Buss, "Couragierter Einsatz," 137–138.
58. Elisabeth Schmitz, "Zur Lage der deutschen Nichtarier," in Manfred Gailus, *Mir aber zerriss es das Herz: Der stille Widerstand der Elisabeth Schmitz* (Göttingen: Vandenhoeck und Ruprecht, 2011), 223–252, esp. 240–242; on Schmitz's early life, see 38–57.
59. Gailus, *Zerriss es das Herz*, 94–95.
60. Barth to Schmitz, January 18, 1934, in Dietgard Meyer, "'Wir haben keine Zeit zu warten': Der Briefwechsel zwischen Elisabeth Schmitz und Karl Barth in den Jahren 1934–1936," *Kirchliche Zeitgeschichte* 22, no. 1 (2009): 343–349.
61. Ziemann, *Niemöller*, 277–280.
62. Martin Greschat, ed., *Zwischen Widerspruch und Widerstand: Texte zur Denkschrift der Bekennenden Kirche an Hitler (1936)* (Munich: Kaiser, 1987), 26–27, 48–49.
63. Ziemann, *Niemöller*, 281.
64. "Die veröffentlichte Denkschrift," in Greschat, *Zwischen Widerspruch und Widerstand*, 157.
65. "Die veröffentlichte Denkschrift," 159.
66. Quoted in Ziemann, *Niemöller*, 283, emphasis in original.
67. On Weissler's imprisonment and murder, see Manfred Gailus, *Friedrich Weissler: Ein Jurist und bekennender Christ im Widerstand gegen Hitler* (Göttingen: Vandenhoeck und Ruprecht, 2017), 145–190, quote at 155. The biblical reference is to Acts 5:29: "We must obey God rather than any human authority."
68. Victoria J. Barnett, "Ecumenical Protestant Responses to the Rise of Nazism, Fascism, and Antisemitism during the 1920s and 1930s," in *Religion, Ethnonationalism, and Antisemitism in the Era of the Two World Wars*, ed. Kevin P. Spicer and Rebecca Carter-Chand (Montreal: McGill-Queen's University Press, 2022), 370–371. On the Oxford conference, see Justin Reynolds, "Against the World: International Protestantism and the Ecumenical Movement between Secularization and Politics, 1900–1952" (PhD diss., Columbia University, 2016), 232–247; and Graeme Smith, *Oxford 1937: The Universal Christian Council for Life and Work Conference* (Frankfurt: Peter Lang, 2004).
69. James Chappel, "The Catholic Origins of Totalitarianism Theory in Interwar Europe," *Modern Intellectual History* 8, no. 3 (2011): 561–590, quote at 568.
70. J. H. Oldham, *Church, Community, and State: A World Issue*, 2nd ed. (London: Christian Student Movement Press, 1935), 38. On Oldham and personalism, see also Terence Renaud, "Human Rights as Radical Anthropology: Protestant Theology and Ecumenism in the Transwar Era," *Historical Journal* 60, no. 2 (2017): 503–506; and Smith, *Oxford 1937*, 117–133.
71. Oldham, *Church, Community, and State*, 14.
72. The preparations of the two German church factions are detailed in Kenneth C. Barnes, *Nazism, Liberalism, and Christianity: Protestant Social Thought in Germany and Great Britain, 1925–1937* (Lexington: University Press of Kentucky, 1991), 106–122.

NOTES TO PAGES 67–70   309

73. Barnett, "Ecumenical Protestant Responses," 370–373; Reynolds, "Against the World," 242–247.

74. "Arbeitstagung des Oekumenischen Arbeitskreises innerhalb der DEK," October 20–22, 1936, EZA 5/4043.

75. Paul Althaus, "Kirche, Volk und Staat," in *Kirche, Volk und Staat: Stimmen aus der deutschen evangelischen Kirche zur Oxforder Weltkirchenkonferenz,* ed. Eugen Gerstenmaier (Berlin: Furche, 1937), 20–21.

76. Erik Wolf, "Bemerkungen zu dem Entwurf für die Diskussionsgrundlage über 'Kirche und Staat,'" March 1937, EZA 5/4045. On Wolf's membership in the Nazi Party, see Faye, *Heidegger,* 197.

77. Heinz-Dietrich Wendland, "'Christliche Freiheit,' kreatürliche Freiheit und totaler Staat," in *Totaler Staat und christliche Freiheit,* ed. Emil Brunner (Geneva: Forschungsabteilung der Ökumenischen Rates für Praktisches Christentum, 1937), 171–174.

78. "Bericht über die Studientagung 'Religion und Recht,'" February 23–24, 1937, BArch Koblenz N 1117/8.

79. Daniela Rüther, *Der Widerstand des 20. Juli auf dem Weg in die Soziale Marktwirtschaft: Die wirtschaftspolitischen Vorstellungen der bürgerlichen Opposition gegen Hitler* (Paderborn: Schöningh, 2002), 195. On Dibelius, see Ziemann, *Niemöller,* 185, 267–268. On Dietze, see Detlef J. Blegsen, "'Widersteht dem Teufel'—Ökonomie, Protestantismus und politischer Widerstand bei Constantin von Dietze (1891–1973)," in *Wirtschaft, Politik und Freiheit: Freiburger Wirtschaftswissenschaftler und der Widerstand,* ed. Nils Goldschmidt (Tübingen: Mohr Siebeck, 2005), 67–90.

80. Hans Böhm, *Kirche, Volk und Staat: Bericht des ökumenischen Ausschusses der Vorläufigen Leitung der Deutschen Evangelischen Kirche* (Stuttgart: Quell, 1948), 11–13.

81. Böhm, *Kirche, Volk und Staat,* 11.

82. Barnes, *Nazism,* 100–101; Matthew D. Hockenos, *Then They Came for Me: Martin Niemöller, the Pastor Who Defied the Nazis* (New York: Basic Books, 2018), 123–125 (quote at 125), 132.

83. Quoted in Renaud, "Human Rights," 509.

84. Tom Lawson, *The Church of England and the Holocaust: Christianity, Memory, and Nazism* (Woodbridge: Boydell and Brewer, 2006), 35–36.

85. Quoted in Paul Hanebrink, "European Protestants between Anti-Communism and Anti-Totalitarianism: The Other Interwar Kulturkampf?," *Journal of Contemporary History* 53, no. 3 (2018): 638.

86. Heinz-Dietrich Wendland, "The Kingdom of God and History," in *The Kingdom of God and History,* ed. H. G. Wood (London: George Allen and Unwin, 1938), 145–194; Werner Wiesner, "The Law of Nature and Social Institutions," in *Christian Faith and the Common Life,* ed. Nils Ehrenström (London: George Allen and Unwin, 1938), 101–142.

87. On Niemöller's imprisonment, see Ziemann, *Niemöller,* 311–356.

88. Barnett, *Soul of the People,* 87; Graf, *Der heilige Zeitgeist,* 469.

NOTES TO PAGES 70–73

89. Barnett, *Soul of the People*, 90–91.
90. Noah Benezra Strote, *Lions and Lambs: Conflict in Weimar and the Creation of Post-Nazi Germany* (New Haven, CT: Yale University Press, 2017), 162–163.
91. Gailus, *Zerriss es das Herz*, 114–120; Helmut Gollwitzer, "Predigt über Lukas 3, 3–14 (Bußtag, 16.11.1938)," *EvTh* 11, no. 4 (1951/52): 145–151, quotes at 147–148.
92. Manfred Gailus identifies only three Protestant pastors and one Catholic church official who spoke out in opposition to the Kristallnacht pogrom. See Gailus, *Gläubige Zeiten*, 105–109, quote at 108.
93. On the Grüber office, see Barnett, *Soul of the People*, 144–146; Gerlach, *Zeugen*, 256–273; and Hartmut Ludwig, *An der Seite der Entrechteten und Schwachen: Zur Geschichte des "Büro Pfarrer Grüber" (1938 bis 1940) und der Ev. Hilfsstelle für ehemals Rassesnverfolgte nach 1945* (Berlin: Logos, 2009).
94. For examples, see Gailus, *Gläubige Zeiten*, 118–127.
95. Gerlach, *Zeugen*, 269–270.
96. Gerlach, *Zeugen*, 326.
97. Helmut Gollwitzer, *Unwilling Journey: A Diary from Russia*, trans. E. M. Delacour (London: SCM Press, 1953), 20. On the criminalization of conscientious objection in Nazi Germany, see Thomas Widera, "Kriegsdienstverweigerung und staatliche Herrschaft—NS-Regime, SED-Staat, Bundesrepublik Deutschland," *Totalitarismus und Demokratie* 5, no. 2 (2008): 397–403.
98. Bergen, *Between God and Hitler*, 113–171. See also Dagmar Pöpping, *Passion und Vernichtung: Kriegspfarrer an der Ostfront 1941–1945* (Göttingen: Vandenhoeck und Ruprecht, 2019).
99. Ziemann, *Niemöller*, 321–330.
100. Günter Brakelmann, "Der Kreisauer Kreis als christliche Widerstandsgruppe," in *Der 20. Juli 1944 und das Erbe des deutschen Widerstands*, ed. Günter Brakelmann and Manfred Keller (Münster: Lit, 2005), 67–85; Maria D. Mitchell, *The Origins of Christian Democracy: Politics and Confession in Modern Germany* (Ann Arbor: University of Michigan Press, 2012), 29–32.
101. On the origins and membership of the Freiburg circle, see Nils Goldschmidt, "Die Entstehung der Freiburger Kreise," *Historisch-politische Mitteilungen* 4, no. 1 (1997): 1–17. Gollwitzer did not attend the meetings of the circle but remained in correspondence with its members while serving on the Eastern Front. See Gollwitzer to Dietze, April 19, 1944; and Gollwitzer to Dietze, July 16, 1944, both ACDP 01-345-005/2. On Erik Wolf's wartime writings, see Faye, *Heidegger*, 186–192.
102. Doris L. Bergen, "Contextualizing Dietrich Bonhoeffer: Nazism, the Churches, and the Question of Silence," in *Interpreting Bonhoeffer: Historical Perspectives, Emerging Issues*, ed. Clifford J. Green and Guy C. Carter (Minneapolis: Fortress Press, 2013), 111–126.
103. Gerhard Ritter, "Kirche und Welt: Eine notwendige Besinnung auf die Aufgaben des Christen und der Kirche in unserer Zeit," in *Gerhard Ritter:*

Ein politischer Historiker in seinen Briefen, ed. Klaus Schwabe and Rolf Reichardt (Boppard: Boldt, 1984), 635–654, quotes at 647, 650, emphasis in original.

104. Constantin von Dietze, *Nationalökonomie und Theologie* (Tübingen: Furche, 1947), quotes at 32, 40; see also Dietze's address to the Freiburg circle, "Stellung und Aufgabe des evangelischen Christen und der evangelischen Kirche in ihrem Verhältnis zum Recht," ACDP 01-345-012/6. On the Society for Protestant Theology, see Ernst Wolf, "Niederschrift über die erste Sitzung des Vorstandes," April 15, 1940, BArch Koblenz N 1367/318.

105. Thielicke to Dietze, August 1, 1941, and Wendland to Dietze, May 28, 1942, both UAF C 100/580; Becker to Dietze, September 12, 1941, UAF C 100/780.

106. George Bell, "Memorandum of Conversations," June 19, 1942, in *Dietrich Bonhoeffer Works*, vol. 16, *Conspiracy and Imprisonment: 1940–1945*, ed. Mark S. Brocker (Minneapolis: Fortress Press, 2006), 319–324; Marsh, *Strange Glory*, 329–331.

107. Rüther, *Widerstand*, 196.

108. Rüther, *Widerstand*, 196–198.

109. Helmut Thielicke, ed., *In der Stunde Null: Die Denkschrift des Freiburger "Bonhoeffer-Kreises"* (Tübingen: Mohr Siebeck, 1979), 73, 78.

110. Thielicke, *In der Stunde Null*, 36–54, quotes at 38–39.

111. Samuel Moyn, *Christian Human Rights* (Philadelphia: University of Pennsylvania Press, 2015), 117; Thielicke, *In der Stunde Null*, 105, 129.

112. Thielicke, *In der Stunde Null*, 58–59.

113. Thielicke, *In der Stunde Null*, 64.

114. Thielicke, *In der Stunde Null*, 78.

115. Thielicke, *In der Stunde Null*, 102–107, quote at 106.

116. Thielicke, *In der Stunde Null*, 107, 129–130.

117. Thielicke, *In der Stunde Null*, 88–89.

118. Barnett, *Soul of the People*, 166–172. For a detailed reconstruction of the debate, see Dagmar Herbrecht, *Emanzipation oder Anpassung: Argumentationswege der Theologinnen im Streit um die Frauenordination in der Bekennenden Kirche* (Neukirchen-Vluyn: Neukirchener Verlag, 2000).

119. Thielicke, *In der Stunde Null*, 146–151.

120. Gerhard Ritter, "Vorwort," in Thielicke, *In der Stunde Null*, 28.

121. Daniela Rüther, "Der Einfluss der Freiburger Kreise auf die Widerstandsbewegung des 20. Juli 1944," in *Die Freiburger Kreise: Akademischer Widerstand und Soziale Marktwirtschaft*, ed. Hans Maier (Paderborn: Schöningh, 2014), 57–70. For an analysis of the Freiburg circle's economic proposals, see Rüther, *Widerstand*, 208–265.

122. On the postwar planning of the Kreisau circle, see Hans Mommsen, *Germans against Hitler: The Stauffenberg Plot and Resistance under the Third Reich*, trans. Angus McGeoch (Princeton, NJ: Princeton University Press, 2003), 42–133.

123. Quoted in Gailus, *Gläubige Zeiten*, 159.

312   NOTES TO PAGES 78–82

124. Beate Kosmala, "'Losgelöst und auf sich gestellt': Helene Jacobs' Hilfe für verfolgte Juden," in Gailus and Vollnhals, *Mit Herz und Verstand*, 191–212; Katrin Rudolph, *Hilfe beim Sprung ins Nichts: Franz Kaufmann und die Rettung von Juden und "nichtarischen" Christen*, rev. ed. (Berlin: Metropol, 2017). Much of the circle was arrested in August 1943 after being denounced to the Gestapo. Kaufmann, a Protestant of Jewish descent, was murdered at Sachsenhausen in February 1944.

125. Blegsen, "'Widersteht dem Teufel,'" 75; Marsh, *Strange Glory*, 375–376.

126. Marsh, *Strange Glory*, 344, 380–390.

127. Dietrich Bonhoeffer, "After Ten Years: An Account at the Turn of the Year 1942–1943," in *"After Ten Years": Dietrich Bonhoeffer and Our Times*, ed. Victoria J. Barnett (Minneapolis: Fortress Press, 2017), 20–21.

128. Marsh, *Strange Glory*, 345–347.

129. Constantin von Dietze to his family, October 28, 1944, ACDP 01-256-059/4.

3. Post-Nazi Justice and Protestant Human Rights

1. Helmut Thielicke, "Die Kirche inmitten des deutschen Zusammenbruchs, ihre Beurteilung der Lage und ihre Ziele" (June 15, 1945), in *Kirche nach der Kapitulation: Das Jahr 1945, eine Dokumentation*, vol. 1, *Die Allianz zwischen Genf, Stuttgart und Bethel*, ed. Gerhard Besier, Jörg Thierfelder, and Ralf Tyra (Stuttgart: Kohlhammer, 1989), 203–209.

2. Quoted in Damian van Melis, "'Strengthened and Purified through Ordeal by Fire': Ecclesiastical Triumphalism in the Ruins of Europe," in *Life after Death: Approaches to a Cultural and Social History of Europe during the 1940s and 1950s*, ed. Richard Bessel and Dirk Schumann (Washington, DC: German Historical Institute, 2003), 233.

3. "Report of Section III: 'The Church and the Disorder of Society,'" in *Man's Disorder and God's Design: The Amsterdam Assembly Series*, vol. 3, *The Church and the Disorder of Society*, ed. World Council of Churches (New York: Harper and Brothers, 1948), 191.

4. Maria D. Mitchell, *The Origins of Christian Democracy: Politics and Confession in Modern Germany* (Ann Arbor: University of Michigan Press, 2012), 35–37, quote at 35.

5. Piotr H. Kosicki, *Catholics on the Barricades: Poland, France, and "Revolution," 1892–1956* (New Haven, CT: Yale University Press, 2018), 152–188.

6. James Chappel, *Catholic Modern: The Challenge of Totalitarianism and the Remaking of the Church* (Cambridge, MA: Harvard University Press, 2018), 144–181; Wolfram Kaiser, *Christian Democracy and the Origins of the European Union* (Cambridge: Cambridge University Press, 2007), 163–190; Mitchell, *Origins of Christian Democracy*, 115–139.

7. Doris L. Bergen, *Twisted Cross: The German Christian Movement in the Third Reich* (Chapel Hill: University of North Carolina Press, 1996), 212.

NOTES TO PAGES 83–84   313

8. The literature on human rights in postwar European and global history is vast. Major works include Marco Duranti, *The Conservative Human Rights Revolution: European Identity, Transnational Politics, and the Origins of the European Convention* (Oxford: Oxford University Press, 2017); Jan Eckel, *The Ambivalence of Good: Human Rights in International Politics since the 1940s,* trans. Rachel Ward (Oxford: Oxford University Press, 2019); and Samuel Moyn, *Not Enough: Human Rights in an Unequal World* (Cambridge, MA: Harvard University Press, 2018). On Christian iterations of human rights, see Samuel Moyn, *Christian Human Rights* (Philadelphia: University of Pennsylvania Press, 2015); and Sarah Shortall and Daniel Steinmetz-Jenkins, eds., *Christianity and Human Rights Reconsidered* (Cambridge: Cambridge University Press, 2020). On the West German case, see Lora Wildenthal, *The Language of Human Rights in West Germany* (Philadelphia: University of Pennsylvania Press, 2013). Wildenthal's discussion of competing "languages of human rights" has been particularly important in framing my analysis.

9. While numerous scholars have addressed the German Protestant opposition to Allied war crimes trials, this episode has not been linked to questions of human rights or the longer transformation of the postwar church. See Hilary Earl, *The Nuremberg SS-Einsatzgruppen Trial, 1945–1958: Atrocity, Law, and History* (Cambridge: Cambridge University Press, 2009), 270–286; Norbert Frei, *Adenauer's Germany and the Nazi Past: The Politics of Amnesty and Reconciliation,* trans. Joel Golb (New York: Columbia University Press, 2002), 98–126; Katharina von Kellenbach, *The Mark of Cain: Guilt and Denial in the Post-War Lives of Nazi Perpetrators* (Oxford: Oxford University Press, 2013), 33–61; Ernst Klee, *Persilscheine und falsche Pässe: Wie die Kirchen die Nazis halfen* (Frankfurt: Fischer Taschenbuch, 1991); Jerome S. Legge Jr., "Resisting a War Crimes Trial: The Malmédy Massacre, the German Churches, and the U.S. Army Counterintelligence Corps," *Holocaust and Genocide Studies* 26, no. 2 (2012): 229–260; Kim Christian Priemel, *The Betrayal: The Nuremberg Trials and German Divergence* (Oxford: Oxford University Press, 2016), 354–362; Steven P. Remy, *The Malmedy Massacre: The War Crimes Trial Controversy* (Cambridge, MA: Harvard University Press, 2017), 180–212; Nicholas John Williams, *"Die Gefangenen leiden sehr unter ihrer Lage": Die Betreuung deutscher NS-Täter durch Hans Stempel und Theodor Friedrich* (Stuttgart: Kohlhammer, 2023); JonDavid K. Wyneken, "Driving Out the Demons: German Churches, the Western Allies, and the Internationalization of the Nazi Past, 1945–1952" (PhD diss., Ohio University, 2007), 336–392; and Ronald Webster, "Opposing 'Victors' Justice': German Protestant Churchmen and Convicted War Criminals in Western Europe after 1945," *Holocaust and Genocide Studies* 15, no. 1 (2001): 47–69.

10. On early Allied planning for postwar Germany, see Jeffrey K. Olick, *In the House of the Hangman: The Agonies of German Defeat, 1943–1949* (Chicago: University of Chicago Press, 2005), 65–94.

11. Sean Brennan, *The Politics of Religion in Soviet-Occupied Germany: The Case of Berlin-Brandenburg, 1945–1949* (Lanham, MD: Lexington Books, 2011).

314 NOTES TO PAGES 84–89

12. Wyneken, "Driving Out the Demons," 80–85.
13. "Bishop of Chichester's Visit to Germany, October 18–30, 1945: Press Conference at the Ministry of Information," November 1, 1945, WCC Archives, 301.43.13/2; George Bell et al., *The Task of the Churches in Germany* (London: SPCK, 1947). See also Tom Lawson, *The Church of England and the Holocaust: Christianity, Memory, and Nazism* (Woodbridge: Boydell and Brewer, 2006), 124–125, 131–133.
14. Stewart W. Herman, *The Rebirth of the German Church* (New York: Harper and Brothers, 1946), quote at xvi; Herman, "Does Germany Need Help?," March 1946, WCC Archives, 301.43.14/8. On Herman, see James Strasburg, *God's Marshall Plan: American Protestants and the Struggle for the Soul of Europe* (Oxford: Oxford University Press, 2021), 79–103, 132–144. On WCC aid to occupied Germany, see also James C. Enns, *Saving Germany: North American Protestants and Christian Mission to West Germany, 1945–1974* (Montreal: McGill-Queen's University Press, 2017), 26–59.
15. Strasburg, *God's Marshall Plan,* 134–135, 152–153; Wyneken, "Driving Out the Demons," 60–73.
16. Christiane Tietz, *Karl Barth: A Life in Conflict,* trans. Victoria Barnett (Oxford: Oxford University Press, 2021), 268–277, 296–297.
17. Karl Barth, "Church and State," in Barth, *Community, State, and Church: Three Essays,* ed. David Haddorff (Eugene, OR: Wipf and Stock, 2004), 101–148. See also Tietz, *Barth,* 281–283.
18. Barth, "Church and State," 130. The biblical verse is Romans 13:1.
19. Barth, "Church and State," 146.
20. Barth, "Church and State," 139 (emphasis in original).
21. Benjamin Ziemann, *Martin Niemöller: Ein Leben in Opposition* (Munich: Deutsche Verlags-Anstalt, 2019), 359–368, quotes at 385.
22. Karl Barth, *The Germans and Ourselves,* trans. Ronald Gregor Smith (London: Nisbet, 1945).
23. Ziemann, *Niemöller,* 388–390.
24. "Message to the Pastors (Brethren Council, August 1945)," in Matthew D. Hockenos, *A Church Divided: German Protestants Confront the Nazi Past* (Bloomington: Indiana University Press, 2004), 181–183.
25. On narratives of inaction in postwar accounts of the Nazi-era churches, see also Doris L. Bergen, "Contextualizing Dietrich Bonhoeffer: Nazism, the Churches, and the Question of Silence," in *Interpreting Bonhoeffer: Historical Perspectives, Emerging Issues,* ed. Clifford J. Green and Guy C. Carter (Minneapolis: Fortress Press, 2013), 111–126.
26. Victoria Barnett, *For the Soul of the People: Protestant Protest against Hitler* (New York: Oxford University Press, 1992), 251–253.
27. Quoted in Hockenos, *A Church Divided,* 48.
28. Ziemann, *Niemöller,* 387, 390–391. On the Treysa conference, see also Hockenos, *A Church Divided,* 42–55.

NOTES TO PAGES 89–92   315

29. "Vorläufige Ordnung der Evangelischen Kirche in Deutschland," in *Protokolle*, vol. 1, *1945/46*, ed. Carsten Nicolaisen and Nora Andrea Schulze (Göttingen: Vandenhoeck und Ruprecht, 1995), 13–14. On Heinemann's participation in the Confessing Church, see Jörg Treffke, *Gustav Heinemann: Wanderer zwischen den Parteien: Eine politische Biographie* (Paderborn: Schöningh, 2009), 76–81.

30. The first woman appointed to the EKD Council was the theologian Gerta Scharffenorth. See Ralf Schick, "Die erste Frau im Rat der EKD," Evangelischer Pressedienst, December 9, 2014, https://www.evangelisch.de/inhalte /111679/09-12-2014.

31. Ernst Forsthoff, "Das Elternrecht: Juristisch beleuchtet," in *Christen und Nichtchristen in der Rechtsordnung: Vorträge der 5. Plenarsitzung der Studiengemeinschaft der Evangelischen Akademie* (Bad Boll: Studiengemeinschaft der Evangelischen Akademie, 1950), 63–83; "Tage der Stille und Besinnung für Juristen vom 1. bis 6. Oktober 1948 im Kurhaus Bad Boll," EABB, Juristentagungen, 1948. For a critical perspective on the founding of the Protestant Academies, see Thomas Mittmann, *Kirchliche Akademien in der Bundesrepublik: Gesellschaftliche, politische und religiöse Selbstverortungen* (Göttingen: Wallstein, 2011), 13–42.

32. Thomas Sauer, *Westorientierung im deutschen Protestantismus? Vorstellungen und Tätigkeit des Kronberger Kreises* (Munich: Oldenbourg, 1999), 54–60.

33. Mittmann, *Kirchliche Akademien*, 14–15.

34. Doris L. Bergen, *Between God and Hitler: Military Chaplains in Nazi Germany* (Cambridge: Cambridge University Press, 2023), 124, 142–143.

35. Claudia Lepp, "Konservativ-christlicher Widerstand: Das Beispiel Gerhard Ritter," *Jahrbuch für badische Kirchen- und Religionsgeschichte* 2 (2008): 77; Gerhard Ritter, "Vorwort," in *In der Stunde Null: Die Denkschrift des Freiburger "Bonhoeffer-Kreises,"* ed. Helmut Thielicke (Tübingen: Mohr Siebeck, 1979), 26–30.

36. Reinhold Schneider, "Geleitwort für die Sammlung 'Das Christliche Deutschland 1933–1945,'" in *"Im Reiche dieses Königs hat man das Recht lieb": Der Kampf der Bekennenden Kirche um das Recht*, ed. Erik Wolf (Tübingen: Furche, 1946), 7.

37. Asmussen to Dietze, Ritter, and Wolf, September 20, 1945, BArch Koblenz N 1166/256.

38. The program and list of attendees are found in "Tagung der Stille und Besinnung für Männer des Rechts und der Wirtschaft, 29. September–12. Oktober 1945," EABB, Juristentagungen, 1945.

39. "Ansprache (D. Wurm) bei der Eröffnung der Juristenfreizeit in Bad Boll am 29. September 1945," EABB, Juristentagungen, 1945.

40. Landgerichtsrat Nestle, "Bericht über die Tagung der Evangelischen Akademie für Männer des Rechts und der Wirtschaft in Bad Boll vom 30. September bis 12. Oktober 1945," EABB, Juristentagungen, 1945.

41. Gerhard Ritter, *Christentum und Selbstbehauptung* (Tübingen: Furche, 1946), 5, 10–12.

NOTES TO PAGES 93–96

42. Constantin von Dietze, "Eigengesetzlichkeit und Verantwortlichkeit in der Wirtschaft," in *Wirtschaftsmacht und Wirtschaftsordnung* (Tübingen: Furche, 1947), 16–17, 25–27, quote at 25.

43. Dietze, "Eigengesetzlichkeit," 20–22.

44. Hockenos, *A Church Divided*, 77–81; Strasburg, *God's Marshall Plan*, 150–152.

45. "Stuttgart Declaration of Guilt (Evangelical Church of Germany council, October 1945)," in Hockenos, *A Church Divided*, 187.

46. Some of the letters are collected in EZA 2/34 and 2/35. See also Hockenos, *A Church Divided*, 84–90.

47. "Hans Asmussens Kommentar zur Stuttgarter Erklärung," in *Die Schuld der Kirche: Dokumente und Reflexionen zur Stuttgarter Schulderklärung vom 18./19. Oktober 1945*, ed. Martin Greschat (Munich: Kaiser, 1982), 132–143.

48. "Helmut Thielicke: Exkurs über Karl Barths Vortrag in Tübingen (8.11.1945)," in Greschat, *Die Schuld der Kirche*, 163–172, quote at 166. See also "Karl Barth: Ein Wort an die Deutschen (2.11.1945)," in Greschat, *Die Schuld der Kirche*, 160–163.

49. Frei, *Adenauer's Germany*, 94. On the shift from the IMT to the subsequent Nuremberg trials, see Priemel, *Betrayal*, 151–161.

50. On the survey, see Mikkel Dack, *Everyday Denazification in Postwar Germany: The Fragebogen and Political Screening during the Allied Occupation* (Cambridge: Cambridge University Press, 2023), quote at 10.

51. For the conviction rates in each zone, see Perry Biddiscombe, *The Denazification of Germany: A History, 1945–1950* (Stroud: Tempus, 2007), 81, 114–115, 151–152, 181.

52. Gary Bass, *Stay the Hand of Vengeance: The Politics of War Crimes Tribunals* (Princeton, NJ: Princeton University Press, 2000), 181–191, 195–196.

53. Francine Hirsch, *Soviet Judgment at Nuremberg: A New History of the International Military Tribunal after World War II* (Oxford: Oxford University Press, 2020), 47; Priemel, *Betrayal*, 60–71.

54. Hirsch, *Soviet Judgment*, 34–39.

55. Lawrence Douglas, "Was damals Recht war . . . *Nulla Poena* and the Prosecution of Crimes against Humanity in Occupied Germany," in *Jus Post Bellum and Transitional Justice*, ed. Larry May and Elizabeth Edenberg (Cambridge: Cambridge University Press, 2013), 44–73; Hirsch, *Soviet Judgment*, 245–319; Devin O. Pendas, *Democracy, Nazi Trials, and Transitional Justice in Germany, 1945–1950* (Cambridge: Cambridge University Press, 2020), 104–137; Priemel, *Betrayal*, 125–136.

56. "3. Sitzung Frankfurt/Main 13. und 14. Dezember 1945: Protokoll," in Nicolaisen and Schulze, *Protokolle*, 1:211–212.

57. Wurm to Amerikanische Militärregierung für Deutschland, April 26, 1946, *KJ* 72–75 (1945–1948): 191–197, quote at 193. On German critiques of denazification, see also Biddiscombe, *Denazification*, 183–216; and Dack, *Everyday Denazification*, 175–180.

58. "Bishop of Chichester's Visit to Germany"; Herman, *Rebirth*, 111–124.

NOTES TO PAGES 96–102

59. Wurm to Amerikanische Militärregierung für Deutschland, 192.
60. "Entschließung des Rates zur Durchführung der Entnazifizierung im deutschen Volk: Treysa, 2. Mai 1946," in Nicolaisen and Schulze, *Protokolle,* 1:504. More broadly on the Protestant campaign against denazification, see Clemens Vollnhals, *Evangelische Kirche und Entnazifizierung: Der Last der nationalsozialistischen Vergangenheit* (Munich: Oldenbourg, 1989).
61. "Evangelische Akademie—Tage der Stille und Besinnung für Juristen vom 2. bis 9. Oktober 1946 im Kurhaus Bad Boll / Freitag, 4. Oktober 1946, nachmittags," EABB, Juristentagungen, 1946, quotes at 15, 33.
62. "Juristentagung der Evangelischen Akademie in Bad Boll," *Deutsche Rechts-Zeitschrift* 1, no. 6 (1946): 190.
63. Erik Wolf, "Biblische Weisung als Richtschnur des Rechts," in *Rechtsgedanke und biblische Weisung* (Tübingen: Furche, 1948), 33–64. See also Lena Foljanty, *Recht oder Gesetz: Juristische Identität und Autorität in den Naturrechtsdebatten der Nachkriegszeit* (Tübingen: Mohr Siebeck, 2013), 137–153.
64. Wolfgang Maasser, "Wolf, Ernst," in *BBKL,* vol. 13, ed. Traugott Bautz (Herzberg: Bautz, 1998), 1495–1496.
65. Jürgen Seim, *Hans Joachim Iwand: Eine Biografie* (Gütersloh: Gütersloher Verlagshaus, 1999), 306–308.
66. On the activities of the Rhineland and Württemberg groups during the Nazi era, see Diethard Buchstädt, *Kirche für die Welt: Entstehung, Geschichte und Wirken der Kirchlichen Bruderschaften im Rheinland und in Württemberg 1945–1960* (Cologne: Rheinland, 1999), 12–42.
67. Karl Barth, "The Christian Community and the Civil Community," in *Community, State, and Church,* 149–189. On the context of Barth's lecture, see Tietz, *Barth,* 321–324.
68. Barth, "Christian Community," 173–179, quote at 175.
69. Barth, "Christian Community," 172.
70. Barth, "Christian Community," 161 (emphasis in original).
71. Barth, "Christian Community," 182.
72. Barth, "Christian Community," 163–165.
73. Barth, "Christian Community," 184.
74. Quoted in Tietz, *Barth,* 323. On Heinemann's role in the founding of the CDU, see Treffke, *Heinemann,* 87–88.
75. Ernst Wolf, "Zur Selbstkritik des Luthertums," in *Evangelische Selbstprüfung: Beiträge und Berichte von der gemeinsamen Arbeitstagung der Kirchlich-theologischen Sozietät in Württemberg und der Gesellschaft für Evangelische Theologie, Sektion Süddeutschland im Kurhaus Bad Boll vom 12. bis 16. Oktober 1946,* ed. Paul Schempp (Stuttgart: Kohlhammer, 1947), 113–135, quote at 132.
76. Hans-Joachim Iwand, "Die Neuordnung der Kirche und die konfessionelle Frage," in Schempp, *Evangelische Selbstprüfung,* 57–68, quotes at 64–65.
77. "Statement by the Council of Brethren of the Evangelical Church of Germany Concerning the Political Course of Our People (Darmstadt Statement,

318 NOTES TO PAGES 102–106

August 1947)," in Hockenos, *A Church Divided,* 193–194. On the meeting that produced the statement, see Ziemann, *Niemöller,* 426–427.

78. Joachim Beckmann, Hermann Diem, Martin Niemöller, and Ernst Wolf, "Das Wort des Bruderrates der Evangelischen Kirche in Deutschland zum politischen Weg unseres Volkes," *Flugblätter der Bekennenden Kirche,* no. 9/10 (Stuttgart: Quell, 1948), 7–9.

79. Hockenos, *A Church Divided,* 125–127.

80. Beckmann et al., "Das Wort des Bruderrates," 13–14.

81. Hockenos, *A Church Divided,* 130–133.

82. Gerhard Ritter, "Luther und die politische Erziehung der Deutschen," *Zeitwende* 18, no. 6 (1947): 592–607.

83. Helmut Thielicke, *Kirche und Öffentlichkeit: Zur Grundlegung einer lutherischen Kulturethik* (Tübingen: Furche, 1947), 37–38.

84. Stewart Herman, "Conversation with Pastor Niemoller in Frankfurt," December 2, 1945, WCC Archives, 301.43.14/9. Herman repeated this accusation in *Rebirth,* 95.

85. "Kanzelabkündigung (Hessen-Nassau)," *KJ* 72–75 (1945–48): 206–208. See also Ziemann, *Niemöller,* 409–412.

86. Buchstädt, *Kirche,* 103–110.

87. "Evangelische Kirche und Entnazifizierung, 14.2.1948: Eine Stellungnahme des Ausschusses der Kirchlich-theologischen Sozietät in Württemberg," in Buchstädt, *Kirche,* 465–469, quote at 469.

88. Karl Heinz Voigt, *Ökumene in Deutschland von der Gründung der ACK bis zur Charta Oecumenica* (Göttingen: Vandenhoeck und Ruprecht, 2015), 64–67. More generally on the Amsterdam Assembly, see Justin Reynolds, "Against the World: International Protestantism and the Ecumenical Movement between Secularization and Politics, 1900–1952" (PhD diss., Columbia University, 2016), 321–337.

89. See Duranti, *Conservative Human Rights,* esp. 215–254, 321–342.

90. Jacques Maritain, *The Rights of Man and Natural Law,* trans. Doris C. Anson (New York: Scribner, 1943), quotes at 64–68; see also 73–83. On Maritain's writings on human rights, see Chappel, *Catholic Modern,* 169–173; and Moyn, *Christian Human Rights,* 65–100.

91. Moyn, *Christian Human Rights,* 54–55, 86–87.

92. On the Dulles commission, see Andrew Preston, *Sword of Spirit, Shield of Faith: Religion in American War and Diplomacy* (New York: Knopf, 2012), 384–409; Michael G. Thompson, *For God and Globe: Christian Internationalism in the United States between the Great War and the Cold War* (Ithaca, NY: Cornell University Press, 2015), 167–189; and Gene Zubovich, *Before the Religious Right: Liberal Protestants, Human Rights, and the Polarization of the United States* (Philadelphia: University of Pennsylvania Press, 2021), 89–119.

93. Ernst Wolf, "Menschenwerdung des Menschen? Zum Thema Humanismus und Christentum," *EvTh* 6, no. 1 (1946/47): 4–25, quote at 23.

NOTES TO PAGES 106–109   319

94. Gerhard Ritter, "Kirche und internationale Ordnung," September 22, 1947, quotes at 10, 16; and Walz to Mitarbeiter und Freunde der Studiengemeinschaft, October 24, 1947, both UAF C 100/568.

95. David Lovekin, *Technique, Discourse, and Consciousness: An Introduction to the Philosophy of Jacques Ellul* (Bethlehem, PA: Lehigh University Press, 1991), 129–132.

96. Ellul would be posthumously recognized as "Righteous among the Nations" by the Israeli Holocaust memorial Yad Vashem. See "Ellul, Jacques," The Righteous among the Nations, Yad Vashem, https://collections.yadvashem .org/en/righteous/4412162.

97. Barth, "Church and State," 101.

98. Jacques Ellul, *The Theological Foundation of Law,* trans. Marguerite Wieser (New York: Seabury Press, 1969), 79–84, quotes at 81.

99. Ernst Wolf, "Naturrecht und Gerechtigkeit: Zum Problem des Naturrechts," *EvTh* 7, no. 7/8 (1947/48): 252–253. See also Reinhard Mumm, "Jesus Christus der Herr alles Rechts," *Die Zeichen der Zeit* 2, no. 7/8 (1948): 255–260; and Heinz-Horst Schrey and Otto Weber, "Wiederkehr des Naturrechts?," *Verkündigung und Forschung* 3 (1946/1947): 215–220. Otto Weber translated Ellul's text into German as *Die theologische Begründung des Rechts* (Munich: Kaiser, 1948).

100. Ellul, *Theological Foundation,* 135–136, emphasis in original.

101. Jacques Ellul, "Note sur le Procès de Nuremberg," *Verbum Caro: Revue théologique et ecclésiastique* 1, no. 3 (1947): 97–112.

102. Lorenz Völker, *"War mein Grossvater ein Nazi?": Ein Enkel auf Spurensuche nach der Geschichte eines Staatsanwalts im Dritten Reich* (Hildesheim: Arete, 2015), 31–37, 66–90, 99–110, 123.

103. On the attendance at the lecture, see "Liste der Teilnehmer an der zweiten Plenarsitzung der Studiengemeinschaft der Evangelischen Akademie vom 19.–22.9.47," EABB, Studiengemeinschaft, 2. Plenarsitzung.

104. Hans Dombois, *Menschenrechte und moderner Staat* (Frankfurt: Lembeck, 1948), 9, 34.

105. Dombois, *Menschenrechte,* 18–19.

106. Dombois, *Menschenrechte,* 13–14, quotes at 47.

107. O. Frederick Nolde, "Freedom of Religion and Related Human Rights," in *Man's Disorder and God's Design,* vol. 4, *The Church and the International Disorder,* ed. World Council of Churches (New York: Harper and Brothers, 1948), 148–149. For the list of member churches, see "Member Churches Represented at the Assembly," in *Man's Disorder and God's Design,* vol. 5, *The First Assembly of the World Council of Churches,* ed. W. A. Visser 't Hooft (London: SCM Press, 1949), 230–236.

108. In addition to the memorandum by Gerhard Ritter cited above, see "Beitrag zum Problem der Menschenrechte von Staatsanwalt Dombois, Frankfurt am Main, April 1948," WCC Archives, 31.015.7/1; "Libertas Christiana (erster Entwurf) von Prof. D. Ernst Wolf, Göttingen, April 1948," WCC Archives,

320   NOTES TO PAGES 109–112

31.016.7/1; and "'Biblische Weisung als Richtschnur des Rechts,' von Prof. Dr. Erik Wolf, Freiburg i.Br., Oktober 1947," WCC Archives, 31.016.7/3.

109. For instance, see the reflections of the Freiburg participants cited in Hans-Georg Dietrich, "Kirche und Welt—Impulse aus Freiburg zur Weltkirchenkonferenz in Amsterdam 1948," *Freiburger Universitätsblätter* 27, no. 102 (1988): 78–80. The German delegates are listed in *Man's Disorder,* 5:239, 249–250.

110. Gerhard Ritter, "Bilanz von Amsterdam," *Der Spiegel,* October 1, 1948. See also Rudolf Smend, "Amsterdam und die Versammlung des Ökumenischen Rates der Kirchen," *Deutsche Universitätszeitung* 3, no. 20 (1948): 6–8.

111. "Die Kirche und die internationale Unordnung: Bericht der Sektion IV," *EvW,* September 15, 1948.

112. "Das Weltgespräch über die Menschenrechte," *EvW,* December 15, 1948; Ha. [Oskar Hammelsbeck], "Die Kirche vor der Frage der Neugestaltung des Rechts," *JK* 10, no. 3–4 (1949): 106–114; Reinhard Mumm, "Um eine evangelische Begründung des Rechts," *JK* 10, no. 3–4 (1949): 79–92.

113. "Universal Declaration of Human Rights," art. 18, United Nations, https://www.un.org/en/universal-declaration-human-rights/; Linde Lindkvist, *Religious Freedom and the Universal Declaration of Human Rights* (Cambridge: Cambridge University Press, 2017), 78–85, 106–110.

114. Mumm, "Evangelische Begründung des Rechts," 91.

115. Hirsch, *Soviet Judgment,* 363–364; "Transcript for NMT 4: Pohl Case," August 25, 1947, 6839, Harvard Law School Library Nuremberg Trials Project, https://nuremberg.law.harvard.edu/transcripts/5-transcript-for-nmt -4-pohl-case.

116. Remy, *Malmedy Massacre,* 198–199. On the torture allegations, see Remy, *Malmedy Massacre,* 82–90, 143–179.

117. "Bischof Wurm zu den Kriegsverbrecherprozessen," *EvW,* June 1, 1948. See also "Wurm fordert eine Berufungsinstanz," *EvW,* July 1, 1948.

118. Wyneken, "Driving Out the Demons," 365–372.

119. Wyneken, "Driving Out the Demons," 363.

120. Earl, *Nuremberg SS-Einsatzgruppen Trial,* 270–272. On Neuhäusler and German Catholic opposition to war crimes trials, see also Frei, *Adenauer's Germany,* 110–119; and Remy, *Malmedy Massacre,* 186–195, 206–212.

121. Legge, "Resisting," 236–238.

122. For the example of SS-Obergruppenführer Oswald Pohl, who reclaimed his Catholic faith in prison, see Kellenbach, *Mark of Cain,* 87–111; and Klee, *Persilscheine,* 104–107.

123. "Ranke, Hansjürg," in *Personenlexikon zum deutschen Protestantismus 1919–1949,* ed. Hannelore Braun and Gertraud Grünzinger (Göttingen: Vandenhoeck und Ruprecht, 2006), 202.

124. Hansjürg Ranke, "Einleitung," in *Frucht der Gefangenenschaft: Eine Zusammenfassung von Berichten aus Kriegsgefangenenlagern in England, Frankreich*

und Russland mit einem Geleitwort von Landesbischof D. Wurm, ed. Oekumenische Commission zur Pastoration der Kriegsgefangenen, Geneva, November 29, 1948, EZA 657/7.

125. "Niederschrift über die 1. Sitzung des Rates der Evangelischen Kirche in Deutschland am 17. und 18. Februar 1949 in Darmstadt," in *Protokolle,* vol. 3, *1949,* ed. Karl-Heinz Fix (Göttingen: Vandenhoeck und Ruprecht, 2006), 54.

126. Ranke to Dibelius, February 12, 1949, in Fix, *Protokolle,* 3:67–69. For the synod debate, see Kirchenkanzlei der EKD, ed., *Bethel 1949: Bericht über die 1. Tagung der 1. Synode der Evangelischen Kirche in Deutschland vom 9.–13. Januar 1949* (Göttingen: Vandenhoeck und Ruprecht, 1953), 82–103, 143–154.

127. Heinz Brunotte, "Zur Einführung," in *Kirche und Recht: Ein vom Rat der Evangelischen Kirche in Deutschland veranlasstes Gespräch über die christliche Begründung des Rechts,* ed. Rat der EKD (Göttingen: Vandenhoeck und Ruprecht, 1950), 3.

128. Ernst Wolf, "Rechtfertigung und Recht," in Rat der EKD, *Kirche und Recht,* 16–17.

129. Martin Otto, "Vom 'Evangelischen Hilfswerk' zum 'Institut für Staatskirchenrecht': Ulrich Scheuner (1903–1981) und sein Weg zum Kirchenrecht," in *Entwicklungstendenzen des Staatskirchen- und Religionsverfassungsrechts: ausgewählte begrifflich-systematische, historische, gegenwartsbezogene und biographische Beiträge,* ed. Thomas Holzner and Hannes Ludyga (Paderborn: Schöningh, 2013), 556–562; Ulrich Scheuner, "Die nationale Revolution: Eine staatsrechtliche Untersuchung," *Archiv des öffentlichen Rechts* NF 24 (1934): 166–220, 261–344. On the involvement of the Evangelisches Hilfswerk in aiding convicted war criminals, see Frei, *Adenauer's Germany,* 122, 140, 181; and Legge, "Resisting," 243.

130. Ulrich Scheuner, "Zum Problem des Naturrechts nach evangelischer Auffassung," in Rat der EKD, *Kirche und Recht,* 43–44.

131. "Thesen," in Rat der EKD, *Kirche und Recht,* 51–52.

132. [Hans] Dombois, "Material zu einem Wort des Rates der EKiD zur Rechtsnot der Gegenwart"; and [Ulrich] Scheuner, "Gedanken zum Thema 'Rechtsnot der Gegenwart,'" both EZA 2/2802. Ranke received both statements by July 1949: Ranke to Vogel, July 30, 1949, EZA 2/2802.

133. "Niederschrift über die Besprechung am 28. Mai 1949 in Heidelberg in den Räumen der Juristischen Fakultät," EZA 2/235. On the Heidelberg circle, see Frei, *Adenauer's Germany,* 121–124.

134. Council of the Evangelical Church in Germany, *Memorandum on the Question of War Crimes Trials before American Military Courts: Published for the Council of the Evangelical Church in Germany by Bishop D. Wurm, Church President D. Niemöller, and Prelate D. Hartenstein* (Stuttgart: Stürner, 1949), 22–23. On the memorandum's distribution, see Brunotte to EKD Council, January 14, 1950, EZA 2/240.

NOTES TO PAGES 113–116

135. Nolde to Kirchliches Aussenamt, August 10, 1949, EZA 2/2491.
136. Stratenwerth to Smend et al., December 1, 1949, EZA 2/2491.
137. "Stellungnahme zu dem Entwurf der UN-Kommission der Menschenrechte für einen Covenant on Human Rights," January 9, 1950, EZA 2/2491. On the report's submission to Nolde, see Stratenwerth to EKD Council, March 9, 1950, EZA 614/66.
138. Eckel, *Ambivalence*, 51–74.
139. "Niederschrift über die Besprechung anläßlich der Übergabe der Kriegsverbrecherdenkschrift der EKD an McCloy am 21. Februar 1950," in *Protokolle*, vol. 4, *1950*, ed. Anke Silomon (Göttingen: Vandenhoeck und Ruprecht, 2007), 162–166.
140. Frei, *Adenauer's Germany*, 145–146; Thomas Alan Schwartz, *America's Germany: John J. McCloy and the Federal Republic of Germany* (Cambridge, MA: Harvard University Press, 1991), 158–162.
141. Niebuhr to McCloy, June 15, 1949, John J. McCloy Papers, series 13A, box HC4, folder 19, Amherst College Archives and Special Collections, Amherst College Library. See also Lawson, *Church of England*, 153–155; and Priemel, *Betrayal*, 368–370.
142. Schwartz, *America's Germany*, 162–163.
143. Stratenwerth to Kaufmann et al., September 15, 1950, EZA 2/2491.
144. The participants are listed in Ranke to Brunotte, November 20, 1950, EZA 2/2491.
145. Vicco von Bülow, *Otto Weber (1902–1966): Reformierter Theologe und Kirchenpolitiker* (Göttingen: Vandenhoeck und Ruprecht, 1999), 98–135, 211–218.
146. Otto Weber, "Geschichtliche und politische Schuld: Zum Problem der westeuropäischen Kriegsverbrecherprozesse," Nachlass Otto Weber, Johannes a Lasco Bibliothek, Emden. Thanks to Vicco von Bülow for providing me with this document.
147. "Schreiben des Rates 'an die Regierungen der beteiligten Länder': Stuttgart, 6. Dezember 1950," in Silomon, *Protokolle*, 4:378–380.
148. "Schreiben des Rates 'an die Kirchen der beteiligten Staaten': Stuttgart, 6. Dezember 1950," in Silomon, *Protokolle*, 4:380–383. Scheuner's draft is found in Silomon, *Protokolle*, 4:398–399.
149. Boegner to Niemöller, December 21, 1950; British Council of Churches, General Secretary to Niemöller, December 28, 1950; Linde to Niemöller, January 5, 1951; Linde to Niemöller, September 6, 1951; and Fuglsang-Damgaard to Kirchliches Aussenamt, October 19, 1951, all in EZA 6/165. On the distribution of the petitions, see "Niederschrift über die 18. Sitzung des Rates der Evangelischen Kirche in Deutschland am 5./6. Dezember in Stuttgart," in Silomon, *Protokolle*, 4:375–376.
150. François-Poncet to Dibelius, December 23, 1950, EZA 6/165.
151. Meiser to Kirchenführer in Westdeutschland, January 15, 1951, EZA 2/2501; "Eine Frage an McCloy," *Christ und Welt*, January 4, 1951.

NOTES TO PAGES 116–121 323

152. Ranke to Brunotte, December 13, 1950, EZA 2/2478.
153. Frei, *Adenauer's Germany,* 164–165.
154. Office of the US High Commissioner for Germany, *Landsberg: A Documentary Report* (Frankfurt: n.p., 1951), 3–4.
155. Rüsam to Ranke, February 14, 1951; and Meiser to Lundquist, March 3, 1951, both EZA 2/2502.
156. Hartenstein to McCloy, February 2, 1951, in *Protokolle,* vol. 5, *1951,* ed. Dagmar Pöpping (Göttingen: Vandenhoeck und Ruprecht, 2005), 139–141.
157. "Niederschrift über die 20. Sitzung des Rates der Evangelischen Kirche in Deutschland am 6. März 1951 in Hannover-Herrenhausen," in Pöpping, *Protokolle,* 5:106.
158. Ranke, "Vermerk," January 26, 1952; and Ranke to Adenauer, January 30, 1952, EZA 2/2479. On Stille Hilfe, see Klee, *Persilscheine,* 107–118.
159. Frei, *Adenauer's Germany,* 203–233.
160. Kristina Meyer, *Die SPD und die NS-Vergangenheit 1945–1990* (Göttingen: Wallstein, 2015), 134–148; Pendas, *Democracy,* 38–56.

4. Families, Schools, and the Battle for the Basic Law

1. "Basic Law of the Federal Republic of Germany (1949/Amendments 1956)," German History in Documents and Images, https://ghdi.ghi-dc.org/sub_document.cfm?document_id=2858.
2. On "third way" proposals in the early postwar years, see Sean A. Forner, *German Intellectuals and the Challenge of Democratic Renewal: Culture and Politics after 1945* (Cambridge: Cambridge University Press, 2014). Such ideas were also present in the earliest programs of the CDU: Maria D. Mitchell, *The Origins of Christian Democracy: Politics and Confession in Modern Germany* (Ann Arbor: University of Michigan Press, 2012), 126–151.
3. Ronald J. Granieri, "Thou Shalt Consider Thyself a European: Catholic Supranationalism and the Sublimation of German Nationalism after 1945," in *Religion und Nation, Nation und Religion: Beiträge zu einer unbewältigten Geschichte,* ed. Michael Geyer and Hartmut Lehmann (Göttingen: Wallstein, 2004), 336–363. On confessional discourses of the *Abendland,* see also Axel Schildt, *Zwischen Abendland und Amerika: Studien zur westdeutschen Ideenlandschaft der 50er Jahre* (Munich: Oldenbourg, 1999), 24–38.
4. Mitchell, *Origins of Christian Democracy,* 76–104.
5. Frank Bösch, *Die Adenauer-CDU: Gründung, Aufstieg und Krise einer Erfolgspartei 1945–1969* (Stuttgart: Deutsche Verlags-Anstalt, 2001), 114–118, 320.
6. Bösch, *Adenauer-CDU,* 109–138; Mitchell, *Origins of Christian Democracy,* 180–191.
7. On the crisis of the family in postwar Germany, see Elizabeth D. Heineman, *What Difference Does a Husband Make? Marriage and the Family in Nazi and Postwar Germany* (Berkeley: University of California Press, 1999), 108–136, 142–155; Dagmar Herzog, *Sex after Fascism: Memory and Morality in*

324 NOTES TO PAGES 121–124

Twentieth-Century Germany (Princeton, NJ: Princeton University Press, 2005), 64–72; Robert G. Moeller, *Protecting Motherhood: Women and the Family in the Politics of Postwar West Germany* (Berkeley: University of California Press, 1993), 8–37; and Alexandria N. Ruble, *Entangled Emancipation: Women's Rights in Cold War Germany* (Toronto: University of Toronto Press, 2023), 15–38. For the broader European context, see Martin Conway, *Western Europe's Democratic Age: 1945–1968* (Princeton, NJ: Princeton University Press, 2020), 236–247; and Dagmar Herzog, *Sexuality in Europe: A Twentieth-Century History* (Cambridge: Cambridge University Press, 2011), 96–132.

8. There is a large literature on Protestants and the social market economy. Major works include Traugott Jähnichen, *Vom Industrieuntertan zum Industriebürger: Der soziale Protestantismus und die Entwicklung der Mitbestimmung (1848–1955)* (Bochum: SWI, 1993); Stephan Holthaus, *Zwischen Gewissen und Gewinn: Die Wirtschafts- und Sozialordnung der "Freiburger Denkschrift" und die Anfänge der Sozialen Marktwirtschaft* (Berlin: Lit, 2015); and Daniela Rüther, *Der Widerstand des 20. Juli auf dem Weg in die Soziale Marktwirtschaft: Die wirtschaftspolitische Vorstellung der bürgerlichen Opposition gegen Hitler* (Paderborn: Schöningh, 2002). For an overview, see Traugott Jähnichen, "Die protestantischen Wurzeln der Sozialen Marktwirtschaft," *Ethik und Gesellschaft* (2010), https://doi.org/10.18156/eug-1-2010-art-3.

9. West Berlin sent five additional nonvoting members. See Jocasta Gardner, "The Public Debate about the Formulation of the Basic Law in the Federal Republic of Germany, 1948–1949" (DPhil diss., Oxford University, 2004), 13.

10. Gustav Radbruch, "Gesetzliches Unrecht und übergesetzliches Recht," *Süddeutsche Juristen-Zeitung* 1, no. 5 (1946): 105–108, quote at 107. On Radbruch's thesis and its reception, see Douglas G. Morris, "Accommodating Nazi Tyranny? The Wrong Turn of the Social Democratic Legal Philosopher Gustav Radbruch after the War," *Law and History Review* 34, no. 3 (2016): 649–688; and Lena Foljanty, *Recht oder Gesetz: Juristische Identität und Autorität in den Naturrechtsdebatten der Nachkriegszeit* (Tübingen: Mohr Siebeck, 2013), 51–95.

11. Noah Benezra Strote, *Lions and Lambs: Conflict in Weimar and the Creation of Post-Nazi Germany* (New Haven, CT: Yale University Press, 2017), 167–171.

12. The most comprehensive discussion is Ernst Christian Helmreich, *Religious Education in German Schools: A Historical Approach* (Cambridge, MA: Harvard University Press, 1959), esp. 39–41, 53–65, 119–125, 153–178, 217–220, 256–259. On the Nazi campaign against confessional schools, see also Lisa Pine, *Education in Nazi Germany* (Oxford: Berg, 2010), 28–29.

13. Frings to Adenauer, October 25, 1948, EZA 2/32.

14. Adolf Süsterhenn, *Wir Christen und die Erneuerung des staatlichen Lebens* (Bamberg: Meisenbach, 1948). On Süsterhenn, see Christoph von Hehl, *Adolf Süsterhenn (1905–1974): Verfassungsvater, Weltanschauungspolitiker, Föderalist* (Düsseldorf: Droste, 2012).

15. Gardner, "Public Debate," 229–230.

NOTES TO PAGES 124–126   325

16. "Die Tagung der Bruderräte in Frankfurt am Main 21.–24. August 1945, I: Oskar Hammelsbeck: Zur Schulfrage," in *Evangelische Schulpolitik in Deutschland 1918–1958: Dokumente und Darstellung,* ed. Sebastian Müller-Rolli and Reiner Anselm (Göttingen: Vandenhoeck und Ruprecht, 1999), 409–410. On Hammelsbeck, see Gottfried Adam, "Oskar Hammelsbeck (1889–1975)," in *Klassiker der Religionspädagogik,* ed. Heinrich Schroerer and Dietrich Zillessen (Frankfurt: Diesterweg, 1989), 236–249.
17. "Hans Meiser: Memorandum zur Neugestaltung des Schulwesens, 22. August 1945," in Müller-Rolli and Anselm, *Evangelische Schulpolitik,* 406–409; Otto Dibelius, *Grenzen des Staates* (Tübingen: Furche, 1949), 87–98.
18. Lilje to Parlamentarischer Rat, March 3, 1949, *Protokolle,* vol. 3, *1949,* ed. Karl-Heinz Fix (Göttingen: Vandenhoeck und Ruprecht, 2006), 148–149.
19. "Heinz Brunotte: Grundsätzliches zur Frage der Schulform sowie praktische Fragen und Folgerungen. (Auszug), März 1948," in Müller-Rolli and Anselm, *Evangelische Schulpolitik,* 484–491.
20. Eberhard Pickart and Wolfram Werner, eds., *Der Parlamentarische Rat 1948–1949: Akten und Protokolle,* vol. 5, *Ausschuß für Grundsatzfragen* (Boppard: Boldt, 1993), 813–825.
21. Gardner, "Public Debate," 242–243.
22. "Die deutschen Bischöfe: Erklärung zum geplanten Grundgesetz der Bundesrepublik Deutschland, Pützchen bei Bonn, 11. Februar 1949," in *Dokumente deutscher Bischöfe,* vol. 1, *Hirtenbriefe und Ansprachen zu Gesellschaft und Politik 1945–1949,* ed. Günter Baadte, Anton Rauscher, and Wolfgang Löhr (Würzburg: Echter, 1986), 289–290; Held to Kanzlei der EKD, April 26, 1949, EZA 2/964.
23. Basic Law, art. 7, para. 4; Hehl, *Süsterhenn,* 417.
24. "Vorschlag der Konferenz der Landeskirchen der britischen Zone für das Grundgesetz," in *Protokolle,* vol. 2, *1947/48,* ed. Carsten Nicolaisen and Nora Andrea Schulze (Göttingen: Vandenhoeck und Ruprecht, 1997), 641–643. For the discussion of the petition at the Parliamentary Council, see Pickart and Werner, *Der Parlamentarische Rat,* 5:633–647.
25. Ehlers's participation is noted in "Aktenvermerk von Harlings," October 26, 1948, in Nicolaisen and Schulze, *Protokolle,* 2:640.
26. Hermann Ehlers, "Menschliches Recht und göttliche Gerechtigkeit, Bremen, 20.4.47," ACDP 01-369-035/5.
27. "Bericht: Am 22. und 23. September 1947 versammelten sich im Johannesstift in Berlin-Spandau auf Einladung der Kanzlei der EKD Referenten der Landeskirchen zu einer Besprechung über die Bedeutung der neuen Länderverfassungen," EZA 2/31. See also Andreas Meier, *Hermann Ehlers: Leben in Kirche und Politk* (Bonn: Bouvier, 1990), 236, 243–247, 253–254.
28. Pickart and Werner, *Der Parlamentarische Rat,* 5:835–836n44.
29. Pickart and Werner, *Der Parlamentarische Rat,* 5:837–838.
30. Christoph Link, *Staat und Kirche in der neueren deutschen Geschichte: Fünf Abhandlungen* (Frankfurt: Peter Lang, 2000), 160–161.

326   NOTES TO PAGES 127–131

31. Basic Law, preamble. On the debate about the invocation of God in the Basic Law, see Gardner, "Public Debate," 203–218; and Strote, *Lions and Lambs*, 171–174.

32. Hermann Ehlers, "Evangelische Erwägungen zu den Grundrechten," *JK* 10, no. 15–16 (1949): 443–452.

33. "Bonner Kompromiß," *EvW*, March 1, 1949.

34. Gerhard Ritter, "Die Menschenrechte und das Christentum," *Zeitwende* 21, no. 1 (1949–50): 1–12.

35. "Die deutschen Bischöfe: Erklärung nach Annahme des Grundgesetzes der Bundesrepublik Deutschland, 23. Mai 1949," in *Dokumente deutscher Bischöfe*, 1:311–316, quote at 315.

36. On anti-positivist legal theory outside the confessional milieus, see Foljanty, *Recht oder Gesetz*, 175–224.

37. Bund Nationalsozialistischer Deutscher Juristen to Rudolf Smend, March 1, 1934, SUBG, Nachlass Rudolf Smend, C 13; Michael Stolleis, *A History of Public Law in Germany, 1914–1945*, trans. Thomas Dunlap (Oxford: Oxford University Press, 2004), 315–316.

38. Stolleis, *History of Public Law*, 279.

39. Konrad Hesse, "In Memoriam Rudolf Smend," in Hesse, *Ausgewählte Schriften*, ed. Peter Häberle and Alexander Hollerbach (Heidelberg: C. F. Müller, 1984), 574–576. Smend notes his distance from the resistance movement around Carl Goerdeler in Smend to Huppenkothen, January 7, 1948, SUBG, Nachlass Smend, C 25.

40. On this cohort, see Frieder Günther, *Denken vom Staat her: Die bundesdeutsche Staatsrechtslehre zwischen Dezision und Integration* (Munich: Oldenbourg, 2004), 159–191.

41. Rudolf Smend, "Staat und Kirche nach dem Bonner Grundgesetz," in *Staatsrechtliche Abhandlungen und andere Aufsätze*, 3rd ed. (Berlin: Duncker und Humblot, 1994), 411–422.

42. Smend, "Staat und Kirche," 416.

43. Smend, "Staat und Kirche," 415.

44. Smend, "Staat und Kirche," 422.

45. Smend, "Staat und Kirche," 419.

46. Christian-Friedrich Menger, "Die Gegenwartslage des Staatskirchenrechts," *Deutsches Verwaltungsblatt* 67, no. 24 (1952): 751–752.

47. Menger, "Gegenwartslage des Staatskirchenrechts," 749–751, quote at 751. See also Werner Weber, *Spannungen und Kräfte im westdeutschen Verfassungssystem* (Stuttgart: Vorwerk, 1951). The Schmitt school is detailed in Günther, *Denken*, 112–158.

48. Ulrich Scheuner, "Auflösung des Staatskirchenrechts?," *Zeitschrift für evangelisches Kirchenrecht* 2, no. 3–4 (1953): 382–393, quotes at 392.

49. Ludwig Raiser, "Christen und Nichtchristen im Recht," in *Rechtsprobleme in Staat und Kirche: Festschrift für Rudolf Smend zum 70. Geburtstag 15. Januar 1952*, ed. Erich Kaufmann, Ulrich Scheuner, and Werner Weber (Göttingen: Schwartz, 1952), 243–252, quote at 251.

NOTES TO PAGES 131–134   327

50. Gerhard Leibholz, "Die Gleichheit vor dem Gesetz und das Bonner Grundgesetz," *Deutsches Verwaltungsblatt* 66, no. 7 (1951): 200.

51. Ulrich Scheuner, "Zur Frage der Kriegsdienstverweigerung," *Evangelische Verantwortung: Politische Briefe des Evangelischen Arbeitskreises der Christlich-Demokratischen / Christlich-Sozialen Union* 3, no. 9 (1955): 6–10.

52. "Wehrbeitrag und christliches Gewissen," in *Kirche und Kriegsdienstverweigerung: Ratschlag zur gesetzlichen Regelung des Schutzes der Kriegsdienstverweigerer,* ed. Rat der EKD (Munich: Kaiser, 1956), 40–42.

53. Justin Collings, *Democracy's Guardians: A History of the German Federal Constitutional Court, 1951–2001* (Oxford: Oxford University Press, 2015), 16.

54. Basic Law, art. 3, para. 2. On the debate in the Parliamentary Council, see Moeller, *Protecting Motherhood,* 38–75; and Ruble, *Entangled Emancipation,* 46–58.

55. Ruble, *Entangled Emancipation,* 16–20.

56. Basic Law, art. 117, para. 1.

57. The biblical verse is Ephesians 5:22.

58. Quoted in Lukas Rölli-Alkemper, *Familie im Wiederaufbau: Katholizismus und bürgerliches Familienideal in der Bundesrepublik Deutschland 1945–1965* (Paderborn: Schöningh, 2000), 47.

59. Rölli-Alkemper, *Familie,* 41–44.

60. On the cases of France, Italy, Portugal, and Spain, see Ann Taylor Allen, *Women in Twentieth-Century Europe* (New York: Palgrave Macmillan, 2008), 82–83. On the evolution of Catholic family ideology in the 1950s, however, see James Chappel, *Catholic Modern: The Challenge of Totalitarianism and the Remaking of the Church* (Cambridge, MA: Harvard University Press, 2018), 188–200.

61. Basic Law, art. 6, para. 1; Moeller, *Protecting Motherhood,* 41.

62. Frank Bosch, "Gleichberechtigung im Bereich der elterlichen Gewalt," *Süddeutsche Juristen-Zeitung* 5, no. 9 (1950): 625–646, quotes at 627–628. On Bosch, see Rölli-Alkemper, *Familie,* 543–545.

63. Rölli-Alkemper, *Familie,* 552–553; Ruble, *Entangled Emancipation,* 88.

64. Walter Dirks, "Soll er ihr Herr sein?," *Frankfurter Hefte* 7, no. 11 (1952): 825–837; Hildegard Krüger, "Gedanken zur Familienrechtsform," *Hochland* 44, no. 8 (1952): 542–551.

65. "Hirtenwort der deutschen Erzbischöfe und Bischöfe zur Neuordnung des Ehe- und Familienrechts, 30. Januar 1953," in *Gleichberechtigung als Verfassungsauftrag: Eine Dokumentation zur Entstehung des Gleichberechtigungsgesetztes vom 18. Juni 1957,* ed. Gabrielle Müller-List (Düsseldorf: Droste 1996), 295–302. On the distribution of the letter, see Rölli-Alkemper, *Familie,* 558–560.

66. Dietrich Pirson, "Evangelische Eheschließung," in *Gesammelte Beiträge zum Kirchenrecht und Staatskirchenrecht* (Tübingen: Mohr Siebeck, 2008), 657–658.

67. Hans Dombois, "Das Problem der Institutionen und die Ehe," in *Familienrechtsreform: Dokumente und Abhandlungen,* ed. Hans Adolf Dombois and Friedrich Karl Schumann (Witten-Ruhr: Luther, 1955), 132–142, quotes at 134, 141.

328 NOTES TO PAGES 134–136

68. Althaus to Ranke, September 27, 1950, EZA 2/4345, emphasis in original. On Althaus's postwar career, see Tanja Hetzer, *"Deutsche Stunde": Volksgemeinschaft und Antisemitismus in der politischen Theologie bei Paul Althaus* (Munich: Allitera, 2009), 213–234.

69. Frieder Günther, "Ordnen, gestalten, bewahren: Radikales Ordnungsdenken von deutschen Rechtsintellektuellen der Rechtswissenschaft 1920 bis 1960," *Vierteljahreshefte für Zeitgeschichte* 59, no. 3 (2011): 353–384. On this cohort, see also Peter C. Caldwell, *Democracy, Capitalism, and the Welfare State: Debating Social Order in Postwar West Germany, 1949–1989* (Oxford: Oxford University Press, 2019), 52–58; and Jens Hacke, *Philosophie der Bürgerlichkeit: Die liberalkonservative Begründung der Bundesrepublik,* 2nd ed. (Göttingen: Vandenhoeck und Ruprecht, 2011), 136–153.

70. On conservative discourses of sexuality in Allied-occupied Germany and the early Federal Republic, see Herzog, *Sex after Fascism,* 72–140.

71. The founding vision of the Christophorus-Stift is outlined in "Erster Jahresbericht des Christophorus-Stifts in Hemer i. Westf. über das Jahr 1948: Erstattet vom Stiftsrat," FEST Archive, box 134.

72. "Bericht über die Sitzung des Ausschusses für Grundfragen des Rechts vom 24.-26. Februar 1950 im Christophorus-Stift zu Hemer," EZA 2/4344; K. A. Bettermann, "Der Grundsatz von der Gleichberechtigung der Geschlechter und das geltende Familienrecht: Gutachten erstattet im Auftrage der Evangelischen Akademie (Christophorus-Stift) in Hemer," FEST Archive, box 671, quote at I.19. On Schumann, see Eckhard Lessing, *Geschichte der deutschsprachigen evangelischen Theologie von Albrecht Ritschl bis zur Gegenwart,* vol. 2, *1918 bis 1945* (Göttingen: Vandenhoeck und Ruprecht, 2004), 71–75.

73. Bettermann, "Grundsatz," II.6–8, II.20–23.

74. Friedrich Karl Schumann, "Grundsätzliche Fragen zum evangelischen Verständnis der Ehe: Theologisches Geleitwort zur Denkschrift über den Gleichberechtigungsartikel des Grundgesetzes," FEST Archive, box 671.

75. Jacques Ellul, *The Theological Foundation of Law,* trans. Marguerite Wieser (New York: Seabury Press, 1969), 76.

76. Karl Barth, *Church Dogmatics,* vol. 3, pt. 4, *The Doctrine of Creation: The Command of God the Creator,* trans. G. T. Thomson (Edinburgh: T&T Clark, 1961), 116–117.

77. Dagmar Herbrecht, *Emanzipation oder Anpassung: Argumentationswege der Theologinnen im Streit um die Frauenordination in der Bekennenden Kirche* (Neukirchen-Vluyn: Neukirchener Verlag, 2000), 57–63, 66–72; Ranke to Wolf, October 2, 1950, EZA 2/4345.

78. Ernst Wolf, "'Evangelisches' Eherecht? Theologische Erwägungen zu einer aktuellen Frage," in Kaufmann, Scheuner, and Weber, *Rechtsprobleme in Staat und Kirche,* 413–431, quotes at 425–426.

79. Emil Brunner, *The Divine Imperative: A Study of Christian Ethics,* trans. Oliver Wyon (New York: Macmillan, 1937), 373–380; Otto Piper, *Sinn und Geheimnis der Geschlechter: Grundzüge einer evangelischen Sexualethik* (Berlin: Furche, 1935), 184–191.

NOTES TO PAGES 136–138   329

80. Till van Rahden, "Fatherhood, Rechristianization, and the Quest for Democracy in Postwar West Germany," in *Raising Citizens in the "Century of the Child": The United States and German Central Europe in Comparative Perspective*, ed. Dirk Schumann (New York: Berghahn Books, 2013), 141–164, quote at 154.

81. Sara Jäger, *Bundesdeutscher Protestantismus und Geschlechterdiskurse 1949–1971: Eine Revolution auf leisen Sohlen* (Tübingen: Mohr Siebeck, 2019), 77; on the role of the Evangelische Frauenarbeit in postwar family law reform, see 62–67.

82. Claudia Koonz, *Mothers in the Fatherland: Women, the Family, and Nazi Politics* (London: Routledge, 1987), 221–264, at 241 on Eyl. See also Heike Köhler, *Deutsch, Evangelisch, Frau: Meta Eyl, eine Theologin im Spannungsfeld zwischen nationalsozialistischer Reichskirche und evangelischer Frauenbewegung* (Neukirchen-Vluyn: Neukirchener Verlag, 2003).

83. Andrea Bieler, *Konstruktionen des Weiblichen: Die Theologin Anna Paulsen im Spannungsfeld bürgerlicher Frauenbewegungen der Weimarer Republik und nationalsozialistischer Weiblichkeitsmythen* (Gütersloh: Kaiser, 1994), 133–138.

84. Köhler, *Deutsch, Evangelisch, Frau*, 310.

85. "Gespräch Frau Bundesminister a.D. Dr. Elisabeth Schwarzhaupt mit Herrn Heribert Koch (Archiv) am 11.3.1976 in Frankfurt/M.," ACDP 01-048-001/2.

86. Generalsekretär to Schwarzhaupt, April 5, 1932, ACDP 01-048-012/5; Elisabeth Schwarzhaupt, *Was hat die deutsche Frau vom Nationalsozialismus zu erwarten?* (Berlin: Deutsche Erneuerung, 1932).

87. Heike Drummer and Jutta Zwilling, "Elisabeth Schwarzhaupt: Eine Biographie," in *Elisabeth Schwarzhaupt (1901–1986): Portrait einer streitbaren Politikerin und Christin*, ed. Hessische Landesregierung (Freiburg: Herder, 2001), 36–37, 51–60.

88. Ranke to Schwarzhaupt, January 20, 1950, EZA 2/2491; Evangelische Frauenarbeit in Deutschland to United Council of Church Women, May 10, 1950, EZA 2/2478.

89. "Vorschlag der Evangelischen Frauenarbeit für eine Reform des Eherechts," July 11, 1950, EZA 2/4344. See also Alexandria N. Ruble, "Creating Postfascist Families: Reforming Family Law and Gender Roles in Postwar East and West Germany," *Central European History* 53, no. 2 (2020): 427.

90. Quote in Elisabeth Schwarzhaupt, "Die Gleichberechtigung von Mann und Frau: Artikel 3, Absatz 2 des Bonner Grundgesetzes," *SdG*, 2, no. 1 (1950): 11–12; see also Schwarzhaupt, "Die Stellung der Frau in Deutschland," *SdG* 1, no. 10 (1949): 11–12.

91. "Gleichberechtigung in biblischer Sicht," *EvW*, October 1, 1951.

92. "Wie sollen die neuen Eherechtsparagraphen lauten?," *EvW*, April 16, 1952. On the Justice Ministry's report, see also Ruble, *Entangled Emancipation*, 82–84.

93. "Stellungnahme des Rates der Evangelischen Kirche in Deutschland zu den Fragen der Revision des Ehe- und Familienrechts (22.3.1952)," in Dombois and Schumann, *Familienrechtsreform*, 9–15.

330 NOTES TO PAGES 138–142

94. "Gegen die Unterordnung der Frau," *EvW,* August 1, 1952. See also "18.11.1952: Stellungnahme der Evangelischen Frauenarbeit in Deutschland zum Gleichberechtigungsgesetz," in Müller-List, *Gleichberechtigung als Verfassungsauftrag,* 263–265. For the debate in the marriage law commission, see "Niederschrift der Eherechtskommission," January 16–17, 1952, EZA 2/4346.

95. Ulrich Scheuner, "Die verfassungsrechtlichen Grundlagen der Familien-rechtsreform," in Dombois and Schumann, *Familienrechtsreform,* 42–56, quotes at 54–56.

96. Friedrich Karl Schumann, "Gleichberechtigung und Eherecht," *EvW,* April 1, 1952.

97. Frings to Dehler, January 12, 1952, in Müller-List, *Gleichberechtigung als Verfassungsauftrag,* 178–183. See also Rölli-Alkemper, *Familie,* 560–562.

98. "Bericht Osterlohs über eine Besprechung im Bundesjustizministerium über Fragen des Eherechts," in *Protokolle,* vol. 6, *1952,* ed. Dagmar Pöpping, Anke Silomon, and Karl-Heinz Fix (Göttingen: Vandenhoeck und Ruprecht, 2008), 132–134.

99. Ranke to Mitglieder der Eherechtskommission, July 14, 1952, EZA 2/4347; Ruble, *Entangled Emancipation,* 87–90.

100. Maria Mitchell, "Imperfect Interconfessionalism: Women, Gender, and Sexuality in Early Christian Democracy," in *Germany and the Confessional Divide: Religious Tensions and Political Culture, 1871–1989,* ed. Mark Edward Ruff and Thomas Großbölting (New York: Berghahn Books, 2022), 179.

101. Moeller, *Protecting Motherhood,* 101–102. On Wuermeling, see also James Chappel, "Nuclear Families in a Nuclear Age: Theorising the Family in 1950s West Germany," *Contemporary European History* 26, no. 1 (2017): 88–95.

102. Ruble, *Entangled Emancipation,* 100–101.

103. "Stellungnahme der Eherechtskommission der Evangelischen Kirche in Deutschland" (December 18, 1953), in Dombois and Schumann, *Familien-rechtsreform,* 28–33.

104. "Gespräch Frau Bundesminister a.D. Dr. Elisabeth Schwarzhaupt mit Herrn Heribert Koch." On the intersection of gendered and confessional divisions in the CDU, see also Mitchell, "Imperfect Interconfessionalism," 170–193. On the CDU Protestant Working Group, see Bösch, *Adenauer-CDU,* 320–337.

105. Bösch, *Adenauer-CDU,* 309; Ruble, *Entangled Emancipation,* 87–88.

106. *VDBT,* 2. Deutscher Bundestag, 15. Sitzung, February 12, 1954, 499.

107. *VDBT,* 2. Deutscher Bundestag, 15. Sitzung, February 12, 1954, 499–501. On West German family wage and tax policies, see Moeller, *Protecting Mother-hood,* 109–141.

108. On the entanglements of East and West German family law reform after the 1953 elections, see Ruble, *Entangled Emancipation,* 97–126.

109. *VDBT,* 2. Deutscher Bundestag, 15. Sitzung, February 12, 1954, 498. On Metzger, see Michael Klein, *Westdeutscher Protestantismus und politische Parteien: Anti-Parteien-Mentalität und parteipolitisches Engagement von 1945 bis 1963* (Tübingen: Mohr Siebeck, 2005), 83–84, 327–329, 339.

NOTES TO PAGES 142–146   331

110. *VDBT,* 2. Deutscher Bundestag, 15. Sitzung, February 12, 1954, 506. The reference is to Galatians 3:28: "There is no longer Jew or Greek; there is no longer slave or free; there is no longer male and female, for all of you are one in Christ Jesus." On Lüders, see Heineman, *Difference,* 140.

111. Kirchenkanzlei der EKD, ed., *Berlin-Spandau 1954: Bericht über die fünfte Tagung der ersten Synode der Evangelischen Kirche in Deutschland vom 14.–19. März 1954* (Hanover: Verlag des Amtsblattes der EKD, 1954), 106–164.

112. Kirchenkanzlei der EKD, *Berlin-Spandau 1954,* 179–201, quote at 200. Schelsky would clash directly with Franz-Josef Wuermeling shortly afterward. On the conflict between the two, see Chappel, "Nuclear Families."

113. "Die Familie in der modernen Gesellschaft und in der christlichen Gemeinde," *EvW,* April 1, 1954.

114. Kirchenkanzlei der EKD, *Berlin-Spandau 1954,* 329. For the synod's discussion of the report, see Kirchenkanzlei der EKD, *Berlin-Spandau 1954,* 292–317, 327–347, 355–359.

115. Ruble, *Entangled Emancipation,* 108–109. For Schwarzhaupt's and Metzger's statements at the final parliamentary reading, see *VDBT,* 2. Deutscher Bundestag, 206. Sitzung, May 3, 1957, 11773–11774.

116. "Beschluss der Eherechtskommission der EKD zur Eherechtsreform vom 24./25. Sept. 1954," in Dombois and Schumann, *Familienrechtsreform,* 61–66; Kirchenkanzlei der EKD, *Berlin-Spandau 1954,* 314, 327–328.

117. Walter Dirks, "Aus dem Schulstreit heraus," *Frankfurter Hefte* 10, no. 3 (1955): 181–186.

118. Adolf Süsterhenn, "Concordat und Grundgesetz: Zum Schulkampf im Südwesten," *Rheinischer Merkur,* November 7, 1952.

119. "Das Schulproblem im werdenden Südweststaat," *EvW,* August 1, 1952; "Unbefriedigende Beschlüsse im Südweststaat," *EvW,* April 1, 1953.

120. "Das hessische Schulverwaltungsgesetz," *EvW,* April 1, 1953; "Was bringen die neuen hessischen Schulgesetze?," *EvW,* November 16, 1953.

121. Joachim Kuropka, "Eine Minderheit in Niedersachsen: Die Katholiken," in *Woher kommt und was haben wir an Niedersachsen,* ed. Joachim Kuropka and Hermann von Laser (Cloppenburg: Runge, 1996), 192.

122. Joachim Kuropka, "'Kulturkampf' in der Nachkriegsära? Zum Konflikt um die Konfessionsschule in Nordrhein-Westfalen und Niedersachsen 1945 bis 1954," in *Kirche, Staat und Gesellschaft nach 1945: Konfessionelle Prägungen und sozialer Wandel,* ed. Bernd Hey (Bielefeld: Luther, 2001), 182–187.

123. Kuropka, "Eine Minderheit in Niedersachsen," 205–209, quote at 208.

124. Nathan Stoltzfus, *Hitler's Compromises: Coercion and Consensus in Nazi Germany* (New Haven, CT: Yale University Press, 2016), 86–102.

125. "Zur schulpolitischen Lage nach den Bundestagswahlen," *EvW,* November 1, 1953.

126. "Der Schulkampf in Niedersachsen," *EvW,* March 1, 1954.

127. Bösch, *Adenauer-CDU,* 133. On the confessional conflict over Lower Saxony's school law, see also Mark Edward Ruff, *The Battle for the Catholic*

332 NOTES TO PAGES 146–149

Past in Germany, 1945–1980 (Cambridge: Cambridge University Press, 2017), 69–71.
128. Kuropka, "Eine Minderheit in Niedersachsen," 209.
129. Ruff, *Battle,* 48; Adolf Süsterhenn, "Concordat und Elternrecht: Das niedersächsische Schulgesetz entfesselt den Kulturkampf," *Rheinischer Merkur,* December 3, 1954.
130. Ruff, *Battle,* 72–73.
131. For instance, Georg Heidingsfelder, "Vom politischen Katholizismus und Klerikalismus," *SdG* 6, no. 9 (1954): 213–216.
132. On Ziegler, see Manfred Gailus, "Vom 'gottgläubigen' Kirchenkämpfer Rosenbergs zum 'christgläubigen' Pfarrer Niemöllers: Matthes Zieglers wunderbare Wandlungen im 20. Jahrhundert," *Zeitschrift für Geschichtswissenschaft* 54, no. 11 (2006): 937–973.
133. Matthäus Ziegler, "Vor dem Karlsruher Konkordatsprozeß," *SdG* 8, no. 11 (1956): 341–344. See also Ziegler, "Gültigkeit und Zweckmäßigkeit des Concordates," *SdG,* special issue, 1956; and Ziegler, "Ist das Hitler-Konkordat ein verpflichtendes Erbe?," *SdG* 8, no. 6 (1956): 173–174.
134. Ziegler, "Vor dem Karlsruher Konkordatsprozeß," 343.
135. Wolfgang Sucker, "Evangelisches Interesse am Reichskonkordat," *Konfessionskundliche Mitteilungen* 3/1956, EZA 2/2342. On Sucker, see Christian Wiese, "Sucker, Wolfgang," *BBKL,* vol. 29, ed. Traugott Bautz (Nordhasen: Bautz, 2008), 1411–1416.
136. "Vertrauliche Besprechung über den Verfassungsstreit zum Concordat zwischen der Bundesregierung und den Landesregierungen von Niedersachsen, Hessen und Bremen," November 15, 1955, EZA 2/2342.
137. Brunotte to Ranke, January 19, 1956, EZA 87/14.
138. Smend to Strauss, May 4, 1956; and Smend to Arndt, May 4, 1956, both SUBG, Nachlass Smend, K29.
139. Rudolf Smend, "Concordat und Schulgesetzgebung," and "Noch einmal: Concordat und Schulgesetzgebung," in *Staatsrechtliche Abhandlungen,* 487–499, quote at 494.
140. On Arndt's early life, see Dieter Gosewinkel, *Adolf Arndt: Die Wiederbegründung des Rechtsstaats aus dem Geist der Sozialdemokratie (1945–1961)* (Bonn: Dietz, 1991), 21–63.
141. Gosewinkel, *Arndt,* 72–77.
142. Adolf Arndt, "Die Evangelische Kirche in Deutschland und das Befreiungsgesetz," *Frankfurter Hefte* 1, no. 5 (1946): 35–46; Arndt, "Die Krise des Rechts," *Die Wandlung* 3, no. 5 (1948): 421–440.
143. Gosewinkel, *Arndt,* 162–163.
144. Adolf Arndt, *Rechtsdenken in unserer Zeit: Positivismus und Naturrecht* (Tübingen: Mohr, 1955); Gosewinkel, *Arndt,* 527–531, 560–562.
145. Adolf Arndt, "Reichskonkordat noch Gültig? Bundesregierung beschwört Gefahr eines Kulturkampfes herauf," *Neuer Vorwärts,* November 19, 1954; Arndt, "Süsterhenn und das Konkordat: Eine Stellungnahme von Dr. Arndt," *Neuer Vorwärts,* December 10, 1954.

NOTES TO PAGES 150–155

146. *VDBT,* 2. Wahlperiode, "Große Anfrage der Abgeordneter Mellies, Dr. Reif, Feller und Genossen betr. Verfassungsklage wegen des Concordats," March 23, 1956.

147. Niemöller to Arndt, May 22, 1956, AdsD, Nachlass Adolf Arndt, box 238.

148. Friedrich Giese and Friedrich August Freiherr von der Heydte, eds., *Der Konkordatsprozess,* vol. 4 (Munich: Isar, 1959), quote at 1470–1472, see also 1491–1499.

149. Giese and Heydte, *Konkordatsprozess,* 4:1445–1448.

150. Giese and Heydte, *Konkordatsprozess,* 4:1554–1555.

151. Giese and Heydte, *Konkordatsprozess,* 4:1565–1566.

152. Giese and Heydte, *Konkordatsprozess,* 3:1216–1217, 1239–1244.

153. Giese and Heydte, *Konkordatsprozess,* 3:1274–1276.

154. Ruff, *Battle,* 80.

155. Giese and Heydte, *Konkordatsprozess,* 4:1660–1664.

156. Günther, *Denken,* 191.

157. Smend to Redaktion der Juristenzeitung, May 14, 1956; Mallmann to Smend, June 18, 1956, both SUBG, Nachlass Smend, K29.

158. Ruff, *Battle,* 83. On dissenting opinions, see Collings, *Democracy's Guardians,* 90.

159. For the full decision, see Giese and Heydte, *Konkordatsprozess,* 4:1669–1712.

160. Giese and Heydte, *Konkordatsprozess,* 4:1674.

161. Basic Law, art. 20, para. 1.

162. Leibholz to Smend, April 2, 1957, SUBG, Nachlass Smend, A502.

163. Smend to Mallmann, April 16, 1957, SUBG, Nachlass Smend, K29; see also Smend to Leibholz, April 26, 1957, SUBG, Nachlass Smend, A502.

164. Scheuner to Ruppel, April 28, 1957, EZA 87/14.

165. Quoted in "Das Urteil im Konkordatsprozess," *EvW,* April 16, 1957.

166. "Das Urteil von Karlsruhe," *Materialdienst des konfessionskundlichen Instituts* 8, no. 2 (1957): 28–31, quote at 31.

167. Adolf Süsterhenn, "Tabula Rasa: Karlsruhe hat mit der Diffamierung des Concordates aufgeräumt," *Rheinischer Merkur,* May 3, 1957.

168. Ruff, *Battle,* 83.

169. Thomas Großbölting, *Losing Heaven: Religion in Germany since 1945,* trans. Alex Skinner (New York: Berghahn Books, 2017), 139–141.

170. Marike Hansen, *Erna Scheffler (1893–1983): Erste Richterin am Bundesverfassungsgericht und Wegbereiterin einer geschlechtergerechten Gesellschaft* (Tübingen: Mohr Siebeck, 2019), 145–158. On Scheffler, see also Till van Rahden, *Demokratie: Eine gefährdete Lebensform* (Frankfurt: Campus, 2019), 69–74.

171. "Urteil des Ersten Senats vom 29. Juli 1959," *Entscheidungen des Bundesverfassungsgerichts* 10 (1960): 63, 80–81.

172. "Urteil des Ersten Senats vom 29. Juli 1959," 84–85.

173. "Urteil des Ersten Senats vom 29. Juli 1959," 72.

174. "Urteil des Ersten Senats vom 29. Juli 1959," 66.

175. "Urteil des Ersten Senats vom 29. Juli 1959," 73–75.

176. "Urteil des Ersten Senats vom 29. Juli 1959," 63.

177. Quoted in van Rahden, *Demokratie,* 70–71.

334 NOTES TO PAGES 155–161

178. Elisabeth Schwarzhaupt, "Patriarchat des Staates?," *Christ und Welt,* October 8, 1959.
179. "Familienpolitik als gesamtkirchliche Aufgabe," *EvW,* October 1, 1959.
180. Van Rahden, *Demokratie,* 77.
181. Van Rahden, *Demokratie,* 78.

5. Rearmament and the Myths of Resistance

1. Theodor Heuss, "Zur 10. Wiederkehr des 20. Juli," in *Widerstandsrecht,* ed. Arthur Kaufmann (Darmstadt: Wissenschaftliche Buchgesellschaft, 1972), 280–290, quote at 283. On the context, see Douglas Peifer, "Commemoration of Mutiny, Rebellion, and Resistance in Postwar Germany: Public Memory, History, and the Formation of 'Memory Beacons,'" *Journal of Military History* 65, no. 4 (2001): 1041.
2. Gerhard Ritter, "Deutscher Widerstand: Betrachtungen zum 10. Jahrestag des 20. Juli 1944," in Kaufmann, *Widerstandsrecht,* 291–304.
3. Karl Barth, "Rede gehalten bei der Gedenkfeier für die Opfer des Krieges und des Nationalsozialismus in Wiesbaden am 14. November 1954," *SdG* 6, no. 3 (1954): 529–539, quotes at 532, 535.
4. Barth, "Rede," 535.
5. For an account focusing on the debate's theological consequences, see Hendrik Meyer-Magister, *Wehrdienst und Verweigerung als komplementäres Handeln: Individualisierungsprozesse im bundesdeutschen Protestantismus der 1950er Jahre* (Tübingen: Mohr Siebeck, 2020).
6. David Clay Large, *Germans to the Front: West German Rearmament in the Adenauer Era* (Chapel Hill: University of North Carolina Press, 1996), 24–25.
7. Meyer-Magister, *Wehrdienst,* 106–107.
8. Large, *Germans to the Front,* 66. See also Michael Geyer, "Cold War Angst: The Case of West-German Opposition to Rearmament and Nuclear Weapons," in *The Miracle Years: A Cultural History of West Germany, 1949–1968,* ed. Hanna Schissler (Princeton, NJ: Princeton University Press, 2001), 376–408.
9. Richard Bessel, "Polizei zwischen Krieg und Sozialismus: Die Anfänge der Volkspolizei nach dem Zweiten Weltkrieg," in *Von der Aufgabe der Freiheit: Politische Verantwortung und bürgerliche Gesellschaft im 19. und 20. Jahrhundert,* ed. Christian Jansen (Berlin: Akademie, 1995), 517–531.
10. David Clay Large, "'A Gift to the German Future?' The Anti-Nazi Resistance Movement and West German Rearmament," *German Studies Review* 7, no. 3 (1984): 509–510.
11. A survey of June 1951 found that 40 percent of West Germans viewed the July 20 conspirators in a positive light, whereas 30 percent viewed them negatively: Jörg Echternkamp, *Postwar Soldiers: Historical Controversies and West German Democratization, 1945–1955,* trans. Noah Harley (New York: Berghahn Books, 2020), 287. On the contested postwar legacies of July 20, see also Echternkamp, *Postwar Soldiers,* 281–301; Large, "Gift," 499–529; and Peifer, "Commemoration," 1028–1044.

NOTES TO PAGES 162–164

12. Jeremy K. Kessler, "A War for Liberty: On the Law of Conscientious Objection," in *The Cambridge History of the Second World War*, vol. 3, *Total War: Economy, Society and Culture*, ed. Michael Geyer and Adam Tooze (Cambridge: Cambridge University Press, 2015), 449–454.

13. Benjamin W. Goossen, *Chosen Nation: Mennonites and Germany in a Global Era* (Princeton, NJ: Princeton University Press, 2017), 48–53, 90–93.

14. Rebecca Ayako Bennette, *Diagnosing Dissent: Hysterics, Deserters, and Conscientious Objectors in Germany during World War One* (Ithaca, NY: Cornell University Press, 2020).

15. Jehovah's Witnesses made up 112 of the 117 men sentenced to death by the Reich Military Court for "demoralization of the armed forces" during the first year of the war alone: Detlef Garbe, *Between Resistance and Martyrdom: Jehovah's Witnesses in the Third Reich*, trans. Dagmar G. Grimm (Madison: University of Wisconsin Press, 2008), 366. See also Thomas J. Kehoe, "The Reich Military Court and Its Values: Wehrmacht Treatment of Jehovah's Witness Conscientious Objectors," *Holocaust and Genocide Studies* 33, no. 3 (2019): 351–372.

16. Alexander Gallus, *Die Neutralisten: Verfechter eines vereinten Deutschland zwischen Ost und West 1945–1990* (Düsseldorf: Droste, 2001), 65–72; Adam Seipp, "A Reasonable 'Yes': The Social Democrats and West German Rearmament, 1945–1956," in *Rearming Germany*, ed. James S. Corum (Leiden: Brill, 2011), 59–63.

17. Patrick Bernhard, *Zivildienst zwischen Reform und Revolte: Eine bundesdeutsche Institution im gesellschaftlichen Wandel 1961–1982* (Munich: Oldenbourg, 2005), 27.

18. Parlamentarischer Rat, *Verhandlungen des Hauptausschusses* (Bonn: Bonner Universitäts-Buchdruckerei Gebr. Scheur, 1949), 545–546.

19. Eberhard Pickart and Wolfram Werner, eds., *Der Parlamentaische Rat 1948–1949: Akten und Protokolle*, vol. 5, *Ausschuß für Grundsatzfragen* (Boppard: Boldt, 1993), 417–422; Parlamentarischer Rat, *Verhandlungen des Hauptausschusses*, 209–210.

20. Basic Law, art. 4, para. 3; Pickart and Werner, *Der Parlamentarische Rat*, 5:760–762. For the final vote, see Parlamentarischer Rat, *Verhandlungen des Hauptausschusses*, 546.

21. Basic Law, art. 4, para. 3.

22. Martin Luther, "Whether Soldiers, Too, Can Be Saved," in *Luther's Works*, vol. 46, *The Christian in Society III*, ed. Robert C. Schultz (Philadelphia: Fortress Press, 1967), 95.

23. "Denkschrift 'Kriegsdienstverweigerung und Friedensdienst,'" in *Protokolle*, vol. 2, *1947/48*, ed. Carsten Nicolaisen and Nora Andrea Schulze (Göttingen: Vandenhoeck und Ruprecht, 1997), 648–657, quote at 654. See also "Zusammenstellung: 'Daten aus der Geschichte der religiösen kriegsgegnerischen Gemeinschaften,'" in Nicolaisen and Schulze, *Protokolle*, 2:657–665.

24. Jochen Eber, "Künneth, Walter," in *BBKL*, vol. 20, ed. Traugott Bautz (Nordhasen: Bautz, 2002), 886–895; Robert P. Ericksen, *Theologians under Hitler:*

336   NOTES TO PAGES 164–167

Gerhard Kittel, Paul Althaus, and Emanuel Hirsch (New Haven, CT: Yale University Press, 1985), 111.

25. Walter Künneth, *Der große Abfall: Eine geschichtstheologische Untersuchung der Begegnung zwischen Nationalsozialismus und Christentum* (Hamburg: Wittig, 1947), 113–116.

26. "Statement by the Council of Brethren of the Evangelical Church of Germany Concerning the Political Course of Our People (Darmstadt Statement, August 1947)," in Matthew D. Hockenos, *A Church Divided: German Protestants Confront the Nazi Past* (Bloomington: Indiana University Press, 2004), 193.

27. See also Michael Geyer, "Resistance as Ongoing Project: Visions of Order, Obligations to Strangers, Struggles for Civil Society," in *Resistance against the Third Reich, 1933–1990*, ed. Michael Geyer and John W. Boyer (Chicago: University of Chicago Press, 1994), 325–350.

28. Characteristically, Wilhelm Niemöller's 1948 history of the Confessing Church devoted only 11 of over 500 pages to the "Jewish question." The only woman mentioned in this section is Meusel, to whom Niemöller incorrectly attributed Schmitz's memorandum. See Wilhelm Niemöller, *Kampf und Zeugnis der Bekennenden Kirche* (Bielefeld: Bechauf, 1948), 453–463. On Wilhelm Niemöller, see also Robert P. Ericksen, "Wilhelm Niemöller and the Historiography of the Kirchenkampf," in *Nationalprotestantische Mentalitäten: Konturen, Entwicklungslinien und Umbrüche eines Weltbildes*, ed. Manfred Gailus and Hartmut Lehmann (Göttingen: Vandenhoeck und Ruprecht, 2005), 433–451.

29. Niemöller, *Kampf*, 526–527.

30. Marguerite Higgins, "Niemoeller for United Reich, Even if It's Red," *New York Herald Tribune*, December 14, 1949. See also Large, *Germans to the Front*, 54.

31. For contrasting assessments, see Matthew D. Hockenos, *Then They Came for Me: Martin Niemöller, The Pastor Who Defied the Nazis* (New York: Basic Books, 2018), 220–225; and Benjamin Ziemann, *Martin Niemöller: Ein Leben in Opposition* (Munich: Deutsche Verlags-Anstalt, 2019), 428–429.

32. Kirchenkanzlei der EKD, ed., *Berlin-Weissensee 1950: Bericht über die zweite Tagung der ersten Synode der Evangelischen Kirche in Deutschland vom 23.–27. April 1950* (Hanover: Schlütersche Verlagsanstalt und Buchdruckerei, 1953), 310–312.

33. Large, *Germans to the Front*, 69–74.

34. Udo Wengst, "Neutralistische Positionen in der CDU und in der FDP in den 1950er Jahren," in *Neutralität—Chance oder Chimäre? Konzepte des Dritten Weges für Deutschland und die Welt 1945–1990*, ed. Dominik Geppert and Udo Wengst (Munich: Oldenbourg, 2005), 36–38.

35. For studies of the anti-rearmament coalition, see Detlef Bald and Wolfram Wette, eds., *Alternativen zur Wiederbewaffnung: Friedenskonzeptionen in Westdeutschland 1945–1955* (Essen: Klartext, 2008); Alice Holmes Cooper, *Paradoxes of Peace: German Peace Movements since 1945* (Ann Arbor: University of Michigan Press, 1996), 25–81; Gallus, *Neutralisten;* and Michael Werner, *Die "Ohne mich"-Bewegung: Die bundesdeutsche Friedensbewegung im deutsch-deutschen Kalten Krieg (1949–1955)* (Münster: Monsenstein und Vannerdat, 2006).

36. Ranke to Mitglieder der Kammer für öffentliche Verantwortung, June 16, 1950, EZA 2/1346.
37. For the group's composition, see "Wiesbaden, 22. März 1949," in *Protokolle,* vol. 3, *1949,* ed. Karl-Heinz Fix (Göttingen: Vandenhoeck und Ruprecht, 2006), 112–113.
38. Walter Künneth, "Thesen zur Frage der Kriegsdienstverweigerung," August 1950, EZA 2/2574.
39. Jörg Treffke, *Gustav Heinemann: Wanderer zwischen den Parteien* (Paderborn: Schöningh, 2009), 106–107; Werner, *"Ohne mich"-Bewegung,* 198–200.
40. On Heinemann's resignation, see Gallus, *Neutralisten,* 76–85; Treffke, *Heinemann,* 105–116; and Werner, *"Ohne mich"-Bewegung,* 189–212.
41. "Handreichung an die Gemeinden zur Wiederaufrüstung," *KJ* 77 (1950): 169–174, quote at 171 (emphasis added). On the leaflet, see also Meyer-Magister, *Wehrdienst,* 144–156.
42. "Offener Brief D. Martin Niemöllers an Bundeskanzler Dr. Adenauer," *KJ* 77 (1950): 174–175.
43. Ziemann, *Niemöller,* 433. On the SED-backed poll, see Werner, *"Ohne mich"-Bewegung,* 267–283.
44. Gustav W. Heinemann, "Was heißt Demokratie?," *SdG* 3, no. 6 (1951): 1–2. The Darmstadt pastor Herbert Mochalski made a similar argument: Mochalski, "Jeder ist Verantwortlich," *SdG* 3, no. 11 (1951): 7–8.
45. Hans Joachim Iwand, "Die Bekennende Kirche gehört in der Opposition," *SdG* 2, no. 6 (1950): 11. See also Iwand, "Seid untertan der Obrigkeit," *SdG* 3, no. 11 (1951): 5–7; and Iwand, "Seid untertan der Obrigkeit—II," *SdG* 4, no. 1 (1952): 9–12.
46. Theodor Dipper, "Was bedeutet das Wort über die Kriegsdienstverweigerung in der Friedensbotschaft der Synode der Evangelischen Kirche in Deutschland?," *SdG* 2, no. 9 (1950): 3–5.
47. Gustav W. Heinemann, "Zur theologischen Bemühung um Politik aus christlicher Verantwortung," *SdG* 3, no. 5 (1951): 5–6.
48. These communications were ongoing by the summer of 1951: Kunst to Dibelius, July 20, 1951, EZA 2/2574.
49. Ranke to Osterloh, October 2, 1951, EZA 2/2575. For the competing positions, see also Eberhard Müller, "Treffen des Leiterkreises der Evangelischen Akademien mit westdeutschen Politikern," October 29, 1951, EZA 2/2575.
50. *1948 Christmas Message of Pope Pius XII* (Washington, DC: National Catholic Welfare Conference), 9. See also Giuliana Chamedes, *A Twentieth-Century Crusade: The Vatican's Battle to Remake Christian Europe* (Cambridge, MA: Harvard University Press, 2018), 246.
51. Fulda'er Bischofskonferenz, "Die christlichen Grundsätze über Krieg und Kriegsdienst," EZA 87/144. Portions of the statement were later published in "Sittlich erlaubt," *Der Spiegel,* November 1, 1950.
52. Ranke to Osterloh, October 11, 1951, EZA 87/144.
53. Niemöller to Osterloh, October 8, 1951, EZA 2/2574.

338 NOTES TO PAGES 170–174

54. Peter Cajka, *Follow Your Conscience: The Catholic Church and the Spirit of the Sixties* (Chicago: University of Chicago Press, 2021), 19–20; Stephan Schaede, "Gewissensproduktionstheorien: Ein Überblick über Gewissenstypen in Positionen reformatorischer und evangelischer Theologie," in *Das Gewissen,* ed. Stephan Schaede and Thorsten Moos (Tübingen: Mohr Siebeck, 2015), 152–157.

55. For instance, Karl Heim, "Krieg und Gewissen," in *Glaube und Leben: Gesammelte Aufsätze und Vorträge* (Berlin: Furche, 1926), 234–265.

56. Walter Dirks, "Man braucht deutsche Soldaten," *Frankfurter Hefte* 6, no. 8 (1951): 533–536; Eugen Kogon, "Die Entscheidung auf Leben und Tod," *Frankfurter Hefte* 5, no. 9 (1950): 907–913.

57. James Chappel, *Catholic Modern: The Challenge of Totalitarianism and the Remaking of the Church* (Cambridge, MA: Harvard University Press, 2018), 232–233.

58. Rachel M. Johnston-White, "A New Primacy of Conscience? Conscientious Objection, French Catholicism, and the State during the Algerian War," *Journal of Contemporary History* 54, no. 1 (2019): 112–138. On traditions of conscience rights in Catholic thought, see also Cajka, *Follow Your Conscience.*

59. "Niederschrift über die 26. Sitzung des Rates der Evangelischen Kirche in Deutschland am 7. Dezember 1951 in Berlin-Spandau," in *Protokolle,* vol. 5, *1951,* ed. Dagmar Pöpping (Göttingen: Vandenhoeck und Ruprecht, 2005), 436. For competing drafts of a public statement on conscientious objection, see "Entwurf einer Antwort Osterlohs auf die Frage: 'Was heißt: 'Kriegsdienstverweigerer um des Gewissens willen?'. [Hannover, 18. Oktober 1951]," in Pöpping, *Protokolle,* 5:424–425; and "Entwurf für eine Stellungnahme des Rates der EKD zu Fragen der Gesetzgebung über Kriegsdienstverweigerung um des Gewissens willen [Hannover, 28. November 1951]," in Pöpping, *Protokolle,* 5:445–447.

60. Gavriel D. Rosenfeld, *The Fourth Reich: The Specter of Nazism from World War II to the Present* (Cambridge: Cambridge University Press, 2019), 114–123, quote at 116.

61. Werner, *"Ohne mich"-Bewegung,* 207–210, quote at 209. On Noack, see Gallus, *Neutralisten,* 153–179.

62. Roman Steinke, *Fritz Bauer: The Jewish Prosecutor Who Brought Eichmann and Auschwitz to Trial,* trans. Sinéad Crowe (Bloomington: Indiana University Press, 2020), 86–105, quotes at 88, 99.

63. Steinke, *Bauer,* 99.

64. Hans Joachim Iwand and Ernst Wolf, "Entwurf eines Gutachtens zur Frage des Widerstandsrechts nach evangelischer Lehre," in *Die im Braunschweiger Remerprozeß erstatteten moraltheologischen und historischen Gutachten nebst Urteil,* ed. Herbert Kraus (Hamburg: Girardet, 1953), 9–18, reprinted in *JK* 13, no. 7–8 (1952): 192–199. On Luther's disputation, see J. Michael Raley, "Martin Luther on the Legitimacy of Resisting the Emperor," *Journal of Law and Religion* 37, no. 1 (2022): 96–132, esp. 110–114.

65. Iwand and Wolf, "Entwurf eines Gutachtens," 18.

66. "Befragung des Prof. D. Iwand durch die Verteidiger Dr. Wehage und Dr. Noack," in Kraus, *Braunschweiger Remerprozeß,* 22–23.

NOTES TO PAGES 174–177 339

67. On the "new peace movement" and its subordination to the SED, see Werner, *"Ohhe mich"-Bewegung,* 131–147.
68. Ziemann, *Niemöller,* 436–440.
69. Large, *Germans to the Front,* 143–153. On the Stalin note, see also Jürgen Zarusky, ed., *Die Stalin-Note vom 10. März 1952: Neue Quellen und Analysen* (Munich: Oldenbourg, 2002).
70. "Die Auseinandersetzungen über die politische Verantwortung der Kirche," *KJ* 79 (1952): 43–48.
71. "Erklärung der 'Kirchlichen Bruderschaft im Rheinland,'" in *Kirche und Kriegsdienstverweigerung: Ratschlag zur gesetzlichen Regelung des Schutzes der Kriegsdienstverweigerer,* ed. Rat der EKD (Munich: Kaiser, 1956), 53.
72. For Gollwitzer's recollections of his Soviet experience, see Helmut Gollwitzer, *Unwilling Journey: A Diary from Russia,* trans. E. M. Delacour (London: SCM Press, 1953). On his return to Bonn, see Friedrich-Wilhelm Marquardt, Wolfgang Brinkel, and Manfred Weber, eds., *Helmut Gollwitzer: Skizzen eines Lebens* (Gütersloh: Kaiser, 1998), 250–251.
73. Helmut Gollwitzer, "Der Christ zwischen Ost und West," in *Forderungen der Freiheit: Aufsätze und Reden zur politischen Ethik* (Munich: Kaiser, 1962), 125–141.
74. Helmut Gollwitzer, *Die christliche Gemeinde in der politischen Welt,* 2nd ed. (Tübingen: Mohr Siebeck, 1955), 31–39. For a selection of reviews that appeared in West Germany, France, the Netherlands, and the United States, see EZA 686 / 9026.
75. Gollwitzer, *Die christliche Gemeinde,* 46.
76. Gollwitzer, *Die christliche Gemeinde,* 44.
77. Helmut Gollwitzer, "Gewissen," in *Evangelisches Soziallexikon,* ed. Friedrich Karrenberg (Stuttgart: Kreuz, 1954), 446.
78. Gollwitzer, *Die christliche Gemeinde,* 49.
79. Josef Müller, *Die Gesamtdeutsche Volkspartei: Entstehung und Politik unter dem Primat nationaler Wiedervereinigung 1950–1957* (Düsseldorf: Droste, 1990), 281–301; Werner, *"Ohne mich"-Bewegung,* 427–439.
80. Large, *Germans to the Front,* 171–172.
81. Werner, *"Ohne mich"-Bewegung,* 430.
82. "Beschluss der Kirchenleitung der Ev. Kirche in Hessen und Nassau zur Frage der Kriegsdienstverweigerung. O.O., 28. September 1953," in *Protokolle,* vol. 7, *1953,* ed. Dagmar Pöpping and Peter Beier (Göttingen: Vandenhoeck und Ruprecht, 2009), 555–556.
83. "Erklärung der Kirchlichen Bruderschaft im Rheinland, Leverkusen," in Rat der EKD, *Kirche und Kriegsdienstverweigerung,* 57–58. For the number of signatories, see Immer to Kirchliche Bruderschaft im Rheinland, March 18, 1955, EZA 2 / 2576. On the collapse of the EDC, see Large, *Germans to the Front,* 205–215.
84. See Scheuner's memorandum to the EKD Commission on Public Responsibility: Ulrich Scheuner, "Zum Problem der Kriegsdienstverweigerung in der Gegenwart," October 4, 1950, EZA 2 / 2574.

340 NOTES TO PAGES 177–181

85. Eivind Berggrav, "Staat und Kirche in lutherischer Sicht," in *Offizieller Bericht der zweiten Vollversammlung des Lutherischen Weltbundes, Hannover, Deutschland, 25. Juli–3. Aug. 1952*, ed. Carl E. Lund-Quist (Hanover: n.p., 1953), 78–86.

86. Ulrich Scheuner, "Begriff und Entwicklung des Rechtsstaats," in *Macht und Recht: Beiträge zur lutherischen Staatslehre der Gegenwart*, ed. Hans Dombois and Erwin Wilkens (Berlin: Lutherisches Verlagshaus, 1956), 78–79.

87. Ulrich Scheuner, "Das Recht auf Kriegsdienstverweigerung," in *Der deutsche Soldat in der Armee von morgen: Wehrverfassung, Wehrsystem, inneres Gefüge*, ed. Institut für Staatslehre und Politik (Mainz: Isar, 1954), 253–281, quotes at 265–266.

88. Theodor Immer, "Bericht über die Aussprache über das Wort zur Kriegsdienstverweigerung der Kirchlichen Bruderschaft in Leverkusen," November 15, 1954, AEKR 5WV018/60.

89. Wolfgang Kraushaar counts over sixty protests, demonstrations, and public meetings against rearmament in the Federal Republic during February 1955 alone. See Kraushaar, *Die Protest-Chronik 1949–1959: Eine illustrierte Geschichte von Bewegung, Widerstand und Utopie*, vol. 2, *1953–1956* (Hamburg: Rogner und Bernhard, 1996), 1120–1145.

90. Alfred Weber et al., *Rettet Einheit, Freiheit, Frieden: Gegen Kommunismus und Nationalismus!* (Frankfurt: Union-Druckerei, 1955), 9–10.

91. Weber, *Rettet Einheit, Freiheit, Frieden*, 5–7.

92. Weber, *Rettet Einheit, Freiheit, Frieden*, 13. On the Paulskirche rally, see also Werner, *"Ohne mich"-Bewegung*, 477–510.

93. Werner, *"Ohne mich"-Bewegung*, 497–503.

94. Large, *Germans to the Front*, 215–220, 232–233.

95. Kirchenkanzlei der EKD, ed., *Espelkamp 1955: Bericht über die erste Tagung der zweiten Synode der Evangelischen Kirche in Deutschland vom 6. bis 11. März 1955* (Hanover: Verlag des Amtsblattes der EKD, 1955), 485–487. Although not formally a commission member, Gollwitzer participated in the drafting of the final memorandum: "Einleitung," in Rat der EKD, *Kirche und Kriegsdienstverweigerung*, 7–8.

96. "Niederschrift über die Verhandlungen der 4. Sitzung des Ausschusses für Fragen der Kriegsdienstverweigerung," November 2, 1955, EZA 2/2596.

97. "Niederschrift über die Verhandlungen des Ausschusses für Fragen der Kriegsdienstverweigerung auf seiner 3. Tagung," September 29, 1955, EZA 2/2596.

98. "Ratschlag zur gesetzlichen Regelung des Schutzes der Kriegsdienstverweigerer," in Rat der EKD, *Kirche und Kriegsdienstverweigerung*, 22–23.

99. "Kirche und Wehrpflicht: Das Echo des 'Ratschlags' der EKD," *EvW*, March 16, 1956. A selection of church members' letters to the *Sonntagsblatt* is printed in "Für und wider die Kriegsdienstverweigerung," *Sonntagsblatt*, January 8, 1956.

100. The March 1956 demonstration pictured in Figure 5.2 is described in Kraushaar, *Protest-Chronik*, 2:1352.

101. Dieckmann to Dibelius, June 11, 1956, EZA 2/2577.

NOTES TO PAGES 182–186   341

102. Deutscher Bundestag, "Stenographisches Protokoll (Sonderprotokoll) der 94. Sitzung des Ausschusses für Verteidigung," June 1, 1956, AdsD, Nachlass Adolf Arndt, box 239. On Kunst's service as a Wehrmacht chaplain, see Dagmar Pöpping, *Passion und Vernichtung: Kriegspfarrer an der Ostfront 1941–1945* (Göttingen: Vandenhoeck und Ruprecht, 2019), 195, 221.

103. Early postwar contacts between the Protestant churches and the SPD are detailed in Michael Klein, *Westdeutscher Protestantismus und politische Parteien: Anti-Parteien-Mentalität und parteipolitisches Engagement von 1945 bis 1963* (Tübingen: Mohr Siebeck, 2005), 323–337.

104. *VDBT,* 2. Deutscher Bundestag, 159. Sitzung, July 6, 1956, 8836–8841, 8850–8852, 8856.

105. For a detailed discussion of Arndt's petitions against the constitutionality of West German rearmament, see Dieter Gosewinkel, *Adolf Arndt: Die Wieder-begründung des Rechtsstaats aus dem Geist der Sozialdemokratie (1945–1961)* (Bonn: Dietz, 1991), 247–362.

106. *VDBT,* 2. Deutscher Bundestag, 159. Sitzung, July 6, 1956, 8838.

107. *VDBT,* 2. Deutscher Bundestag, 159. Sitzung, July 6, 1956, 8856. See also Large, *Germans to the Front,* 256–257.

108. "Wehrpflichtgesetz vom 21. Juli 1956," *Bundesgesetzblatt,* July 24, 1956, 657 (emphasis added).

109. "Aus der Evangelischen Kirche in Deutschland," *JK* 17, no. 19–20 (1956): 515; Scheuner to Kirchenkanzlei der EKD, August 23, 1956, EZA 2/2577.

110. "Der Kriegsdienstverweigerung im deutschen Wehrpflichtgesetz," *Herder Korrespondenz* 10, no. 12 (1956): 576–580.

111. Bernhard, *Zivildienst,* 50–59.

112. "BVG-Urteil zum Wehrpflichtgesetz erneut verschoben," *Badische Neuste Nachrichten,* October 14, 1960, in BArch Freiburg BW 1/94601. On the right of individual petition, see Justin Collings, *Democracy's Guardians: A History of the German Federal Constitutional Court, 1951–2001* (Oxford: Oxford University Press, 2015), xxvi, 49.

113. Quoted in Marc Cioc, *Pax Atomica: The Nuclear Defense Debate in West Germany during the Adenauer Era* (New York: Columbia University Press, 1988), 42. On the New Look plan, see Cioc, *Pax Atomica,* 21–37.

114. "Das 'Göttinger Manifest' von 18 Atomwissenschaftlern. 12.4.1957," in *Atomwaffen und Ethik: Der deutsche Protestantismus und die atomare Aufrüstung 1954–1961,* ed. Christian Walther (Munich: Kaiser, 1981), 36. See also Holger Nehring, *Politics of Security: British and West German Protest Movements and the Early Cold War, 1945–1970* (Oxford: Oxford University Press, 2013), 93–96.

115. Helmut Thielicke, "Was heißt Verantwortung im Atomzeitalter? Hamburg, 13.5.1957," in Walther, *Atomwaffen und Ethik,* 40–48.

116. Cioc, *Pax Atomica,* 117–119; Nehring, *Politics of Security,* 66–67.

117. Meyer-Magister, *Wehrdienst,* 399–400, 420.

118. Treffke, *Heinemann,* 155–158.

342 NOTES TO PAGES 186–191

119. Cioc, *Pax Atomica*, 121.
120. Helmut Gollwitzer, "Die Christen und die Atomwaffen," in *Forderungen der Freiheit*, 289–301.
121. "Anfrage an die Synode der EKiD zur atomaren Bewaffnung," in *Königsherrschaft Christi: Der Christ im Staat*, ed. Werner Schmauch and Ernst Wolf (Munich: Kaiser, 1958), 67–70.
122. On the synod debate, see Meyer-Magister, *Wehrdienst*, 501–507.
123. "Beschluß der 3. Tagung der 2. Synode der EKD. Berlin, 30.4.1958," in Walther, *Atomwaffen und Ethik*, 139.
124. "Theologische Erklärung," in *Christusbekenntnis im Atomzeitalter? Im Auftrag des Arbeitskreises Kirchlicher Bruderschaften*, ed. Ernst Wolf, Heinz Kloppenburg, and Helmut Simon (Munich: Kaiser, 1959), 15–16.
125. Ernst Wolf, "Die Königsherrschaft Christi und der Staat," in Schmauch and Wolf, *Königsherrschaft Christi*, 20–61, esp. 29–46.
126. "Thesen," in Schmauch and Wolf, *Königsherrschaft Christi*, 66.
127. Gosewinkel, *Arndt*, 407–417.
128. Cioc, *Pax Atomica*, 139–140.
129. For a detailed reconstruction of the commission's work, see Meyer-Magister, *Wehrdienst*, 513–539.
130. "'Heidelberger Thesen' der Atomkommission der Evangelischen Studiengemeinschaft. Herbst 1959," in Walther, *Atomwaffen und Ethik*, 142–148, quotes at 146, 148.
131. Cioc, *Pax Atomica*, 114.
132. For alternative perspectives on the transformation of the SPD, see Julia Angster, *Konsenskapitalismus und Sozialdemokratie: Die Westernisierung von SPD und DGB* (Munich: Oldenbourg, 2003); and Terence Renaud, *New Lefts: The Making of a Radical Tradition* (Princeton, NJ: Princeton University Press, 2021) 173–205.
133. Angster, *Konsenskapitalismus*, 368.
134. On Erler's ties to left-wing Protestantism, see Klein, *Westdeutscher Protestantismus*, 82, 283–285.
135. Adolf Arndt, "Christentum und freiheitlicher Sozialismus," in Arndt, *Politische Reden und Schriften*, ed. Horst Ehmke and Carlo Schmid (Berlin: Dietz, 1976), 113–133, quote at 131. See also Arndt, "Das Toleranzproblem aus der Sicht des Staates," in *Politische Reden und Schriften*, 134–149.
136. Arndt to Bundesverfassungsgericht Erster Senat, August 10, 1956, BArch Freiburg BW 1/313599.
137. Arndt to Bundesverfassungsgericht Erster Senat, January 23, 1957, BArch Freiburg BW 1/313599.
138. Arndt to Bundesverfassungsgericht Erster Senat, March 16, 1959, BArch Freiburg BW 1/49163.
139. Arndt to Bundesverfassungsgericht Erster Senat, March 16, 1959.
140. Arndt to Bundesverfassungsgericht Erster Senat, December 10, 1957, BArch Freiburg BW 1/49163.
141. Arndt to Bundesverfassungsgericht Erster Senat, March 16, 1959.

NOTES TO PAGES 192–198 343

142. Heinemann and Posser to Bundesverfassungsgericht, November 22, 1956, BArch Freiburg BW 1/94602.

143. Löffler to Bundesverfassungsgericht, July 27, 1956, BArch Freiburg BW 1/94602. On Löffler, see Reinhart Ricker, "Martin Löffler," in *Juristen im Portrait: Verlag und Autoren in 4 Jahrzehnten*, ed. Hans Dieter Beck (Munich: Beck, 1988), 531–537.

144. Susanne Király, *Ludwig Metzger: Politiker aus christlicher Verantwortung* (Darmstadt: Hessische Historische Kommission, 2004), 302–304; Hartmut Soell, *Fritz Erler: Eine politische Biographie*, vol. 1 (Berlin: Dietz, 1976), 224–225.

145. Angster, *Konsenskapitalismus*, 415–430.

146. "Grundsatzprogramm der Sozialdemokratischen Partei Deutschlands, beschlossen auf dem außerordentlichen Parteitag in Bad Godesberg, 1959," in *Programmatische Dokumente der deutschen Sozialdemokratie*, ed. Dieter Dowe and Kurt Klotzbach (Berlin: Dietz, 1984), 366. On Arndt's role, see Gosewinkel, *Arndt*, 542–557.

147. "Grundsatzprogramm," 377. On Heinemann's role, see Treffke, *Heinemann*, 171.

148. "Grundsatzprogramm," 368.

149. Herbert Werner, "SPD—wohin?," *SdG* 12, no. 1 (1960): 21–24; and *SdG* 12, no. 3 (1960): 77–80.

150. On left socialism at the Godesberg Congress, see Geogor Kritidis, *Linkssozialistische Opposition in der Ära Adenauer* (Hanover: Offizin, 2008), 429–446.

151. Cooper, *Paradoxes*, 98–101.

152. "BVerwG, Urteil v. 3.10.1958," *JuristenZeitung* 14, no. 5/6 (1959): 159–162.

153. For the list of cases considered in the judgment, see Bundesverfassungsgericht Erster Senat to Bundesminister für Verteidigung, April 12, 1960, BArch Freiburg BW1/94601.

154. "Beschluß vom 20. Dezember 1960," in *Entscheidungen des Bundesverfassungsgerichts*, vol. 12 (Tübingen: Mohr, 1962), 45–61, quotes at 54, 60; "Urteil des Ersten Senats vom 18. April 1961," in *Entscheidungen des Bundesverfassungsgerichts*, 12:311–318.

155. On postwar debates about judicial review, see Collings, *Democracy's Guardians*, 16–17.

156. Gustav W. Heinemann, "Der Verfassungsstreit um die Kriegsdienstverweigerung," *JK* 22, no. 9 (1961): 553–555.

157. Theodor Michaltscheff, "Die Fehlbarkeit einer unfehlbaren Entscheidung," *SdG* 13, no. 3 (1961): 81–84. On Michaltscheff, see Werner, *"Ohne mich"-Bewegung*, 301–302.

6. The Eastern Border and the Bounds of Reconciliation

1. Rat der EKD, ed., *Die Lage der Vertriebenen und das Verhältnis des deutschen Volkes zu seinen östlichen Nachbarn: Eine evangelische Denkschrift* (Hanover: Verlag des Amtsblattes der EKD, 1965), 29.

2. For a detailed account of the expulsions, see R. M. Douglas, *Orderly and Humane: The Expulsion of the Germans after the Second World War* (New Haven,

344 NOTES TO PAGES 198–203

CT: Yale University Press, 2013). On war memory in postwar West Germany, see Gilad Margalit, *Guilt, Suffering, and Memory: Germany Remembers Its Dead of World War II*, trans. Haim Watzman (Bloomington: Indiana University Press, 2010); and Robert G. Moeller, *War Stories: The Search for a Usable Past in the Federal Republic of Germany* (Berkeley: University of California Press, 2001). On expellee narratives in particular, see Peter N. Gengler, "Constructing and Leveraging 'Flight and Expulsion': Expellee Memory Politics and Victimhood Narratives in the Federal Republic of Germany, 1944–1970" (PhD diss., University of North Carolina, Chapel Hill, 2019).

3. Annika Elisabet Frieberg, *Peace at All Costs: Catholic Intellectuals, Journalists, and Media in Polish–German Reconciliation* (New York: Berghahn Books, 2019); Manfred Kittel, *Vertreibung der Vertriebenen? Der historische deutsche Osten in der Erinnerungskultur der Bundesrepublik (1961–1982)* (Munich: Oldenbourg, 2007), 31–57.

4. On the disjuncture between official expellee politics and popular memory, see Andrew Demshuk, *The Lost German East: Forced Migration and the Politics of Memory, 1945–1970* (Cambridge: Cambridge University Press, 2012).

5. Ian Connor, "The Protestant Churches and German Refugees and Expellees in the Western Zones of Germany after 1945," *Debatte: Journal of Contemporary Central and Eastern Europe* 15, no. 1 (2007): 43–63. For a detailed study of the Evangelisches Hilfswerk, see Hartmut Rudolph, *Evangelische Kirche und Vertriebene 1945 bis 1972*, vol. 1, *Kirche ohne Land* (Göttingen: Vandenhoeck und Ruprecht, 1984), 39–175. On Catholic aid to German expellees, see Sabine Vosskamp, *Katholische Kirche und Vertriebene in Westdeutschland: Integration, Identität und ostpolitischer Diskurs 1945 bis 1972* (Stuttgart: Kohlhammer, 2007), 43–55, 61–78.

6. Vosskamp, *Katholische Kirche und Vertriebene*, 229–232; Robert Żurek, *Zwischen Nationalismus und Versöhnung: Die Kirchen und die deutsch-polnischen Beziehungen 1945–1956* (Cologne: Böhlau, 2005), 183–213.

7. Peter N. Gengler, "'New Citizens' or 'Community of Fate'? Early Discourses and Politics on 'Flight and Expulsion' in the Two Postwar Germanies," *Central European History* 53, no. 2 (2020): 314–334. On the formation of the expellee organizations, see Pertti Ahonen, *After the Expulsion: West Germany and Eastern Europe, 1945–1990* (Oxford: Oxford University Press, 2003), 24–38.

8. Margalit, *Guilt*, 190–194. On the treaty, see also Katarzyna Stokłosa, *Polen und die deutsche Ostpolitik 1945–1990* (Göttingen: Vandenhoeck und Ruprecht, 2011), 76–79.

9. "Charta der Heimatvertriebenen (August 1950)," in *Das Recht auf die Heimat: Vorträge und Aussprachen*, vol. 1, ed. Kurt Rabl (Munich: Lerche, 1958), 117–118; Hartwig Bülck, "Das Recht auf Heimat," *Jahrbuch für internationales und ausländisches öffentliches Recht* 3 (1950/1951): 58–84; Rudolf Laun, *Das Recht auf die Heimat* (Hanover: Schroedel, 1951). On Laun, postwar West Germany's most prominent specialist in international law, see Lora Wildenthal, *The Language of Human Rights in West Germany* (Philadelphia: University of Pennsylvania Press, 2013), 45–62.

NOTES TO PAGES 203–206   345

10. On these organizations, see Rudolph, *Evangelische Kirche und Vertriebene*, 1:390–403, 412–432.
11. "Universal Declaration of Human Rights," art. 13, para. 2, United Nations, https://www.un.org/en/universal-declaration-human-rights/; Laun, *Recht auf die Heimat*, 35.
12. Vosskamp, *Katholische Kirche und Vertriebene*, 232–233. For an example of the Catholic approach, see Julius Doms, *Gedanken zum Recht auf Heimat* (Troisdorf: Wegweiser, 1953).
13. Kurt Rabl, *Das Selbstbestimmungsrecht der Völker* (Munich: Korn, 1963). On Rabl, see Wildenthal, *Language of Human Rights*, 121, 238n122.
14. Walter Künneth, "Die Frage des Rechts auf die Heimat in evangelischer Sicht," in *Recht auf die Heimat*, 1:11–40, quotes at 17, 38.
15. Vosskamp, *Katholische Kirche und Vertriebene*, 45, 257–258.
16. Frieberg, *Peace*, 28–29.
17. Karl Barth, *Church Dogmatics*, vol. 3, pt. 4, *The Doctrine of the Creation: The Command of God the Creator*, trans. G. T. Thomson (Edinburgh: T&T Clark, 1961), 285–323.
18. Friedrich Spiegel-Schmidt, *Lernprozess: Ein Leben zwischen Kirche und Politik*, vol. 1, *1912–1950* (Vienna: Evangelischer Presseverband in Österreich, 1992), 71–72.
19. Rudolph, *Evangelische Kirche und Vertriebene*, 1:597; Spiegel-Schmidt, *Lernprozess*, 1:134–142, 177–190.
20. Friedrich Spiegel-Schmidt, "Der evangelische Christ und seine Heimat," *EvTh* 14, no. 3 (1954): 105–119, quotes at 113, 118–119.
21. Heinz-Horst Schrey, "Heimat—Theologisch gesehen," in *Evangelisches Soziallexikon*, ed. Friedrich Karrenberg (Stuttgart: Kreuz, 1954), 483–484. See also Heinz-Horst Schrey, Hans Hermann Walz, and W. A. Whitehouse, *The Biblical Doctrine of Justice and Law* (London: SCM Press, 1955).
22. Herbert Girgensohn, "Das Recht auf Heimat als Menschenrecht," *Der Remter: Blätter ostdeutscher Besinnung* 1, no. 4 (1955): 21–26. On Girgensohn, see "Girgensohn, Herbert," in *Personenlexikon zum deutschen Protestantismus 1919–1949*, ed. Hannelore Braun and Gertraud Grünzinger (Göttingen: Vandenhoeck und Ruprecht, 2006), 87.
23. On church–state conflict in 1950s East Germany, see Martin Greschat, *Protestantismus im Kalten Krieg: Kirche, Politik und Gesellschaft im geteilten Deutschland 1945–1963* (Paderborn: Schöningh, 2010), 195–250.
24. Frieberg, *Peace*, 36–37; Peter Morré, "Allies against the Imperial West: Josef L. Hromádka, the Ecumenical Movement and the Internationalization of the Eastern Bloc since the 1950s," in *Globalisierung der Kirchen: Globale Transformation und ökumenische Erneuerung des Ökumenischen Rates der Kirchen in den 1960er- und 1970er-Jahren*, ed. Katharina Kunter and Annegreth Schilling (Göttingen: Vandenhoeck und Ruprecht, 2014), 170–174; Victoria Smolkin, *A Sacred Space Is Never Empty: A History of Soviet Atheism* (Princeton, NJ: Princeton University Press, 2018), 70–74. Khrushchev relaunched the antireligious campaign in the Soviet Union in 1958.

346   NOTES TO PAGES 207–210

25. Frieberg, *Peace*, 41–46. On the Polish October, see also Stokłosa, *Polen*, 80–94.
26. Herbert Mochalski, "Polen–im February 1957," *SdG* 9, no. 6 (1957): 177–180; Mochalski, "Neun Millionen bezahlen!," *SdG* 9, no. 7 (1957): 201–204, quote at 202.
27. Erica Küppers, "Was sagte Niemöller zur Oder-Neiße-Linie?," *SdG* 9, no. 8 (1957): 237–240.
28. "Bandaufnahme Gespräch Niemöller—Walter am 8. April 1957," *SdG* 9, no. 8 (1957): 249–252; Renate Riemeck, "Zum Problem der Oder-Neiße-Linie," *SdG* 9, no. 10 (1957): 305–310.
29. Greschat, *Protestantismus*, 374–375. On the formation of the Christian Peace Conference, see also Claudia Lepp, *Tabu der Einheit: Die Ost-West-Gemeinschaft der evangelischen Christen und die deutsche Teilung (1945–1969)* (Göttingen: Vandenhoeck und Ruprecht, 2005), 469–472; and Gerhard Lindemann, "'Sauertieg im Kreis der gesamtchristlichen Ökumene': Das Verhältnis zwischen der Christlichen Friedenskonkferenz und dem Ökumenischen Rat der Kirchen," in Gerhard Besier, Armin Boyens, and Gerhard Lindemann, *Nationaler Protestantismus und Ökumenische Bewegung: Kirchliches Handeln im Kalten Krieg (1945–1990)* (Berlin: Duncker und Humblot, 1999), 654–684.
30. Lindemann, "'Sauertieg,'" 658–659; Jürgen Seim, *Hans Joachim Iwand: Eine Biografie* (Gütersloh: Gütersloher Verlagshaus, 1999), 485–486, 495–497.
31. Morré, "Allies," 174–176. See also Helena Tóth, "Dialogue as a Strategy of Struggle: Religious Politics in East Germany, 1957–1968," *Contemporary European History* 29, no. 2 (2020): 171–186.
32. Bradley F. Adams, *The Struggle for the Soul of the Nation: Czech Culture and the Rise of Communism* (Lanham, MD: Rowman and Littlefield, 2004), 265–274; Morré, "Allies," 178–179.
33. Heinrich Vogel, "The Call of Hiroshima," in *Elige Vitam: The Second Meeting of the Christian Peace Conference, Prague, April 16th to 19th, 1959* (Prague: Christian Peace Conference, 1959), 10–19.
34. Helmut Gollwitzer, "Christianity and War," in *Elige Vitam*, 27–42.
35. Władysław Śliwka-Szczerbic, "Wie uns ein Pole sieht," *SdG* 9 (1957): 425–428, 465–468, 501–504, 525–528.
36. H. J. Iwand, "The Situation in Western Germany," in *Elige Vitam*, 59–61.
37. Ahonen, *After the Expulsion*, 147–154.
38. R. Gerald Hughes, "Unfinished Business from Potsdam: Britain, West Germany, and the Oder-Neisse Line, 1945–1962," *International History Review* 27, no. 2 (2005): 279–282.
39. Seim, *Iwand*, 580.
40. Herbert Girgensohn, "Das Recht auf Heimat als seelsorgerliches Problem der Gegenwart," *Der Remter* 5, no. 4 (1959): 197–202; Friedrich Spiegel-Schmidt, "Selbstbestimmungsrecht und Heimatrecht," *Der Remter* 5, no. 4 (1959): 219–227.
41. Kurt Rabl, "Diskussion um das Heimatrecht," *Der Remter* 5, no. 4 (1959): 203–212, quote at 211.

NOTES TO PAGES 210–215   347

42. "Entschließung des Konvents der zerstreuten evangelischen Ostkirchen," in *Das Recht auf die Heimat*, vol. 4, ed. Kurt Rabl (Munich: Lerche, 1959), 162–163. For the theses of the 1949 Göttingen conference, see "Thesen," in *Kirche und Recht: Ein vom Rat der Evangelischen Kirche in Deutschland veranlasstes Gespräch über die christliche Begründung des Rechts*, ed. Rat der EKD (Göttingen: Vandenhoeck und Ruprecht, 1950), 51–52.

43. Hans J. Iwand, "Das Recht auf Heimat," *JK* 20, no. 10 (1959): 477–481; Friedrich Spiegel-Schmidt, "Stellungnahme zum Wort des Ostkirchenausschusses über das Heimatrecht," EZA 17/528; Leiterkonferenz der Kirchlichen Bruderschaften in Deutschland to Mitglieder der Synode der Evangelischen Kirche in Deutschland, January 12, 1961, EZA 613/15.

44. Hans Joachim Iwand, letter to the editor of *Die Welt*, September 18, 1959, reprinted as "Tag der Heimat: Moralische Unverfrorenheit," *JK* 20, no. 10 (1959): 481.

45. "Karl Barth: Stelle uns folgende Sätze zur Verfügung," *Der Remter* 6, no. 3 (1960): 140.

46. Seim, *Iwand*, 342–346.

47. Iwand, "Tag der Heimat." The controversy over Iwand's letter is documented in letters to *Junge Kirche:* "Das Recht auf Heimat," *JK* 20, no. 10 (1959): 481–487; and "Briefe an Professor Iwand," *JK* 20, no. 12 (1959): 613–633.

48. Quoted in Konrad Raiser, *Von der politischen Verantwortung des Nichtpolitikers: Ein Lebensbild meines Vaters Ludwig Raiser* (Norderstedt: Books on Demand, 2020), 20.

49. Raiser, *Verantwortung*, 20–23, 46–55.

50. Raiser, *Verantwortung*, 61, 84; see also 62–68.

51. Raiser, *Verantwortung*, 104.

52. Raiser, *Verantwortung*, 111–116.

53. For instance, Ludwig Raiser, "Vorwort," in *Christen und Nichtchristen in der Rechtsordnung: Vorträge der 5. Plenarsitzung der Studiengemeinschaft der Evangelischen Akademie* (Bad Boll: Studiengemeinschaft der Evangelischen Akademie, 1950), 1–2.

54. Raiser, *Verantwortung*, 164; "Wehrbeitrag und christliches Gewissen," in *Kirche und Kriegsdienstverweigerung: Ratschlag zur gesetzlichen Regelung des Schutzes der Kriegsdienstverweigerer*, ed. Rat der EKD (Munich: Kaiser, 1956), 40–42.

55. Carl Friedrich von Weizsäcker, "Vorwort," in Ludwig Raiser, *Vom rechten Gebrauch der Freiheit: Aufsätze zu Politik, Recht, Wissenschaft und Kirche*, ed. Konrad Raiser (Stuttgart: Klett-Cotta, 1982), 10.

56. See Chapter 4 of this volume.

57. For the participants at the initial meeting, see Hans Dombois, ed., *Recht und Institution: Eine Fortsetzung des Göttinger Gesprächs von 1949 über die christliche Begründung des Rechts* (Witten-Ruhr: Luther, 1956), 7. The subsequent meetings are documented in EZA 87/171–172.

58. "Thesen 1957," in *Recht und Institution*, vol. 2, *Arbeitsbericht und Referate aus der Institutionenkommission der Evangelischen Studiengemeinschaft*, ed. Hans

348 NOTES TO PAGES 215–219

Dombois (Stuttgart: E. Klett, 1969), 62. For an overview of the group's work, see Rolf-Peter Calliess, "Institution und Recht: Bericht über das Rechtsgespräch in der Institutionenkommission der Evangelischen Studiengemeinschaft in der Zeit von 1956 bis 1961," in *Recht und Institution*, 2:11–60.

59. Ludwig Raiser, "Institution und Rechtsnorm: Referat für die Institutionen- kommission der Evangelischen Studiengemeinschaft," October 19–20, 1959, EZA 87/171.

60. Wolfgang Schweitzer, *Dunkle Schatten, helles Licht: Rückblick auf ein schwieriges Jahrhundert* (Stuttgart: Radius, 1999), 108–109, 152–155, 210–233.

61. "Niederschrift der Sitzung der von der Kanzlei der Evangelischen Kirche in Deutschland einberufenen Eigentumskommission," November 29–30, 1957, EZA 2/1504.

62. Erwin Metzke, "Vorwort," in *Marxismus-Studien*, vol. 1, ed. Iring Fetscher (Tübingen: Mohr, 1954), vi.

63. For instance, see the minutes for the session "Eigentum und Gerechtigkeit, 2. Folge," March 6–8, 1961, FEST Archive, box 709.

64. Ernst Wolf, "Eigentum und Existenz," *ZEE* 6 (1962): 1–17, quotes at 11, 17.

65. On the composition of the Tübingen Memorandum, see Martin Greschat, "'Mehr Wahrheit in der Politik!' Das Tübinger Memorandum von 1961," *Vierteljahreshefte für Zeitgeschichte* 48, no. 3 (2000): 491–513; and Andrea Strübind, "Das Tübinger Memorandum: Die politische Verantwortung der Nichtpolitiker," *Kirchliche Zeitgeschichte* 24, no. 2 (2011): 360–395. On Klaus von Bismarck, see also Frieberg, *Peace*, 82–106.

66. "Das Tübinger Memorandum," *KJ* 89 (1962): 75–78.

67. Strübind, "Tübinger Memorandum," 385–386.

68. Quote in "Protestanten kritisieren die Bonner Politik," *Deutsche National- Zeitung*, February 24–25, 1962. See also "Acht gegen Bonn: Tübinger Memorandum, eine Grundsatzfrage der Willensbildung in der Demokratie," *Bayerische Staatszeitung und Bayerischer Staatsanzeiger*, March 2, 1962; and Gerhard Wirsing, "Ein Schuß ins Leere," *Christ und Welt*, March 2, 1962. Press reactions to the Tübingen Memorandum are collected in BArch Koblenz N 1287/60.

69. Helmut Gollwitzer, "Zur Einführung," in *Forderungen der Freiheit: Aufsätze und Reden zur politischen Ethik* (Munich: Kaiser, 1962), xxvii. See also "Erklärung des 'Beienroder Konvents,'" *KJ* 89 (1962): 85–86.

70. "Laien am Werk," *Der Spiegel*, March 7, 1962; Marion Gräfin Dönhoff, "Lobbyisten der Vernunft: Das Memorandum der Acht: Eine kritische Bestandaufnahme der Bonner Politik," *Die Zeit*, March 2, 1962; W. E. Süskind, "Nicht zuständig für Politik," *Süddeutsche Zeitung*, March 2, 1962.

71. Wilkens to Raiser, February 26, 1962, EZA 2/1353.

72. "Niederschrift über die Verhandlungen der Kammer für öffentliche Verantwor- tung," February 16, 1963, EZA 2/1354.

73. "Niederschrift über die 16. Sitzung des Rates der Evangelischen Kirche in Deutschland," January 17–18, 1963, EZA 2/1807.

NOTES TO PAGES 219–221

74. The exception was the Spandau Prison in West Berlin, where three Nazi leaders convicted at the Nuremberg International Military Tribunal remained incarcerated after 1957.

75. Marc von Miquel, "Explanation, Dissociation, Apologia: The Debate over the Criminal Prosecution of Nazi Crimes in the 1960s," in *Coping with the Nazi Past: West German Debates and Generational Conflict, 1955–1975*, ed. Philipp Gassert and Alan E. Steinweis (New York: Berghahn Books, 2006), 51–56. On the Schörner trial, see also "Wer half Schörner?," *Der Spiegel*, October 15, 1957.

76. Devin O. Pendas, *The Frankfurt Auschwitz Trial, 1963–1965: Genocide, History, and the Limits of the Law* (Cambridge: Cambridge University Press, 2006), 53–79.

77. On the press and public reactions to the trials, see Frank Biess, *German Angst: Fear and Democracy in the Federal Republic of Germany* (Oxford: Oxford University Press, 2020), 170–184; and Pendas, *Frankfurt Auschwitz Trial*, 249–287.

78. Matthew D. Hockenos, *A Church Divided: German Protestants Confront the Nazi Past* (Bloomington: Indiana University Press, 2004), 160. On the German Protestant mission to the Jews, see Christopher M. Clark, *The Politics of Conversion: Missionary Protestantism and the Jews in Prussia, 1728–1941* (Oxford: Oxford University Press, 1995).

79. "Message Concerning the Jewish Question (Council of Brethren of the Evangelical Church, Darmstadt, April 8, 1948)," in Hockenos, *A Church Divided*, 195–197. On the context of the statement, see also Hockenos, *A Church Divided*, 157–163.

80. Josef Foschepoth, *Im Schatten der Vergangenheit: Die Anfänge der Gesellschaften für Christlich-Jüdische Zusammenarbeit* (Göttingen: Vandenhoeck und Ruprecht, 1993), 61–79, 134–140, 164–177.

81. Noah Benezra Strote, "Sources of Christian–Jewish Cooperation in Early Cold War Germany," in *Is There a Judeo-Christian Tradition? A European Perspective*, ed. Emmanuel Nathan and Anya Topolski (Berlin: De Gruyter, 2016), 75–100.

82. Atina Grossmann, "Where Did All 'Our' Jews Go? Germans and Jews in Post-Nazi Germany," in *The Germans and the Holocaust: Popular Responses to the Persecution and Murder of the Jews*, ed. Susanna Schrafstetter and Alan E. Steinweis (New York: Berghahn Books, 2015), 150.

83. Quoted in Willehad Eckert, "Christlich-jüdische Begegnungen in Deutschland nach 1945," *Freiburger Rundbrief* 12, no. 49 (1960): 7. I elaborate on postwar Christian–Jewish dialogue in Brandon Bloch, "In the Presence of Absence: Transformations of the Confessional Divide in West Germany after the Holocaust," in *Germany and the Confessional Divide: Religious Tensions and Political Culture, 1871–1989*, ed. Mark Edward Ruff and Thomas Großbölting (New York: Berghahn Books, 2022), 216–241.

84. Gerhard Gronauer, *Der Staat Israel im westdeutschen Protestantismus: Wahrnehmungen in Kirche und Publizistik von 1948 bis 1972* (Göttingen: Vandenhoeck und Ruprecht, 2013), 139–142, 179–190. On Scharf's role in the Confessing Church, see Wolf-Dieter Zimmermann, *Kurt Scharf: Ein Leben zwischen Vision und Wirklichkeit* (Göttingen: Vandenhoeck und Ruprecht, 1992), 22–52.

350　　NOTES TO PAGES 221–225

85. On the group's formation, see Gabriele Kammerer, *In die Haare, in die Arme: 40 Jahre Arbeitsgemeinschaft "Juden und Christen" beim Deutschen Evangelischen Kirchentag* (Gütersloh: Gütersloher Verlagshaus, 2001), 9–27.

86. Robert Raphael Geis, "Der Auftrag Israels an die Völker," in *Der ungekündigte Bund: Neue Begegnungen von Juden und christlicher Gemeinde,* ed. Dietrich Goldschmidt and Hans-Joachim Kraus (Stuttgart: Kreuz, 1962), 57–62. On the reception of Geis's lecture, see Kammerer, *In die Haare,* 33–37.

87. On Goldschmidt, see Michael Becker, "Dietrich Goldschmidt, 'Educator and Political Activist': Über einen fast vergessenen Soziologen und Intellektuellen," in *Erkundungen im Historischen: Soziologie in Göttingen,* ed. Oliver Römer and Ina Alber-Armenat (Wiesbaden: Springer VS, 2019), 203–245.

88. Goldschmidt to Raiser, January 14, 1963; and Goldschmidt to Harder and Scharf, January 14, 1963, both EZA 2/1354.

89. "Bumke schwieg," *Der Spiegel,* December 12, 1961.

90. "Niederschrift über die Verhandlungen der Kammer für öffentliche Verantwortung," February 16, 1963, EZA 2/1354.

91. *Statement of the Council of the EKD on the Trials of Nazi Criminals* (Frankfurt: Kirchliches Außenamt der Evangelischen Kirche in Deutschland, 1963), 2–6.

92. "Echo der Erklärung des Rates der EKD zu den NS-Prozessen," *EvW,* June 1, 1963.

93. "Sonderdrucke der Betheler Erklärung des Rates der EKD," *EvW,* April 16, 1963.

94. "EKD-Wort zu den NS-Prozessen dreisprachig," *EvW,* June 1, 1963.

95. "Echo der Erklärung." For the critical response to the statement, see also the letters to the EKD chancellery collected in EZA 2/2487.

96. Ludwig Raiser, "Kommentar zum Wort des Rates der Evangelischen Kirche in Deutschland zu den NS-Kriegsverbrecherprozessen," Norddeutscher Rundfunk, May 4, 1963, EZA 2/2480.

97. Erwin Wilkens, *NS-Verbrechen: Strafjustiz, deutsche Selbstbesinnung* (Berlin: Lutherisches Verlagshaus, 1964), 25. On Wilkens, see Valentin Schmidt, "'Eine prägende Gestalt des Nachkriegsprotestantismus,'" Evangelische Kirche in Deutschland, January 29, 2000, https://www.ekd.de/11975.htm.

98. Zimmermann, *Scharf,* 56, 88–91.

99. Hartmut Rudolph, *Evangelische Kirche und Vertriebene,* vol. 2, *Kirche in der neuen Heimat,* 97–104, quote at 98. See also Bismarck to Scharf, March 12, 1963, EZA 2/1353.

100. Spiegel-Schmidt, *Lernprozess,* vol. 2, *1950–1992* (Vienna: Evangelischer Presseverband in Österreich, 1992), 166–169.

101. "Protokoll über die Sitzung der Kammer für öffentliche Verantwortung," November 29, 1963, EZA 2/1354. See also Wolfgang Schweitzer, "Ideologisierung des 'Rechts auf Heimat'? Dargestellt im Zusammenhang mit den Auseinandersetzungen um das 'Tübinger Memorandum der Acht' vom November 1961/Februar 1962," *ZEE* (1963): 36–61, and the critical replies to Schweitzer: Joachim Freiherr von Braun, "Deutschlands Ostproblem: Eine

Antwort an Wolfgang Schweitzer," *ZEE* 7 (1963): 234–245; and Kurt Rabl, "Diskussionsbeitrag zum Thema 'Recht auf Heimat,'" *ZEE* 7 (1963): 245–262.

102. "Protokoll über die Sitzung," November 29, 1963. For the theses of Schweitzer's group, see "Die Versöhnung in Christus und die Frage des deutschen Anspruchs auf die Gebiete jenseits der Oder und Neiße: Eine vom Bielefelder Arbeitskreis der Kirchlichen Bruderschaften zur Diskussion gestellte Thesenreihe," *JK* 24, no. 12 (1963): 718–723, quote at 721.

103. "Niederschrift über die Sitzung der Kammer für öffentliche Verantwortung," February 21–22, 1964, EZA 2/1354.

104. Erwin Wilkens, "Das Recht auf Heimat," EZA 2/1356.

105. "Kurzprotokoll über die Sitzung der Kammer für öffentliche Verantwortung," October 2–3, 1964, EZA 2/1357; Wilkens to EKD Council, October 13, 1964, EZA 2/1356.

106. "Kurzprotokoll über die Sitzung der Kammer der EKD für öffentliche Verantwortung," December 18–19, 1964, EZA 2/1357.

107. Rat der EKD, *Lage der Vertriebenen*, 26–29. The authorship of the memorandum is discussed in Rudolph, *Evangelische Kirche und Vertriebene*, 2:138–139.

108. Rat der EKD, *Lage der Vertriebenen*, 33–34.

109. Rat der EKD, *Lage der Vertriebenen*, 42–43.

110. Rat der EKD, *Lage der Vertriebenen*, 38.

111. Lepp, *Tabu der Einheit*, 520–522.

112. Noel D. Cary, "Reassessing Germany's Ostpolitik. Part I: From Détente to Refreeze," *Central European History* 33, no. 2 (2000): 235–262; Benedikt Schoenborn, *Reconciliation Road: Willy Brandt, Ostpolitik and the Quest for European Peace* (New York: Berghahn Books, 2020).

113. For detailed overviews of the reception, see Reinhard Henkys, "Die Denkschrift in der Diskussion," in *Deutschland und die östlichen Nachbarn: Beiträge zu einer evangelischen Denkschrift*, ed. Reinhard Henkys (Stuttgart: Kreuz, 1966), 33–91; and Rudolph, *Evangelische Kirche und Vertriebene*, 2:150–210.

114. Margalit, *Guilt*, 211.

115. Quoted in Henkys, "Denkschrift," 35. For a collection of critical responses, see Peter Nasarski, ed., *Stimmen zur Denkschrift der EKD: Die Lage der Vertriebenen und das Verhältnis des deutschen Volkes zu seinen östlichen Nachbarn* (Cologne: Verlag Wissenschaft und Politik, 1966).

116. "'Das sagt man doch als guter Deutscher nicht,'" *Der Spiegel*, November 16, 1965; Ludwig Raiser, "Blick nach Osten," *Die Zeit*, March 18, 1966.

117. Henkys, "Denkschrift," 62–65.

118. Quoted in Henkys, "Denkschrift," 65.

119. Quoted in Henkys, "Denkschrift," 58–59.

120. Henkys, "Denkschrift," 47–52.

121. Henkys, "Denkschrift," 52–55.

122. On the Bensberg Circle of left Catholic intellectuals, which emerged from the Pax Christi movement, see Frieberg, *Peace*, 143–147.

352   NOTES TO PAGES 230–235

123. "Polish Bishops' Appeal to Their German Colleagues," in *German Polish Dialogue: Letters of the Polish and German Bishops and International Statements* (Bonn: Edition Atlantic-Forum, 1966), 7–19, quotes at 15, 18.

124. "German Bishops' Reply to Their Polish Colleagues," in *German Polish Dialogue*, 21–26.

125. Stokłosa, *Polen*, 137. On the exchange, see also Frieberg, *Peace*, 135–143.

126. Stokłosa, *Polen*, 133–136.

127. Renate Riemeck, "Zur Ost-Denkschrift der EKD," *SdG* 17, no. 22 (1965): 675–676; Helmut Thielicke, "Was geht denn das die Kirche an?," *Sonntagsblatt*, October 31, 1965.

128. "Erklärung der in Berlin-Spandau zu ihrer Tagung vom 13. bis 18. März 1966 versammelten Mitglieder der Synode der Evangelischen Kirche in Deutschland vom 18. März 1966," in *Vertreibung und Versöhnung: Die Synode der EKD zur Denkschrift "Die Lage der Vertriebenen und das Verhältnis des deutschen Volkes zu seinen östlichen Nachbarn*," ed. Erwin Wilkens (Stuttgart: Kreuz, 1966), 59–63.

129. Ahonen, *After the Expulsion*, 243–256.

130. Ahonen, *After the Expulsion*, 155–200; Demshuk, *Lost German East*, 232–262.

131. Quoted in Raiser, *Verantwortung*, 217.

132. Wolfgang Schweitzer, "Die Ostdenkschrift der EKD von 1965 in der Perspektive von 1985," *ZEE* 29 (1985): 269. See also Erwin Wilkens, *Vertreibung und Versöhnung: Die Ostdenkschrift als Beitrag zur deutschen Ostpolitik* (Hanover: Lutherhaus, 1986).

133. "Huber zum 40. Jahrestag der Ostdenkschrift in Warschau," Evangelische Kirche in Deutschland, October 5, 2005, https://www.ekd.de/pm196_2005 _rv_warschau_ostdenkschrift.htm.

134. On Catholicism and West European integration, see Wolfram Kaiser, *Christian Democracy and the Origins of European Union* (Cambridge: Cambridge University Press, 2007).

7. Emergencies of Democracy

1. Wolfgang Kraushaar, "Furcht vor einem 'neuen 33': Protest gegen die Notstandsgesetzgebung," in *Streit um den Staat: Intellektuelle Debatten in der Bundesrepublik 1960–1980*, ed. Dominik Geppert and Jens Hacke (Göttingen: Vandenhoeck und Ruprecht, 2008), 139.

2. Helmut Schauer, ed., *Notstand der Demokratie: Referate, Diskussionsbeiträge und Materialien vom Kongreß am 30. Oktober 1966 in Frankfurt am Main* (Frankfurt: Europäische Verlagsanstalt, 1967), 13–14.

3. Thomas Großbölting, *Losing Heaven: Religion in Germany since 1945*, trans. Alex Skinner (New York: Berghahn Books, 2017), 107. On the factors behind religious change in 1960s West Germany, see Großbölting, *Losing Heaven*, 105–132; and Detlef Pollack, "Religiöser und gesellschaftlicher Wandel in den 1960er Jahren," in *Religion und Lebensführung im Umbruch der langen 1960er Jahren*, ed. Claudia Lepp, Harry Oelke, and Detlef Pollack (Göttingen:

NOTES TO PAGES 235–237   353

Vandenhoeck und Ruprecht, 2016), 31–63. For a comparative perspective, see Hugh McLeod, *The Religious Crisis of the 1960s* (Oxford: Oxford University Press, 2007).

4. While recent studies of the West German New Left have foregrounded the neglected roles of women, conservative students, and international students, religion has remained a marginal theme. See Timothy Scott Brown, *West Germany and the Global Sixties: The Antiauthoritarian Revolt, 1962–1978* (Cambridge: Cambridge University Press, 2013); Anna von der Goltz, *The Other '68ers: Student Protest and Christian Democracy in West Germany* (Oxford: Oxford University Press, 2021); Christina von Hodenberg, *The Other '68: A Social History of West Germany's Revolt,* trans. Rachel Ward (Oxford: Oxford University Press, 2024); Martin Klimke, *The Other Alliance: Student Protest in West Germany and the United States in the Global Sixties* (Princeton, NJ: Princeton University Press, 2010); and Quinn Slobodian, *Foreign Front: Third World Politics in Sixties West Germany* (Durham, NC: Duke University Press, 2012). Several scholars, however, have explored productive exchanges between religious thinkers and the West European New Left. See, for instance, Pascal Eitler, *Gott ist tot—Gott ist rot: Max Horkheimer und die Politisierung der Religion um 1968* (Frankfurt: Campus, 2009); Udi Greenberg, *The End of the Schism: Catholics, Protestants, and the Remaking of Christian Life in Europe, 1880s–1970s* (Cambridge, MA: Harvard University Press, 2025), 228–279; Dagmar Herzog, "The Death of God in West Germany: Between Secularization, Postfascism, and the Rise of Liberation Theology," in *Die Gegenwart Gottes in der modernen Gesellschaft: Transzendenz und religiöse Vergemeinschaftung in Deutschland,* ed. Michael Geyer and Lucian Hölscher (Göttingen: Wallstein, 2006), 431–466; and Gerd-Rainer Horn, *The Spirit of Vatican II: Western European Progressive Catholicism in the Long 1960s* (Oxford: Oxford University Press, 2015). For a detailed study of the EKD's engagement with the New Left, focused on intra-church developments, see Alexander Christian Widmann, *Wandel mit Gewalt? Der deutsche Protestantismus und die politisch motivierte Gewaltanwendung in den 1960er und 1970er Jahren* (Göttingen: Vandenhoeck und Ruprecht, 2013).

5. On intergenerational dialogue and conflict around 1968, see also A. Dirk Moses, *German Intellectuals and the Nazi Past* (Cambridge: Cambridge University Press, 2007), 186–198; and Terence Renaud, *New Lefts: The Making of a Radical Tradition* (Princeton, NJ: Princeton University Press, 2021), 234–275.

6. Boris Spernol, *Notstand der Demokratie: Der Protest gegen die Notstandsgesetze und die Frage der NS-Vergangenheit* (Essen: Klartext, 2008), 12–17.

7. See also Frank Biess, *German Angst: Fear and Democracy in the Federal Republic of Germany* (Oxford: Oxford University Press, 2020), 184–194; and Karrin Hanshew, *Terror and Democracy in West Germany* (Cambridge: Cambridge University Press, 2012), 57–67.

8. Spernol, *Notstand der Demokratie,* 15–18.

354   NOTES TO PAGES 237–242

9. Biess, *German Angst,* 107–116.

10. Von Harling to Bundesinnenministerium, May 31, 1963, EZA 2/4662.

11. Udi Greenberg, *The Weimar Century: German Émigrés and the Ideological Foundations of the Cold War* (Princeton, NJ: Princeton University Press, 2014), 172–187, 198–204.

12. Basic Law, art. 21, para. 2; Greenberg, *Weimar Century,* 205–206; Sebastian Ullrich, *Der Weimar-Komplex: Das Scheitern der ersten deutschen Demokratie und die politische Kultur der frühen Bundesrepublik 1945–1959* (Göttingen: Wallstein, 2009), 357–376.

13. Ullrich, *Weimar-Komplex,* 364–365.

14. Dieter Gosewinkel, *Adolf Arndt: Die Wiederbegründung des Rechtsstaats aus dem Geist der Sozialdemokratie (1945–1961)* (Bonn: Dietz, 1991), 493–497. On the Lüth decision, see also Justin Collings, *Democracy's Guardians: A History of the German Federal Constitutional Court* (Oxford: Oxford University Press, 2015), 54–61.

15. Spernol, *Notstand der Demokratie,* 13.

16. Adolf Arndt, "Demokratie—Wertsystem des Rechts," in Adolf Arndt and Michael Freund, *Notstandsgesetz—Aber wie?* (Cologne: Verlag Wissenschaft und Politik, 1962), 17–30, quote at 23. See also Gosewinkel, *Arndt,* 417–431.

17. Arndt, "Demokratie," 13.

18. Arndt, "Demokratie," 41–43.

19. Spernol, *Notstand der Demokratie,* 21–22.

20. Arndt, "Demokratie," 44–46.

21. Geogor Kritidis, *Linkssozialistische Opposition in der Ära Adenauer* (Hanover: Offizin, 2008), 477–493; Renaud, *New Lefts,* 225–228.

22. For instance, Wolfgang Abendroth, "Der deutsche politische Widerstand gegen das 'Dritte Reich,'" *SdG* 16, no. 14/15 (1964): 425–432; Ossip K. Flechtheim, "Gefahren der Notstandsgesetzgebung," *SdG* 14, no. 23 (1962): 713–718. On Abendroth and Flechtheim, see Renaud, *New Lefts,* 212–220.

23. Holger Nehring, *Politics of Security: British and West German Protest Movements and the Early Cold War, 1945–1970* (Oxford: Oxford University Press, 2013), 71–73. On the Easter Marches, see also Karl A. Otto, *Vom Ostermarsch zur APO: Geschichte der ausserparlamentarischen Opposition in der Bundesrepublik 1960–1970* (Frankfurt: Campus, 1977).

24. Martin Greschat, *Protestantismus im Kalten Krieg: Kirche, Politik und Gesellschaft im geteilten Deutschland* (Paderborn: Schöningh, 2010), 211–218.

25. Karl Barth, "Letter to a Pastor in the German Democratic Republic," in Karl Barth and Johannes Hamel, *How to Serve God in a Marxist Land* (New York: Association Press, 1959), 45–80, quote at 68. On the reception of Barth's letter, see Gerhard Besier, "Karl Barths 'Brief an einen Pfarrer in der DDR' vom Oktober 1958: Kontext, Vor- und Wirkungsgeschichte," in *Die evangelische Kirche in den Umbrüchen des 20. Jahrhunderts: Gesammelte Aufsätze* (Neukirchen-Vluyn: Neukirchener Verlag, 1994), 177–189.

26. Besier, "Barths 'Brief,'" 185.

NOTES TO PAGES 242–246

27. Greschat, *Protestantismus,* 206–210, 216–217.
28. Otto Dibelius, "'Obrigkeit'? Eine Frage an den 60jährigen Landesbischof von Otto Dibelius, Berlin 1959," in *Violett-Buch zur Obrigkeitsschrift von Bischof Dibelius: Dokumente zur Frage der Obrigkeit,* ed. Martin Fischer, 3rd ed. (Frankfurt: Stimme, 1963), 21–31, quote at 29.
29. "Kein Mord im Dom," *Der Spiegel,* November 11, 1959; Greschat, *Protestantismus,* 237. Additional newspaper coverage of the controversy is collected in BArch Koblenz N 1367/309.
30. Helmut Gollwitzer, "Unser Antrag zur Obrigkeitsfrage," *Junge Kirche* 21, no. 4 (1960): 186–192.
31. "Die Christen und ihre Obrigkeit," July 4, 1960, EZA 686/8672. On the meetings that led to the statement, see Diethard Buchstädt, *Kirche für die Welt: Entstehung, Geschichte und Wirken der Kirchlichen Bruderschaften im Rheinland und in Württemberg 1945–1960* (Cologne: Rheinland, 1999), 393–396, 401–405, 421.
32. "Das Rundfunkgespräch zwischen Bischof Dibelius, Landesbischof Lilje und Professor Scheuner," in Fischer, *Violett-Buch zur Obrigkeitsschrift,* 48–58, quotes at 50, 53–54.
33. Rolf Schönfeldt, "Die Deutsche Friedens-Union," in *Parteien-Handbuch: Die Parteien der Bundesrepublik Deutschland 1945–1980,* vol. 1, ed. Richard Stöss (Opladen: Westdeutscher Verlag, 1983), 852–859.
34. Greschat, *Protestantismus,* 309.
35. Albert Vinzens, *Renate Riemeck: Historikerin, Pädagogin, Pazifistin (1920–2003)* (Göttingen: Wallstein, 2023), 153–155, 175–176.
36. Heike Amos, *Die SED-Deutschlandpolitik 1961 bis 1989: Ziele, Aktivitäten und Konflikte* (Göttingen: Vandenhoeck und Ruprecht, 2015), 225–233; Vinzens, *Riemeck,* 230.
37. Schönfeldt, "Deutsche Friedens-Union," 860.
38. Ullrich, *Weimar-Komplex,* 284–285, 394–395. The 5 percent threshold was introduced at the state level in 1949 and at the national level in 1953.
39. Flechtheim, "Gefahren."
40. For Riemeck's and other critiques of emergency laws from within the milieu of the Church Brethren Societies, see "Notstandsgesetz? Nein," *SdG* 14, no. 21 (1962): 645–652.
41. Vinzens, *Riemeck,* 66–67, 164–167, 187–190.
42. Kirchliche Bruderschaft in Hessen und Nassau, ed., *3 Vorträge gehalten auf der Landestagung 1961* (Frankfurt: Stimme, 1962), 5.
43. Fritz Bauer, "Widerstandsrecht und Widerstandspflicht des Staatsbürgers," in Kirchliche Bruderschaft in Hessen und Nassau, *3 Vorträge,* 41–64, quotes at 56, 58.
44. Heinrich Hannover, "Die Verteidigung des Staates als Gewissensfrage," in Kirchliche Bruderschaft in Hessen und Nassau, *3 Vorträge,* 29–40, quote at 40.
45. Heinrich Hannover, *Politische Diffamierung der Opposition im freiheitlich-demokratischen Rechtsstaat* (Dortmund: Pläne, 1962).

356 NOTES TO PAGES 246–249

46. "Möglichkeit des Widerstandes," in Heinrich Hannover, *Zum Entwurf eines "Gesetzes über den Zivildienst im Verteidigungsfall" (Zivildienstgesetz)* (Offenbach am Main: Verband der Kriegsdienstverweigerer—Geschäftsstelle, 1962). On the vote, see Spernol, *Notstand der Demokratie,* 25.

47. Heinz Kloppenburg, "Beschlüsse der Leiterkonferenz der Kirchlichen Bruderschaften," November 26, 1962; and Kloppenburg to Vorsitzenden der Kirchlichen Bruderschaften, December 21, 1962, both EZA 613/16. On Kloppenburg, see Hannelore Braun, "Kloppenburg, Heinrich," in *BBKL,* vol. 4, ed. Traugott Bautz (Herzberg: Bautz, 1992), 73–78.

48. "Einstimmig beschlossene Erklärung der Leiterkonferenz der Kirchlichen Bruderschaften vom 4. Januar 1963 zur Notstandsgesetzgebung," EZA 613/16. Arndt's reply is included in Martin Rohrkrämer, "Kirchliche Bruderschaft im Rheinland: Rundbrief Nr. 2/1963," June 1963, AEKR 6HA016/10.

49. See also Hanshew, *Terror and Democracy,* 78–82.

50. Peter C. Caldwell, *Democracy, Capitalism, and the Welfare State: Debating Social Order in Postwar West Germany* (Oxford: Oxford University Press, 2019), 52–58. See especially Ernst Forsthoff, *Verfassungsprobleme des Sozialstaates* (Münster: Aschendorff, 1954).

51. Konrad Hesse, "Der Rechtsstaat im Verfassungssystem des Grundgesetzes," in *Staatsverfassung und Kirchenordnung: Festgabe für Rudolf Smend zum 80. Geburtstag am 15. Januar 1962,* ed. Konrad Hesse, Siegfried Reicke, and Ulrich Scheuner (Tübingen: Mohr, 1962), 71–95; Ulrich Scheuner, "Die neuere Entwicklung des Rechtsstaats in Deutschland," in *Hundert Jahre deutsches Rechtsleben: Festschrift zum hundert jährigen Bestehen des Deutschen Juristentages 1860–1960,* ed. Ernst von Caemmerer, Ernst Friesenhahn, and Richard Lange (Karlsruhe: C. F. Müller, 1960), 229–262.

52. Michael Frey, *Vor Achtundsechzig: Der Kalte Krieg und die Neue Linke in der Bundesrepublik und in den USA* (Göttingen: Wallstein, 2020), 199–259; Matthew G. Specter, *Habermas: An Intellectual Biography* (Cambridge: Cambridge University Press, 2010), 5–8.

53. Specter, *Habermas,* 73–84.

54. Almut Röse and Wolf Röse, *Helmut Simon: Recht bändigt Gewalt: Eine autorisierte Biografie* (Berlin: Wichern, 2011), 111–119, quote at 114; Helmut Simon, *Leben zwischen den Zeiten: Von der Weimarer Republik bis zur Europäischen Union—Vom Bauernbub zum Verfassungsrichter und Kirchentagspräsidenten,* ed. Peter Becker and Heide Simon (Baden-Baden: Nomos, 2020), 24–26, 32–33.

55. Helmut Simon, *Der Rechtsgedanke in der gegenwärtigen deutschen evangelischen Theologie unter besonderer Berücksichtigung des Problems materialer Rechtsgrundsätze* (Bonn: n.p., 1952).

56. Helmut Simon, *Katholisierung des Rechts? Zum Einfluss katholischen Rechtsdenkens auf die gegenwärtige deutsche Gesetzgebung und Rechtsprechung* (Göttingen: Vandenhoeck und Ruprecht, 1962), esp. 12–13, 31, 33–38, 46–47.

57. Simon, *Leben zwischen den Zeiten,* 85–92. See also Helmut Simon, "Artikel 4, Absatz 3 des Grundgesetzes, sein Inhalt und seine Auslegung," in Friedrich

NOTES TO PAGES 249–253   357

Delekat et al., *Evangelische Stimmen zur Frage des Wehrdienstes* (Stuttgart: Kreuz, 1956), 43–57.

58. For instance, Helmut Simon, "Die evangelischen Christen vor der Frage nach dem Naturrecht," in *Hören und Handeln: Festschrift für Ernst Wolf zum 60. Geburtstag,* ed. Helmut Gollwitzer and Hellmut Traub (Munich: Kaiser, 1962), 358–361.

59. "Consensus?," *Kirche in der Zeit* 15, no. 11 (1960): 378–381, quotes at 380. See also Helmut Simon, "Vorentwurf zur Frage nach dem Verhalten der Christen zum Kommunismus und zum kommunistischen Staat," EZA 686/8672.

60. Quoted in Frank Bösch, "Später Protest: Die Intellektuelle und die Pressefreiheit in der frühen Bundesrepublik," in Geppert and Hacke, *Streit um den Staat,* 104–105.

61. Diether Posser, "Recht und Politik in der Spiegel-Affäre," *SdG* 14, no. 22 (1962): 689–694, quote at 689. On the *Spiegel* affair and its fallout, see also Biess, *German Angst,* 186–187; and Collings, *Democracy's Guardians,* 80–83.

62. Helmut Simon, "Ist in der theologischen Ethik Platz für den Rechtsstaat? Die *Spiegel*-Affäre als Lehre und Aufgabe," in *Via viatorum: Für Karl Kupisch,* ed. Heinrich Albertz (Berlin: Käthe Vogt, 1963), 62–76, quote at 68–69. For Simon's critique of emergency laws, see Horst Dahlhaus, ed., *Notstandsrecht und Demokratie: Notwendigkeit oder Gefahr?* (Stuttgart: Kreuz, 1963), 15, 20–21, 25–26.

63. Helmut Simon, "Der Rechtsstaat: Fragen des Juristen an die Theologie," Deutschlandfunk, May 22, 1963, AEKR 6HA017/3, quotes at 12, 15.

64. "Kirchliche Bruderschaft im Rheinland: Rundbrief Nr. 2/1963."

65. "Kirchliche Bruderschaft im Rheinland: Rundbrief Nr. 2/1963"; Simon, *Leben zwischen den Zeiten,* 133.

66. Linke to Arbeitskreis der kirchlichen Bruderschaften, October 6, 1963, EZA 613/16.

67. Ulrich Scheuner, "Die rechtsstaatliche Ordnung des Grundgesetzes," in *Der Rechtsstaat: Angebot und Aufgabe: Eine Anfrage an Theologie und Christenheit heute,* ed. Ernst Wolf (Munich: Kaiser, 1964), 11–27, quote at 19.

68. Scheuner, "Die rechtsstaatliche Ordnung," 21–22, 26–27.

69. Ernst Wolf, "Die rechtsstaatliche Ordnung als theologisches Problem," in Wolf, *Der Rechtsstaat,* 28–63, esp. 38–48, quote at 55.

70. "Der Rechtsstaatsgedanke in der Rechtsprechung: Zusammengestellt von Helmut Simon," in Wolf, *Der Rechtsstaat,* 71–79.

71. For an example of the conflict, see "Protokoll der Leiterkonferenz der Bruderschaften," May 24–25, 1961, EZA 613/15.

72. Gustav W. Heinemann, "Der demokratische Rechtsstaat als theologisches Problem," in *Plädoyer für den Rechtsstaat: Rechtspolitische Reden und Aufsätze* (Karlsruhe: C. F. Müller, 1969), 9–21, quotes at 17.

73. Heinemann, "Der demokratische Rechtsstaat," 20.

74. In addition to the sources by Heinemann, Simon, and Wolf cited above, see Heinz Kloppenburg, "Die Bundesrepublik—Unsere politische Verantwortung," *JK* 26, no. 2 (1965): 88–92; and Karl Linke, "Der Rechtsstaat—Verfassung,

358 NOTES TO PAGES 253–257

Ideologie, Wirklichkeit: Zur Jahrestagung der Kirchlichen Bruderschaft," *SdG* 16, no. 5 (1964): 137–142.

75. This trope had gained prominence among Catholic as well as Protestant conservatives in the early 1950s. See Axel Schildt, *Zwischen Abendland und Amerika: Studien zur westdeutschen Ideenlandschaft der 50er Jahre* (Munich: Oldenbourg, 1999), 39–82.

76. Hanshew, *Terror and Democracy,* 63.

77. "Neuer Professoren-Appell," *SdG* 18, no. 8 (1966): 251–254. The number of signatories appears in Werner to signatories, October 6, 1966, EZA 613 / 186. On the so-called drawer laws (*Schubladengesetze*), see Biess, *German Angst,* 187–188.

78. Heinrich Hannover, "Normenkontrollklage gegen sechs Notstandsgesetze," *SdG* 18, no. 6 (1966): 170–175.

79. Schauer, *Notstand der Demokratie,* 13–14.

80. Maus and Ridder to Kloppenburg, July 15, 1966, EZA 613 / 186.

81. Nick Thomas, *Protest Movements in 1960s West Germany: A Social History of Democracy and Dissent* (Oxford: Bern, 2003), 91.

82. Thomas, *Protest Movements,* 91–93.

83. Ekkehart Stein, "Notstandsgesetze und Gewissensfreiheit," in Schauer, *Notstand der Demokratie,* 163–177. On Stein, see Götz Frank and Heiki Stintzing, "Ekkehart Stein," *JuristenZeitung* 64, no. 5 (2009): 252–254.

84. "Aus der Diskussion," in Schauer, *Notstand der Demokratie,* 177–181. Similar arguments for civil disobedience were advanced in the Congress's concluding resolution. See "Schlußerklärung des Kuratoriums 'Notstand der Demokratie' zum Kongreß," in Schauer, *Notstand der Demokratie,* 209–211.

85. Arbeitsgemeinschaft Kirche und Demokratie, "Presseinformation"; and Werner to signatories, October 6, 1966, both EZA 613 / 186.

86. On the international contexts of the West German student movement, see especially Klimke, *The Other Alliance;* and Slobodian, *Foreign Front.*

87. For instance, von der Goltz, *Other '68ers;* Hodenberg, *Other '68;* Renaud, *New Lefts.*

88. Dagmar Herzog, *Sex after Fascism: Memory and Morality in Twentieth-Century Germany* (Princeton, NJ: Princeton University Press, 2005), 148–152. On the European context of the sexual revolution, see Dagmar Herzog, *Sexuality in Europe: A Twentieth-Century History* (Cambridge: Cambridge University Press, 2011), 133–175.

89. James F. Tent, *The Free University of Berlin: A Political History* (Bloomington: Indiana University Press, 1988), 160–164, 288–289. See also Ben Mercer, *Student Revolt in 1968: France, Italy and West Germany* (Cambridge: Cambridge University Press, 2020), 131–136.

90. "Großer Topf," *Der Spiegel,* July 20, 1969.

91. Claudia Lepp, "Helmut Gollwitzer als Dialogspartner der sozialen Bewegungen," in *Umbrüche: Der deutsche Protestantismus und die sozialen Bewegungen in den 1960er und 70er Jahren,* ed. Siegfried Hermle, Claudia Lepp, and Harry Oelke (Göttingen: Vandenhoeck und Ruprecht, 2007), 226–246.

NOTES TO PAGES 257–260   359

92. On Dutschke's Protestant background, see Wolfgang Kraushaar, "Rudi Dutschke: Protestant und Inbegriff einer Protest-Generation," in *Protestantische Impulse: Prägende Gestalten in Deutschland nach 1945,* ed. Siegfried Hermle and Thomas Martin Schneider (Leipzig: Evangelische Verlagsanstalt, 2021), 29–35.

93. Karl-Behrnd Hasselmann, *Politische Gemeinde: Ein kirchliches Handlungsmodell am Beispiel der Evangelischen Studentengemeinde an der Freien Universität Berlin* (Hamburg: Furche, 1969), 11. Hasselmann offers a sympathetic account of the Free University's Protestant Student Community from the perspective of one of its pastors.

94. Mercer, *Student Revolt,* 178–192, quote at 190.

95. Hasselmann, *Politische Gemeinde,* 24–29.

96. Kraushaar, "Dutschke"; Renaud, *New Lefts,* 235–239.

97. Foreign students in West Germany had pushed for a more international focus years before Dutschke became the leader of the SDS, however. See Slobodian, *Foreign Front,* 17–50.

98. Thomas, *Protest Movements,* 69–85.

99. Nehring, *Politics of Security,* 276; Spernol, *Notstand der Demokratie,* 75–76.

100. Nehring, *Politics of Security,* 252.

101. Richard Shaull, "The Revolutionary Challenge to Church and Theology," *Theology Today* 23, no. 4 (1967): 470–480, quote at 473. On the context of the Geneva conference, see Justin Reynolds, "Apostles of Secularization: The Ecumenical Movement and the Making of a Postcolonial Protestantism in the 1950s and 1960s," in *Decolonization and the Remaking of Christianity,* ed. Elizabeth A. Foster and Udi Greenberg (Philadelphia: University of Pennsylvania Press, 2023), 12–31.

102. For a list of the West German participants, see Wilkens to Krüger, January 30, 1967, EZA 6/5950.

103. "World Conference on Church and Society, July, 1966. Section II: Officers and Staff for Sub-Sections," May 25, 1966, WCC Archives, 243.7.2. For the group's report, see *Christians in the Technical and Social Revolutions of Our Time: World Conference on Church and Society, Geneva, July 12–26, 1966* (Geneva: World Council of Churches, 1966), 101–106, quote at 103.

104. Helmut Gollwitzer, "Must a Christian Be a Socialist?," in W. Travis McMaken, *Our God Loves Justice: An Introduction to Helmut Gollwitzer* (Minneapolis: Fortress Press, 2017), 169–186. On Gollwitzer's evolution, see Benedikt Brunner, "Avantgardist Christi? Helmut Gollwitzer als Prototyp eines progressiven Protestanten im 20. Jahrhundert," *Kirchliche Zeitgeschichte* 35, no. 2 (2022): 357–362.

105. On Scharf's election as bishop, see Wolf-Dieter Zimmermann, *Kurt Scharf: Ein Leben zwischen Vision und Wirklichkeit* (Göttingen: Vandenhoeck und Ruprecht, 1992), 114–118.

106. Hanshew, *Terror and Democracy,* 97–107.

107. Kurt Scharf, "Wort an die Berliner," in Scharf, *Für ein politisches Gewissen der Kirche: Aus Reden und Schriften 1932 bis 1972,* ed. Wolfgang Erk (Stuttgart: Steinkopf, 1972), 247. See also Zimmermann, *Scharf,* 127–129.

NOTES TO PAGES 260–263

108. Helmut Gollwitzer, "Ansprache bei der Überführung des Sarges von Benno Ohnesorg am Zehlendorfer Kleeblat am 8.6.67," in Friedrich-Wilhelm Marquardt and Helmut Gollwitzer, *Was wollen die Studenten?* (Berlin: Lettner, 1967); "Votum von Professor D. Helmut Gollwitzer in einer Fernsehdiskussion im Dritten Programm vom 14.6.1967," in *Materialsammlung über die Unruhen an den Universitäten, das politische Mandat der Studentenschaft und die Stellung der Evangelischen Studentengemeinde,* ed. Berliner Arbeitsgemeinschaft für kirchliche Publizistik (Berlin: Evangelisches Publizistisches Zentrum, 1968), 13–14.

109. Quoted in Biess, *German Angst,* 222.

110. Kurt Scharf, "Brief an die Gemeindeglieder, die zu den studentischen Demonstrationen Stellung genommen und dabei am Verhalten der Kirche Kritik geübt haben," in *Für ein politisches Gewissen,* 252–257. On this episode, see Hasselmann, *Politische Gemeinde,* 66–73; Widmann, *Wandel mit Gewalt,* 167–169; and Zimmermann, *Scharf,* 132–134. On Engelbrecht, see also Anne Jelena Schulte, "Manfred Engelbrecht (geb. 1927)," *Tagesspiegel,* December 20, 2013, https://www.tagesspiegel.de/berlin/manfred-engelbrecht-geb-1927-2356045.html.

111. Scharf, "Brief an die Gemeindeglieder."

112. Jacques Schuster, *Heinrich Albertz: Der Mann, der mehrere Leben lebte: Eine Biographie* (Berlin: Alexander Fest, 1997), 222–226. On Albertz's participation in the Confessing Church, see Schuster, *Albertz,* 27–33.

113. Schuster, *Albertz,* 237–247.

114. These events are described in Gemeindkirchenrat der Kaiser-Wilhelm-Gedächtnis-Kirche, *Was ist geschehen? Dokumentation zu den Störungen der Gottesdienste in der Kaiser-Wilhelm-Gedächtnis-Kirche in Berlin am Heiligen Abend und in der Silvesternacht 1967* (Berlin: Büxenstein, 1968), 4–6, 20–22; and Zimmermann, *Scharf,* 138–139. Letters to Scharf's office are collected in Evangelisches Landeskirchliches Archiv in Berlin, 1/2912.

115. "Berliner Kirchenleitung verurteilt Störungen der Gottesdienste," in Berliner Arbeitsgemeinschaft für kirchliche Publizistik, *Materialsammlung über die Unruhen,* appendix, 12.

116. "'Mit den Führern radikaler Gruppen sprechen," in Berliner Arbeitsgemeinschaft für kirchliche Publizistik, *Materialsammlung über die Unruhen,* appendix, 12.

117. Helmut Gollwitzer, "Noch einmal: Heiligabend in der Kaiser-Wilhelm-Gedächtniskirche," *Junge Kirche* 29, no. 2 (1968): 103–105.

118. "Zum Jahresbeginn an die Kirchengänger der Kaiser Wilhelm Gedächtniskirche zu Berlin, Anfang 1968," EZA 686/832.

119. "Vermittlungsversuch der Kirche gescheitert," *Der Tagesspiegel,* February 17, 1968. Press coverage of the church's response to the 1968 protests in West Berlin can be found in EZA 686/829–831. On the International Vietnam Congress, see also Klimke, *Other Alliance,* 91–100.

120. "Evangelische Kirchenleitung zum Vietnam-Kongreß," *Der Tagesspiegel,* February 21, 1968.

NOTES TO PAGES 263–267   361

121. "Studentische Protestdemonstration im Hamburger 'Michael,'" in Berliner Arbeitsgemeinschaft für kirchliche Publizistik, *Materialsammlung über die Unruhen,* appendix, 12–13. These events are described in "Mookt wi," *Der Spiegel,* January 21, 1968.

122. "Thielicke gegen Diskussionen im Gotteshaus," in Berliner Arbeitsgemeinschaft für kirchliche Publizistik, *Materialsammlung über die Unruhen,* appendix, 14–15.

123. "Platte abgelaufen," *Der Spiegel,* January 28, 1968.

124. "Ergebnisse der Diskussionen im Audimax der TU zur Frage der Gewalt," *Evangelische Studentengemeinde-Nachrichten* 38 (1968): 26.

125. On the Dutschke shooting and the resulting protests, see Thomas, *Protest Movements,* 165–181.

126. Quotes in "Scharf: Aus Gewalt kann nicht Gutes kommen," *Die Welt,* April 16, 1968. See also Zimmermann, *Scharf,* 147–148.

127. Helmut Gollwitzer, "Studentenunruhen," *Der Tagesspiegel,* April 21, 1968. See also the report on the protests in *Berliner Sonntagsblatt: Die Kirche,* April 21, 1968.

128. Gollwitzer, "Studentenunruhen." On the criticisms in the West Berlin Senate, see "Nur im Prinzip war man sich einig," *Die Welt,* April 19, 1968; and "Ein Hauch von Weimar," *Berliner Morgenpost,* April 19, 1968.

129. The full statement is reprinted in Hasselmann, *Politische Gemeinde,* 101–103.

130. Hanshew, *Terror and Democracy,* 65–66; Spernol, *Notstand der Demokratie,* 28.

131. Heinemann, "Vorsorge für den Notfall," in *Plädoyer für den Rechtsstaat,* 57–61.

132. Kraushaar, "Furcht," 139–140; Thomas, *Protest Movements,* 194. For the statement of the West Berlin Protestant Student Community on the march, see Hasselmann, *Politische Gemeinde,* 105–106.

133. Quote in "Studenten besetzen Rektorat," *Frankfurter Allgemeine Zeitung,* May 28, 1968. See also "Die Aktion der Gegner der Notstandsgesetze in der Bundesrepublik," *Frankfurter Allgemeine Zeitung,* May 28, 1968; and Thomas, *Protest Movements,* 195.

134. For instance, see the announcement of the Bonn protest march by the Committee on the Emergency of Democracy: Wolfgang Abendroth, Werner Hoffmann, Heinrich Düker, and Helmut Ridder, "Aufruf," April 1968, BArch Koblenz N 1367/49.

135. Renaud, *New Lefts,* 248.

136. Helmut Gollwitzer, "Leichenrede auf das Grundgesetz," *SdG* 20, no. 13 (1968): 397–400.

137. Basic Law, art. 20, para. 4; art. 79, para. 3.

138. Christoph Böckenförde, "Die Kodifizierung des Widerstandsrechts im Grundgesetz," *JuristenZeitung* 25, no. 5–6 (1970): 171. On the constitutional debate about the right of resistance, see also David Johst, *Begrenzung des Rechtsgehorsams: Die Debatte um Widerstand und Widerstandsrecht in Westdeutschland 1945–1968* (Tübingen: Mohr Siebeck, 2016), 213–226.

139. *VDBT,* 5. Deutscher Bundestag, 175. Sitzung, May 16, 1968, 9451.

362   NOTES TO PAGES 268–270

140. Thomas, *Protest Movements*, 202–204.

141. Ulrike Meinhof, "From Protest to Resistance," in *Everybody Talks about the Weather . . . We Don't: Writings of Ulrike Meinhof*, ed. Karin Bauer (New York: Seven Stories Press, 2011), 239–243.

142. Jutta Ditfurth, *Ulrike Meinhof: Die Biografie* (Berlin: Ullstein, 2007), 64–70, 105; Vinzens, *Riemeck*, 57–59, 116–117.

143. Gerd Koenen, *Vesper, Ensslin, Baader: Urszenen des deutschen Terrorismus* (Cologne: Kiepenheuer und Witsch, 2003), 92–94. Despite the voluminous literature on the RAF, this connection has yet to be explored in depth.

144. Heinrich Albertz et al., *"Pfarrer, die dem Terror dienen"? Bischof Scharf und der Berliner Kirchenstreit 1974: Eine Dokumentation* (Hamburg: Rowohlt, 1975); Vinzens, *Riemeck*, 310–311.

145. Hasselmann, *Politische Gemeinde*, 148; Widmann, *Wandel mit Gewalt*, 280–281.

146. On the Uppsala conference, see Annegreth Schilling, "1968 und die Ökumene: Die Vollversammlung des ÖRK in Uppsala als Beginn einer neuen Ära?," in *Globalisierung der Kirchen: Globale Transformation und ökumenische Erneuerung des Ökumenischen Rates der Kirchen in den 1960er- und 1970er-Jahren*, ed. Katharina Kunter and Annegreth Schilling (Göttingen: Vandenhoeck und Ruprecht, 2014), 89–120. On Sölle and the Political Night Prayer, see Benjamin T. Shannon, "The Political Night Prayer and the Politicization of Religion in West Germany, 1968–1972" (PhD diss., University of Wisconsin-Madison, 2020).

147. On this conflict, see Zimmermann, *Scharf*, 149–150. See also Hasselmann, *Politische Gemeinde*, 159–165.

148. Widmann, *Wandel mit Gewalt*, 65–66, 279.

149. "Beschlüsse der ausserordentliche Provinzialsynode Berlin-Brandenburg (Regionale Synode in Berlin West)," in *Berlin Studenten Christen: Überlegungen und Stellungnahmen zur politischen Diakonie*, ed. Berliner Arbeitsgemeinschaft für kirchliche Publizistik (Berlin: Büxenstein, 1968), 77–81.

150. Helmut Gollwitzer, "Die Weltverantwortung der Kirche in einem revolutionären Zeitalter," in *Die Zukunft der Kirche und die Zukunft der Welt: Die Synode der EKD 1968 zur Weltverantwortung der Kirche in einem revolutionären Zeitalter*, ed. Erwin Wilkens (Munich: Kaiser, 1968), 69–96, quotes at 69–70, 94–95.

151. Helmut Thielicke, "Diskussion zu 'Weltverantwortung der Kirche,'" in Wilkens, *Zukunft der Kirche*, 167–169; Hans-Otto Wölber, "Antwort auf den Bericht von Walter Kreck," in Wilkens, *Zukunft der Kirche*, 161–163.

152. Widmann, *Wandel mit Gewalt*, 282.

153. Helmut Gollwitzer, "Antwort an Hans-Otto Wölber," in Wilkens, *Zukunft der Kirche*, 163–165.

154. Wölber, "Antwort," 161–163.

155. Raiser to Werner, May 5, 1966; Raiser to Scharf, June 5, 1967; and Raiser to Heipp, June 26, 1967, all in BArch Koblenz N 1287 / 185.

NOTES TO PAGES 270–276   363

156. Quote in Ludwig Raiser, "Entwurf," EZA 2/1360. See also Raiser to Wilkens, August 20, 1968; and Helmut Aichelin and Ludwig Raiser, "Erklärung des Rates der Evangelischen Kirche in Deutschland zur Unruhe unter der jungen Generation, zweiter Entwurf," both EZA 2/1360.
157. Helmut Simon, *Freiheitliche Verfassung und Demonstrationsrecht: Vortrag gehalten am 31. Januar 1969* (Berlin: Lettner, 1969).
158. Only a shortened version was published by the EKD Council in January 1969 as a press release: "Zur Unruhe in der jungen Generation," *KJ* 96 (1969): 111–112. See also Widmann, *Wandel mit Gewalt,* 288–289.
159. Evangelische Akademikerschaft in Deutschland, "Zur gegenwärtigen Lage in der Bundesrepublik," April 12, 1969, AEKR 5WV003/96.
160. Gollwitzer, "Weltverantwortung," 69; Raiser, "Entwurf."
161. On the division, see Claudia Lepp, *Tabu der Einheit: Die Ost-West-Gemeinschaft der evangelischen Christen und die deutsche Teilung (1945–1969)* (Göttingen: Vandenhoeck und Ruprecht, 2005), 790–850.
162. Nehring, *Politics of Security,* 70–71, 122–126, 212, 281–282. More broadly on the gender politics of 1968 in West Germany, see Hodenberg, *Other '68,* 92–135.

Conclusion

1. Benjamin Ziemann, *Martin Niemöller: Ein Leben in Opposition* (Munich: Deutsche Verlags-Anstalt, 2019), 497–511.
2. Frieder Günther, *Denken vom Staat her: Die bundesdeutsche Staatsrechtslehre zwischen Dezision und Integration* (Munich: Oldenbourg, 2004), 159.
3. Alexander Christian Widmann, *Wandel mit Gewalt? Der deutsche Protestantismus und die politisch motivierte Gewaltanwendung in den 1960er und 1970er Jahre* (Göttingen: Vandenhoeck und Ruprecht, 2013), 345–349, 406–408.
4. Mark Edward Ruff, *The Wayward Flock: Catholic Youth in Postwar West Germany, 1945–1965* (Chapel Hill: University of North Carolina Press, 2005), esp. 48–85.
5. Thomas Großbölting, *Losing Heaven: Religion in Germany since 1945,* trans. Alex Skinner (New York: Berghahn Books, 2017), 215–222. On this concept, see Grace Davie, "Resacralization," in *The New Blackwell Companion to the Sociology of Religion,* ed. Bryan S. Turner (Malden, MA: Wiley-Blackwell, 2010), 160–177. For a critique in the West German context, see Detlef Pollack, "Religiöser und gesellschaftlicher Wandel in den 1960er Jahren," in *Religion und Lebensführung im Umbruch der langen 1960er Jahren,* ed. Claudia Lepp, Harry Oelke, and Detlef Pollack (Göttingen: Vandenhoeck und Ruprecht, 2016), 31–63.
6. James Chappel, *Catholic Modern: The Challenge of Totalitarianism and the Remaking of the Church* (Cambridge, MA: Harvard University Press, 2018), 232–239; Großbölting, *Losing Heaven,* 119–129.

NOTES TO PAGES 276–278

7. A pioneering work of sociology in this vein was Gerhard Schmidtchen, *Protestanten und Katholiken: Soziologische Analyse konfessioneller Kultur* (Bern: Francke, 1973). See also Großbölting, *Losing Heaven*, 105–111; and Benjamin Ziemann, *Encounters with Modernity: The Catholic Church in West Germany, 1945–1975*, trans. Andrew Evans (New York: Berghahn Books, 2014), 24–62.

8. Florian Bock, "The Churches and Changes in Missionary Work: Biconfessionalism and Developmental Aid to the 'Third World' since the 1960s," in *Germany and the Confessional Divide: Religious Tensions and Political Culture, 1871–1989*, ed. Mark Edward Ruff and Thomas Großbölting (New York: Berghahn Books, 2022), 300–323; Udi Greenberg, *The End of the Schism: Catholics, Protestants, and the Remaking of Christian Life in Europe, 1880s–1970s* (Cambridge, MA: Harvard University Press, 2025), 213–227, quote at 226.

9. Doris L. Bergen, "Contextualizing Dietrich Bonhoeffer: Nazism, the Churches, and the Question of Silence," in *Interpreting Bonhoeffer: Historical Perspectives, Emerging Issues*, ed. Clifford J. Green and Guy C. Carter (Minneapolis: Fortress Press, 2013), 124–125.

10. N. Peter Levinson, "Internationale 'Holocaust'-Konferenz in Hamburg: Der Holocaust und seine Lehren heute," *Freiburger Rundbrief* 27, no. 101–104 (1975): 24–25. On the impact of the *Holocaust* miniseries, see Jacob S. Eder, *Holocaust Angst: The Federal Republic of Germany and American Holocaust Memory since the 1970s* (Oxford: Oxford University Press, 2016), 30–37.

11. Helga Kuhlmann, "Protestantismus, Frauenbewegung und Frauenordination," in *Umbrüche: Der deutsche Protestantismus und die sozialen Bewegungen in den 1960er und 70er Jahren*, ed. Siegfried Hermle, Claudia Lepp, and Harry Oelke (Göttingen: Vandenhoeck und Ruprecht, 2007), 147–162; Simone Mantei, *Nein und Ja zur Abtreibung: Die evangelische Kirche in der Reformdebatte um §218 StGB 1970–1976* (Göttingen: Vandenhoeck und Ruprecht, 2004); Kornelia Sammet, "Feministische Theologie und die Politisierung evangelischer Theologinnen," in *Die Politisierung des Protestantismus: Entwicklungen in der Bundesrepublik Deutschland während der 1960er und 70er Jahre*, ed. Klaus Fitschen et al. (Göttingen: Vandenhoeck und Ruprecht, 2011), 168–190; Benjamin T. Shannon, "The Political Night Prayer and the Politicization of Religion in West Germany, 1968–1972" (PhD diss., University of Wisconsin–Madison, 2020), 119. For the results of these discussions, see *Die Denkschriften der Evangelischen Kirche in Deutschland*, vol. 3, pt. 1, *Ehe, Familie, Frauen und Männer* (Gütersloh: Gütersloher Verlagshaus, 1993).

12. Michael Schüring, "West German Protestants and the Campaign against Nuclear Technology," *Central European History* 45, no. 4 (2012): 744–762. More broadly on the second antinuclear movement, see Frank Biess, *German Angst: Fear and Democracy in the Federal Republic of Germany* (Oxford: Oxford University Press, 2020), 290–330; and Stephen Milder, *Greening Democracy: The Anti-Nuclear Movement and Political Environmentalism in West Germany and Beyond, 1968–1983* (Cambridge: Cambridge University Press, 2017).

NOTES TO PAGES 279–280 365

13. Biess, *German Angst,* 301–304; Justin Collings, *Democracy's Guardians: A History of the German Federal Constitutional Court, 1951–2001* (Oxford: Oxford University Press, 2015), 208.
14. Biess, *German Angst,* 314–315.
15. Helmut Simon, *Leben zwischen den Zeiten: Von der Weimarer Republik bis zur Europäischen Union—Vom Bauernbub zum Verfassungsrichter und Kirchentagspräsidenten,* ed. Peter Becker and Heide Simon (Baden-Baden: Nomos, 2020), 178.
16. Collings, *Democracy's Guardians,* 208–210. On the Protestant influence on the decision, see Oliver Lepsius and Anselm Doering-Manteuffel, "Die Richterpersönlichkeiten und ihre protestantische Sozialisation," in *Der Brokdorf-Beschluss des Bundesverfassungsgerichts 1985,* ed. Anselm Doering-Manteuffel, Bernd Greiner, and Oliver Lepsius (Tübingen: Mohr Siebeck, 2015), 167–224.
17. Helmut Simon, "Vom Nutzen protestantischer Einmischung in die Politik," *Zeitschrift für dialektische Theologie* 9, no. 2 (1993): 117–127, quotes at 123–124. See also Simon, "Protestantismus und Protest: Vortrag auf dem 21. Deutschen Evangelischen Kirchentag in Düsseldorf," *Junge Kirche* 46, no. 6 (1985): 312–321.
18. Dolf Sternberger, "Verfassungspatriotismus," in *Verfassungspatriotismus* (Frankfurt: Insel, 1990), 13–16. On the conceptual history of constitutional patriotism, see Jan-Werner Müller, *Constitutional Patriotism* (Princeton, NJ: Princeton University Press, 2007), 15–45.
19. For instance, the philosopher Jürgen Habermas, a key theorist of constitutional patriotism, maintained connections to the postwar Protestant milieu that have been overlooked in the vast scholarship on his oeuvre. Habermas's early career included participation in the Marxism commission of the Heidelberg-based Protestant Research Center and exchanges with Protestant theologians including Jürgen Moltmann and Dorothee Sölle. See "Marxismus und Rechtsordnung," March 10–11, 1960, and "Eigentum und Gerechtigkeit 2. Folge," March 6–8, 1961, both in FEST Archive, box 709; Jürgen Habermas, ed., *Observations on "The Spiritual Situation of the Age": Contemporary German Perspectives,* trans. Andrew Buchwalter (Cambridge, MA: MIT Press, 1984); and Dorothee Sölle, ed., *Religionsgespräche: Zur gesellschaftlichen Rolle der Religion* (Darmstadt: H. Luchterhand, 1975). On the Protestant adoption of constitutional patriotism, see also Arnulf von Scheliha, *Protestantische Ethik des Politischen* (Tübingen: Mohr Siebeck, 2013), 198–200.
20. Rat der EKD, *Evangelische Kirche und freiheitliche Demokratie: Der Staat des Grundgesetzes als Angebot und Aufgabe* (Frankfurt: Evangelischer Pressedienst, 1985), 22–23.
21. Rat der EKD, *Evangelische Kirche und freiheitliche Demokratie,* 33. On the memorandum, see Hans-Michael Heinig, ed., *Aneignung des Gegebenen: Entstehung und Wirkung der Demokratie-Denkschrift der EKD* (Tübingen: Mohr Siebeck, 2017); and Scheliha, *Protestantische Ethik,* 214–218.

NOTES TO PAGES 280–283

22. On these criticisms, see Wolfgang Huber, "Demokratie wagen: Der Protestantismus im politischen Wandel 1965–1985," in Hermle, Lepp, and Oelke, *Umbrüche*, 385–386.
23. Simon, *Leben zwischen den Zeiten*, 135–136.
24. Rita Chin, *The Guest Worker Question in Postwar Germany* (Cambridge: Cambridge University Press, 2007), 144–157. On family migration, see also Lauren Stokes, *Fear of the Family: Guest Workers and Family Migration in the Federal Republic of Germany* (Oxford: Oxford University Press, 2022), at 101–102 for statistics.
25. Chin, *Guest Worker Question,* quote at 105, see also 204; David Rüschenschmidt, "Der christlich-islamische Dialog als Integrationsgeschehen? Historische Perspektiven auf die 1970er und 80er Jahre," in *Christliche Willkommenskultur? Die Integration von Migranten als Handlungsfeld christlicher Akteure nach 1945,* ed. Claudia Lepp (Göttingen: Vandenhoeck und Ruprecht, 2020), 168–175.
26. Chin, *Guest Worker Question,* 99–105, 139–140, 202–205.
27. A growing literature addresses the influence of the Protestant and Catholic churches on discourses of Muslim integration in contemporary Germany. See Schirin Amir-Moazami, *Interrogating Muslims: The Liberal-Secular Matrix of Integration* (London: Bloomsbury, 2022), 54–60, 87–110; Sultan Doughan, "Teaching Tolerance: Citizenship, Religious Difference, and Race in Contemporary Germany" (PhD diss., University of California-Berkeley, 2019), esp. chap. 4; Großbölting, *Losing Heaven,* 228–258; Thomas Mittmann, "Säkularisierungsvorstellungen und religiöse Identitätsstiftung im Migrationsdiskurs: Die kirchliche Wahrnehmung 'des Islams' in der Bundesrepublik Deutschland seit den 1960er Jahren," *Archiv für Sozialgeschichte* 51 (2011): 267–289; and Birgit Rommelspracher, *Wie christlich ist unsere Gesellschaft? Das Christentum im Zeitalter von Sekularität und Multireligiosität* (Bielefeld: transcript, 2017), 365–377.
28. "Verfassungsmäßigkeit der christlichen Gemeinschaftsschule," *Neue Juristische Wochenschrift* 29, no. 21/22 (1976): 947–950; "Verfassungsmäßigkeit des Schulgebets an bekenntnisfreien Gemeinschaftsschulen außerhalb des Religionsunterrichts," *Neue Juristische Wochenschrift* 33, no. 11 (1980): 575–579.
29. Historiography on this theme is just beginning to emerge. See Rita Chin and Heide Fehrenbach, "German Democracy and the Question of Difference, 1945–1995," in Rita Chin et al., *After the Nazi Racial State: Difference and Democracy in Germany and Europe* (Ann Arbor: University of Michigan Press, 2009), 102–136; Michelle Lynn Kahn, *Foreign in Two Homelands: Racism, Return Migration, and Turkish-German History* (Cambridge: Cambridge University Press, 2024); and Christopher A. Molnar, "Asylum Seekers, Antiforeigner Violence, and Coming to Terms with the Past after German Reunification," *Journal of Modern History* 94, no. 1 (2022): 86–126.
30. On the case, see Beverly Weber, "Cloth on Her Head, Constitution in Hand: Germany's Headscarf Debates and the Cultural Politics of Difference," *German Politics and Society* 72, no. 3 (2004): 33–64.
31. "Lehrerin mit Kopftuch," *Neue Juristische Wochenschrift* 56, no. 43 (2003): 3111–3117.

NOTES TO PAGES 283–286

32. Weber, "Cloth on Her Head," 44. Headscarf bans in schools were forbidden in a subsequent Constitutional Court decision of 2015, but implementation of the decision has been uneven and the issue continues to be contested in German courts. See Gabriele Boos-Niazy, "Der Geist des Grundgesetzes und die gesellschaftliche Praxis: Facetten struktureller Diskriminierung muslimischer Frauen, dargestellt an Praxisbeispielen: Kopftuchverbot und Diskriminierung von Frauen mit Kopftuch," in *Der Islam und die Geschlechterfrage: Theologische, gesellschaftliche, historische und praktische Aspekte einer Debatte,* ed. Silvia Horsch et al. (Frankfurt: Peter Lang, 2019), 109–136.

33. Rita Chin, *The Crisis of Multiculturalism in Europe: A History* (Princeton, NJ: Princeton University Press, 2017), 217–220; Joan Wallach Scott, *The Politics of the Veil* (Princeton, NJ: Princeton University Press, 2007), 151–174.

34. "Lehrerin mit Kopftuch," 3113.

35. For instance, Wolfgang Huber, *Kirche und Öffentlichkeit* (Stuttgart: Klett, 1973); Wolfgang Huber and Heinz Eduard Tödt, *Menschenrechte: Perspektiven einer menschlichen Welt* (Stuttgart: Kreuz, 1977). See also Philipp Gessler, *Wolfgang Huber: Ein Leben für Protestantismus und Politik* (Freiburg: Kreuz, 2012), 100–111.

36. Gessler, *Huber,* 112–119.

37. Quoted in Gessler, *Huber,* 222.

38. Rat der EKD, ed., *Klarheit und gute Nachbarschaft: Christen und Muslime in Deutschland: Eine Handreichung des Rates der Evangelischen Kirche in Deutschland* (Hanover: Kirchenamt der EKD, 2007), 22.

39. Rat der EKD, *Klarheit und gute Nachbarschaft,* 15–21, quote at 17.

40. Rat der EKD, *Klarheit und gute Nachbarschaft,* 36–42.

41. Rat der EKD, *Klarheit und gute Nachbarschaft,* 21.

42. Rat der EKD, *Klarheit und gute Nachbarschaft,* 64–65.

43. For instance, "'Die AfD tritt das christliche Menschenbild mit Füßen,'" Evangelische Kirche in Deutschland, March 19, 2024, https://www.ekd.de/die-afd-tritt-das-christliche-menschenbild-mit-fuessen-83384.htm; Wolfgang Huber, "Zwischen Terror und Integration," *Tagesspiegel,* January 17, 2016, https://www.tagesspiegel.de/politik/zwischen-terror-und-integration-5465350.html; Angela Merkel, "Speech Given by Federal Chancellor Dr Angela Merkel in Lutherstadt Wittenberg on 31 October 2017 on the Occasion of the 500th Anniversary of the Reformation," The Federal Chancellor, https://www.bundesregierung.de/breg-en/service/archive/archive/speech-given-by-federal-chancellor-dr-angela-merkel-in-lutherstadt-wittenberg-on-31-october-2017-on-the-occasion-of-the-500th-anniversary-of-the-reformation-798224; Wolfgang Schäuble, *Protestantismus und Politik* (Munich: Claudius, 2017); Frank-Walter Steinmeier, "Eröffnung des 38. Deutschen Evangelischen Kirchentages," Der Bundespräsident, June 7, 2023, https://www.bundespraesident.de/SharedDocs/Reden/DE/Frank-Walter-Steinmeier/Reden/2023/06/230607-Evangelischer-Kirchentag-Nuernberg.html.

ACKNOWLEDGMENTS

This book took shape over many years, and I am humbled to recognize the people and institutions whose support made it possible. I was fortunate to begin the work that became this book among a dedicated community of historians and Europeanists at Harvard University. I am tremendously grateful to Peter Gordon, who saw the potential in this topic from an early stage and has shown endless dedication to my development as a scholar. Peter is a model of scholarly rigor and generosity whose joy in academic life continues to inspire me. His own work poses profound questions about the meanings of secularization and the religious sources of modern political thought that can be heard in the background of these pages. Alison Frank Johnson encouraged me to articulate the project's larger stakes and has been a source of sage counsel on all matters of Central Europe and historical writing. Samuel Moyn's move to Harvard was a stroke of good luck, and our conversations helped me work through key methodological issues. Like many before me, I benefited from Charles Maier's hard questions and prodigious knowledge of European history. Doris Bergen generously participated in an early discussion of this work, offering vital feedback that fundamentally shaped my revision process.

Conversations with David Armitage, James Kloppenberg, Mary Lewis, Kevin Madigan, and Terry Martin fostered my growth as a historian. Workshops in Harvard's History Department and Center for European Studies provided the first testing ground for my arguments. For their feedback in these venues and their camaraderie, my thanks go to Colleen Anderson, Tomasz Blusiewicz, Charles Clavey, John Gee, Benjamin Goossen, Erin Hutchinson, Gili Kliger, Ian Kumekawa, James McSpadden, and Sarah Shortall. I owe a debt of gratitude to Liat Spiro for believing in this project, encouraging me to have confidence in my scholarship, and helping me hone my ideas in many spirited conversations. The path to this book began at the University of Pennsylvania, where Warren Breckman, Antonio Feros, and Ronald Granieri guided my earliest attempts at historical research and provided both clear-eyed advice and encouragement on pursuing a career in this field. Some of the questions from which this book arises were born in a seminar with Ellen Kennedy, whose insight into German political thought and its protagonists brought the material to life.

370 ACKNOWLEDGMENTS

The research and writing of this book were enabled by generous support from funding institutions: the Berlin Program for Advanced German and European Studies at the Free University of Berlin; the German Academic Exchange Service; the Edmond J. Safra Center for Ethics and Minda de Gunzburg Center for European Studies at Harvard University; and the Wisconsin Alumni Research Foundation, Office of the Vice Chancellor for Research and Graduate Education, and Institute for Research in the Humanities at the University of Wisconsin–Madison. For helping me access resources, and for fostering stimulating intellectual communities at the academic centers where this project developed, I would like to acknowledge Katie Apsey, Elizabeth Covington, Karin Goihl, and Elizabeth Johnson.

This book draws on documents from thirteen church, government, party, and university archives, whose staff play vital roles in historical research. Several archivists went out of their way to introduce me to the richness of German Protestant history and guide me through the collections of their archives: Peter Beier of the Protestant Central Archive in Berlin; Stefan Flesch of the Rhineland Protestant Church Archive in Düsseldorf; and Armin Roether of the Protestant Academy in Bad Boll. A special thanks to Klaus Vogler and the staff at the Protestant Central Archive for accommodating my seemingly endless requests for files with good cheer. Librarians at the Harvard Divinity School Library made available extensive periodical collections and obtained key documents. Pastors Dagmar Pruin and Siegfried Virgils met with me early in my research in Germany to share their perspectives on their church's history and contemporary role.

Many colleagues in German history and beyond shared their insight in seminars and conference panels where portions of this project were presented, and met with me to discuss my work. They include Julia Ault, Matthew Berg, Jeremy Best, Bastiaan Bouwman, Thomas Brodie, Benedikt Brunner, James Chappel, Mikkel Dack, Skye Doney, John Eicher, Sebastian Gehrig, Michael Geyer, Alice Goff, Paul Hanebrink, Felix Jiménez-Botta, Rachel Johnston-White, Michelle Kahn, Melissa Kravetz, Douglas Morris, Dirk Moses, Paul Nolte, Michael O'Sullivan, Till van Rahden, Justin Reynolds, Julia Roos, Amy Rutenberg, Matthew Specter, Lauren Stokes, Noah Strote, and Jonathan Wiesen. Scholars of German religious history on both sides of the Atlantic, whose groundbreaking studies form the foundation for this book, gave generously of their time to guide a newcomer to the field and warn me of pitfalls: Victoria Barnett, Lukas Bormann, Doris Bergen, Robert Ericksen, Manfred Gailus, Michael Germann, Thomas Großbölting, Siegfried Hermle, Susannah Heschel, Hans-Michael Heinig, Maria Mitchell, Mark Ruff, and Klaus Tanner. Mark Ruff has served as a valued colleague and mentor, and the seminars he convened at the German Studies Association, along with Thomas Großbölting and Maria Mitchell, expanded my methodological horizons. Stefanie Woodard and Patrick Holschuh brightened many long days at the *Evangelisches Zentralarchiv*. Sultan Doughan, Frances Tanzer, Teresa Walch, and Brian van Wyck provided solidarity in navigating the early stages of an academic career and helped me think through ideas in this book.

The History Department and Center for European Studies at the University of Wisconsin–Madison have offered an embarrassment of riches since I arrived in 2020.

My colleagues Laird Boswell, Giuliana Chamedes, Kathryn Ciancia, Lynn Nyhart, Jennifer Ratner-Rosenhagen, Lou Roberts, and Marc Silberman thoughtfully engaged with drafts of the manuscript and made valuable suggestions on strengthening its arguments. Francine Hirsch not only provided detailed comments on the manuscript but has been a dedicated mentor throughout my time as a junior faculty member. Carl Caldwell and Udi Greenberg participated in a book workshop supported by UW-Madison's Center for the Humanities and offered generative feedback at a crucial stage in the revision process. Other colleagues who welcomed me to Madison, and from whose mentorship I have benefited, include Thomas Broman, Ashley Brown, Suzanne Desan, Sonja Klocke, Emma Kuby, David McDonald, Tony Michels, Viren Murthy, Adam Nelson, Pamela Potter, Ulrich Rosenhagen, Daniel Stolz, Daniel Ussishkin, Lee Wandel, and Louise Young. Department chairs Anne Hansen, Neil Kodesh, and Leonora Neville have been unfailingly supportive of my research. My friends and fellow assistant professors Mou Banerjee, Allison Powers Useche, and Matthew Villeneuve cheered me on and offered welcome respites from writing. History department staff including Leslie Abadie, Todd Anderson, Scott Burkhardt, and Jen Schumacher made my transition to Madison as seamless as possible; Iain McLoughlin went above and beyond to ensure that images for this book could be obtained.

My writing has benefited immeasurably from the sharp editorial eye of Emily Silk, who has been a champion of this project from our first meeting and a true partner in bringing this book to fruition. Two anonymous reviewers for Harvard University Press, one of whom later identified himself as Sean Forner, brought deep knowledge of the subject and carefully considered the manuscript's structure and argumentation. Their trenchant—and timely—feedback has made this a much better book. My thanks also go to Melody Negron at Westchester Publishing Services, and to Jillian Quigley, Stephanie Vyce, and the art and marketing teams at the Press. Joan Wong created a striking cover design of which I am undeservedly proud.

Family and friends never doubted that I would finish this book, even when the endpoint seemed out of sight. New friends have made Madison a second home; a special thanks to Yash Babar, Joshua Braver, Keith Levin, Priya Mukherjee, and Ramya Vinayak for helping me reach the finish line. My life is richer for the companionship of friends who have known me long before the idea for this book was born. I would like to acknowledge in particular Michael Adelson, Jason Fishman, Michael Fox, Andrew Kener, Anirudha Majumdar, Jordan Maidman, and Itai Stein for supporting this project and its author through many phases.

A delight in the process of completing this book has been sharing the joys and frustrations of writing with my wife, Liana Hershey-Nexon. Liana has learned more about the German Protestants than she ever expected to know, lifted me up in moments of doubt, and brightened my life with her kindness, humor, and wit. My parents, Myra Adelmann and Frank Bloch, created a home where reading and debate were valued and gave me the foundations to pursue an academic career. I thank them for providing much-needed encouragement and motivation at critical junctures over the years it took to complete this book. My sister Ilyssa Hecht, my aunt Myrna Bloch, and my extended family made me laugh and reminded me to take breaks from writing. My late cousin, Jonathan Adelman, took great interest in my academic pursuits and provided critical professional advice. I dedicate this book to the memory of my grandparents, whose creativity, integrity, and zest for life leave a legacy that I cherish.

Portions of Chapter 3 were first published in "'The Limits of Human Jurisdiction': Protestantism, War Crimes Trials, and Human Rights in Occupied Germany," *Journal of Modern History* 93, no. 2 (2021): 363–400. Portions of Chapter 5 were first published in "Democratic Illusions: The Protestant Campaign for Conscientious Objection in the Early Federal Republic of Germany," *Central European History* 56, no. 1 (2023): 71–91.

INDEX

Note: Page numbers in italics refer to illustrations

Abendland (Occident), 120, 249, 252, 253
Abendroth, Wolfgang, 216, 241, 246, 254, 267
Adenauer, Konrad, 120, 146, 158, 174, 180, 184, 238; Erhard and, 121, 253; on family law reform, 139; GDR, not recognizing, 209, 216; rearmament plans, 159, 165–169, 185
Albertz, Heinrich, 261–262
Albertz, Martin, 230
All-German People's Party (GVP), 176–177, 184, 186, 213, 243–244
Allied Control Council, 84, 94, 111
Althaus, Paul, 22, 23–24, 46–47, 76, 79, 164; Barth as a critic of, 42, 56, 60; on marriage, 134, 136; *Theology of Orders,* 60–61; total state, as a proponent of, 51–52, 67–68, 90; Weimar Republic, hostility toward, 33–36, 39, 40, 41
Ansbach memorandum, 60
antisemitism, 11, 12, 50, 212; Christian–Jewish dialogue on, 220–221, 273, 277; Confessing Church opposition to, 63–65; in the EKD, 83, 110, 116, 118; of the Freiburg circle, 74, 77–78; in the German Empire, 8–9; Nazi antisemitism, 56, 59; neglecting to address, 56, 68, 73, 98; in the Weimar Republic, 24, 35–36; of the Young Reformation movement, 52–53, 55
Arndt, Adolf, 148–149, 178, 188, 238–239, 275; on the Concordat, 149–153, 156,

282; conscientious objection, defending, 182–185, 190–191, 194; emergency laws, supporting, 234, 239–240, 244, 246; at the Godesberg Congress, 192, 249; on the right of resistance, 267
Asmussen, Hans, 64, 89, 92, 94, 97

Baader, Andreas, 268
Bad Boll, 90–93, 96–97, 100, 108, 170
Baden Theological Society, 249
Barmen Declaration, 58–59, 61, 62, 63, 68, 101, 129, 169, 182, 253, 270, 272; Ansbach memorandum on, 60; Barmen synod, 56, 87, 89, 98, 221; fifth thesis of, 58–59, 188
Barth, Karl, 20, 23–24, 42–43, 64, 71, 102, 126, 158, 169, 191, 208, 248–249, 275; "Christian Community and the Civil Community" lecture, 98–100, 164, 175–176, 211; Dahlemites, influence on, 82, 85–87, 98–101, 106–107, 124, 187–188; dialectical theology of, 28–31; early life, 27–28; on the GDR, 241–242, 243; on German guilt, 93–94; "Gospel and Law" lecture, 62, 135; "Justification and Justice" lecture, 86, 107; on marriage, 135–136, 138, 141; National Socialism, response to, 56, 58–59; natural theology, critiquing, 59–60; on the "right to the homeland," 204–206, 208, 210–211

Basic Law, 18, 119, 139, 148, 169, 184, 188, 200, 236, 238; Arndt as interpreting, 149, 151, 183, 239–240, 249; Article 3 on women's equality, 132, 133, 138; Article 4 on conscientious objection, 159–160, 162–163, 166, 177, 181, 185, 191–192, 194–195; Article 6 on protection of marriage, 133, 155; Article 7 on religious education, 125; Article 8 on right of assembly, 279; Article 20 on the "democratic and social federal state," 247–248, 267; Article 123 on preexisting treaties, 145; church–state relations in, 125–126, 128–131; and the Concordat decision, 152–154, 282; drafting of, 122–127; "funeral oration for the Basic Law" speech, 265–266; occupational freedom, guaranteeing, 254; parents' rights and, 124–125, 127, 144, 282–283; and the Rechtsstaat, 247–254; reunification, goal anchored in, 228

Bauer, Fritz, 172–173, 219, 245

Bäumler, Alfred, 30

Becker, Karl-Heinz, 63, 74

Beckmann, Joachim, 43, 98, 102, 180, 217, 269

Bell, George, 69, 70, 74, 76, 84, 85, 93, 96, 114

Berggrav, Eivind, 177

Bettermann, Karl August, 135, 257

Bild-Zeitung (periodical), 264

Bismarck, Klaus von, 217

Bismarck, Otto von, 8, 9, 22, 34

Bismarck, Philipp von, 224–225

Blätter für religiösen Sozialismus (journal), 31

Bloch, Ernst, 254, 258

Bodelschwingh, Friedrich von, 55

Böhler, Wilhelm, 139

Bonhoeffer, Dietrich, 55, 68, 70, 74, 78–80, 86, 176, 188, 270

Bosch, Frank, 133, 134–135, 155

Brandt, Willy, 190, 229, 231, 275

Brethren Council, 58, 97–98, 101–103, 117, 125, 131, 137, 171, 172, 206; conscientious objectors, supporting, 177, 182, 187; first postwar meeting, 87–88, 124; "Message concerning the Jewish Question," 220; "Message to the Pastors," 87–88, 101; Niemöller as a leader of, 61, 65, 87, 151, 164–165, 174; resistance narrative, 98, 158, 165, 169; SPD, dialogue with, 142, 182; women and the council, 58, 77, 88, 98

Brokdorf decision, 279, 280

Brüning, Heinrich, 41, 44–45, 46, 237

Brunner, Emil, 59–60, 136

Brunotte, Heinz, 277

Brunstäd, Friedrich, 32–33, 36, 40, 45

Bundestag, 176, 180, 188, 192, 217, 231, 238, 240, 279; Civil Code, reform of, 132, 139, 141–142, 143; conscription statute, discussion of, 182–184; defense committee, 181, 182, 191; Ehlers as president, 127, 175; emergency laws, discussion of, 246, 250, 254, 265, 266–267; 5 percent threshold for entry, 176, 244; Gerstenmaier as president, 229

Caritas relief agency, 199–200

Catholic Church. *See* Catholic social teaching; Center Party; Concordat; Frings, Josef; Fulda Bishops Conference; Hirschmann, Johannes; Kulturkampf; Neuhäusler, Johannes; Pius XII, Pope

Catholic social teaching, 37–39, 59, 66, 99–100, 104, 123–124, 214–215; on just war, 170–171, 182, 184, 187; on marriage, 132–133

Center Party, 25, 41, 42, 54, 122, 124, 126, 239; Catholic membership, 9, 23, 38, 120; on parents' rights, 125

Central Apologetic Institute, 41, 51

Charter of Expellees, 203

Christian Democratic Union (CDU), 12, 16, 72, 82, 120, 122, 128, 149, 153, 156, 193, 276, 279; Barth as critiquing, 100; and Christian–Jewish dialogue, 221; confessional schools, favoring, 20, 124, 125, 126, 130, 146–148, 150, 249; on conscientious objection, 163, 169, 177,

181, 184, 249; elections and, 139, *140*, 176, 186, 190, *201*, 217, 228, 237; emergency laws, supporting, 237, 240; on family law, 132, 133, 139, 142, 143, 214, 249; FDP-CDU coalition, 142, 180, 186, 253; Niemöller as critiquing, 165, 170; on the Oder–Neisse Line, 203, 218, 229; Protestant Working Group, 131, 141; rearmament, supporting, 166–168, 183, 185, 213; SPD-CDU relations, 238, 258; in the Soviet zone, 84; Women's Committee, 141

Christian–Jewish dialogue, 211, 220–222, 223, 224, 273, 277

Christian Peace Conference, 207–209, 215, 244

Christian Social People's Service (CSVD), 44–45

Christian Social Union (CSU), 122, 250

Christian Social Workers' Party, 8

Christophorus-Stift research institute, 134, 135, 136, 177, 189, 214, 215, 216

Christ und Welt (periodical), 116, 155, 218, 228

Church Brethren Societies, 242, 247, 270, 275, 281; antinuclear advocacy, 185–188, 189, 235–236, 238, 249, 269; anti-rearmament stance, 168, 174, 176–177, 180, 195; Cold War neutrality, commitment to, 243–244; Eastern bloc, contacts with, 206–209; emergency laws, opposing, 240–241, 245–246, 254, 265, 266; on the Oder-Neisse Line, 218, 225, 226; Rhineland society, 98, 174–175, 177, 178, 180, 217, 248, 269; Simon as member, 248–251; Working Group of, 188, 208, 210, 246, 249, 251–253, 273

church emergency law, 61, 187

Church-Theological Working Group, Württemberg, 98, 100, 103

Clay, Lucius, 96

Commission on a Just and Durable Peace, 105

Committee for Church Aid to Prisoners, 111

Committee on the Emergency of Democracy, 234, 265

Communist Party of Germany, 122, 203, 238, 244, 252

Concordat: Arndt as arguing against, 148–152, 182–183, 190, 191, 238–239; Nazi state-Catholic Church relations, as regulating, 54, 61, 123, 129; 1956 decision, 152–153, 155, 194, 282, 284; postwar debate about, 144–146; Protestant critics of, 146–148, 153–154, 275

Confessing Church, 2, 50, 56, 58, 81, 82, 84, 87, 164, 181, 191, 245; Bad Oeynhausen synod, 64; Bonhoeffer's critique of, 79–80; Church Brethren Societies as successors to, 98, 168, 206–207; Dahlem synod, 61; *Evangelische Theologie*, publishing, 60, 62–63, 70, 98, 205; Gestapo arrests of Confessing Church pastors, 69; Hitler, memorandum to, 64–65; Jewish persecution, stance on, 64, 71, 78; legacy of, 21, 272, 273, 278, 281–282, 284; Oxford conference, contribution to, 68–69; pastors of, as military chaplains in the Wehrmacht, 71; resistance narrative, 50, 66, 85, 129, 149, 169, 199, 236, 274, 277, 286; women members, 63, 76–77, 88, 98, 101, 136, 137, 165, 277. *See also* Barmen Declaration; Barth, Karl; Dahlemites; Freiburg circle; Gollwitzer, Helmut; Niemöller, Martin

confessional schools, 39, 125, 154, 156, 159, 199, 249; Basic Law, as nonbinding under, 152, 282; Catholic defense of, 20, 130, 144, 230; Concordat as guaranteeing protection of, 54, 123, 144; Federal Constitutional Court ruling against, 121, 249; freedom of conscience, as violating, 124, 147, 150; parents' right to, 124, 153; postwar debate about, 144–146, 170

Congress on the Emergency of Democracy, 254–255

376 INDEX

conscientious objection, 6, 178, 189, 212, 258, 275, 279, 286; Arndt as defending, 183, 184–185, 190–192, 194; Basic Law as guaranteeing, 159, 162–163; Catholic stance on, 170; CDU restriction of, 169, 181, 184; Church Brethren Societies as upholding, 174–175, 185, 187, 249, 252; Dahlemite support for, 160, 164, 168–171, 177, 180, 195–196; EKD synod commission on, 181–182; Gollwitzer on, 175–176; Künneth on, 167; Nazi regime as banning, 71, 162; and the right of resistance, 245–246; SPD as supporting, 182, 184, 186, 193, 235, 240; Weissensee synod on the right of, 166, 168, 169, 180; West Berlin as a haven for conscientious objectors, 257
constitutional theory, 36–40, 127–31, 149, 247–53
Convention of Dispersed Eastern Protestant Churches, 203, 210
Cyrankiewicz, Józef, 231

Dahlemites, 149, 157, 175, 199, 214, 215, 223, 236, 245, 269, 272; anti-Catholic stance, 121, 141, 144, 146–147, 156; Barth as influencing, 82, 85–87, 98–99, 100, 124, 135, 241; as a Confessing Church faction, 61–72, 64–65, 66, 69, 72, 75; conscientious objection, supporting, 159, 160, 164, 171, 174, 177, 178, 180, 195, 196; denazification, critiquing, 103; human rights stance, 105–106, 107, 109, 112; on marriage, 135, 136, 142; resistance narrative, 88, 98, 101, 158, 164–165, 173, 277; on the "right to the homeland," 204, 205–207, 210–212, 231, 232. *See also* Darmstadt statement; *Junge Kirche* (journal); *Stimme der Gemeinde* (journal)
Darmstadt statement, 101–102, 164–165, 206
Dehn, Günther, 30
Delekat, Friedrich, 74, 112, 216
Der Remter (journal), 206, 211

Der Spiegel (periodical), 2, 218, 228, 243, 250, 263
dialectical theology, 29–31, 32, 33, 36, 41, 56, 59, 106
Dibelius, Otto, 26, 45, 49, 89, 109; Barth as critiquing, 42, 56; Berlin-Brandenburg, as bishop of, 125, 242, 259; Confessing Church leadership, 48, 68, 74; Lilje, letter on political authority to, 242–243, 249
Die Christliche Welt (journal), 27, 31
Diem, Hermann, 100, 102, 103, 178, 220
Dietze, Constantin von, 68, 79–80, 92–93, 109, 180, 275; as a Freiburg circle member, 72, 73–74, 76–77, 78, 91–92
Die Zeit (periodical), 218, 225, 228
Dipper, Theodor, 169
Dirks, Walter, 204
Dombois, Hans, 36, 109, 111, 112, 113, 115, 214, 215; on family law, 134–135, 139; on human rights, 107–108; Marxism commission membership, 216
Dönhoff, Marion, 225
Dulles, John Foster, 105
Dutschke, Rudi, 1, 2, 256, 257–258, 260–261, 264, 267

Easter March movement, 193, 241, 273, 277
Eastern Memorandum, 20–21, 197–199, 232–233, 259; origins of the memorandum, 211–219; public reception of, 227–232; reconciliation, calling for, 224–227
Ehlers, Hermann, 15, 126, 127, 141, 175
Elert, Werner, 32, 60
Ellul, Jacques, 106–108, 112, 113, 115, 135
emergency laws, 21, 234–236, 250, 270, 272–273; Arndt, stance on, 234, 239–240, 244–246; CDU proposals for, 237; Church Brethren Societies and, 240–241, 246, 254, 265; EKD Council recommendations on, 237–238;

opposition to, 244–246, 254–255, 265–268; SPD proposals for, 240, 245, 253–254, 258, 267

Enabling Act, 234, 244, 273

Engelbrecht, Manfred, 261

Ensslin, Gudrun, 268

Equal Rights Act, 143, 154, 155, 194

Erhard, Ludwig, 121, 253–254, 258

Erler, Fritz, 182, 190, 192

Eucken, Walter, 72, 121

European Defense Community (EDC), 174, 176, 177

Evangelische Frauenarbeit, 136–138, 142, 143, 214

Evangelische Kirche in Deutschland (EKD), 12, 18, 102, 103, 125, 132, 156–157, 160, 235, 241, 255, 272, 273, 282, 287; Commission on Public Responsibility, 167, 171, 218–219, 222–227, 229, 233, 270, 275, 280; conscientious objection, supporting, 20, 163, 166, 181–182, 184, 189, 212; conservative wing, 14, 90, 173, 181, 204, 211, 213, 263; Dahlemite wing, 124, 144, 165, 236; Democracy Memorandum, 280–281, 284; denazification, campaign against, 96, 149; Eastern Church Committee, 203, 205, 206, 218, 226; EKD chancellery, 92, 93–94, 108, 134, 136, 137, 138, 139, 147, 163, 169, 223, 277; EKD Foreign Office, 89, 113, 114, 115–116, 137, 223, 281; EKD synod, 143, 167, 180, 187, 189, 229–231, 270; *Evangelische Welt* as an EKD newspaper, 109, 127; Institute for Confessional Research, 147, 154; Institute for Protestant Church Law, 112, 128, 210; Islam, 2006 memorandum on, 284–286; marriage law commission, 135, 138, 139, 143, 155; Ranke as EKD administrator, 111–112, 169–170; statement on Nazi trials (1963), 222–224; war crimes trials, campaign against, 109–118, 199, 213, 220. *See also* Brethren Council; Eastern Memorandum; Evangelische

Frauenarbeit; Evangelisches Hilfswerk; Stuttgart Declaration

Evangelische Theologie (journal), 60, 62–63, 70, 98, 105, 205, 275

Evangelisches Hilfswerk, 112–113, 130, 199–200

Extra-Parliamentary Opposition, 258, 264–265, 267, 268, 273

Eyl, Meta, 136, 137

Federal Constitutional Court, 121, 127, 131, 143, 156–157, 188, 247, 254, 272–273, 282–283; Brokdorf decision, 279; Concordat case before, 146, 148–152; Concordat decision, 152–154; conscientious objection rulings, 160, 184, 186, 190–191, 192, 194; Equal Rights Act, decision on, 152–156; SRP and Communist party, banning, 238, 252

Federal Republic of Germany (FRG): 1949 elections in, 120, 139; 1953 elections in, 139, 141, 176; 1957 elections in, 186, 190, 209; 1961 elections in, 217, 239, 244–245; 1965 elections in, 253–254; 1969 elections in, 231; ethnic Germans living in, 198, 203; Foreign Ministry, 209; formation of, 110–111, 119–120; Interior Ministry, 135, 139, 240, 249, 254; Justice Ministry, 135, 138, 139, 154; migration to, 21, 281–283; Nazi Reich, as legal successor to, 144–145, 146, 152, 161; nuclear war preparedness, 185, 250; Office for the Protection of the Constitution, 238; Protestant population of, 12, 119–120. *See also* Basic Law; Bundestag; Christian Democratic Union (CDU); Federal Constitutional Court; Social Democratic Party (SPD)

Federation of Expellees, 209, 218, 228

Federation of Germans, 176, 244

Fight Against Atomic Death, 186, 188, 190, 241, 278

Flechtheim, Ossip K., 241, 244

Forsthoff, Ernst, 51, 90, 111, 134, 247
François-Poncet, André, 116
Frankfurter Hefte (journal), 133, 144, 171, 204
Free Democratic Party (FDP), 125, 126, 138, 142, 154, 163, 258, 266; CDU-FDP coalition, 180, 186, 253; SPD-FDP coalition, 145, 146
Free University, 2, 158, *260;* Berlin Model of governance, 256–257; Dutschke, enrolling in, 257–258; Protestant Student Community of, 257, 259, 264, 268
Freiburg circle, 72–80, 81, 83, 90, 121, 220
Freiburg memorandum, 74, 75, 77, 79, 91–93, 97, 134
Freikorps, 30, 52, 212
Freisler, Roland, 78
Friedrich Wilhelm III, Kaiser, 8
Frings, Josef, 124, 127, 137, 170, 171, 230, 276
Fulda Bishops Conference, 124, 170

Gablentz, Otto Heinrich von der, 257
Geis, Robert Raphael, 221
Gerlach, Wolfgang, 277
German Civil Code, 131–132, 135, 136–138, 139, 141–142, 143, 155, 214
German Democratic Republic (GDR), 12, 249; Adenauer, refusal to recognize, 209, 216; Christians in, 120, 206, 224, 241–242, 243; Eastern border, recognizing, 203, 227; formation of, 119; League of Protestant Churches in, 272; women's equality in, 132
German Manifesto, 178, *179*
German National People's Party (DNVP), 29, 31, 32, 36, 39, 44, 46, 52, 72, 258
German Peace Union (DFU), 243–244, 245, 251, 256
German People's Party (DVP), 137, 176, 186, 213, 243–244
German Protestant Association, 8, 10, 103
German Protestant Church (DEK), 56, *57,* 58, 61, 67–68, 87, 111, 137

German Protestant Church Federation, 35, 41
Gerstenmaier, Eugen, 15, 72, 229
Girgensohn, Herbert, 206, 210
Godesberg Congress, 190, 193, 237; Godesberg program, 190, 192–93, 195, 231, 240, 249, 252; left socialist disillusion with, 193, 240, 246; post-Godesberg SPD, 228, 238–240, 245, 267
Goerdeler, Carl, 78, 79
Gogarten, Friedrich, 27, 32, 43
Goldschmidt, Dietrich, 218, 222, 225, 229, 234
Gollwitzer, Helmut, 2–3, 15, 178, 216, 218, 270, 272, 275; antinuclear efforts, 186–187, 189, 208; Barth, as a student of, 30, 86, 175; Christian–Jewish dialogue, participation in, 221; as a Confessing Church member, 71, 72, 73; conscientious objectors, support for, 175–177, 180; emergency laws, opposition to, 234, 254–255, 265–267; student protesters, sympathizing with, 257, 259–260, 262, 264–265, 268
Gomułka, Władysław, 207
Göttingen Manifesto, 185, 186, 188, 217
Gradl, Johann Baptist, 229
Grüber, Heinrich, 71, 78, 221

Habermas, Jürgen, 216, 248
Hammelsbeck, Oskar, 124, 151, 178, 244
Handy, Thomas, 116
Hannover, Heinrich, 245–246, 254, 255
Häring, Bernhard, 171
Harlan, Veit, 239
Harnack, Adolf von, 22, 23, 27, 64
Hartenstein, Karl, 116–117
Heidelberg jurists circle, 113, 115, 117
Heinemann, Gustav, 44, 89, 100, 171, 190, 251, 268, 275; conscientious objectors, defending, 184–185, 191–192, 194, 195; EKD synod, as president of, 167, 180; GVP, co-founding, 176, 186; as justice minister, 234, 265; on rearmament, 168–169, 172, 178;

"Rechtsstaat as a Theological Problem" address, 252–253
Held, Heinrich, 125
Hennis, Wilhelm, 239
Herder Korrespondenz (journal), 184
Herman, Stewart, 85, 93, 96, 103
Herrmann, Wilhelm, 27, 28
Herzog, Roman, 279
Hesse, 162, 243, 283; Arndt as representing, 148, 150, 182; interconfessional schools in, 123, 145, 146, 150–151; Niemöller as a Protestant leader in, 103, 145, 147, 150, 177, 245
Hesse, Konrad, 247, 279
Heuss, Theodor, 126, 158, 159, 164, 180
Hindenburg, Paul von, 41, 46, 48, 59
Hirsch, Emanuel, 29, 30
Hirschmann, Johannes, 181, 182, 184
Hitler, Adolf, 41, 49, 54, 59, 60, 69, 70, 137, 161, 244; assassination attempt, 74, 78, 86, 158; Bonhoeffer, ordering execution of, 78–79; chancellor, appointment as, 46, 48, 55, 237; Confessing Church memorandum to, 64–65, 75; continental expansion, 169, 197; oath to Hitler as required for employment, 62, 212–213
Hoffmann, Adolph, 25
Holl, Karl, 22, 23, 31, 33
Hossenfelder, Joachim, 48–49
Hromádka, Josef, 207–208
Huber, Wolfgang, 232, 284, 286
Hugenberg, Alfred, 44
human rights, 14, 17, 18, 19, 20, 83, 126, 274, 284; Catholic theories of, 104–105; and Christian–Jewish dialogue, 220, 224; in the Freiburg memorandum, 76–77; Protestant critiques of, 105–108; and the "right to the homeland," 203, 206, 210, 212; war crimes trials, in the campaign against, 110–111, 113–115, 117–118, 122, 199, 220; and the WCC, 105, 108–109, 259

Immer, Karl, 62
International Military Tribunal (IMT), Nuremberg, 94, 95, 107, 110, 117
Iwand, Hans Joachim, 52, 109, 217, 261; and the Christian Peace Conference, 208–209; as a Confessing Church member, 70, 98; Darmstadt statement, authoring, 101–102, 164–165; as a nationalist, 30, 36, 212; rearmament, opposing, 169, 171, 175, 178; on the right of resistance, 173–174; on the "right to the homeland," 210–211

Jacobs, Helene, 78, 165
Jehovah's Witnesses, 162, 163, 164, 191
Judenmission, 8, 220
Junge Kirche (journal), 55, 70, 109, 127, 173, 184, 195, 241, 262
Jungnationale Stimmen (journal), 30, 36, 41, 44
JuristenZeitung (journal), 148, 152, 153
Just-Dahlmann, Barbara, 222

Kaiser Wilhelm Memorial Church, 1–2, 3, *4, 5*, 21, 262, 263
Kapp Putsch, 30
Karwehl, Richard, 42–43
Kaufmann, Erich, 37, 78, 115
Kempner, Robert, 110
Kerrl, Hanns, 64, 67
Khrushchev, Nikita, 206, 207, 209
Kierkegaard, Søren, 28
Kiesinger, Kurt Georg, 258
King, Martin Luther, Jr., 264
Kirchentag (lay assembly), 35, 42, 68, 175, 221, 222, 229, 279, 284
Kloppenburg, Heinz, 64, 178, 221, 234, 246, 253, 254, 267
Knappen, Marshall, 85
Koch, Eckhard, 150
Kominek, Bolesław, 230
Kommune I, 261
Kopf, Hinrich Wilhelm, 145
Kreisau circle, 72, 74, 78, 213
Krippendorff, Ekkehart, 257
Kristallnacht pogrom, 71, 73, 224

380 INDEX

Kuby, Erich, 257
Kulturkampf, 9–10, 129, 146, 149
Künneth, Walter, 41–42, 64, 67, 212, 214, 269; on conscientious objection, 164, 167, 171, 173, 182; *Nation before God,* 52–53, 55; on the "right to the homeland," 204; Young Reformation movement, founding, 51–52, 54, 90
Kunst, Hermann, 180, 181–182, 184, 191, 217, 218, 225

Lampe, Adolf, 72, 74, 78
Law Against the Enemies of Democracy, 238
League of National Socialist German Jurists, 128, 137
League of Protestant Churches in the GDR, 272
Lehr, Robert, 72, 139, 172
Leibholz, Gerhard, 45–46, 70, 131, 152, 153
Leo XIII, Pope, 38–39
Life and Work movement, 36, 66, 67, 69, 103
Lilje, Hanns, 51, 89, 90, 109, 125, 145–146, 181, 242, 243
Loewenstein, Karl, 238
Löffler, Martin, 192
Los von Rom (Away from Rome) initiative, 9
Ludendorff, Erich, 34–35
Lüders, Marie-Elisabeth, 142, 154
Ludin, Fereshta, 283–284
Lüth, Erich, 239, 247, 248, 249
Luther, Martin, 8, 22, 34, 57, 72, 79, 170; Luther renaissance, 31–32, 42, 43, 50; two-kingdoms doctrine, 14, 73, 102, 163, 164, 176; *Volk* concept and, 10, 35; Wolf as a Luther scholar, 30, 60, 100–101, 173

Malmédy massacre, 110–111
Mangoldt, Hermann von, 163
Marahrens, August, 56–57, 61, 62
Maritain, Jacques, 66, 104–105, 107
Mausbach, Joseph, 133
McCloy, John, 114, 116, 117

Meinhof, Ulrike, 248, 256, 268, 275
Meiser, Hans, 56, 58, 89, 96, 116, 125
Mennonites, 162, 163, 164
Metzger, Ludwig, 142, 143, 149, 182, 190, 192, 218
Meusel, Margarete, 63, 66, 165
Michaltscheff, Theodor, 195
militant democracy, 235, 236–240, 243–244, 247, 248, 255, 271
Mitzenheim, Moritz, 241
Mochalski, Herbert, 207, 243, 244, 251
Moltke, Helmuth James von, 72, 74, 78
Muench, Aloisius, 154
Müller, Eberhard, 90–91, 97, 259
Müller, Ludwig, 56, 57, 58
Mussolini, Benito, 40, 43, 54

NATO alliance, 1, 66; nuclear defense program, 185, 187, 188, 193, 278, 279; West German membership, 178, 180, 182, 186, 236
natural law, 53, 73, 75, 100, 127–128, 133, 152, 204, 230; Arndt on, 149, 239, 267; Barthian critique of, 61, 62, 99–100, 206, 249; and family law reform, 132–133, 139, 143, 149, 154–155; human rights and, 104–105, 107, 108, 113, 118, 210; Protestant critiques of, 60, 112–113, 126, 156, 214–215, 216; Provisional Church Administration and, 68–69; Smend as critiquing, 40, 45. *See also* Catholic social teaching
natural theology, 59–60, 61
Nauheim circle, 172
Naumann, Friedrich, 10, 11, 25, 26
Neuhäusler, Johannes, 111, 116
Neu-Westend Church, 1, 260–261
Niebuhr, Reinhold, 114
Niemöller, Martin, 20, 48, 65, 66, *88,* 93, 109, 146, 167, 172, 175, 181, 208, 220, 230, 256, 275, 276; Adenauer, critiquing, 165, 168; Berlin-Dahlem parish of, 61, 63, 68, *88,* 175; Brethren Council membership, 87, 151, 165; Committee on the Emergency of Democracy, on executive board, 234, 254; as a

Confessing Church pastor, 49, 62, 64, 70, 178; Dahlemite faction, leader of, 61, 87, 138; Darmstadt statement, signing, 102, 164; EKD Foreign Office, heading, 89; German Peace Union, as a founding member, 244; Hesse-Nassau church, leading, 103, 145, 147, 150, 177, 245; imprisonment of, 49, 61, 69, 70, 71–72, 87; on the Oder-Neisse territories, 207, 209; Pastors' Emergency League and, 56, 58, 221; rearmament, opposing, 165, 166, 169, 171, 195; Soviet Union visit, 174, 206; in Young Reformation movement, 51–52, 55

Niemöller, Wilhelm, 165

Noack, Ulrich, 172, 174, 176

Nolde, Frederick, 105, 109, 113

"No Other Gospel" movement, 269

Oberländer, Theodor, 209, 211

Oder-Neisse Line, *201*, 215–216, 225, 244, 275; Church Brethren Societies on, 207, 209; government stance against, 204, 209, 216–217, 229; West German recognition of, 199, 231. *See also* Eastern Memorandum; Tübingen Memorandum

Ohnesorg, Benno, 1, 259–260, 262

Oldham, Joseph H., 67–68, 70

Osterloh, Edo, 139

Ostpolitik (Eastern policy), 199, 227, 231, 272

Oxford conference, 66–68, 69–70, 103, 105

Papen, Franz von, 46, 54

parents' rights, 124–125, 127, 131, 132, 142, 144, 147

Parliamentary Council, 119, 122–127, 132–133, 144, 145, 162–163, 169

Pastors' Emergency League (PEL), 56, 58, 221

Paulsen, Anna, 136–137, 138

Paulskirche (Saint Paul's Church), 178, *179*, 180

Peters, Hans, 130, 150

Piper, Otto, 44, 136

Pius XI, Pope, 38

Pius XII, Pope, 54, 81, 105, 118, 133, 170, 171, 204

Pohl, Oswald, 116

Political Night Prayer, 268–269, 277–278

Posser, Diether, 176, 184–185, 192, 194

Potsdam Agreement, 102, 197, 198

Potsdam Conference, 84, 95, 160

Protestant Academies, 6, 134, 135, 163, 170, 211, 213, 214; in Arnoldshain, 190, 204, 282; in Bad Boll, 90, *91*, 92–93, 96–97, 100–101, 108, 170; human rights concerns, 107, 117–118; Simon lecturing before, 270–271

Protestant League, 9, 30, 147

Protestant Research Center (FEST), 189, 214–217, 218, 224, 233, 284

Protestant Student Communities, 1, 257, 259, 262, 264, 265, 268

Provisional Church Administration, 61, 62, 63, 64–66, 67, 68–69, 70, 101

Prussian Constitution, 25, 39

Prussian Union of Churches, 8, 25, 39, 77

Quakers, 163, 164

Quervain, Alfred de, 30

Rabehl, Bernd, 258

Rabl, Kurt, 204, 210

Radbruch, Gustav, 122, 127

Rade, Martin, 31

Ragaz, Leonhard, 28

Raiser, Ludwig, 112, 113, 131, 143, 212–217, 228, 231, 234, 259, 275; atomic commission, leading, 189, 216; Commission on Public Responsibility, as chair of, 218–219, 222–226; in intergenerational dialogue, 270, 271, 272

Ranke, Hansjürg, 111–115, 116, 117, 147, 169–170, 214–215, 216, 259

Rechtsstaat (rule-of-law state), 65, 191, 245, 256, 258, 259, 270, 271; Church Brethren Societies in affinity with, 247, 248, 251–253, 281; Protestants as affirming values of, 177, 236, 250–251, 253, 265, 272

382 INDEX

Red Army Faction (RAF), 268, 275
Reich Church. *See* German Protestant Church (DEK)
Remer, Otto Ernst, 172–174
Rheinischer Merkur (periodical), 145, 155, 228
Ridder, Helmut, 154, 254, 255, 267
Riemeck, Renate, 207, 230, 244–245, 255, 256, 268, 272, 275
right to the homeland *(Recht auf die Heimat)*, 199–211, 212, 218, 219, 225–226
Ritter, Gerhard, 72, 73, 78, 102, 127, 167, 250, 275; Freiburg memorandum, authorship of, 74–76, 91–92; on human rights, 106, 108, 109; on resistance, 158, 159, 164, 173
Rosenberg, Alfred, 53, 61, 64, 147, 212–213

Scharf, Kurt, 221, 222, 224, 227, 259, 260, 261–262, 263, 264, 267, 268, 275
Scheffler, Erna, 154
Schelsky, Helmut, 134, 142–143
Scheuner, Ulrich, 112–113, 115, 130–131, 156, 189, 243; on the Concordat, 147, 153; on conscientious objection, 167, 170, 177–178, 180, 184, 194; on family law, 138, 155; on the Rechtsstaat, 247, 251; at the University of Bonn, 130, 249, 275
Schlatter, Adolf, 31, 33
Schmitt, Carl, 37, 130, 251; as a Nazi sympathizer, 38, 45, 95–96, 134, 247; total state theory, 43–45, 46, 50–51, 66; on the Weimar Constitution, 39–40
Schmitz, Elisabeth, 64, 66, 71, 165
Schörner, Ferdinand, 219
Schrey, Heinz-Horst, 206
Schröder, Gerhard, 229, 237, 272
Schumacher, Kurt, 162, 190
Schumann, Friedrich Karl, 67, 135, 138–139, 214, 215
Schutzstaffel (SS), 57, 90, 94, 116, 117, 204, 205, 219
Schwarzhaupt, Elisabeth, 137–138, 147–148, 155, 156, 275; as a CDU

parliamentarian, 15, 141–142, 143; Commission on Public Responsibility membership, 218, 225, 229
Schweitzer, Wolfgang, 215, 225–226, 231
Seeberg, Reinhold, 10, 11, 23, 31, 33
Seifert, Jürgen, 248, 254
Shaull, Richard, 259
Siegmund-Schultze, Friedrich, 181
Simon, Helmut, 248–251, 252, 253, 255, 259, 267, 270–271, 272; as a Federal Constitutional Court judge, 273, 279–280
Śliwka-Szczerbic, Władysław, 209
Smend, Rudolf, 23–24, 41, 46–47, 68, 142, 192, 213, 214, 253, 275, 280; Arndt, as inspired by, 149, 239; on the Basic Law, 129–130, 148, 151, 155, 156, 240; on the Concordat debate, 148, 150–151, 152, 153, 190, 194, 282; Confessing Church membership, 128–129; EKD Council membership, 89, 109, 113, 128; Institute for Protestant Church Law, as founder, 112, 128, 210; Leibholz, association with, 45–46, 70, 131, 152, 153; "Protestantism and Democracy" essay, 44–45, 128; Smend school, 193, 239, 247–249, 251, 254; on the Weimar Constitution, 37, 39–40
Social Democratic Party (SPD), 10, 125, 142, 149, 151–152, 154, 156, 261, 275, 279; Barth as member, 43; Concordat, opposing, 145–146, 153; conscientious objection, stance toward, 159, 162–163, 182–184, 186, 191–193, 195; emergency laws, supporting, 238–240, 244–245, 253, 258, 265, 267; Fight Against Atomic Death, backing, 186, 188, 241; Heinemann as member, 186, 251–252; on the Oder-Neisse Line, *202*, 203, 217, 229, 231; rearmament, opposing, 162, 167, 174, 176, 178, 180, 183. *See also* Arndt, Adolf; Godesberg Congress
Socialist German Student League (SDS), 1, 240–241, 257–258, 263, 268, 270, 273
Socialist Reich Party (SRP), 172, 173, 174, 238, 252

Socialist Unity Party (SED), 12, 84, 142, 161, 168, 176, 206, 241, 242, 244
Societies for Christian–Jewish Cooperation, 211, 221
Society for Protestant Theology, 73, 98, 100
Sölle, Dorothee, 268
Sonntagsblatt (periodical), 181, 223
Spiegel-Schmidt, Friedrich, 205–206, 210, 225, 226
Stalin, Joseph, 95, 174, 206, 209
Stauffenberg, Claus von, 78
Sternberger, Dolf, 280
Stille Hilfe, 117
Stimme der Gemeinde (journal), 138, 147–149, 168–169, 193, 195, 207, 209, 241, 244, 250
Stoecker, Adolf, 8–9
Strauss, Franz Josef, 185, 250
Sturmabteilung (SA), 48, 49, 56, 108, 112, 147, 212
Stuttgart Declaration, 93–94, 148
Sucker, Wolfgang, 147
Süddeutsche Zeitung (periodical), 133, 218
Süsterhenn, Adolf, 124, 125, 126, 139, 144–145, 146, 149, 154

Tag der Heimat (Homeland Day), 209, 211
Teufel, Fritz, 261
Thielicke, Helmut, 2–3, 81, 94, 102, 108, 189, 263, 270, 275; on atomic weapons, 185–186, 189; Eastern Memorandum, favoring, 230; Freiburg circle participation, 74
Tillich, Paul, 31
Treaty of Görlitz, 203
Treaty of Moscow, 231
Treaty of Warsaw, 231
Treysa conference, 89, 90, 92, 97
Troeltsch, Ernst, 26, 27
Tübingen Memorandum, 217, 218, 223, 225, 233, 238
two-kingdoms doctrine, 33, 73, 102, 163, 164, 176

Union of Christian German Students, 90
United Nations Commission on Human Rights, 105, 109, 113, 114
United Nations Universal Declaration of Human Rights, 109, 115, 203

Versailles Treaty, 26, 33, 36, 71, 75, 94, 147
Vogel, Heinrich, 208
völkisch movement, 34–36, 41–43, 53, 55, 56, 67–68

War Resisters International, *183*, 195
Weber, Helene, 125, 142
Weber, Otto, 115
Weber, Werner, 130–131, 134, 247
Weimar Constitution, 25, 31, 38, 46, 48, 123, 239; Basic Law and, 126–127, 129; presidential emergency powers in, 237, 246; Schmitt on, 39–40; Smend on, 37, 39–40, 41; women's suffrage in, 34, 132
Weissensee synod, 166, 168, 169, 180
Weissler, Friedrich, 65, 68
Weizsäcker, Carl Friedrich von, 185, 189, 217
Wendland, Heinz-Dietrich, 36, 41, 44, 46, 52, 53, 67–68, 69, 74, 216, 259
Werner, Herbert, 193, 243
Wessel, Helene, 176
Wilhelm I, Kaiser, 3
Wilhelm II, Kaiser, 3, 22
Wilkens, Erwin, 218, 224, 225, 226–227
Wilm, Ernst, 223
Wölber, Hans-Otto, 263, 270
Wolf, Erik, 53, 67, 68, 72, 74, 76, 92, 109, 111
Wolf, Ernst, 102, 106, 107, 109, 136, 141, 178, 188, 190, 214, 216, 222; "Church and Law" commission, as member, 112–115; Committee on the Emergency of Democracy, on executive board, 234, 254; *Evangelische Theologie,* as founder and editor, 60, 63, 98, 105, 275; as a Luther scholar, 30, 100–101, 173; Society for Protestant Theology, as founder, 73, 98, 100; Working Group of Church Brethren Societies, as speaker, 188, 251–252, 253

Working Group on Jews and Christians, 221, 222, 229

World Council of Churches (WCC), 105, 106, 113–114, 115, 208, 215, 223, 276, 277; Amsterdam Assembly, 81–82, 103–104, 108–109, 166; Herman as delegate of, 85, 93; Uppsala conference, 268–269; World Conference on Church and Society, 258–259

Wuermeling, Franz-Josef, 139, 142, 143

Wurm, Theophil, 89, 96, 97, 109, 112, 114; as bishop of Württemberg, 56, 58, 74, 78, 92, 103; Malmedy defendants, campaigning for, 110–111

Young National League, 36, 52, 98, 108

Young Reformation movement, 51–52, 54, 55, 56, 90, 125

Zeitschrift für evangelisches Kirchenrecht (journal), 129, 130–131, 225, 275

Zeitwende (journal), 102, 158

Ziegler, Matthäus, 147

Zwischen den Zeiten (journal), 29, 30, 42–43, 46, 56, 59